THE AGE OF CIVIL WAR
AND RECONSTRUCTION,
1830-1900

A Book of Interpretative Essays

THE DORSEY SERIES IN AMERICAN HISTORY

COLE   *An Interpretive History of American Foreign Relations*

CRONON (ed.)   *Twentieth Century America: Selected Readings* Volumes I and II

CROWE (ed.)   *The Age of Civil War and Reconstruction, 1830–1900: A Book of Interpretative Essays*

FILENE (ed.)   *American Views of Soviet Russia, 1917–1965*

FULLINWIDER   *The Mind and Mood of Black America: 20th Century Thought*

GLAAB   *The American City: A Documentary History*

KAPLAN   *Recent American Foreign Policy: Conflicting Interpretations*   rev. ed.

NEWBY (ed.)   *The Development of Segregationist Thought*

PESSEN   *Jacksonian America: Society, Personality, and Politics*

QUINT, CANTOR & ALBERTSON (eds.)   *Main Problems in American History*   3d ed.   Volumes I and II

SALE & KARN   *American Expansion: A Book of Maps*

SHAFER   *A Guide to Historical Method*

TAGER & GOIST (eds.)   *The Urban Vision: Selected Interpretations of the Modern American City*

VAN TASSEL & HALL (eds.)   *Science and Society in the United States*

WILSON (ed.)   *Darwinism and the American Intellectual: A Book of Readings*

THE AGE OF CIVIL WAR AND RECONSTRUCTION, 1830-1900

A Book of Interpretative Essays

Edited by
CHARLES CROWE
University of Georgia

1966

THE DORSEY PRESS
Homewood, Illinois

First Printing, September, 1966

Second Printing, May, 1967

Third Printing, September, 1968

Fourth Printing, July, 1969

Fifth Printing, December, 1969

Sixth Printing, July, 1970

Seventh Printing, October, 1972

Library of Congress Catalog Card No. 66–27454

PRINTED IN THE UNITED STATES OF AMERICA

For Joyce and Thad

Preface

The remoteness of textbooks from contemporary scholarship and their failure to present history as a complex, evolving discipline, rich in intellectual demands and rewards, suggest very strongly the need for specific teaching remedies. As early as the 1930s scholars who recognized these difficulties began to publish "problem" and "crisis" anthologies. Unfortunately and perhaps unavoidably the anthology editors, with an air of total impartiality, often assumed the existence of an impossible freedom from value judgments and limited the utility of their books by reducing the most complex historical situations to simple "either/or" categories. While the discipline could not exist without explanations, they need not be slogan-like formulae and implausibly over-simplified categories which obscure or falsify the richness of collective human experience of the past. Nor does the need for the scholar to follow the standard rules on evidence, and to be on guard against some of the more arbitrary moralizations and subjective statements, invalidate the fact that history is always written by individuals from within a particular culture and era. The historian is himself in history, viewing the past from a constantly moving vantage point. From time to time old lines of inquiry become irrelevant, conventional solutions fade into implausibility, and modern sensibilities interacting with changing events reveal new patterns of research and bring to the foreground insights unavailable to earlier generations. It is also possible that the discipline itself progresses as scholars find new approaches and better uses for old ones. I wish to make available to students the best scholarship of present times in a way that will reveal the most probable conclusions as well as the plastic context from which they emerge. It seems self-defeating for those who wish to depart from the narrow vistas of the textbook world to assign students, without adequate explanation, and as if the scholarship of the various generations existed on the same plane of meaning, the more precise, sophisticated and thoughtful work of leading contemporary scholars such as Kenneth M. Stampp, John Hope Franklin and C. Vann Woodward, side by side with essays by James Ford Rhodes, William A. Dunning, and Ulrich B. Phillips from the high era of racism and imperialism of fifty years ago. Such a procedure is unhistorical; just as it misses the point that the historian is in history, so it fails to grasp the fact that historical writing becomes in time a part of intellectual history. The scholar who assumes a democracy of authorities and sources tells us something about his mind and culture, but he does not provide a valid scholarly technique. Will anyone argue that Ulrich B. Phillip's book of 1918 on slavery, immersed as it was in conceptions we know to be false and assumptions we can no longer accept, is somehow "equal" in authority during the 1960s to Kenneth M. Stampp's book of 1956 which is singularly free of those conceptions and assumptions?

Undoubtedly historians of our times fall into transgressions which future generations will be quick to pounce upon. Such a statement can be taken for granted in a discipline which seems to be moving toward a greater awareness of complexity, paradox, ambiguity, and irony; fully aware of the probability of our own errors, we look back across the past half a century with a certain wryness at all the banners of "scientific" history waving from the fortresses of doubtful, false, and malicious values, assumptions, double standards of judgment, sympathies, hostilities, and interpretative myths. Yet it would be unwise to dismiss all explanations as "myths," and the man who insists that all explanations are equal simply ceases to function as a historian. That history bears some resemblance to philosophy, where questions can disappear before they are dismissed and conclusions be abandoned before they are disproved, we can readily admit without surrendering the historical quest. Still, a consciousness of these conditions may both improve the discipline and enable the historian to bury his own dead past. To suggest today as a topic for scholarly inquiry, whether or not slavery was a benevolent institution, would be an implausible notion, a bogus act of inquiry. Thus, we might try to abandon implausible inquiries and to seek plausible ones.

My goal has been to present modern scholarship as it emerged from its own antecedents and precedents; to provide key interpretative essays and major presentations of new evidence from both senior and junior scholars on the grand issues of Civil War and Reconstruction. Like many of my contemporaries I have been much impressed by a sense of *déja vu,* by the interplay of present sensibilities and past events, and by the fact that all histories pre-suppose at least a few very fundamental value judgments. Few professors will agree with the choice of every single essay, but I hope that the collection in general will be useful to American historians. I am indebted to Professor James P. Shenton of Columbia University for a critical reading and helpful suggestions. I also owe a debt of thanks to Professor Jack P. Greene of The Johns-Hopkins University, not for specific aid on the era of Civil War and Reconstruction but for many discussions through the years on the discipline of history—on what historians do, what we think we are doing, what we might do, and what we ought to do. Certainly, my greatest debt is to my wife for giving her time and thought so generously to a great variety of tasks from typing and proofreading to discussions about and criticisms of the chapter introductions.

Croatan, Va.   CHARLES CROWE
September, 1966

Table of Contents

CHAPTER 1

Background to Conflict

The grand drama of sectional conflict between "the North" and "the South" began in the 1770s. The authors of the Declaration of Independence and the Constitution concentrated on the process of creating a new nation but not to the extent of abandoning sectional disputes. Regional hostilities affected the party battles of the Jeffersonian era and gave rise to so fiery a controversy over the admission of Missouri as a slave state in 1819 that Thomas Jefferson was reminded of "a fire bell in the night" tolling the death knell of the Union. If conflict slumbered for a decade, the abolitionists broke that sleep rudely with an uncompromising campaign against "the peculiar institution." The great debate over newly acquired territories in the 1840s fed the springs of sectional hostility, which increased steadily until the outbreak of the Civil War in 1861. Not even military victory and defeat destroyed the pattern of conflict, and at times during the three decades after 1865 Reconstruction yielded more bitter recriminations than the war itself. Sectional disputes, which receded after 1900 without ever completely disappearing, came to the center of the political stage again in our own time under the impact of a new and militant civil rights movement.

The central drama in the long history of dissension was, of course, Civil War and Reconstruction. Two leading theories about the nature of the war, developed in the 1920s and '30s, held that the conflict was either a struggle between the industrial North and the agricultural South or that it was a "needless war" over illusory issues brought on by fanatics and irresponsible politicians. Both interpretations dismissed slavery as a major issue. The scholars argued that "the peculiar institution" came to the political foreground only in the 1850s when it was doomed to extinction in the Old South as an unprofitable institution and could not possibly have survived in the arid wastes of the new Western territories. Yet, the "irresponsible fanatics" of abolition, too impatient to allow slavery to run its "doomed" course, took upon themselves a heavy burden of guilt by provoking war with their "incendiary propaganda." Historians who criticized the abolitionists so sharply tended to deal with the South and slavery in "neutral" or positive terms and to absolve Southerners of any substantial burden of responsibility. Most of the textbooks written between 1900 and 1950 reflected these value judgments and gave the impression that, while slavery had serious faults, the institution did serve as a more or less benevolent "training school" to introduce untutored savages to American culture. The "needless war" school refused to dwell on slavery as a moral issue or as a major issue of any kind; expansion, settlement, and the growth of the American economic system provided the *real* issues in contrast to the relatively inconsequential distractions of slavery and abolition. The general consensus of the textbooks suggested that when war came, the South fought with exceptional valor for home, state, and "a way of life." After the war Southerners, relieved to be rid of the problem of slavery, granted the error of secession and sought to return to their normal status as American citizens—only to be thwarted by the "fanatical and self-seeking acts" of the Radical Republicans who "cynically" sought to sustain their power "at bayonet point" through Negro and carpetbagger domination. The South struggled for "honest government and home rule" until Northerners, tiring of Radical schemes, conflict, and social chaos, agreed to remove federal troops and to allow home rule. With the basic issues satisfactorily settled, both Northerners and Southerners traveled the "road to reunion" and the broken nation once again became whole.

A changed climate of opinion, along with the new research and ideas of the past 20 years, has challenged almost every major point in the traditional explanatory patterns. Recent scholarship has given us a vivid sense of slave oppression and of the extent to which slavery became a pressing moral question in the antebellum era. The ordeal of slavery has been compared by one historian to the experience of survivors in the Nazi death camps; and several scholars have discovered in the slave songs symbols of alienation, terror, and a bitter longing for transcendent freedom. After more than a half century of abuse the abolitionists have at last gained a host of defenders who recognize their honest and complete commitment to democratic and Christian values. The Civil War no longer seems to have been a monolithic struggle of Northern industrial forces and Southern "agrarianism," but rather an incredibly intricate matrix of economic and social forces in which slavery played a large part. Kenneth M. Stampp analyzed the manner in which historians over many decades created a "tragic legend" by describing the Reconstruction struggle for Negro citizenship as "the age of hate," "the hour of national shame," and "the tragic era." Stampp related the old and the new explanatory patterns to the racist ideas which prevailed a generation ago. In the 1890s virtually the entire Western world believed in the biological inferiority and the proper subordination of Asians and Africans to Europeans. In such an intellectual milieu it is not surprising that American historians of Reconstruction often found "Negro domination" offensive and welcomed the return of "home rule" under Southern white men. According to Stampp, romanticizing the Civil War was a harmless pastime compared to the more dangerous legends about Reconstruction which could be used to justify the continuing subordination of Negroes. Yet on closer examination it would appear that Americans have devised a series of unfortunate myths about the Civil War, Reconstruction, slavery, abolition, and national values which have proved equally harmful to the Negro and to American democracy.

In the last two decades scholars have attempted to grapple more closely with the nature of power and its particular uses in the age of Civil War and Reconstruction. It is now obvious that slavery was far more than the legal code and the system of economic exploitation which came to an end in 1865. If this point cannot be granted, then the stormy controversies of Reconstruction and the modern drive for Negro freedom and equality are incomprehensible. After applying modern historical and social science research it becomes clear that no Negro in antebellum America was really free. Even "prejudice" turns out to be a vastly inadequate word to describe the phenomenon of caste domination. As Leon F. Litwack indicated in 1958, the federal government gave support to slavery and caste status in many ways, and most Northerners including a majority of Republicans, believed firmly in white supremacy. American society from the lowest to the highest levels of culture registered hostility toward men on the other side of the color line. Popular jokes, songs, and cartoons spoofed the Negro, and the minstrel show emerged as a standing recognition of the fact that most men regarded any basic claims to human dignity by black men as grotesque and absurd. Although racial prejudice penetrated even the anti-slavery camp, the abolitionists nevertheless waged a determined war against caste as well as against slavery and initiated a drive for freedom and equality which gathered great momentum before collapsing in the 1880s and '90s. At the turn of the century when the scholars began to piece together a detailed history of the Civil War era, caste ideas once again stood in high favor. William A. Dunning approached the study of Reconstruction with fresh assurance from all quarters on the Negro's racial inferiority. In fact, books of "the Dunning School" became a part of the caste controls which helped to reassure Americans about the color line. Thus the historian is himself in history, and his investigations often have political consequences during his own times.

These militant racial animosities seem to cry out for explanation. Scholars have often debated the relationship of prejudice and slavery, and one school of thought ascribed the whole history of racist ideas and practices to the long shadow of slavery. Oscar and Mary Handlin suggested in 1950 that the first Negroes in America lived neither in bondage nor under great bias and were only very gradually enslaved; but nine years later Carl N. Degler made a case for the existence of an early and strong prejudice against black men which became a major cause of enslavement. In 1962 Winthrop D. Jordan insisted that the ambiguous evidence did not establish either position and argued that both slavery and prejudice were interacting "species of a general debasement of the Negro." It is possible to accept Jordan's general line of reasoning and still maintain that the prejudice of the early seventeenth century was only a somewhat stronger form of the hostility toward all "aliens" from Irishmen to Africans. By the end of the American colonial period, however, "prejudice" all through the Western world had undergone a change which would be more sharply underscored by developments of the nineteenth century. Just exactly when one may justifiably speak of "racism" may be open to debate, but certainly a great many eighteenth-century writers spoke with distaste and hostility of black men as subhuman, or as a separate species.

Dante A. Puzzo in 1964 gave the most plausible explanation for racism. There had always been, Puzzo reasoned, categories of insiders and outsiders, generally based on culture and religion after the fashion of Jew and Gentile, Greek and barbarian, Roman citizen and all the others, Christian and pagan. The almost simultaneous emergence of European nationalism and imperialism made possible the fury of modern racism. The Christian Middle Ages had been largely free of color arrogance but the conquest over several centuries of darker skinned peoples by Europeans ultimately produced a rigid association of culture and color which duly noted the superiority of the powerful, "civilized," and victorious white men over all yellow, brown, and black peoples. Newspapers, magazines, textbooks, and popular culture expressed the sense of superiority in a variety of ways. In 1964 Ruth M. Elson explored the major modes of racist expression in a study of nineteenth-century textbooks. A characteristic textbook device was the "Races of Man" chart which used Apollo Belvedere to personify the Western white man, presented the European as the norm and the highest form of humanity, and depicted a descending scale of esthetic degeneracy down to the the presumably ugly and barbarous black man. Harold R. Isaacs in a study of 1963 demonstrated the nature of the psychological havoc wreaked by white supremacist claims and values on nonwhites. Naturally enough, hostile evaluations in the United States of Negroes, Orientals, and Latin Americans reached their greatest intensity simultaneously with the climax of Western imperial power. Modern American equalitarianism is also related to the reemergence of Africa and Asia during the years following World War II, and the anti-colonialist movement had a clear impact on American Negroes and the civil rights movement.

Until recently historians paid scant attention to the power of racial ideologies, appeared unaware of international implications, and were generally prisoners of their own racial and ethnic presuppositions. Now a number of scholars have become more conscious of slavery and caste and of the world context of antagonism and conflict in which they exist. For nearly three centuries Americans fought the Indians and held a position of ascendancy over Negroes, which gave rise to an imperious pride and a heightened sense of power. Yet the American creed helped to muffle and obscure this pride and power in a fashion which created vast areas of incoherence in American history. In 1963 Thomas F. Gossett provided a simplified summary of the main contours of American racism. Hostility toward Indians and Orientals in the West often approached in intensity and virulence the responses of the white Southerner toward his black subordinate. American society has been justly celebrated for its power to gradually accommodate various immigrant groups, but in many cases the myth of accomplishment has been substituted for the reality of conflict and rejection. The threads of violent reaction which run through the national pattern have received little attention in the "liberal" and "consensus" chronicles, which have often failed to distinguish between aspirations and accomplishments and between myth and reality.

Major historical events are complex, ambiguous, and often contain baffling elements which are not easily described in the format of most American textbook explanations. One of the great and tragic ambiguities which has marked the history of the Republic from the beginning is the fact that the nation harboured both the highest expressions of enlightened liberalism and some of the cruelest events in the history of Western imperialism. The Founding Fathers who dreamed of political institutions to protect "life, liberty, and the pursuit of happiness" also contributed to the process of conquest and expansion which threatened the destruction of the American Indians. The Republic was in the beginning a slave power which perpetuated ancient traditions of despotism and simultaneously announced the advent of universal liberty and equality. In the eighteenth century Americans earnestly sought new forms of religious toleration and group accommodation while they also engaged in the bloody and destructive international and domestic slave trade. "The father of our country" who spoke so eloquently of a government without bigotry or persecution was capable of selling a recalcitrant slave "down the river" to the West Indies; and Andrew Jackson, the grand old leader of popular democracy, was not the only President who wished extermination on the Indian peoples. The same imperial techniques which European powers used to conquer, exploit, and often demoralize most of the globe also dominated the history of the New World. The conquest of the American Indians, the bloody and destructive international slave trade, and American slavery were all surely among the great catastrophes in the modern history of humanity. In the American microcosm of European expansion, men developed a great consciousness of "race" which led them into restrictions and denials of the Republican creed.

If human catastrophes and tragic ambiguities have played a large part in the nation's chronicles, so have the great struggles against caste and class, bondage and oppression. The American past has its own moral grandeur in the effort to make from so many divergent human elements one people in a just society. No other theme illuminates so many aspects of American and world history as the struggle for Negro freedom and equality in the era of the Civil War and Reconstruction. The Republic has been strangely marked by both dismal savagery and the brightest and most unexpected turns of event. Who in 1859 could have predicted with confidence the early end of slavery? Who in the fall of 1865 would have forecast the great human efforts which were soon to be channeled into Reconstruction? Who in 1950 could have imagined the Negro freedom movement which came into being only a few years later?

BIBLIOGRAPHY

Books and Articles Referred to in the Chapter Introduction

Kenneth M. Stampp, *The Era of Reconstruction, 1865–1877* (1965).
Leon F. Litwack, *North of Slavery: The Negro in the Free States, 1790–1860* (1961).
William A. Dunning, *Reconstruction, Political and Economic, 1865–1877* (1907).
Oscar and Mary Handlin, "Origins of the Southern Labor System," *William and Mary Quarterly* (1950).

Carl N. Degler, "Slavery and the Genesis of American Race Prejudice," *Comparative Studies in Society and History* (1959); and Chapter I, *Out of Our Past* (1959).

Ruth M. Elson, *Guardians of Traditions: American Schoolbooks of the Nineteenth Century* (1964).

Thomas F. Gossett, *Race: The History of an Idea in America* (1963).

Suggested Readings

Much has been said by American historians about "sectionalism" and the reader may wish to pursue traditional explanations of the topic in standard reference books such as the *Harvard Guide to American History* (1954), edited by Oscar Handlin and others. The best bibliography on the Civil War era is in James G. Randall and David Donald, *The Civil War and Reconstruction* (1961). John R. Alden made a very cogent presentation of early Southern sectionalism in *The First South* (1961); and Robert McColley in *Slavery and Jeffersonian Virginia* (1964) argued that the early South was not very "liberal" but rather a section in which slavery was a dynamic, rapidly expanding institution. Thomas N. Bonner presented a concise summary of the "needless war" interpretations of the Civil War: see "Civil War Historians and the 'Needless War' Doctrine," *Journal of the History of Ideas* (1956).

For other books and articles on the causes of the Civil War see the references in Chapter VII; on Southern sectionalism, Chapter II; on color, race, and status, Chapter IV; on interpretative myths of antislavery, Chapter V; on traditional notions of Reconstruction, Chapter VIII. Winthrop D. Jordan has written several articles which relate to color, status, and the origins of slavery. He traced New England slavery to the example of the West Indies in "The Origins of New England Slavery," *William and Mary Quarterly* (1961); and he compared attitudes toward color in British North America and the British West Indies in "American Chiaroscuro: The Status and Definition of Mulattoes in the British Colonies," *William and Mary Quarterly* (1962). For an interesting document on eighteenth-century Virginia color attitudes, see Emory G. Evans, "A Question of Complexion," *Virginia Magazine of History and Biography* (1963). David B. Davis explored the ways in which general prejudice served American society in "Some Ideological Functions of Prejudice in Ante-Bellum America," *American Quarterly* (1963). For evidence contrary to Puzzo's thesis about the uniqueness of modern racism, see Katherine George, "The Civilized West Looks at Primitive Africa, 1400–1800: a study in Ethnocentrism," *Isis* (1958).

The rigid North American belief in only two color distinctions can be contrasted with the elaborate status hierarchies of Central and South America. See Charles Wagley, *Race and Class in Rural Brazil* (1952); Irene Diggs, "Color in Colonial Spanish America," *Journal of Negro History* (1953); Lloyd Braithwaite, "Social Stratification in Trinidad," *Social and Economic Studies* (1953); Charles Wagley and Marvin Harris, *Minorities in the New World* (1958); and Vera Rubin, "Culture, Politics, and Race Relations: Brown vs. Black," *Social and Economic Studies* (1962). The most adequate survey of American racism is Gossett's book which was listed earlier. The extent of racial hostility in pre-Revolutionary and early national America is not commonly acknowledged, but see Milton Cantor, "The Image of the Negro in Colonial Literature," *New England Quarterly* (1963); John C. Greene, "The American Debate on the Negro's Place in Nature, 1780–1815," *Journal of the History of Ideas* (1954). On antebellum "scientific" racism, see William R. Stanton, *The Leopard's Spots: Scientific Attitudes Toward Race in America, 1815–1859* (1960). On the later "scientific" racism, see John C. Greene, "Biology and Social Theory in the Nineteenth Century," in Marshall Clagett, *Critical Problems in the History of Science* (1959); and George W. Stocking, Jr., "Lamarckianism in American Social Science, 1890–1915," *Journal of the History of Ideas* (1962).

The best book on the contemporary world implications of white supremacy attitudes is Isaacs' book listed earlier. Also see J. Saunders Redding, *The Lonesome Road: The*

Story of the Negro's Part in America (1958) for an idea of the impact of hostile historical stereotypes on modern Negroes. Jacques Voegeli explored the extensive racial hostilities of the old Northwest in "The Northwest and the Race Issue 1861–1862," *Mississippi Valley Historical Review* (1963). For an interesting account of the historian as a participant in history see Eric Dardel, "History and our Times," *Diogenes* (1958), and for a discussion of historical myths see Alfred Stern, "The Irreversibility of History," *Diogenes* (1962). Gerhard Masur analysed the "provincialism" of Western ethnocentric "world" histories in "Distinctive Traits of Western Civilization: Through the Eyes of Western Historians," *American Historical Review* (1961). For a good account of the Lockean-Jeffersonian "prison" of presuppositions in which American scholars have written, see Roland Van Zandt, *The Metaphysical Foundations of American History* (1959). For an interpretation of the preconceptions of Progressive-liberal scholarship, see Charles Crowe, "The Emergence of Progressive History," *Journal of the History of Ideas* (1966). Several scholars have analyzed the more primitive racist distortions in textbooks: see Patrick J. Groff, "The Abolitionist Movement in High School Textbooks," *Journal of Negro Education* (1963); Mark M. Krug, "On Rewriting the Story of Reconstruction in the U.S. History Textbooks," *Journal of Negro History* (1961); and Robert Cruden "James Ford Rhodes and the Negro: A Study in the Problem of Objectivity," *Ohio History* (1962).

For two extremely perceptive recent studies which cast new light on slavery, prejudice, the origins of anti-slavery, etc., see David B. Davis, *The Problem of Slavery in Western Culture* (1966), and Winthrop D. Jordan, *White over Black: Development of American Attitudes toward the Negro* (1967). Two recent articles on the color attitudes of Northerners are worth mentioning; see Eric Foner, "Racial Attitudes of the New York Free Soilers" and "Politics and Prejudice: The Free Soil Party and the Negro, 1849–1852" in *New York History* (1965).

1958

The Federal Government and Racism[*]

LEON F. LITWACK

In the absence of any clear constitutional or judicial directive, the federal government and the individual states separately defined the legal status of antebellum free Negroes. Prior to the Fourteenth and Fifteenth Amendments, each state determined their political and educational rights. In many cases, this resulted in disfranchisement, immigration restrictions, and public school segregation. Various branches of the federal government also confronted problems involving the constitutional rights of free Negroes, an aspect of federal policy that historians have generally neglected.

During the Missouri controversy of 1819–21, Congress exhaustively debated the Negro's legal status but failed to clarify it. Not until 1857, when the Supreme Court settled the Dred Scott case, did the federal government finally resolve the question. By then, Chief Justice Roger B. Taney could turn to federal legislation and "the conduct of the Executive Department" for precedents.

II

Reflecting the popular conception of the United States as a white man's country, early congressional legislation frequently excluded Negroes from federal rights and privileges. In 1790, Congress limited naturalization to "any alien, being a white per-

[*] Leon F. Litwack, "The Federal Government and the Free Negro, 1790-1860," *The Journal of Negro History* Vol. XLIII, No. 4 (October 1958), 261–78.

son"; in 1792, it organized the militia and restricted enrollment to "each and every free, able-bodied white male citizen"; in 1810, it excluded Negroes from carrying the United States mails; in 1820, it authorized the citizens of Washington, D.C., to elect "white" city officials and to adopt a code governing free Negroes and slaves.[1] It repeatedly approved the admission of states whose constitutions severely limited the legal rights of Negroes.[2] On one occasion, however, the House of Representatives momentarily recognized Negro citizenship when it resolved in 1803 "to enquire into the expediency of granting protection to such American seamen citizens of the United States, as are free persons of color."[3]

These measures elicited only minor discussion. But after 1821 legislation affecting the legal position of Negroes frequently involved Congress in lengthy and bitter debates. As abolition sentiment and agitation increased, southern and "Doughface" congressmen seized upon opportunities to show the inconsistency of pronouncements on equality and freedom with the treatment accorded free Negroes in the North. In the famous exchange between Daniel Webster and Robert Hayne, for example, the South Carolina senator defended Negro bondage and charged that slaves were induced to leave their masters and go North where they were treated as outcasts and assigned to "the dark and narrow lanes, and obscure recesses" of the cities. "Sir," he cried, "there does not exist on the face of the earth, a

population so poor, so wretched, so vile, so loathsome, so utterly destitute of all the comforts, conveniences, and decencies of life, as the unfortunate blacks of Philadelphia and Boston."[4] Senator Felix Grundy of Tennessee observed in 1830 that the treatment of Negroes in the free western states proved that "general notions about the liberation of slaves are idle and visionary."[5] In denouncing northern interference with slavery, a Virginia Representative asked, "Do you permit the black man to sit on juries, to enter the learned professions, and to associate with you upon an equal footing, or, to worship by your side in the house of God? It is notorious you permit none of these things. . . . Go home, and emancipate your free negroes. When you do that, we will listen to you with more patience."[6]

III

After 1840, southern congressmen could assert that the federal government itself offered authoritative proof of the benign influence of slavery on Negroes. The Sixth Census of the United States, released in 1841, enumerated for the first time the mentally diseased and defective—or "insane and idiots" as they were then officially described—and contained the startling revelation that their prevalence among free Negroes was about 11 times higher than among slaves. In the southern states, the ratio of insane or idiotic among the Negro population stood at one to every 1,558; in the northern states, it was one to every 144.5.[7] In fact, the frequency of these afflic-

---

[1] *Appendix to the Annals of Congress,* 1 Cong., 2 Sess., 2 Cong., 1 Sess., 1392; 11 Cong., 1 and 2 Sess., 2569; 16 Cong., 1 Sess., 2600–10; 18 Cong., 2 Sess., 91.

[2] Charles H. Wesley, "Negro Suffrage in the Period of Constitution Making 1787–1865," *Journal of Negro History,* XXXII (1947), 154. Vermont (1790), Kentucky (1792), and Tennessee (1796) made no provision in their constitutions excluding Negroes from the suffrage. With Maine (1819), they were the only states which entered the Union, prior to the admission of Nebraska in 1867, which did not restrict the suffrage to whites. Kentucky and Tennessee subsequently enacted such a restriction.

[3] *Journal of the House of Representatives,* 8 Cong., 1 Sess., 224.

[4] *Register of Debates,* 21 Cong., 1 Sess., 47.
[5] *Ibid.,* 215.
[6] *Congressional Globe,* 30 Cong., 1 Sess., 602; 29 Cong., 2 Sess., 349.
[7] Albert Deutsch, "The First U.S. Census of the Insane (1840) and Its Use as Pro-Slavery Propaganda," *Bulletin of the History of Medicine,* XV (1944), 469–82. Aside from the Deutsch article, I am indebted for suggested references to William R. Stanton, *The Leopard's Spots: Science and the American Idea of Equality, 1815–1860* (Ph.D. dissertation, Brown University, 1955),

tions among Negroes decreased from Maine to Louisiana with virtual mathematical precision. For example, it was found that in Maine every 14th Negro was either a lunatic or an idiot; in New Hampshire every 28th; in Massachusetts every 43rd; in Connecticut every 184th; in New York every 257th; and in New Jersey every 297th. This was in sharp contrast with the South where the proportion ranged from one in 1,299 in Virginia and one in 2,477 in South Carolina to one in 4,310 in Louisiana.[8]

Such statistics not only offered obvious moral lessons but gave official credence to popular "scientific" ideas about the peculiar suitability of Negroes for slavery. One northern observer, in a letter to a New York business journal, explained that the prevalence of insanity among local Negroes resulted from "the rigors of a northern winter, which have no influence on the temperament of the whites," but "which affect the cerebral organs of the African race." He admitted, however, that slavery undoubtedly lessened such occurrences.[9] The *Southern Literary Messenger* printed the insanity returns, declared that the sectional disparity resulted from "moral causes, arising from their situation, and in no degree the effect of climate," and concluded "that where slavery has been longest extinguished, the condition of the colored race is worse." It painted a dark picture of what would happen in the event of emancipation. "Let us then suppose," it remarked, "a half of a million of free negroes suddenly turned loose in Virginia, whose propensity it is, constantly to grow more vicious in a state of freedom. . . . Where should we find Penitentiaries for the

thousands of felons? Where, lunatic asylums for the tens of thousands of maniacs? Would it be possible to live in a country where maniacs and felons met the traveller at every cross road?"[10] In Congress, a Mississippian used the census tables to contrast "the happy, well-fed, healthy, and moral condition of the southern slaves, with the condition of the miserable victims and degraded free blacks of the North." Such must be the case, he declared, for "idiocy and lunacy . . . in the lower classes, had been shown by medical men to be invariably caused by vice and missery."[11]

These remarkable statistics eventually found their way into the diplomatic crisis over Texas. The British government, in a communication to Secretary of State Abel Upshur in 1844, had expressed a desire to see slavery abolished in Texas and throughout the world. John C. Calhoun, Upshur's successor, replied that slavery in Texas was the concern of neither the British nor the federal government, but was a local matter. Calhoun nevertheless lectured the English foreign secretary on the relative merits of slavery and freedom for the Negro population, and he used the latest statistics to support his argument. "The census and other authentic documents," he declared, "show that, in all instances in which the States have changed the former relation between the two races, the condition of the African, instead of being improved, has become worse. They have been invariably sunk into vice and pauperism, accompanied by the bodily and mental inflictions incident thereto— deafness, blindness, insanity and idiocy— to a degree without example."[12]

87–100. For the original returns, see *Compilation of the Enumeration of the Inhabitants and Statistics of the United States, as Obtained at the Department of State, from the Returns of the Sixth Census* (Washington, D.C., 1841), 4–104.

8 "Reflections on the Census of 1840," *Southern Literary Messenger*, IX (1843), 341; Edward Jarvis, "Insanity among the Coloured Population of the Free States," *American Journal of the Medical Sciences*, VII (1844), 71–83.

9 "Table of Lunacy in the United States," *Hunt's Merchants' Magazine and Commercial Review*, VIII (1843), 460–61.

10 Reflections on the Census of 1840," 342, 344, 346–47.

11 *Congressional Globe*, 28 Cong., 1 Sess., 239.

12 John C. Calhoun to Lord Richard Pakenham, April 18, 1844, "Proceedings of the Senate and Documents Relative to Texas," *Senate Document*, 28 Cong., 1 Sess., no. 341 (1844), 50–53. This letter also appears in Richard K. Cralle (ed.), *The Works of John C. Calhoun* (6 vols.; New York, 1853–55), V, 333–39. In a subsequent communication, Calhoun denied that he had defended slavery in his previous letter. His intention had simply been to demonstrate "from unquestionable

But Calhoun's "unquestionable sources" were already seriously challenged by Dr. Edward Jarvis, a Massachusetts-born physician and specialist in mental disorders, and a founder of the American Statistical Association.[13] In his first reaction to the returns on insanity and idiocy, Jarvis remarked that slavery must have "a wonderful influence upon the development of moral faculties and the intellectual powers."[14] Upon more careful investigation, however, he found that the errors in these returns were nearly as startling as the statistics themselves, and in January, 1844—four months prior to Calhoun's first letter—he thoroughly refuted the census findings. Contrasting the population returns with the insanity figures, Jarvis found that in numerous northern towns insane Negroes were enumerated where no Negro population existed, and that in others they exceeded the reported number of Negro residents. He concluded that "the sixth census has contributed nothing to the statistical nosology of the free blacks" and was, "in respect to human ailment, a bearer of falsehood to confuse and mislead."[15]

Similar objects were raised throughout the North. A Boston newspaper examined the returns and concluded that "the remarkable prevalence of insanity among the colored people of the free States . . . exists only in the error of the census."[16] The *North American Review* regretted that the census was "vitiated by carelessness in regard to the statistics of insanity."[17] In a letter to the *New York Tribune,* a Negro leader declared, "Freedom has not made us mad; it has strengthened our minds by throwing us upon our own resources, and has bound us to American institutions with a tenacity which nothing but death can overcome."[18]

Demands arose for a correction of the census. Jarvis declared that it was "due to the honour of our country, to medical science, and to truth." The American Statistical Association sent a memorial to Congress enumerating the errors.[19] A group of New York Negroes met "to consider the calumnies recently uttered against the free people of color by John C. Calhoun," and memorialized Congress to reexamine the returns in view of the many glaring inaccuracies.[20]

In Congress, Representative John Quincy Adams of Massachusetts demanded a correction. On February 26, 1844, the House directed the Secretary of State, who was responsible for the conduct of the census, to inform them "whether any gross errors"

---

sources" the depraved condition of Negroes in those states which had abolished the institution. Calhoun to Pakenham, April 27, 1844, "Proceedings of the Senate and Documents Relative to Texas," 65–67, and Cralle (ed.), *Works,* V, 343–47.

[13] Jarvis went to Louisville, Kentucky to practice in 1837 but his antipathy to slavery prompted his return to Massachusetts six years later. He became a leading statistician, served for 31 years as president of the American Statistical Association, and helped to prepare the census of 1850, 1860, and 1870. For further biographical information, see William R. Leonard, "Edward Jarvis," in Allen Johnson and Dumas Malone (eds.), *Dictionary of American Biography* (22 vols.; New York, 1928–44), IX, 621–22, and Robert W. Wood, *Memorial of Edward Jarvis, M.D.* (Boston, 1885).

[14] Edward Jarvis, 'Statistics of Insanity in the United States," *Boston Medical and Surgical Journal,* XXVII (1842), 116–21, as quoted in Stanton, *The Leopard's Spots,* 87–88. Neither Deutsch nor Wood, in their studies of Jarvis' efforts to correct the census, mention his first reaction.

[15] For example, in Maine where every fourteenth Negro was supposedly insane, the census listed six such Negroes in Scarsboro but no Negro population, and credited Dresden with twice as many insane Negroes as Negro residents. In

Worcester, Massachusetts, the census found 133 insane out of a Negro population of 161. Actually, this former number represented the white patients in the state hospital for the insane at Worcester. *Compilation of the Enumeration of the Inhabitants and Statistics of the United States,* 5, 7, 9, 11; Deutsch, "The First U.S. Census of the Insane," 475–76.

[16] Boston *Daily Advertiser and Patriot,* as reprinted in *The Liberator,* August 18, 1843.

[17] "Review of Edward Jarvis, 'What Shall We Do With The Insane,' *North American Review,* LVI (1843), 172–73n.

[18] James McCune Smith to the Editor of the New York *Tribune,* January 29, 1844, as reprinted in *The Liberator,* February 23, 1844.

[19] "Errors in Sixth Census," *House Report,* 28 Cong., 1 Sess., no. 580 (1844), 1–9.

[20] *The Liberator,* May 10, 31, 1844. See also Herbert Aptheker (ed.), *A Documentary History of the Negro People in the United States* (New York, 1951), 238–43.

were discovered, but Calhoun evaded the inquiry by finding a technical error in the resolution.[21] Adams then called on Calhoun and was told "that where there were so many errors they balanced one another, and led to the same conclusion as if they were all correct."[22] In June the House committee, to which the memorial of the American Statistical Association had been referred, reported that they "have no reason to doubt the correctness of the statements in the memorial, and feel that they destroy the utility of the printed census, so far as the subjects referred to are concerned and render completely nugatory any conclusions which may be based upon them." The committee hoped that no such errors would appear in the next census.[23]

But Calhoun remained adamant. In response to a new House resolution, he stated that the "gross and glaring errors" imputed by the memorialists had been given a "full and thorough examination," and "the result would seem fully to sustain the correctness of the census." While errors could be expected in any such undertaking, they did not, he declared, alter the conclusion that a far greater prevalence of the diseases of insanity, blindness, deafness, and dumbness existed among northern Negroes. This fact, Calhoun asserted, "stands unimpeachable."[24]

In the absence of any revision, the census of 1840 continued to serve the purposes of anti-abolition orators and editors. In fact, a Georgia congressman reportedly admitted to Jarvis that the census contained numerous errors but he added, "It is too good a thing for our politicians to give up. They had prepared speeches based on it, which they could not afford to lose."[25]

IV

The congressional debates on slavery expansion in the 1840s and 1850s had little significance for the political or economic progress of northern Negroes. Most proponents of slavery restriction tried to make it clear that their concern was not for the plight of the Negro but for the welfare of the white race. When Representative David Wilmot of Pennsylvania introduced his proviso to exclude slavery from the territories acquired from Mexico, he carefully explained that he did not propose to interfere with southern institutions, and that he possessed "no squeamish sensitiveness upon the subject of slavery, no morbid sympathy for the slave." What he wanted were free states for free white men. "I plead the cause and the rights of white freemen," he declared in 1847. "I would preserve to free white labor a fair country, a rich inheritance, where the sons of toil, of my own race and own color, can live without the disgrace which association with negro slavery brings upon free labor."[26] The following year, a New York representative proposed that Congress "inquire into the expediency of setting apart a portion of the public lands for the exclusive use and possession of free black persons."[27]

In order to reserve the new territories for whites, Negroes would have to be barred from the benefits of federal land policy. The Senate attempted this in 1841 when it voted to confine the privileges of the new preemption law to whites. Augustus Porter of Michigan, the lone dissenter, observed that no previous act had embodied such a clause and that it conflicted with the right to buy and dispose of property. While Negroes enjoyed no political rights in his state, they were entitled, he declared, to all the civil rights conferred by the Constitution, including that of holding property. By "general

21 Charles F. Adams (ed.), *Memoirs of John Quincy Adams, Comprising Portions of His Diary from 1795-1848* (12 vols.; Philadelphia, 1875), XII, 22-23.

22 *Ibid.*, 29.

23 "Errors in Sixth Census," 1. A Senate committee reached identical conclusions. See *Senate Document*, 28 Cong., 1 Sess., no. 146 (1845), 1-2.

24 *Niles' National Register*, June 7, 1845.

25 Wood, *Memorial of Edward Jarvis*, quoted in Deutsch, "The First U.S. Census of the Insane," 478.

26 *Appendix to the Congressional Globe*, 29 Cong., 2 Sess., 317.

27 *Congressional Globe*, 30 Cong., 1 Sess., 778.

consent," the Senate deleted the restriction from the bill before its final passage.[28] But it still required an opinion from the Attorney General's office to qualify Negroes for the benefits of the act. In the 1850s Congress frequently tacked amendments onto land and homestead bills excluding Negroes from their provisions, because granting them land would encourage and prolong "their common residence in this Confederacy" with white people.[29]

The Dred Scott decision dealt a severe blow to the Negro's preemption rights. The Secretary of the Interior had previously written a New York Negro that "there is nothing in the laws of the United States which would prevent you, as a Freeman of African descent, from settling upon land in the Territory of Minnesota, and acquiring a right of pre-emption." Soon after the Supreme Court ruling, however, the commissioner of the General Land Office announced that since Negroes were not citizens, they could not qualify for preemption benefits.[30]

V

As early as 1810 the federal government excluded Negroes from the postal service. Postmaster General Gideon Granger, in "a private representation" to Senator James Jackson of Georgia, declared in 1802 that objections existed to Negroes handling the mail, "of a nature too delicate to engraft into a report which may become public, yet too important to be omitted or passed over without full consideration." Granger feared that they would use the postal service to coordinate insurrectionary activities, particu-

larly in the southern states. "Every thing which tends to increase their knowledge of natural rights," he warned, "of men and things, or that affords them an opportunity of associating, acquiring, and communicating sentiments . . . and of establishing a chain or line of intelligence" must excite alarm. As post riders, Negroes would mix with other people, acquire information, and "learn that a man's rights do not depend on his color."[31] Congress responded in 1810 by providing "that no other than a free white person shall be employed in conveying the mail."[32] Postmaster General John McLean instructed his deputies in 1828 to adhere strictly to this regulation. If Negro labor was required "to lift the mail from the stage into the postoffice," it must be "performed in the presence and under the immediate direction of the white person who has it in custody."[33]

Not until 1862 did Congress attempt to abrogate the restriction. In that year the Senate passed Charles Sumner's bill to revoke the clause, and thereby caused the Boston *Journal* to remark that it was the first time, within their recollection, "that any bill having the negro in it, directly or indirectly, has been passed by the Senate without debate." But the House tabled the bill after Schuyler Colfax, Republican chairman of the post office committee, objected to it on the grounds that no public demand exised for its repeal, that it would qualify Negroes and Indians as mail contractors and even officers in the department, and that the Postmaster General had not recom-

[28] *Ibid.*, 26 Cong., 2 Sess., 77, 114; *Appendix*, 27.

[29] For examples, see *Congressional Globe*, 31 Cong., 1 Sess., 33 Cong., 1 Sess., 1057–58, 1071–73. Frederick Douglass and Rep. Gerrit Smith strongly condemned the "white" restriction in the Homestead Bill of 1854. *Frederick Douglass' Paper*, March 17, 1854.

[30] New York *Daily Times*, August 21, 1857; *Annual Reports of the American Anti-Slavery Society, . . . for the years ending May 1, 1857, and May 1, 1858* (New York, 1859), 130.

[31] *American State Papers. Documents, Legislative and Executive, of the Congresses of the United States* . . . (38 vols., Washington, D.C., 1832–61), Class VII: Post Office, 27.

[32] The restriction was reenacted without change in 1825. *Appendix to the Annals of Congress*, 11 Cong., 1 and 2 Sess., 2569; 18 Cong., 2 Sess., 91.

[33] William Jay, "A View of the Action of the Federal Government in Behalf of Slavery," in *Miscellaneous Writings on Slavery* (Boston, 1853), 233; William C. Nell, *The Colored Patriots of the American Revolution, with Sketches of Several Distinguished Colored Persons: To which is added a Brief Survey of the Condition and Prospects of Colored Americans* (Boston, 1855), 312.

mended passage and did not regard it in "the best interests of the Department."[34]

VI

In citing "the conduct of the Executive Department" as a precedent for his opinion, Chief Justice Taney referred specifically to the refusal of the State Department to grant passports to Negroes. Actually, Negroes secured passports in several cases as late as 1854.[35] However, the Secretary of State rejected the application of a Philadelphia Negro in 1839 on the grounds that the newly revised Pennsylvania Constitution did not recognize Negroes as citizens.[36] In 1847 Secretary of State James Buchanan clarified this policy when he declared that it was customary to grant free Negroes "not a passport, in the ordinary form, recognizing them as citizens, but a certificate suited to the nature of the case."[37] His successor, John M. Clayton, stated two years later that passports "are not granted by this department to persons of color, and that protections are only given to them when they are in the service of diplomatic agents, etc., of the United States going abroad."[38] This prompted one observer to write that "the colored man is not only insulted and wronged at home, and in half the Union is

utterly defenceless, but if he would leave this cruel country he must go abroad as an outlaw."[39] Severely censured by several newspapers, Clayton justified his action with the assertion that this has been the "settled regulation of the Department."[40]

In the late 1840s and in the 1850s, numerous Negro leaders sought passports for England where they planned to lecture and raise money for the abolitionist cause, but in most cases their applications were rejected. The hardening of State Department policy was evident in an official letter accompanying the refusal of passports to 11 northern Negroes in 1856. It declared that the question of Negro citizenship "has repeatedly arisen in the administration of both the national and State governments," and it cited the opinion of Attorney General William Wirt in 1821 that free Negroes were not citizens under the Constitution. According to this interpretation, the letter continued, free Negroes "cannot be regarded, when beyond the jurisdiction of the Government, as entitled to the full rights of citizens." The department was willing, however, to grant certificates "that they were born in the United States, are free, and that the government thereof would regard it to be its duty to protect them if wronged by a foreign government, while within its jurisdiction for a legal and proper purpose."[41]

Following the Dred Scott decision, the State Department relied on Taney's ruling as proper and sufficient grounds for rejecting Negro applicants. But Secretary of State Lewis Cass went so far as to assert that "a passport being a certificate of citizenship, has never since the foundation of

[34] *Congressional Globe*, 37 Cong., 2 Sess., 1260, 1390, 1626, 2231–32, 2262–63; Charles Sumner, *The Works of Charles Sumner* (15 vols.; Boston, 1870–83), VI, 385–88.

[35] For example, the State Department issued passports to Robert Purvis in 1834; Peter Williams in 1836; William Wells Brown in 1849; and John Remond in 1854. Arnold Buffum to Roberts Vaux, May 16, 1834, Historical Society of Pennsylvania, Philadelphia; *The Liberator*, April 16, 1858.

[36] Sarah M. Grimke to Elizabeth Pease, August 25, 1839, in Gilbert H. Barnes and Dwight L. Dumond (eds.), *Letters of Theodore Dwight Weld, Angelina Grimke Weld and Sarah Grimke, 1822–1844* (2 vols.; New York, 1934), II, 792–93. The Pennsylvania Constitutional Convention of 1837–38 restricted the suffrage to white males.

[37] James Buchanan to N. H. Davis, March 8, 1847, in John Bassett Moore (ed.), *The Works of James Buchanan* (12 vols.; Philadelphia, 1908–11), VII, 236.

[38] *The North Star*, July 20, August 24, 1849. See also *The Non-Slaveholder*, IV (1849), 191, and *Eighteenth Annual Report, presented to the Massachusetts Anti-Slavery Society, ... January 23, 1850* (Boston, 1850), 44–45.

[39] *The Non-Slaveholder*, IV (1849), 191.

[40] John M. Clayton to the Editor of the Salem *Register*, in The [10th] *Annual Report of the American and Foreign Anti-Slavery Society, presented at New York May 7, 1850, ...* (New York, 1850), 128–29.

[41] *The Liberator*, November 28, 1856; Edward Bates to Salmon P. Chase, November 29, 1862, in *Official Opinions of the Attorneys General of the United States . . .* (38 vols., Washington, D.C., 1791–1948), X, 404. The letter, written by Assistant Secretary J. A. Thomas, conveyed the opinion of Secretary of State William L. Marcy.

the Government, been granted to persons of color."[42] Several newspapers thereupon enumerated for Cass's edification those passports that had been granted to free Negroes.[43] "If the statement is a blunder on the part of General Cass, it betrays reprehensible ignorance," a Cleveland newspaper declared; "if a deliberate falsification, it is deserving of the severest censure."[44] One rejected Negro applicant remarked that his only hope now was "to go to some foreign country, and through the assistance of friends, claim its protection, or else, through their assistance, get permission to travel as an American outlaw!"[45] The Massachusetts Legislature decided that since the Dred Scott decision "virtually denationalized" the state's Negro citizens, it would authorize its own secretary of state to grant passports to any citizen of the Commonwealth "whatever his color may be."[46] In 1861, the new secretary, William H. Seward, reversed State Department policy.

VII

The opinions of the attorneys general demonstrated that differences did exist in the federal interpretation of Negro citizenship. In 1821, William Wirt ruled that free Negroes in Virginia were not citizens of the United States and, therefore, could not command vessels according to the acts regulating the foreign and coasting trade. However, since Wirt defined "citizens of the United States" as "those only who enjoyed the full and equal privileges of white citizens in the State of their residence," he implied that Negroes could be so considered.[47] Two years later, Wirt ruled that Negro soldiers were entitled to the bounty lands promised them for service in the War of 1812, although he felt "that it was not the

intention of Congress to incorporate negroes and people of color with the army any more than with the militia of the United States."[48]

In 1822, the South Carolina legislature passed the first in a series of southern acts which provided for the imprisonment of free Negro seamen while their vessels remained in port. After formal protests by the British government, Wirt advised that the acts violated "the Constitution, treaties, and laws of the United States" and were "incompatible with the rights of all nations in amity with the United States."[49] Seven years later, however, Attorney General John Berrien found the acts to be a lawful exercise of state police powers.[50] Upon the receipt of another British protest in 1831, Secretary of State Edward Livingston asked the new attorney general, Roger Taney, for his opinion. Taney's reply, although never completed for publication, clearly anticipated his decision 25 years later as chief justice. "The African race in the United States even when free," he wrote, "are everywhere a degraded class, and exercise no political influence. The privileges they are allowed to enjoy, are accorded to them as a matter of kindness and benevolence rather than of right. . . . And where they are nominally admitted by the law to the privileges of citizenship, they have no effectual power to defend them, and are permitted to be citizens by the sufferance of the white population and hold whatever rights they enjoy at their mercy." Negroes were "a separate and degraded people to whom the sovereignty of each state might accord or withhold such privileges as they deemed proper." Consequently, the framers of the Constitution had not regarded them as citizens and they "were evidently

---

[42] New York Times, April 12, 1858.
[43] "The Oppression of the Buchanan Administration Towards Colored Citizens," Boston Daily Bee, reprinted in The Liberator, April 16, 1858.
[44] Cleveland Leader, April 20, 1858.
[45] Ibid., May 4, 1858.
[46] The Liberator, April 24, 1857.
[47] Official Opinions, I, 506–9.

[48] Ibid., I, 602–3. The acts of Congress under which these Negro troops were raised called for "able-bodied, effective" men (1811) and "free, effective, able-bodied men" (1814). Wirt decided that Negroes could satisfy either of these requirements and therefore must receive the promised bounties.
[49] Ibid., I, 659–61.
[50] Ibid., II, 426–42.

not supposed to be included by the term *citizens*."[51]

Attorney General Hugh Legare decided in 1843 that free Negroes were neither aliens nor citizens but occupied an intermediate position. When asked whether they were entitled to the benefits of the new preemption act, Legare replied that they had previously been admitted to the benefits of these laws and he saw nothing in the new act "that necessarily excludes them." The "plain meaning" of the act was to exclude aliens and to grant preemption rights "to all denizens"; any foreigner who filed his intention of citizenship could thus qualify for its benefits. "Now, free people of color are not aliens," Legare advised, "they enjoy universally . . . the rights of denizens. . . . How far a political *status* may be acquired is a different question, but his *civil* status is that of a complete denizenship."[52] However, this newly discovered legal position for the free Negro did not meet the approval of a later attorney general, Caleb Cushing. He charged in 1856 that Legare "had . . . been carried away in argument by a generous disposition to protect in the given case the claim of a free African, without admitting him to be a citizen of the United States." A free Negro could be entitled to preemption rights, Cushing asserted, only if Wirt's opinion was first overruled, and he had no intention of doing this.[53]

The constitutional rights of free Negroes were finally recognized during the Civil War. Attorney General Edward Bates advised in 1862 that citizenship was "*not* dependent nor coexistent" with color, race, "the degradation of a people," or the legal right to vote and hold office. "Free men of color, if born in the United States, are citizens of the United States."[54] Six years later, the Fourteenth Amendment confirmed this opinion.

---

[51] Carl Brent Swisher, *Roger B. Taney* (New York, 1935), 154.
[52] *Official Opinions*, IV, 147–48.
[53] *Ibid.*, VII, 751–73.
[54] *Ibid.*, X, 382–413.

VIII

If any confusion existed in the federal government prior to 1857 on the constitutional rights of Negroes, it was finally dispelled by the decision of the Supreme Court in *Dred Scott* v. *Sanford*. The Missouri Compromise and Negro citizenship were both found to be unconstitutional.

Chief Justice Taney constructed his opinion on a review of the historical status of the Negro population, and he placed particular emphasis on their legal position at the time of the Constitutional Convention of 1787. For more than a century prior to that convention, Taney declared, Negroes had "been regarded as beings of an inferior order, and altogether unfit to associate with the white race, either in social or political relations; and so far inferior, that they had no rights which the white man was bound to respect." Colonial legislation demonstrated the extent of public antipathy toward Negroes. Although the northern states abolished slavery, this resulted not from "any change of opinion in relation to this race" but from its unprofitability in the northern climate and economy. That no moral revolution had occurred, Taney continued, was nowhere more clearly demonstrated than in the laws passed by several states to control free Negroes.[55] "It cannot be supposed," he stated, that the framers of the Constitution intended to grant Negroes "rights, and privileges, and rank, in the new political body throughout the Union, which every one of them denied within the limits of its own dominion." Consequently, Negroes were "not intended to be included, and formed no part of the people who framed and adopted" the Declaration of Independence and the Constitution.[56]

---

[55] Taney cited as examples the Massachusetts and Rhode Island laws forbidding interracial marriages (1786 and 1822); the Connecticut law prohibiting the establishment of any school for the instruction of Negroes not inhabitants of the state (1833), and the decision of a Connecticut court upholding that law (1834); and the New Hampshire act barring Negroes from the militia (1815).
[56] *Dred Scott* v. *Sanford*, 19 Howard 407–10, 412–16.

State and federal citizenship must not be confused, Taney asserted, for while a state can legally naturalize its own inhabitants, it has no power to secure to them the rights and privileges of citizens in other states or in the United States. Since Congress alone possesses the right to establish a uniform rule of naturalization, states are prohibited from introducing any new members "into the political community created by the Constitution," and "for the same reason" they "cannot introduce any person, or description of persons, who were not intended to be embraced in this new political family." That this applied to Negroes was abundantly clear to the chief justice. Had not Congress restricted naturalization to "free white persons"? Subsequent legislation and the practices of the Executive Department, Taney believed, confirmed his conclusion that Negroes "are not included, and were not intended to be included, under the word 'citizens' in the Constitution, and can therefore claim none of the rights and privileges which that instrument provides for and secures to citizens of the United States."[57]

Two justices joined Taney in his opinion on Negro citizenship, four avoided the issue, and two others—John McLean and Benjamin R. Curtis—wrote vigorous dissents. Curtis contended that the right to confer citizenship rested with the states and that the federal government could only specify the manner in which an alien's disabilities might be removed. Free native-born citizens of each state were thus citizens of the United States. Curtis denied that the Constitution was a white man's document. At the time of the ratification of the Articles of Confederation, he pointed out, free Negroes were not only citizens in five states—New Hampshire, Massachu-

setts, New York, New Jersey, and North Carolina—but actually exercised the right of suffrage on equal terms with whites. The framers of the Articles must have known this, Curtis declared, for they rejected a move by South Carolina to restrict the privileges and immunities clause to white persons. Negroes, he concluded, "were not only included in the body of 'the people of the United States,' by whom the Constitution was ordained and established, but in at least five of the States they had the power to act, and doubtless did act, by their suffrages, upon the question of its adoption." They were thus clearly entitled to its privileges and immunities.[58]

While many northern political leaders and newspaper editors assailed Taney's decision, they indicated more concern over its repudiation of that sacred sectional compact, the Missouri Compromise, than over the constitutional rights of Negroes. However, the Negro community bitterly condemned the ruling. One protest meeting called it "a palpably vain, arrogant assumption, unsustained by history, justice, reason or common sense."[59] Frederick Douglass declared that "the National Conscience" would not be silenced "by such an open, glaring, and scandalous tissue of lies as that decision is, and has been, over and over, shown to be."[60] But Robert Purvis, a colored abolitionist, warned his people not to comfort themselves with the thought that this decision was unconstitutional. It was, he declared, "in perfect keeping with the treatment of the colored people by the American Government from the beginning to this day."[61] This sentiment was shared by other Negro leaders who, while condemning the decision, expressed no great surprise. After all, one Negro protest declared, it was but "final confirmation of

---

[57] *Ibid.*, 404–6. Federal practices and legislation cited by Taney included the militia law of 1792; an act of 1813 prohibiting employment on vessels to "any person or persons except citizens of the United States, or persons of color, natives of the United States"; the Washington, D.C., administrative act of 1820; the opinions of Attorneys General Wirt and Cushing; and the passport policy of the State Department.

[58] *Ibid.*, 572–82.

[59] *The Liberator*, July 9, 1858. Meeting of New Bedford Negroes on June 16, 1858.

[60] "The Dred Scott Decision, Speech delivered before the American Anti-Slavery Society, New York, May 11, 1857," reprinted in Philip S. Foner (ed.), *The Life and Writings of Frederick Douglass* (4 vols.; New York, 1950–55), II, 411.

[61] *The Liberator*, April 10, 1857.

the already well known fact that under the Constitution and Government of the United States, the colored people are noth-

ing, and can be nothing but an alien, disfranchised and degraded class."[62]

[62] *Ibid.*

1962

Did Slavery Create Prejudice?*

WINTHROP D. JORDAN

Thanks to John Smith we know that Negroes first came to the British continental colonies in 1619.[1] What we do not know is exactly when Negroes were first enslaved there. This question has been debated by historians for the past 70 years, the critical point being whether Negroes were enslaved almost from their first importation or whether they were at first simply servants and only later reduced to the status of slaves. The long duration and vigor of the controversy suggest that more than a simple question of dating has been involved. In fact certain current tensions in American society have complicated the historical problem and greatly heightened its significance. Dating the origins of slavery has taken on a striking modern relevance.

During the nineteenth century historians assumed almost universally that the first Negroes came to Virginia as slaves. So close was their acquaintance with the prob-

lem of racial slavery that it did not occur to them that Negroes could ever have been anything but slaves. Philip A. Bruce, the first man to probe with some thoroughness into the early years of American slavery, adopted this view in 1896, although he emphasized that the original difference in treatment between white servants and Negroes was merely that Negroes served for life. Just six years later, however, came a challenge from a younger, professionally trained historian, James C. Ballagh. His *A History of Slavery in Virginia* appeared in the *Johns Hopkins University Studies in Historical and Political Science,* an aptly named series which was to usher in the new era of scholarly detachment in the writing of institutional history. Ballagh offered a new and different interpretation; he took the position that the first Negroes served merely as servants and that enslavement did not begin until around 1660, when statutes bearing on slavery were passed for the first time.[2]

There has since been agreement on dating the statutory establishment of slavery, and differences of opinion have centered

* Winthrop D. Jordan, "Modern Tensions and the Origins of American Slavery," *Journal of Southern History*, XXVIII (May 1962), 18–30. Copyright 1962 by the Southern Historical Association. Reprinted by permission of the Managing Editor.

[1] "About the last of August came in a dutch man of warre that sold us twenty Negars." Smith was quoting John Rolfe's account. Edward Arber and A. G. Bradley (eds.), *Travels and Works of Captain John Smith . . .* (2 vols.; Edinburgh, 1910), II, 541.

[2] Philip A. Bruce, *Economic History of Virginia in the Seventeenth Century* (2 vols.; New York, 1896), II, 57–130; James C. Ballagh, *A History of Slavery in Virginia* (Baltimore, 1902), 28–35.

on when enslavement began in actual practice. Fortunately there has also been general agreement on slavery's distinguishing characteristics: service for life and inheritance of like obligation by any offspring. Writing on the free Negro in Virginia for the Johns Hopkins series, John H. Russell in 1913 tackled the central question and showed that some Negroes were indeed servants but concluded that "between 1640 and 1660 slavery was fast becoming an established fact. In this twenty years the colored population was divided, part being servants and part being slaves, and some who were servants defended themselves with increasing difficulty from the encroachments of slavery."[3] Ulrich B. Phillips, though little interested in the matter, in 1918 accepted Russell's conclusion of early servitude and transition toward slavery after 1640. Helen T. Catterall took much the same position in 1926. On the other hand, in 1921 James M. Wright, discussing the free Negro in Maryland, implied that Negroes were slaves almost from the beginning, and in 1940 Susie M. Ames reviewed several cases in Virginia which seemed to indicate that genuine slavery had existed well before Ballagh's date of 1660.[4]

All this was a very small academic gale, well insulated from the outside world. Yet despite disagreement on dating enslavement, the earlier writers—Bruce, Ballagh, and Russell—shared a common assumption which, though at the time seemingly irrelevant to the main question, has since proved of considerable importance. They assumed that prejudice against the Negro was natural and almost innate in the white man. It would be surprising if they had felt otherwise in this period of segregation statutes, overseas imperialism, immigration restriction, and full-throated Anglo-Saxonism. By the 1920s, however, with the easing of these tensions, the assumption of natural prejudice was dropped unnoticed. Yet only one historian explicitly contradicted that assumption: Ulrich Phillips of Georgia, impressed with the geniality of both slavery and twentieth-century race relations, found no natural prejudice in the white man and expressed his "conviction that Southern racial asperities are mainly superficial, and that the two great elements are fundamentally in accord.[5]

Only when tensions over race relations intensified once more did the older assumption of natural prejudice crop up again. After World War II American Negroes found themselves beneficiaries of New Deal politics and reforms, wartime need for manpower, worldwide repulsion at racist excesses in Nazi Germany, and growingly successful colored anti-colonialism. With new militancy Negroes mounted an attack on the citadel of separate but equal, and soon it became clear that America was in for a period of self-conscious reappraisal of its racial arrangements. Writing in this period of heightened tension (1949) a practiced and careful scholar, Wesley F. Craven, raised the old question of the Negro's original status, suggesting that Negroes had been enslaved at an early date. Craven also cautiously resuscitated the idea that white men may have had natural distaste for the Negro, an idea which fitted neatly with the suggestion of early enslavement. Original antipathy would mean rapid debasement.[6]

---

[3] John H. Russell, *The Free Negro in Virginia, 1619–1865* (Baltimore, 1913), 29.

[4] *Ibid.*, 23–39; Ulrich B. Phillips, *American Negro Slavery* (New York, 1918), 75–77, and *Life and Labor in the Old South* (Boston, 1929), 170; Helen T. Catterall (ed.), *Judicial Cases Concerning American Slavery and the Negro* (5 vols.; Washington, 1926–37), I, 54–55, 57–63; James M. Wright, *The Free Negro in Maryland, 1634–1860* (New York, 1921), 21–23; Susie M. Ames, *Studies of the Virginia Eastern Shore in the Seventeenth Century* (Richmond, 1940), 100–6. See also T. R. Davis, "Negro Servitude in the United States," *Journal of Negro History*, VIII (July, 1923), 247–83, and Edgar T. Thompson, "The Natural History of Agricultural Labor in the South" in David K. Jackson (ed.), *American Studies in Honor of William Kenneth Boyd* (Durham, N.C., 1940), 127–46.

[5] Phillips, *American Negro Slavery*, viii.

[6] Wesley F. Craven, *The Southern Colonies in the Seventeenth Century, 1607–1689* (Baton Rouge, 1949), 217–19, 402–3.

In the next year (1950) came a sophisticated counterstatement, which contradicted both Craven's dating and implicitly any suggestion of early prejudice. Oscar and Mary F. Handlin in "Origins of the Southern Labor System" offered a case for late enslavement, with servitude as the status of Negroes before about 1660. Originally the status of both Negroes and white servants was far short of freedom, the Handlins maintained, but Negroes failed to benefit from increased freedom for servants in mid-century and became less free rather than more.[7] Embedded in this description of diverging status were broader implications: Late and gradual enslavement undercut the possibility of natural, deep-seated antipathy toward Negroes. On the contrary, if whites and Negroes could share the same status of half freedom for 40 years in the seventeenth century, why could they not share full freedom in the twentieth?

The same implications were rendered more explicit by Kenneth M. Stampp in a major reassessment of Southern slavery published two years after the Supreme Court's 1954 school decision. Reading physiology with the eye of faith, Stampp frankly stated his assumption "that innately Negroes *are*, after all, only white men with black skins, nothing more, nothing less."[8] Closely following the Handlins' article on the origins of slavery itself, he almost directly denied any pattern of early and inherent racial antipathy: ". . . Negro and white servants of the seventeenth century seemed to be remarkably unconcerned about their visible physical differences." As for "the trend toward special treatment" of the Negro, "physical and cultural differences provided handy excuses to justify it."[9] Distaste for the Negro, then, was in the beginning scarcely more than an appurtenance of slavery.

These views squared nicely with the hopes of those even more directly concerned with the problem of contemporary race relations, sociologists and social psychologists. Liberal on the race question almost to a man, they tended to see slavery as the initial cause of the Negro's current degradation. The modern Negro was the unhappy victim of long association with base status. Sociologists, though uninterested in tired questions of historical evidence, could not easily assume a natural prejudice in the white man as the cause of slavery. Natural or innate prejudice would not only violate their basic assumptions concerning the dominance of culture but would undermine the power of their new Baconian science. For if prejudice was natural there would be little one could do to wipe it out. Prejudice must have followed enslavement, not vice versa, else any liberal program of action would be badly compromised. One prominent social scientist suggested in a UNESCO pamphlet that racial prejudice in the United States commenced with the cotton gin![10]

Just how closely the question of dating had become tied to the practical matter of action against racial prejudice was made apparent by the suggestions of still another historian. Carl N. Degler grappled with the dating problem in an article frankly entitled "Slavery and the Genesis of American Race Prejudice."[11] The article appeared in 1959, a time when Southern

[7] *William and Mary Quarterly*, s. 3, VII (April, 1950), 199–222.

[8] Kenneth M. Stampp, *The Peculiar Institution: Slavery in the Ante-Bellum South* (New York, 1956), vii–viii, 3–33.

[9] *Ibid.*, 21–22.

[10] Arnold Rose, "The Roots of Prejudice" in UNESCO, *The Race Question in Modern Science* (New York, 1956), 224. For examples of the more general view see Frederick G. Detweiler, "The Rise of Modern Race Antagonisms," *American Journal of Sociology*, XXXVII (March, 1932), 743; M. F. Ashley Montagu, *Man's Most Dangerous Myth: The Fallacy of Race* (New York, 1945), 10–11, 19–20; Gunnar Myrdal, *An American Dilemma: The Negro Problem and Modern Democracy* (New York, 1944), 83–89, 97; Paul Kecskemeti, "The Psychological Theory of Prejudice: Does it Underrate the Role of Social History?" *Commentary*, XVII (October, 1954), 364–66.

[11] *Comparative Studies in Society and History*, II (October, 1959), 49–66. See also Degler, *Out of Our Past: The Forces that Shaped Modern America* (New York, 1959), 26–39.

resistance to school desegregation seemed more adamant than ever and the North's hands none too clean, a period of discouragement for those hoping to end racial discrimination. Prejudice against the Negro now appeared firm and deep-seated, less easily eradicated than had been supposed in, say, 1954. It was Degler's view that enslavement began early, as a result of white settlers' prejudice or antipathy toward the first Negroes. Thus not only were the sociologists contradicted but the dating problem was now overtly and consciously tied to the broader question of whether slavery caused prejudice or prejudice caused slavery. A new self-consciousness over the American racial dilemma had snatched an arid historical controversy from the hands of an unsuspecting earlier generation and had tossed it into the arena of current debate.

Ironically there might have been no historical controversy at all if every historian dealing with the subject had exercised greater care with facts and greater restraint in interpretation. Too often the debate entered the realm of inference and assumption. For the crucial early years after 1619 there is simply not enough evidence to indicate with any certainty whether Negroes were treated like white servants or not. No historian has found anything resembling proof one way or the other. The first Negroes were sold to the English settlers, yet so were other Englishmen. It can be said, however, that Negroes were set apart from white men by the word *Negroes*, and a distinct name is not attached to a group unless it is seen as different. The earliest Virginia census reports plainly distinguished Negroes from white men, sometimes giving Negroes no personal name; and in 1629 every commander of the several plantations was ordered to "take a generall muster of all the inhabitants men woemen and Children as well *Englishe* as Negroes."[12] Dif-

ference, however, might or might not involve inferiority.

The first evidence as to the actual status of Negroes does not appear until about 1640. Then it becomes clear that *some* Negroes were serving for life and some children inheriting the same obligation. Here it is necessary to suggest with some candor that the Handlins' statement to the contrary rests on unsatisfactory documentation.[13] That some Negroes were held as slaves after about 1640 is no indication, however, that American slavery popped into the world fully developed at that time. Many historians, most cogently the Handlins, have shown slavery to have been a gradual development, a process not completed until the eighteenth century. The complete deprivation of civil and personal rights, the legal conversion of the Negro into a chattel, in short slavery as Americans came to know it, was not accomplished overnight. Yet these developments practically and logically depended on the practice of hereditary lifetime service, and

---

C. Hotten (ed.), *The Original Lists of Persons of Quality . . .* (New York, 1880), 169–265.

[13] "The status of Negroes was that of servants; and so they were identified and treated down to the 1660's." ("Origins," 203.) The footnote to this statement reads, "For disciplinary and revenue laws in Virginia that did not discriminate Negroes from other servants, see Hening, *Statutes*, I, 174, 198, 200, 243, 306 (1631–1645)." But pp. 200 and 243 of William Waller Hening (ed.), *The Statutes at Large; Being a Collection of All the Laws of Virginia . . .* (2d ed. of vols. 1–4; New York, 1823), I, in fact contain nothing about either servants or Negroes, while a tax provision on p. 242 specifically discriminates against Negro women. The revenue act on p. 306 lists the number of pounds of tobacco levied on land, cattle, sheep, horses, etc., and on tithable persons, and provides for collection of lists of the above so that the colony can compute its tax program; nothing else is said of servants and tithables. To say, as the Handlins did in the same note, that Negroes, English servants, and horses, etc., were listed all together in some early Virginia wills, with the implication that Negroes and English servants were regarded as alike in status, is hardly correct unless one is to assume that the horses were sharing this status as well. (For complete bibliographical information on Hening [ed.], *Statutes*, see E. G. Swem, *Virginia Historical Index* [2 vols.; Roanoke, Va., 1934–36], I, xv–xvi.)

---

[12] H. R. McIlwaine (ed.), *Minutes of the Council and General Court of Colonial Virginia, 1622–1632, 1670–1676* (Richmond, 1924), 196. See the lists and musters of 1624 and 1625 in John

it is certainly possible to find in the 1640s and 1650s traces of slavery's most essential feature.[14]

The first definite trace appears in 1640 when the Virginia General Court pronounced sentence on three servants who had been retaken after running away to Maryland. Two of them, a Dutchman and a Scot, were ordered to serve their masters for one additional year and then the colony for three more, but "the third being a negro named John Punch shall serve his said master or his assigns for the time of his natural life here or else where." No white servant in America, so far as is known, ever received a like sentence.[15] Later the same month a Negro was again singled out from a group of recaptured runaways; six of the seven were assigned additional time while the Negro was given none, presumably because he was already serving for life.[16] After 1640, too, county court records began to mention Negroes, in part because there were more of them than previously—about 2 percent of the Virginia population in 1649.[17] Sales for life, often including any future progeny, were recorded in unmistakable language. In 1646 Francis Pott sold a Negro woman and boy to Stephen Charlton "to the use of him . . . forever." Similarly, six years later William Whittington sold to John Pott "one Negro girle named Jowan; aged about Ten yeares and with her Issue and produce duringe her (or either of them) for their Life tyme. And their Successors forever"; and a Maryland man in 1649 deeded two Negro men and a woman "and all their issue both male and Female." The executors of a York County estate in 1647 disposed of eight Negroes—four men, two women, and two children—to Captain John Chisman "to have hold occupy posesse and inioy and every one of the aforementioned Negroes forever[.]"[18] The will of Rowland Burnham of "Rapahanocke," made in 1657, dispensed his considerable number of Negroes and white servants in language which clearly differentiated between the two by specifying that the whites were to serve for their "full terme of tyme" and the Negroes "forever."[19] Nor did anything in the will indicate that this distinction was exceptional or novel.

In addition to these clear indications that some Negroes were owned for life, there were cases of Negroes held for terms far longer than the normal five or seven years.[20] On the other hand, some Negroes served only the term usual for white servants, and others were completely free.[21] One Negro freeman, Anthony Johnson,

[14] Latin-American Negroes did not lose all civil and personal rights, did not become mere chattels, yet we speak of "slavery" in Latin America without hesitation. See Frank Tannenbaum, *Slave and Citizen: The Negro in the Americas* (New York, 1947), and Gilberto Freyre, *The Masters and the Slaves: A Study in the Development of Brazilian Civilization* (New York, 1946).

[15] "Decisions of the General Court," *Virginia Magazine of History and Biography*, V (January, 1898), 236. Abbot Emerson Smith in the standard work on servitude in America, *Colonists in Bondage: White Servitude and Convict Labor in America, 1607–1776* (Chapel Hill, 1947), 171, says that "there was never any such thing as perpetual slavery for any white man in any English colony." There were instances in the seventeenth century of white men sold into "slavery," but this was when the meaning of the term was still indefinite and often equated with servitude.

[16] "Decisions of the General Court," 236–37.

[17] *A Perfect Description of Virginia* . . . (London, 1649), reprinted in Peter Force (ed.), *Tracts* . . . (4 vols.; Washington, 1836–46), II.

[18] These four cases may be found in Northampton County Deeds, Wills &c. (Virginia State Library, Richmond), No. 4 (1651–54), 28 (misnumbered 29), 124; *Archives of Maryland* (69 vols.; Baltimore, 1883–1961), XLI, 261–62; York County Records (Virginia State Library), No. 2 (transcribed Wills & Deeds, 1645–49), 256–57.

[19] Lancaster County Loose Papers (Virginia State Library), Box of Wills, 1650–1719, Folder 1656–59.

[20] For examples running for as long as 35 years, see *William and Mary Quarterly*, s. 1, XX (October, 1911), 148; Russell, *Free Negro in Virginia*, 26–27; Ames, *Eastern Shore*, 105. Compare the cases of a Negro and an Irish servant in *Calendar of Virginia State Papers* . . . (11 vols.; Richmond, 1875–93), I, 9–10, and *Maryland Archives*, XLI, 476–78; XLIX, 123–24.

[21] Russell, *Free Negro in Virginia*, 24–41. See especially the cases in *Virginia Magazine of History and Biography*, V (July, 1897), 40; York County Deeds, Wills, Orders, etc. (Virginia State Library), No. 1 (1633–57, 1691–94), 338–39.

himself owned a Negro.[22] Obviously the enslavement of some Negroes did not mean the immediate enslavement of all.

Further evidence of Negroes serving for life lies in the prices paid for them. In many instances the valuations placed on Negroes (in estate inventories and bills of sale) were far higher than for white servants, even those servants with full terms yet to serve. Since there was ordinarily no preference for Negroes as such, higher prices must have meant that Negroes were more highly valued because of their greater length of service. Negro women may have been especially prized, moreover, because their progeny could also be held perpetually. In 1645, for example, two Negro women and a boy were sold for 5,500 pounds of tobacco. Two years earlier William Burdett's inventory listed eight servants (with the time each had still to serve) at valuations ranging from 400 to 1,100 pounds, while a "very anntient" Negro was valued at 3,000 and an eight-year-old Negro girl at 2,000 pounds, with no time-remaining indicated for either. In the late 1650s an inventory of Thomas Ludlow's large estate evaluated a white servant with six years to serve at less than an elderly Negro man and only one-half of a Negro woman.[23] The labor owned by James Stone in 1648 was evaluated as follows:

	lb tobo
Thomas Groves, 4 yeares to serve	1300
Francis Bomley for 6 yeares	1500
John Thackstone for 3 yeares	1300
Susan Davis for 3 yeares	1000
Emaniell a Negro man	2000
Roger Stone 3 yeares	1300
Mingo a Negro man	2000[24]

Besides setting a higher value on the two Negroes, Stone's inventory, like Burdett's,

failed to indicate the number of years they had still to serve. It would seem safe to assume that the time remaining was omitted in this and similar documents simply because the Negroes were regarded as serving for an unlimited time.

The situation in Maryland was apparently the same. In 1643 Governor Leonard Calvert agreed with John Skinner, "mariner," to exchange certain estates for 17 sound Negro "slaves," 14 men and 3 women between 16 and 26 years old. The total value of these was placed at 24,000 pounds of tobacco, which would work out to 1,000 pounds for the women and 1,500 for the men, prices considerably higher than those paid for white servants at the time.[25]

Wherever Negro women were involved, however, higher valuations may have reflected the fact that they could be used for field work while white women generally were not. This discrimination between Negro and white women, of course, fell short of actual enslavement. It meant merely that Negroes were set apart in a way clearly not to their advantage. Yet this is not the only evidence that Negroes were subjected to degrading distinctions not directly related to slavery. In several ways Negroes were singled out for special treatment which suggested a generalized debasing of Negroes as a group. Significantly, the first indications of debasement appeared at about the same time as the first indications of actual enslavement.

The distinction concerning field work is a case in point. It first appeared on the written record in 1643, when Virginia pointedly recognized it in her taxation policy. Previously tithable persons had been defined (1629) as "all those that worke in the ground of what qualitie or condition soever." Now the law stated that all adult men and *Negro* women were to be tithable,

[22] John H. Russell, "Colored Freemen As Slave Owners in Virginia," *Journal of Negro History*, I (July, 1916), 234–37.

[23] York County Records, No. 2, 63; Northampton County Orders, Deeds, Wills, &c., No. 2 (1640–45), 224; York County Deeds, Orders, Wills, &c. (1657–62), 108–9.

[24] York County Records, No. 2, 390.

[25] Apparently Calvert's deal with Skinner was never consummated. *Maryland Archives*, IV, vii, 189, 320–21. For prices of white servants see *ibid.*, IV, 31, 47–48, 74, 78–79, 81, 83, 92, 98, 108–9, 184, 200, 319.

and this distinction was made twice again before 1660. Maryland followed a similar course, beginning in 1654.[26] John Hammond, in a 1656 tract defending the tobacco colonies, wrote that servant women were not put to work in the fields but in domestic employments, "yet som wenches that are nasty, and beastly and not fit to be so imployed are put into the ground."[27] Since all Negro women were taxed as working in the fields, it would seem logical to conclude that Virginians found them "nasty" and "beastly." The essentially racial nature of this discrimination was bared by a 1668 law at the time slavery was crystallizing on the statute books:

Whereas some doubts, have arisen whether negro women set free were still to be accompted tithable according to a former act, *It is declared by this grand assembly* that negro women, though permitted to enjoy their ffreedome yet ought not in all respects to be admitted to a full fruition of the exemptions and impunities of the English, and are still lyable to payment of taxes.[28]

Virginia law set Negroes apart in a second way by denying them the important right and obligation to bear arms. Few restraints could indicate more clearly the denial to Negroes of membership in the white community. This action, in a sense the first foreshadowing of the slave codes, came in 1640, at just the time when other indications first appear that Negroes were subject to special treatment.[29]

Finally, an even more compelling sense of the separateness of Negroes was revealed in early distress concerning sexual union between the races. In 1630 a Virginia court pronounced a now famous sentence: "Hugh Davis to be soundly whipped, before an assembly of Negroes and others for abusing himself to the dishonor of God and shame of Christians, by defiling his body in lying with a negro."[30] While there were other instances of punishment for interracial union in the ensuing years, fornication rather than miscegenation may well have been the primary offense, though in 1651 a Maryland man sued someone who he claimed had said "that he had a black bastard in Virginia."[31] There may have been nothing racial about the 1640 case by which Robert Sweet was compelled "to do penance in church according to laws of

---

[26] Hening (ed.), *Statutes*, I, 144, 242, 292, 454. The Handlins erroneously placed the "first sign of discrimination" in this matter at 1668 ("Origins," 217n). For Maryland, see *Maryland Archives*, I, 342; II, 136, 399, 538–39; XIII, 538–39.

[27] John Hammond, *Leah and Rachel, or, the Two Fruitfull Sisters Virginia, and Mary-land: Their Present Condition, Impartially Stated and Related* . . . (London, 1656), reprinted in Force (ed.), *Tracts*, II.

[28] Hening (ed.), *Statutes*, II, 267. The distinction between white and colored women was neatly described at the turn of the century by Robert Beverley, *The History and Present State of Virginia*, Louis B. Wright, ed. (Chapel Hill, 1947), 271–72.

[29] Hening (ed.), *Statutes*, I, 226, and for the same act in more detail see *William and Mary*

Quarterly, s. 2, IV (July 1924), 147. The Handlins discounted this law: "Until the 1660's the statutes on the Negroes were not at all unique. Nor did they add up to a decided trend." ("Origins," 209.) The note added to this statement reads, "That there was no trend is evident from the fluctuations in naming Negroes slaves or servants and in their right to bear arms. See Hening, *Statutes*, I, 226, 258, 292, 540; Bruce, *Institutional History*, II, 5 ff., 199 ff. For similar fluctuations with regard to Indians, see Hening, *Statutes*, I, 391, 518." But since the terms "servants" and "slaves" did not have precise meaning, as the Handlins themselves asserted, fluctuations in naming Negroes one or the other can not be taken to mean that their status itself was fluctuating. Of the pages cited in Hening, p. 258 is an act encouraging Dutch traders and contains nothing about Negroes, servants, slaves, or arms. Page 292 is an act providing that fifteen tithable persons should support one soldier; Negroes were among those tithable, but nothing was said of allowing them to arm. Page 540 refers to "any negro slaves" and "said negro," but mentions nothing about servants or arms. In the pages dealing with Indians, p. 391 provides that no one is to employ Indian servants with guns, and p. 518 that Indians (not "Indian servants") are to be allowed to use their own guns; the two provisions are not contradictory. Philip A. Bruce, *Institutional History of Virginia in the Seventeenth Century* (2 vols.; New York, 1910), II, 5 ff., indicates that Negroes were barred from arming in 1639 and offers no suggestion that there was any later fluctuation in this practice.

[30] Hening (ed.), *Statutes*, I, 146. "Christianity" appears instead of "Christians" in McIlwaine (ed.), *Minutes of the Council*, 479.

[31] *Maryland Archives*, X, 114–15.

England, for getting a negroe woman with child and the woman whipt."[32] About 1650 a white man and a Negro woman were required to stand clad in white sheets before a congregation in Lower Norfolk County for having had relations, but this punishment was sometimes used in ordinary cases of fornication between two whites.[33]

It is certain, however, that in the early 1660s when slavery was gaining statutory recognition, the colonial assemblies legislated with feeling aganist miscegenation. Nor was this merely a matter of avoiding confusion of status, as was suggested by the Handlins. In 1662 Virginia declared that "if any christian shall committ ffornication with a negro man or woman, hee or shee soe offending" should pay double the usual fine. Two years later Maryland prohibited interracial marriages:

forasmuch as divers freeborne English women forgettfull of their free Condicōn and to the disgrace of our Nation doe intermarry with Negro Slaves by which alsoe divers suites may arise touching the Issue of such woemen and a great damage doth befall the Masters of such Negros for prevention whereof for deterring such freeborne women from such shamefull Matches. . . .

strong language indeed if the problem had only been confusion of status. A Maryland act of 1681 described marriages of white women with Negroes as, among other things, "always to the Satisfaccōn of theire Lascivious & Lustfull desires, & to the disgrace not only of the English butt allso of many other Christian Nations." When Virginia finally prohibited all interracial liaisons in 1691, the assembly vigorously denounced miscegenation and its fruits as "that abominable mixture and spurious issue."[34]

One is confronted, then, with the fact that the first evidences of enslavement and of other forms of debasement appeared at about the same time. Such coincidence comports poorly with both views on the causation of prejudice and slavery. If slavery caused prejudice, then invidious distinctions concerning working in the fields, bearing arms, and sexual union should have appeared only after slavery's firm establishment. If prejudice caused slavery, then one would expect to find such lesser discriminations preceding the greater discrimination of outright enslavement.

Perhaps a third explanation of the relationship between slavery and prejudice may be offered, one that might fit the pattern of events as revealed by existing evidence. Both current views share a common starting point: They predicate two factors, prejudice and slavery, and demand a distinct order of causality. No matter how qualified by recognition that the effect may in turn react upon the cause, each approach inevitably tends to deny the validity

---

H. R. McIlwaine (ed.), *Legislative Journals of the Council of Colonial Virginia* (3 vols.; Richmond, 1918–19), I, 262. The Handlins wrote ("Origins," 215), "Mixed marriages of free men and servants were particularly frowned upon as complicating status and therefore limited by law." Their citation for this, Hening (ed.), *Statutes*, II, 114 (1661/ 62), and Marcus W. Jernegan, *Laboring and Dependent Classes in Colonial America, 1607–1783* (Chicago, 1931), 55, 180, gives little backing to the statement. In Virginia secret marriage or bastardy between whites of different status got the same punishment as such between whites of the same status. A white servant might marry any white if his master consented. See Hening (ed.), *Statutes*, I, 252–53, 438–39; II, 114–15, 167; III, 71–75, 137–40. See also James C. Ballagh, *White Servitude in the Colony of Virginia* (Baltimore, 1895), 50. For Maryland, see *Maryland Archives*, I, 73, 373–74, 441–42; II, 396–97; XIII, 501–2. The Handlins also suggested that in the 1691 Virginia law, "spurious" meant simply "illegitimate," and they cited Arthur W. Calhoun, *A Social History of the American Family from Colonial Times to the Present* (3 vols.; Cleveland, O., 1917–19), I, 42, which turns out to be one quotation from John Milton. However, "spurious" was used in colonial laws with reference only to unions between white and black, and never in bastardy laws involving whites only. Mulattoes were often labeled "spurious" offspring.

---

[32] Hening (ed.), *Statutes*, I, 552; McIlwaine, *Minutes of the Council*, 477.

[33] Bruce, *Economic History of Virginia*, II, 110.

[34] Hening (ed.), *Statutes*, II, 170; III, 86–87; *Maryland Archives*, I, 533–34; VII, 204. Opinion on this matter apparently was not unanimous, for a petition of several citizens to the Council in 1699 asked repeal of the intermarriage prohibition.

of its opposite. But what if one were to regard both slavery and prejudice as species of a general debasement of the Negro? Both may have been equally cause and effect, constantly reacting upon each other, dynamically joining hands to hustle the Negro down the road to complete degradation. Mutual causation is, of course, a highly useful concept for describing social situations in the modern world.[35] Indeed it has been widely applied in only slightly altered fashion to the current racial situation: Racial prejudice and the Negro's lowly position are widely accepted as constantly reinforcing each other.

This way of looking at the facts might well fit better with what we know of slavery itself. Slavery was an organized pattern of human relationships. No matter what the law might say, it was of different character than cattle ownership. No matter how degrading, slavery involved human beings. No one seriously pretended otherwise. Slavery was not an isolated economic or institutional phenomenon; it was the practical facet of a general debasement without which slavery could have no rationality. (Prejudice, too, was a form of debasement, a kind of slavery in the mind.) Certainly the urgent need for labor in a virgin country guided the direction which debasement took, molded it, in fact, into an institutional framework. That economic practicalities shaped the external form of debasement should not tempt one to forget, however, that slavery was at bottom a social arrangement, a way of society's ordering its members in its own mind.

[35] For example, George C. Homans, *The Human Group* (New York, 1950).

1964

The Origins of Racism*

DANTE A. PUZZO

The revolution in expectations, carburetor of the engine of change now roaring through Asia, Africa, and Latin America, owes much in precept and example to the United States, the classic land of the common man. It is therefore altogether fitting that the final assault on the last important stronghold of colonialism—that which exists within the nation and rests on race—should occur in America. For the American Negro the affluent has also been the closed society. His awakening to new and great expectations marks the end of an era, an era through which racism coursed black, broad, and mighty, like the Mississippi on a moonless night.

Gaetano Salvemini, the great Italian historian, once remarked that "the historical sense is a kind of sixth sense which we cannot fail to acquire as we breathe the intellectual atmosphere of our times."[1] Salvemini was undoubtedly right, the twentieth century is the most historically minded of all the centuries. Perhaps this is so because with us the present is almost unendurable

* Dante A. Puzzo, "Racism and the Western Tradition," *Journal of the History of Ideas* (1964), 579–86.

[1] Gaetano Salvemini, *Historian and Scientist* (Cambridge, Mass., 1939), 28.

and the future quite uncertain. Yet, unlike other dominant ideological forces in modern society, such as nationalism and even socialism, racism is more often viewed sociologically than historically. It might be useful to consider how and in what circumstances this fateful idea first arose, attained a Mephistophelian respectability, and fell into discredit.

Racism rests on two basic assumptions: that a correlation exists between physical characteristics and moral qualities; that mankind is divisible into superior and inferior stocks. Racism, thus defined, is a modern conception, for prior to the sixteenth century there was virtually nothing in the life and thought of the West that can be described as racist. To prevent misunderstanding a clear distinction must be made between racism and ethnocentrism. The term ethnocentrism—of comparatively recent coinage—is derived from the Greek. While *ethnos* meaning race or nation and *ethos* meaning character or tradition are related words, ethnocentrism serves to describe the identification of oneself with one's own people as against the rest of mankind, indiscriminately. The ancient Hebrews, in referring to all who were not Hebrews as Gentiles, were indulging in ethnocentrism, not in racism. For there was nothing in their attitude to suggest that they believed that a relationship existed between physical characteristics and moral qualities. So it was with the Hellenes who denominated all non-Hellenes—whether the wild Scythians or the Egyptians whom they acknowledged as their mentors in the arts of civilization—barbarians, the term denoting that which was strange or foreign.

This is not to imply that the ancients were unaware of or uninterested in the physical differences which distinguish the varieties of man. On the contrary, many of the ancient authors reflect a keen appreciation of the differences, both physical and cultural, which separate and group mankind. Xenophanes, for example, in a passage concerning the gods declared that if animals, like men, had hands and could paint and produce works of art they would represent their gods as animals, oxen as oxen, horses as horses, etc., adding that the Ethiopians made their gods black and snubnosed, the Thracians gave theirs red hair and blue eyes.[2] Herodotus filled his pages with rich descriptions of the physical appearance, the dress, manners, and customs of the peoples of whom he had a direct or indirect knowledge, declaring that Ethiopia produced the most handsome, tallest, and longest-lived men.[3] Caesar and Tacitus provided excellent descriptions of the Gauls and Germans. Caesar held the Belgae to be the bravest of the Gauls, ascribing their warlike qualities to their proximity to the Germans with whom they were in constant conflict and to their greater distance than other Gauls from the enervating influences which emanated from the Roman Province.[4] Tacitus expressed admiration for the height and strength and chaste ways of the Germans, while he saw the facial features of the Sarmatians (a people living to the east of the Germans) as ugly.[5] Tacitus, too, believed the Germans to be a pure stock, "untainted by intermarriage with other peoples."[6] At first blush it would seem that in Tacitus we encounter an ancient author who was extremely "race-conscious" and much taken with the Germans. However, a closer reading reveals that Tacitus was something of a moralist. In his concern to reflect the laxity and corruption of Roman society in the mirror of German virtue he was, perhaps, rather lavish with the quicksilver. Be that as it may, his "race-consciousness" never became racism and it is fallacious to see in his discussion of the Germans—as it was once fashionable to do—an anticipation of the theories of the Count de Gobineau.

It was Aristotle who made what was

---

[2] See Werner Jaeger, "Xenophanes and the Beginnings of Natural Theology," in A. A. Roback (ed.), *The Albert Schweitzer Jubilee Book* (Cambridge, Mass., 1945), 411.

[3] Herodotus, *The Histories*, iii. 19. 23.

[4] Caesar, *The Conquest of Gaul*, 1. 1.

[5] Tacitus, *Germania*, 18. 19. 20. 46.

[6] *Ibid.*, 4.

probably the most racist statement to come out of the ancient world. Depicting the Orientals as quick-witted but weak of spirit and the northern barbarians as strong of spirit but dull-witted, Aristotle held that the Hellenes, inhabiting a middle region and combining quickness of mind with strength of spirit, were superior to both.[7] It is of interest that Houston Stewart Chamberlain, despite many references to Aristotle, ignores him on this score but extracts full measure from Tacitus' observations.[8]

However, Tacitus' moral zeal and Aristotle's penchant for the golden mean notwithstanding, it remains true that the ancient world was free of racist dogma. Allusions to color and other physical characteristics were usually made within an ethnocentric frame of reference and did not imply the "scientific" relationships which are integral to modern racism. Even Aristotle proved himself a poor racist in the end by amending his observation to the effect that only some Hellenic peoples possessed both intelligence and spirit, other Hellenic peoples tending to approximate in their attributes either northern barbarians or Orientals.[9] It is one thing, then, to describe a people as longheaded and brave or as roundheaded and philosophical; it is quite another to aver that because a people is longheaded it is brave or because it is roundheaded it is given to philosophy.

In the period following the fall of Rome, during the so-called Dark Ages, there was as little evidence of racist sentiment as in classical times, and this despite the barbarian invasions which saw Germans and Romano-Celts sharply divided into conquerors and the conquered. The collapse of Roman power and the establishment of numerous barbarian kingdoms on the soil of the old empire found Germans and Romano-Celts under the single rule of various Germanic kings and princelings, but living apart, each people abiding by its own laws and seeking to preserve its own customs. In many instances, intermarriage between the victors and the vanquished was forbidden. However, the motivations which underlay these policies were not even remotely racist but ethnocentric and, more to the point, a matter of the Germans seeking to consolidate their hold on the newly acquired territories and to insure for themselves the spoils of victory.

The passage of time and the conversion of the Germans to Christianity saw a fusion of Germans and Romano-Celts. During the Middle Ages race, both as a concept and as a program of action, lay outside the ken of Western man. This was a time when religious faith served to define man's basic loyalties. Christianity had been, in its historicity, and remained, quintessentially, a creed open to all men and women regardless of origin or station in life. Thus, the Roman Catholicism professed by all the Western European peoples gave them a common locus of allegiance. The relative isolation and backwardness of Western Europe insured the continuance of established attitudes.

However, the Crusades, the revival of trade and the growth of urban life, the Scholastic movement and the Renaissance —in a word, war, trade, and learning— restitched the torn garment of the Mediterranean world. The end of Europe's isolation marked the beginning of Europe's phenomenal rise to wealth and power. The expansion of Europe thrust white men out toward nearly every point of the compass, across seas and continents, down rivers, through forests, over deserts, plains, and mountains, saw them struggling against the forces of nature, among themselves, and with strange breeds of men, red, yellow, brown, and black, for mastery of a vastly expanded world. But while caravels sailed uncharted seas and armed, casqued men penetrated distant jungles Europe itself cracked the crust of Church and Empire and emerged not one but many. The voyages of discovery and exploration, the

---

[7] Aristotle, *Politics*, vii. 7. 1–3. See also Aristotle, *Ethics*, iii. 7.

[8] Houston Stewart Chamberlain, *The Foundations of the Nineteenth Century* (London and New York, 1911), I, 496, *passim*.

[9] Aristotle, *Politics*, vii. 7. 4.

Protestant Reformation, the rise of the dynastic state and the beginning of national sentiment, and the struggle for empire were not only to change the face and character of Europe but were to furnish the elements of a calculus—not really understood by the ancients and quite unknown to the Middle Ages—by means of which the worth of color was measured and determined.

The quick, violent, overwhelming intrusion of the white man into the colored man's world was an act of epic drama beside which the conquest of the Aegean world by the ancient Hellenes was a paltry affair. To the colored man the white man must have seemed the embodiment of elemental force. Yet, while less dramatic and not as immediately felt, the impact of the colored man on the white man proved both real and significant. Races and nations which heretofore had been completely unknown or had been but exotic names, the stuff of legends, the stock-in-trade of travelers and storytellers such as Marco Polo and John Mandeville, soon became quite familiar not only to European sailors and traders but to Europe itself. In the presence of variety and contrast, as it were, there developed a greater self-awareness. It can be said that race-consciousness—in the modern sense of the term—was carried back to Europe, along with gold and silver, silks and spices, dyestuffs and furs, in European bottoms.

Whatever the ultimate achievements of the Protestant Reformation with respect to the emancipation of the human spirit—and these are considerable—the rise of Protestantism served initially to diminish and to militate against the universality of the Christian religion. For an immediate result of the spread of Protestantism was the establishment of new and antagonistic loci of allegiance, this militant parochialism nurturing a weed-like growth of mutual intolerance in what had been the Christian common. This development, confluent with the impact of Europe's expansion on Europe's self-awareness, strengthened a growing sense of difference and separateness among the Europeans themselves.

The claims to spiritual and temporal suzerainty over Europe of Pope and emperor, respectively, were relegated to limbo by the Treaty of Westphalia that ended the Thirty Years' War (1618–1648), the last and bloodiest of the so-called religious wars. In the attempt to curtail the privileges and autonomy of the feudal nobility and the Church, prince and merchant had found themselves to be natural allies. Thus the dynastic state had been born of the union of royal pretension and burgher ambition, with gunpowder, American treasure, Protestantism, and the printing press acting as so many midwives. National sentiment, if it can be said to have existed at all at this time, was expressed in terms of the king and his dynasty. However, when the great and growing middle class sought to limit royal power, national sentiment began to acquire the direction, as well as the breadth and depth, of modern nationalism, and the dynastic state became the nation-state. What is germane and important in all this is that while the absolute monarch might have denied or ignored papal and imperial claims to suzerainty, he remained, essentially, a feudal expression. Well might he declare that "I am the State," yet the state continued to be his fief from God. In theory, and to a considerable extent in practice as well, the entire range of his power and ambition was contained in that relationship. But if the *mystique* of the dynastic-state led ultimately to God, the *mystique* of the nation-state began and ended with the nation itself.

The moral self-sufficiency of the nation-state proved of salient importance. For, in the circumstances engendered by the struggle for empire, it gave powerful impetus to the natural tendency of nationalism to become chauvinism. And chauvinism, perverting to its uses the new sciences, could become and, where conditions were propitious, did become racism. The interaction between colonialism and this nationalism provided the necessary *milieu* for the emergence and development of racism. Racism, then, resulted from the conjunction of certain historical developments, ranging from the end of Europe's isolation through the emergence of the secular, national state to the struggle for empire. It is this unique set of circumstances which serves not only to account for the rise of racism but to set it off from earlier ethnocentric notions and simple patriotism.

From the Spaniard's declaration that "todos blancos son caballeros"[10] to the American Southerner's "Jim Crow" is a long but straight road. Racism provided a simple, direct, apparent-to-the-eye explanation of the most complex and perplexing phenomenon of modern times, to wit, the rise of a comparatively small, poor, and backward Western Europe to undisputed dominion over the world. Racism, too, provided the Europeans with a moral rationale for their subjugation and exploitation of "inferior" peoples. There were, basically, two directions that this line of reasoning could take: one, that just as God had created the beasts to serve man, to provide him with food and to haul his burdens, so "inferior" breeds of men should serve the "white," "Christian," "superior" European; two, that the "white," "Christian," "superior" European must serve as mentor and guide to "inferior" peoples. Both these lines of argument were pursued from the beginning of the expansion of Europe, with the first more popular with the tough-minded and

during periods calling for repression of native dissidence, and the second more popular with the mission-minded and in relatively tranquil times.

This is not to imply, of course, that if the situation had been diametrically different, that if instead of the expansion of Europe the expansion of Asia or Africa or America had come to pass, the treatment meted out to the Europeans would have been different from that in fact received by Asians, Negroes, and Indians. On the contrary, it is reasonable to suppose that it would not have been, for man's inhumanity to man is not a monopoly of the Western world. However, what concerns us is not a supposition but a fact. That racism, in the sense in which the term has been used here, bears the stamp of European manufacture admits of no doubt. Moreover, that racist notions continued to enjoy wide popularity and to sell well in the political marts even after they were shown to be shoddy and without basis in scientific fact is beyond cavil to a generation whose experience encompasses Auschwitz, South Africa's apartheid, and Birmingham. This is not really surprising, for racism is, in the final analysis, a political device, an instrument of national or class power.

Nordicism is simply a late and peculiar development of European racism. The growth in wealth, power, and civilization of the nations of northern Europe, coupled with the relative decline of the Mediterranean region, served as the *mise en scène* for the appearance of the Nordic myth. Some forty years after the Battle of Waterloo the Count de Gobineau published his four-volume work, *Essai sur l'inégalité des races humaines*. Now Gobineau, like other thinkers with whom certain ideas are associated, had his precursors. Long before the 1850s there had been hints and suggestions to the effect that the tall, blond, blue-eyed people who originally dwelled along the shores of the Baltic sea constituted a race possessing markedly superior qualities not only in comparison with colored peo-

10 Montesquieu refers amusingly to the racial pride of the *Conquistadores* in his *Persian Letters*. He writes: "Those who dwell in the Indies are . . . elated by the consideration that they have the sublime merit to be, as they say, white-skinned men. There was never in the seraglio of Grand Seigneur, a sultana so proud of her beauty, as the oldest and ugliest rascal among them is of his complexion of pale olive, when in a Mexican town he sits at his own door with his arms folded. A man of such importance, a creature so perfect, would not work for all the wealth of the world; and could never persuade himself to compromise the honor and the dignity of his color by vile mechanic industry." See C. de Montesquieu, *Persian Letters* (Philadelphia, n.d.), Vol. II, No. 78, pp. 7–12.

ples but also in comparison with fellow Caucasoids of the brunette type. In the eighteenth century Montesquieu, for example, had declared that the Germanic peoples possessed a unique capacity for self-government and leadership.[11] However, it remained for Gobineau to convert these hints and suggestions into a full-blown philosophy of race that came to be known as Nordicism. The year following the publication of Gobineau's fourth and last volume of *Essai sur l'inégalité des races humaines* (1855) a German edition of his work appeared. With the defeat of the French by the Germans in the Franco-Prussian War of 1870–71, Nordicism received a tremendous fillip. By the end of the century it had secured a strong hold on the thinking and feelings of millions not only east of the Rhine, across the Channel, and beyond the Atlantic (north of the Rio Grande) but also in many other places where the Nordic type was less in evidence. With the advent to power of the Nazis in Germany in 1933 Nordicism became the official doctrine of a powerful and important European state.

Now Nordicism, like the more general European racism out of which it arose, served a twofold purpose: it supplied a facile explanation for the recent successes enjoyed by northern European peoples, while it furnished a moral rationale for the contemplated subjection of the European continent to German rule. Thus Nordicism —more self-consciously, perhaps—was to the struggle to dominate Europe what European racism had been to the establishment of European hegemony over America, Africa, and Asia. But Nordicism was by no means exclusively a German affair, and it had still other uses. Both in Europe and elsewhere, it was an instrument of class as well as national power. Indeed, early Nordicists, such as Gobineau himself, saw the revolutionary struggle in Europe that pitted bourgeois against aristocrat as essentially a *Rassenkampf*.[12]

The defeat of the Germans in World War II, to which, it should be noted, "inferior" Slavs contributed importantly, the precipitate decline of the power and prestige of Great Britain, and the emergence of the United States as the foremost power in the world have so altered the pattern of political, economic, and military realities out of which Nordicism arose, that without doubt the Nordic myth can no longer be nourished by the "facts" of life, that is, by subjective evaluations of objective circumstances. A complete disengagement from reality is not a characteristic of the normal mind. It becomes increasingly difficult for Germans, Englishmen, and others to continue to hold to notions of superiority as it becomes ever more evident that Germany and Great Britain are today what Spain and Italy have been for centuries and France for decades—stars of second and even third magnitude in the constellation of world powers.

But what of the United States? Are not the Americans the most powerful people in the world today? And is not Nordicism a prevalent mode of thinking and feeling in America? Concerning the vast wealth and power of the United States there can be no question. It must be conceded, too, that America has been, and remains, a land plagued by racist and Nordic notions and discriminatory practices. The history of the Negro (and of the Indian) in America is eloquent on this score, as is the history of selective immigration policies which sought, and seek, to preserve the Nordic character of the country. No less significant is the very real if veiled hierarchism that serves to separate the sheep from the goats along the highways and byways of American life.

Yet, for all that, there are certain factors in American life which have had, and are increasingly having, a restraining and a most salutary influence on racial prejudice. To begin with, America is a melting pot of many nationalities and races. In terms of racist thinking, the American is

---

[11] C. de Montesquieu, *The Spirit of Laws* (Cincinnati, 1873), I, 308–10, passim.

[12] A. de Gobineau, *Essai sur l'inégalité des*

races humaines (Paris, 1853), II, 445. See also *ibid.*, I, 167–69.

becoming a very elusive fellow. With immigration now reduced to a trickle and with intermarriage of persons of diverse national and ethnic origins proceeding apace, the "mongrelization" of the American people —which Hitler believed to be already sufficiently advanced to bring into question the Nordic status of the United States[13]— must ultimately result in the abandonment of all racist notions and discriminatory practices in America. To the extent that racism (including Nordicism) is a pseudo-anthropological extension of a nationalism become chauvinism, to that extent it is already a patent absurdity in America.

Then, too, American politics, with respect to both the main postulates of democratic ideology and the practical necessities of the democratic process, have provided a comparatively poor soil for the growth of racist sentiment into an above-the-ground, full-blown, officially watered and manured racist philosophy. This can be seen at the ideological level in the crisis of conscience that has plagued a growing number of Americans down through the years. Although some Americans have managed it (thanks to a watertight compartmentalization of their ideas), others have found it intellectually and morally agonizing to be democrats and racists at one and the same time. At the practical level of politics—save, of course, where the dominant majority constitutes a compact, homogeneous mass—even the dullest precinct captain is aware that in view of universal suffrage and the heterogeneity of the

---

[13] *Hitler's Table Talk*, trans. N. Cameron and R. H. Stevens (London, 1953), 186–88.

population it would be the greatest folly for an aspirant to political office to make an open avowal of racism. Indeed, if words alone can be said to comprise reality, election time is the season that finds the flower of democratic equality in full bloom in America.

While all this can give but cold comfort to the Negro, the Indian, the Oriental, the Puerto Rican, the Jew, the eastern or southern European who finds himself the victim of racist or Nordic discrimination, it remains nonetheless a valid description of important tendencies within American life. Who can gainsay that, morally, the most significant and compelling struggle in America today is that of the Negro to achieve complete equality? And who can doubt that, ultimately, he will be successful? Buttressing equalitarian tendencies within American life are the realities of a newly fashioned world.

If, then, Nordicism, which reached a crescendo of fury in the late thirties and early forties, is moribund in today's world, European racism, which was antecedent to and generative of Nordicism, is quite dead for all practical purposes. The rise to power and importance of erstwhile colonial peoples, coupled with the political decline of Europe, has cut the ground from under the European's claim to a superiority attested to and supported by the "facts" of life. Inevitably, the calculus of color will be thrust, as were alchemy and astrology, into the limbo of false sciences. When this happens, the West will be free of a fateful idea that, appearing late in its history, was incompatible with its best traditions.

1963

Black and White in the World Context[*]

HAROLD R. ISAACS

The white races are but one-third of the population of the globe—or one of them to two of us—and it cannot much longer continue that two-thirds will passively submit to the universal domination of this one-third.

These words were spoken to a convention of free Negroes 108 years ago, in 1854, by Martin R. Delany, a physician, author, and leading figure among free Negroes in New York.[1]

On February 6, 1866, Charles Sumner of Massachusetts, arguing in the United States Senate for the full grant of civil rights to the freedmen, summoned up the same world view that Delany had grasped 12 years earlier and spoke these words:

The population of the earth—embracing Caucasians, Mongolians, Malays, Africans, and Americans—is about thirteen hundred millions, of whom only three hundred and seventy-five million are "white men," or little less than one-fourth, so that in claiming exclusive rights for "white men," you degrade nearly three-quarters of the human family, made in the "image of God" and declared to be of "one blood" while you sanction a caste offensive to religion, an oligarchy inconsistent with Republican government, and a monopoly which has the whole world as its footstool.

Against this assumption, I protest with mind, soul, and heart. It is false in religion, false to statesmanship, and false in economy. . . . You cannot deny these rights without impiety. And so has God linked the national welfare with national duty, you cannot deny these rights without peril to the Republic."[2]

It has taken just about a century for events to confirm these remarkably prophetic insights. In the world, the two-thirds *have* stopped passively submitting to the domination of the one-third. In the United States these rights were persistently denied until now and this denial has much to do with the peril in which the Republic now stands.

From the time of the signing of the Emancipation Proclamation until only a few years ago, the American society was able to deny civil and human rights to millions of its members because of their "race" and yet keep on seeing itself as a striving democracy of free men. For nearly three-quarters of a century, it proved possible to sweep this gross contradiction under the national rug. But the circumstances favoring this massive deception and self-deception began to evaporate about 25 years ago. As Sumner Welles observed in 1944: "The thesis of white supremacy could only exist so long as the white race actually proved

---

[*] Harold R. Isaacs, *The New World of Negro Americans* (New York: John Day Co.) Copyright 1963 by Massachusetts Institute of Technology. Reprinted by permission of The John Day Company, Inc., publisher.

[1] Quoted by Howard H. Bell, "Negro Emigration Movement, 1849–54, A Phase of Negro Nationalism," *Phylon*, 2d quarter, 1959, p. 141.

[2] Quoted by John A. Davis, *et al.*, "Foreign Reactions to American Racial Problems," Unpub. MS, American Information Committee on Race and Caste (New York, 1955), p. 5.

to be supreme."[3] That thesis was built into the superstructure of Western white-world power; it was used to rationalize and justify on racial grounds the Western white man's sovereignty over the whole of the globe. That system of power and sovereignty had been weakening for decades, barely managed to survive World War I, began to fall apart with the onset of World War II, and finally came tumbling down in the years of its aftermath. The empires that white Europe had established in Asia and Africa over some 300 years were almost completely dissolved in the 15 years between 1945 and 1960 and were replaced by some 40 new nation-states. To be sure, life-and-death power over the world remained in the hands of the nuclear superpowers and economic power likewise remained heavily concentrated in Western hands, but this was something quite different from the intimate and direct rulership of Western whites over Asian and African nonwhites which was the substance of imperial political sovereignty. The whole basis of their relationship now had to be revised.

For with the collapse of its underpinning political power, the whole superstructure of Western white supremacy began to waver and fall. It has been in these years like watching a slow-motion film of the collapsing of a dynamited building: slowly it falls out into the air, parts of it retaining form and structure even as they sink and are gradually obscured by the dust and rubble into which they fall. Because it is slow motion, some can imagine that these slabs of the familiar facade are still standing there in the air and are not falling at all. But this is illusion becoming delusion, for here they are coming down all around us—all the assumptions we made about each other, about ourselves and about other human beings, about our own and other groups and kinds, "races," peoples, cultures. Here, coming apart amid their fallen power props, are all the myths of white superiority and nonwhite inferiority, all the

[3] Sumner Welles, *Time of Decision* (New York, 1944), pp. 297–98.

deeply imbedded notions and emotions, all the patterns of long-practiced behavior. All are being displaced and have to be replaced. All that was *given*, in a word, is now being taken away. Whether we will it, or know it, or like it, or not, we are all participants in this great continental rearrangement of power and human relationships. All Western white men have to get rid of the habits of mastery, and all nonwhites the habits of subjection. This is now the common and nearly universal experience. There is hardly a corner of national or international life now that is not touched by it and hardly anyone, white or black or whatever, who is not now faced by its demands.

In Asia and Africa where the colonies have become nation-states, this process of revision in relationship and mutual image can at least begin with a transfer of political power and thus throw around the new confusions a screen of formal new status relationship. The styles of this transfer have varied greatly—the hasty but relatively skillful improvising of the British, the myopic but brief resistance of the Dutch, the myopic and prolonged resistance of the French, the pell-mell panicking of the Belgians—but the result in every case creates a new formal situation. A new state is proclaimed, a new flag raised, a new government established, a new "power" is established, and from here on out at least the externals of behavior are governed by the protocol of diplomacy and the needs of policy. Seemingly in a twinkling, yellow and brown and black men, only yesterday despised and relegated to the orders of inferiority, now take *their* places in the seats of the mighty. They walk the red carpets of privilege, enjoy all the perquisites of sovereignty, are wooed and pressured instead of dominated and, wherever they can, begin to do a little dominating themselves. The old badges of inferiority are torn off, the signs of discrimination and debasement come down, the exclusive places and modes of behavior are abolished; the Queen now dances with the black prime minister, and the Duke with the prime minister's black wife. To be sure, behind this facade the new situation remains a jumble of old rancors, guilts, and shames, all of which have to be accommodated to the new needs. The shedding of colonial power does not at a stroke relieve the old colonial master of the whole burden of his beliefs about himself, nor Western white people generally of the legacy of what their whole culture taught them for so long about these matters. Similarly, political independence does not at a stroke free either the new nation or its people from *their* legacy of subjection, imposed inferiority, dependence, and self-rejection. But at least now the power of government is in the hands of one's own kind and the most egregious forms of subordination to foreign rulership are forced to disappear. The new national power, no matter how weak, is at least strong enough to put a prohibitive tariff on the return of this kind of foreign domination and under its protection to produce (to resurrect, recreate, or create as the case may be) a new national, cultural, or even "racial" identity on which indigenous self-respect can begin to thrive.

In American society, on the other hand, the end of white supremacy has to be signaled not by *separation* but by *integration*. Here there is no simple initial solution like changing the signs at a boundary line and raising a new flag. Here the issue remains locked in the society's unfulfilled promise of democratic pluralism. This promise is perhaps our greatest and most unique virtue and our failure to fulfill it may be our costliest failure, for we have been overtaken by it at last. The gulf between our profession and our practice has become an abyss to whose edge the world has pushed us.

The downfall of the white supremacy system in the rest of the world made its survival in the United States suddenly and painfully conspicuous. It became our most exposed feature and, in the swift unfolding of the world's affairs, our most vulnerable weakness. It was like being caught naked in a glaring spotlight alone on a great stage in a huge theater filled with people we had not known were there. Here we were now, our vulnerability so highly visible that when hundreds of millions of people all around the world looked in our direction it seemed to be all that they could see.

This was because the "world" in which we now live is no longer the dominant white Atlantic world in which most of us were born. It is a rudely enlarged place that includes Asia and Africa on a wholly new footing. Most of the millions whose scrutiny we are now feeling are the nonwhite peoples coming so dramatically into view with the scars of Western white dominance still heavily marked upon them. These great masses of Asians and Africans turn out to be, moreover, people whose future has become a critical factor in the American future, not to say American survival. For the world power struggle between the United States and the Soviet Union now turns not only on the balance of economies or weapons, on systems of production or control of strategic resources and territories, but also on the shape of man's political future, the institutions he will choose or be led to build, the conceptions of freedom or unfreedom he will embrace or be embraced by in the next few decades. Unless it is dissolved by resort to the Bombs, the coming shape of things will be largely decided by the choices made by precisely these "new" Asian and African peoples. If, as we insist, the power struggle is not only a confrontation of Bombs and systems of production, but also a confrontation of fundamentally different ways of relating man to his society, then the nature of the American democracy itself becomes a critical issue in this struggle.

The facts are that the American democracy housed slavery for its first 75 years, then freed the slaves and promised them the same constitutional rights enjoyed by all citizens, and then proceeded for nearly another hundred years to deny Negroes those rights. It comes now into this new revolutionary epoch faced abruptly with the need to establish new and more mutually respectful relations with the nonwhite peoples of the earth without being able to show that it has given to its own nonwhite citizens even a minimum measure of the dignity and freedom on which it bases its philosophy and its whole case against the totalitarians. The democratic system itself produced no sufficient self-correction of this profound anomaly. Only the slow trickle of cases through the courts gave evidence of any inward capacity for change, and it was hardly moving at all until it was washed over by the great flood of world events.

So the end of white supremacy in the United States is finally being forced by the end of white supremacy in the rest of the world. We now have to abandon racist practices because we simply can no longer afford to cling to them, any more than we can cling to the idea that there is any security left in continental isolation. No doubt it would have been far better to have reached this point through the working out of the democratic belief in the equality of rights of all citizens or the Christian belief in human brotherhood. It may be that the democratic process works not only as slowly but also as mysteriously as Providence is reputed to do. Nevertheless, both isolationism and racism have had to be blasted out of their deeply imbedded places in American life and history by nothing less than the great world explosions of our time, the technological and political explosions that have transformed all human affairs in this century. Isolationism could not survive the scientific advances that made the globe itself the smallest viable unit of political and social change. White supremacy in America cannot survive the political overturns that have brought to an end the Western white man's sovereignty over the rest of the world. It may be possible to imagine white racist systems persisting in an isolation protected by Super-Bombs. But such systems, even assuming they could survive in a hopelessly hostile world environment, could not remain even nominally democratic. This is what makes the persistence of isolationists and racists among us so perilous and their grip on crucial sections of our national life

a drag that threatens to carry us all down with them as they disappear.

There is a certain awesome, almost Biblical irony in the way things have worked out. It is not really very much of an exaggeration to say that as matters stand now, "democrats" must finally become democratic (and "Christians" Christian) or die.

The intimate interaction between surviving American racism and American relations with the world became steadily more visible and more continuous year after year following World War II. Every racial episode in the United States was instantly reported around the globe and reaction came bouncing back like radar signals from almost every direction. At each eruption the federal government was galvanized, its spokesmen forced to keep on finding the words with which to counter these hostile and damaging views of what America is and what it does. The record of this interaction has become a fat file indeed. A study of foreign press comment on American race issues, covering only certain countries for the period 1949 to 1954, filled nearly a thousand pages of typescript.[4] It would take many times that number again even for bare summaries of the world press, radio, and television coverage of all that has happened since then. The news files have bulged year after year with names of persons that became familiar everywhere and of places suddenly ringed on the whole world's maps. In 1955 it was the murder of Emmett Till in Mississippi. Beginning that same year and carrying over into 1956, the whole world watched walking Negroes boycott the buses in Montgomery. That year it was also the case of Autherine Lucy's attempt to enter the University of Alabama and the dynamiting of the high school by segregationists at Clinton, Tennessee. The echoes of these events had barely begun to die away when the first major battle over enforcement of the school desegregation decision erupted at Little Rock in 1957 in circumstances that car-

---

[4] Davis *et al., op. cit.*

ried awareness of American race issues into the world's most obscure places and finally caused the whole American nation to feel the heat of the world's new interest in its most private affairs. . . .

* * * * *

What came new out of Africa in the late 1950s for a great many Negro Americans was indeed the chance for the first time to identify in a positive way with the continent of their black ancestors. Instead of looking away from it, many began to look at it. In place of indifference, rejection, and shame, they began to feel a rise of interest, acceptance, and pride. This change began to set in with the approach of independence in Ghana and the appearance of Kwame Nkrumah as the first new African world figure, followed in a quick few years by the great swarm of new African states and the coming of other African black men to places of power. What came out of these events was not only the spectacle of white power fallen or falling but the new and even more gratifying image of black men acquiring dignity and commanding attention and respect. Africa became visible, and black men moved into positions where they could be seen by all and where the white world at last had to take account of their presence. This in itself was enough to establish *something* where—it had seemed for so long—there had been *nothing*, a quickening sense of importance where there had been that deadening feeling of insignificance. Africa offered the Negro American a new place not only in the here and now but also in history; a new link to his past and the part played by his forebears in the unfolding story of man. The African emergence dramatized in these peculiarly personal ways the new leverage in world affairs working on the affairs of the Negro in America.

These new sensations started up at many different points and varied greatly in shape and intensity in different individuals and among different layers of people. They began to show themselves in a new rush of written and spoken communication about

Africa and in outcroppings of many kinds of new behavior and experiences: crowds roaring welcomes to visiting African leaders on parade in the big cities; the elect discovering the feel of red carpet beneath their feet as they more and more commonly joined in social events honoring Africans at the Waldorf, at the delegations and embassies, or at the White House; leaders forming the American Negro Leadership Conference on Africa, adopting resolutions on matters of American policy in Africa and being received at the White House to present their views to the President; intellectuals forming the American Society of African Culture to promote the new mutual rediscovery on a high cultural plane, others forming organizations to enjoy the new opportunities on many other planes (Americans of African Ancestry, Afro-American Cultural Society, Friends of Ghana, African Heritage, etc.); nationalist and chauvinist groups enjoying the spur of having their prophecies of the rising of the black man coming true at last and winning national and international visibility by their demonstration at the United Nations in February, 1961, during the great and passionate confusions surrounding the murder of Patrice Lumumba in the Congo; ordinary folk reading about these things or following the heavy budget of news from Africa in their newspapers, by radio, or watching on their television screens the reappearance of Kenyatta in Kenya, Luthuli accepting a Nobel Prize in Stockholm, a great sudden flow of documentary reports by word and film of country after country in Africa, and dignitaries or interviewers facing a succession of newly distinguished African visitors, Mboya, Touré, Nyerere, Balewa, Senghor, Houphouet-Boigny—all of this in a great flood dislodging a mass of old images of Africa that still filled most minds, undercutting old emotions and fixed ideas, and creating a floating tangle of old and new ideas out of which a new order of things would not quickly be made.

This great jumble of new impulses, sensations, moods, and experiences remains in constant motion. It can hardly be seen whole or even easily caught in part. Great numbers of people are passing from one set of notions and emotions to another, and each one makes this passage in his own unique way, traveling with his own special mixture of what he brings to these exposures and what he takes from them. Of all this I can here make only a modest report, a series of glimpses and vignettes which suggest how the matter was seen by certain individuals at certain moments. These glimpses are of value, I believe, partly because of the identity of these individuals and because the moments in which we catch them here all fell at various times between 1958 and 1961 when these impacts were at their newest and the changes only beginning to show. The first cluster of these vignettes is drawn from the interviews I conducted in the United States during this time, and the second from conversations with Negroes I encountered in West Africa during the summer of 1960.

As Seen From Afar

The range of views begins with a very small number which believed that the Negro "man in the street" still had no interest in Africa at all. Two examples:

He would say: "What've I got to do with Africa or Africans?" He's as removed from interest in Africa as the white man in the street is from interest in Rumania!

I think the man in the street has the same ideas I have about it, no interest, too far away from his own problems, getting a living, housing, desegregation.

Others felt a clear sense of change taking place:

Now he's interested in finding out about it. Two years ago he would have said: "I couldn't care less." Four years ago he would have shown a rejection of Africa and anything it stood for, including black people and Negroid characteristics.

A few years ago, if asked about Africans, he would have laughed and said: "A funky bunch of niggers!" Now there is pride.

A considerable majority, however, already saw this change in views as an emphatic shift to the affirmative side.

Many Negroes are still ashamed of being identified with Africa, but I've heard men on the street corner right here on 135th Street say that they can hold their heads up higher since Nkrumah and Azikiwe came up.

I would expect the man in the street to say: "It's wonderful!" I'd expect him to know the names of the important places and the names of some of the leaders. This has all happened since Ghana's independence. It would not have been so, much more than five years ago.

It's changing and exploding, a new and revived interest in Africa. The Negro never could escape being thought of, consciously or unconsciously, as a relative of Africans. He now can at least be proud of what is happening there and get increased status for himself by identifying with it.

I heard an uneducated woman say: "Those Africans standing up there in the UN, they make me proud!"

A query about the "black bourgeois" response to the African emergence brought some answers that strongly reflected Franklin Frazier's characterization of that upper economic group, e.g.:

This type of Negro is not too emotionally involved, not at all wrought up about it. He is too caught up in the Cadillac-mink coat culture.

Africa has become quite fashionable lately; Many have become interested because of moneymaking opportunities out there.

Just a few years ago, Africa would have been the last place in the world people would have thought to go to; now it's a tourist spot.

But Professor Frazier himself, when we talked about this, put the matter on quite a different level:

I believe that in a way the African is helping the Negro to find his world. With independent states in Africa, there is greater recognition of Negroes here. As Negroes in America increasingly accept an identification with Africa, it will mean something different to them from what it meant in the past.

Africa was already coming to mean something strongly different to many of these individuals. Its emergence in world affairs, its importance in politics, its mere presence in the day's news, had already begun to make this difference. There were many examples of the feeling that what was good for the African in Africa was going to be good for the Negro in America. Here is how the matter was put by the editor of a major Negro weekly:

We are giving more and more emphasis to what is taking place in Africa. Ghana's independence was the starting point of this. . . . This is all good news for the Negro because it gives him a sense of pride. I feel that if the African is successful in winning respect for the African personality, he will help me in terms of my own status. If he fails, I am inclined to believe I fail along with him. I share in the disdain with which black people are regarded. If black people anywhere in the world make a significant impact and thereby win respect and status, I share in some of it.

A New York editor:

I am happy and proud when Africans reach their potential, because I believe this will automatically help me. The African in the next 25 years will do more to ease the stigma of color than the American Negro has done in the past 99 years he has been free . . . What they do in remote Africa has a direct bearing on me . . . the feeling that they are fighting there, and we are fighting here, and someday in the never-never they will and we will win and then things will be great.

A government official:

Africa provides me today with a kind of proud identification with ancestors. It can cause you to swell with pride just to see an African on the podium of the UN, Africans who have to be consulted in the decision-making process in the world. The kind of pride other peoples have had, of being recognized. It gives the Negro American something outside of himself and this little world of discrimination. He gains some kind of feeling of importance. When a Negro wants to go somewhere to feel that he can be somebody, he doesn't go to Paris anymore, he goes to Ghana.

A Southern businessman:

I think I am getting a new respect for the African, reorienting myself entirely. You see pictures of the prime ministers in *Time* magazine, face to face. I declare, you never expected anything like this. The Southern papers never carried pictures like that. We are getting a better feeling of kinship. Instead of thinking of Nkrumah as an African, I think of him as another Negro. . . . Events have given me a new appreciation of Africa. I am now overcoming the rejection which made me recoil from it.

A leader of a major Negro organization:

It is the feeling of importance. The average Negro sees that the whole world is forced to recognize and readjust its attitudes toward the colored world; the rising black man is the theme of his thinking. . . . The enthusiasm about Ghana has tended to submerge that kind of irritation [we used to feel]. Now everything African is welcome. Ghana independence parties were held everywhere. For the first time American Negroes found those robes admirable instead of quaint or embarrassing.

Finally, a senior Negro leader:

There is a new feeling that Africa is becoming a great force and the Negro in America takes pride in this. This is more than a bandwagon interest. It has an element of a reach for survival. So long as there is an Africa, this assures the Negro his historic continuity, his place in history.

These were all responses to Africa in the large and from afar, with Ghana still standing in the foreground as a symbol for the whole. They came, moreover, in the first flush of the emergence and reflected the fine first glow of the ideas of *freedom* and *independence* not yet complicated by the development of authoritarian politics or the confusion over the events in the Congo, and only to a limited extent by actual contact with Africans. But by this time a growing number of Negroes had gone to Africa to have a look for themselves—of those I interviewed 30 had already done so—and had begun to experience more directly the adjustment of their old views to the new actualities. . . .

CHAPTER 2

Modern Images of the South

The South has been defined in many ways, most frequently as the rural home of cotton and plantations, but also in terms of political peculiarities or climate and geography. Yet these definitions tend to break down under critical scrutiny. Other regions were also rural—wheat ruled the Dakotas as firmly as cotton ever dominated Dixie, and cotton did not create "Southern" towns in California. Certainly "ninety degrees in the shade" failed to prevent Miami from becoming a "Northern enclave," and all the mills of Richmond and Raleigh did not destroy local identity. Nor can one find much validity in the ancient argument of special devotion to "states rights" as a defining force. "States rights" has been at various times the instrument of New England merchants and Mississippi planters, New York racists and antislavery equalitarians, and all the evidence indicates that it was the legalistic strategy of minority groups rather than a creed to be taken literally. As for the old notions about a strong loyalty to low tariffs, not even Karl Marx who always looked for the immediate economic grounds of identity and social conflict supposed that the tariff was a crucial issue in Southern hearts or a serious sectional grievance in the crisis of disunion. Even the song "Dixie," a popular symbol of unity and an unofficial "anthem," ironically originated as a blackface walk-around in a "Yankee" minstrel show.

Nearly four decades ago Ulrich B. Phillips, granting the inadequacy of all standard definitions of his native region, provided his own formulation of "The Central Theme in Southern History." Phillips found the touchstone of Southern identity in the common "indomitable resolve" maintained with "the patrician's quietude" as well as "the frenzy of a demagogue" to preserve the South as "a white man's country." During the era of Civil War and Reconstruction and in modern times, he explained with obvious approval, Southerners were preoccupied with "the maintenance of Caucasian civilization" and "the problem of race control" over an inferior race unfit even to govern itself. A goodly number of scholars and writers shared Phillips' assumptions and values but disliked his "oversimplification," "distortion," and perhaps his candor.

In the first half of the twentieth century both the world of scholarship and the realm of popular culture reflected the enormous popularity of myths which cast the image of a civilized and graceful social world marked by economic plenty and populated by kindly masters and their faithful black retainers. A more sophisticated version of the old myth was provided by the "Nashville Agrarians," who came to prominence in the 1930s. In 1930 Frank L. Owsley, the professional historian among the Agrarians, told a dramatic tale of sectional conflict between the coarse materialism and the "egocentric sectionalism" of the industrial North and the humane traditions of the Southern "agrarian ideal . . . the old and accepted manner of life for which Egypt, Greece, Rome, England, and France stood." In Owsley's antebellum Eden the generally benevolent institution of slavery was "one element and not an essential one" of "the agrarian system" rather than an oppressive institution energetically defended by the South through four bloody and destructive years of conflict.

The sectional conflict which reached a climax in the Civil War has been commonly characterized by schools of thought with distinctly different orientations as a struggle between the "agrarian South" and the emerging industrialism of the North. However, as Thomas P. Govan suggested in 1964, the explanation leaned heavily on "agrarian," a term extraordinarily rich in ambiguity. If the word can be equated with "agricultural," it is too vague and general to be useful—the great majority of antebellum Northerners were also farmers. Modern Asiatic peasants, prosperous New Jersey truck farmers, Soviet collective farm managers, and quasi-feudal landlords of Peru can all be described as "agrarians." Obviously many definitions have been attached to the term. Several meanings are completely contradictory; others defended the South by reviving portions of the proslavery argument; and some served to avoid or to confuse discussions about the harsher aspects of American experience not easily reconciled with the national democratic creed. By making the South the major carrier of Jacksonian and Jeffersonian "democracy" and by describing the North as the seedbed of robber barons and the forerunner of industrial plutocracy, the dominant scholarly interpretation even characterized the slaveowner as the defender of democratic values against the Free Soil and Republican challengers of "democracy"! In the days since the defenders of the "agrarian" tradition and the school of Ulrich B. Phillips dominated the intellectual scene, the context of interpretation has changed a great deal. Scholars no longer speak of "Caucasian civilization" or "the white man's burden." The plantation myth often appeared in the context of an explicit or implicit defense of white supremacy and has not survived the demise of ideological racism. The very word "Southerner" has generally meant "white Southerner" with the implication that Negroes did not belong to the South or were in some sense unworthy of consideration. ("Southerner" will be used in this book in the conventional way, but with the realization that it is in a sense a technical term.) New perspectives for the study of white and black people were made possible by the decline of explanations which were tied to agrarian and plantation myths.

Before the defeat of Reconstruction and the rise of the plantation myth during the 1880s and '90s, the dominant tradition of interpretation portrayed the slave South as the oppressive citadel of human bondage. From the turn of the century critics began to accuse this "abolitionist-Radical-Republican" tradition of improbable moralism, exaggeration, and excessive propaganda; and the increasingly powerful imperialist and racist concepts of the times lent plausi-bility to the charges. During our own era, as the plantation myth declined and ideological racism approached its nadir, both trends joined with the current political events to alter American sensibilities. After 1954 the school desegre-gation drive in the South encountered an annual September Saturnalia of de-fiance and mob action, and the Negro Freedom Movement of the early 1960s with its demonstrations, freedom rides (and its excursions into the racial ghet-toes of Northern cities) met an even greater response of violence and hate. Racial oppression was not peculiar to our own era, and racial violence had received national publicity in earlier generations, but the reemergence of Asia and Africa, the extensiveness of public discussion, the growth of equalitarian feeling, and most importantly the civil rights movement itself, created a new situation. Changing events made possible new insights, and scholars began to make comparisons between abolitionists and freedom riders, and between Reconstruction laws and recent civil rights legislation.

Long before the civil rights movement, the rise of a major body of literature in the writings of William Faulkner and others had suggested the existence of a tormented South sorely afflicted by a great web of racial injustice. Images from the realm of literature were reinforced by the daily newspapers of the early sixties, which brought frequent news of midnight assassinations, the bombing of churches, and the uncontrolled rage of mobs. The more violent police officials and citizens of the lower South did not remind anyone of chivalrous plantation "Cavaliers," and stereotypes of the past as well as the present came under attack from those who asked if the romantic images of the antebellum South might not conceal realities even more sinister than those of modern times. Certainly the portraits drawn by several scholars did not reassure one about either the modern or the antebellum South. James W. Silver in 1964 presented a social world in Mississippi which did indeed appear to be a "closed society," organized for the defense of white supremacy and capable of vast quantities of self-deception. Later during the same year (but in a dif-ferent context), Clement Eaton summarized several decades of his research and thought by concluding that there had been "little of . . . liberalism" in an Old South marked by "extreme conservatism; a spirit of intolerance; a powerful religious orthodoxy; an intense attachment . . . to local community; and a powerful race feeling." It was also difficult to imagine "liberalism" at-tached to the "militant South," which was presented to historians by John Hope Franklin in 1956. On the contrary, the region seemed to be excessively inclined to the celebration of martial virtues, the play of unbridled and aggressive egos, and the tendency to settle disputes with weapons rather than courts and laws.

Yet racial violence also existed in the North, and after reading Robert F. Durden's report of 1957 on racism in the early Republican party, one might feel a certain caution about drawing very sharp contrasts between Southern racial attitudes and Northern "equalitarianism." One school of thought stressed the fact that the Southerner, whatever his vices and virtues, was also an American with national experiences and a common acceptance of the same political creed. Charles G. Sellers, Jr., suggested in 1960 that it was precisely this indoctrination in American concepts of liberty and equality which divided the minds of Southerners and left them tragically torn between pleasure in the gains of slavery and the inner taunts of democratic and Christian ideals. However much Southerners might worship at the shrine of slavery they were nonetheless reminded that the national creed called men to the temple of liberty. The Civil War was a mad flight from "their essential natures as Southerners, liberals, Christians, and Americans."

Much of the debate over regional identity involved the modern South or the South generally. In 1963 Dewey W. Grantham, Jr., reasoned that the image of a monolithic and conservative South completely given over to political reaction and racial demagoguery must be tempered by the reality of a liberal tradition. Grantham argued that every major reform movement affected the South, and that Wilson's New Freedom and Roosevelt's New Deal had strong Southern support and local manifestations. Even the Dixie demagogues who flourished so dramatically in the era between the two world wars represented something more than violent Negrophobia and surrender to large property interests—Hoke Smith of Georgia, Huey Long of Louisiana, and others had sponsored authentic reform programs for white citizens.

When scholars applied this line of thought to the antebellum era, they generally stressed the diversity of the region and the "Americanness" of the men who lived there. In several Southern states during the 1850s politicians came to power who represented the common white man. Conceptions of "Jacksonian democracy" vary, but by any definition Southerners were participants. Ameliorative and moral reforms such as poor relief, school drives, temperance campaigns, and moral improvement societies also existed in Southern states. Sellers' "tragic Southerner" was persuasively drawn, and his account of the Southern mind was strengthened by Ralph E. Morrow's thesis of 1961. Morrow reasoned that the proslavery argument came packaged for home consumption and often implied an audience which was by no means completely convinced about the justice of slavery.

William R. Taylor in 1961 explored another approach in tracing Cavalier myths to antebellum origins and questioning the reasons for their creation. Taylor indicated that during the first four decades of the nineteenth century, Southern fiction tended to be a means of self-admonition and reconciliation rather than the militant advocacy of a Southern cause against all comers. The Southern gentleman was indeed "synthetic" and embraced by Southerners not so much because they believed in him but because they needed him so badly. Moreover, the Cavalier was the invention of both Northerners and Southerners to fill the common need for codes and creeds which were not bound to the bustling, acquisitive materialism of nineteenth-century American society.

BIBLIOGRAPHY

Books and Articles Referred to in the Chapter Introduction

Karl Marx and Frederick Engels, *The Civil War in the United States* (3rd ed., 1961).
   Ulrich B. Phillips, "The Central Theme of Southern History," *American Historical Review* (1928).

Frank L. Owsley *et al.*, *I'll Take My Stand* (1930).
Clement Eaton, *The Mind of the Old South* (1964).
Robert F. Durden, *James Shepherd Pike, Republicanism and the American Negro, 1850–1882* (1957).
Dewey W. Grantham Jr., *The Democratic South* (1963).

Suggested Reading

For the idea that the South as a distinctive region dates back to the 1770s, see John R. Alden, *The First South* (1961); and for the argument that this "first South" was *not* characterized by declining slavery and Jeffersonian liberals, see Robert McColley, *Slavery and Jeffersonian Virginia* (1964). E. James Ferguson traced some economic origins of sectionalism in "Public Finance and the Origins of Southern Sectionalism," *Journal of Southern History* (1962). Margaret K. Latimer argued that the flush of "nationalism" that hit South Carolina was based on a cotton boom, "South Carolina, a Protagonist of the War of 1812," *American Historical Review* (1956). For a Marxist view of "the central theme," see Herbert Aptheker, *Toward Negro Freedom* (1956). On the exaggerations and confusions of the "agrarians," see Anne Ward Amacher, "Myths and Consequences: Calhoun and Some Nashville Agrarians," *South Atlantic Quarterly* (1960); Edward M. Moore, "The Agrarians of the 1930's," *Sewanee Review* (1963); and I. A. Newby, "The Southern Agrarians: A View After Thirty Years," *Agricultural History* (1963). On class differences among Southern whites as affected by slavery, see Wilbert E. Moore, "Slave Law and the Social Structure," *Journal of Negro History* (1941); Wilbert E. Moore and Robin W. Williams, "Stratification in the Ante-Bellum South," *American Sociological Review* (1942); Rudolf Heberle, "The Changing Social Stratification of the South," *Social Forces* (1959); Nancy C. Roberson, "Social Mobility in Ante-Bellum Alabama," *Alabama Review* (1960); George R. Woolfolk, "Taxes and Slavery in the Ante Bellum South," *Journal of Southern History* (1960). The whole question of the antebellum South has, of course, been tied to discussions of the South in general and of the modern South. Arthur S. Link, "The Progressive Movement in the South, 1870–1914," *North Carolina Historical Review* (1946), and Fletcher M. Green, "Democracy in The Old South," *Journal of Southern History* (1946), suggested new possibilities for inquiry into the Old and the New South. Dewey W. Grantham, Jr., has argued for a "liberal South" in *The Democratic South* (1963), and earlier in *Hoke Smith and the Politics of the New South* (1958). Grantham's case was strengthened by Anne F. Scott in "A Progressive Wind from the South, 1906–1913," *Journal of Southern History* (1963). Grantham traced the roots of the modern South neither to the Confederates nor to the Radicals but to the laissez-faire, pro-business "Redeemers" in "The Southern Bourbons Revisited," *South Atlantic Quarterly* (1961). Nash K. Burger and John Bettersworth, without rejecting the trends discussed by Grantham, took a more sympathetic stance toward the "Brigadiers" and Confederates in *South of Appomattox* (1957). Allen J. Going in *Bourbon Democracy in Alabama* (1959) criticized the "Redeemers" as an increasingly selfish and irresponsible oligarchy vulnerable to the victorious attacks of the Dixie demagogues and the "rednecks." On this turn of events, see Albert D. Kirwan, *Revolt of the Rednecks; Mississippi Politics, 1876–1925* (1951); and V. O. Key, *Southern Politics in State and Nation* (1949). Grantham analyzed the racist elements of national Progressivism in "The Progressive Movement and the Negro," *South Atlantic Quarterly* (1955), and continued to argue that a democratic tradition existed even among some of the Dixie demagogues. T. Harry Williams has sustained Grantham in the case of Huey Long, and discussed the "realistic" and "romantic" aspects of Dixie politics. See Williams, *Romance and Realism in Southern Politics* (1961). Frank E. Vandiver analyzed the more absurd popular myths about the Confederacy in "The Confederate Myth," *Southwest Review* (1961) and "The Confederacy and the American Tradition," *Journal of Southern History* (1962). See also Vandiver's discussion of Southern "extremism" in *The Idea of the South* (1964). George B. Tindall wrote an interesting account of myths in "The Benighted South: Origins of a Modern Image," *Virginia Quarterly Review* (1964), but one fears that all "reality" has been dissolved in "myth" and that all "myths" are created equal. Even more stimulating is Burl Noggle, "Variety and Ambiguity: The Recent Approach to Southern History," *Mississippi Quarterly* (1963–64). Still the scholar who surrenders completely to "Variety and Ambiguity" may cease to function. Wilma Dykeman once again followed the central theme of Southern history to race in "The Southern Demagogue," *Virginia Quarterly Review* (1957). Grantham provided a resume of the debate to 1964 in "Interpreters of the Modern South," *South Atlantic Quarterly* (1964). The central problem for this chapter is, of course, the question of "democratic" and "American" elements in the antebellum South. The chief work on this theme is Charles G. Sellers, Jr., *The Southerner as American* (1960). Sellers suggested a more complex South by arguing that town and professional people played a large role in the Southern Whig party, "Who Were the Southern Whigs?" *American Historical Review* (1953). Grady McWhiney gave a negative answer to the question "Were the Whigs a Class Party in Alabama?" *Journal of Southern History* (1957). See also Fletcher M. Green, "Listen to the Eagle Scream: One Hundred Years of the Fourth of July in North Carolina, 1776–1876," *North Carolina Historical Review* (1954). Wilfred B. Yearns traced strong Whig influence into *The Confederate Congress* (1960).

1964

Those Mysterious Southern Agrarians*

THOMAS P. GOVAN

Agarian and agrarianism are words commonly used by historians to describe particular aspects of American life, but despite, or perhaps because of, wide usage, it is often difficult to know what the words are intended to convey. They have something to do with farming, that much seems sure, but some farmers, apparently, are not agrarians. They live in the wrong part of the country, in New England or the middle states; for, though there are farms all over the nation, most of the agrarians are in the South and West. The words also carry a penumbra of

undefined meaning, an implication of hostility to industry, commerce, and finance, and the persons to whom they are applied are described, in most instances, as innocent victims of an unfair economic system, exploited by others, not dangerous radicals or revolutionaries.

No hint of opprobrium, no pejorative implication, accompany the twentieth-century use of the terms, and it is somewhat puzzling to read in the 1874 "Declaration of the Purposes of the National Grange" that "In our noble order, there is no communism, no agrarianism."[1] It is likewise confusing to learn that President James Madison thought

* Thomas P. Govan, "Agrarian and Agrarianism: A Study in the Use and Abuse of Words," *Journal of Southern History,* XXX (February 1964), 35–47. Copyright 1964 by the Southern Historical Association. Reprinted by permission of the Managing Editor.

[1] Henry S. Commager (ed.), *Documents of American History* (2 vols. in 1; New York, 1958), II, 80.

agrarianism a dangerous doctrine that must be guarded against, a product of the "levelling spirit" that had already appeared in Shays' Rebellion. "No agrarian attempts have yet been made in this country," he said in the Constitutional Convention in 1787, but, unless preventive measures were taken, he was certain they would be. He also said that if elections in Great Britain "were open to all classes of people, the property of the landed proprietors would be insecure [and] an agrarian law would soon take place"; and Thomas Jefferson, in 1813, praised the American Congress because it had provided "protection to wealth against the agrarian and plundering enterprises of the majority of the people."[2]

Agrarian, to them, meant the forced equalization of the ownership of cultivated land, "spoliation under the name of division or redistribution." It had entered the language as a translation of *lex agraria*, the agrarian law, that provided for the equal division of public lands, *ager publicus*, in ancient Rome, and its "socialistic" connotation was confirmed by its use in James Harrington's utopian study, the *Commonwealth of Oceana* (1656). "An equal agrarian," Harrington wrote, "is a perpetual law establishing and preserving the balance of dominion," and to bring this political equilibrium about he proposed an "agrarian law" that would limit landed estates to those with annual rents of no more than 2,000 pounds. He later attributed the collapse of the commonwealth to its failure to confiscate the large estates, and, of all his proposals, the agrarian law encountered the sharpest contemporary criticism.[3]

Such a coerced redistribution of land, in the opinion of John Adams, was unnecessary in the United States because, as he noted with pride in 1787, "The agrarian"— by which he meant, simply, cultivated land —"is divided among the common people in every state"; and Jefferson, in an 1811 letter to Dupont de Nemours, wrote, "We are all the more reconciled to the tax on importations, because it falls exclusively on the rich, and with the equal partition of intestates' estates, constitutes the best agrarian law." Their use of the word, without a connotation of forced equalization, was apparently the sense of Noah Webster's definition in the first American dictionary (1806), in which he gave a nonradical, at least noncoercive, meaning to the word by defining it simply as "relating to an equal division of lands." But he may have meant more; he clearly did in the 1828 edition where he quoted Edmund Burke's admonition that "An *agrarian* distribution of land or property would make the rich, poor, but would not make the poor, rich."[4]

Burke knew, however, that the great inequities in land distribution, particularly in his native Ireland, were a source of dangerous, but justifiable, discontent, and he warned the British that such landed possessions as those held by the Duke of Bedford were "irresistibly inviting to an agrarian experiment."[5] He wanted economic reforms to prevent a future outbreak of violence, and here, surprisingly, he joined one of his most persistent antagonists, the radical revolutionary, Thomas Paine. In a 1797 pam-

---

[2] Charles C. Tansill (ed.), *Documents Illustrative of the Formation of the Union of the American States* (Washington, 1927), 280, 811; Thomas Jefferson to John Adams, October 28, 1813, in Thomas Jefferson, *Writings*, Andrew A. Lipscomb and Albert E. Bergh (eds.) (20 vols.; Washington, 1907), XIII, 397.
[3] Robert G. Latham (ed.), *A Dictionary of the English Language* (2 vols.; London, 1872); James A. H. Murray and others (eds.), *A New English Dictionary on Historical Principles* . . . (10 vols.; Oxford, 1888–1928); James Harrington, *The Oceana and Other Works* . . . (London,

1737), 57–58; Will and Ariel Durant, *The Age of Louis XIV* (New York, 1963), 564–66; H. F. Russell Smith, *Harrington and His Oceana; a Study of a 17th Century Utopia and Its Influence in America* (Cambridge, 1914), 118.
[4] John Adams, *Works*, Charles Francis Adams, ed. (10 vols.; Boston, 1850–56), IV, 359; Sir William Craigie and James R. Hulbert (eds.), *A Dictionary of American English* . . . (4 vols.; Chicago, 1938–44); Jefferson to Dupont de Nemours, April 15, 1811, in Jefferson, *Writings*, XIII, 39; Noah Webster, *A Compendious Dictionary of the English Language* . . . (Hartford, 1806); *A Dictionary of the English Language* . . . (London, 1832).
[5] Edmund Burke, *Works* (12 vols.; London, 1899), V, 217.

phlet, *Agrarian Justice*, addressed to "the Legislature and the Executive Directory of the French Republic," Paine suggested a way whereby the inequities and injustices perpetuated by oligarchic control of the land could be remedied without confiscation and redistribution. He advocated the establishment of a fund, through a ground rent paid by the owners of land, that would provide a stated sum to all young persons as they entered adult life and pay pensions to the old, no longer able to work; but no government of the time, certainly not the one to which the proposal was addressed, considered adopting this precursor of the single tax and social security.[6]

Paine's friends in America, the Jeffersonian Republicans, were as uninterested as the French Directory, and it was not until the early years of Andrew Jackson's administration that any American became a convert to this point of view. Sometime in the late 1820s, George Henry Evans, a leader of the New York Workingmen's party and editor of the *Workingman's Advocate*, read *Agrarian Justice* and in his paper began advocating this kind of agrarianism as well as shorter hours and better conditions of work. Like most New York reformers during these years, Evans was an opponent of Tammany Hall and the Albany Regency (the Jackson party in the city and state), and in 1830 the Albany *Argus*, an administration newspaper, denounced those who, "as Anti-Masons, as Working-men, as Agrarians, as Fanny Wright men," were hostile to that which should be advocated by "sound, discreet and honest citizens."[7]

Included in this indictment was not Evans alone but also another predomi-

nantly antiadministration group of men in western New York, who, in 1827, had organized the Agrarian Convention of the Holland Purchase. These self-styled agrarians did not want to expropriate the lands owned by the Dutch-controlled Holland Land Company. Their purpose was rather to persuade the New York legislature to levy taxes on the unimproved lands of the company to finance the building of schools, roads, and other public improvements, but Martin Van Buren's Albany Regency, which controlled legislative action, refused to comply. The convention dissolved in 1835, without accomplishing its purpose, but the denunciation of this group—and of Evans—by the Jacksonians gave currency to *agrarian* as an opprobrious term, a name, as Hermann von Holst noted in 1879, to be given to opponents "to make them an abomination in the eyes of all those who took any interest in law or social order."[8]

Thus a word that in eighteenth-century America had been unambiguously used in regard to an equal or more equitable distribution of ownership of cultivated land became little more than a rubbery epithet, a loose, ambiguous term of denunciation and abuse. Its use in this way had been originated by Jacksonians in New York. Elsewhere, however, it was used against the Jacksonians; in 1835, for example, George McDuffie, governor of South Carolina, despairingly predicted that "the agrarianism, which is but another name for the Jackson party, will permanently maintain the ascendency, and God only knows how soon it will come to pass that the multitude will claim the right to live upon private plunder, as their leaders do upon the public offices."[9]

Van Buren's alliance with the Locofoco Democrats, Frances Wright, Robert Dale

[6] Thomas Paine, *Life and Works*, William M. Van der Weyde, ed. (10 vols.; New Rochelle, N.Y., 1925), X, 1–37.

[7] Hans Sperber and Travis Trilteschuh, *American Political Terms; an Historical Dictionary* (Detroit, 1962); Mitford M. Mathews, *A Dictionary of Americanisms on Historical Principles* (Chicago, 1951); Fred E. Haynes, "George Henry Evans," *Dictionary of American Biography*, VI, 201–2; Lee Benson, *The Concept of Jacksonian Democracy; New York As a Test Case* (Princeton, 1961), 33–40.

[8] Paul D. Evans, *The Holland Land Company* (Buffalo, 1924), 354–89; Hermann von Holst, *The Constitutional and Political History of the United States* (8 vols.; Chicago, 1876–1892), II, 397.

[9] George McDuffie to Nicholas Biddle, January 26, 1835, in Nicholas Biddle Papers (Library of Congress).

Owen, and other proponents of "agrarianism and infidelity" in 1837 increased the virulence of the Whig attacks, and Mordecai M. Noah—once a Jackson editor who had been rewarded with public office but, in 1838, an opponent of Jackson's successor—charged that "2,000 radicals, agrarians, Fanny Wright men and Locofocos" had "thrown themselves on the bounty of Van Buren." James Silk Buckingham, an English observer, quoted Noah's use of the term and explained to his readers that " 'Agrarian' is the name . . . given to people who . . . recommend to Government to keep the revenue in safe custody, in treasuries of their own." But then, with an irony that did not quite come off, he stated that "In other countries this term is usually, though erroneously, applied to those who are supposed to desire that the public lands and public wealth should be taken from the rich and divided among the poor."[10]

Through the remaining years of the nineteenth century, most Americans used the word as a disparaging epithet, usually descriptive of those who would subvert the existing property structure; and, when the Grangers, in 1874, joined communism and agrarianism, they were doing what came naturally to their generation. In other countries, the usage varied. The German adjective *agrarisch* and the French *agrarien*, though translated into English as *agrarian*, were generally used as if they were exactly synonymous with *agricultural*, and in Germany, the late nineteenth-century *Bund der Landwirte* (the Agrarian League), has been described as the most conservative and reactionary group within the empire.[11]

Historians of Great Britain, conversely, continued to use *agrarian* as a term referring to controversies—sometimes, but not always, connected with radicalism and violence—that arose over the ownership and use of cultivated land. Two monographic essays, published in the *Cambridge Modern History* in 1910, illuminate this difference in national usage. One, written by a German, Hermann Oncken, said that despite the development of manufacturing in Germany, "it would be an exaggeration to speak of the transformation of an agrarian into an industrial state"; but in the second, Robert Dunlop, an Englishman, wrote of the "agrarian problem" in Ireland and of the "agrarian outrages" that occurred during the "agrarian war" between landlords and tenants.[12]

Another British historian, Richard H. Tawney, in *The Agrarian Problem in the Sixteenth Century* (1912) used the word to describe both the peaceful and violent changes in land ownership and use in Tudor England, and a similar usage is to be found in an article written by Joseph B. Ross, an American agricultural historian, "Agrarian Changes in the Middle West" (1910). Ross wrote of "the present agrarian revolution in the Middle West" that had been brought about by "the growth of large estates," the "shifting of land values," and "the increasing number of tenant farmers." Robert Preston Brooks employed the word similarly in *The Agrarian Revolution in Georgia, 1865–1912* (1914), a study of the changes in land tenure after the Civil War.[13]

This use of the word as a precise technical term, referring specifically to land distribution, tenure, and use, has continued.

---

[10] Mathews, *Dictionary of Americanisms;* James Silk Buckingham, *America, Historical, Statistic and Descriptive* (2 vols.; New York, 1841), I, 124.

[11] As examples see Johann Croner, *Die Geschichte der agrarischen Bewegung in Deutschland* (Berlin, 1909), and Edgard Milhaud, "Le mouvement agrarien en Allemagne," *Revue de Paris,* VII, pt. 2 (April, 1900), 785–816. On the *Bund der Landwirte* see Robert H. Fife, Jr., *The German Empire Between Two Wars* . . . (New York, 1916), 120–21, 128, 149.

[12] A. W. Ward and others (eds.), *The Cambridge Modern History* (13 vols.; Cambridge, 1902–11), XII, 65–90, 134–73.

[13] Joseph B. Ross, "Agrarian Changes in the Middle West," *Political Science Quarterly,* XXV (December, 1910), 637; "The Agrarian Revolution in the Middle West," *North American Review,* CXC (September, 1909); Robert Preston Brooks, *The Agrarian Revolution in Georgia, 1865–1912, Bulletin of the University of Wisconsin,* No. 639, History Series, III, No. 3 (Madison, 1914).

The 1959 edition of the *Encyclopaedia Britannica*, for example, spoke of the agrarian associations in Italy, Latvia, and Bulgaria that sought more equitable land distribution after World War I; and a 1963 issue of *Time* said, "Practicing what [Cardinal] Silva Henríquez preached about agrarian reform, the Roman Catholic Church in Chile undertook its own land-distribution program."[14] The "agrarian reforms" brought about under General Douglas MacArthur in Japan after World War II are another example of this use of the word, and it was likewise the meaning intended by those American diplomats who, unfortunately for their future careers, described the Chinese Communists as "agrarian reformers."

In most American usage during the twentieth century, however, *agrarian* has had little connection with land tenure or distribution. Rather it has been fitted into varying contexts, almost existentially or nominalistically, according to the will and definition of the particular author. In 1920, Louis Bernard Schmidt, describing "Some Significant Aspects of the Agrarian Revolution in the United States," wrote that by "agrarian revolution" he meant "the transformation of agriculture from a primitive, pioneer, largely self-sufficing type of industry into a modern business organized on a scientific, capitalistic, commercial basis."[15] But a more widely known work by Solon J. Buck, published the same year, used the word with a different connotation. Buck's was a study of agricultural discontent in the late nineteenth century, in which the Grangers, who, we have seen, repudiated agrarianism along with communism, are described as participants in an agrarian crusade.

Another writer, James Christy Bell, used the word similarly in 1921 in describing "Agrarian Discontent in the Mississippi Valley, 1840–1850."[16] To him and to Buck, *agrarian* was a synonym for *agricultural;* but, since the farmers they were writing about were discontented protestors against existing economic conditions, some of whom were active in politics, their definition of the word became inextricably connected with another that had been devised, only a few years before, by Charles A. Beard in *An Economic Interpretation of the Constitution* (1913). The Constitution and the controversies concerning its ratification, according to Beard, were the product of "a deep-seated conflict between a popular party based on paper money and agrarian interests, and a conservative party centered in towns and resting on financial, mercantile, and personal property interest generally." He never explicitly stated what these "agrarian interests" were, apparently believing them self-evident, but he made his meaning somewhat clearer two years later in the *Economic Origins of Jeffersonian Democracy* (1915), when he wrote that Jefferson "declared the battle to be between agrarianism and capitalism," that he "consciously and purposely [directed] his public policies and his political appeal to the agricultural sections of the population," and that "this alignment of the agrarian mass against the capitalistic class . . . was likewise accepted by the leading Federalists as fundamental."[17]

Jefferson, it is obvious, did not call himself an agrarian. He had no sympathy with "agrarian and plundering enterprises." He also was a capitalist in the customary meaning of the term. Never once did he challenge the private ownership of the means of production or their operation for profit,

14 *Time*, August 23, 1963, 20.

15 Louis Bernard Schmidt, "Some Significant Aspects of the Agrarian Revolution in the United States," *Iowa Journal of History and Politics*, XVIII (July, 1920), 371–95. Another historian, David M. Potter, in "The Enigma of the South," *Yale Review*, LI (October, 1961), 142–51, states that this transformation of agriculture was a departure from an agrarian economy rather than being the agrarian revolution.

16 Solon J. Buck, *Agrarian Crusade* (New Haven, 1920), 18, 38, 39, 60, 87, 90, 97, 110, 125; James Christy Bell, *Opening a Highway to the Pacific, 1838–1846* (New York, 1921), 116–31.

17 Charles A. Beard, *An Economic Interpretation of the Constitution* (New York, 1913), 292, and *Economic Origins of Jeffersonian Democracy* (New York, 1915), 358, 427–28.

and on his own farm, he not only shifted from one crop to another—from tobacco to wheat and back again—in accordance with market conditions but also built a factory in which to manufacture nails for sale through merchants at Milton, Charlottesville, and Staunton. He would have been surprised, even offended, at being connected with "a party based on paper money," since one of his principal objections to the policies of Alexander Hamilton was the conviction, recorded in the *Anas*, that Hamilton, through the Bank of the United States, had contrived a system "for deluging the states with paper money instead of gold and silver." Jefferson believed that a paper currency, no matter how issued, would necessarily be abused, and that specie—gold and silver—was the only safe medium of exchange.[18]

[18] Dumas Malone, *Jefferson and the Ordeal of Liberty* (Boston, 1962), 201, 205, 217-20; Jefferson, *Writings*, I, 209; XIII, 430. Andrew Jackson, another President frequently described as an agrarian, also desired an exclusively metallic currency, and his and Jefferson's opposition to paper money has led to some confusion as to what the agrarian position on this question can be said to be. E. James Ferguson, *The Power of the Purse; a History of American Public Finance, 1776–1790* (Chapel Hill, 1961), 335, 342, states that "Nearly all the states carried over from colonial times a predilection for currency finance methods. Accustomed to these modes, which suited agrarian circumstances, most people regarded specie payment as signifying permanent debts, heavy taxes—in a word, oppression." He also writes concerning Hamilton that "Rejecting agrarian modes, he [by insisting on specie payment] pledged the central government to high finance, and in this he had the overwhelming approval of the Congress."

Charles Sellers and Henry May, *A Synopsis of American History* (Chicago, 1963), 142–43, take a directly opposite view, writing in one place that "Jackson and many of his principal followers were 'hard-money' men who wanted all bank notes driven from circulation, leaving only gold and silver as a circulating medium. Their attack on the national bank was only the first step in their deflationary, agrarian-minded program" and in another that "The hard money men could only shout futile warnings. Their Jeffersonian constitutional scruples prevented them from attempting direct federal regulation of the state banks. Regulation at the state level was equally impossible because the uneasy alliance between hard-money (or agrarian-minded) Democrats and enterprise-minded Democrats began breaking down."

Vernon L. Parrington, an intellectual historian who had little interest in currency, also described Jefferson as an anticapitalist agrarian. "The sharp struggle between Jefferson and Hamilton," he wrote in *Main Currents in American Thought* (1927), "must be reckoned, in part at least, a conflict between the rival principles of Quesnay and Adam Smith, between an agrarian and a capitalist economy."[19] This statement connecting agrarianism with the economic teachings of Quesnay added some content to the term, but Parrington made no attempt to explain how farmers, owning land and producing crops for sale in markets in all parts of the world, could be considered outside the capitalist economy or hostile to its principles.

His work, though that of a liberal, progressive reformer, a sympathizer with socialism, was well received by Donald Davidson of Vanderbilt University in Nashville, a spokesman not only for the genteel, aristocratic, and noncommercial tradition of the South but also for a group of writers who were soon to put *agrarian* and *agrarianism* in the vocabulary of every intellectual. Davidson had no sympathy with Arthur M. Schlesinger, Sr., and other "progressive historians" of what he called "the Beard school," but he thought Parrington's book "a judicial, clarifying force" that would enable the South to overcome the "equalitarian idealism" of Jefferson by a return to its true tradition: Calhoun's "Greek-like conception of society based on economic realism," that had been derived from the writings of John Taylor of Caroline, "an almost forgotten 'philosopher and statesman of agrarianism.' "[20]

The same point of view was present three years later in *I'll Take My Stand: The South and the Agrarian Tradition* (1930), in which Davidson and 11 other

[19] Vernon L. Parrington, *Main Currents in American Thought* (3 vols.; New York, 1927–30), I, 346.

[20] Donald Davidson, *The Spyglass; Views and Reviews, 1924–1930*, John Tyree Fain, ed. (Nashville, 1963), 131–37, 227.

Southerners argued for the restoration of a gentler, less competitive way of life. They were tired of progress, of go-getting, of bigness, of mechanization, and nostalgically sought a return to the "antique conservatism" of the South. They defended the "Southern way of life against what may be called the American or prevailing way," and the phrase they selected to express the distinction, as foreshadowed in Davidson's review of Parrington, was "Agrarian versus Industrial." The agrarian society, they said, "is hardly one that has no use for industries, for professional vocations, for scholars and artists and the life of cities. Technically perhaps, an agrarian society is one in which agriculture is the leading vocation. . . . The theory of agrarianism is that the culture of the soil is the best and most sensitive of vocations, and that therefore it should have the economic preference and enlist the maximum number of workers."[21]

These Agrarians, it seems almost needless to say, were not themselves farmers and did not make their own living from the land. They were teachers and writers—historians, philosophers, economists, poets, novelists, and critics—who milked no cows, shoveled no manure, and picked no cotton or peas. Through their influence, however, *agrarian* spread outside the ranks of historians and economists into general scholarly and literary use, but now in an almost idealized sense as a word somehow particularly descriptive of the South, though also of the West, and as an antonym of industrial. It also became connected with the economic and political views of John Taylor and thus helped confirm an unuttered assumption, shared by Beard, Parrington, and many other American students, that there was a fundamental conflict between the economic interests of farmers and the economic interests of all other vocational groups.

This basic dichotomy was accepted axiomatically by these twentieth-century writers, as it had been by Taylor, Jefferson, Madison, and many others; but, despite the wide acceptance of the view, it is not, and has never been, an accurate description of the economic situation of farmers in the United States. The sources from which this mistaken view was derived were the writings of European political economists, the Physiocrats and others, who accurately described the conflict of interest between the commercial and landed classes found on the continent of Europe and Great Britain. Most European and British landlords, not themselves farmers, were collectors of fixed rents from farmers, so that a rising level of prices and an increase of economic activity, though as advantageous to the growers and sellers of crops as to merchants, manufacturers, shippers, and bankers, tended to decrease the relative income of those who had inherited or purchased the right to collect money rents.

This fundamental conflict of interest between the landed and commercial classes has never existed in the United States. American farmers, though they would not use the name, have been entrepreneurs, engaged in the production of goods for sale, and their quarrels with merchants, bankers, manufacturers, shippers, and other farmers were and are over such matters as the objects of taxation, the division of profits (the costs of services), and which should receive the larger share of governmental bounty and support. Agriculture, in intention at least, has been a profit-making enterprise in an economy made up of such enterprises —a truth that became so obvious by the mid-twentieth century that most writers abandoned the use of *agrarian* when describing the large, mechanized, governmentally subsidized American farms. The shepherds of Arcady could not compete with combines, tractors, and cotton pickers, and not even the Nashville Agrarians could describe the operation of these machines as "the best and most sensitive of vocations." Some signs of dissatisfaction with the

[21] Twelve Southerners, *I'll Take My Stand: The South and the Agrarian Tradition* (New York, 1930), ix, xviii–xix, 3.

confused and differing definitions also appeared. Earle D. Ross and Robert L. Tontz, agricultural economists at Iowa State University, in 1948 wrote that "The word 'agrarian' has a particular meaning which no legitimate usage can make synonymous with 'agricultural' "; and the present writer, in 1955, questioned the validity of the agrarian-capitalist dichotomy, particularly as used to distinguish the South from the North. Robert E. Brown, in addition to making severe strictures on Beard's method of inquiry and conclusions in *Charles Beard and the Constitution* (1956), protested against the loose and ambiguous manner in which *agrarian* was used.[22]

In recent years, nevertheless, the meaning of the word has clouded rather than cleared. Richard Hofstadter, though an admirer of Beard and a defender of his work, used a different, almost an opposite, definition of *agrarian* in the *Age of Reform* (1955). Agrarians, in Beard's view, were farmers, motivated in their political actions by what they considered their economic advantage, but to Hofstadter, agrarians, throughout most of American history, were not farmers at all. They were reactionary traditionalists loyal to the values of a society that had disappeared. The only true agrarians were subsistence farmers, relying on barter for the few necessities they did not produce. But then without stating when or where any substantial number of such farmers were to be found, either in the British colonies or the subsequently formed United States, he wrote, "While early American society was an agrarian society, it was fast becoming more commercial, and commercial goals made their way among the agricultural classes almost as rapidly as elsewhere. The more commercial this so-ciety became, however, the more reason it found to cling in imagination to the non-commercial agrarian values."[23]

Another definition, even more subjective than Hofstadter's, is found in Lee Benson's *Turner and Beard* (1960), which denied any necessary connection between agrarianism and the vocation of farming. This writer first made a distinction between "agrarian-minded" men and those who were "commercial-minded," and then stated that "The terms do not denote classes, socioeconomic status groups, or occupations—they denote ways of thinking. Thus farmers with no intention or prospect of changing their occupations may have been commercial-minded, and men not engaged in farming may have been agrarian-minded. In short, our terms suggest the philosophy and ethos that men wanted to prevail in the United States."[24]

Benson said that his intention was "to paraphrase and extend" Beard's economic interpretation of American political controversies; but, in this instance, as in other parts of his work, he has followed the example of Marx in regard to Hegel: he has turned Beard upside down. He has transformed what Beard described objectively and materialistically as a conflict between groups with different economic interests—farmers and debtors, on the one hand, urban capitalists, on the other—into a conflict that is entirely subjective and ideological in character.

This almost total reversal in meaning should not be surprising, for once a word ceases to be connected with preceding usages and definitions, no other principle of limitation can be found. Its users enter the bewildering world of Alice and Humpty Dumpty:

"When *I* use a word," Humpty Dumpty said, in rather a scornful tone, "it means just

---

[22] Earle D. Ross and Robert L. Tontz, "The Term 'Agricultural Revolution' As Used by Economic Historians," *Agricultural History*, XXII (January, 1948), 33; Thomas P. Govan, "Was the Old South Different?" *Journal of Southern History*, XXI (November, 1955), 447–55; Robert E. Brown, *Charles Beard and the Constitution* (Princeton, 1956), 108, 187, 189, 190.

[23] Richard Hofstadter, *The Age of Reform: From Bryan to F.D.R.* (New York, 1955), 23–24.

[24] Lee Benson, *Turner and Beard: American Historical Writing Reconsidered* (Glencoe, Ill., 1960), 215–18.

what I choose it to mean—neither more nor less."

"The question is," said Alice, "whether you *can* make words mean so many different things."

"The question is," said Humpty Dumpty, "which is to be master—that's all."[25]

And the word now has many masters. A college president writes of "the transfer of much of our higher education from agrarian settings to urban centers," and a master's candidate, of the "agrarian bourgeoisie." There are "agrarian Reds" and "agrarian Bakunists," also the "agrarian middle class"; and, though the demand for railroad regulation in the late nineteenth century is deemed part of the "agrarian revolt," it is also described as not coming from "oppressed agrarians" but rather from dissatisfied business groups in the cities. So confused is the situation that it is now necessary for each speaker or writer to define the word every time it is used, and it has thus lost most of its usefulness as a historical term.

What is needed is an "agrarian reform," perhaps an "agrarian revolution," that would enable historians and other writers to continue their use of the word by confining it to controversies concerning land tenure and land reform, where no semantic confusion or ambiguity exists. Ordinary words are available—farm, farmer, farming; agriculture, agriculturist, agricultural; even plantation, planter, planting—to express every meaning that Beard and other objective materialists wanted to convey; and equally precise words and phrases can be found by subjective idealists, such as Hofstadter and Benson, to describe an ideology or value system that continues to influence action long after the circumstances to which it was a response have passed away.

A precedent for such action is to be found in the language of botany, where *agrarian* means today what it always has meant, "growing wild in the fields"; but such consistency is perhaps impossible in the language of history. Historians, having little power of self-discipline, should have an academy, a setter of rules for the use of words; but, unfortunately, the anarchism which makes such an institution needed would probably prevent them from accepting this desirable constraint. They will, it seems certain, continue to use *agrarian* and *agrarianism* in any way they think fit, as part of their freedom to be, like Humpty Dumpty, existential nominalists, masters of their words.

---

[25] Charles Lutwidge Dodgson, *The Complete Works of Lewis Carroll* (London, 1939), 196.

1964

The Oppressive Mississippians*

JAMES W. SILVER

Between 1938 and 1947 three Mississippi professors, Percy Lee Rainwater, John K. Bettersworth, and Vernon L. Wharton, published scholarly volumes which laid great stress on Mississippi's poverty-stricken leadership in secession, Civil War, and Reconstruction to 1890. It is quite likely that if these studies were put on the market today, their authors would be run out of the state.

The search for historical truth has become a casualty in embattled Mississippi where neither the governor nor the legislature, in their hot pursuit of interposition, indicates any awareness that Mississippians were Americans before they were Southerners or that Magnolia State politicians once stood firm against nullification and secession. The state's present-day exploiters of federal munificence, however, should applaud the cleverness of their ancestors in the 1850s who interpreted state rights as requiring the use of national power to destroy local self-government in the territories and to thwart Northern state nullification of the fugitive slave law.

The striking parallel between people and events of the 1850s and the 1950s reminds us that Mississippi has been on the defensive against inevitable social change for

* James W. Silver, "Mississippi: The Closed Society," *Journal of Southern History* (1964). An expanded version of the presidential address delivered at the annual meeting of the Southern Historical Association at Asheville, North Carolina, November 7, 1963. Copyright 1963 by James W. Silver.

more than a century, and that for some years before the Civil War it had developed a closed society with an orthodoxy accepted by nearly everybody in the state. The all-pervading doctrine then and now has been white supremacy—whether achieved through slavery or segregation—rationalized by a professed adherence to state rights and bolstered by religious fundamentalism. In such a society a never ceasing propagation of the "true faith" must and has gone on relentlessly with a constantly reiterated demand for loyalty to the united front demanding that nonconformists be hushed, silenced with a vengeance, or in crisis situations driven from the community. Violence and the threat of violence have reinforced the presumption of unanimity.

By 1861 Mississippians had been thoroughly prepared for secession by their short-sighted politicians, their chauvinistic press, their political preachers, and their blind philosophers, all operating within the authoritarian society. Even to the present generation the people have been paying for and *eulogizing* their most unwise decision of all time. In fact the romanticism associated with the Old South, the glorification of the Confederacy, and the bitter remembrances of Reconstruction have played their witless and powerful role in preserving a social order based on neither fact nor reason. According to Citizens Council literature, Mississippi is now the innocent victim of a second vicious Reconstruction from which its stalwart citizenry, demonstrating ancestral courage, will emerge triumphant as it did in 1875.

One of today's little sophistries asserts that equality must be earned, can never be achieved by force or law. The forgotten truth is that between 1875 and 1890 *inequality* was effected by force and regularized by law. By the end of the century Negroes had long since learned that Mississippi freedom included neither political nor any other kind of equality. The caste system had once and apparently for all [time] been substituted for slavery, the Negro was in his place, and the society was once more closed and sacrosanct.

No meaningful challenge to the caste system was possible in Mississippi in the first half of the twentieth century. In public life no white man, demagogue or patrician, proposed to do anything constructive about the Negro. Preferring corrupt and inefficient government to participation by the black man, the whites got a one-party system without competition between recognizable groups, with no continuity of existence even of factions, and no means of checking the wild-eyed—in sum, a series of Bilbonic plagues and Barnett blights. Whether The Man Bilbo was just the "slick little bastard" described by his admirers, or represented "nothing save passion, prejudice, and hatred," as claimed by Fred Sullens, is of small importance as compared with his career as symptomatic of the chaos and bankruptcy of Mississippi politics and its social order. In such a demoralized wasteland the sharp-eyed Snopeses have grasped their petty gains, to the greater glory of laissez faire, which ironically has in turn produced the much damned transfer of state functions to the federal government and a diminution of state sovereignty.

Today the totalitarian society of Mississippi imposes on all its people an obedience to an official orthodoxy almost identical with the proslavery philosophy—this in the teeth of the nearly universal dissipation of whatever intellectual sanction white supremacy had among the enlightened at the turn of this century. Every Mississippi politician not only denies the validity of the Fourteenth Amendment but in his heart hungers for the negative days of the Articles of Confederation. Governor Ross Barnett, whose personal constitution stops with the Tenth Amendment, is conveniently ignorant of the incompatibility of state rights and modern industrialization.

On the racial question, the Governor's views are now well known. "If we start off with the self-evident proposition," Barnett says, "that the whites and colored are different, we will not experience any difficulty in reaching the conclusion that they are not and never can be equal." It was his appointee to the Mississippi Supreme Court, Justice Tom Brady, who became for awhile the metaphysician of the master racists with the publication of the hastily written and scholastically barren *Black Monday* (1955). In turn this was outmoded by *Race and Reason* (1961) by Carleton Putnam, Roosevelt biographer and successful airline executive, become, by his own admission, expert theologian, psychologist, and anthropologist within a two-year period. To the enchantment of Mississippians, Putnam exposed the Franz Boas conspiracy which, he asserted, had held the scientific world in a climate of terror and fear of persecution for half a century. Mississippians did not read the book (they just sent it to their friends, as instructed by the Citizens Council), else they would have discovered that, even by Putnam's logic, the white race was already doomed inasmuch as more than half the country's Negroes lived in integrated situations. But who would argue with the new messiah? With a flourish of trumpets he was brought to Jackson on October 26, 1961 (proclaimed by the Governor as Race and Reason Day), and feted at a $25-a-plate dinner attended by 500 patriots.

There was no Dickens to point out that there never had been another such day in Mississippi. It could, Barnett believed, "mark the turning point in the South's struggle to preserve the integrity of the white race." Putnam had indeed provided an Article of Faith that Mississippians could live by. Denouncing the "left-wing pseudo-scientists" for creating the fallacy that "has gained complete possession of the Northern and Western mind," he designated Mississippi as "the heartland of the struggle for racial integrity" and in his best Bryan manner exclaimed, "You don't crucify the South on a cross of equalitarian propaganda." Calling on the South to produce more Barnetts, Putnam identified equalitarianism with Communism and segregation with Christianity.

In one respect Putnam's racist argument was not anachronistic. At the very time when the Negro was in the lengthy process of becoming a civilized being, he appeared to be and demonstrably *was* a cultural inferior, carefully trained for that status by every controllable factor in his environment. Faulkner has the Mississippian say: "We got to make him a nigger first. He's got to admit he's a nigger." From birth to death the Negro was exposed to an irresistible pressure for deferential behavior, and when he failed to conform he was driven out or even killed. By and large he played the role of Sambo well, giving little indication of any hope or desire to share in the white man's privileges.

One of the privileges he has seldom had in Mississippi is that of voting. In the twentieth century never so much as 10 percent and normally less than 5 percent of the Negro voting population has been allowed to register. Governor Barnett has repeatedly asserted that Negroes in Mississippi just don't want to vote, that they could if they so desired. Since 1954, Mississippi law, Barnett to the contrary, has required the voter applicant to read and write *and* interpret any section of the state constitution and (since 1960) to be of good moral character and to have his name and address published in a local newspaper for two weeks. At the moment, a substantial Negro vote would embarrass any white candidate in Mississippi. But the future is also plain. As Senator Bilbo once reminded an organizer for the Amalgamated Clothing Workers, "Son,

when you can show me that you can control any sizable number of voters in Mississippi, I'll be the damnedest champion you've ever had."

Gradual improvement of white schools has until very recently been shared by the Negroes only to a remote degree. But, as James K. Vardaman had understood, *any* Negro education spelled the eventual doom of the caste system. There may have been rumblings before, but the summer of 1954 brought a shock from which Mississippi's Old Guard will never recover. Having checked with his retinue of Uncle Toms, Governor Hugh White called in a hundred Negroes to get their anticipated endorsement for "separate but equal" school facilities. But a few young Negro radicals arranged for a caucus the night before the big meeting and after a heated debate carried the timid along with them.

Speaker Walter Sillers opened the momentous conference. Governor White spoke of the amicable race relations of the past. As planned, when the preliminaries were over, Charlie Banks got the floor and argued for the abolition of segregation. Five or six others followed suit. A conservative Negro publisher made a last stand for the old regime but was roundly denounced by a woman delegate as being a classic example of the effects of segregation. In desperation, Sillers called on another known friend of the white man, the Reverend H. H. Humes. As he walked to the front of the room the old minister was the center of all attention. "Gentlemen," he told the Governor and his friends, "you all should not be mad at us. Those were nine *white* men that rendered that decision. Not one colored man had anything to do with it. The real trouble is that you have given us schools too long in which we could study the earth through the floor and the stars through the roof." At this point, Governor White, mumbling that you couldn't trust Negroes any more, called the meeting to an end. It was also the end of an era. "For the first time," one of the delegates later said, "I was really proud to be a Negro in Mississippi."

Yet in the years since 1954 the state's Negroes have made few gains. The Establishment is entrenched so strongly that without the help of external forces (channeled through the federal government) Mississippi Negro leadership is for the short run in a helpless position. For, with varying degrees of enthusiasm, the makers of the orthodoxy —the press, the pulpit, the politicians, the philosophers, and the patriots—have since the Brown decision rushed to the successful defense of their way of life.

Moderation is expressed in the daily newspapers of Greenville, Tupelo, and McComb, and in an occasional weekly; nevertheless, the Mississippi press as a whole mounts vigilant guard upon the closed society. Happy with what a news director of a Jackson television station called "their home grown version of news management," the Hederman family newspapers manipulate information with little regard for accuracy or integrity. Negro crime and immorality in the North, Negro complicity in Communism, even Negro support for Barnett are given the headlines day after day. Shotgun blasts fired into a Negro home become a NAACP plot, the assassination of Medgar Evers is turned into a sacrificial offering to rekindle racial unrest, Mississippi is victimized by hate peddlers jealous of the state's economic progress. The Jackson *Clarion-Ledger* makes a revealing historical comparison: "Never was Hitler, nor Mussolini, nor the Mikado, nor even Kaiser Wilhelm attacked so venomously" as Mississippi—which invariably represents the South, with the South always a solid and unfaltering unit. But this leading state newspaper will find it difficult to approach ever again the imagination of its most famous headline, inspired by the arrest of Byron de la Beckwith, scion of an old Delta family, born on the Pacific coast but who had lived in Mississippi for 38 years: "CALIFORNIAN IS CHARGED WITH MURDER OF MEDGAR EVERS."

To such editors and their heavy-handed associates the Fifth Circuit Court becomes "the nine judicial baboons in New Orleans,"

President Kennedy "regards himself as a Jesus whose infinite wisdom represents mankind's only real hope of salvation," and Ross Barnett is twisted into a modern combination of David, Horatius, and Leonidas. Tougaloo College, a center of integrationist activity, is rechristened "Cancer College," with a new summer course in "Rapid Hate," and the slanderous *Rebel Underground*, having recommended the execution of the President of the United States, emerges as "an innocuous handbill." By March, 1963, the Jackson *Daily News* adds up the "price tag" on the federal invasion of Mississippi as coming to $14 million because of 130 bonus accidental deaths on the state's highways attributed to "a frame of mind, an atmosphere of anger, a period of bayonet-point frustration" which lowered the morale of the highway patrol. For the university faculty members who had the temerity to treat James Meredith as a human being, editor Jimmy Ward predicts crushed spirits, bitterness, even self-imposed tragedy.

In times of trial the Jackson papers lose all semblance of perspective. For example, on the day that Judge Sidney Mize ordered Meredith enrolled in the university, the *Daily News* front page carried these headlines:

ROSS RISKS JAIL TO HALT MIXING

Note Bares Negro Plan to Agitate
Hattiesburg Agitation Order [photostat]
We Support Gov. Barnett [editorial]
Negroes Purchased Shot, Says Mayor
President Deplores Shooting in State
Judge Mize Issues Permanent Injunction
   [bulletin]
Meredith Effigy Hanged at Oxford
Barnett During and After Broadcast
   [pictures]
Moses' Automobile [picture]
Editor's Column: All Loyal Mississippians Support Him [Barnett]

There was still room for a small cartoon about a Mississippi College football game and the index.

The role of the church since 1954 is more

difficult to assess than is that of the press. Some churches have taken exceptional action, notably the Mississippi diocese of the Episcopal Church which issued a general call for support of the Supreme Court's decision and eventual integration. And in the past year many preachers and a few ministerial groups have made courageous stands. But the church as a whole has remained loyal to the *status quo*. Ministers who led the discussion about segregation were for it, prompted no doubt by "an echo from the pew." In annual session, the Mississippi Baptist convention refused to endorse a series of resolutions reaffirming "our intelligent good will toward all men" and calling upon Christians to pray "that we may live consistent with Christian citizenship." A Baptist missionary, second cousin of Governor Barnett, wrote from Nigeria that Mississippians were making her work extremely difficult: "You send us out here to preach that Christ died for all men. Then you make a travesty of our message by refusing to associate with some of them because of the color of their skin. You are supposed to be holding the lifelines for us, and you are twisting them into a noose of racism to strangle our message. Communists do not need to work against the preaching of the Gospel here; you are doing it quite adequately." The missionary's mother expressed regret: "Antonina doesn't understand that Ross has been doing the best he can."

Other groups in Mississippi society, supporters of the orthodoxy, hold a position comparable to their predecessors of the Civil War period. The conservative men of large property holdings considered secession a doubtful though perfectly legal remedy for their troubles; it was a much larger group of active, restless lawyer-politicians, petty planters, and small-town editors, successful enterprisers on the make, who took Mississippi out of the Union in 1861. After World War II another crowd of "new men," bold entrepreneurs enamored as their forefathers had been of the prevailing social order, too busy making money to think deeply about changes bound to accompany progress, pleased with the "right-to-work" principle embedded in the constitution and with a colossal program of state socialism to entice the Yankee carpetbagger industrialist, sat by quietly and acquiesced in the building of the Citizens Council juggernaut.

Constitutional questions, on which so much controversy has centered since 1954, continue to bring a response in keeping with the quality of Mississippi leadership. There seems to be some confusion in the minds of the state's lawyers and jurists as to whether Mississippians must obey the law of the land as interpreted by the federal courts. Dean Robert J. Farley of the Ole Miss law school repeatedly warned in public that lawyers were acting irresponsibly in permitting by their silence the Citizens Council and irreconcilable politicians to interpret the law for them. The chief dereliction, it seems clear, came in *allowing the people of Mississippi to believe that they could get away with an outright defiance of the courts.* "We as Mississippians," declared Justice Brady in 1959, "will not bow down to a court of nine old men whose hearts are as black as their robes." Brady castigated Governor Coleman, who had frowned upon interposition as so much "legal poppycock," as a moderate—"a man who is going to let a little sewage under the door." But the classic statement regarding law and order came in 1963 from the very top of Mount Olympus. Indignant over the "sickening" conduct of Negro parents and ministers in Birmingham in permitting boys and girls to run "afoul" of the law by "using these children for ignoble and loathesome ends and deliberately and contemptuously inciting them to become juvenile delinquents," Governor Barnett declared in a burst of emotion: "What do these degenerates know of freedom? True freedom consists of and is founded upon the observance of law and the power of law to make those who would break the law conform to it. History tells us that freedom can exist only under the protection of constitutional law. These agitators seek to defy constitutional law under the name of freedom." Once again Ross was doing the best he could.

The new legislature convening in January, 1962, was met by a request from the Governor to (1) outlaw the Communist party (years before, the FBI had found one Communist in Mississippi), (2) pass "an enforceable sedition act," and (3) compel state employees to take an oath of allegiance to the United States and Mississippi. (Barnett did not explain whether this could be accomplished in a single oath.) In any event, when Mississippi legislators get together their herd instinct drives them to resolving the fate of the world. If they hate Hodding Carter or the President of the United States, or love Elvis Presley, Dizzy Dean, the Mississippi State basketball team, or South Africa, or feel that a former Miss America is an accomplished actress, they are not inhibited from saying so. Senator Hugh Bailey, who had ridden a bull from Canton to Jackson to fulfill a campaign promise, offered a resolution urging the United States to substitute turnip seed for cash in the foreign aid program. Such action, he asserted, "would relieve pressure in this country's economy and give the world's population necessary vitamins, minerals, and bulk." A mere handful of the seed would feed a hundred people and could be mailed overseas for planting.

Legislators spend much of their time devising legal subterfuges to keep the Negro in his place. When it appeared that the number of "smart alecks" telephoning "white ladies" had reached "epidemic stages," the House voted a $10,000 fine and five years' imprisonment for cursing into the telephone. Objection to such stiff punishment brought the assurance that judges would know how to use the law. The House unanimously called for a constitutional amendment barring from voting persons guilty of vagrancy, perjury, and child desertion, and concurred in the addition of adultery, fornication, larceny, gambling, and crimes committed with a deadly weapon. A still further addition of habitual drunkenness was defeated when a member suggested that it "might even get

some of us." There was some objection, also, to the inclusion of adultery. Reprisal legislation is common, like that bill which the committee chairman said was "concerned with a woman editor who has been writing things which don't go along with the feelings in the community" or another condemning land belonging to Campbell College after Representative McClellan explained, "Jackson has had a cancer in its midst long enough." The cancer will be removed to Mound Bayou in 1964.

One legislator was sorely impressed with the power of the Citizens Council:

It's hard for us sometimes to consider a bill on its merits if there is any way Bill Simmons [executive secretary of the Citizens Council] can attach an integration tag. For instance, a resolution was introduced in the House to urge a boycott of Memphis stores because some of them have desegregated. I knew it was ridiculous and would merely amuse North Mississippians who habitually shop in Memphis. The resolution came in the same week that four Negroes were fined in court for boycotting Clarksdale stores. Yet the hot eyes of Bill Simmons were watching. If we had voted against the resolution he would have branded us. So there we were, approving a boycott while a Mississippi court was convicting Negroes for doing what we lawmakers were advocating. It just didn't make sense.

As is characteristic of a closed society, the schools, too, are pressured by organized voices of the orthodoxy: the Citizens Council, the American Legion, and the patriotic ladies' groups. A case in point was the withdrawal of a film called "The High Wall," donated to the state by the Anti-Defamation League and shown in Mississippi schools for more than six years. The Citizens Council interpreted the film as teaching "children to pity their prejudiced parents who did not enjoy the enriching experience of intermingling with persons of different racial, ethnic and cultural backgrounds." At the end of the film the Council was saddened to find "Americans and Poles walk arm-in-arm into the setting sun." An "alert state senator" sounded the alarm, a private exhibition was given for Council and Mississippi Sovereignty Commission officials who agreed "The High Wall" was "unfit for showing to Mississippi school children," and the menace was removed.

The state Daughters of the American Revolution have time and again gone directly to the legislature, predictably with the encouragement of the Governor who comes down hard for cleaning up the books "so that children can be truly informed of the southern way of life." The *Daily News* was acutely disturbed by such "oblique propaganda as 'gives evidence that Negro people have done much to develop themselves.' " The DAR is understandably unhappy when first-graders are no longer exposed to "the story of the squirrel storing nuts," since it "helped to make America a great nation populated by men and women steadfast in their ability to put into effect their early training for adult life." All but the headiest fans of Lord Keynes may look upon such a lament with sympathy. But listen to what the Citizens Council officially suggests for the third and fourth grades:

God wanted the white people to live alone. And He wanted colored people to live alone. The white men built America for you. White men built America so they could make the rules. George Washington was a brave and honest white man. The white men cut away big forests. The white man has always been kind to the Negro. We do not believe that God wants us to live together. Negro people like to live by themselves. Negroes use their own bathrooms. They do not use white people's bathrooms. The Negro has his own part of town to live in. This is called our Southern Way of Life. Do you know that some people want the Negroes to live with white people? These people want us to be unhappy. They say we must go to school together. They say we must swim together and use the bathroom together. God had made us different. And God knows best. Did you know that our country will grow weak if we mix the races? White men worked hard to build our country. We want to keep it strong and free.

And some recommendations for the fifth and sixth grades:

The Southern white man has always helped the Negro whenever he could. Southerners were always their best friends. The South went to war to prevent the races from race-mixing. If God had wanted all men to be one color and to be alike, He would not have made the different races. One of the main lessons in the Old Testament of our Bible is that your race should be kept pure. God made different races and put them in different lands. He was satisfied with pure races so man should keep the races pure and be satisfied. BIRDS DO NOT MIX. CHICKENS DO NOT MIX. A friend had 100 white chickens and 100 reds. All the white chickens got to one side of the house, and all the red chickens got on the other side of the house. You probably feel the same way these chickens did whenever you are with people of a different race. God meant it to be that way.

With the makers of the ideology in control and economic opportunity at a minimum, it is not strange that large numbers of the most ambitious Mississippians, the ablest and the most adaptable to change, have left the state year after year. Such constant attribution of potential leadership (proven by the eminence achieved by Mississippi exiles) must be a major reason for the people's unwillingness to discard their ancient folkways. One cannot help speculating as to what degree Mississippi's story would have been more heartening if a sizable proportion of those thousands of bright, perceptive *natural leaders* among the men and women who have left the state had in some miraculous way found it possible to remain.

Some of those who have left had no choice. They were victims of a state now deservedly famous for its incredible past of police brutality and for the harassment, even to death, of those who defy the code. The state retains a good deal of the frontier recklessness toward human life found by William Howard Russell who noted that casual Mississippi conversations had "a smack of manslaughter about them." In the year after the Brown decision, four Negroes were openly slain, with no conviction for any crime; it would almost seem that when these atrocities had served their purpose, murder as an instrument of policy was then put in cold storage for a time.

On March 31, 1963, the Voter Education Project of the Southern Regional Council released a chronological list of 64 acts of violence and intimidation against Negroes since January, 1961. The 30-page indictment of man's inhumanity to man, with its accusations of whippings, shootings, murder, and outrageous debasement of the courts, admittedly came from an interested party, but it is characterized by understatement.

Mississippi acts of savagery have often been publicized throughout the world, some beyond their merit. The following examples of harassment by the closed society have been examined with caution and some thoroughness.

For twelve years Eugene Cox and Dr. David Minter, both Southerners, had worked closely together as manager and physician for the white and black families making up the Providence Cooperative, a 2,700-acre farm in Holmes County. On September 27, 1955, at a mass meeting called by leading members of the Citizens Council, Cox and Minter were ordered out of the community, mainly on the basis of evidence recorded in two hours of questioning by Council and county officials of four Negro boys accused of making obscene remarks about a white girl. Allegations of the intermingling of the races at the farm were denied, though it was conceded freely that white and Negro patrons did attend meetings of the credit union together. Threats of violence were made against both men and their families, and, Minter's patients having been intimidated, his medical practice fell off about 50 percent. An economic boycott was less effective. Professional segregationist Edwin White said, "We just can't afford to have them up there teaching what they are teaching—which will lead to violence unless it is stopped." At the mass assembly Cox admitted his belief that segregation is un-Christian. A planter whose father had been a minister spoke out, "This isn't a Christian meeting." Cox and Minter continued to deny all accusations and offered to make their records available for investigation. White commented, "I do not say these men are Communists, but I do say they are following the Communist line." With threats of arson increasing, and a roadblock arranged by the sheriff, Cox sat up, a rifle across his knees, from midnight to dawn for ten straight nights. Minter stuck it out until July, 1956. Cox left for Memphis a month later. In their joint Christmas greeting that year, they recalled: "Only two members of our church wrote to us. A few others have voiced their faith in us, but above these small voices is the frightening SILENCE. It is frightening—not only for us, but for any Christian and American who may wake up some morning to find himself persecuted because of his beliefs, or for unfounded rumors and 'guilt by association.' "

When James Meredith made his painful entry into Ole Miss, the "forgotten man" who had tried to break down the Mississippi education racial barrier without federal aid was languishing in the state penitentiary at Parchman, having been sentenced to a seven-year term for stealing by proxy $25 worth of chicken feed. Much of the evidence points to the conclusion that Clyde Kennard was "framed," though no one seems to know who did it. Born in Hattiesburg, moved to Chicago at 12, discharged from paratroop service in Korea and Germany in 1952, Kennard meritoriously attended the University of Chicago for three years. Upon the death of his stepfather, he returned to Mississippi to help his mother run a chicken farm in Forrest County. For years he discussed with the president of Mississippi Southern University his possible admission on a voluntary basis. In 1958 he turned down Governor Coleman's offer of education outside the state but obligingly agreed to delay his formal application until after the 1959 Democratic primary. On September 15 he was officially refused admission in a 15-minute interview witnessed by the chief investigator for the Sovereignty Commission. Within minutes Kennard was arrested for speeding, then fined for possession of liquor (probably planted) in his car. By 1961 when the Mississippi Supreme Court disposed of this summary justice, Kennard had been convicted as an accessory in the theft of three bags of chicken feed and sentenced to one year's imprisonment for each $3.57 worth of feed allegedly stolen. At most the penalty, assuming guilt, would normally have been 90 days. The illiterate boy who made the theft, if there was one, continued in his job with the feed cooperative.

Though President William D. McCain refused Kennard's application on specious claims of "irregularities" and "questionable" moral character, and is alleged to have said that he could do more to "develop honesty, culture, and individual integrity as president of Mississippi Southern than he can in a silly martyrdom for one Negro," Kennard himself refused to believe that McCain "had anything to do with what happened to me." The subsequent career of Clyde Kennard is a sad one. It includes surgery for cancer at the University Hospital in Jackson in June, 1962, unconscionable treatment at Parchman in the months following his operation when he was refused periodic checkups recommended by University doctors, the rapid development of his malignancy, an eight-hour operation in the Billings Hospital at the University of Chicago, and his death in the early summer of 1963. Not long before he died, Kennard was planning to return to his chicken farm and, as he saw it, to help Mississippi "coordinate" her race relations. One of his last statements was, "I still think there are a few white people of good will in the state and we have to do something to bring this out."

The most likely candidate in Mississippi for the next Medgar Evers treatment is the president of the state NAACP, Aaron Henry, one time porter and shoeshine boy in the Old Cotton Bowl Court Hotel in Clarksdale and now owner of a drugstore on Fourth Street. He walks the earth with the sure step and upright carriage of a younger version of another Mississippian, Archie Moore, and he is not likely to be run out of Coahoma County. He does not know how many times the windows in his place of business have been smashed, but the last time, in March, 1963, he left for all to see the bricks, the broken glass, and the displays —one of the Declaration of Independence and the other of the Emancipation Proclamation. In 1962 he was convicted of leading a boycott of Clarksdale stores after it had been determined there would be no Negro float in the Christmas parade.

In March, Henry was fined $500 and sentenced to six months in jail by an 80-year-old justice of the peace for allegedly molesting a white hitchhiker. According to the *Daily News* reporter, the Bolivar County attorney "during the final arguments, took the Mississippi statute and read to Judge Rowe the disturbing the peace law, explained it to him and told him the maximum sentence and fine." Before defining the sentence, the judge said, "The evidence shows this young man could not have described the interior of the defendant's car unless he was in it." There was no other witness.

When Henry accused the county attorney and police chief of plotting the charge against him, they countered with a libel suit in the Coahoma Circuit Court where the jury awarded them damages of $40,000. All these cases are still in the higher courts. On March 13, 1963, Henry's living room picture window was demolished and his home set afire at two in the morning by gasoline bombs thrown by two young thugs who said they were "just having fun" and were not aware of being in the Negro section of town.

Not only did they admit the bombing, but a filling station attendant heard them planning the attack and commenting afterward that Henry "was lucky to be alive." The first man tried was acquitted of arson by an all-white jury which deliberated for 15 minutes, and an identical charge against the other was dropped. One of those involved later asked Henry's forgiveness, saying he had been tricked into the nasty business.

In May, 1963, the Henry drugstore was rocked by an explosion which ripped a hole in the roof. Sheriff Ross and Deputy State Fire Marshal Hopkins investigated and found that the blast "was caused by a bolt of lightning." Henry wrote: "I am not really sure as to the cause. The hole on top of the roof is much smaller than the rupture in the ceiling. The experts I have talked with contend that lightning does not act that way." It would appear that Henry is not only courageous but more literate than his opposition.

Harassment by the closed society can be savage even when it is not violent. Twenty-eight young Methodist ministers, feeling that they had "a particular obligation to speak," issued by way of the *Mississippi Methodist Advocate* of January, 1963, a "Born of Conviction" statement that still has the state and church in an uproar. They affirmed their belief in the freedom of the pulpit, the brotherhood of man, an unalterable opposition to the closing of the public schools, and an unflinching antagonism toward Communism. Within two weeks the Mississippi Association of Methodist Ministers and Laymen, displaying more churchmanship than religion, had repudiated the "Born of Conviction" pastors, submitted their own "declaration of conscience on racial matters" (drawn up by Medford Evans, Citizens Council consultant, and published in the January issue of the *Citizen*), and called for a secret referendum on whether or not Methodists wanted their church integrated. Later these conservatives declared integration a "crime against God." The lament of one of the young ministers, that "The power clique which dominates the conference has aligned itself with the Methodist Ministers and Laymen and with the Citizens Council," was corroborated by subsequent events.

The closed society battered the outspoken young preachers upon the anvil of public opinion. By summer ten had left the state, and at least half a dozen more were shifted to urban pulpits. At least half volunteered the feeling that they had not been sufficiently supported by their superintendents and their bishop. Methodists in general, with professional assistance, were reflecting

an opinion that had driven from Mississippi 68 of their seminary-trained men since 1954. Dr. W. B. Selah, for 18 years pastor of the largest Methodist congregation in the state, who had supported the "Born of Conviction" statement and had declared "there can be no color bar in a Christian church," resigned in protest when five Negroes were refused admission to his church.

The Mississippi Advisory Committee to the United States Commission on Civil Rights made, in January, 1963, a report on the administration of justice within the state. In a period of 14 months it had held six open meetings in which a hundred or so Mississippians had testified, though "actively opposed by agents and instrumentalities of the State Government." The legislature in 1960 "passed an act," the committee stated, "to intimidate persons who might wish to assert their rights as citizens by altering the requirement of proof for prosecution of perjury solely in cases where the defendant has testified before this Committee."

In its published findings, the committee declared that "in all important areas of citizenship, a Negro in Mississippi receives substantially less than his due consideration as an American and as a Mississippian." They found that "a pattern exists in our State that leads to the denial of Constitutional rights and, in some instances, to brutality and terror. From the moment a Negro adult is hailed as 'boy' or 'girl' by a police officer, through his arrest, detention, trial—during which his Negro lawyer is treated with contemptuous familiarity by the judge and other officers of the court— and eventual imprisonment, he is treated with a pernicious difference. This difference is incompatible with Christian ideals about the dignity of man and with principles of Anglo-Saxon criminal law." Declaring that "justice under law is not guaranteed for the Negro in Mississippi in the way that it is for the white man," the committee reported that "42.3% of the citizens of this State must either accept an inferior station in life and an attitude of servility or endanger themselves and their families by protesting. We find that terror hangs over the Negro in Mississippi and is an expectancy for those who refuse to accept their color as a badge of inferiority; and terrorism has no proper place in the American form of government." The committee found that "in general the press is failing to meet its obligation to our society. The people of Mississippi are largely unaware of the extent of illegal official violence and the press is partly to blame. . . . When a State disregards a large segment of its population, the Federal Government is compelled to intervene in behalf of the victims."

And the federal government *has* intervened at the state's best known institution of higher learning, the University of Mississippi. The university has had its moments of greatness, its faculty and administrators of integrity and virtue, and a long history of genteel poverty. In the presidency of Alfred B. Butts (1935–46) Ole Miss began a precarious climb from the depths of depression despair and the shame of the Bilbo spoliation. For at least a decade after World War II, under the leadership of Chancellor John D. Williams, the university seemed on the verge of living up to the dreams and hopes of its founders and directors of exactly a century before. A tremendous building program on the already beautiful, wooded campus, an expansion of libraries and laboratories, the addition of new departments, and, most exciting of all, the gathering together of an excellent faculty dedicated to good teaching and fruitful research, all of these developments and more were taking place. The new chancellor was adept not only at selling the university to the people but in making it an integral part of many schemes designed to raise the horizons of a long submerged society.

It was increasingly evident in the middle fifties, however, that changes were taking place in the state that would adversely affect the university. In a series of crises from Kershaw (1955) to Kerciu (1963), the administration became more and more appeasement-minded, more and more involved (like a woman constantly professing her virtue) in presenting the Ole Miss story to the state as if it were a bar of soap.

More serious was a 1955 edict of the board of trustees requiring the screening of all speakers brought to the campus, a ruling steadfastly opposed by the chancellor at its inception but stoutly defended some years later when he refused even to pass along to the board a petition of the AAUP calling for an end to the screening. A clergyman was turned away from Religious Emphasis Week when it became known that he had contributed to the NAACP, and the incoming president of the Southern Historical Association was paid his full fee for not delivering a history lecture after the shocking disclosure that his wife had written in the *Saturday Evening Post* of her teaching experiences with Negro students in Atlanta.

The handling of absurd charges of apostasy and subversion against 14 members of the university community in 1958 was brought off expeditiously and with a flair for public relations. Faculty members involved in this tempest, which was kept going in the press for almost a year, were asked to remain silent (which most of them did) while the chancellor affirmed his belief in the Bible, an omnipotent God, immortality of the soul, state sovereignty, segregation, and the right of private property. In August, 1959 the board dismissed the allegations against the chancellor and the faculty and stated its policy that "there should prevail at our universities and colleges an atmosphere of freedom in their research, teaching programs and services and that there should be no political or subversive propagandizing in the academic program."

In the past year or so the University of Mississippi has desperately needed the help of all those concerned with its welfare, but, far from being consulted, these friends have been told that things were under control, the situation was returning to normal, enrollment was holding up in great style, just a few professors were leaving. On the anniversary of the insurrection, the director of the University News Service insulted "some few professors" by accusing them of having leveled "bitter attacks" against it to "make national headlines" for the purpose of securing better positions, and it belittled the intelligence of those who remained by stating that "the vast majority" of these had refused more lucrative job offers elsewhere. In a state where higher education is expendable, this bowing before and in fact anticipating every wind may have had a soothing effect on the legislature, but it also indicated a chronic inability to face reality. After all, General Ulysses S. Grant has been the only man in history to make a positive decision *not* to destroy the university.

Until 1962 the university successfully avoided integration. In that year, on June 26, almost exactly 18 months after he had first written to the registrar, James Howard Meredith, the "man with a mission and with a nervous stomach," was ordered admitted to the University of Mississippi. Speaking for the Fifth Circuit Court in New Orleans Judge John Minor Wisdom later said that "A full review of the record leads the Court inescapably to the conclusion that from the moment the defendants discovered Meredith was a Negro they engaged in a carefully calculated campaign of delay, harassment, and masterly inactivity. It was a defense designed to discourage and defeat by evasion tactics which would have been a credit to Quintus Fabius Maximus." Tartly reprimanding Judge Sidney Mize of the United States District Court for the Southern District of Mississippi for "continuances of doubtful propriety and unreasonably long delays," Judge Wisdom viewed the case as one "tried below and argued here in the eerie atmosphere of never-never land." He might have added, "of the closed society." The contention of the board of trustees and of university officials, accepted as fact by Judge Mize, "that the University is not a racially segregated institution" and that "the state has no policy of segregation

. . . defies history and common knowledge." There was nothing in the case "reaching the dignity of proof" to make the court think otherwise. "We find that James Meredith's application for transfer to the University of Mississippi was turned down solely because he was a Negro."

Many members of the faculty expressed dismay when Ole Miss officials made uncalled-for affirmations which the court deemed frivolous and when they followed "a determined policy of discrimination by harassment" and assigned as a reason for rejecting Meredith "a trumped-up excuse without any basis except to discriminate." It was hard, too, to comprehend why an administrator would deny that "he understands and interprets the policy of the State of Mississippi as being that negroes and whites are educated in separate institutions of higher learning." More than a hundred years ago Chancellor F. A. P. Barnard had declared that the University's destiny was "to stamp upon the intellectual character of Mississippi the impress it is to wear. . . ."

From September 13, 1962, when Mississippi's long court battle against Meredith reached "the end of the road" in Judge Mize's sweeping injunction and Governor Barnett read his antiquarian interposition proclamation, it was evident to all that the showdown was imminent. In those last hectic days the "power structure" of the state made a rather impressive attempt to control the Barnett juggernaut, but it was too late, and the people were largely unaware of the effort. Moderate statements by Oxford ministers appeared in the Memphis but not the Jackson papers which thundered about taking note "of those who stand with courage in an hour of crisis." The closed society was operating efficiently and almost automatically, as it does in times of great stress, as if it were some malicious Frankenstein monster.

On the Ole Miss campus was circulated a broadside, *The Liberty Bulletin*, urging students to "Place yourself under the direction of Gov. Barnett. Do not engage yourself in force or violence unless he calls for it." *Clarion-Ledger* columnist Hills reported that "the governor will watch with a jaundiced eye any attempt to apply punitive action against Mississippi's patriots. College presidents are standing ready to fight alongside the governor, or else."

In the upper house of the legislature on September 25, Senator E. K. Collins arose to remark, "We must win this fight regardless of the cost in time, effort, money and in human lives." Senator Hayden Campbell thought "they would have to open the doors to murder and rape." Senator Hilbun barked that "these are the same people who won't let our children pray in school." In Washington, Senator Eastland was sure that the next few days would "determine whether a judicial tyranny as black and hideous as any in history exists in the United States."

On Thursday, September 27, the *Clarion-Ledger* carried a sensational headline to the effect that a "gunbattle" was possible at the university. Representative Walter Hester told the UPI it was "likely" that state officials would attempt to fight off the marshals if they tried to enroll Meredith, but he did not prophesy an all-out insurrection. The situation was "extremely tense and there are some people who don't mind dying for an honorable cause." Either Senator McLaurin or Senator Yarbrough told Senator Lambert that "they were going to provoke the Kennedys into sending troops into Mississippi." Months later, Attorney General Patterson called McLaurin and the "CC & Co." a "little band of would-be ruthless dictators seeking to promote all-out riot and bloodshed on the campus by encouraging the people of Mississippi to pick up their rifles, shotguns and sling-shorts and go to fight it out with the armed forces of the United States." This could result only in "bloodshed, death, destruction and heartaches."

Barnett talked about jailing any federal officer attempting to arrest a state official. The *Daily News* was accused by the campus paper, the *Mississippian*, of distortion, fabrication, "screaming and sensational stories." On the day of the Ole Miss-Vanderbilt football game the hysteria whipped up in Jackson was unbelievable. The press and radio added their bluster to the normal uproar of a conference game. At the halftime ceremonies that night when he still might have turned the populace aside from its madness, the Governor achieved his greatest triumph of oratorical lunacy: "I love Mississippi—I love her people—I love her customs!" Understandably, the man was overcome by his own hoarse eloquence and the reasonless, incoherent, delirious response. He could not go on. The people were bewildered. Television carried the infection statewide, and former Major General Edwin Walker was on his way to Oxford.

The propaganda machine never faltered. The next day, the Sunday that began so peacefully, a joint legislative committee pronounced nine frivolous reasons for denying Meredith admission and cunningly announced that his registration would jeopardize the accreditation of the university to the point of expulsion from the Southern Association of Colleges. In the afternoon and early evening, fatigued students were driving back to the campus, listening to their blaring radios tuned to the appeals of the Citizens Council to "form a human wall around the mansion" to protect the Governor from arrest by federal marshals. Thousands of citizens swarmed the streets of Jackson. Few knew that the Governor, called by an Episcopal priest the "living symbol of lawlessness," had already sold out his closest advisers. Word came that planeloads of marshals had flown out of Memphis. For some time their destination was in doubt. Unknown to most Mississippians, Meredith was, before supper, unpacking his bag in his room in Baxter Hall on the Ole Miss campus.

It was impossible that he could stay without help from the federal government. When Mississippi officials blocked by physical might on four separate occasions Meredith's court-ordered enrollment, and the Fifth Circuit Court wearily acknowledged that it had come to the end of its resources, the President was faced with the alternative of acceptance of the breakdown of law or the employment of force. The admission of Meredith was not negotiable. Kennedy performed his constitutional obligation in the same spirit George Washington had exhibited in the Whisky Rebellion. Having apparently learned the lesson of Little Rock, he insisted upon the use of civilian federal marshals rather than paratroopers. Certainly there had been no stated objection to marshals accompanying Meredith on those expeditions when they had been overcome by superior state power. Whatever "deals" he may have made with the Governor behind the scenes, the President gently and eloquently appealed to the patriotism and sense of sportsmanship of Mississippi citizens in asking them to obey unpopular court decrees. But former Major General Walker having called for 10,000 volunteers to go to the aid of Barnett, and it being general knowledge that hundreds and perhaps thousands were converging on Oxford, there would have been a serious evasion of responsibility had the Army high command not prepared for the emergency. Troops were moved to Memphis. The President earnestly hoped that the job could be done by civilians, and the United States Army was not ordered to the University of Mississippi until it became evident that the marshals were fighting for their lives, and the Army's first contingent arrived just in time to prevent a disaster.

From the arrival of the marshals at the Lyceum Building shortly before five o'clock until the firing of the tear gas at eight, it became increasingly apparent that there was a serious lack of liaison between federal and state officials on the scene. At six the chancellor (at this time not much more than a spectator himself) believed the deal had been made and the game would have to be played out, and the gathering students and faculty were so informed. By seven all observers knew that for whatever reason, the Mississippi Highway Patrol had abandoned its enforcement of law and or-

der and was in fact in some cases encouraging the restless crowd to demonstrate against the marshals. Twice these agents of the federal government donned their masks as the crowd closed in. The campus chief of police and four highway patrolmen had moved back part of the surly crowd (which promptly surged forward again when the officers left that part of the scene) and were achieving some little success in front of the Lyceum Building when the marshals opened fire with gas and drove what almost instantly became a howling mob back to the Confederate monument. Whether Chief Marshal McShane was justified in giving the order to fire at precisely the moment he did is a question for the professionals to answer. It is relevant, however, that two score of faculty members and their wives later testified that the marshals had undergone for at least an hour a constant harassment of obscene language and an increasingly heavy barrage of lighted cigarette butts, stones, bottles, pieces of pipe, and even acid. It is a small matter whether the gas should have come 15 minutes earlier or later, but rather ironic that a full-scale insurrection should get under way at the exact moment that the President was appealing to Mississippians for fair play in the name of Lucius Quintus Cincinnatus Lamar.

Before the work was done that night the Army brought more troops to Mississippi than General Sherman had had in the environs of Oxford exactly a hundred years before. Several hundred reporters soon concentrated on the Mississippi campus to ferret out the facts about what actually had taken place and to inquire into the background for the state's turmoil. By and large the reportage was accurate and the interpretation sound and temperate. Those who have wished to know have had spread before them a reasonably trustworthy record of events.

This is true for all the world except Mississippi. With its long history of being on the defensive against outside criticism and a predisposition to believe their own leaders can do no wrong, the people have been almost completely sold on a palpable and cynical hoax. The closed society immediately projected (in fact, it had foreshadowed) the orthodox version that the insurrection resulted from federal encroachment, deliberately planned by the Kennedys and callously incited by McShane when he called for tear gas. What did happen in front of the Lyceum Building in that crucial hour before eight o'clock on the night of September 30? Truth cries out that the orthodox Mississippi view is false, that cleverness in shifting the culpability for defiance of law from those creating the violence to those enforcing the law could succeed only among a people suffering from a touch of paranoia.

The genesis of the deception which shifted the blame for the insurrection from Mississippians to federal officials came from the university administration. A singularly inaccurate story blaming the "trigger-happy, amateurish, incompetent" marshals and suggesting examples of diabolical brutality toward male and female students was in the hands of Barnett and Eastland within an hour or so of the firing of the gas. These opportunists took up and grossly exaggerated the cry and called for state and federal investigations. By October 2, David Lawrence was to devote his syndicated column to the "official" view of the university. Long after it was made abundantly clear that many faculty members had witnessed the inception of the riot and knew for a certainty about the fraud against the federal government, the administration did not deviate from its original position but, on the contrary, continued to search for evidence condemning the marshals.

On the morning of October 1, Governor Barnett ordered the Mississippi flag at half-mast because "there had been an invasion of our state resulting in blood." The riot, he said, had been touched off by those "inexperienced, nervous and trigger-happy" marshals who had "deliberately inflamed" the people "in order that the resulting resistance can be cited as justification for mili-

tary force against a sovereign state." Next day the *Clarion-Ledger* headline, "Eastland, Others Charge [⅜ in.]/Marshals Set Off Ole Miss Rioting [⅞ in.]" was serenity itself compared to a featured column which elaborated the official view: "Our state is labeled insurrectionist because it does not care to be negroid in totality." The columnist did admit a temporary defeat: "So watch the peace-lovers come to the fore, grab a nigger-neck and start bellowing brother love."

The Mississippi Junior Chamber of Commerce distributed almost a half-million copies of a 24-page pamphlet entitled *Oxford: A Warning for Americans*, which put the blame for the insurrection squarely on the shoulders of John and Robert Kennedy. The most specious implication of the pamphlet was that Meredith would have been allowed to enroll peacefully if only the Attorney General had awaited "the completion of the judicial processes," a most unlikely result in a state which had already indulged in so much legal quackery and whose Governor had made it so evident that he would never accept the desegregation of the university. John Satterfield, probable author of the pamphlet and certainly an intimate counselor of Barnett, was now apparently defending his own bad advice which in part came straight from John C. Calhoun. Satterfield has tried to place the mantle of respectability on Barnett's unlawful conduct and to cast doubt on the legality and propriety of the United States government's actions. He threw his weight as past president of the American Bar Association and a prime mover in the Citizens Council into the intellectual propaganda barrage directed at Mississippians, who were unlikely anyhow to pay attention to the statement made on October 2 by the incumbent president of the ABA: "The paramount issue was whether or not the judgment of the court was to be upheld. The executive branch had a clear duty to see that the courts were sustained."

Mr. Satterfield maintained an Olympian objectivity compared to Judge W. M.

O'Barr, who in his charge to the LaFayette County grand jury investigating the death of two persons on the night of the insurrection, spoke of the United States Attorney General as "stupid little brother" and described the Supreme Court as made up of "political greedy old men" who "together with the hungry, mad, ruthless, ungodly, power-mad men [in Washington] would change this government from a democracy to a totalitarian dictatorship." The grand jury responded appropriately with an indictment of McShane for precipitating the riot, and for good measure taunted university professors (who had previously defended the marshals) for talking too much.

Support for the state administration came, too, just one month after the insurrection, from Mississippi's Women for Constitutional Government. One of the state's more active groups, they were assembled in Jackson by the sister of the speaker of the House of Representatives to adopt a "bill of grievances" against the "unwarranted and unlawful use of military force" and the alleged violation of Mississippians' civil rights resulting from "the collusion of the President of the United States, the Justice Department, and the Federal courts." The high-flown language of "the thousand angry women" obscured, for Mississippians at least, their exquisitely imaginative account of what had taken place at the university.

In the months after the insurrection, many engaged in the pleasant pastime of guessing whether the Governor was at the moment taking instructions from the "resistance to the death" counselors (the White Muslim clique in the Citizens Council) or from the more cautious who, as one observer put it, had planned only a little riot, who didn't really want to see anybody killed. The Council sent up trial balloons suggesting the closing of the university, called upon faculty moderates (to Simmons, "gutless liberals") to accept segregation or resign, and conducted a postcard campaign directing the board to fire "quislings and scalawags [who] betray our

state and our people in the time of crisis." The extent of the council's responsibility for open defiance of university authorities by extremist students who returned from weekends at home with suitcases filled with cherry bombs and minds filled with rebellion is still an open question. The Oxford council, whose leaders were dedicated if not brilliant, distributed a mimeographed list of faculty members who were to be harassed with anonymous telephone calls—which did cause some inconvenience because the sleeping habits of the daring dialers did not mesh with those of their victims.

The Mississippi Municipal Association prepared a model speech to be used in winning friends and thwarting enemies. After touching lightly on the notion that court decisions, after all, are not the law of the land and warning of the danger of centralization, the orator was then to rise eloquently to the defense of Mississippi's official conduct: "This action is not a defiance of the law or the courts. Such action is an exercise of the heritage of freedom and liberty under the law preserved for us by our fathers." Although it was not suggested, the more gifted ambassadors could also have sung some lines from the "Ballad of the Ole Miss Invasion":

They came rolling down from Memphis and
    dropping from the skies
With bayonets for our bellies and tear gas for
    our eyes
Some resisted them with brickbats, while
    others ran and hid,
Some tangled with the marshals—who can
    blame them if they did?

For months it was believed that the General Legislative Investigating Committee would quietly abandon its inquiry into the insurrection as it ran into more and more unpalatable material. Having sent investigators from Washington, Senator Stennis made no report and Senator Eastland shifted his effort to the collection of tall tales by disgruntled students against their instructors. The Mississippi Senate of course did not need facts to plead with the country to "join our State in defiance of all who would destroy our freedoms, heritage and constitutional rights." Only one senator called for secession, a few more demanded Kennedy's impeachment, while others galloped up and down the land to warn their countrymen of the coming of the orange-jackets, those federal fiends whose savage brutalities at Oxford had "stopped short of Nazi atrocities only in that there were no deaths."

The legislative committee took six months to put together from the sworn statements of more than 90 witnesses its masterpiece of sententious fiction. For reasons never explained, faculty witnesses and even legislators who had been at Ole Miss with the federalized national guard had not been called upon to testify. There was no minority report. How scores of the world's crack reporters had been kept from seeing the blundering and the repeated brutalities and "planned physical torture" of the marshals, the women students hit by projectiles fired at point-blank range, the deliberate gassing of seven dormitories, the "torture slab," the army truck set on fire by "a folded paper airplane," and dozens of other Alice-in-Wonderland concoctions will remain one of the mysteries of twentieth-century journalism. It was the sad commentary of an eyewitness that the "young gentlemen of the New Confederacy," who were able to glorify insurrectionist conduct as "freedom fighters" in the "Brick and Bottle Brigade"—attacking the armed forces of their own country—would have small compunction about lying to a legislative investigating committee, especially one that made perfectly clear what it wanted to hear.

The legislative report was "verified" in advance by a documentary film, "Oxford, U.S.A.," depicting "how the federal government violated the constitution in the invasion of Mississippi last fall." Just before he sold three copies to the Sovereignty Commission for almost $7,000, the producer asserted the picture was "based strictly on the Constitution" and had been endorsed by Governors Barnett and Wal-lace. According to billboard advertising, it "EXPOSES FEDERAL ATROCITIES." Actually, about half of the 50-minute extravaganza is taken up with poorly filmed statements from Barnett, Johnson, Attorney General Patterson, Chief of the Highway Patrol Birdsong, and a legislator who makes some disparaging and untrue remarks about the university and Meredith. The opening action shot shows motorized troops moving into Oxford, which they did —about eight hours after the beginning of the insurrection. By implication the viewer gets the impression that marshals had fired shotguns (which they did not have) at innocent students and even that they had killed the French reporter. Altogether the film is a shabby conglomeration of falsehood, distortion, and political dissemblance unlikely to convince the fair-minded who may be left in the membership of the Citizens Council.

The people of Mississippi have thus once again been victimized, this time by a gigantic hoax perpetrated on them by their own timeserving leaders whose sense of loyalty is only to the false orthodoxy of the closed society.

The closed society is never the absolute society. There always have been and there always will be the dissenters, the doubters who point to the road not taken. In the past year more than 50 professors have departed from the University of Mississippi, many of them literally driven from the state. The best of them, particularly the native Mississippians, would have remained if there had been any prospect of an atmosphere of freedom or a decent chance to fight for one.

No, the closed society is not absolute. In Mississippi there are legislators, editors, lawyers, labor leaders, educators, and ordinary citizens who sometimes protest against the prevailing orthodoxy. The day that Barnett let loose his interposition blast, Ira Harkey pointed out in the Pascagoula *Chronicle* that it was not the Kennedys but "the United States of America, democracy itself, the whole of humanity" that was making demands upon Mississippi. In a series of five short, logical articles, Representative Karl Wiesenburg demonstrated conclusively that Barnett's course was "the road to riot," that the Governor had violated his oath of office, that the bloodshed on September 30 was the "price of defiance," and that states have responsibilities as well as rights. The *Mississippi Methodist Advocate* accepted for the church part of the guilt for the riot.

Three days after the insurrection, the Ole Miss chapter of the American Association of University Professors adopted a ringing statement protesting the fraud against the marshals. Without a campaign in its favor more than 70 faculty members signed the document as their way of "standing up to be counted." A professor of anthropology made his protest by putting into writing the conclusions of those in his profession concerning the validity of Putnam's *Race and Reason*, and this was serialized in the Pascagoula *Chronicle*. The exemplary conduct of more than 3,000 federalized Mississippi national guardsmen is worth the scrutiny and praise of all Americans. General W. P. Wilson said, "There were absolutely no incidents of any individual wilfully refusing to report for mobilization." George Fielding Eliot paid high tribute to the state guard: "In its ranks are men who, as citizens, share some of the views and even the prejudices of their fellow Mississippians. But when the call to duty came, they laid all else aside. After that they were soldiers of the United States, summoned by the President to aid in enforcing the laws of the Union, as the Constitution provides." One guardsman who had suffered rough treatment at the hands of the hoodlums went right to the heart of the matter: "It was just the matter of an oath I took."

There are many thousands of "men of good will" in Mississippi, mild-mannered people for the most part, who in their day-to-day affairs do what they can to ameliorate the difficult conditions imposed upon

their fellowmen by the closed society. But because of a strong desire to live in peace or because of one kind of fear or another, these men will not openly protest what they know in their hearts are gross evils all about them. These are the individuals who, when one of their own number speaks out or in some little way defies the orthodoxy and is pilloried as a result, shrug their shoulders and say, "Well, he asked for it."

Men of good will are not enough. In his article in the *Saturday Evening Post* after the riot, John Faulkner professed surprise at a plea to return to law and order: "this to us, the responsible people of Oxford, who raised no finger against any man." In high indignation he refused to see the need for penitence: "If all the sin I have to answer for is my part in bringing on what happened here Sunday and Monday, then I relinquish my place to someone more needful of forgiveness than I." Perhaps Mr. Faulkner said more than he intended, perhaps he was speaking for all the good men who to whatever degree had abandoned the feeling of accountability for conditions in Mississippi. These same men were shocked to learn, probably at Leslie's drugstore, the price of defiance as well as the fact that some of their neighbors were throwing rocks at other neighbors in the uniform of the United States government. But they were not moved by the riot—they were solidified. They had forgotten, if they had ever known, that it was not Gavin Stevens who had prevented the lynching of Lucas Beauchamp, but Miss Habersham, Chick Mallison, and Aleck Sander.

The more embattled the closed society becomes, the more monolithic, the more corrupt, and the more willing to engage in double-think and double-talk. There is Mississippi's institutionalized hypocrisy that the Negro can freely vote and freely attend the university of his choice. There is the casuistry of Governor Barnett that he is preserving law and order and upholding the Constitution by physically obstructing the execution of an explicit directive of the Fifth Circuit Court of Appeals of the United States. There is the legislature shamefully passing laws which the judges "will know how to handle" or for the purpose of "getting" certain individuals. The idea that this is a nation of laws and not of men, constantly reiterated within the state, has a hollow ring in Mississippi. How few of its leaders can come into court with clean hands!

Hostility to authority and disrespect for law are commonplace in Mississippi. How could it be otherwise in a state which tolerates the cynical disregard of prohibition and collects the black-market tax? How can anything else be expected when the state itself brazenly tells the world it has achieved "separate but equal" school facilities, when in 1959–60 local school expenditures were $81.86 for the white child as against $21.77 for the colored? Or when, as in 1951, the county superintendents of education, looking greedily toward the allocation of equalization funds, reported 895,779 children of educable age (6–20) while the United States census of 1950 listed the number of children from 5 to 19 as only 651,600? What respect can there be for the legal process when one standard of justice prevails when a Negro commits a crime against a Negro, another when a Negro commits a crime against a white, still another when a white commits a crime against a white, and a fourth when a white commits a crime against a Negro?

What can be said about the morality of a social order that sends a teen-age colored girl to a long term in an institution for delinquents because, by walking from school to the courthouse, she is held to have violated an injunction against demonstrations? And, when questioned, justifies the exorbitant penalty on the basis of previous abortions—which up to the time of her sentence the society had ignored? Which is immoral, the girl or the society?

In spite of the closed society the Negro has made *some* gains since his emancipation a century ago. In the same period, the white man, determined to defend his way of life at all costs, has compromised his old virtues, his integrity, his once unassailable character. He has so corrupted the language itself that he says one thing while meaning another. He no longer has freedom of choice in the realm of ideas because they must first be harmonized with the orthodoxy. New currents of thought he automatically distrusts, and if they clash with the prevailing wisdom he ruthlessly rules them out. He cannot allow himself the luxury of thinking about a problem on its merits. In spite of what he claims, the white Mississippian is not even conservative—he is merely negative. He grows up being against most things other men at least have the pleasure of arguing about. All his life he spends on the defensive. The most he can hope for is to put up a good fight before losing. This is the Mississippi way, this is the Mississippi heritage. It will ever be thus as long as the closed society endures.

Although there have been moments of enlightenment, the spiritual secession of Mississippi from history has never ended. For more than a century Mississippians have refused to be bound by the national will. Perhaps this recalcitrance could be borne with in the past, as have been many other excesses of democracy. But with the sanctuary provided by the oceans gone, the national interest, the instinct for survival, demand discipline. They demand also that attitudes or "principles" growing out of racial situations not be allowed to intrude themselves into the country's policy making decisions. Since Reconstruction Mississippians have had no real reason to believe that they were not free to handle the race question as they wished, without meaningful interference from the federal government; and, when they now discover that all their bluster and subterfuge and intransigence will avail them nothing, they have little to fall back on except blind rage and fierce hatred.

In committing itself to the defense of the biracial system, Mississippi has erected a totalitarian society which to the present moment has eliminated the ordinary processes by which change may be channeled. Through its police power, coercion and force prevail, instead of accommodation, and the result is social paralysis. Thus, the Mississippian who prides himself on his individuality in reality lives in a climate where nonconformity is forbidden, where the white man is not free, where he does not dare to express a deviating opinion without looking over his shoulder. Not only is the black man not allowed to forget that he is a nigger, but the white moderate must distinctly understand that he is a "nigger-lover."

Mississippi has long been a hyperorthodox social order in which the individual has no option except to be loyal to the will of the white majority. And the white majority has subscribed to an inflexible philosophy which is not based on fact, logic, or reason. Nonwhite Mississippians and all others are outlanders. Close contiguity with a large repressed population and fear of what these "inferior" people might do have held the society near the point of unanimity. Especially in times of stress the orthodoxy becomes more rigid, more removed from reality, and the conformity demanded to it more extreme. Today the advocacy or even the recognition of the inevitability of change becomes a social felony, or worse. Mississippi is the way it is not because of its views on the Negro—here it is simply "the South exaggerated"—but because of its closed society, its refusal to allow freedom of inquiry or to tolerate "error of opinion." The social order that refuses to conform to national standards insists upon strict conformity at home. While complaining of its own persecuted minority station in the United States, it rarely considers the Negro minority as having rights in Mississippi.

Perhaps the greatest tragedy of the closed society is the refusal of its citizens to believe that there is any view other than the orthodox. In recent years there has been a hardening attitude among college students who do not want to hear the other side. In such a twilight of nondiscussion, minds not only do not grow tough, they do not grow at all. Intelligent men with ideas are isolated from the rest of the community, and what little interracial communication existed in the past is now destroyed. One reason the Ole Miss faculty failed to protest an ugly situation before the insurrection was that through one means or another freedom of speech had long since been curtailed. This was at least a partial cause for from eight to ten members of the history department leaving in the two years *before* the troubles of last year. The jolt of the violence on the campus and the obvious fraud against the federal government initiated a spurt of resistance to ignorance, stupidity, and conformity. For the moment many of the faculty developed a healthy scorn for expediency and security. In the light of Mississippi's history it was probably already too late to expect anything more than an occasional stand, such as that put up by the ministers who were willing to count the cost and pay the price. With the great silence from the men of goodwill, and the disposition of the good people to let things run their course, there can be little hope for anything constructive in Mississippi in the next decade.

It can be argued that in the history of the United States democracy has produced great leaders in great crises. Sad as it may be, the opposite has been true in Mississippi. As yet there is little evidence that the society of the closed mind will ever possess the moral resources to reform itself, or the capacity for self-examination, or even the tolerance of self-examination. Inasmuch as a nation marching swiftly in the direction of the fulfillment of the promise of the Declaration of Independence and the Emancipation Proclamation is at the same time fighting for survival against Communism, it will not much longer indulge the frustration of its will. Nevertheless, it would seem that for the foreseeable future the people of Mississippi will plod along the troubled road of resistance, violence, anguish, and injustice, moving slowly until engulfed in the predictable cataclysm.

And yet, in spite of all that has been presented in this paper, it seems inescapable that Mississippians one day will drop the mockery of the late Confederacy and resume their obligations as Americans. It is just that there is small reason to believe that they will somehow develop the capability to do it themselves, to do it, as William Faulkner said, in time. If not, the closed society will become the open society with the massive aid of the country as a whole, backed by the power and authority of the federal government.

1956

The Militant Southerner*

JOHN HOPE FRANKLIN

. . . By 1860 the South claimed to be the fountainhead of martial spirit in the United States. It argued that it had turned the tide of battle in the nation's wars and had been the training ground for the soldiers of the country. America's soldiers had even been schooled in the art and science of war by treatises written by Southerners. Major D. H. Hill boasted that the Southern scholar had evinced the section's military spirit just as forcefully as had the soldier. "The books on Infantry Tactics we use, were prepared by Scott, of Virginia and Hardee, of Georgia. The Manual of Artillery Tactics in use is by Anderson, of Kentucky. The only works in this country on the Science of Artillery, written in the English language are by Kingsbury and Gibbon of North Carolina." Mordecai of South Carolina was the leading authority on gunpowder, while Mahan of Virginia had published the best works in military engineering. "These gentlemen are all graduates of West Point and are officers in the Army, but the South claims them as her own."[1]

The South's reputation for fighting—and winning—was secure. This reputation was more firmly established in the minds of Southerners than anywhere else, to be sure; but people in other places took cognizance of the South's claims and were willing to make some concessions regarding its military spirit.

Wars, however, had their limitations in strengthening the military reputation of Southern men, for there were years in which there was no resort to arms against the British, Indians, or Mexicans. But day-to-day experiences kept them in practice. Many were hotheaded and high-tempered, and, in personal relations, conducted themselves as though each were a one-man army exercising and defending its sovereignty.

* Reprinted by permission of the publishers from John Hope Franklin, *The Militant South* (Cambridge, Mass.: Harvard University Press. Copyright 1956 by the President and Fellows of Harvard College).

[1] Major D. H. Hill, "Essay on Military Education," *North Carolina Journal of Education*, IV (April, 1861), 115.

Duels were as "plenty as blackberries" in Mississippi in 1844.[2] Traveling in the Southwest in the 1830s, Ingraham saw and heard about much violence. In New Orleans, "the rage for duelling is at such a pitch that a jest or smart repartee is sufficient excuse for a challenge. . . ." What manner of men were these who could refer to an appointment for a duel "with the *nonchalance* of an invitation to a dinner or supper party?"[3]

When there was not dueling, there was fighting. The public walks were arenas for sport among the rustics, most of whom carried weapons and "counted on the chance of getting into difficulty."[4] This violence was described with a mixture of jest and disgust by an Alabama editor:

The Summer Sports of the South, as Major Noah calls them, have already commenced in Huntsville. On Monday last, in the Court Square, and during the session of Court, too, a man by the name of Taylor stabbed another by the name of Ware in such a shocking manner that his life is despaired of . . . this stabbing and dirking business has become so common and fashionable, that it has lost all the horror and detestation among . . . our population. . . .[5]

In Florida, Bishop Henry Whipple found the fighting spirit prevalent even among the community's more responsible members. On one occasion a member of the grand jury went outside where he found his son of eight or nine years of age fighting with another boy. "The father looked coolly on until it was ended and then said, 'now you little devil, if you catch him down again bite him, chaw his lip or you never'll be a man.'" The Bishop said that the father's attitude was "only one of the numerous specimens of this fighting spirit only to be found in the South."[6]

The fighting spirit was no respector of class or race, and the willingness of Negroes to resort to violence shows the extent to which such conduct pervaded the entire community. Free Negroes fought slaves, whites, and each other. Fearful of losing the few privileges that freedom accorded them and dogged by the vicissitudes that the struggle of such an anomalous position involved, they frequently outdid other members of the community in manifesting a proclivity to fight.[7] There were fights among slaves and revolts and rumors of revolts. Owners and overseers, moreover, occasionally met foul play as they undertook to supervise and punish their slaves. The people of Louisiana were excited in 1845 over the murder of a Caddo Parish mill superintendent by a Negro whom he sought to chastise. What was more, the *New Orleans Bee* complained, "instances of this kind are becoming quite numerous. It was only a few months since that a Negro was hanged in Greenwood for attempting the life of his overseer; and but a few weeks or so since in the . . . County of Harrison, Texas a Mr. Wilson met with the most distressing death by the hands of his own slaves."[8]

Southerners could have done no better job of establishing a reputation for violence and fighting had they sought to do so by formal dramatization. Visitors from the North and from Europe did much to spread the South's reputation for militancy. But the alacrity with which Southerners displayed their bellicosity and the boastful pride with which they discussed it contributed significantly to the general impression that Southerners were a pugnacious lot. They were not being merely theatrical, although they had their moments of sheer

[2] J. E. Walmsley, "The Presidential Campaign in Mississippi," *Publications of the Mississippi Historical Society*, IX, 195.

[3] Ingraham, *The Southwest*, I, 208.

[4] *Southern Literary Messenger*, XXI (January, 1855), 2.

[5] *Southern Advocate*, May 9, 1828.

[6] Henry Benjamin Whipple, *Bishop Whipple's*

Southern Diary, 1843–1844, ed. by Lester Burrell Shippee (Minneapolis, 1937), 24–25.

[7] John Hope Franklin, *The Free Negro in North Carolina, 1790–1860* (Chapel Hill, 1943), 100.

[8] Quoted in *Plantation and Frontier Documents, 1649–1863,* ed. by Ulrich B. Phillips (Cleveland, 1909), II, 120.

acting. The flow of blood and the grief produced suggest a deep, pervading quality that could not be overlooked. Violence was inextricably woven into the most fundamental aspects of life in the South and constituted an important phase of the total experience of its people.

Fighting became a code by which men lived. Southerners themselves were apt to explain their dueling and other fighting propensities by pointing to the aristocratic character of their society; but this explanation seems somewhat flattering. The aristocratic element was much too inconsequential to give a tone of manners to the whole community; and the widespread existence of violence, even where there was no semblance of aristocratic traditions, suggests influences other than those of the select. The prevalence of violence was due, in part at least, to the section's peculiar social and economic institutions and to the imperfect state of its political organization. The passions that developed in the intercourse of superiors and inferiors showed themselves in the intercourse with equals, for, observed Stirling, "the hand of the violent man is turned against itself."[9] Far from loathing violence, the man of the South was the product of his experiences as a frontiersman, Indian fighter, slaveholder, self-sufficient yeoman, poor white, and Negro. He gladly fought, even if only to preserve his reputation as a fighter. . . .

[The Northern boy] went into law or politics; and could enjoy travel, the excitement of urban life in the North or abroad, or select the best that the South had to offer as diversion. But few Southerners had such opportunities, and few of the alternatives in a sluggish social and economic order were very attractive. As boys, even the average could hunt; as men they could join some local military outfit and seek the glory attached to successful forays against the Indians. A boy with such experiences might decide on a military career; even if he did not, the marks left by an early military or

semimilitary experience were lasting. From this frontier atmosphere, a combination of monotony and conflict, emerged a tense, sensitive fighting man. . . .

It was easy for such . . . [attitudes] to ripen into contempt for control and to render the further development of law and government even more difficult. While this attitude never succeeded in completely destroying government, it did make for distrust of all authority beyond the barest minimum essential to the maintenance of the political and social organism. Cash has aptly observed that the South "never developed any such compact and effective unit of government as the New England town. Its very counties were merely huge, sprawling hunks of territory, with almost no internal principle of cohesion. And to the last day before the Civil War, the land remained by far the most poorly policed section of the nation."[10]

There were, moreover, certain concepts of chivalric conduct that were involved in the reaction of the Southerner to crisis situations. However seriously or lightly he may have taken other rules of life—such as religion and morality—the Southerner was convinced that life should be ordered by certain well-defined codes of conduct that were a part of the cult of chivalry. Horsemanship and skill in the use of arms, so indispensable to successful living in the South, fitted conveniently and prominently into the cult of chivalry. Respect for and protection of white women were aspects that seemed to increase in importance as the problem of sex and race became more complicated and as the maintenance of racial integrity became a part of the program. Other attributes and trappings of the chivalric cult ranged from flamboyant oratory to lavish hospitality.[11] But through them all, and affecting them all, ran a concept of honor that was of tremendous importance

---

[9] Stirling, *Letters from the Slave States*, p. 271.

[10] W. J. Cash, *The Mind of the South* (New York, 1941), pp. 34–35.

[11] See the discussion in Rollin J. Osterweis, *Romanticism and Nationalism in the Old South* (New Haven, 1949), pp. 82–102.

in regulating and determining the conduct of the individual.

While the concept of honor was an intangible thing, it was no less real to the Southerner than the most mundane commodity that he possessed. It was something inviolable and precious to the ego, to be protected at every cost. It promoted extravagance, because of the imputation of poverty which might follow retrenchment. It sanctioned prompt demand for the redress of grievance, because of the imputation of guilt that might follow a less precipitate policy. It countenanced great recklessness of life, because of the imputation of cowardice that might follow forgiveness of injuries. The honor of the Southerner caused him to defend with his life the slightest suggestion of irregularity in his honesty or integrity; and he was fiercely sensitive to any imputation that might cast a shadow on the character of the women of his family. To him nothing was more important than honor. Indeed, he placed it above wealth, art, learning, and the other "delicacies" of an urban civilization and regarded its protection as a continuing preoccupation.

This Southern concept of honor discouraged the growth of strong law enforcement agencies. (The individual insisted on the right to defend his own honor.) To him it was a peculiarly personal thing in which the rest of the community could have little more than a casual interest. And his peers upheld him, realizing that they might play a similar role. The community, going beyond mere acceptance of vigorous defense of honor, regarded such action with hearty approval. The man who killed his adversary in a personal quarrel (while showing some regard for the amenities), need not fear public disgrace. The chances were excellent that his conduct would be judged as self-defense. Only in the case of some flagrant violation of the rules of a fair fight might he expect an indictment and conviction.

The idea of honor contained certain elements that encouraged its excessive application. Whenever a difficulty arose in which there was a *possibility* that honor was involved, it was usually decided—just to be on the safe side—that it *was* involved. Alexander Mackay saw this phenomenon among the people of Richmond and was shocked at its consequences. "Their code of honour," he remarked, "is so exceedingly strict that it requires the greatest circumspection to escape its violation. An offence which elsewhere would be regarded as one of homeopathic proportions, is very apt to assume in Richmond the gravity of colossal dimensions; even a coolness between parties is dangerous as having a fatal tendency speedily to ripen into a deadly feud. . . ."[12] It was only natural that such an atmosphere would lead to an excessive amount of violence in personal relations that caused a Southerner to "pop over an antagonist from a sense of duty much as he would a turkey, or a 'pa-atridge,' from a sense of pleasure." It has been suggested, with some reason, that these excesses in violence, growing out of the code of honor, actually created a "cult of murder" in the South from which sprang feuds between families as well as between individuals.[13]

The feeling of personal responsibility in defending himself, together with the deep appreciation for the idea of honor, created in each Southerner a sense of "personal sovereignty." Ruler of his own destiny, defender of his own person and honor, keeper and breaker of the peace, he approached a personal imperiousness that few modern men have achieved. Not since the days of the medieval barons, perhaps, had there been such individual sovereignty as was found in the antebellum South. Whenever a Southerner fought another, he was, in a very real sense, engaged in war. The honor and dignity at stake were no less important to the individual than they would be to an embattled nation.

---

[12] Alexander Mackay, *The Western World*, I, 254.

[13] Thomas Cooper DeLeon, *Belles, Beaux, and Brains of the 60's* (New York, 1909), pp. 11–12; and William O. Stevens, *Pistols at Ten Paces; The Story of the Code of Honor in America* (Boston, 1940), p. 108.

No single class had a monopoly on these sentiments and attitudes. While the planters refined the notion of honor and set the pattern for adhering to certain rules of conduct in personal warfare, this concept and that of personal sovereignty descended to other groups as they assimilated the interests and points of view of the dominant element of the community.[14] The sense of personal insecurity in the absence of law and order was an important factor in the lives of *all* Southern whites, and violence was to be found at every level of the social scale. If there were distinctions, they were in the relative crudeness in the violence of the lower classes in contrast to the refinement in that of the upper.

The reckless disregard for life and the consequent violence in evidence throughout the South and Southwest greatly alarmed Harriet Martineau, who called it the most savage in the world. Where else, in the nineteenth century, she asked, were there such practices as "burning alive, cutting the heart out, and sticking it on the point of a stick, and other such diabolical deeds?"[15] The countryside and the towns vied in their production of violent incidents. Violence could be predicted whenever there was any considerable assemblage of persons for a militia muster, protracted meeting, or a similar gathering. On such occasions there were numerous fights, some to avenge an alleged wrong, others merely for sport. It was hardly possible to distinguish by observation between the sport and the "blood fight." Even if it began in good humor as a display of physical prowess, there was a good chance that it would end on a more serious and, sometimes, deadly note.

In some communities there were men who, by their own appointment or by popular consensus, were the champion fighters of their respective bailiwicks. Such champions "strutted, bragged, and issued challenges" that were frequently accepted.[16] These local heroes provided diversion for spectators and anxious moments for their opponents who felt compelled to defend not only their manhood but their lives. Bishop Whipple was disgusted to find that in Florida in 1843, people were witnessing public fights in which "those who ought to be gentlemen descend to the common bully" but admitted that there were moments of levity. At the trial of a judge he was quite amused to hear the details of how the defendant had whipped another judge; but he was "surprised to hear such scurrility and vulgarity allowed in a court of justice as was used by one of the parties."[17]

The most refined defense of honor found expression in dueling which was widespread throughout the antebellum South. In Prussia and other militaristic European countries the duel was based on the principle of self-regulation by which the military sought to protect itself from civilian intervention.[18] In the South it was the manner of settling personal disputes by which "gentlemen," reflecting the strong influence of the European military tradition, sought to draw some line of behavioral distinction between themselves and others. Men of any class could—and did—fight; but dueling should be confined to those who claimed to be "gentlemen." The practice was defended "on the ground that it tended to preserve the amenities of life, that it was an incentive to virtue, and a shield of personal honor. . . ."[19]

While the duel was not an outgrowth of slavery, it was the most convenient and proper way for a slaveholder to settle a dispute involving honor. Accustomed to the use of firearms and the exercise of almost

---

[14] See Frank L. Owsley, *Plain Folk of the Old South* (Baton Rouge, 1949), pp. 117–18; and H. C. Brearley, "The Pattern of Violence" in William T. Couch, *Culture in the South* (Chapel Hill, 1934), pp. 685–88.

[15] Harriet Martineau, *Society in America*, II, 329.

[16] Everett Dick, *Dixie Frontier* (New York, 1948), p. 140.

[17] Whipple, *Southern Diary*, pp. 26–27.

[18] Alfred Vagts, *A History of Militarism, Romance and Realities of a Profession* (New York, 1937), pp. 185–86.

[19] Rosser H. Taylor, *Ante-Bellum South Carolina* (Chapel Hill, 1942), 47.

unlimited power over his dependents, "he could not endure contradiction, he would not brook opposition. When one lord ran against another in controversy, if the feelings were deeply engaged the final argument was the pistol."[20] Governor Hammond of South Carolina vigorously denied any connection between slavery and dueling. Admitting that "the point of honor is recognized throughout the slave region and that disputes of certain classes are frequently referred for adjustment to the 'trial by combat,' " it was not, he insisted, caused by slavery, "since the same custom prevails in France and England." But he failed to give a satisfactory explanation of its causes. . . .[21]

[Southern politicians sometimes] set out to chastise their critics by caning, pistol-whipping, or some other form of corporal punishment. In the contest over the House speakership in the winter of 1855–56, Horace Greeley went to Washington to support the candidacy of Nathaniel P. Banks. He criticized and probably helped to defeat a House resolution presented by Albert Rust of Arkansas calling for all candidates to withdraw. At their next encounter Rust and Greeley exchanged a few words, and Rust began to strike Greeley on the head with his cane. They were separated, but a few minutes later Rust met Greeley again and resumed the lashing. Once more they were separated by bystanders.[22]

In general, the South approved the summary chastisement of those who offended it or censured its leaders. When, in 1856, Representative Preston Brooks of South Carolina beat Charles Sumner into insensibility with a cane because of Sumner's severe strictures against South Carolina in his "Crime Against Kansas" speech, the South was delighted. Even the next day Brooks could write his brother that the "fragments of the stick are begged for as *sacred relics.*"[23] Southern newspapers lavishly praised Brooks's deed and numerous groups, among them the student body of the University of Virginia, passed resolutions endorsing it.[24] A leading Richmond paper rejoiced that a Southern gentleman had the courage to register his objections to Sumner's "insults" and to "cow-hide bad manners *out* of him, or good manners into him." Later, when it was reported that a few Southern editors expressed disapproval of Brooks's action, the fiery Richmond editor called them "mealy mouthed pharisees of the press."[25] All over the South Brooks was praised by editors, student groups, and citizens' mass meetings. In Columbia, South Carolina, even the slaves collected a handsome purse for him, much to the disgust of a Charleston editor, who felt that the South did not need the assistance of its slaves to show the North the extent of its resentment as well as its unity.[26] When Brooks resigned and returned to South Carolina—to be triumphantly reelected— he was given a hero's welcome. In Columbia an enormous crowd greeted him, and the mayor presented him a silver pitcher, a goblet, and a "fine hickory cane," with a handsome gold head. In Charleston the citizens presented him a cane with the inscription, "Hit Him Again," while his constituents in the Fourth District gave him one that was inscribed, "Use Knock-Down Arguments."[27]

[20] James Ford Rhodes, *History of the United States* (New York, 1928), I, 362; see also Osterweis, *Romanticism and Nationalism*, 97.

[21] James H. Hammond, "Governor Hammond's Letters on Slavery—No. 2," *De Bow's Review*, VII (December, 1849), 491.

[22] *New York Times*, January 30, 31, 1856, and Glyndon G. Van Deusen, *Horace Greeley, Nineteenth Century Crusader* (Philadelphia, 1953), pp. 201 ff. During these years there were numerous altercations of a similar nature, both in and out of the Congress. For an engaging account of several of them see Benjamin Perley Poore, *Perley's Reminiscences of Sixty Years in the National Metropolis* (Philadelphia, n.d.) I, 466, 532 ff.

[23] Preston Brooks to J. H. Brooks, May 23, 1856, in Robert Meriwether (ed.), "Preston Brooks on the Caning of Charles Sumner," *South Carolina Historical and Genealogical Magazine*, LII (January, 1951), 3.

[24] *Daily Richmond Enquirer*, June 14, 1856. These students presented Brooks with a goblet.

[25] *Ibid.*, May 29, 1856; June 3, 1856.

[26] *Charleston Mercury*, May 28, 1856; May 29, 1856.

[27] Columbia Citizens, *Reception and Speech*

No class of Southerner, perhaps, went to the field of honor more frequently than newspaper editors.[28] Of course, there were some editors who never had the opportunity to settle their disputes with their readers in such a formal manner. If the offense was grave enough and the aggrieved person impulsive enough, the latter might well storm into the editor's office or meet him on the streets and start shooting. Editors enjoyed neither the immunity that a member of Congress could invoke—although no real gentleman would—nor the claim of misquotation that an oral purveyor could make. The written word by which he was compelled to stand made him especially vulnerable; and the occasions on which he was called to defend, by pistol or sword, his words are so numerous that it is not possible to make more than a brief reference to some of them. . . .

Fanny Kemble, after marrying a Southern planter, was greatly disturbed by what her oldest child's superior position was doing. With dismay, she saw how the little girl's "swarthy worshiper . . . sprang to obey her little gestures of command. She said something about a swing, and in less than five minutes head man Frank had erected it for her, and a dozen young slaves were ready to swing little 'missus'—think of learning to rule despotically your fellow-creatures before the first lesson of self-government has been well spelt over!" Miss Kemble said that the habit of command, developed so early among Southerners, seemed to give them a certain self-possession and ease. This, she believed, was rather superficial, and upon closer observa-

tion the vices of the social system became apparent. The "haughty, overbearing irritability, effeminate indolence, reckless extravagance, and a union of profligacy and cruelty" of the slaveholders were the immediate result of their "irresponsible power over their dependents." These traits became apparent upon intimate acquaintance with Southern character, she asserted.[29]

That slavery tended to create tyranny in the South was not merely abolitionist prattle. For years it had been the considered judgment of some responsible white Southerners that a powerful socio-political absolutism was a significant consequence of the institution of slavery. In the debate on the question of the importation of slaves, Colonel George Mason of Virginia told the Federal Convention in 1787 that slaves produced "a most pernicious effect on manners" and that every master was a "born petty tyrant."[30] Ulrich B. Phillips said that the actual regime "was one of government not by laws but by men." In fact, he continued, each slave was under a paternalistic despotism, "a despotism in the majority of cases benevolent but in some cases harsh and oppressive, a despotism resented and resisted by some . . . but borne with light-heartedness, submission and affection by a huge number of blacks."[31]

The amount of benevolence, if any, in the despotism depended on the individual's relationship with his slaves. The system provided the despot with extensive prerogatives and ample opportunities for their abuse. The master had almost unlimited personal authority over his slaves as long as they were guilty of no flagrant violations of the rights of whites or of the feebly enforced state laws. For all practical purposes he was the source of law on the plantation; and, in the rare instances when he resorted to the law of the state to invoke his right

---

(n.p., n.d.), pp. 4–5; and James E. Campbell, "Sumner—Brooks—Burlingame," *Ohio Archaeological and Historical Quarterly*, XXXIV (October, 1925), 453 ff. In the controversy that followed the caning, Brooks challenged three Northern offenders, all of whom declined. For congressional reaction to this altercation, see the *Congressional Globe*, 34th Cong., 1st sess., Appendix, *passim*.

28 For a comprehensive discussion of the duels of southern editors, see Frederic Hudson, *Journalism in the United States from 1690 to 1872* (New York, 1873), pp. 761–68.

29 Fanny Kemble, *Residence on a Georgia Plantation*, pp. 57–58, 305.

30 Max Farrand, *Records of the Federal Convention* (New Haven, 1927), II, 370.

31 Ulrich B. Phillips, *Race Problems, Adjustments and Disturbances in the Ante-Bellum South* (Richmond, 1909), p. 200.

over his human property, its interpretation and enforcement were in his control. If the government of the plantation was not by laws but by men, its stability rested on force or the threat of force. Believing that slavery could be sustained by force and violence exercised against the slave, or against the challenges of free men, owners had no qualms about resorting to force and violence.

The planter regarded arms as a necessary adjunct to the machinery of control. The lash was used generously or sparingly, depending on the temperament of the master and the tractability of the slave. If the slave resisted the "mild" discipline of the lash or undertook to return blow for blow, how else could the master maintain his complete authority except through the use of, or the threat to use, more deadly weapons whose possession was forever denied the slave? Arming themselves with knives and guns became habitual with some masters and overseers. In moments of anger, they sometimes turned their weapons against each other. This was to be expected among an aggregation of armed lords having no superimposed discipline. The rule of tyranny by which they lived fostered independence and self-sufficiency—almost an individual sovereignty—that occasionally burst out in their quarrels.

The relationship between master and slave was that of superior and subordinate, despot and subject, or victor and vanquished. A spirit approaching the martial pervaded the entire plantation atmosphere. The conduct of the master toward the slave was determined by rules and considerations not unlike those of the military. Slaves enjoyed no well-defined rights: infractions brought summary punishment from which there was no appeal. A vigorous antislavery tract pointed out that the plantation was

"the seat of a little camp, which over-awes and keeps in subjection the surrounding peasantry." The master could claim and exercise over his slaves all the rights of a victorious warrior over a vanquished foe.[32]

The connection between slavery and the martial spirit was almost universally recognized. If the observer were an implacable foe like Charles Sumner, he could see only its bad effects; to him the result was a criminal distortion of the values and notions regarding the fighting spirit. In the South, the swagger of the bully was called chivalry, a swiftness to quarrel was regarded as courage. The bludgeon was adopted as a substitute for argument; and assassination was lifted to a fine art.[33] If the observer were an apologetic friend, he could be proud of the fact that Southerners had been bred under the influences of an institution "which, with its admitted evils, was calculated to foster the martial spirit and give force of character."[34]

The slave was never so completely subjugated as to allay all fears that he would make a desperate, bloody attempt to destroy the institution which bound him. Slaveholders could never be quite certain that they had established unquestioned control; fear and apprehension were always present. Judgment insisted on the strictest vigilance with no relaxation—the only policy consistent with the maintenance of the institution. . . .

---

[32] Richard Hildreth, *Despotism in America* . . . (Boston, 1840), p. 37.

[33] Charles Sumner, "The Barbarism of Slavery," speech delivered in the U.S. Senate, June 4, 1860 (Washington, 1860), p. 13.

[34] H. S. Fulkerson, *Random Recollections of Early Days in Mississippi* (Vicksburg, 1885), p. 143. See also the account of the planter who was seriously considering putting his slaves in uniform and providing drill music for them. MS fragment, Nov. 8, 1853, in the Mary Eliza Fleming Papers, Duke University Library.

1960

The Tragic Southerner[*]

CHARLES GRIER SELLERS, JR.

The American experience knows no greater tragedy than the Old South's twistings and turnings on the rack of slavery. Others suffered more from the "peculiar institution," but only the suffering of white Southerners fits the classic formula for tragedy. Like no other Americans before or since, the white men of the antebellum South drove toward catastrophe by doing conscious violence to their truest selves. No picture of the Old South as a section confident and united in its dedication to a neofeudal social order, and no explanation of the Civil War as a conflict between "two civilizations," can encompass the complexity and pathos of the antebellum reality. No analysis that misses the inner turmoil of the antebellum Southerner can do justice to the central tragedy of the southern experience.[†]

The key to the tragedy of southern history is the paradox of the slaveholding South's devotion to "liberty." Whenever and wherever Southerners sought to invoke their highest social values—in schoolboy declamations, histories, Fourth of July orations, toasts, or newspaper editorials— "liberty" was the incantation that sprang most frequently and most fervently from their lips and pens. "The love of liberty had taken deep root in the minds of carolinians [sic] long before the revolution," explained South Carolina's historian David Ramsay in 1809. The "similarity of state and condition" produced by the early settlers' struggle to subdue the wilderness had "inculcated the equality of rights" and "taught them the rights of man."[1]

The Revolutionary struggle made this implicit colonial liberalism explicit and tied it to patriotic pride in the new American Union. From this time on, for Southerners as for other Americans, liberty was the end for which the Union existed, while the Union was the instrument by which liberty was to be extended to all mankind. Thus the Fourth of July, the birthday of both liberty and Union, became the occasion for renewing the liberal idealism and the patriotic nationalism which united Americans of all sections at the highest levels of political conviction. "The Declaration of Independence, and the Constitution of the United States—Liberty and Union, now and forever, one and inseparable," ran a Virginian's toast on July 4, 1850. The same sentiment and almost the same phrases might have been heard in any part of the South in any year of the antebellum period.[2]

Now "liberty" can mean many things, but

---

[*] Reprinted from Charles G. Sellers, Jr., *The Southerner as American* (Chapel Hill, N.C.: University of North Carolina Press, 1960).

[†] My interpretation of the Old South draws heavily on the brilliant insights of Wilbur J. Cash in *The Mind of the South* (New York, 1941), and also on Clement Eaton's *Freedom of Thought in the Old South* (Durham, 1940).

[1] David Ramsay, *The History of South-Carolina, from Its First Settlement in 1670, to the Year 1808* (2 vols.; Charleston, 1809), II, 384.

[2] Fletcher M. Green, "Listen to the Eagle Scream: One Hundred Years of the Fourth of July in North Carolina (1776–1876)," *North Carolina Historical Review*, XXXI (July, October, 1954), 36, 534.

the Old South persistently used the word in the universalist sense of the eighteenth-century Enlightenment. At Richmond in 1826 John Tyler eulogized Jefferson as "the devoted friend of man," who "had studied his rights in the great volume of nature, and saw with rapture the era near at hand, when those rights should be proclaimed, and the world aroused from the slumber of centuries." Jefferson's fame would not be confined to Americans, said Tyler, for his Declaration of Independence would be known wherever "man, so long the victim of oppression, awakes from the sleep of ages and bursts his chains." The conservative, slaveholding Tyler would soon be indicted by northern writers as a leader of the "slave power conspiracy" against human freedom; yet in 1826 he welcomed the day "when the fires of liberty shall be kindled on every hill and shall blaze in every valley," to proclaim that "the mass of mankind have not been born with saddles on their backs, nor a favored few booted and spurred to ride them. . . ."[3]

Although a massive reaction against liberalism is supposed to have seized the southern mind in the following decades, the Nullifiers of the thirties and the radical southern sectionalists of the forties and fifties did not ignore or reject the Revolutionary tradition of liberty so much as they transformed it, substituting for the old emphasis on the natural rights of all men a new emphasis on the rights and autonomy of communities. It was ironic that these slaveholding defenders of liberty against the tyranny of northern domination had to place themselves in the tradition of '76 at all, and the irony was heightened by their failure to escape altogether its universalist implications. Even that fire-eater of fire-eaters, Robert Barnwell Rhett, declaimed on "liberty" so constantly and so indiscrimi-

nately that John Quincy Adams could call him "a compound of wild democracy and iron bound slavery."[4]

Indeed the older nationalist-universalist conception of liberty remained very much alive in the South, and Southerners frequently used it to rebuke the radical sectionalists. Denouncing nullification in 1834, a Savannah newspaper vehemently declared that Georgians would never join in this assault on America's Revolutionary heritage. "No!" said the editor, "the light of the 4th of July will stream across their path, to remind them that liberty was not won in a day. . . ." Even a Calhounite could proudly assure an Independence Day audience in Virginia a few years later that American principles were destined "to work an entire revolution in the face of human affairs" and "to elevate the great mass of mankind." In North Carolina in the forties, citizens continued to toast "The Principles of the American Revolution—Destined to revolutionize the civilized world"; and editors rejoiced that the Fourth sent rays of light "far, far into the dark spots of oppressed distant lands." In Charleston itself a leading newspaper proclaimed that Americans were "the peculiar people, chosen of the Lord, to keep the vestal flame of liberty, as a light unto the feet and a lamp unto the path of the benighted nations, who yet slumber or groan under the bondage of tyranny."[5]

Throughout the antebellum period the South's invocation of liberty was reinforced by its fervent devotion to the Union. "America shall reach a height beyond the ken of mortals," exclaimed a Charleston orator in the 1820s; and through the following decades Southerners continued to exult with other Americans over their country's unique advantages and brilliant destiny. The Old South's Americanism sometimes had a sur-

---

[3] *A Selection of Eulogies Pronounced in the Several States, in Honor of Those Illustrious Patriots and Statesmen, John Adams and Thomas Jefferson* (Hartford, 1826), 6–7. For an indication of the currency of similar sentiments, see Green, "Listen to the Eagle Scream," *North Carolina Historical Review*, XXXI, 303, 305, 548.

[4] Laura A. White, *Robert Barnwell Rhett, Father of Secession* (New York, 1931), 50–52; Merle Curti, *The Roots of American Loyalty* (New York, 1946), 137–38, 153–54.

[5] Curti, *American Loyalty*, 68, 154; R. M. T. Hunter, *An Address Delivered before the Society of Alumnia of the University of Virginia . . . on the 4th of July, 1839* (Charlottesville, 1839), 4.

prisingly modern ring, as when a conservative Georgia newspaper called on "True Patriots" to join the Whigs in defending the "American Way" against the "Red Republicanism" of the Democratic party. Even that bellwether of radical Southernism, *De Bow's Review*, printed article after article proclaiming the glorious destiny of the United States.[6]

To the very eve of the Civil War the Fourth of July remained a widely observed festival of liberty and union in the South. By 1854, a hard-pressed orator was complaining that there was nothing fresh left to say: "The Stars and Stripes have been so vehemently flourished above admiring crowds of patriotic citizens that there is hardly a rhetorical shred left of them. . . . The very Union would almost be dissolved by eulogizing it at such a melting temperature." The rising tide of sectional antagonism did somewhat dampen Independence Day enthusiasm in the late fifties, but even after the Civil War began, one southern editor saw "no reason why the birth of liberty should be permitted to pass unheeded wherever liberty has votaries. . . . The accursed Yankees are welcome to the exclusive use of their 'Doodle' but let the South hold on tenaciously to Washington's March and Washington's Principles and on every recurring anniversary of the promulgation of the Declaration, reassert the great principles of Liberty."[7]

What are we to make of these slaveholding champions of liberty? Was the antebellum Southerner history's most hypocritical casuist? Or were these passionate apostrophes to the liberty of distant peoples a disguised protest against, or perhaps an escape from, the South's daily betrayal of its liberal self? Southerners were at least subconsciously aware of the "detestable paradox" of "our every-day sentiments of liberty" while holding human beings in slavery, and many Southerners had made it painfully explicit in the early days of the republic.[8]

A Virginian was amazed that "a people who have declared 'That all men are by nature equally free and independent' and have made this declaration the first article in the foundation of their government, should in defiance of so sacred a truth, recognized by themselves in so solemn a manner, and on so important an occasion, tolerate a practice incompatible therewith." Similarly, in neighboring Maryland, a leading politician expressed his astonishment that the people of the Old Free State "do not blush at the very name of Freedom." Was not Maryland, asked William Pinkney, "at once the fair temple of freedom, and the abominable nursery of slaves; the school for patriots, and the foster-mother of petty despots; the asserter of human rights, and the patron of wanton oppression?" "It will not do," he insisted, "thus to talk like philosophers, and act like unrelenting tyrants; to be perpetually sermonizing it with liberty for our text, and actual oppression for our commentary."[9]

Still another leading Marylander pointed out that America's Revolutionary struggle had been "grounded upon the *preservation of those rights* to which God and nature entitled *us*, not in *particular*, but in common with *all the rest of mankind*." The retention of slavery, declared Luther Martin in 1788, was "a solemn mockery of, and insult to, that God whose protection we had then implored, and could not fail to hold us up to detestation, and render us contemptible to every true friend of liberty in the world." During the Revolution, said Martin, "when our liberties were at stake, we warmly felt for the common rights of men."[10]

Martin did not exaggerate the inclusive-

[6] Curti, *American Loyalty,* 41, 43, 61, 72, 102–3, 152; Horace Montgomery, *Cracker Parties* (Baton Rouge, 1950), 3.

[7] Green, "Listen to the Eagle Scream," *North Carolina Historical Review,* XXXI, 314, 319–20, 534–36.

[8] Daniel R. Goodloe, *The Southern Platform: or, Manual of Southern Sentiment on the Subject of Slavery* (Boston, 1858), 91.

[9] William S. Jenkins, *Pro-Slavery Thought in the Old South* (Chapel Hill, 1935), 37–38.

[10] Goodloe, *Southern Platform,* 94.

ness of the liberal idealism that had accompanied the Revolutionary War in the southern states. Many of the Revolutionary county committees had denounced slavery, and Virginia's Revolutionary convention of 1774 had declared its abolition to be "the greatest object of desire in those colonies where it was unhappily introduced in their infant state." The implications of universalist liberalism for slavery were recognized most clearly, perhaps, by the Georgia county committee which resolved early in 1775 "to show the world that we are not influenced by any contracted motives, but a general philanthropy for all mankind, of whatever climate, language, or complexion," by using its best endeavors to eliminate "the unnatural practice of slavery."[11]

It is well known that the South's great statesmen of the Revolutionary generation almost unanimously condemned slavery as incompatible with the nation's liberal principles. Though these elder statesmen proved incapable of solving the problem, Thomas Jefferson consoled himself with the thought that it could safely be left to the "young men, grown up, and growing up," who "have sucked in the principles of liberty, as it were, with their mother's milk."[12] Such young men did indeed grow up, and they kept most Southerners openly apologetic about slavery for 50 years following the Declaration of Independence.

When, in the mid-thirties, John C. Calhoun declared on the floor of the Senate that slavery was "a good—a great good," one of Jefferson's protégés and former law students was there to denounce "the obsolete and revolting theory of human rights and human society by which, of late, the institution of domestic slavery had been sustained and justified by some of its advocates in a portion of the South." Slavery was "a misfortune and an evil in all circumstances," said Virginia's Senator William C. Rives, and he would never "deny, as has been done by this new school, the natural

freedom and equality of man; to contend that slavery is a positive good." He would never "attack the great principles which lie at the foundation of our political system," or "revert to the dogmas of Sir Robert Filmer, exploded a century and a half ago by the immortal works of Sidney and Locke."[13]

Though open antislavery utterances grew infrequent after the 1830s, the generation which was to dominate southern life in the forties and fifties had already come to maturity with values absorbed from the afterglow of Revolutionary liberalism. On the eve of the Civil War *De Bow's Review* was to complain that during these earlier years, "when probably a majority of even our own people regarded the existence of slavery among us as a blot on our fair name . . . our youth [were allowed] to peruse, even in their tender years, works in which slavery was denounced as an unmitigated evil."[14] Some of these youngsters had drawn some vigorous conclusions. "How contradictory" was slavery to every principle of "a republican Government where liberty is the boast and pride of its free citizens," exclaimed the son of a slaveholding family in South Carolina. Similarly a 15-year-old Tennessee boy called slavery "a foul, a deadly blot . . . in a nation boasting of the republicanism of her principles" and owing allegiance to "the sacred rights of man."[15]

A whole generation cannot transform its

---

[11] *Ibid.*, 3–5.

[12] Hinton Rowan Helper, *The Impending Crisis of the South: How to Meet It* (New York, 1860), 197.

[13] *Register of Debates*, 24th Cong., 2d Sess., 719–23. Almost as significant as Rives' own position is the fact that he touched Calhoun at a tender point when he associated him with the anti-libertarian Filmer. The South Carolinian "utterly denied that his descendants had any thing to do with the tenets of Sir Robert Filmer, which he abhorred." "So far from holding with the dogmas of that writer, he had been the known and open advocate of freedom from the beginning," Calhoun was reported as saying. "Nor was there any thing in the doctrines he held in the slightest degree inconsistent with the highest and purest principles of freedom."

[14] Russel B. Nye, *Fettered Freedom: Civil Liberties and the Slavery Controversy, 1830–1860* (East Lansing, Mich., 1949), 72.

[15] Lillian A. Kibler, *Benjamin F. Perry, South Carolina Unionist* (Durham, 1946), 31; Pulaski *Tennessee Beacon and Farmers Advocate*, June 16, 1832.

most fundamental values by a mere effort of will. Though Southerners tended during the latter part of the antebellum period to restrict their publicly voiced libertarian hopes to "oppressed distant lands," the old liberal misgivings about slavery did not die. Instead they burrowed beneath the surface of the southern mind, where they kept gnawing away the shaky foundations on which Southerners sought to rebuild their morale and self-confidence as a slaveholding people.

Occasionally the doubts were exposed, as in 1857, when Congressman L. D. Evans of Texas lashed out at the general repudiation of liberalism to which some defenders of slavery had been driven. The doctrine of human inequality and subordination might do for the dark ages of tyranny, he declared, "but emanating from the lips of a Virginia professor, or a statesman of Carolina, it startles the ear, and shocks the moral sense of a republican patriot." But Evans only illustrated the hopelessness of the southern dilemma by his tortured argument for transforming slavery into a kind of serfdom which would somehow preserve the slave's "natural equality," while gradually evolving into a state of "perfect equality."[16]

The same year a Charleston magazine admitted that "We are perpetually aiming to square the maxims of an impracticable philosophy with the practice which nature and circumstances force upon us." Yet on the very eve of war, few Southerners were ready to resolve the dilemma by agreeing with the writer that "the [liberal] philosophy of the North is a dead letter to us."[17]

If the Southerner had been embarrassed by his devotion to liberty and Union alone, he would have had less trouble easing his mind on the subject of slavery. But as a Virginia legislator exclaimed in 1832, "This, sir, is a Christian community." Southerners "read in their Bibles, 'Do unto all men as you would have them do unto you'; and this golden rule and slavery are hard to reconcile."[18] During those early decades of the nineteenth century, when the South was confessing the evils of slavery, it had been swept by a wave of evangelical orthodoxy. Though the wave crested about the time some Southerners, including some clergymen, began speaking of slavery as a positive good, it does not follow that the evangelical reaction against the eighteenth century's religious ideas contributed significantly to the reaction against the eighteenth century's liberalism with regard to slavery.

On the contrary, the evangelical denominations had strong antislavery tendencies. Methodists, Quakers, and Baptists nurtured an extensive abolitionist movement in the upper South during the twenties, when the rest of the country was largely indifferent to the slavery question; and the Presbyterians were still denouncing slavery in Kentucky a decade later. It would be closer to the truth to suggest that as Southerners wrestled with their consciences over slavery, they may have gained a firsthand experience with the concepts of sin and evil that made them peculiarly susceptible to Christian orthodoxy. At any rate, as late as 1849, a proslavery professor at the University of Alabama complained to Calhoun that no one had yet published a satisfactory defense of slavery in the light of New Testament teachings. The "many religious people at the South who have strong misgivings on this head," he warned, constituted a greater threat to the peculiar institution than the northern abolitionists.[19]

Even the irreligious found it hard to resist the claims of simple humanity or to deny that slaves, as one Southerner put it, "have hearts and feelings like other men." And those who were proof against the appeals to Revolutionary liberalism, Christianity, and humanity, still faced the arguments of Southerners in each succeeding generation that slavery was disastrous to

---

[16] W. G. Bean, "Anti-Jeffersonianism in the Ante-Bellum South," *North Carolina Historical Review*, XII (April, 1935), 111.

[17] John Hope Franklin, *The Militant South, 1800–1861* (Cambridge, 1956), 222.

[18] Goodloe, *Southern Platform*, 49.

[19] E. Mitchell to John C. Calhoun, February 5, 1849, John C. Calhoun Papers (Clemson College Library).

the whites. Jefferson's famous lament that the slaveholder's child, "nursed, educated, and daily exercised in tyranny . . . must be a prodigy who can retain his manners and morals undepraved," was frequently echoed. George Mason's lament that slavery discouraged manufactures, caused the poor to despise labor, and prevented economic development, found many seconders in Virginia's slavery debate of 1831–32 and received elaborate statistical support from Hinton Rowan Helper in the fifties. The seldom mentioned but apparently widespread practice of *miscegenation* was an especially heavy cross for the women of the South. "Under slavery we live surrounded by prostitutes," wrote one woman bitterly. ". . . Any lady is ready to tell you who is the father of all the mulatto children in everybody's household but her own. . . . My disgust sometimes is boiling over."[20]

It is essential to understand that the public declarations of Southerners never revealed the full impact of all these antislavery influences on the southern mind. Fear of provoking slave insurrections had restrained free discussion of slavery even in the Revolutionary South, and an uneasy society exerted steadily mounting pressure against antislavery utterances thereafter. Only when Nat Turner's bloody uprising of 1831 shocked Southerners into open debate over the peculiar institution did the curtain of restraint part sufficiently to reveal the intensity of their misgivings. Thomas Ritchie's influential Richmond *Enquirer* caught the mood of that historic moment when it quoted a South Carolinian as exclaiming, "We may shut our eyes and avert our faces, if we please, but there it is, the dark and growing evil at our doors; and meet the question we must, at no distant day. . . . What is to be done? Oh! my God, I do not know, but something must be done."[21]

Many were ready to say what had to be done, especially a brilliant galaxy of the liberty-loving young Virginians on whom the dying Jefferson had pinned his hopes. "I will not rest until slavery is abolished in Virginia," vowed Governor John Floyd; and during the winter of 1831–32 a deeply earnest Virginia legislature was wrapped in the Old South's only free and full debate over slavery. Not a voice was raised to justify human servitude in the abstract, while a score of Virginians attacked the peculiar institution with arguments made deadly by the South's endemic liberalism and Christianity. Two years later a Tennessee constitutional convention showed a tender conscience on slavery by admitting that "to prove it to be an evil is an easy task." Yet in both states proposals for gradual emancipation were defeated.[22]

The outcome was no surprise to the editor of the Nashville *Republican*. Few would question the moral evil of slavery, he had written back in 1825, "but then the assent to a proposition is not always followed by acting in uniformity to its spirit." Too many Southerners believed, perhaps from "the exercise of an interested casuistry," that nature had ordained the Negro to slavery by giving him a peculiar capacity for labor under the southern sun. Furthermore, southern white men would have to "be convinced that to labor personally is a more agreeable, and desirable occupation, than to command, & superintend the labor of others." Consequently, "as long as slavery is conceived to advance the pecuniary interests of individuals, they will be slow to relish, and reluctant to encourage, any plan for its abolition. They will quiet their consciences with the reflection that it was entailed upon us—that it has grown up with the institutions of the country—and that the establishment of a new order of things would be attended with great difficulty, and might be perilous."[23]

[20] Goodloe, *Southern Platform*, 49; Helper, *Impending Crisis*, 195, 208–9; John J. Flournoy, *An Essay on the Origin, Habits, &c. of the African Race* . . . (New York, 1835), 25; Kenneth M. Stampp, *The Peculiar Institution: Slavery in the Ante-Bellum South* (New York, 1956), 356.

[21] Joseph C. Robert, *The Road from Monti-*

cello: *A Study of the Virginia Slavery Debate of 1832* (Durham, 1941), 17–18, and *passim*.

[22] Charles H. Ambler, *The Life and Diary of John Floyd* (Richmond, 1918), 172; Jenkins, *Pro-Slavery Thought*, 88n.

[23] Nashville *Republican*, October 22, 1825.

Thus when Nat Turner frightened Southerners into facing squarely the tragic ambiguity of their society, they found the price for resolving it too high. The individual planter's economic stake in slavery was a stubborn and perhaps insurmountable obstacle to change; and even Jefferson's nerve had failed at the task of reconstituting the South's social system to assimilate a host of Negro freedmen.

The whole South sensed that a fateful choice had been made. Slowly and reluctantly Southerners faced the fact that, if slavery were to be retained, things could not go on as before. The slaves were restive, a powerful antislavery sentiment was sweeping the western world, and southern minds were not yet nerved for a severe struggle in defense of the peculiar institution to which they were now committed. The South could no longer ease its conscience with hopes for the eventual disappearance of slavery, or tolerate such hopes in any of its people. "It is not enough for them to believe that slavery has been entailed upon us by our forefathers," proclaimed Calhoun's national newspaper organ. "We must satisfy the consciences, we must allay the fears of our own people. We must satisfy them that slavery is of itself right—that it is not a sin against God—that it is not an evil, moral or political. . . . In this way, and this way only, can we prepare our own people to defend their institutions."[24] So southern leaders of the Calhoun school began trying to convince themselves and others that slavery was a "positive good," while southern legislatures abridged freedom of speech and press, made manumission difficult or impossible, and imposed tighter restrictions on both slaves and free Negroes. The Great Reaction was under way.

Yet the Great Reaction, for all its formidable facade and terrible consequences, was a fraud. Slavery simply could not be blended with liberalism and Christianity, while liberalism and Christianity were too deeply rooted in the southern mind to be torn up overnight. Forced to smother and distort their most fundamental convictions by the decision to maintain slavery, and goaded by criticism based on these same convictions, Southerners of the generation before the Civil War suffered the most painful loss of social morale and identity that any large group of Americans has ever experienced.

The surface unanimity enforced on the South in the forties and fifties by the Great Reaction concealed a persistent hostility to slavery. It is true that large numbers of the most deeply committed antislavery men left the South. They were usually men of strong religious conviction, such as Levi Coffin, the North Carolina Quaker who moved to Indiana to become the chief traffic manager of the Underground Railroad, or Will Breckinridge, the Kentucky Presbyterian who declared, "I care little where I go—so that I may only get where every man I see is as free as myself." In fact the national banner of political antislavery was carried in the forties by a former Alabama slaveholder, James G. Birney, who had rejected slavery for the same reasons that bothered many other Southerners—because it was "inconsistent with the Great Truth that all men are created equal . . . as well as the great rule of benevolence delivered to us by the Savior Himself that in all things whatsoever ye would that men should do unto you do ye even so to them."[25]

Many zealous antislavery men remained in the South, however, to raise their voices wherever the Great Reaction relaxed its grip. If this almost never happened in the lower South, a dissenter in western Virginia could exult in 1848 that "anti-slavery papers and anti-slavery orators are scattering far and wide the seeds of freedom, and an immense number of persons are uttering vaticinations in contemplation of a day of emancipation"; while the reckless courage of Cassius Clay and his allies kept the anti-

---

[24] Washington (D.C.) *United States Telegraph,* December 5, 1835.

[25] Walter B. Posey, "The Slavery Question in the Presbyterian Church in the Old Southwest," *Journal of Southern History,* XV (August, 1943), 319; Betty Fladeland, *James Gillespie Birney: Slaveholder to Abolitionist* (Ithaca, 1955), 83.

slavery cause alive in Kentucky. "The contention of planter politicians that the South had achieved social and political unity," concludes the ablest student of the peculiar institution, "appears, then, to have been the sheerest of wishful thinking."[26]

Far more significant than outright antislavery opinion was the persistent disquietude over slavery among the many white Southerners who found the new proslavery dogmas hard to swallow. The official southern view held that slaveholders "never inquire into the propriety of the matter . . . they see their neighbors buying slaves, and they buy them . . . leaving to others to discuss the right and justice of the thing." In moments of unusual candor, however, the proslavery propagandists admitted the prevalence of misgivings. Calhoun's chief editorial spokesman thought the principal danger of northern abolitionism was its influence upon "the consciences and fears of the slave-holders themselves." Through "the insinuation of their dangerous heresies into our schools, our pulpits, and our domestic circles," Duff Green warned, the abolitionists might succeed in "alarming the consciences of the weak and feeble, and diffusing among our own people a morbid sensitivity on the question of slavery."[27]

Slavery's apologists were particularly irritated by the numerous instances "in which the superstitious weakness of dying men . . . induces them, in their last moments, to emancipate their slaves." Every manumission was an assault on the peculiar institution and a testimony to the tenacity with which older values resisted the proslavery dogmas. "Let our women and old men, and persons of weak and infirm minds, be disabused of the false . . . notion that slavery is sinful, and that they will peril their souls if they do not disinherit their offspring by emancipating their slaves!" complained a

Charleston editor in the fifties. It was high time masters "put aside all care or thought what Northern people say about them."[28]

Yet the manumissions went on, despite mounting legal obstacles. The census reported more than 3,000 for 1860, or one manumission for every 1,309 slaves, which was double the number reported ten years before. If this figure seems small, it should be remembered that these manumissions were accomplished against "almost insuperable obstacles"—not only southern laws prohibiting manumission or making it extremely difficult, but also northern laws barring freed Negroes. The evidence indicates that there would have been many more manumissions if the laws had been more lenient, and if masters had not feared that the freed Negroes would be victimized.[29]

The explanations advanced by men freeing their slaves illustrate the disturbing influence of liberalism and Christianity in the minds of many slaveholders. A Virginia will affirmed the testator's belief "that slavery in all its forms . . . is inconsistent with republican principles, that it is a violation of our bill of rights, which declares, *that all men are by nature equally free;* and above all, that it is repugnant to the spirit of the gospel, which enjoins universal love and benevolence." A North Carolinian listed four reasons for freeing his slaves: (1) "Agreeably to the rights of man, every human being, be his colour what it may, is entitled to freedom"; (2) "My conscience, the great criterion, condemns me for keeping them in slavery"; (3) "The golden rule directs us to do unto every human creature, as we would wish to be done unto"; and (4) "I wish to die with a clear conscience, that I may not be ashamed to appear before my master in a future World." In Tennessee, one man freed his slave woman because he wanted her to "Enjoy Liberty the birthright of all

[26] Kenneth M. Stampp, "The Fate of the Southern Antislavery Movement," *Journal of Negro History,* XXVIII (January, 1943), 20, 22, and *passim.*

[27] Stampp, *Peculiar Institution,* 422–23; Washington (D.C.) *United States Telegraph,* December 5, 1835.

[28] Stampp, *Peculiar Institution,* 234, 423.

[29] Clement Eaton, *Freedom of Thought in the Old South* (2d ed.; New York, 1951), xii–xiii; J. Merton England, "The Free Negro in Ante-Bellum Tennessee," *Journal of Southern History,* IX (February, 1943), 44–45. Cf. Stampp, *Peculiar Institution,* 234–35.

Mankind." Another not only believed "it to be the duty of a Christian to deal with his fellow man in a state of bondage with humanity and kindness," but also feared that his own "happiness *hereafter*" depended on the disposition he made of his slaves. Still another, after ordering two slaves freed, hoped that "no one will offer to undo what my conscience tole me was my duty," and that "my children will consider it so and folow the futsteps of their father and keep now [no] slaves longer than they pay for their raising and expenses."[30]

But conscience was a problem for many more Southerners than those who actually freed their slaves, as the proslavery philosophers were compelled to recognize. "I am perfectly aware that slavery is repugnant to the *natural* emotions of men," confessed William J. Grayson on the eve of the Civil War. James H. Hammond was one of many who sought to quiet the troublesome southern conscience by picturing slavery as an eleemosynary institution, maintained at considerable cost by generous slaveholders. Southerners must content themselves, said Hammond, with "the consoling reflection, that what is lost to us is gained to humanity." Grayson, on the other hand, despaired of quieting conscience and concluded grimly that conscience itself must be discredited. "I take the stand on the position that our natural feelings are unsafe guides for us to follow in the social relations."[31]

But a host of Southerners, perhaps including Grayson and Hammond, could neither satisfy nor ignore their consciences. One troubled master confided to his wife, "I sometimes think my feelings unfit me for a slaveholder." A North Carolina planter told his son that he could not discipline his slaves properly, believing that slavery was a violation of "the natural rights of a being who is as much entitled to the enjoyment of liberty as myself." In the rich Mississippi

Delta country, where many of the largest slaveholders remained loyal to the Union in 1861, one man had long sought "some means . . . to rid us of slavery, because I never had any great fondness for the institution although I had been the owner of slaves from my youth up." Another Mississippi slaveholder was "always an abolitionist at heart," but "did not know how to set them free without wretchedness to them, and utter ruin to myself." Still another "owned slaves & concluded if I was merciful & humane to them I might just as well own them as other Persons . . . [but] I had an instinctive horror of the institution." How many masters held such opinions privately can never be known, but observers at the close of the Civil War noted a surprisingly general feeling of relief over the destruction of slavery. An upcountry South Carolinian certainly spoke for many Southerners when he said, "I am glad the thing is done away with; it was more plague than pleasure, more loss than profit."[32]

The nub of the Southerner's ambivalent attitude toward slavery was his inability to regard the slave consistently as either person or property. Slaves "were a species of property that differed from all others," James K. Polk declared as a freshman congressman, "they were rational; they were human beings."[33] The slave's indeterminate status was writ large in the ambiguity of the whole structure of southern society. A sociologist has analyzed the institutional features of slavery as lying along a "rationality-traditionalism range," whose polar points were mutually contradictory. At one pole lay the economic view. Since slavery was a labor system employed in a highly competitive market economy, a minimum of rational efficiency was necessarily prescribed for

---

[30] Eaton, *Freedom of Thought*, 18–19; Stampp, *Peculiar Institution*, 235–36; England, "Free Negro," *Journal Southern History*, IX, 43–44.

[31] Jenkins, *Pro-Slavery Thought*, 236; Stampp, *Peculiar Institution*, 383.

[32] Stampp, *Peculiar Institution*, 424; Eaton, *Freedom of Thought*, 19; Frank W. Klingberg, *The Southern Claims Commission* (Berkeley and Los Angeles, 1955), 11, 108; J. W. De Forest, "Chivalrous and Semi-Chivalrous Southrons," *Harper's New Monthly Magazine*, XXVIII (January, February, 1869), 200.

[33] *Register of Debates*, 19th Cong., 1st Sess., 1649.

economic survival. This called for a "sheerly economic" view of slavery, one which regarded the slave as property, which gave the master unlimited control over the slave's person, which evaluated the treatment of slaves wholly in terms of economic efficiency, which structured the slave's situation so that his self-interest in escaping the lash became his sole motivation to obedience, which sanctioned the domestic slave trade and demanded resumption of the foreign slave trade as essential mechanisms for supplying and redistributing labor, and which dismissed moral considerations as both destructive of the labor supply and irrelevant. Though the plantation system tended during the latter part of the slavery period to approach the ideal type of a purely commercial economic organization, especially with the geographical shift to the new lands of the Southwest, few if any Southerners ever fully accepted this "sheerly economic" view of slavery.

At the other pole lay a "traditional" or "familial" view, which regarded the slave more as person than property and idealized "the patriarchial organization of plantation life and the maintenance of the family estate and family slaves at all costs." Both the "sheerly economic" and the "familial" views of slavery were sanctioned by southern society; economics and logic drove Southerners toward the former, while sentiment, liberalism, and Christianity dragged them in the other direction.[34]

This fundamental ambivalence was most clearly apparent in the law of slavery. Early colonial law had justified the enslavement of Negroes on the ground that they were heathens, so that the conversion of slaves to Christianity raised a serious problem. Though the Negro was continued in bondage, the older conviction that conversion and slave status were incompatible died hard, as was demonstrated by the succes-

sive enactments required to establish the new legal definition of slavery on the basis of the Negro's race rather than his heathenism. Even then problems remained. Not all Negroes were slaves, and the South could never bring itself to reduce free Negroes to bondage. Moreover the slave's admission to the privilege of salvation inevitably identified him as a person. But slavery could not be viewed as a legal relationship between legal persons; in strict logic it had to be a chattel arrangement that left the slave no legal personality.

Was the slave a person or merely property in the eyes of the law? This question southern legislatures and courts never settled. He could not legally marry, own property, sue or be sued, testify, or make contracts; yet he was legally responsible for crimes he committed, and others were responsible for crimes committed against him. The ambiguity was most striking in the case of a slave guilty of murder; as a person he was responsible and could be executed; but he was also property, and if the state took his life, his owner had to be compensated. "The slave is put on trial as a *human being*," declared a harassed court in one such case. "Is it not inconsistent, in the progress of the trial, to treat him as property, like . . . a horse, in the value of which the owner has a pecuniary interest which makes him incompetent as a witness?"[35]

The Southerner's resistance to the legal logic of making slavery a simple property arrangement is amply illustrated in court decisions. "A slave is not in the condition of a horse," said a Tennessee judge. "He has mental capacities, and an immortal principle in his nature." The laws did not "extinguish his high-born nature nor deprive him of many rights which are inherent in men." Similarly a Mississippi court declared that it would be "a stigma upon the character of the State" if a slave could be murdered "without subjecting the offender to the highest penalty known to the criminal

---

[34] Wilbert E. Moore, "Slavery, Abolition, and the Ethical Valuation of the Individual: A Study of the Relations between Ideas and Institutions" (Ph.D. dissertation, Harvard University, 1940), 193–212.

[35] Wilbert E. Moore, "Slave Law and the Social Structure," *Journal of Negro History*, XXVI (April, 1941), 171–202.

jurisprudence of the country. Has the slave no rights, because he is deprived of his freedom? He is still a human being, and possesses all those rights of which he is not deprived by the positive provision of the law."[36]

The anguish induced by the legal logic of slavery was expressed most clearly in a North Carolina decision. Recognizing the objectives of slavery to be "the profit of the master, his security and the public safety," and recognizing the slave to be "doomed in his own person, and his posterity, to live without knowledge, and without the capacity to make any thing his own, and to toil that another may reap the fruits," the court concluded that, "Such services can only be expected from one . . . who surrenders his will in implicit obedience to that of another. . . . The power of the master must be absolute." The judge felt "as deeply as any man can" the harshness of this proposition. "As a principle of moral rights, every person in his retirement must repudiate it. . . . It constitutes the curse of slavery to both the bond and the free portions of our population. But it is inherent in the relation of masters and slaves."[37]

The slave's indeterminate status was not just a legal problem, but a daily personal problem for every master. "It is difficult to handle simply as property, a creature possessing human passions and human feelings," observed Frederick Law Olmsted, "while, on the other hand, the absolute necessity of dealing with property as a thing, greatly embarrasses a man in any attempt to treat it as a person." Absentee owners and the masters of large, commercially rationalized plantations might regard their field hands as economic units, but few of them could avoid personalizing their relationships with house servants in a way that undercut the sheerly economic conception of the peculiar institution. The majority of slaveholders, moreover, were farmers who

lived and worked closely with their slaves, and such masters, according to D. R. Hundley, "seem to exercise but few of the rights of ownership over their human chattels, making so little distinction between master and man, that their Negroes [are] . . . in all things treated more like equals than slaves."[38]

The personalized master-slave relationship was a direct threat to the peculiar institution, for slavery's stability as an economic institution depended upon the Negro's acceptance of the caste line between himself and the white man. Sociologists tell us that such caste systems as India's were stabilized by the fact that "those goals and value-attitudes which were legitimate for the dominant caste had no implications concerning their legitimacy for the subordinate caste." In the South, however, where the values of the dominant caste produced personalized master-slave relationships, and where Negroes could view manumission as the crucial product of personalization, members of the subordinate caste learned to regard the value system and goals of the dominant caste as at least partly valid for themselves. The presence of free Negroes in southern society meant that the caste line did not coincide completely with the color line, and the overlap made liberty a legitimate goal even for the slave. Thus the slave's passion for freedom, manifested in countless escapes and insurrection plots, was not "lit up in his soul by the hand of Deity," as a Virginia legislator thought, but was implanted by the white man's own inability to draw the caste line rigidly.[39]

Though Southerners could guard against the dangers of personalization in the abstract, as when legislatures prohibited manumission, the individual master, face to face with his human property, found it harder to

---

[36] Stampp, *Peculiar Institution*, 217; Helper, *Impending Crisis*, 223–24.

[37] Moore, "Slavery and Ethical Valuation," Ph.D. dissertation (Harvard), 187–88.

[38] Stampp, *Peculiar Institution*, 193; D. R. Hundley, *Social Relations in Our Southern States* (New York, 1860), 193.

[39] Moore, "Slavery and Ethical Valuation," 233–35; Wilbert E. Moore and Robin M. Williams, "Stratification in the Ante-Bellum South," *American Sociological Review*, VII (June, 1942), 348–51; Robert, *Road from Monticello*, 103.

behave in accordance with the sheerly economic view of slavery. Economic efficiency demanded "the painful exercise of undue and tyrannical authority," observed a North Carolina planter; and the famous ex-slave Frederick Douglass testified that kind treatment increased rather than diminished the slave's desire for freedom. Consequently humanity and the profit motive were forever struggling against each other in the master's mind. While the profit motive frequently won out, humanity had its victories too. "I would be content with much less . . . cotton if less cruelty was exercised," said a disturbed planter in Mississippi. "I fear I am near an abolition[i]st." Most often, perhaps, the master's humanitarian and economic impulses fought to a draw, leaving him continually troubled and frustrated in the management of his slaves. Slaveholding, concluded one master, subjected "the man of care and feeling to more dilemmas than any other vocation he could follow."[40]

Certainly southern opinion condemned thoroughgoing economic rationality in the treatment of slaves. This was most apparent in the low social status accorded to slave traders and overseers, when by normal southern canons of prestige their intimate relation with the peculiar institution and their control over large numbers of slaves should have given them a relatively high rank. Both groups were absolutely essential to the slavery system, and both bore a purely economic relation to it. The overseer, who was judged primarily by the profits he wrung out of slave labor, typified the sheerly exploitative aspects of slavery; while the slave trader, who presided over the forcible disruption of families and the distribution of slaves as marketable commodities, was the most conspicuous affront to the familial conception of the peculiar institution. These men certainly developed a cynical attitude toward the human property they controlled, but they did not uniformly exhibit the dishonesty, greed, vulgarity, and

general immorality that southern opinion ascribed to them. By thus stereotyping these exemplars of the sheerly economic aspects of slavery, southern society created scapegoats on whom it could discharge the guilt feelings arising from the necessity of treating human beings as property.[41]

These guilt feelings seem to have increased during the final years of the antebellum period, as slavery approximated the sheerly economic pattern on more and more plantations. Never had Southerners regaled themselves and others so insistently with the myth of the happy slave. A European traveler met few slaveholders who could "openly and honestly look the thing in the face. They wind and turn about in all sorts of ways, and make use of every argument . . . to convince me that the slaves are the happiest people in the world, and do not wish to be placed in any other condition." At the same time there developed a strong movement to extend and implement the paternalistic-personalistic pattern. Some states amended their slave codes to prescribe minimum standards of treatment, and there was agitation for more fundamental reforms—legalization of slave marriages, protection against disruption of slave families, and encouragement of Negro education.[42]

Especially significant was the crusade for religious instruction of slaves. "We feel that the souls of our slaves are a solemn trust, and we shall strive to present them faultless and complete before the presence of God," declared that high priest of southern Presbyterianism, Dr. James Henley Thornwell. The argument for religious instruction was also a justification of slavery, and the only one that effected any kind of real accommodation between the peculiar institution and the white Southerner's innate disposition to regard the slave as a human being. It was precisely for this reason that the religious in-

[40] Stampp, *Peculiar Institution*, 89–90, 141, 191.

[41] Moore, "Slavery and Ethical Valuation," 194–95; Moore and Williams, "Stratification," 345–46.

[42] Stampp, *Peculiar Institution*, 423; Herbert Aptheker, *American Negro Slave Revolts* (New York, 1943), 59–60.

terpretation of slavery quieted more south-ern qualms than any other facet of the pro-slavery argument. "However the world may judge us in connection with our institution of slavery," said Georgia's Bishop Stephen Elliott, "we conscientiously believe it to be a great missionary institution—one ar-ranged by God, as he arranges all the moral and religious influences of the world so that the good may be brought out of the seem-ing evil, and a blessing wrung out of every form of the curse."

Yet the religious argument was ultimately subversive of slavery. By giving the slave's status as person precedence over his status as property, and by taking as its mission the elevation of the slave as a human being, the movement for religious instruction nec-essarily called into question the inherent beneficence and permanence of the institu-tion. Dr. Thornwell resolutely argued that slavery could end only in heaven, because only there could the sin that produced it end; meanwhile the Christian's duty was to mitigate its evils. Bishop Elliott, on the other hand, believed that by giving the slaves re-ligious instruction "we are elevating them in every generation" here on earth, and he spoke for many another southern church-man when he conceded that this implied ulti-mately some change in the slaves' worldly status. Thus, by the close of the slavery era, the religious defense of the institution was bringing the South back toward its old co-lonial doubts about the validity of continued bondage for converted men and women.[43]

Nowhere, in fact, was the South's painful inner conflict over slavery more evident than in the elaborate body of theory by which it tried to prove (mainly to itself) the beneficence of its peculiar social system. "It has not been more than . . . thirty years since the abolition of slavery was seriously debated in the legislature of Virginia," ob-served the *Southern Literary Messenger* on the eve of the Civil War. "Now, on the con-trary . . . the whole Southern mind with an unparalleled unanimity regards the institu-tion of slavery as righteous and just, or-dained of God, and to be perpetuated by Man." Yet the stridency with which south-ern unanimity was ceaselessly proclaimed stands in suggestive contrast to the private views of many Southerners. "To expect men to agree that Slavery is a blessing, social, moral, and political," wrote a North Caro-lina congressman to his wife, "when many of those who have all their lives been ac-customed to it . . . believe exactly the re-verse, is absurd." Even the fire-eaters con-fessed privately that outside South Caro-lina most slaveholders were "mere negro-drivers believing themselves wrong and only holding on to their negroes as something to make money out of." South Carolinians themselves had "retrograded," wrote Rob-ert W. Barnwell in 1844, "and must soon fall into the same category."[44]

Close examination of the superficially im-pressive proslavery philosophy reveals, as Louis Hartz has brilliantly demonstrated, a "mass of agonies and contradictions in the dream world of southern thought." The peculiar institution could be squared theo-retically with either the slave's humanity or democratic liberalism for whites, but not with both. Thus the necessity for justifying slavery, coupled with the white South's in-ability to escape its inherited liberalism or to deny the common humanity it shared with its Negro slaves, inspired "a mixture of pain and wild hyperbole."[45]

Recognizing that the religious argument by itself was a threat to the peculiar institu-tion, one school of proslavery philosophers

[43] Jenkins, *Pro-Slavery Thought*, 214–18.

[44] Jay B. Hubbell, "Literary Nationalism in the Old South," in David K. Jackson (ed.), *American Studies in Honor of William Kenneth Boyd* (Dur-ham, 1940), 183n.; David Outlaw to Mrs. David Outlaw, July [28], 1848, David Outlaw Papers (Southern Historical Collection, University of North Carolina); Robert W. Barnwell to Robert Barnwell Rhett, November 1, 1844, Robert Barn-well Rhett Papers (Southern Historical Collec-tion, University of North Carolina).

[45] Louis Hartz, *The Liberal Tradition in Amer-ica: An Interpretation of American Political Thought since the Revolution* (New York, 1955), 145–200.

sought to preserve both slavery and the slave's humanity by sacrificing democratic liberalism and falling back to a neofeudal insistence on the necessity of subordination and inequality in society. "Subordination rules supreme in heaven and must rule supreme on earth," asserted Bishop Elliott, and he did not attempt to disguise the repudiation of democratic liberalism that followed from this principle. Carried away by Revolutionary fervor, Southerners along with other Americans had "declared war against all authority and against all form"; they had pronounced all men equal and man capable of self-government. "Two greater falsehoods could not have been announced," Elliott insisted, "because the one struck at the whole constitution of civil society as it had ever existed, and because the other denied the fall and corruption of man."[46]

George Fitzhugh, the most logical and impressive of the proslavery philosophers and the leading exponent of southern neofeudalism, would have preserved the humanity of the Negroes but denied freedom to the white masses by making both subject to the same serf-like subordination. Only thus could men be saved from the frightful corruption and turbulence of "free society." But southern planters were too much bourgeois capitalists and southern farmers were too much Jacksonian democrats to entertain the neo-feudalists' vituperation at "free society." "Soon counties, neighborhoods, or even individuals will be setting up castles," commented a sarcastic Alabamian.[47] Fitzhugh and his fellow intellectuals might talk all they pleased about reducing the masses, white and black, to serfdom, but practical politicians and publicists knew better than to fly so directly in the face of the South's liberal bias.

At the hands of men like James H. Hammond, therefore, neo-feudalism became a racial "mud-still" theory, which divided society along the color line, relegating Negroes to bondage and reserving democratic liberalism for white men only. In the late forties a school of southern ethnologists arose to declare the Negro a distinct and permanently inferior species; and by 1854 Mississippi's Senator Albert G. Brown could invite Northerners to his state "to see the specimen of that equality spoken of by Jefferson in the Declaration of Independence." Nowhere else in the Union, said Brown, was there such an exemplification of Jefferson's beautiful sentiment. "In the South all men are equal. I mean of course, white men; negroes are not men, within the meaning of the Declaration."[48]

The racist argument was attacked with surprising vehemence by both religionists and feudalists. At least one Southerner went far beyond most northern abolitionists in asserting that "the African is endowed with faculties as lofty, with perceptions as quick, with sensibilities as acute, and with natures as susceptible of improvement, as we are, who boast a fairer skin." Indeed, said this Virginian, if Negroes were "operated upon by the same ennobling impulses, stimulated by the same generous motives, and favored by the same adventitious circumstances, they would, as a mass, reach as high an elevation in the scale of moral refinement, and attain as great distinction on the broad theatre of intellectual achievement, as ourselves."[49]

While few Southerners would go as far as this, the religionists did maintain stoutly "that the African race is capable of considerable advance." Religious instruction of slaves would have been pointless without some such assumption, but the churchmen objected more fundamentally to the racist argument because it robbed the slave of his essential humanity. The feudalists, too, rejected the idea of racial inferiority, with Fitzhugh arguing that "it encourages and incites brutal masters to treat negroes, not as weak, ignorant and dependent brethren, but as wicked beasts, without the pale of

[46] Jenkins, *Pro-Slavery Thought*, 239–40.

[47] Ollinger Crenshaw, *The Slave States in the Presidential Election of 1860* (Baltimore, 1945), 253.

[48] *Congressional Globe*, 33rd Cong., 1st Sess., Appendix, 230.

[49] Goodloe, *Southern Platform*, 93.

humanity." The Negro was essential to the web of reciprocal duties and affections between superiors and subordinates that was supposed to knit the idyllic neo-feudal world together. "The Southerner is the negro's friend, his only friend," said Fitzhugh. "Let no intermeddling abolitionist, no refined philosophy dissolve this friendship."[50]

The debate between the religionists and feudalists, on the one hand, and the racists, on the other, defined the old South's central dilemma. The first two championed personalism and the familial view of the peculiar institution. The religionists were willing to question the beneficence and permanence of slavery in order to assert the slave's humanity; and the feudalists were willing to surrender democratic liberalism in order to retain a personalized system of servitude. The racists, on the other hand, denied the slave's full human status in order to reconcile slavery with democratic liberalism for whites. The South's ingrained liberalism and Christianity, in short, were continually thwarting the logic-impelled effort to develop a fully rationalized, sheerly economic conception of slavery, warranted by the racist argument.

It was this inner conflict which produced the South's belligerent dogmatism in the recurrent crises of the fifties. The whole massive proslavery polemic had the unreal ring of logic pushed far beyond conviction. "I assure you, Sir," Fitzhugh confessed in a private letter, "I see great evils in Slavery, but in a controversial work I ought not to admit them."[51] If the South's best minds resolutely quashed their doubts, it is small wonder that crisis-tossed editors and politicians took refuge in positive and extreme positions.

The final open collision between the two contradictory tendencies in the South's thinking about slavery came on the very eve of the Civil War, when some Southerners relentlessly pursued the logic of slavery's

beneficence to the conclusion that the foreign slave trade should be reopened. "I would sweep from the statute-book every interference with slavery," shouted a fire-eating South Carolina congressman. "I would repeal the law declaring the slave trade piracy; I would withdraw our slave squadron from the coast of Africa; and I would leave slavery unintervened against, wherever the power of the country stretches."[52]

Despite the lip service paid to the "positive good" doctrine, majority southern opinion was deeply shocked by its logical extension to sanction the foreign slave trade. Few Southerners were willing "to roll back the tide of civilization and christianity of the nineteenth century, and restore the barbarism of the dark ages," declared a Georgia newspaper, and churchmen denounced the proposal with special vehemence. Even one of its original advocates turned against it when he witnessed the suffering of the Negroes aboard a captured slave ship. This "practical, fair evidence of its effects has cured me forever," confessed D. H. Hamilton. "I wish that everyone in South Carolina, who is in favor of re-opening of the Slave-trade, could have seen what I have been compelled to witness. . . . It seems to me that I can never forget it."[53] This was the agony of the proslavery South under the shadow of Civil War.

How, then, did the fundamentally liberal, Christian, American South ever become an "aggressive slavocracy"?* How

---

[50] Jenkins, *Pro-Slavery Thought*, 281; Harvey Wish, *George Fitzhugh: Propagandist of the Old South* (Baton Rouge, 1943), 111.

[51] Wish, *Fitzhugh*, 111.

[52] Harold S. Schultz, *Nationalism and Sectionalism in South Carolina, 1852–1860: A Study of the Movement for Southern Independence* (Durham, 1950), 182.

[53] Stampp, *Peculiar Institution*, 278; Schultz, *Nationalism and Sectionalism*, 158–59.

* The viewpoint of the present essay is not to be confused with the interpretation of the Civil War in terms of a "slave power conspiracy." Chauncey S. Boucher has demonstrated convincingly that the South was incapable of the kind of concerted action necessary for conspiracy. "In Re That Aggressive Slavocracy," *Mississippi Valley Historical Review*, VIII (June-September, 1921), 13–79. He is less persuasive, however, in demonstrating the equal inappropriateness of the

did it bring itself to flaunt an aristocratic social philosophy? To break up the American Union? To wage war for the purpose of holding four million human beings in a bondage that violated their humanity? The answer is that Southerners did not and could not rationally and deliberately choose slavery and its fruits over the values it warred against. Rather it was the very conflict of values, rendered intolerable by constant criticism premised on values Southerners shared, which drove them to seek a violent resolution.

Social psychologists observe that such value conflicts—especially when they give rise to the kind of institutional instability revealed by the ambiguities of southern slavery—make a society "suggestible," or ready to follow the advocates of irrational and aggressive action.† Thus it was fateful

that the Old South developed an unusually able minority of fire-eating sectionalists, who labored zealously, from the 1830s on, to unite the South behind radical measures in defense of slavery. Though a majority of Southerners remained profoundly distrustful of these extremists throughout the antebellum period, their unceasing agitation steadily aggravated the South's tensions and heightened its underlying suggestibility. By egging the South on to ever more extreme demands, the Calhouns, Rhetts, and Yanceys provoked violent northern reactions, which could then be used to whip the South's passions still higher. At length, in 1860, capitalizing on intrigues for the Democratic presidential nomination, the fire-eaters managed to split the Democratic party, thus insuring the election of a Republican President and paving the way for secession.

Inflammatory agitation and revolutionary tactics succeeded only because Southerners had finally passed the point of rational self-control. The almost pathological violence of their reactions to northern criticism indicated that their misgivings about their moral position on slavery had become literally intolerable under the mounting aboli-

designation "aggressive slavocracy." Boucher does admit (p. 30) that many Southerners "took a stand which may perhaps best be termed 'aggressively defensive.' " This is not too far from the attitude of the present essay, especially in view of Boucher's tantalizing suggestion (p. 70) that when Southerners talked of slavery as a divinely ordained institution, they were in the position of "saying a thing and being conscious while saying it that the thing is not true . . . but a position forced upon them by necessity of circumstances for their own immediate protection."

† Hadley Cantril, *The Psychology of Social Movements* (New York, 1941), 61–64. The social sciences have much to contribute to southern historical scholarship; in fact, the essential key to understanding the Old South seems to lie in the area of social psychology. Though Harry Elmer Barnes asserted as much nearly 40 years ago, scholarly efforts in this direction have hardly moved beyond the naïve enthusiasm of Barnes' suggestion that "southern chivalry" was "a collective compensation for sexual looseness, racial intermixture, and the maltreatment of the Negro." —"Psychology and History: Some Reasons for Predicting Their More Active Cooperation in the Future," *American Journal of Psychology*, XXX (October, 1919), 374. A psychologist has interpreted southern behavior in terms of defense mechanism, rationalization, and projection.— D. A. Hartman, "The Psychological Point of View in History: Some Phases of the Slavery Struggle," *Journal of Abnormal Psychology and Social Psychology*, XVII (October-December, 1922), 261– 73. A psychoanalyst has traced the white South's treatment of the Negro to the general insecurities of Western man uprooted by industrialism, and to an unconscious sexual fascination with the Negro as "a symbol which gives a secret gratification to

those who are inhibited and crippled in their instinctual satisfaction."—Helen V. McLean, "Psychodynamic Factors in Racial Relations," *Annals of the American Academy of Political and Social Science*, CCLIV (March, 1946), 159–66. And a sociologist has sought to explain the South in terms of a concept of "social neurosis."—Read Bain, "Man Is the Measure," *Sociometry: A Journal of Inter-Personal Relations*, VI (November, 1943), 460–64.

These efforts, while suggestive, seem hardly more systematic and considerably less cautious than the historian's unsophisticated, commonsense way of trying to assess psychological factors. Yet Hadley Cantril's *Psychology of Social Movements* has demonstrated that the infant discipline of social psychology can, even in its present primitive state, furnish the historian with extremely useful concepts. Historians of the Old South have special reason for pressing their problems on their brethren in social psychology, while the social psychologists may find in historical data a challenging area for developing and testing hypotheses. Especially rewarding to both historians and social scientists would be a collaborative study of antebellum southern radicalism and its peculiar locus, South Carolina.

tionist attack. "The South has been moved to resistance chiefly . . . by the popular dogma in the free states that slavery is a crime in the sight of GOD," said a New Orleans editor in the secession crisis. "The South, in the eyes of the North, is degraded and unworthy, because of the institution of servitude."[54]

Superimposed on this fundamental moral anxiety was another potent emotion, fear. John Brown's raid in October, 1859, created the most intense terror of slave insurrection that the South had ever experienced; and in this atmosphere of dread the final crisis of 1860–61 occurred. The press warned that the South was "slumbering over a volcano, whose smoldering fires, may at any quiet starry midnight, blacken the social sky with the smoke of desolation and death." Southerners believed their land to be overrun by abolitionist emissaries, who were "tampering with our slaves, and furnishing them with arms and poisons to accomplish their hellish designs." Lynch law was proclaimed, and vigilance committees sprang up to deal with anyone suspected of abolitionist sentiments. A Mississippian reported the hanging of 23 such suspects in three weeks, while the British consul at Charleston described the situation as "a reign of terror."[55]

Under these circumstances a large part of the southern white population approached the crisis of the Union in a state of near-hysteria. One man thought that "the minds of the people are aroused to a pitch of excitement probably unparalleled in the history of our country." "The desire of some for change," reported a despairing Virginian, "the greed of many for excitement, and the longing of more for anarchy and confusion, seems to have unthroned the reason of men, and left them at the mercy of passion and madness."[56]

Just as important as the hysteria which affected some Southerners was the paralysis of will, the despair, the sense of helplessness, which the excitement created in their more conservative fellows. Denying that the southern people really wanted to dissolve the Union, a Georgia editor saw them as being "dragged on, blindfolded, to consummation of the horrid act." A "moral pestilence" had "swept over the South," said a prominent North Carolinian, "dethroning reason, & paralyzing the efforts of the best Union men of the country." But even some who decried the hysteria felt that "no community can exist & prosper when this sense of insecurity prevails," and concluded that almost any alternative was preferable to the strain of these recurrent crises. It was this conviction, more than anything else, which caused moderate men to give way to the bold and confident radicals.[57]

From the circumstances of the secession elections—the small turnouts, the revolutionary tactics of the fire-eaters, the disproportionate weighting of the results in favor of plantation areas, the coercive conditions under which the upper South voted, and the hysteria that prevailed everywhere—it can hardly be said that a majority of the South's white people deliberately chose to dissolve the Union in 1861. A member of South Carolina's secession convention frankly admitted that "the common people" did not understand what was at stake. "But whoever waited for the common people when a great movement was to be made?" he asked. "We must make the move and force them to follow. That is the way of all revolutions and all great achievements."[58]

The leaders made the move, and the people followed, but with what underlying misgivings the sequel only too plainly demonstrated. The first flush of enthusiasm was rapidly supplanted by an apathy and a grow-

---

[54] Dwight L. Dumond (ed.), *Southern Editorials on Secession* (New York, 1931), 315–16.

[55] Crenshaw, *Slave States*, 100, 103, 106; Laura A. White, "The South in the 1850's as Seen by British Consuls," *Journal of Southern History*, I (February, 1935), 44.

[56] Crenshaw, *Slave States*, 111; Robert C. Gun-

derson, "William C. Rives and the 'Old Gentlemen's Convention,' " *Journal of Southern History*, XXII (November, 1956), 460.

[57] Crenshaw, *Slave States*, 111n., 237; Klingberg, *Southern Claims Commission*, 13. Cf. Cantril, *Psychology of Social Movements*, 61.

[58] White, *Rhett*, 177n.

ing disaffection which historians have identified as major factors in the Confederacy's failure. During the dark winter of 1864–65, North Carolina's Governor Zebulon Vance commented on the supineness with which the southern population received the invading Sherman. It was evidence, said Vance, of what he had "always believed, that *the great popular heart* is not now, and never has been in this war! It was a revolution of the *Politicians*, not the *People*."[59]

And when the cause was lost, Southerners abandoned it with an alacrity which underscored the reluctance of their original commitment. It was left for a leading ex-fire-eater to explain why they returned to the Union of their fathers with so little hesitation. Standing before the Joint Congressional Committee on Reconstruction in 1866, James D. B. De Bow attested in all sincerity the South's willingness to fight once again for the flag of the Union. "The southern people," he said "are Americans, republicans."[60]

---

[59] Klingberg, *Southern Claims Commission*, 138.

[60] *Report of the Joint Committee on Recon-*

Yet it is idle to wonder whether secession represented the deliberate choice of a majority of white Southerners, or to speculate about the outcome of a hypothetical referendum, free from ambiguity, coercion, and hysteria. Decisions like the one that faced the South in 1860–61 are never reached in any such ideal way. And even had the South decided for the Union, its and the nation's problem would have remained unsolved, and a violent resolution would only have been postponed. Slavery was doomed by the march of history and by the nature of Southerners themselves, but so deeply had it involved them in its contradictions that they could neither deal with it rationally nor longer endure the tensions and anxieties it generated. Under these circumstances the Civil War or something very like it was unavoidable. It was also salutary, for only the transaction at Appomattox could have freed the South's people—both Negro and white—to move again toward the realization of their essential natures as Southerners, liberals, Christians, and Americans.

---

struction, at the First Session, Thirty-Ninth Congress (Washington, 1866), 133.

1961

Was the Proslavery Argument for Home Consumption?*

RALPH E. MORROW

The ideological conflicts of the twentieth century have provided convincing evidence that "the enemy" is not always the target

* Ralph E. Morrow, "The Proslavery Argument Revisited," *The Mississippi Valley Historical Review*, XLVIII (June, 1961), 70–94.

of propaganda. The efforts of totalitarian regimes to insure "right thinking" on the part of their people or, closer to home, of citizens' councils to influence the thinking of local constituents, demonstrate that propaganda is likely to be beamed at the people of a nation or region from which it originates. Commonplace as this observation may be, it nevertheless suggests the advisability of another look at the arguments evolved in defense of slavery in the last three decades before the Civil War. Historians usually have discussed these arguments in juxtaposition to the abolitionist attack and construed the former as counterpropaganda addressed primarily to an audience north of the Mason and Dixon line. The standard account of southern thought on slavery asserts, for example, that "The South . . . without apology, presented her case to the world tribunal,"[1] and the context prompts the inference that the people of the North constituted a large part of the "world tribunal." On another level, the explanation that the proslavery argument was a species of counterfirc aimed at northerners has been presented to several generations of students through the medium of college textbooks in American history. "The more strongly the winds of abolitionism swept down from the North," says a sprightly recent text, "the more . . . savagely [the South] struck back at its tormentors."[2]

The view that proslavery propaganda was directed toward proselytizing the people of the North or, at least, combating abolitionists apparently has grown in vitality in the years since the end of the Civil War. The antebellum southern writers themselves did not consistently entertain such sanguine expectations. In the pioneering days of the "positive good" theory, William Harper remarked on "the indisposition of the rest of the world to hear anything more on this subject." The North, he complained, "seems unaware that there is a reason to be encountered or an argument to be answered."[3] Better than some who

came after them Harper and a number of his contemporaries appreciated the formidable obstacles to the effective persuasion of outsiders. Southern propagandists largely were denied access to media that would give their opinions national dissemination. The South had no newspapers whose geographical coverage compared to that of the northern metropolitan journals, its few periodicals were of restricted circulation, and southern booksellers complained of insufficient outlets even in their own section. If the complaints of some of the apologists were well founded, difficulties were compounded by the uncooperative policies of northern publishing houses. Although the North, unlike the South, did not attempt formal censorship of unwanted ideas, results were not wholly different. Thornton Stringfellow, James H. Hammond, Josiah C. Nott, and Iverson L. Brookes, apologists for slavery, all admitted to learning that a New York, Philadelphia, or Boston publisher, although reluctant to offend the South, was not eager to advertise its cause.[4]

If the North was a hard audience to reach it was an even harder one to convince. Because of its remoteness it might be won to forbearance toward slavery but hardly to sympathetic acceptance of the institution. Chancellor Harper, again anticipating many who followed him, asserted that "there seems to be something in this subject [of slavery] which blunts the perceptions, and darkens and confuses the understandings of men." Present the ablest arguments in defense of slave society to one who was not part of it, he said, and "you have done nothing."[5] Harper's judgment was con-

[1] William S. Jenkins, *Pro-Slavery Thought in the Old South* (Chapel Hill, 1935), 89.

[2] Thomas A. Bailey, *American Pageant* (Boston, 1957), 370.

[3] William Harper, "Slavery in the Light of Social Ethics," E. N. Elliott (ed.), *Cotton Is King, and Pro-Slavery Arguments: Comprising the Writings of Hammond, Harper, Christy, Stringfellow, Hodge, Bledsoe, and Cartwright on This Important Subject* (Augusta, Ga., 1860), 550–51.

[4] Thornton Stringfellow, "The Bible Argument: or, Slavery in the Light of Divine Revelation," Elliott (ed.), *Cotton Is King*, 519; Joseph Ficklin to James H. Hammond, July 24, 1845, James H. Hammond Papers (Manuscript Division, Library of Congress); Josiah C. Nott to Ephraim G. Squier, February 14, 1849, Ephraim G. Squier Papers (Manuscript Division, Library of Congress); Iverson L. Brookes, *A Defense of the South against the Reproaches and Encroachments of the North* . . . (Hamburg, S.C., 1850).

[5] Harper, "Slavery in the Light of Social Ethics," Elliott (ed.), *Cotton Is King*, 553.

firmed by the adventures of two redoubtable champions of slavery, James H. Hammond and George Fitzhugh. In 1845, Hammond attempted to draw the patron of reform, Lewis Tappan, into an argument about the merits of slavery by sending him a copy of *Letters on Slavery*. Tappan refused the engagement with the excuse that no "rational person" could sincerely uphold the views expounded by Hammond in his pamphlet.[6] A decade later, Fitzhugh celebrated the publication of *Sociology for the South* by lecturing at New Haven, Connecticut. A reporter of the event noticed "much fog and much nonsense" in Fitzhugh's remarks, and estimated, probably correctly, that "no one was convinced by his attempted arguments." Fitzhugh subsequently confessed to his failure to dent opinion in the North by reproaching its press for treating his *Sociology* with "the affectation of silent contempt." "Why the devil," he asked pretentiously, "don't someone abuse me?"[7]

These failures, however, did not diminish the impulse to defend slavery. On the contrary, the difficulties of convincing the North aggravated the awareness that the security of slave property depended upon those closest to it. Nearly every major apology for slavery, from Thomas R. Dew's essays on the debates in the Virginia legislature in 1831–32 to the diffuse polemics of Fitzhugh, explicitly showed concern for the state of southern opinion. Authors sometimes sought only the coercion, intimidation, or strengthening of the thought of their fellow southerners and regarded the conversation of northerners as merely extra dividends. Josiah Nott, readying one of his broadsides for publication, wrote: "All the articles I have written on *niggerology* have been eagerly sought for at the South, and in the present excited state of the political world, I think the thing will go well."[8] Southern intellectuals were assuredly in the forefront of the propaganda campaign, but with a certain constancy their foes seemed to be "the mawkish sensibilities and the imbecile ignorance of many within [their] own borders."[9]

The scattering of historians who have interpreted the patterns in proslavery literature as a reflex of the tensions within the South have emphasized the conflict between the planter and nonslaveholder. With the rise of radical sentiment in the North the spectral results of abolitionism were conjured up to paralyze effective action by southern antislavery elements and to frighten nonslaveholders into submitting to the continued rule of the gentry.[10] This hypothesis helps to explain some peculiar features of the proslavery crusade. Virginia, for instance, contributed more lustrous names to the roster of defenders than did any other state. It was also the last of the southern states to engage in official debate on emancipation, and even thereafter it was remarked for the persistent antislavery sentiment concentrated in the western counties where the slave population was sparse. Thomas R. Dew, who is credited with switching the South onto the "positive good" track, won his reputation by his exertions against southern displays of abolitionism. His *Review of the Debates in the Virginia Legislature* was pitched specifically toward western Virginia and generally toward the nonslaveholder. Nor did Dew bury the concern about the attitudes of many Virginians toward slavery. The Fredericksburg *News,* a newspaper to which Fitzhugh contributed, warned its readers periodically that "In Virginia are to be found some of the most detestable abolitionists in the

---

[6] Lewis Tappan to Hammond, June 6, 1845, Hammond Papers.

[7] New Haven *Daily Palladium*, March 22, 1855, quoted in Harvey Wish, *George Fitzhugh: Propagandist of the Old South* (Baton Rouge, 1943), 133; Richmond *Examiner*, October 26, 1855; Fitzhugh to George F. Holmes, April 11, 1855, George F. Holmes Papers (Southern Historical Collection, University of North Carolina Library).

[8] Nott to Squier, May 4, 1850, Squier Papers.

[9] *Southern Literary Messenger* (Richmond), XVIII (December, 1852), 724.

[10] See especially William B. Hesseltine, "Some New Aspects of the Pro-Slavery Argument," *Journal of Negro History* (Washington), XXI (January, 1936), 1–15.

Union."[11] In the general body of proslavery writing it seems apparent that the repetition of certain themes can be fitted into the courtship of the yeoman. The reiterations of the pervasive economic advantages of slavery, the slaveholder as the living illustration of the gospel of success, race as a guarantor of status, and miscegenation as the consequence of emancipation were suited to the hardheaded interest or ego needs of the nonslaveholder.[12]

Class antagonism, however, was only one of the southern impulses that produced the proslavery argument. Furthermore, it was one to which apologists for slavery attached decreasing significance. Worry among southern intellectuals over the yeoman and nonslaveholding population was much more evident in the 1830s than it was 20 years later. For all that the hypothesis of yeoman alienation tells us about proslavery polemics it has, in its literalness, a resemblance to the older view which sees only the North as the target of southern propaganda. Both regard proslavery writing as a simple response to antislavery elements and seem to agree that the object of the writing was to counter the activity of those elements. Differences arise only over the location of the danger. One finds it in the North; the other among the nonslaveholders of the South. Neither fully appreciates the disquietude of proslavery writers over the state of mind among southerners who entertained no hostility to the institution, or who even were committed to its preservation, and the extent to which the theoretical defenses of slavery were attuned to the needs of these people. But therein lies another dimension of the proslavery argument.

The milieu in which the proslavery writers worked is more fully understood by disregarding the venerable convention of dividing the socio-intellectual history of the antebellum South into sharply distinguishable periods. What was increasingly called "the southern way of life" consisted not merely of institutions and affirmative beliefs concerning those institutions but of traditions and memories of enduring vitality. Much in this tradition was summed up in the historical figure of Jefferson. The Jeffersonian legacy included not only a set of positive views on man and society but also a habit of candid inquiry into the forms of social organization. It flourished on "a happy variety of minds." Whether the tradition unequivocally condemned slavery is less important than its refusal to foreclose discussion of the matter.[13] Although the thinking symbolized by Jefferson may have left most southerners untouched, the mood implicit in it reached beyond a narrow clique of disciples. A Georgia contributor to De Bow's Review in 1854, although harshly critical of this Jeffersonian tradition, testified to the radius of its influence. She recalled the textbooks that boldly presented the pros and cons of slavery, the schoolboys who declaimed against it at commencement exercises, and the monotony with which local debating societies mulled over the merits of the institution. It was a tradition of open inquiry, she rightly noted, that regularly involved members of affluent families.[14]

While this tradition held slavery to be a subject open for discussion, another put it under the condemnation of the Christian conscience. Evangelical religion in the South of the earlier nineteenth century had a strain of antislavery sentiment as strong as that of Jeffersonianism. Before 1830 local or national assemblies of Methodists, Baptists, and Presbyterians, the denominations which included the bulk of churchgoing southerners, had placed slaveholding or the practices associated with it outside the pale of holy living.[15] The stand taken

---

[11] Quoted in Wish, *George Fitzhugh*, 112.

[12] The standard summary of these arguments is James D. B. De Bow *et al., Interest in Slavery of the Southern Non-Slaveholder* (Charleston, 1860).

[13] Daniel J. Boorstin, *The Lost World of Thomas Jefferson* (New York, 1948), 92–98, 119–27.

[14] *De Bow's Review* (New Orleans), XVI (January, 1854), 22–23.

[15] William W. Sweet (ed.), *Religion on the American Frontier* (4 vols.; New York and Chicago, 1931–1946), I, *The Baptists*, 78–88; II, *The*

by the churches was made more effectual by clerical participation in the struggling antislavery movement in the South and by a current of emancipationist sympathy rising from the rank and file of evangelical communicants. Among the later censors of southern ecclesiastical thought on slavery were children of evangelical pioneers who had entertained strong reservations about the godliness of the institution.[16] Inherent in the evangelical heritage were compulsions of a particularly powerful character; the apocalyptic framework of sin, evil, and redemption within which the issues were discussed admitted of little evasion or compromise.

The affirmations which constituted the proslavery argument contradicted but did not obliterate the antislavery traditions which Jeffersonian and evangelical thought had fostered. The common use of Jefferson as a foil in the vindication of slavery and the indignant repudiation of evangelical excesses by a later generation of southern clergymen are as suggestive of the persistence of the older tradition as of its liquidation. Figuratively, these ancient attitudes constituted the South's conscience, and this conscience helped to condition southern reactions to the sweep of nineteenth-century history. Antislavery developments in Europe and the United States had a special meaning, not only because they menaced vested economic or social interests, but because they seemed expressive or norms once espoused or tolerated by the South but later rejected or denied. The abolition of slavery in the dependencies and nations of the New World was a forceful reminder of the correctness of Jefferson's view that the status of slavery was not beyond the purview of change. The preeminently moral arguments

of the abolitionists stung another vein of sensitivity embedded in the experience of southerners. Charges of the sinfulness of slaveholding harked back to the earlier days of southern evangelicalism, and the South's reaction was not unlike that of a righteous person accused of philandering. An effect of the outside pressures was to intensify the conflict between the two personalities of the South. One embodied a set of beliefs that had been fashioned by past conditions; the other grew from the estimated needs of the succeeding age.

The foregoing diagnosis finds support in the works of several eminent proslavery writers. In 1856 William A. Smith, president of Randolph-Macon College, authored a publication intended to supplement existing college texts in moral philosophy inasmuch as their treatment of slavery implanted in "the minds of young men . . . a fatal direction both as regards the principles of the institution and the institution itself." The opening pages of Smith's book included a lucid exposition of the South's dilemma. "There are . . . not a few," he wrote, "spread through our Southern states . . . whose minds are in a state of great embarrassment on this subject [of slavery]." And, even more significantly, he believed that this "secret doubt of the mortality of African slavery" had affected "many of [the South's] best citizens." The "painful . . . suspicion that there must be something wrong in the principle of domestic slavery" Smith blamed on the persistence of "prior views of religion" and "the great abstract doctrine of Mr. Jefferson, that the principle of African slavery is *per se* sinful."[17] Contradicting this doctrine, however, was the observable reality that "slavery has become more and more practical—a fixed fact in this country." The incompatibility of the persisting ideal and the "fixed fact," Smith said, had set "men against themselves."[18] "Pressed on the one hand by what is assumed to be correct principle, and on

Presbyterians, 110–15; Wade C. Barclay, *Early American Methodism* (2 vols.; New York, 1950), II, 1–12.

16 John B. McFerrin, *History of Methodism in Tennessee* (3 vols., Nashville, 1883), II, 463–95; Henry Little to Absalom Peters, July 21, 1825, and Harvey Woods to Peters, June 29, 1836, American Home Missionary Society Papers (Hammond Theological Seminary, Chicago).

17 William A. Smith, *Lectures on the Philosophy and Practice of Slavery* (Nashville, 1856), 15, 17, 28.

18 *Ibid.,* 26.

the other by . . . the necessity of governing and providing for their slaves . . . they really find themselves in a most embarrassing situation, from which they sigh to be released."[19]

By thus identifying the problem, Smith clarified the function of the proslavery argument. It aimed to resolve the "interminable strife between antagonistic principles" and had as its end the psychological adjustment of southerners—slaveholders perhaps more than nonslaveholders—to the external conditions of their existence. Thornton Stringfellow also owned that his attempts "to prove slavery a lawful relation among men" were intended "to satisfy the conscientiousness of Christians."[20] Others with associations less intimately clerical avowed the same purpose of putting the South at peace with herself by bringing moral values into line with social practice. The debates in the state legislature during 1831–32 prompted another Virginian, Benjamin Watkins Leigh, "to address a few remarks to those who have conscientious scruples about the holding of slaves, and therefore, consider themselves under an obligation to flee to a land where this evil does not exist."[21] Later, in the tumultuous decade of the 1850s when the South was supposed to have achieved a new moral equilibrium, George F. Holmes, professor at the University of Virginia and literary czar of major southern periodicals, asserted that "this affair of conscience must be decided promptly." He asked southern intellectuals to overcome the "speculative doubts by which slaveholders [were] troubled" by assisting them to "a clear comprehension of the reasons by which slavery is justified and proved to be right." Even Holmes's admiring correspondent, George Fitzhugh, interrupted the dismal descriptions of free society and proposals for the universalization of slavery in his *Cannibals All* to point out the vulnerability of the South's moral position. The belief enter-

tained by many in the South that "slavery, in the general . . . is morally wrong and against common right" had compromised the defense of southern society, and as a remedy Fitzhugh urged that "we must vindicate [the] institution in the abstract."[22]

The exhortations of Smith, Leigh, and Holmes about the moral needs of the slave-owner disclose the orientation in proslavery literature often overlooked. Although propaganda was not unanimously trimmed to the needs of a single socio-economic group, members of the corps of defenders had convincing reasons for their solicitous interest in the slaveholding population. The defenders' own associations often were of a type to encourage familiarity with the minds and feelings of the more propertied classes. Many writers were connected to slavery either through ownership or family ties. Those academicians, clergymen, litterateurs, and publicists without primary ties to slavery nonetheless had regular contact with the homegrown aristocracy in the latter's various capacities as patrons, governors of educational and religious institutions, students, and parishioners. The intercourse with slaveholders which made writers party to the thinking in top social echelons also promoted concern about the quality of that thought, because the perpetuation of slavery rested first of all upon the unflinching fidelity of those who were involved in the peculiar property and who possessed much of the power to make decisions for the South. The consequences of irresolution, many propagandists were disposed to argue, grew more dangerous as one ascended the social pyramid.

These factors left a mark on proslavery writing. In the principal works produced after 1850, concern for the mind of the slaveholder is as great if not greater than concern for any other element of the southern population. Holmes believed that the

---

19 *Ibid.*, 57–58.
20 Stringfellow, "The Bible Argument," Elliott (ed.), *Cotton Is King*, 522.
21 Richmond *Enquirer*, February 4, 1832.

22 *Southern Literary Messenger*, XIX (June, 1853), 324; *De Bow's Review*, XXI (August, 1856), 132; George Fitzhugh, *Cannibals All! or, Slaves without Masters* (Richmond, 1857), 294–95.

dangerous dispersion of flabby opinions on slavery was attributable to those whose stake in its maintenance was largest. In an article prepared for the *Southern Literary Messenger* in 1853, he condemned "the weak minds and vacillating fancies of many . . . slaveholders." Their lukewarm, shilly-shally convictions," he said, had "armed . . . Abolition adversaries with firebrands" which "they were hurling into the South's combustible materials." To Holmes the conduct of many aristocrats bordered "on treason . . . to the South."[23] Concern about attitudes common among employers of slave labor often brought prescriptions for correct reading. One review of Fitzhugh's *Sociology* enumerated the occupational groups likely to benefit from the book and placed planters at the head of the list. Another commentator recommended the volume as a cure for "the painful sense of inferiority" contracted by planters "on visits to Northern cities with their splendor, animation, and crowded population."[24] In a summary of 25 years of proslavery literature the editor of the *Southern Literary Messenger*, John R. Thompson, concluded that most of the barrage had been served up "to strengthen and confirm the convictions of the slaveholder."[25]

The therapy suggested by proslavery writers unfolded in two directions. One form, instead of coming to grips with the roots of the conflict, tended to facilitate escape into a world of unreality. A clerical apologist declared that "if masters could be prevailed upon to . . . perform their whole duty to their servants . . . all the objections to slavery . . . in reasonable minds, would be silenced thereby."[26] This belief, like other arguments for better treatment of the slaves, was easily made part of a larger image of the unalloyed benignity of the southern system

of bondage. The wish gave way to an illusion. The vein of sentimentalism in proslavery literature offered an avenue of flight from the doubts arising from the theory or workings of the peculiar institution. Warm public responses to romanticized treatments of slave society indicate both the depth of the South's disturbances and the success with which they were exploited. William J. Grayson's *Hireling and the Slave,* which appeared in 1856, chiefly impresses as a transmutation of the mottled relationships of slavery into a vision of a paradisical order. Yet a reviewer for a leading southern periodical proclaimed: "There is nothing unreal . . . in the scenes and incidents depicted. . . . It is a living representation of things as they are."[27]

Despite the popularity of the literature of escape, many polemicists saw in it a dead end. Holmes condemned "the writers of replicant romances" as "quacks" who had "injured the South" because they anesthetized the conscience without relieving it of painful antagonisms.[28] Only by planting the institution "on the firm basis of philosophical reasoning, historical testimony, and social experience" could the South be "rid . . . of the superstition that slavery is a cleaving mischief."[29] The satisfaction of this need to believe sent southern authors on heroic searches for the certitude that would dissolve guilt and doubt. John Thompson exclaimed: "Let this subject be understood . . . and we need not fear to stand alone."[30] The need to believe in slavery was inseparably wedded to the intellectual content of the proslavery argument. The finely reasoned cases by which God, nature, and history vindicated slavery were offered as assurances. One reader congratulated James Hammond on his pamphlet because the author had not left "a thread of doubt" to

---

[23] *Southern Literary Messenger*, XIX (June, 1853), 325.

[24] Charleston *Mercury*, April 21, 1855; *De Bow's Review*, XIX (October, 1855), 463.

[25] *Southern Literary Messenger*, XXIII (October, 1856), 245.

[26] C. F. Sturgis, "Melville Letters," *Duties of Masters to Servants* (Charleston, 1851), 54.

[27] *De Bow's Review*, XVIII (April, 1855), 460.

[28] *Southern Literary Messenger*, XIX (June, 1853), 324.

[29] *Ibid.*, XXI (March, 1855), 129; XXIII (October, 1856), 244.

[30] *Ibid.*, XXIII (October, 1856), 242.

"unhinge minds upon the moral merits of slavery."[31]

The increasing barrage of propaganda obviously did much to scatter and demoralize southern antislavery elements. But the suppression of dissent was looked upon as an essentially negative achievement, depreciated by many of slavery's most vocal advocates. When Fitzhugh said that "agitation for the South and her institutions [was] . . . the obvious duty of every patriot" he was calling for more than the mere dispersion of heretics.[32] Those who agreed with Fitzhugh hoped to people the South with true believers—defenders of slavery who would make competition in affirming their faith the test of orthodoxy. Although the term "positive good" was coined to describe the intellectual content of the proslavery argument, it also has a profound psychological meaning. It afforded ground for overcoming anxiety and doubt by the activity of belief. James P. Holcombe, Holmes's colleague at the University of Virginia, urged alumni of the institution to bold measures in behalf of the South, assuring them that the "final sentence of impartial history" would pronounce slavery "consistent with the purest justice, commended by the highest expediency and sanctioned by a[n] . . . enlightened humanity."[33]

The effort to rest the southern defense upon a firm ideological base turned the attention of many authors to the developing sciences of nature and society. The increasing resort to the empirical sciences was accompanied by some faint suspicions, though largely unspoken, about the validity of Scriptural evidence in controversies over social policy. It is possible to attribute fondness for the newer hypotheses concerning man and society merely to the intellectual satisfaction which they afforded southern thinkers who, like those elsewhere in the Western World, were attracted to them as offering a more rational understanding of man's behavior. Nonetheless, the choice of argumentative weapons was sometimes legitimated by referring to their anticipated effect upon public opinion in the South. The persuasiveness of the empirical sciences, it was contended, surpassed that offered by divine revelation. The Biblical defense, although it sometimes went so far as to proclaim that "God himself instituted human slavery,"[34] was not always convincing. The Bible, one critic declared, did not contain "anything which would show . . . that the master commits any offense in holding slaves" but, he added, neither did it furnish the means of effectively buttressing the institution. Chancellor Harper still more emphatically discounted the use of Scripture in defenses of slavery. Slavery, he wrote, "is a civil institution with which religion has no concern."[35]

The justifications manufactured from Biblical material comprised a large part of the proslavery output, but in the 15 years before the Civil War most authors of more than local reputation subordinated or disregarded Biblical sources to draw upon the natural and social sciences. Few notable propagandists were other than impeccably proper in their public religious observances, but their religious beliefs were generally separated from their discussions of public affairs. An exception in his outspoken enmity to religious orthodoxy was the erratic Mobile physician, Josiah Nott. Nott often justified his attitude toward revealed religion in the language of intellectual progress. He refused, he said, "to allow those worn out legends to obstruct the path of science."[36] Nott, nonetheless, was a propagandist as well as a scientist, and he admitted that the homage he paid to the "invincible voice of nature" bore a relationship to his concern for southern morale. Believing, as he once

[31] Thomas J. Butler to Hammond, July 1, 1845, Hammond Papers.

[32] Richmond *Enquirer*, March 27, 1856.

[33] *Southern Literary Messenger*, XXVII (November, 1858), 419.

[34] Brookes, *A Defense of the South*, 8.

[35] *De Bow's Review*, XIX (January, 1855), 552; Harper, "Slavery in the Light of Social Ethics," Elliott (ed.), *Cotton Is King*, 552.

[36] Nott to Squier, August 19, 1848, Squier Papers.

asserted, that slavery was "one of those importunate questions which . . . religion can never decide," he placed large hopes in biology and anthropology and predicted that the exploitation of these fields would bring "public opinion [on slavery] over to me in the South."[37]

Despite their eagerness to toughen the psychological fiber of the South, Nott and many of his collaborators usually wore a mask of complete indifference to the outcome of their inquiries into the constitution of society. Their assumed attitude was that of the objective analyst; but their professions of intellectual aloofness had a necessary connection with the problem of effective persuasion. As positivism preached, truth was the product of objectivity and objective procedures were defined as those in which human reason, undisturbed by any values or bias of the investigator, sorted and arranged the measurable evidence to arrive at conclusions of the highest degree of probability. Holmes proclaimed repeatedly that "if slavery is right let it be maintained at all costs; it it is wrong let it be abolished at all costs." And Albert T. Bledsoe, in his *Liberty and Slavery,* protested that he had eschewed appeals to "passion and interest" and consulted "neither the pecuniary interests of the South nor the prejudices of the North."[38] These claims of utter detachment may have been bows to intellectual convention, but they also served to call the reader's attention to the reliability of the author's work. From an "impartial investigation of the various aspects of slavery," such as that which Holmes professed to undertake, would come the certainty "that the policy finally adopted will prove . . . unquestionably right." And what one "impartial" investigator discovered, the others stood ready to confirm. The monopoly which professional advocates of slavery held over the review columns of southern journals pro-

vided a continuing forum for mutual endorsement. The credentials given to Bledsoe were not exceptional. The Virginia mathematician was advertised as "a genius of polemics," the conqueror of "princes of philosophical theology," and "unmatched by any person in [the] country in logical encounter." These talents, enlisted in the cause of the South, said a critic, had resulted in a book that "left standing no . . . semblance of an argument against slavery."[39]

Internal strains, whether they are traced to class antagonisms or to the conflict between tradition and practical need, were not the only influences arising within the South to give stimulus and direction to the apologists for slavery. In the fulfillment of their community function southern authors found private satisfactions that were, in different degrees, distinguishable from any larger interest. No biography of a major southern controversialist offers a basis for the assertion that he rode the flood of agitation merely for self-advantage, but writers attested to the personal compensations which lent encouragement to their work. Admirers often told James Hammond, who constantly discovered unsuspected delights in authorship, that his literary industry was certain to bring political rewards. "If you continue to strike," one of them told him, "your day must come."[40] Hammond was becomingly modest in his replies, but he confessed to William Gilmore Simms that "I am ambitious for power." The most gratifying way of attaining this power, he said, was "to send from your chest words that reach the hearts and reason of men."[41]

Josiah Nott, a curious compound of ingeniousness, opportunism, and large ambition, was likewise clearly aware of the opportunities for advancement furnished by the crisis. In commenting on the forward position he had taken in the slavery contro-

---

[37] Nott to Hammond, July 25, 1845, Hammond Papers.

[38] *De Bow's Review,* XXI (August, 1846), 133; Albert T. Bledsoe, *An Essay on Liberty and Slavery* (Philadelphia, 1856), 12.

[39] *De Bow's Review,* XXI (August, 1856), 135, 142.

[40] James M. Walker to Hammond, June 11, 1845, Hammond Papers.

[41] Hammond to William Gilmore Simms, July 14, 1845, *ibid.*

versy he declared: "My experience has taught me that if a man wants to get on fast, he must kick up a damned fuss generally. . . . A man must get notoriety in some way or the tide will run by him." At different times, Nott identified his accrued benefits as "popularity," "money," and "professional reputation."[42] Although Nott's capabilities were not of first rank, his inclinations were intellectual and his considerable reputation, derived from works on race and slavery, suggests that the warfare of ideas opened doors to those who aspired to the life of the mind.

In later years critics have said that the South's preoccupation with the defense of slavery stifled the creativity of her intelligensia and constricted their efforts. Antebellum southerners, however, reckoned the results differently. Holmes noticed that the "necessities of society in a great measure . . . give birth to . . . its literature." From this premise he reached the conclusion that southern writers were "indebted to the continuance and asperity of this slavery controversy for the creation of a genuine Southern literature." From the "avidity for information on slavery" had "sprung literary activity and the literary movement."[43] Holmes's definition was broad enough to take in most endeavor cataloged under the humanities and the social sciences. John Thompson agreed with the analysis. The peril of the South, said Thompson, had brought genuine respect for talents that once were taken lightly. Men had been raised from obscurity to the centers of southern life because they possessed gifts which might previously have gone unheralded, but which now had relevance in an age of controversy. On the supposition that the South would furnish bread for its defenders, Thompson advised southern authors that "the field for their labors [was] wide."[44]

While some of the writers could total up personal rewards of self-advancement, adulation, and public influence, others who tested their mettle in controversy found satisfactions that were wholly independent of any public appreciation of their work. Nagged, like other southerners, by the moral dilemmas which slavery posed, some found in authorship a vehicle of relief from their nettlesome uncertainties. James Hammond, although alert to the tangible rewards of proslavery agitation, nevertheless averred that as he wrote his first polemic his "opinions constantly gained strength." By the time he had finished he had become certain "that slaveholding is not a sin."[45] William Gilmore Simms guessed that Hammond's experience was not unique. Simms's assertion that the re-examination of slavery had "resulted in moral reassurance . . . and in relieving . . . all that doubt, that morbid feeling of weakness" applied to authors and readers alike. And significantly, the adversaries identified by Simms—"doubt" and "that morbid feeling of weakness"—were located within the South and even within southerners themselves.[46]

If southern propagandists accurately gauged feeling in their section when they accented the conquest of guilt and doubt, an important aspect of the proslavery writing evidently has not received the attention it merits. The great body of the historical writing on the subject is primarily an analysis of the various proslavery lines of argument, with little attention to the psychological needs of the reading public. The more one studies the latter, however, the greater the temptation grows to conclude that the impact of proslavery dialectics inhered less in the quality of the presentation than in the processes of its assimilation. In other words, the satisfaction of believing in the morality of slavery was more decisive than the substance of anything believed.

---

42 Nott to Squier, February 14, 1849, March 26, 1851, Squier Papers; Nott to Hammond, June 3, August 12, September 4, 1845, Hammond Papers.

43 De Bow's Review, XXI (August, 1846), 133.

44 Southern Literary Messenger, XXIII (October, 1856), 242.

45 Hammond to Lewis Tappan, April 8, 1845, Hammond Papers.

46 William G. Simms, "The Morals of Slavery," The Pro-Slavery Argument: As Maintained by the Most Distinguished Writers of the Southern States . . . (Charleston, 1852), 179.

The common incidence of the themes of guilt and doubt raises questions, too, as to conclusions about the impulse to proslavery writing. Usually emphasized are the South's conviction" of the justice of a condition of slavery, the "challenging temper" in which her case was delivered, and the confidence "that the verdict would be an entire vindication of her course in perpetuating her peculiar institution."[47] This view, which rules out a large body of contrary testimony, evidently supposes that the North alone was responsible for provoking the activity of slavery's apologists. Without the abolitionist crusade the intellectual talents of many southerners admittedly would have been without employment. But once the gauntlet was thrown down proslavery writers believed that the South must look first to herself and they were never quite content with

the state of psychological preparedness which they found. Their immediate worry was not over those with an announced enmity to slavery but over the many southerners who asserted no hatred of the institution and often were slaveowners. Propagandists frequently denied discovering among the latter the relentless certainty commonly ascribed to them. The protestations of the "positive good" of slavery measured not only the vigor of northern abolitionism's attacks but the anxiety over the vulnerability of the South's psychological armor. Yet, it is one of the ironies of American history that southern intellectuals helped to aggravate the condition they wanted to alleviate. The propaganda fusillade caught the South in a vicious circle. Agitation heightened fear and uncertainty which seemingly called for still more agitation. A trial by arms was not an illogical exit from this cycle, for the strength that supposedly came from righteousness could then be definitely asserted.

[47] Jenkins, *Pro-Slavery Thought in the Old South*, 89; Robert E. Riegel, *Young America, 1830–1840* (Norman, 1953), 292–93.

1961

The Synthetic Southern Gentleman*

WILLIAM R. TAYLOR

By the summer of 1861 the subdued, candid and reasonable exchange of views which had taken place between Jefferson and John Adams some 45 years before seemed to belong to another, faraway age.[1] Early that

* George Braziller, Inc.—from *Cavalier and Yankee* by William R. Taylor reprinted with the permission of the publisher. © 1957, 1961, by William Robert Taylor.
[1] [For an interesting letter on secession] See Representative David Clopton of Alabama to Senator Clement C. Clay, Dec. 13, 1860, in Clem-

year, as every schoolboy knows, a separate Southern government had been organized in Montgomery, Alabama. Fort Sumter had fallen in April, a peace conference in Washington had collapsed and by July the United States were at war with themselves. Historians agree that the vast majority of people in the North and South had not wanted secession, to say nothing of war, but events

ent Eaton, *A History of the Southern Confederacy* (New York, 1954), p. 12.

swept them up in a whirlwind of excitement and precipitant action over which no one, finally, could exercise control.

In the South the move to separate had at first received massive support. Of those who hung back, some, perhaps most, were genuinely undecided, others confused or indifferent, and still others afraid to acknowledge their secret convictions. Little recourse was left open for moderation. The choice, to use the language of the time, lay between "secession" and "submission." The insurgents, capitalizing on the fears inspired by Lincoln's election and emboldened by their confidence in the invincibility of the united South, had moved ahead, heedless of dissenting views.

One by one the "erring sisters" had departed "in peace"—South Carolina on December 20; Mississippi, Alabama, Georgia, and Louisiana during the month of January, and Texas on February 1. Not until late spring or early summer did Tennessee, North Carolina, and Arkansas finally secede. Only on April 17, and after Lincoln had called upon her for her militia, did Virginia, the historical leader of Southern opinion, pass an ordinance of secession. Missouri, Maryland, and Kentucky, although tragically divided, chose to remain with the Union.

Along this middle tier of states, which separated New England and the Northwest from the lower South, a resolution of conflicting loyalties was arrived at only after agonizing and prolonged reflection and debate. Lincoln correctly gauged the mood which existed in these still uncommitted parts of the South when he inserted into his Inaugural Address, delivered in March of that year, a pointed reference to Hamlet's Third Act soliloquy. Was the South, he asked, contemplating suicide?

Will you hazard so desperate a step while there is any possibility that any portion of the ills you fly from have no real existence? Will you, while the certain ills you fly to are greater than all the real ones you fly from,

will you risk the commission of so fearful a mistake?[2]

In the state capitals, county seats, in village assemblies and in individual families, anguishing, seldom unanimous, decisions were made, and by midsummer the peoples of the North and South, sometimes with reluctance and sometimes in a fever of excitement, were beginning to array themselves on opposite sides of the battle lines. In a poem written that year, one of the Union's warmest advocates caught the sense of the moment in a few lines of verse.

Beat! beat! drums!—blow! bugles! blow!
Make no parley—stop for no expostulation,
Mind not the timid—mind not the weeper or
    prayer. . . .[3]

The most memorable war in American history was about to begin.

Historians have long debated the causes which precipitated this rapid series of events, and doubtless they always will. Much has been learned about the subtle shifts of opinion which occurred within various Southern states between John Brown's raid on Harper's Ferry in October, 1859, and Lincoln's fateful decision in April, 1861, to send supplies to the beleaguered garrison at Fort Sumter. Careful studies have been made of the parochial political circumstances which heightened the sensitivity of parts of the South to sectional issues and made the election of Abraham Lincoln, as the Northern President backed by a Northern party, a nightmarish prospect. The list of Southern grievances against the federal government, it has been made clear, had been growing since the debates over Missouri in 1819–20; and the constitutional arguments employed at the time of secession have a history almost as long as the Union itself. The growth of the Southern movement for inde-

[2] Richard Hofstadter (ed.), *Great Issues in American History: A Documentary Record* (New York, 1958), p. 392.

[3] Walt Whitman, "Beat! Beat! Drums!" *Complete Poetry and Selected Prose and Letters* (ed.), Emory Holloway (London, n.d.), p. 260.

pendence has been traced back to the statements of its earliest proponents in the thirties. It is the importance of this idea of Southern nationality, the popular supposition that Southerners and Northerners were distinct and different peoples, which has prompted the present study. If this idea had not been firmly embedded in the consciousness of extremists on both sides and vaguely present in the thinking of countless others, it seems doubtful that secession and Civil War would have taken place at the time and in the way that they did.

No one, of course, will ever be able to recapture in their totality the elusive feelings of individual Southerners in the face of these bewildering events, but it is clear that a significant shift in attitude took place after 1859. For a time during the early fifties the threat of open rebellion seemed to have disappeared. Problems there were, and some of them very grave, but concessions had been made. The South was enjoying flush times with cotton and slave prices at an all-time high, and Democrats responsive to Southern opinions were in control of the government in Washington. Then came the brief rehearsal for civil war, between Northerners and Southerners fighting over the corpse of "bleeding Kansas," the appearance on the scene of a sectional party with growing strength, a sudden and disastrous economic depression and Lincoln's highly publicized "House Divided" speech, made during his senatorial campaign in 1858. Lincoln himself conceded that some kind of crisis lay ahead, and a great many people who saw eye to eye with him on little else were inclined to agree. Then, in quick succession, came two events which shattered what little complacency remained in the South. Miscalculation of the significance of these dramatic moments was in the spirit of the times, rumors consciously launched grew rapidly out of control and genuinely conciliatory gestures on the part of the North slipped by unnoticed.

The first shock was provided by John Brown's Private War, as C. Vann Woodward has called it. This brief but highly publicized skirmish began near Harper's Ferry on the night of October 16, 1859, when Brown and 18 cohorts captured a federal arsenal. The struggle was of short duration, and it collapsed in a matter of hours. It left in its wake some 15 dead, a great mass of documents compromising Brown's supporters in the North and one of the most controversial prisoners ever to be arrested and executed by an American state. For many Southerners who took the documents at face value and let their imaginations play over the potential consequences of a massive conspiracy of this kind, John Brown personified Northern predatory intentions which they all along had suspected lurked behind the reasonable and accommodating gestures of Northern statesmen. His name evoked almost everything hateful about the Yankee character: destructiveness, conspiracy, and hypocrisy. Upon this one man for a time were focused the emotions which for close to 30 years had been gathering around the figure of the Yankee. Brown's defense by a few New Englanders such as Emerson and Thoreau, who looked upon him as a saint and a martyr, only quickened Southern response. The possibility that he may have been mad was dismissed by his attackers and supporters alike. The fact that certain of his defenders, like the Reverend Theodore Parker of Boston, were actively implicated in his conspiracy led to gross exaggerations of his real support in New England and the magnitude of his enterprise generally. Although not a single slave rose in rebellion and Brown's action was deplored in Washington and by all but a few extremists in the North, the South in a matter of weeks was thrown into a state of panic and one of the worst witch-hunts in American history occurred as eccentrics and "suspicious characters" of all kinds, many of them innocent strangers passing through, were mobbed, beaten, and tarred and feathered in a vigilante effort to root out Yankees and potential Southern subversives. No relaxation of tension followed. Rumors of slave insurrections swept the South during the next year. Finally, the election of Lincoln, who was popularly believed to be the pawn of abolitionists, and the anticipated prominence in his coming administration of William Seward of "Irrepressible Conflict" fame provided the finishing touches to the picture of a Northern conspiracy about to be launched against the South.[4]

The state of feeling that existed in the South during these fateful months can be suggested in a series of brief tableaux. In Washington Southern congressmen, and in the South, federal judges, began to resign their offices; some like Senator James H. Hammond with hesitation, some with feelings of vindictiveness and triumph. Northerners who happened to be stranded in the South were threatened, mistreated, and even mobbed, and most of them rapidly headed for home. Daniel Hundley, a Southerner living in Chicago, fled the city under cover of night out of fear for his life. There was in fact a general exodus of Southerners from Northern cities. On December 22, 1859, a trainload of students from Philadelphia arrived in Richmond, marched past the stately capitol designed by Jefferson, and assembled before the governor's mansion to hear a speech from Governor John A. Wise on Southern self-sufficiency. "Let Virginia call home her children!" the governor told them, and he went on to advocate self-sacrifice and austerity. "Let us," he said, "dress in the wool raised on our own pastures. Let us eat the flour from our own mills, and if we can't get that, why let us go back to our old accustomed corn bread."[5] Troops of "Minute Men" wearing the blue cockade drilled before admiring Negroes who caught only the holiday spirit of color and display. Everywhere the hated Yankee became a figure of ridicule and contempt. He was a conspirator and a hypocrite, but he was also a coward. He would never fight, and he could certainly never win.

The move to dissociate the South from every contaminating northern influence had reached almost hysterical proportions by the time of Lincoln's inauguration. The capital was almost empty of its former official occupants. Southern politicians and their ladies, including many of the city's most prominent hostesses, had departed for home, leaving the incoming Northern administration to run the country and—such as it was—Washington society. It was all a little mad, Senator Hammond, himself once an ardent secessionist, frankly conceded—and suicidal too. "It is an epidemic and very foolish," he wrote in December, 1860. "It reminds me of the Japanese who when insulted rip open their own bowels."[6]

By the following summer, then, communications between North and South had broken down—even the mail had stopped moving across the Potomac—and many leading spokesmen of both sections now regarded one another suspiciously and hostilely as symbols of alien cultures. To Mrs. Chesnut, who was inclined to see things somewhat melodramatically and—like Lincoln—in familial terms, it was also a question of a divided household and a marriage gone bad. "We separated," she wrote in her diary, "because of incompatibility of temper; we are divorced, North from South, because we have hated each other so."[7] "And for so long a time," she might have added without greater exaggeration than she had already employed, since the hatred to which she referred had been slowly intensifying for over 30 years, and along with it the awakening sense of a divided culture.

Two English astronomers, Charles Mason and Jeremiah Dixon, in an effort to settle a boundary dispute, had run a line between Pennsylvania and Maryland in the 1760s, but no one had then conceived of such a boundary as dividing a North from a South. Jefferson had seen the danger of such a distinction at the time of the Missouri Compromise, but a popular belief in a precise demarcation between North and

---

[4] C. Vann Woodward, "John Brown's Private War," *The Burden of Southern History* (Baton Rouge, 1960), pp. 41–68.

[5] Eaton, *Confederacy*, p. 1.

[6] *Ibid.*, pp. 9–10.

[7] Mary Boykin Chesnut, *A Diary from Dixie* (Boston, 1949), p. 20; cited by Eaton, *Confederacy*, p. 17.

South was a development of the decades which followed, and the frontier was still indistinct even after secession. Maryland, immediately south of the line, remained loyal and other so-called slave states like Missouri and Kentucky, both of them in some measure Southern in their traditions and style of life, remained officially in the North. If there was a line, and increasingly Americans agreed that there was, it possessed no geographical definition. It was a psychological, not a physical division, which often cut like a cleaver through the mentality of individual men and women everywhere in the country.

The shift in attitude which occurred during the fifties and the alignment which rapidly appeared during the tense months following Lincoln's election in 1860, much as they owe to particular contemporary events, are deeply rooted in an equally significant but much less easily defined reorientation of American mentality which had been taking place at least since the thirties. If separation as a political and social fact was the immediate result of the political pressures, miscalculations and excited activism of these tumultuous months, the idea of a coherent South, of a distinct and diffierent Southern civilization was not new in 1850, to say nothing of 1859; yet it was an idea which would have startled both Jefferson and Adams in 1816, and did in fact alarm Jefferson when he caught the first intimation of it in 1820.

Neither Jefferson nor Adams, furthermore, had thought of the natural aristocrat —their choice for the republican leader—as possessing any particular regional traits. Neither, certainly, would have localized either lower-class villainy or aristocratic honor and virture in any North or South which they knew. Adams, with his alertness to the danger of a false aristocracy in New England and with his keen sense of fallibility, saw evil and ambition lurking in every man's heart. He probably would have found the fully developed idea of the Yankee laughable and yet a little appealing, but he scarcely would have looked for better human materials south of the Potomac. Jefferson would have looked upon the full-blown Cavalier ideal with something like loathing and seen in its currency the undoing of much that he had worked to accomplish. Yet some three decades were sufficient to bring about these changes and to usher in a whole new set of assumptions concerning the history, cultural background, and racial composition of the two regions from which these two men had sprung—and for which they had made themselves the spokesmen. The nature of these changes is implicit in the preceding chapters, but the pattern of change is a somewhat complicated one and perhaps deserves brief reiteration.

The Southern Cavalier Redivivus

The first quarter of the nineteenth century had not passed before a significant number of Americans in both the North and the South had begun to express decided reservations about the direction progress was taking and about the kind of aggressive, mercenary, self-made man who was rapidly making his way in their society. In everyone's eyes this type of parvenu came to express a worrisome facet of the national character, to symbolize, in fact, both the restless mobility and the strident materialism of new world society. In the face of the threat which seemed to be posed by this new man, Americans—genteel and would-be genteel—began to develop pronounced longings for some form of aristocracy. They longed for a class of men immune to acquisitiveness, indifferent to social ambition and hostile to commercial life, cities, and secular progress. They sought, they would frankly have conceded, for something a little old-fashioned.

Writers like Cooper, Sarah Hale, and Paulding, themselves representative spokesmen of a much larger group, were particularly attracted by the idea of a conservative country gentry such as England possessed —or, at least, had possessed—only purer and better. The equalitarian character of life in the North provided an unsuitable terrain in which to locate, even in fantasy, an aristocracy of this kind. By the 1830s the legendary Southern planter, despite reservations of one kind or another, began to seem almost perfectly suited to fill the need. His ample estates, his spacious style of life, his Cavalier ancestry and his reputed obliviousness to money matters gained him favor in the eyes of those in search of a native American aristocracy. More and more, he came to be looked upon *the* characteristic expression of life in the South. Meanwhile, the acquisitive man, the man on the make, became inseparably associated with the North and especially with New England. In the end, the Yankee—for so he became known—was thought to be as much the product of the North as the planter-Cavalier of the South. By 1850 these two types—the Cavalier and the Yankee—expressed in the popular imagination the basic cultural conflict which people felt had grown up between a decorous, agrarian South and the rootless, shifting, money-minded North.

No such absolute division, of course, ever really existed between the North and the South. Southerners engaged in business, speculated on real estate, sought profits, lived in towns and cities, voted for the same national parties and subscribed to many of the same ideals and values as other Americans. What differences they developed, as over the issue of Negro slavery, did not lead many of them to formulate a totally different set of social objectives; these differences simply complicated their response to objectives which they already in large measure had accepted. Thus, in crying out against the Yankee North, Southerners who did so were, in a sense, striking out at part of themselves. By 1860 they had become self-divided, frustrated in their hopes and wishes, increasingly unrealistic in their social aspirations and ripe for some kind of bloody showdown.

The problem for the self-conscious South finally lay in the need which it felt to isolate —to quarantine—itself from the contaminating influence of the Yankee North, which it both feared and envied—and which, finally, was so much a part of itself. The result was the creation of an exclusively Southern historical, and even racial, heritage. Outvoted or overruled in national affairs, outgrown in population, outproduced and, as many Southerners at least secretly felt, outraged on the justice of slavery, the South in 1860 sought some kind of redemption in separateness, only to set up a Confederate government which was not essentially different, even in its constitutional details, from the federal republic from which it had just seceded.

The "Southern" problem was, then, for these men a condition of paralysis brought on by conflicting loyalties—they finally could not believe in either their own regional ideals or those of the country as a whole. Belief in the one conflicted with belief in the other; the result was confusion, indecision, and a kind of gnawing dispiritedness. By the 1850s, certainly, they no longer believed wholeheartedly in the effectiveness of the Cavalier gentleman, since they, too, came to measure achievement by financial success and the gentleman planter was, almost by definition, born to fail. But neither could they worship success, since it was measured in dollars and cents rather than in honor and cultural elevation. The improvident, generous-hearted gentleman planter for them became increasingly a symbol of a Lost Cause—an insurgent, a dueler, a fighter against overwhelming odds—in short, a figment of a utopian social world which was doomed to be submerged under a tide of middle-class materialism.

Without quite acknowledging it, many Southerners during these years had been waging a kind of war with themselves. Increasingly their ideal of a stable social order came into conflict with the social and political realities with which they were confronted. The lowly, whether white or black, gave clear evidence that they did not wish to remain lowly and feudally dependent upon the planter's goodwill. Even women were beginning to speak out in their own names, and some of the things they said represented a distinct challenge to the patriarchal role which the planter had assumed for himself and to many of the values which he thought of himself as embodying. Meanwhile, in the larger sphere of political events, the planter class in the Southern states, divested of the support of the West and challenged at home by its own yeomanry, found its power threatened both in Washington and in state legislatures. And what was an aristocrat who did not possess the power to order his own home, to say nothing of ruling over the national councils, especially when he was beginning to question some of the sanctions upon which his power had been based?

The Alabaman, Daniel Hundley,[8] for example, expressed his ambivalent attitude toward the force of the Cavalier ideal in his *Social Relations in our Southern States,* the book which he published on the eve of the war. In it he drew an ominous picture of the aristocrat in the South surrounded by predatory, or at least more forceful, social types, who seemed destined to overthrow his cultural and political domination. His book contained chapters devoted to the Southern Yankee, the southern bully, the poor white, and the enterprising and forward-looking representative of the new middle class. While he argued for the aristocratic ethos of the Southern gentleman, his confidence in his effectiveness clearly wavered before the vision of a rising Southern bourgeoisie.

Few figures in Southern history exemplify better than Edmund Ruffin the tensions and frustrations felt by those who had long battled for the Lost Cause. Ruffin, for years one of the South's leading agricultural scientists and an advocate of a diversified farm economy, was never reconciled to the defeat of the Cavalier ideal. Toward the end of his life, weary and partly deaf, he became obsessed by the idea of an independent, uncontaminated South and fought every inroad of what he regarded as Yankeeism. Dressed—rather conspicuously—in coarse Southern homespun; or, in 1859, at the age

of 63, attending John Brown's hanging clad in the uniform of a VMI cadet; or, as a volunteer in the Palmetto Guards, pulling the lanyard that sent one of the first shells toward Fort Sumter, he became a kind of Lanny Budd of the Old South, his every act a symbolic representation of Southern intransigeance before the Yankee North.

Few men more keenly sensed or more deeply resented the obstacles with which true Southernism was confronted within the South itself; no one, certainly, lashed out at the Yankee with greater bitterness or, finally expressed his feelings of frustration and self-defeat more melodramatically. As an agitator he repeatedly faced indifferent Southern audiences and, poor speaker that he was, he constantly reproached himself for his failure to bring the South to a boil. Virginia he early abandoned as reprobate; he was appalled to find the large planters in Kentucky holding strong Unionist views; and even South Carolina constantly disappointed him by her unwillingness, as in 1850, to take deliberate action. On a visit to White Sulphur Springs in August, 1859, he was astonished to find himself virtually alone among some 1600 Southern guests in calling for secession. For a time after John Brown's raid he hoped "the sluggish blood of the South" would be stirred,[9] and he personally sent pikes with which Brown had intended to arm the slaves to the governors of all the Southern states; but once again he was disappointed in his expectations. Even when confronted with the virtual certainty of Lincoln's election, no state except South Carolina expressed a willingness to take the initiative in seceding. The election of 1860, in which the more moderate Bell triumphed over Breckinridge within the South by a majority of 136,875, only confirmed his fear that the South would never act.

Then, as Southern states began to pass ordinances of secession, his hopes soared one final time. After a lifetime of ceaseless struggle, his dream of an independent South

---

[8] Hundley is discussed at greater length in another section.

[9] Avery Craven, *Edmund Ruffin Southerner: A Study in Secession* (New York, 1932), p. 171.

seemed about to become a reality. Once the exciting days of Fort Sumter were over, even these hopes were dashed as Jefferson Davis neglected former secessionists and formed a government dominated by moderates and men Ruffin regarded as would-be reunionists. Davis himself, furthermore, seemed slow to move and indecisive, and left Southern extremists generally dissatisfied with his leadership. But for Ruffin—as for most Southerners—the most crushing blow, one which destroyed for all time the myth of Southern invincibility, was the military defeat of the South by the Northern armies that swarmed across his beloved Virginia, destroying his plantation "Beechwood" and leaving obscene graffiti scrawled on the walls of his house. His plantation a shambles, deserted by his slaves, his hearing gone, and the alien North on his very doorstep, he had little left to him that he valued save his sense of honor, his bitterness, and his pride, to which he regularly gave expression in a diary kept through these trying years.

On June 17, 1865, after he had digested the news from Appomattox, he made this entry in the diary:

I here declare my unmitigated hatred to Yankee rule—to all political, social and business connections with the Yankees and to the Yankee race. Would that I could impress these sentiments, in their full force, on every living Southerner and bequeath them to every one yet to be born! May such sentiments be held universally in the outraged and downtrodden South, though in silence and stillness, until the now far-distant day shall arrive for just retribution for Yankee usurpation, oppression and atrocious outrages, and for deliverance and vengeance for the now ruined, subjugated and enslaved Southern States! . . . And now with my latest writing and utterance, and with what will be near my latest breath, I here repeat and would willingly proclaim my unmitigated hatred to Yankee rule—to all political, social and business connections with Yankees, and the perfidious, malignant and vile Yankee race.[10]

Almost before the ink of this entry had dried the old man performed his most symbolic act. Seating himself erectly in his chair, he propped the butt of his silver-mounted gun against a trunk at his feet, placed the muzzle in his mouth and, as his son reported in a letter to members of the family, "pulled the trigger with a forked stick."[11]

Coda

With Edmund Ruffin's suicide and the collapse of the Confederacy which it symbolized, the Old South as a concrete entity passed beyond history and into legend. One prolonged attempt to establish and sustain an aristocratic ideal in the face of obstacles of the kind invariably thrown up by American circumstances had ended. It was not the first such attempt, as colonial historians have shown,[12] nor was it to be the last, as those familiar with elitist groups at the end of the century can testify;[13] but perhaps, because of its bearing on the course of American history before 1861 and because of its more general consequences for the development of our cultural self-awareness, it has been the most important.

The Cavalier ideal was predestined to fail, as some of its earliest proponents secretly knew. The men who originated it were not aristocrats in any sense which Europeans would have recognized. Often they themselves were self-made men, provincial in their outlook and historically naïve, who possessed no sure sense of any cultural tradition. I have spoken, principally as a matter of convenience, of "the South" and "the planter class" in assigning a specific locus

[10] *Ibid.*, p. 259. The information about Ruffin, except for the details of his death, derives entirely from Professor Craven's biography.

[11] Edmund Ruffin, Jr., to his sons, June 20, 1865, in "Death of Edmund Ruffin," *Tyler's Quarterly Historical and Genealogical Magazine*, V (January, 1924), 193.

[12] Bernard Bailyn, "Politics and Social Structure in Virginia," *Seventeenth-Century America: Essays in Colonial History* (ed.), James Morton Smith (Chapel Hill, 1959), pp. 90–115.

[13] Barbara Miller Solomon, *Ancestors and Immigrants: A Changing New England Tradition* (Cambridge, Mass.; 1956); Arthur Mann, *Yankee Reformers in The Urban Age* (Cambridge, Mass., 1954).

to the kind of thinking which I have been describing; but at no time, I suspect, was the Cavalier ideal as it was defined by Beverley Tucker, for example, widely understood or embraced by Southern planters in general, to say nothing of other people living within the South. Such an ideal was significant because it exemplified an important American cultural problem and because it defined a tendency in Southern thought which ultimately affected political events.

As it moved toward implementation, of course, the ideal was repeatedly and necessarily compromised. The constitution of no Southern state, not even that of South Carolina, provided for anything more than a kind of modified planter oligarchy; most of the older states within the South yielded to democratic pressures before the war; and the newer states of the Southwest were no more exclusive in their political arrangements than comparable states in the North. The Confederate constitution, finally, despite its explicit recognition of slavery, was in no sense meant to set up an aristocracy, and in certain ways it provided more assurance of popular government than the federal Constitution.

The legacy left behind by the Cavalier ideal is a little difficult to define; a careful consideration of it would require a study in itself. The close of the war did not mean, certainly, that some kind of aristocratic ideal ceased to form a part of Southern thinking, nor did it mean, once Reconstruction was over, that some kind of planter class ceased to dominate Southern politics. Quite the contrary. The century had virtually ended before the old dominant groups in the South

and their new business allies received any substantial challenge from the majority of Southerners, whose affairs they had historically directed. After the war, as everyone knows, the legend, far from dying away, was given a new lease on life and, in the North, probably enjoyed greater popularity and evoked more interest than at any other time. Its vitality, it seems apparent enough, has not yet exhausted itself today after more than a century of discussion and dramatic reembodiment. The nostalgia felt by Americans for the antebellum South and for the drama of the Civil War is a phenomenon which continues to startle those unfamiliar with our culture, with our collective anxieties about the kind of civilization we have created, and with our reservations concerning the kind of social conformity which, it appears, it has been our destiny to exemplify before the world. Some of our greatest writers—Henry Adams and Henry James within the nineteenth century—have employed the Cavalier legend as a means of defining and measuring the failures and limitations of our culture at large. It seems scarcely necessary to add that this same concern has characteristically engaged the imagination of William Faulkner. But for the great mass of Americans, even those who take their impression exclusively from popular novels, television plays, and Civil War centennials, the Old South has also become an enduring part of our sense of the past. At odd moments probably even the most skeptical of us allow our thoughts to play over this lingering social image, and to concede with mingled pride and wonderment: "Once it was *different* down there."

CHAPTER 3

Is Southern History Unique?

Ulrich B. Phillips has few disciples today. Many scholars doubt that white supremacy was "the central theme" of a distinctive Southern history, and an even larger number of historians reject the context of racist opinions which permeated Phillips' explanation. Questions of a different order are now commonly asked: Was the antebellum South really "different" or "unique"? If so, did those differences persist? Will they exist in the future? In 1958 the Arkansas journalist, Harry S. Ashmore, traced the locus of regional distinctiveness to slavery and segregation and predicted that as the gap closed between the South and the rest of the nation in urbanism, industrialism, and stress on segregation, the Southerners' sense of identity would gradually fade away. Indeed, many scholars in the 1950s and '60s were much more inclined to discuss the Southerner "as an American" rather than to seek out provincial differences. (See Chapter II.)

C. Vann Woodward, undaunted by the skeptics, sought in 1960 to explore another way of defining Southern distinctiveness. Many of the appalling differences, "the one-horse farmer, one-crop agriculture, one-party politics, the sharecropper, the poll tax, the white primary, the Jim Crow car, and the lynching bee" could be buried with relief, but should the South welcome all the products of bulldozers and mass culture down to "the threat of becoming 'indistinguishable,' " under the "national steam roller" of "conformity"? Woodward hastened to assure Southerners that even after the "nationalization" of the region, they would still retain a unique historical experience based on an intimate knowledge of defeat, poverty, and social evil. Other Americans inherited affluence and a basic optimism. Never having known a major frustration to the collective will, they could embrace a luxurious confidence in their invincibility and fall back upon the faith of innocent and virtuous souls that every evil has a cure and every social problem a solution. Southerners, who shared "a long and quite un-American experience with poverty" and the evils of slavery, were not inclined to worship the gospel of progress or to tinker with Utopian social schemes. Southerners added another note of difference by bringing a vivid sense of time and place to a nation in which human experience usually had an abstract and disconnected quality. The singular contribution of

Southern history became even clearer after the application of Reinhold Niebuhr's concept of historical irony.

According to Niebuhr the gospel of progress and success gave Americans a conviction about their virtuous innocence until the rise to world prominence compelled the United States to use its new power in a way which brought an end to innocence and covered Americans with guilt. Consequently it was necessary to live with these incongruities of assumed innocence and guilty power, the illusion of near omnipotence and the reality of limited security. Woodward reasoned that antebellum Southerners, after a fashion similar to the Cold War surrender of American ideals to chauvinism and McCarthyism, abandoned both democratic conscience and the unhappy dilemma of slavery to enter a never-never land of imagined Southern perfection or to the dream world of a great slave empire yet to come. The contrast between romantic Southern rhetoric and the grim reality of slavery, between the visions of a future golden age and the bitter experience of defeat, provide the ironic incongruities of Southern history from which the nation in modern times might well learn a lesson.

In 1961 David M. Potter made his contribution to the debate by suggesting that Woodward's comments on poverty, defeat, and guilt were really discussions of qualities which impinged on a still unknown essence. The essential distinctiveness of the South, it seemed, could be found in "a folk culture," a relation of people to land more "direct and primal" and valued for its concrete sense of experience, for the texture and tempo of satisfying life. Southern ways had won attention and interest because the larger society suffered from the lack of relatedness, meaning, and fulfillment of individual personality.

At times Potter did not seem too remote from the point which Woodward had discussed in an essay entitled "The Search For Southern Identity," *The Burden of Southern History* (1960). Certainly one might put questions to both Potter and Woodward in exploring their views. First a scholar might note, as Charles Sellers did in 1960, that the word Southerner has almost always been used to indicate "white Southerner." Having considered this point one might ask if Woodward's generalizations covered both sides of the color line: was not the defeat of the white Southerners in the Civil War a victory for black Southerners? If "defeat" applied to both sides, was not the defeat of black Southerners a more pervasive, continual, and complex defeat? How would an American Negro respond to the ironic national incongruities between the rhetoric of a democratic society and the often bitter realities of his own life? As for Potter, had he not also risked the hazard of "universal" statements that were not actually comprehensive? Were the "folk" Southerners more prone to rigid conformity and social habits which limited human freedom and individual personality? Was there so little bitterness and dehumanizing deprivation in the lives of so many impoverished white Southerners (not to speak of Negroes living under vastly worse conditions)? Did not many of the qualities stressed by Potter really spring from the rural ways which dominated most of nineteenth-century America? After all the questions have been weighed and judged, was the South actually so very "different" or distinct, and if so, was that distinctiveness so prized a possession?

Some of these questions were raised in 1964 by Howard Zinn. At one time Zinn had attributed reality to "the Southern mystique" of "the mysterious and terrible South soaked in blood and history" and peopled by unfathomable Negroes and white men with incomprehensible and violent racial hatreds. Later he changed his line of thought and set out to refute the notions he had once accepted. The South was indeed "racist, violent, hypocritically pious, xenophobic, false in its elevation of women, nationalistic, conservative, and it harbors extreme poverty in the midst of ostentatious wealth." Yet, after a brief account of the racial hatreds which had often characterized the North and the West, Zinn concluded that "the United States as a civilization embodies all of these same qualities" and that the South was merely a mirror of the Republic which reflected national images more vividly and sharply. He also suggested that the tendency of Americans to be overawed by history acted as a barrier to the social change which must come in the future.

"We created the mystery of the South, and we can dissolve it," Zinn concluded. Woodward moved to meet this attack on "exceptionalism" by arguing that "with the best will in the world for sharing guilt, paranoia, and tragedy, the doctrine of anti-exceptionalism cannot be stretched to endow the North with the South's past." Here Woodward stressed the idea that Negroes like white Southerners were another American minority rooted in an "un-American experience of history." Nonviolent tactics, for example, did not come from white intellectuals nor even from India but from "the anguish of an encounter with the white man through the centuries of his greatest power and arrogance." No one, and certainly not the American Negro in the midst of nearly revolutionary change could afford to lose the strength which men draw from the past: "To hear Mahalia Jackson sing, or Fanny Lou Hamer speak, or Martin Luther King preach is to be overwhelmed with the elemental impact of the past on the present." Here, at least for the moment, the debate rested.

BIBLIOGRAPHY

Books and Articles Referred to in the Chapter Introduction

Ulrich B. Phillips, "The Central Theme of Southern History," *American Historical Review* (1928).
Harry S. Ashmore, *An Epitaph for Dixie* (1958).
C. Vann Woodward, *The Burden of Southern History* (1960).

Suggested Reading

For an extremely influential account of Southern distinctiveness, see W. J. Cash, *The Mind of the South* (1941). Rollin G. Osterweis portrayed a South excessively given over to an exaggerated romantic nationalism in *Romanticism and Nationalism in the Old South* (1949). Thomas P. Govan gave a general summary of the debate on Southern uniqueness in "Was the Old South Different?" *Journal of Southern History* (1955); Carl N. Degler discussed the same question in "There Was Another South," in *American Heritage* (1960); and David M. Potter more recently in "On Understanding the South," *Journal of Southern History* (1964). Much discussion on the uniqueness of the South has sprung from accounts of modern Southern literature. See Louis Rubin, "The South and the Faraway Country," *Virginia Quarterly Review* (1962), and Cleanth Brooks, "Regionalism in American Literature," *Journal of Southern History* (1960). On sociological definitions, see Rupert B. Vance, "The Sociological Implications of Southern Regionalism," *Journal of Southern History* (1960). For a general discussion of all aspects of the question, see George B. Tindall, "The Status and Future of Regionalism—A Symposium," *Journal of Southern History* (1960). On the point of religious distinctiveness in the modern South see Kenneth Bailey, *Southern White Protestantism in the Twentieth Century* (1964). The currently changing South was analyzed by Thomas D. Clark in *The Emerging South* (1961); and Robert B. Highsaw (ed.), *The Deep South in Transformation* (1964). A distinctively oppressive South emerged from the study of the sociologist John Dollard on *Caste and Class in a Southern Town* (1937). Louis E. Lomax gave a report on the protest movements against Southern caste in *The Negro Revolt* (1962).

1961

A Distinctive Folk Culture*

DAVID M. POTTER

Among the many flourishing branches of American historical study during the last half-century, one of the most robust has been the history of the South. Fifty years ago, there was already one large body of literature on the Southern Confederacy, especially in its military aspects, and another on the local history of various Southern states, but the history of the South as a region—of the whole vast area below the Potomac viewed as a single entity for the whole time from the settlement of Jamestown to the present—is largely a product of the last five decades. Today, a multivolume history, a number of college textbooks, a quarterly journal, and a substantial library of monographic studies all serve as measures of the extent of the development in this field.

Anyone who seeks an explanation for this interest in Southern history must take account of several factors. To begin with, the study of American regions is a general phenomenon, embracing not only the South but also New England, the Middle West, and the great physiographic provinces beyond the Mississippi. In a nation as vast and as diverse as ours, there is really no level higher than the regional level at which one can come to grips with the concrete realities of the land. But apart from this regional aspect, the Southern theme has held an unusual appeal for the people of the South because of their peculiarly strong and sentimental loyalty to Dixie as their native land, and for Americans outside the South because of the exotic quality of the place and because it bears the aura of a Lost Cause. Union generals, for some reason, have never held the romantic interest that attached to Stonewall Jackson, Jeb Stuart, George Pickett, Bedford Forrest, and, of course, Robert E. Lee.

* David M. Potter, "The Enigma of the South," *The Yale Review* (1961). Copyright Yale University Press.

Today, the predilection of Yankee children for caps, flags, and toys displaying the Rebel insignia bears further witness to the enduring truth that lost causes have a fascination even for those who did not lose them.

But it seems unlikely that either the South as an American region, or the South as Dixieland, or the South as a Lost Cause could hold so much scholarly and popular attention in focus if the South were not also an enigma. To writers for more than half a century the South has been a kind of sphinx on the American land.

To some who viewed it, this sphinx has seemed a great insensate monolith, a vast artifact of the past with no meaning behind its inscrutable expression. Its domain has been just what H. L. Mencken said it was— a cultural desert, a Sahara of the Bozart. But to others this sphinx has seemed to hold a secret, an answer to the riddle of American life.

To many people today, who think of the South in terms of Freedom Riders and lunch-counter sit-ins, of Tobacco Road and Central High School in Little Rock, of robed Klansmen and burning crosses, and perhaps of a Monkey Trial at Dayton, Tennessee, it may seem hard to believe that not long ago the South was regarded by many thoughtful and liberal-minded people as a kind of sanctuary of the American democratic tradition. What is now deplored as the "benighted South," or the "sick South," was, until recently, regarded by many liberals as the birthplace and the natural bulwark of the Jeffersonian ideal—a region where agrarian democracy still struggled to survive, fighting a gallant rearguard action against the commercialism and the industrial capitalism of the Northeast.

It would be a major undertaking to trace the evolution of this concept. The general idea that American democracy is essentially frontier democracy—which closely resembles agrarian democracy—is forever linked with Frederick Jackson Turner, but Turner gave it a Western rather than a Southern orientation. Certainly one of the earliest writers to apply it to the South was William

E. Dodd. In 1911, when Dodd had been but recently appointed to the University of Chicago, and 22 years before Franklin Roosevelt sent him as our unswervingly democratic ambassador to Hitler's Berlin, he wrote a sketchy little book, now largely forgotten, entitled *Statesmen of the Old South,* with the significant subtitle, *From Radicalism to Conservative Revolt.* The statesmen whom he treated were Jefferson, Calhoun, and Jefferson Davis, and the theme which he developed was that the democratic or radical South of Thomas Jefferson—an equalitarian South of small subsistence farmers—had been subverted by the increasingly aristocratic and hierarchical South of the great slaveholders whose property interests found embodiment in Calhoun and Davis.

In three brief and seemingly artless chapters, Dodd achieved two very subtle effects: first, he defined to suit himself what may be called a normative South—the South of Thomas Jefferson—and thus established an arbitrary basis for identifying all future developments of a Jeffersonian tenor as truly or intrinsically Southern, and rejecting all conservative or hierarchical developments as aberrations of Southernism. Using this device, he then proceeded to dispose of the whole conservative, slaveholding South of antebellum fame as a kind of deviation or detour in the true course of Southern history. Thus he finessed the basic question whether the true and realistic image of the South might not be a dualism, with as much of Calhoun as of Jefferson in it, or even whether the true South, historically, is not hierarchical and conservative rather than radical and equalitarian.

In justice to Dodd, one must recognize that his version of Southernism was by no means without foundations. Jeffersonianism, as well as Jefferson, did have distinctively Southern origins, and at almost every decisive turning point in the advancement of American democracy—whether at the time of Jackson, or Bryan, or Wilson, or Franklin Roosevelt—the South has thrown crucial weight on the domestic side. Still, there was something of a tour de force about the way in which Dodd reconciled his love for his native South and his commitment to democracy and, with very little disclosure of the wishful thinking which was involved, identified the land he loved with the values he cherished.

Whether later writers were directly influenced by Dodd or not, the theme of agrarianism has persisted ever since in the literature of the South, sometimes with the most startling implications. Thus when Charles and Mary Beard came to write about the Civil War in their *Rise of American Civilization* (1927), they pictured it as a conflict between Southern agrarianism and Northern industrialism; in this way, the defenders of slavery were transmuted into democrats, more or less, since agrarianism was, in the Beards' lexicon, by definition democratic, and industrialism was an antidemocratic. Again, at the hands of the Beards and of the late Howard K. Beale, in his *The Critical Year,* published in 1930, Reconstruction was not primarily a contest over the rights of Negro freedmen, but rather a series of coups by industrial capitalism to consolidate its ascendancy and to retain its wartime gains, consisting of tariffs, subsidies, and a monetary system favorable to creditors. The Fourteenth Amendment was not a Magna Charta of freedmen's rights but rather a bulwark for property interests, disguised as a Negro rights measure in order to catch votes. Again, the implications were ironic: for instance, under this formula, Andrew Johnson, a onetime slaveowner and an obdurate foe of Negro rights, appeared as a champion of democracy against the predatory capitalists. Thus Johnson received ecstatic praise in a biography (1929) by that archliberal attorney, Lloyd Paul Stryker, who later became a crusading spokesman for Negro rights.

Through all of these treatments there runs a persistent implied affirmation of Dodd's cleverly articulated premise: that which is agrarian in the South is truly Southern; anything not in the agrarian tradition is somehow extraneous—a cowbird's egg in the Southern nest. Almost automatically, this formula reduced the factor of biracialism and caste to secondary importance, or even kept it out of sight altogether. Again, some interesting results follow in the literature. For instance, when Howard W. Odum and his associates at Chapel Hill prepared their great compendium, *Southern Regions of the United States* (1936), they deployed no less than 600 maps and charts to show that the agricultural South, despite its rich natural resources, was worse off in almost every measurable respect than the rest of the country. That is, they mapped, measured, and charted the plight of the agricultural South. But not one graph, map, or chart showed the relatively worse plight of the Negroes within the South. In other words, the most careful reader of this encyclopedic survey of Southern economic and social conditions could almost have overlooked the fact that a biracial system prevailed in the South and that under this system the Negroes experienced adverse differentials in almost every respect. No doubt Odum and his associates chose this presentation deliberately, and certainly not because of any blind agrarianism, for they advocated economic diversification for the South. Their purpose may even have been to avoid dulling the concern of white Southerners about differentials by admitting that these differentials fell more heavily upon the Negro rather than upon the white component in the Southern population. Or, they may have wished to treat Negroes and whites indiscriminately alike as being handicapped by regional differentials. But in any case, their survey of Southern problems left out the greatest problem of all. Like the doctrinal agrarians with whom they disagreed, they presented an image of the South which emphasized the plight of farmers rather than the plight of Negroes.

In quite a different way, the agrarian premise shows itself also in many of the writings of C. Vann Woodward, the foremost historian of the modern South. In Woodward's biography, *Tom Watson* (1938), for instance, the protagonist of the drama is Watson, the agrarian, and the antagonists are the Bourbon Democrats who have betrayed the interests of the South to the forces of industrial capitalism. Or alternately, one could say, the protagonist is the earlier Watson, who championed Populism and defended Negro rights, while the antagonist is the later Watson, a reactionary racist who betrayed the ideals of his youth. Though Woodward's treatment is deeply subtle and sensitive to complexities, while Dodd's was superficial and grossly oversimplified, both are alike in regarding the agrarian South as, almost a priori, the true South, and any force within the South which runs counter to it as an aberration. This is, of course, quite a different thing from merely favoring the agrarian cause.

Although a whole generation of writers have made this tempting equation between Southernism and agrarianism, it requires only a limited analysis to see that, in many respects, the Southern economy and the Southern society have not been agrarian at all—in fact, have embodied almost the antithesis of agrarianism. Agrarianism implies an escape from the commercialism of the money economy, but Southern cotton and tobacco and sugar cultivators have consistently been agricultural businessmen producing for market and for cash income. Agrarianism implies production for use rather than production for sale, and therefore diversification rather than specialization, but the Southern agriculturist stuck to his one-crop system in the past as tenaciously as he clings to segregation at the present. It implies the independence of a husbandman who looks to no one else either for his access to the land or for the necessities of his living, but the Southern cultivator has been historically either a slave or a sharecropper, without land and often without opportunity even to grow his own turnip greens in a garden patch. Meanwhile the Southern landowner, whether an absentee planter or a mortgage-holding bank, frequently failed to follow the ennobling agrarian practice of laboring in the earth. To one who is impressed by these aspects, it may seem realistic to regard Calhoun rather than

Jefferson as the typical leader of the South; the plantation producing raw materials for the textile industry, rather than the subsistence farm producing for use, as the typical economic unit; hierarchy rather than equality as the typical social condition; and conservatism rather than radicalism as the typical mode of thought.

One man who was long the leading historian of the South saw the region to some extent in these terms. This was Ulrich B. Phillips, who began his career around the turn of the century with studies of Southern political history and the history of Southern transportation. But wherever his investigations began, they always led him, as he himself said, back to one feature of life in the South which was constant both before emancipation and after, namely the presence of Negroes and whites whose destinies were inextricably intertwined but whose paths in life were separated by a biracial system. Accordingly, Phillips gave only slight attention to the agrarian theme. Instead he concentrated on the staple-crop economy with its plantation units and its slave labor. With supreme thoroughness in research, he made what remains the basic study of slavery as a system of labor (*American Negro Slavery,* 1918). Later, he developed an artistry in writing which matched his soundness in research, and achieved a felicitous conjunction of both talents in a study of the society and economy of the antebellum period (*Life and Labor in the Old South,* 1929).

When Phillips looked at the Southern economy, the image which seemed visible to him was not an independent husbandman laboring in the soil but a Negro field-hand picking cotton. The persistence of this figure, either as a slave or as a sharecropper, and the persistence of the system which kept him in his subordinate role led Phillips, five years before his death in 1934, to write an essay. "The Central Theme of Southern History," in which he stated what he had found at the core of distinctive Southernism. This was not some agrarian ideal, but rather a fixed purpose on the part of the Southern whites to preserve biracialism, or as he said, in unvarnished terms, to assure that the South "shall be and remain a white man's country."

Although Phillips' stature is still recognized even by his critics, liberal historians have been reluctant to accept his views. Kenneth Stampp has written a new account of slavery (*The Peculiar Institution,* 1956), which emphasizes, as Phillips never did, the harsh and exploitative aspects of the system; Richard Hofstadter has criticized Phillips for giving too much attention to the plantation, and not enough to the slaves held in small holdings; and at least two writers have questioned the "Central Theme."

It is in some ways ironical for liberals, concerned as they are with the "sick South," to reject a formula which explains so cogently the chronic nature of the illness. But what they found fault with was not in fact the accuracy of Phillips' conclusion; it was rather the lack of moral indignation in his statement of it. By asserting that the policy of bi-racialism is and will continue to be a central aspect of Southernism, without personally repudiating this policy, he made it difficult for liberals to identify with him. When Harry Ashmore, more recently, has said in *An Epitaph for Dixie* (1958) that the South will cease to be the South when it ceases to be segregated, the statement was almost identical with that of Phillips, but liberals could accept Ashmore's because he expects the South, in the old sense, to vanish (hence "an epitaph"), whereas they could not accept Phillips', because he seemingly expected the South to survive, with the implied corollary that efforts at integration must fail. Moreover, in the case of liberals who want to love the South, as some do, but who find it psychologically impossible to love an embodiment of bi-racialism, the only recourse is a resort to Dodd's original formula: dispose of the factor which is troublesome (in this case the bi-racialism) by treating it as a great aberration. Here even so excellent a book as Vann Woodward's *Strange Career of Jim Crow* (1955) is a case in point, for though it was intended to emphasize a thoroughly valid observation—

namely, that the patterns of bi-racialism have varied and are not immutable—it lends itself to being read as a statement that caste does not have very deep roots in the South. The preface to the paperback edition (1957) showed that Woodward was himself concerned that his work had been taken too much in this way.

When one considers the degree of hardheadedness and realism which went into Phillips' view that bi-racialism lay at the core of Southernism, and the vulnerability of the doctrine that agrarianism was the heart of the matter, it seems strange that writers have been so abstinent in accepting the former and so addicted to the latter. Clearly, the agrarian interpretation has drawn its strength from something other than the sheer weight of evidence, and it is worth pondering what the real basis of its acceptance is. In the purely historical literature, this basis is hard to detect, for the historian purports merely to be describing the agrarianism which he finds in the past—not to be advocating it. But in 1930, agrarianism enjoyed open advocacy at the hands of a group of writers, all centered at Vanderbilt University, in the famous manifesto entitled *I'll Take My Stand.* The 12 Southerners who joined in this profession of faith categorically rejected the industrial way of life, which they regarded as the prevailing or American way, and with equal conviction they subscribed to an agrarian way, which they identified as a Southern way. They hoped to carry this Southern way to the nation through "a national agrarian movement."

In the extensive and often heated discussion which followed, attention was focused very heavily upon the operative-practicability of their proposals. They were accused of medievalism and of quixotically renouncing all the benefits of modern science and technology. They were also accused, with somewhat more justice, of being in disagreement among themselves as to whether agrarianism was designed to provide a livelihood for dirt farmers or to restore cultural amenities for the landed gentry. Whether they advocated populism or elitism, no one could quite make out. While controversy raged between them and their assailants, not much attention was given to the ideological implications of agrarianism, nor to the question why this particular line of thought had appeared at this particular time. Indeed, the historical significance of agrarian thought has still never been adequately analyzed.

But it is clearly evident that agrarianism appealed to many liberals, both before and after the Nashville group, partly because they were looking for an alternative to the prevailing American way of life. Some writers, like Charles A. Beard so enthusiastically used agrarianism as a stick with which to beat capitalism that it had some of the appearance of a disguised Marxism. But its real significance lay in the fact that it offered an alternative to Marxism. Here, in fact, was a way in which a man could renounce industrial capitalism and all its works without becoming a Marxist. This is perhaps why the agrarian ideal held so much attraction for such a large number of social thinkers. It gave them a chance to express their dissent from the prevailing system without going outside the American tradition in order to do so.

Another significant feature in making agrarianism attractive was its affirmation that the South had something of value in its tradition to offer to the nation. The Nashville group really felt convinced that the Southern sphinx did have an answer to the riddle, if not of the universe, at least of American life. Their affirmation came at a time when it was being asserted by critics like Mencken that the Southern tradition amounted to little more than a sterile, backward-looking form of ancestor worship. Now suddenly men were saying in a fresh and arresting way that the Southern tradition was not merely a pressed flower in the nation's scrapbook of memories but rather an urgent message which Americans, deafened by the roar of progress, had failed to hear. To Southerners who yearned to believe that there was some element of validity in the history of their region, this idea seemed immensely appealing.

The continued acceleration of industrial growth and the failure of the Nashville group to rally a popular following soon showed that agrarianism had no future, but it was still widely believed to have a past, and historians continued to apply it to the interpretation of American history. Henry Bamford Parkes made brilliant use of it in his *The American Experience* (1947), and as recently as 1949, Frank L. Owsley, in his *Plain Folk of the Old South*, delineated the structure of antebellum society in terms in which large slaveholders and plain farmers were practically indistinguishable. In these and many other writings, a number of time-honored propositions continued to find acceptance: that American democracy has been nourished primarily from agrarian roots; that agrarian attitudes are inherently democratic; and that the South peculiarly embodies the agrarian tradition.

But of late, the first two of these propositions have come under criticism, and the agrarian view has been attacked, for the first time, at its foundations. As long ago as 1945, Arthur Schlesinger, Jr., in his *Age of Jackson*, offered the then heretical view that Jacksonian democracy owed more to the East and to class-conscious urban workingmen than to the frontier and its coonskin equality. More recently, Richard Hofstadter, in his *Age of Reform* (1955), has gone even further by arguing that Populism had little affinity with liberal democracy, and was in fact a seedbed for such illiberal manifestations as prohibition, nativism, immigration restriction, Red-baiting, and the like. Thus, according to Schlesinger, democracy was not agrarian, and according to Hofstadter, agrarianism was not democratic.

In literal form, the agrarian formula fitted the South remarkably badly. It envisioned a subsistence economy, agricultural diversification, a wide distribution of small landholdings, a large class of independent husbandmen, and an unstratified society. The cold fact is that none of these features has even been dominant in the South. In the light of these flaws, as well as of recent criticisms, the whole idea of the South as an agrarian society now seems more and more an illusion, nourished by a wish. But once it is discarded, the question reverts to the enigma of the South. All theory aside, is the South, at a purely descriptive level, distinguishable? And if it is, does the distinction lie in anything more than the fact that bi-racialism takes a form in the South differing from the form it takes elsewhere?

This is a question which the literature of the future will perhaps explore further. Vann Woodward, in *The Burden of Southern History* (1960), has already moved in this direction with incisive and fertile arguments that certain distinctive experiences of the South have put their mark upon the Southern people: the experience of defeat and frustration, in an America of monotonous, taken-for-granted success; the experience of guilt because of the Negro, in an America with a cult of Adamic innocence; the experience of poverty, in an America with abundance which has caused people to confuse life with a standard of living. But though Woodward discusses these factors as experiences impinging upon the Southern culture, we still need a dissection of the culture itself upon which they impinge.

On the face of it, it seems a matter of observation and not of theory to say that the culture of the folk survived in the South long after it succumbed to the onslaught of urban-industrial culture elsewhere. It was an aspect of this culture that the relation between the land and the people remained more direct and more primal in the South than in other parts of the country. (This may be more true for the Negroes than for the whites, but then there is also a question whether the Negroes may not have embodied the distinctive qualities of the Southern character even more than the whites.)

Even in the most exploitative economic situations, this culture retained a personalism in the relations of man to man which the industrial culture lacks. Even for those whose lives were narrowest, it offered a relationship of man to nature in which there was a certain fulfillment of personality. Every culture is, among other things, a system of relationships among an aggregate of people, and as cultures differ, the systems of relationship vary. In the folk culture of the South, it may be that the relation of people to one another imparted a distinctive texture as well as a distinctive tempo to their lives.

An explanation of the South in terms of a folk culture would not have the ideological implications which have made the explanation in terms of agrarianism so tempting and at the same time so treacherous. But on the other hand, it would not be inconsistent with some of the realities of Southern society, such as bi-racialism and hierarchy, whereas agrarianism is inconsistent with these realities. The enigma remains, and the historian must still ask what distinctive quality it was in the life of the South for which Southerners have felt such a persistent, haunting nostalgia and to which even the Yankee has responded with a poignant impulse. We must now doubt that this nostalgia was the yearning of men for an ideal agrarian utopia which never existed in reality. But if it was not that, was it perhaps the yearning of men in a mass culture for the life of a folk culture which did really exist? This folk culture, we know, was far from being ideal or utopian, and was in fact full of inequality and wrong, but if the nostalgia persists was it because even the inequality and wrong were parts of a life that still had a relatedness and meaning which our more bountiful life in the mass culture seems to lack?

Dissolving the Southern Mystique*

HOWARD ZINN

Deep-set in the Southern mystique is the notion that the South is more than just "different," that it is distinct from the rest of the nation—a sport, a freak, an inexplicable variant from the national norm. The South, so it goes, does more than *speak* differently; it *thinks* differently. Its apartness goes deeper than the visible elements of soil and sun and large black populations, into the innermost values of the region, into what Wilbur J. Cash called "The Mind of the South." The South—and we are drawn to agree by each ugly headline—has its own set of characteristics. Racism tops the list, of course. But the South is also proverbial, conservative, fundamentalist, nativist, violent, conformist, militarist. It is a stranger to the nation, and not even four years of bloodletting could wash away that strangeness.

Such is the American mystique about the South; and it feeds self-righteousness in the North, defiance below the Mason-Dixon Line. It is supported (deliberately, or unwittingly) by legions of writers, by William Faulkner, by Erskine Caldwell, by Tennessee Williams. And it stands so firmly and so high on a ledge of truth that one must strain to see the glitter of deception in its eye.

For the South, I am about to argue, far from being utterly different, is really the *essence* of the nation. It is not a mutation born by some accident into the normal, lovely American family; it has simply taken

the national genes and done the most with them. It contains, in concentrated and dangerous form, a set of characteristics which mark the country as a whole. It is different because it is a distillation of those traits which are the worst (and a few which are the best) in the national character. Those very qualities long attributed to the South as special possessions are, in truth, *American* qualities, and the nation reacts emotionally to the South precisely because it subconsciously recognizes itself there. The mystery is that attached to the bastard child, whose father disavows his act. But a paternity test, I suspect, would destroy the charge of bastardy and reveal the United States as the true father of the Southern region.

Because the South embarrasses us, we try to disown it, apologize for it, hold it at a distance, pretend it is an abnormal growth on the national body. Once, however, we face the truth—that the South crystallizes the defects of the nation—there may be some value in the acknowledgment. In this part, I shall examine a number of these traits alleged to be peculiarly Southern. Then I shall suggest how candid self-recognition by the nation can be an occasion not for shame, but for insight, and how the South, miserable and rejected, may yet turn out to be the savior of the American dream.

We start, of course, with racism. The ugliest bastions of racist thought and action are in the South: that is undisputed. But when the white Southerner tries to lighten

---

the burden of his guilt by pointing to prejudice and discrimination in the North, the equalitarians, while continuing to denounce the South, become uneasy, for they know how much truth is in the accusation. Although the symptoms show mostly in the South, the entire mind and body of the American nation are afflicted. And it may be important, exactly at this moment in our history, when the South is going through the early stages of a kind of shock therapy, for the rest of the nation to understand that it stands by not as an administering doctor but as the next patient in line. The South turned out to be a convenient place—a kind of Fort Knox of prejudice—where the nation has always stored the bulk of its bigotry, while the rest has circulated—though sometimes stealthily—all over the country.

Slavery, because of favorable agricultural conditions, was concentrated in the American South, but it existed everywhere in the American colonies for over a hundred years. Slaves worked on the land in Rhode Island and New York by the thousands. In the mid-seventeenth century, around the same time that slavery had become a legal institution in Virginia and Maryland, it was legitimized in New York, and it was a fact of life in every Northern colony. On the eve of the Revolution, New York had over 15,000 slaves, roughly 10 percent of the population. New York law in the eighteenth century provided that any slave caught traveling 40 miles above Albany would be executed upon the oath of two credible witnesses. In 1712, a slave uprising took place in New York, when a group of armed Negro slaves killed nine white men. Awaiting capture by the militia, four cut their own throats and one shot his wife and then himself. Twenty-one were executed. A woman was hanged; one man was broken on the wheel and quartered; some were burned to death.

New York again became the scene of race terror in 1741 when a series of fires led to wild rumors of insurrection and to a hysterical trial, which convicted a hundred Negroes and four whites of conspiracy to take over the city. The four whites, one of whom was accused of wanting to establish a monarchy in New York with himself as king and a Negro named Caesar as governor, were hanged. Eighteen Negroes were hanged. Thirteen other Negroes were burned alive. One account reads: "At the rate of two every week, one hanged, and one burned alive, the victims were executed amid prayers, imprecations, and shrieks of agony."

New Jersey, 24 years after the Declaration of Independence, had 1,000 slaves; in 1741 the state burned two Negroes at the stake for setting fire to seven barns in Hackensack. Pennsylvania, the Quaker State, famed for its tolerance of Negroes, had 3,700 slaves in 1790. Negroes were tried by special courts in that state, and were not allowed to assemble in groups of more than four.

In New England, the source of so much abolitionist agitation, slavery was well-established in the first generation of colonization. Those celebrating the heritage of Puritan New England speak fondly of the "Body of Liberties" adopted in Massachusetts in 1641. This prohibited slavery "unless it be lawful captives taken in just wars, and such strangers as willingly sell themselves or are sold to us." In other words, the enslavement of people was obnoxious—except through war or commerce. It is as clear an example of Puritan hypocrisy as we have, and a striking example of the emptiness of Northern moralizing.

When Southerners, stung by Northern posturing, retorted that their slaves had been brought to them by Yankee traders, they were telling the truth. It was an accident of geography and economics, rather than a different attitude of mind or a different capacity to tolerate evil, that kept the number of slaves relatively low in the North. It was the immediate situation—particularly the spur of profit—rather than any persistent difference in regional history or psychology, that determined the extent of enslavement.

The state-by-state abolition of slavery in the North after the Revolution did not signify the abolition of racism; it merely ended one special form of it. For the key factor which ended slavery in the North was not a significant breaking down of racial attitudes, but a set of circumstances which made slavery unprofitable and inconvenient. That these circumstances were heightened by some of the ideological ferment of the Declaration of Independence and the Revolution I would not deny, but ideology played, I believe, only a marginal role. Certainly, moral considerations may tip the scales of social decision, but their weight is usually so slight that they can do this only when the scales are already closely balanced by harder considerations of self-interest. Specifically, it was in the interest of winning the war that the Continental Army enlisted 5,000 Negroes, promising freedom to many after victory over England.

Differences existed between the sections. Abolitionists could not operate at all in the South after the 1830s. In the North they could speak and print—but at the risk of their lives. Garrison was mobbed in Boston, Phillips was stoned throughout the North, and Lovejoy was murdered in Illinois.

* * * * *

[Thus, the differences between the sections are differences of degrees whether they relate to violence, racism, or fundamentalism.] There is *more* Baptist emotionalism in the preaching that goes on in the South, more religious revivalism, more faith healing, more Bible quoting, more downright religious hypocrisy. But this is only an intense form of what has gone on for so long in the whole nation; in the North it has managed to duck below the level of absurdity just often enough to steer the chuckles and jibes of the rationalists toward the harassed South.

If anyone can convince us that there is something about the South which naturally leads it to religious primitivism, it is Cash, who writes in *The Mind of the South* of the Southerner's sense of sin, his fear of damnation: "The world he knew, the hot sting of the sun in his blood, the sidelong glance of the all-complaisant Negro woman—all

these impelled him irresistibly to joy. But even as he danced, and even though he had sloughed off all formal religion, his thoughts were with the piper and his fee."

And it is the physical world of the South, Cash stresses, that enhances this mood:

There are days when the booming of the wind in the pines is like the audible rushing of time—when the sad knowledge of the grave stirs in the subconsciousness and bends the spirit to melancholy. . . . And there are those days, too, when the earth whimpers in dread, when the lightning clicks in awful concatenation with continuous thunder, and hurricanes break forth with semi-tropical fury; days when this land which, in its dominant mood wraps its children in soft illusion, strips them naked before terror. . . . What our Southerner required . . . was a faith as simple and emotional as himself. . . . A faith, not of liturgy and prayer book, but of primitive frenzy and the blood sacrifice. . . .

But Cash is not so carried away that he does not utter the exact truth a paragraph later: "What was demanded here, in other words, was the God and the faith of the Methodists and the Baptists, and the Presbyterians. These personal and often extravagant sects, sweeping the entire American country with their revivals in the first half of the nineteenth century, achieved their greatest success in the personal and extravagant South." The South, Cash tells us here clearly, saw sectarian, primitive religion at its most intense. But the phenomenon itself was a national one. Both statements are true. The second one, however, has been glossed over in the fond romanticism of the South as an area apart from the rest.

And was it only in the South that the forest pressed close, its darkness spawning wild thoughts in the brain? "The edge of the wilderness was close by. The American continent stretched endlessly west, and it was full of mystery for them. It stood, dark and threatening over their shoulders night and day, for out of it Indian tribes marauded from time to time. . . ." This is Arthur Miller's description of seventeenth-century Salem, Massachusetts, in *The Crucible*.

New England was the birthplace of revivalism, through the voice of Jonathan Edwards. In 1741 when he delivered his masterpiece in Enfield, Massachusetts, "Sinner in the Hands of an Angry God," his listeners moaned, shrieked, cried out, until he had to pause. It was the beginning of The Great Awakening, and it soon got out of hand. Perry Miller wrote in *Jonathan Edwards:* "The land was filled with enthusiasm, not just the faintings of 1740, and orgies too fantastic to be credible mounted, while the bastardy rate began to rise."

Shortly after the American Revolution, revivalist religion seems to have sprung up North and South, and especially along the western frontier of both sections. When the wall of a church collapsed at Jones' Hole, Virginia, in 1787, in the midst of a revival, the frenzied dancing and shouting continued through the rain of bricks until everyone was exhausted. Violent religious meetings spread through Kentucky and Tennessee in the early nineteenth century. Twenty thousand people attended one five-day camp meeting in Kentucky. An observer wrote: "Some of the people were singing, others praying, some crying for mercy in the most piteous accents, while others were shouting most vociferously. . . . At one time I saw at least five hundred swept down in a moment, as if a battery of a thousand guns had been opened upon them, and then immediately followed shrieks and shouts that rent the very heavens."

These scenes were easily matched in western New York in the 1820s, where Charles G. Finney started on a rampage of revival meetings that carried him into major cities of the East and Midwest. The religious excitement at those meetings reached points of frenzy induced by Finney's verbal pictures of the terror of hell. It was The Great Revival, and it spread, North and South and West into the antebellum period. The ones held on Long Island perhaps never matched those held in Georgia, one of which is described by Alice Felt Tyler in *Freedom's Ferment:* "The grandeur of the night meeting in the forest, the eight fine altars, the

campfires of resinous wood, the superb singing of the thousands of Negroes, the wails of the penitent, the thunder and lightning of an approaching storm. . . ." But despite differences in tone and style, the camp meeting, and the religious primitivism it represented, were national phenomena.

Dwight Moody, the colorful evangelist of the late nineteenth century, was from Massachusetts. Although he stressed love and mercy rather than hellfire and damnation, his approach was a fundamentalist one. The Bible Institute he established remains in Chicago. Around the same time, the Jehovah's Witnesses group originated with the followers of Charles Russell, a Pennsylvanian who did much of his work in New York City and who preached a fundamentalism as stark as anything seen in the South. We might note too that, although Tennessee gave us the famous *Scopes Case* by passing a law that barred evolutionist teaching which contradicted the Bible, the man who acted as chief witness for the Tennessee Bible crowd was William Jennings Bryan, son of the Midwest. Evangelist Billy Sunday was also a Midwesterner. Historically, fundamentalism is ingrained in the religious tradition of the entire nation, and it leads to a perpetual tension over the constitutional requirement that church and state be separated.

The fact that the social gospel idea, which attracted a tiny part of the American clergy in the early twentieth century, existed mostly in the North, has been used to create an illusion of religious progressiveness in the North and conservation in the South. More accurate is the statement that religion throughout the nation has been a conservative force with no more than a few voices, anywhere, trying to be heard above the pious din. The geographic location of the social gospelers has shifted, depending on where there was a rising movement of general social protest, for the church latched onto going movements more often than it started its own. It was the Progressive swell of the turn of the century, concentrated in the North, that encouraged the rise of the social gospel idea there. The second coming of the social gospel has been in the South, in our own era, represented by the Martin Luther Kings, the Ralph Abernathys, and other militants of the Negro churches.

Stow Persons, in his *American Minds,* notes how little real hold the social gospel movement took in the religious life of the nation, despite bursts of fervor and the momentary attention that the outcries of protest received. "In no denomination did the group of social-gospel advocates constitute more than a small minority, albeit a vocal one." He points out that the social gospelers "were more than balanced by fundamentalist wings that continued to stress the old individualistic evangelical piety. By midtwentieth century, it was apparent that no denomination had in any substantial way been transformed by the social gospel."

There is an undeniable reality about the Bible Belt which stretches through the South. But it does not end there. It winds into the Midwest, and touches every corner of the nation, though not as solidly, or as confidently, as in the South. The placing of Bibles in hotel rooms is a national practice, and there are no indications that the Gideon Society favors any one section. Although the Bible undoubtedly plays an obtrusive role in the public education of the South, most of the Supreme Court cases involving the use of public facilities for religious education have originated in Northern communities.

Jesus lived and died well before the rise of modern nations, and God presumably is not only international, but interplanetary, hardly noticing from his distant post those peculiar boundaries which on our earth mark off nations. But the churches of the United States are national and nationalist. This has been even more true of churches in other nations (the Roman Catholic Church in Italy, the Protestant churches under Hitler, the Russian Orthodox Church, the Church of England), and I mention this because if I am claiming religiosity as a national characteristic, I should note that there is a reverberation between church and nation which often makes the former more national and the latter more pious.

Our society, Max Lerner says in *America As a Civilization,* is a striking mixture of religion and secularism, but he goes on to say what a strong hold religion has on the American character. There is "less and less room for the 'godless' in America, since godlessness is usually associated with Communism and depravity." We are a "Christian country" and, Lerner says: "There is no candidate for even minor political office in America today who would dare to mock religion or alienate any of the denominations. In every major speech a President is likely to indicate what Franklin Roosevelt used to call the 'God stuff.' " And indeed, the speeches of Eisenhower and Kennedy were heavily sprinkled with references to God. The separation of church and state in America is largely a theoretical postulate.

Xenophobia is widespread in the South, as anyone who moves into the region, or travels through it, soon recognizes. It is one of the curious paradoxes of Southern life that suspicion of strangers, of outsiders, goes along with what is called "Southern hospitality." The answer to the paradox is that there is a line of demarcation which separates the accepted person from the unaccepted. Within that line, the warmth is almost overwhelming. But outside it, the coolness can become hostility to the point of violence. The foreign-born is almost always outside that line in the South, as is, of course, the Negro. So Southern hospitality exists, but within rigidly defined limits.

But isn't this true, though to a lesser extent, of the nation? Americans are considered generally to be warm and friendly people, unlike, let us say, the English. If other peoples criticize us, it is rather for being overbearingly friendly rather than withdrawn. We welcomed, let us recall, tens of millions of people from other countries to our shores, with virtually no restriction, for most of our history. But we too laid down our lines, and once laid down, those outside them were treated as coldly, as suspiciously, as any Yankee traveler in the Southern hills.

We began in 1882, with the Chinese, whom we had eagerly sought right after the Civil War as cheap labor to work on the railroads and in the mines, but who later were wanted neither by the industrialists nor the labor unions. The result was the Chinese Exclusion Act of that year. That inaugurated a period of 70 years during which we said very plainly to Asians, in the stiff words of a legislative enactment, that we wanted none of their kind in this country. Our national attitude toward Orientals was one reason for increasing irritation in our relations with Japan all through the early twentieth century up to Pearl Harbor. And our policy toward the immigration of Orientals today, as expressed in the McCarran-Walter Act of 1952, is hardly more friendly: we will admit a hundred Japanese a year, a hundred Chinese, a hundred Indonesians, as compared to tens of thousands for each major country in Western Europe. The message reads clearly to them: in the United States Asians are not wanted.

Our quotas are higher for Europeans, but still there are quotas. Nativism as a private action goes back to the early nineteenth-century resentment of the Irish immigrant; as a public policy it was first written into the law in the 1920s, and it remains on our national statute books in the quota system of the McCarran-Walter Act. The line remains drawn against most foreigners, though the placement of the line varies, depending on where the stranger comes from. Hospitality—in the law—goes first to the English, Irish, and Germans. The Italians, Greeks, and Eastern Europeans are definitely secondhand recipients of welcome. Africans and Asians are last.

Oscar Handlin's sympathetic study of immigrants, *The Uprooted,* which won a Pulitzer Prize, represents the more enlightened thinking in America on the subject of the foreign-born. But more Americans, I suspect, have gone along with the attitude of another historian, Samuel Orth, who wrote a study of immigrants called *Our Foreigners.* Orth saw the people of the Revolutionary epoch—Scotch, English, Irish, German, Dutch—as the "basic American stock." He then said:

Leadership . . . is the gift of but few races; and in the U.S. eminence in business, in statecraft, in letters and learning can with singular directness be traced in preponderating proportion to this American stock. . . . The Puritan, Cavalier, Quaker, Scotch-Irish, Huguenot, and Dutch pioneers were not ordinary folk in any sense of the term. They were, in a measure, a race of heroes. Their sons and grandsons inherited their vigor and their striving. It is not at all singular that every president of the United States and every chief justice of the Federal Supreme Court has come from this stock. . . .

Orth's views were set down in the early part of this century, but public-opinion polls of recent years indicate that the population is not much different today. A 1950 study by Hyman and Sheatsley concluded: "The majority of Americans appear to deny still another traditional feature of democracy, that of offering political asylum and refuge to homeless and oppressed peoples. Faced with the simple proposition of whether or not to admit a certain number of displaced persons from Europe, less than one person in four approved."

The same study found that most Americans who were given a list of seventeen nationalities found only five of these "as good as we are in all important respects." These were: the Canadians, English, Dutch, Scandinavians, and Irish. The rest were judged "not quite as good" or "definitely inferior."

Nativism not only keeps people out: it affects our relationship with those who have come in. And from the Alien Acts of 1798 to the Alien Registration Act of 1940 and the McCarran-Walter Act of 1952, our national policy has been to look with suspicion on the non-citizen.

Aliens must register every year with the government. An alien, in American judicial doctrine, is not entitled to the same constitutional rights accorded a citizen. An alien, for instance, can be deported for an act which has been made a crime ex post facto, though the Constitution bars ex post facto laws to punish Americans. Because aliens are tied in with foreign policy, an area where the national government has almost unlimited powers, Congress has broad legislative authority over them to an extent not true of citizens.

Even a person who has already become a citizen through naturalization is not looked upon by our government as an equal with all other United States citizens. According to the McCarran-Walter Act of 1952, if a naturalized citizen is convicted of contempt of Congress for refusing, within ten years of his naturalization, to testify before a congressional committee on his "subversive" activities, he may be deported. In other words, the Fifth Amendment provision against self-incrimination, and the First Amendment (which in some cases protects against political interrogation), cannot protect the naturalized citizen in any event, so long as the law remains what it is.

Until our national policies—on immigration, on aliens, on naturalization—are changed, until our national attitudes get closer to our oratorical claims, it ill becomes us to let the South bear the burden of the charge of nativism or xenophobia.

The deification of Southern womanhood, more a subject for bemused wonder than for intellectual analysis, has brought both admiration and ridicule. Cash calls it "downright gyneolatry." He says:

She was the South's Palladium, this Southern woman—the shield-bearing Athena gleaming whitely in the clouds, the standard for its rallying, the mystic symbol of its nationality in face of the foe. She was the lily-pure maid of Astolat and the hunting goddess of the Boeotian hill. And—she was the pitiful Mother of God. Merely to mention her was to send strong men into tears—or shouts. There was hardly a sermon that did not begin and end with tributes in her honor, hardly a brave speech that did not open and close with the clashing of shields and the flourishing of swords for her glory. At the last, I verily believe, the ranks of the Confederacy went rolling into battle in the misty conviction that it was wholly for her that they fought.

When Georgia celebrated her 100th anniversary in the 1830s, the toast was cheered 20 times: "Woman! The center and circumference, diameter and periphery, sine, tangent, and secant of all our affections!" And into the twentieth century the basic romantic myth remains the same: in the South the woman is enobled and glorious—only Robert E. Lee stands higher on his pedestal than she does.

Once the florid oratory is set aside, however, the elevation of woman—at least as a surface phenomenon—is seen to be a fact of national life. Tocqueville watched it in the North in the 1830s, and travelers from Europe and the Far East in this century show wonder at the degree of equality between men and women. The growing role of the President's wife, transformed from social accessory to thinking companion, is symbolic of what has been happening in this country: as total personalities, Eleanor Roosevelt and Jacqueline Kennedy were unmatched by president's wives of earlier centuries.

And then there is Marilyn Monroe. Deification moves from metaphor to reality with her, for she was a goddess to the American public, and her death was received as an almost religious mystery. Hollywood has supplied the nation with feminine objects of worship in a continuous stream, from Mary Pickford through Jean Harlow, Greta Garbow, Ingrid Bergman, and the wide-eyed Marilyn.

But now that we've paid obeisance to the tradition of glorification, we need to bring the analysis somewhat closer to the truth, both for the South and the nation. There were several crucial limitations to the Southern attitude. Remember, the phrase is really "Southern *white* womanhood." And *rich* white womanhood, too—for the poor white wife was hardly an object of worship in the South, then or now, bred in poverty, who spends much of her time in labor bearing children, and the rest of her time in labor between childbirths, is a thousand times more numerous than Scarlett O'Hara.

And even the white aristocratic woman,

back in slavery days—how genuine was the veneration, how deep the reverence, when the man of the house rushed as often as he could into sexual union with brown and black women? The existence of millions of tan and fair Negroes in America belies the image of the glorified Southern white woman. What more damning reminder is there of the emptiness of that claim that the white woman was the "center and circumference . . ." of affection than the fact that so often she waited at the periphery while her man was having sexual relations with a darker woman? The hurtful fact about the woman on the pedestal is that she is quite alone.

For the nation, as for the South, the fuss about womanhood has always been somewhat dishonest. The Southern veneration was circumscribed with modifications— whiteness, aristocratic birth, wealth, idleness; so was this true in the United States as a whole. In the country at large, to be considered superior a woman must have certain qualifications: beauty or talent, foremost. Brains alone, however, are not enough for a woman to gain genuine recognition. Mental agility, superior intelligence, bring tolerance and respect, but nothing like idolization; that is reserved for Venus or Diana, not for the lady Ph.D.

The difference in accent, North and South, the soft consonant and prolonged vowels of the Southern woman, conceal the essential similarity of the position of women in the nation, regardless of geographic section. The haughty Daughter of the Confederacy with the big hat at the garden club in Charleston, South Carolina, can hardly be distinguished, except in speech, from the equally haughty, equally big-hatted Daughter of the American Revolution at a lawn party in Newport, Rhode Island. Women in the textile mills, North and South, wear the same slacks, the same bandannas, and the same look of alienation from life.

Cash speaks of the "suppression of class feeling" in the South, both before the Civil War and after Reconstruction. He attributes this "social solidity" to the existence of the Negro as a drain for the ego of the Southern white, drawing off what might have been a natural hostility to the rich, Southern white man. And true, it was only *before* the cotton gin magnified and solidified slavery in the nineteenth century that occasional violent class explosions shook the South.

Bacon's Rebellion of 1676 was only one of many signs of sharp hostility between the frontier farmers and the seaboard aristocracy in Virginia and Maryland. And a century later, the Regulator Movement in the Carolinas expressed, by force of arms, resentments of the poor against the wealthy. In that hundred years between, many clashes of a class nature took place in the Southern colonies. What was said by a contemporary of Bacon was true of much of the South during that period: "Indigent People as had no benefits from the Taxes groaned under our being thus overborn."

No doubt the Negro, as slave before the Civil War and as semi-slave after the War, formed some sort of a block between the downtrodden white and the Southern aristocracy and diverted attention from obvious differences in wealth. Up North, in the same years when Nat Turner's insurrection was fresh in Virginia minds, working men were organizing in the cities of New York and Philadelphia. And the year 1877, which for the South meant preoccupation with the restoration of white supremacy, was the year when gunfire sounded along the railroad lines of the Northeast, and railway workers fought bloody battles against employers over wages and working conditions.

I am trying, in these paragraphs, to do justice to the real difference between North and South in the matter of class conflict and class consciousness, before I move to what I think is the larger truth and the more significant one for our national history: that such differences between North and South have been matters of degree, based on time and circumstance. In the longer perspective, both sections—Americans as a whole— despite periods of sporadic conflict, have moved into a semi-happy narcosis in which consciousness of class has been dulled.

That the South is perfectly capable of *class* violence is shown by the revolts referred to above in the colonial period and by isolated situations, like the Gastonia textile strike of the 1920's, as bitter in its own way as was the Lawrence, Massachusetts, textile strike of a decade earlier. That the South is also capable of subordinating race to class is shown in that brief interlude of the Populist period in the South, when there was some evidence that white and black farmers could be drawn together by common grievances against "the interests." And we get a glimmer of the possible in the South's embrace of Franklin D. Roosevelt during the depression.

True, the North between 1877 and 1940 (such a short span in our history, really!) was the scene of our most intense labor struggles, but this can be laid to the circumstances that brought industrial growth to that area first. And it is in the first agony of such growth (almost as peasants revolted against the Soviet collectivization of the thirties before settling down to live with it) that rebellion occurs. But there is nothing in "the Southern mind," no mystical quality of the Southern temper, which prevents the Southerner from feeling class hostility. As racism erodes and industrialization develops in the South, that chance may come.

True, our national class grievances are nowhere near as sharp as they might be; the distribution of wealth in Latin America, in the Middle East, is unspeakably more uneven. Yet we do have our poor. A substantial part of the nation has to battle every day to keep the family fed, clothed, sheltered, and alive. But the hurt is not so keen, apparently, that it cannot be suppressed by an injection of nationalism; this has always been the salve for internal discomfort, and it has never been available in such gross quantities as now.

Nationalism, manifested extremely in patriotism and superpatriotism, has often been seen as a distinctive Southern trait—oddly juxtaposed with the South's own jealous sectionalism. Aside from those few years around the Civil War, the South has been recognized as the most jingoistic of the sections, the most loudly reverent of the country, flag, national honor. After all, the Daughters of the American Revolution go further back than the Daughters of the Confederacy and are especially strong in the South. A formidable quintet of Virginians— Washington, Jefferson, Madison, Monroe, John Marshall—founded our nation and dominated those early patriotic years.

Southern estrangement from the nation during the Civil War soon ended, and when we fought Spanish armies in Cuba, the Gray stood alongside the Blue. After Appomattox, as before Bull Run, Southern men were especially prominent in the national military establishment. So the emphasis has continued to this day on the idea of a particularly "militant South."

And it is true. Yet, to dwell on that obscures another truth, perhaps more necessary to sober us in today's world; that militant nationalism has been a persistent United States tradition.

Today, sprawled comfortably across the continent from ocean to ocean, our eyes on the galaxies, we are bemused and irritated at what seems a petulant nationalism in the new nations of Africa and Asia. But we were quite feverish in those first decades after the Revolution—eyeing Canada and Florida, snapping at England, France, and Spain, finally devouring half of Mexico in a burst of indignation. Tocqueville had written, in Jackson's time: "Nothing is more embarrassing in the ordinary intercourse of life than this irritable patriotism of the Americans."

Still, nationalism was contained within the continent through most of the nineteenth century; we left Europe and Asia alone. Even after the Spanish-American War, perhaps because we were full of moralistic protestations, perhaps because the European powers were dividing up the world, we still had a look of innocence. This was not easy to maintain, because now we were firmly planted, not only in the Caribbean, but on the other side of the Pacific Ocean.

When we did enter European affairs in

World Wars I and II, it was with grand pronouncements. We fought to make the world safe for democracy the first time, to save the world from Hitlerism the second time; the idea that national interest—imagined in the first instance and real in the second—lay behind it all, was kept obscure. The $16 billion we gave through the Marshall Plan after the war was seen, not as a power move sweetened with good intention, but as nothing more than a sincere effort on our part to help the fallen world. That Asia, Africa, and Eastern Europe were more fallen but less politically susceptible was overlooked.

In the 1960s, if it was not clear before, it is now: Americans as a whole are hot for patriotism, armed and challenging and as self-glorifying as any Southern orator ever was.

Edmund Wilson, in *Patriotic Gore*, points out that the South, in the Civil War, always had its "Great Alibi" for retrogression and that the North has had its "Treasury of Virtue," which "has enabled us to carry along into all our subsequent wars . . . the insufferable moral attitudes that appeared to us first to be justified by our victory over the Confederacy in 1865."

The same goes for conservatism. It was the South that always talked of defending its "way of life." The nation was young, vigorous, forward-looking, the legend goes, and the South was recalcitrant, hugging its traditions, fearful of progress. Supporting this is the fact of our revolutionary tradition. Did not Tocqueville have to explain our rash radicalism, our equalitarianism, our upstart ideas, to the conservatives of Metternichean Europe? The reality of that revolutionary spirit is gone, but its aura remains, with which we find it convenient to belabor the "conservative South."

Today, however, it is the United States that talks of defending "its way of life" against revolutionary threats all over the world. We are now the conservative nation, trying to maintain the *status quo* against what appears to be a torrent of change threatening Western civilization. I am not attempting to assess the quality of our revolutionary ideals of the past as against the quality of the present upsurge, but only to assert that we stand fast, guarding the present, with as much nervous fear as any Southern politician has who holds on to what he is sure of, against the uncertainties of transformation.

The South is poor. Franklin D. Roosevelt called it the "Number One economic problem" of the United States. In 1959, when the median income for the United States was $5,600, in Mississippi it was $2,800, exactly half. While in that year 13 percent of the nation's families earned under $2,000, the percentage for Alabama was 26 percent, for Georgia 22 percent, for Mississippi 37 percent. Poverty marks the South today as clearly as cotton once did.

I do not want to challenge the fact that the South is poorer than the rest of the nation. But I do want to point to something which has been often overlooked (though in the year 1963, notice began to be taken): that there are large and numerous pockets of poverty in the United States as shocking as that one which is the South; that the idea of a rich North and a poor South is demolished by the statistics and the stories of human despair which come out of the cities of the North, out of the rundown little towns of New England and the Midwest. The divisions of rich and poor in this country do not run along sectional lines but exist, to different degrees, in every section of the country.

We reject poverty as a national problem when we relegate it to the South, with the implication that this is a startling divergence from the general United States picture of prosperity. A more accurate image is of a land where thin threads of wealth run through all the sections, along with broad shaded areas representing middle-class, mortgaged affluence, and of millions of people *everywhere,* fighting to meet the basic requirements of life for themselves and their children.

The realities of life are obscured under meaningless statistics when we measure the wealth of people in huge aggregates, pushing all people into one section or taking a national average. To say that the national average income is $5,600 is impressive in giving a picture of a quite well-off nation, but it doesn't do justice to the distinctions by group. When we move slightly closer to piecemeal examination, more light is shed on the subject of income distribution: in 1960, the lowest fifth of the United States population averaged about $1,500 a year in income and the highest fifth averaged about $15,000. And this is only the beginning of the process of making distinctions within the national average, only the first step toward a truly human appraisal of the extent of poverty in the United States. The details themselves have been well told in Michael Harrington's *The Other America* and Leon Keyserling's *Poverty and Deprivation in the U.S.*

Let me go back over my argument. The South is everything its revilers have charged, and more than its defenders have claimed. It is racist, violent, hypocritically pious, xenophobic, false in its elevation of women, nationalistic, conservative, and it harbors extreme poverty in the midst of ostentatious wealth. The only point I have to add is that

the United States, as a civilization, embodies all of those same qualities. That the South possesses them with more intensity simply makes it easier for the nation to pass off its characteristics to the South, leaving itself innocent and righteous.

In any truth which is knotted and complex, we can choose what strand we want to graps. To pick out the South has the advantage of focusing attention on what is worst; but it has the disadvantage of glossing over the faults of the nation. It is particularly appropriate in this time, when the power of the United States gives it enormous responsibility, to focus our critical faculties on those qualities which mark—or disfigure—our nation. With this approach, the South becomes not damnable, but marvelously useful, as a mirror in which the nation can see its blemishes magnified, so that it will hurry to correct them. In effective psychotherapy, the patient is at first disturbed by self-recognition, then grateful for the disclosure. It is the first step toward transformation, and in the 1960s, this nation, with its huge potential for good, needs to take another look in the mirror. We owe this to ourselves, and to our children.

BIBLIOGRAPHICAL NOTES

Since this book is primarily a speculative essay based on personal experience, I have not drawn up a formal bibliography. Nevertheless, I do want to call attention to certain books and articles that have stimulated my thinking, provided supporting facts, or otherwise had an effect on what has gone into this book.

In Part One, "Is the Southern White Unfathomable?" what started as a germ of an idea based on observation and experience became strengthened as I began to read the literature of post-Freudian psychology and certain works of sociology and history. Stanley Elkins's *Slavery* (University of Chicago Press, 1959), besides providing provocative insights, helped me to find a direction for my own thoughts. In one of the classics of sociological literature, E. A. Ross's *Social Control* (Macmillan, 1901), I found a perceptive set of distinctions relating to the attitudes of people involved in social change, and a very useful discussion of the relative weights of moral sentiment and self-interest in activating people. Another sociologist of the same generation, Charles H. Cooley, in *Social Organization* (Scribner's, 1909), made some interesting observations on conformity and its social uses. Karl Mannheim's *Ideology and Utopia* (Harcourt, Brace, 1940), is rich in comments on the participating intellectual, and the possibility of the social scientist being both a scholar and an activist. Robert K. Merton's *Social Theory and Social Structure* (Free Press, 1949) strengthened the conviction that the accuracy of social analysis depends on *social controls*. Melvin Tumin, in *Desegregation: Resistance and Readiness* (Princeton University Press, 1958), gives solid support, it seems to me, to the importance of distinguishing between idea and *action* in the attitudes and behavior of white Southerners. Sociologist Arnold M. Rose, in his article "The Influence of Legislation on Prejudice" in *Common Ground* (1949), showed early the value of firm authority in changing social practices. Among the social psychologists, there is, first, Harry Stack Sullivan, who, in *The Interpersonal Theory of Psychiatry* (Norton, 1953), buttresses optimism about the capacity of the white Southerner (and the white Northerner) to change his behavior swiftly. Kurt Lewin, in *Field Theory in Social Science* (Harper, 1951), goes into great detail to describe the effects of the *present* field on human behavior. Dorwin Cartwright continued Lewin's experimentation and reports on some of this in his article "Achieving Change in People," *Human Relations* (1951). I found particularly stimulating Gardner Murphy's *Personality*, and its discussion of "situationism" and "role." A good survey of the whole subject is in J. A. C. Brown's *Freud and the Post-Freudians* (Penguin Books, 1961). In Herbert Marcuse's *Eros and Civilization* (Beacon Press, 1955) and Norman O. Brown's *Life Against Death* (Wesleyan University Press, 1959), we have two brilliant arguments against what Marcuse calls "neo-Freudian revisionism." The social psychologist who has applied "situationist" theories most closely to the present race problem in America is Thomas Pettigrew, as in his article "Social Psychology and Desegregation Research," in *American Psychologist* (1961). A strong influence along the same lines is Gordon Allport, *The Nature of Prejudice* (Beacon Press, 1954). For a fresh view of race relations in the postbellum South, I drew upon C. Vann Woodward, *The Strange Career of Jim Crow* (Oxford University Press, 1957). Also a new Southern view is that of Dewey Grantham, *The Democratic South* (University of Georgia Press, 1963).

Part Two, "The 'Mysterious' Negro," is even more of a personal commentary than the first part of the book, and so does not come, at least directly, from other published works. Perhaps the best single dispeller of mistique about the Negro is W. E. B. DuBois's beautiful book, *Souls of Black Folk* (A. C. McClung, 1922). And I found many keen observations about Negro society today in E. Franklin Frazier's *Black Bourgeoisie* (Free Press, 1959). I was spurred to think about causation by reading in the philosophy of history, and found some support in E. H. Carr's *What Is History?* (Knopf, 1962), which advances something like the idea of "operable" cause which I set forth in this section.

Part Three, "Albany, Georgia: Ghost in the Cage," is based on personal experience and observation, interviews, and the newspaper reports during the Albany, Georgia, crises of 1961 and 1962, collected while I was doing my reports for the Southern Regional Council in Atlanta. The legal argumentation in this chapter utilizes material from the volume *Justice* put out in 1961 by the U.S. Commission on Civil Rights. I found Jack Greenberg's *Race Relations and American Law* (Columbia University Press, 1959) an indispensable reference work.

In Part Four, "The South as a Mirror," my starting point was Wilbur J. Cash's *The Mind of the South* (Knopf, 1946), a beautifully written book which captures so much of the South, past and present, and yet which also may have a narcotic effect on one's will for change. For the early history of the Negro in America, I have depended on John Hope Franklin, *From Slavery to Freedom* (Knopf, 1956). Valuable for the nineteenth century is Fanny Kemble's *Journal* (Carey, Lea, and Blanchard, 1835). Some of the material on abolitionism and on revivalism is drawn from Alice Felt Tyler's *Freedom's Ferment* (University of Minnesota, 1944). The reference to Richard Hofstadter's comment on the Emancipation Proclamation comes from one of the great books written by this generation of historians, his *The American Political Tradition* (Knopf, 1948). Material on anti-Negro attitudes in Michigan during Reconstruction came from an unpublished work by Ida Meltzer, *The Negro in Michigan 1865–70*. The brief comments on the social gospel movement are based on Stow Persons's *American Minds* (Holt, 1958).

1965

Southern History as Burden and Heritage[*]

C. VANN WOODWARD

The making of Southern mythology has not been an exclusively regional enterprise. No doubt Southerners themselves have been the most prolific contributors, but they have had too much assistance from outside to claim exclusive authorship. Northern contributions derive in part from felt needs and deprivations of Yankee culture that have sought fulfillment in compensatory fantasy. They include a secret yen for aristocracy and the associated airs of grace and decorum, an abiding nostalgia for an America that never really was. William R. Taylor, in *Cavalier and Yankee,* has shown to what a large extent the Cavalier myth was a Yankee creation and that few if any Southerners "really believed in the Cavalier—only in the need for him." Other components of the Northern contribution derive from an uneasy national conscience and the availability of the South as a repository for undischarged guilt as well as a convenient target for aggression. The dark legend of the Gothic South, land of evil, bad blood, degeneracy, and violence, owes much to this source.

Southern contributions to the myth grow out of more conventional needs for defense, self-flattery, and intersectional polemics. And on a more serious level they are part of the unending struggle to make the collective experience intelligible and meaningful. Whatever differences may exist between Northern and Southern sources and their respective handiwork, on one point there is general agreement—that the South is "different." And whether the differences are regarded with dismay and abhorrence or with pride and complacence, they are commonly described as deep and probably ineradicable.

Throughout the confrontation between North and South over school desegregation, civil rights, and voter registration there has been a mounting impatience among friends of the Negro movement with the uses to which the national mythology about the South have too frequently been put. The myth of a mysterious distinctiveness beyond the reach of reason and impervious to change has been employed as a fog to hide realities, an excuse for inaction, evasion, and postponement. It has helped to slow Deliberate Speed to a halt, to rationalize tokenism, and to justify defeatism. It is common to the thinking of liberals and moderates as well as conservatives and reactionaries. It is a mainstay of Southern defiance and a salve for Northern conscience.

Under these circumstances it is not surprising that a recent Northern work on Southern mythology should take the form of iconoclasm. This is a book by Howard Zinn that he chooses to call *The Southern Mystique*. It is clear that he means *myth* instead of

* C. Vann Woodward, "Southern Mythology," reprinted from *Commentary* (May, 1965), by permission; copyright 1965 by the American Jewish Committee.

mystique. A mystique is entirely the creation and possession of an ingroup. One can speak of the mystique *of* a group and a myth *about* a group. But one cannot properly write, as Mr. Zinn does, of "the American mystique about the South," or "the mystique with which Americans have always surrounded the South." The distinction is important because he is talking about a national credo, not a regional dogma. "We created the mystery of the South," he declares, "and we can dissolve it." "We," meaning Americans of all sections.

The avowed purpose of the book is "to dispose of the myth of Southern exceptionalism," to do it in, the whole thing, once and for all. Mystery in any department is anathema and must be banished. Mr. Zinn's method is not to deny the South the formidable array of characteristics traditionally attributed to it but to concede them and at the same time to claim them all as American characteristics. The South is simply America exaggerated, "the essence of the nation." The South is different without being distinctive. "It is different because it is a distillation of those traits which are the worst (and a few which are the best) in the national character." The South "crystallizes the defects." Instead of glossing over national faults by attributing them all to the South, Americans should regard the South "as a mirror in which the nation can see its blemishes magnified." To do so would be to turn self-flattery into self-recognition and insight of therapeutic value. The nation is thus not seen as the doctor, "but the next patient in line." We are all sick.

In the long roster of its revilers the South has rarely had so genial and disarming a critic. What has poisoned the North-South colloquy for a century and a half has been the standing indictment of self-righteousness and hypocrisy. The classic riposte of the South under attack is *tu quoque*: you're another—what about Harlem? Mr. Zinn's strategy is to smother the question with concessions. Harlem is "as terrible as any colored section of a Deep South city." Racism afflicts "the entire mind and body of the

American nation" and forms a "basic community of interest of all sections of the United States, reaching back to our earliest history." He obligingly documents these concessions with chapter and verse. New Jersey burned two Negroes at the stake for setting fire to barns in 1711, and in the same year New York hanged eighteen and burned thirteen alive—two a week, one hanged, one burned. And so on through the appalling record of the two centuries that followed, including the shameful timidity, vacillation, and compromise of the Civil War and Reconstruction, and the betrayal, desertion, and oppression of the years since. The conclusion is that "there is no part of the United States where Negroes as a group have ever stood equal with whites." The South remains, however, the main bastion of racism, "a kind of Fort Knox of prejudice—where the nation has always stored the bulk of its bigotry, while the rest has circulated—though sometimes stealthily—all over the country." The failure of national policy against racial discrimination and injustice is, nevertheless, attributed to "national weakness rather than to Dixie strength."

Having thus disposed of the myth of racist exceptionalism in the South, Mr. Zinn turns to other alleged Southern peculiarities in the same spirit of iconoclasm. These include such themes as violence, fundamentalism, xenophobia, nativism, chauvinism, absence of class feeling, prevalence of poverty, and what W. J. Cash called "downright gyneolatry," the cult of Southern womanhood. Like racism these are all conceded to be Southern traits, but at the same time the South is denied exclusiveness in their possession. They, too, are American. Mr. Zinn does not tackle all the myths, and the best he can do for his thesis in some cases is to maintain that the Southern characteristic is "only an intense form of what has gone on for so long in the whole nation," or that "such differences between North and South have been matters of degree, based on time and circumstances." Of course a sufficient difference in degree can produce a noticeable difference in kind. For all that, it is as well to have some towering pretensions toppled and a sense of proportion, not to say humor, restored.

One conspicuous omission among Mr. Zinn's targets of Southern exceptionalism is the historical experience of the region. This is not an oversight. With the best will in the world for sharing guilt, paranoia, and tragedy, the doctrine of anti-exceptionalism cannot be stretched to endow the North with the South's past. Other Americans are fortunate enough not to share two-and-a-half centuries of chattel slavery, a wild and disastrous adventure in secession and independence ending in crushing defeat, and another century begun with an abortive reconstruction and ending in a second one still in progress. Yet this is the only authentic basis of the South's claim to a distinctive heritage. That heritage can be, often has been, abused, but its distinctiveness cannot be denied.

Mr. Zinn, a historian, does not deny it. He dismisses it. His conviction is that we have an "overly heavy sense of history," and that "we are too much impressed with the power of the past. . . . Transfixed by the past, we escape responsibility for acting in the present. Thus history has become a burden rather than a guide. . . ." He would have us throw off the incubus of history, a 19th-century obsession, and dwell upon "all the possibilities for purposive social change in that old political adage which says that the public has a poor memory." It is only because 20th-century examples are "obnoxious to us" that we ignore the social lessons of "Hitler transforming the German people, the Communists burying centuries in Russia and millennia in China." All of which prove that "the past need not rest heavily on a determined people."

Along with the past, Mr. Zinn would cast off the burden of Freudian psychology, which he considers as much of an incubus upon the individual as history is upon society. Like history, this school of psychology, with its stress on the long arm of the past, especially the determinants of early childhood experience upon lifelong behavior, has "led to a pervasive pessimism about man and society." He embraces instead the "situational psychology" of men like Gardner Murphy, who hold that "the present situation may be far more important than any past experience" in determining behavior anr personality. "Given a changed situation, there is a changed role and consequently a changed personality." According to this school, human nature is so malleable that it will adapt "almost like a chameleon" to manipulated environment.

As test and proof of his hypotheses regarding history and psychology, Mr. Zinn offers testimony of his personal experiences in the Southern race crisis. No summer soldier in the Southern campaigns, he taught for seven years at a Negro college (Spelman) in Atlanta and took active part in sit-in and desegregation demonstrations there and at Albany, Georgia, and observed the movement in other states. As late as 1958 Atlanta was a tightly segregated city with an apparently solid white support behind the slogan, "Never." The change that followed was striking:

By 1963: the busses had desegregated; so had the public libraries, the rail and bus terminals, a number of theaters and restaurants downtown, the department store cafeterias, the opera, the municipal auditorium, the legitimate theater, the public schools, the colleges (public and private), several hotels, the plainclothes squad of the Police Department, the Fire Department, the baseball team, the tennis courts, the parks, the golf courses, the public swimming pools, the Chamber of Commerce, several professional organizations, the county committee of the Democratic party and even the Senate of the Georgia General Assembly!

This was all done without violence in a city with 350,000 white people, the overwhelming majority of whom preferred a segregated society, who could have prevented most of the change *"if they had cared enough."* The point is they did not care enough when it came to a showdown. They would have readily responded to yes-or-no questions of a public opinion pollster with a percentage of "no's" that would have made change appear hopeless. But a real-life situation is quite different from an abstract situation such as an opinion poll. In real life there were multiple choices, none of them perfect: riding an integrated bus or walking, and so with restaurants, parks, schools, etc. Or it might be as simple as a choice between creating a scene or passively submitting—with whatever grace and murderous emotional reservations. It is not the reservations or the emotions that are significant, we are told, but the behavior. And it is not personality or history that are the significant determinants of behavior, but the immediate circumstances, the expected "role." It is "the *situation,* rather than instinct or tradition," that is the key to the revolution, and the situation is "susceptible to manipulation." It is thus assumed that "in spite of the feelings of the Southern white, he can be induced to change his behavior, overnight," by skillful manipulation of sociological circumstances.

Our social engineer will take advantage of a number of human failings, now known as behavioral principles. One, already mentioned, is that "the public has a poor memory." Another is the individual's "need to conform to society at large." A third is "the need to meet the approval of a few people whose influence—consciously or unconsciously felt—is potent and continuous." A fourth is Mr. Zinn's own contribution growing out of personal experience, a doctrine heavily stressed and often repeated, that "the universal detergent for race prejudice is *contact*—massive, prolonged, equal, and intimate contact" between races.

Indiscriminate endorsement of this whole colorful assortment of psychological and sociological doctrines is asking a good deal. But one does not have to go that far to acknowledge the relevance of some of the insights provided. For one thing, they point up the fallacy in the pessimism founded on the opinion polls that register overwhelming percentages saying "Never," or the pessimism based on the solidarity of support for politicians dedicated to Massive Resistance. For another thing, they deal one more blow to the myth of incorrigible and immutable

Southern folkways and their imperviousness to rational appeal and legislative action. The plain and demonstrable fact is that in the last few years, in response to judicial decision and legislative enactments, the South has changed. It has changed deeply, widely, and rapidly. It has not changed as much as many would like or as much as it must to comply with the law or to live up to its own standards of justice. But it has changed. Southern whites and Southern Negroes and the relations between them have changed, and the changes are acknowledged and understood by both.

The analysis and theory of change and the technique of engineering it proposed by Mr. Zinn, however, are open to considerably more question. If change is to be accomplished at the cost of some sort of prefrontal lobotomy on society that blocks off the past irretrievably from the present, the cure may be worse than the malady. If change is only accomplished in contrived circumstances of the "immediate situation," upon individuals whose personality alters automatically with temporarily assigned "roles," the stability of the new order is in some doubt. The chameleon is, after all, proverbially adaptable. The situation may change again—"overnight"— and along with it our transmogrified white Southerner. And if all this is to be done by skilled social manipulation, one would wish to know a little more about the manipulator and his ultimate purposes. And one is reminded that the next manipulator may not be so benevolent in his purposes.

The panacea of massive contact as "the universal detergent for race prejudice" also leaves something to be desired. In the first place, the hypothesis is embarrassed for want of illustrative examples. The one illustration Mr. Zinn offers was shortly to prove singularly unfortunate—"Harlem, or Bedford-Stuyvesant, at the fringes of all-Negro neighborhoods, where whites and Negroes live as cordial neighbors." In the second place, the hypothesis embodies a self-fulfilling prophecy. If the contact is indeed "massive, prolonged, equal, and intimate," the obstacle of race prejudice will necessarily have been removed as a precondition. The segregationist panacea was that strict separation of the races would produce racial harmony. This has been proved false. It does not follow, however, that the opposite hypothesis is necessarily true.

Little comfort is to be derived from the alleged success of the great Twentieth-century experiments in obliterating the past that have been conducted in Russia, Germany, and China. It remains to be seen how much of the past has actually been obliterated, and the long-range cost of the experiments is still to be reckoned. It is true that these experiments are pronounced "obnoxious" by Mr. Zinn, but he shows a disturbing willingness to learn from their techniques of burying or manipulating the past.

It is difficult to imagine where the civil rights movement and the Negro Revolution would be, or how they could be at all, without the past and without constant reference to the past. The white man is not the only Southerner with a history. The Negro is another American minority with a distinctive, un-American experience of history. And that experience has informed and colored every phase of the present movement and endowed it with its basic philosophy. Nonviolence is not an invention of white intellectuals, or whites of any sort, nor was it borrowed from India. It was born out of the anguish of an encounter with the white man through the centuries of his greatest power and arrogance. It saw the Negro through slavery, Civil War, and Reconstruction, in all of which he rejected the bloody tactics urged by well-wishers. And his steadfast adherence to the wisdom of his historic experience explains in large part why he, and not the red Indian, is the center of attention today.

But there is more of the past in the present than philosophy. There are also the music and the rhythm and the words, the songs the people sing and the way they sing them and the meaning behind them, the unfathomable simplicity and the sly pun, the inexhaustible patience and the unflagging purpose, songs of King Jesus and the weary blues, the

imagery and rhetoric of the speeches and the shouted response of the audience. To hear Mahalia Jackson sing, or Fannie Lou Hamer speak, or Martin Luther King preach is to be overwhelmed with the elemental impact of the past on the present. Cut these people off from the past and they would be struck mute.

There are, of course, other potent reminders of the past, the sort of past without which the savagery and brutality of Oxford and Birmingham and Selma are unimaginable. That is the Southern white past according to the historiography of Professor Mink Snopes and his patron, Ross Barnett. If that is accepted as the authentic reading of Southern history we really had better turn it all over to the sanitation department of the social engineers. Fortunately there are rival readings of Southern history that do not square with the Snopes version. They expose its sham, its hypocrisy, and its self-deception. The Southerner will find liberation instead of bondage in his true history. He will find in it persuasive evidence of the futility of erecting blockades against new ideas and attempting to stop the clock of history. He will recognize what obscene caricatures some of his present spokesmen have made of the best in his tradition. And he can gain some degree of immunity from the American myths of success and affluence and innocence and invincibility, which have little foundation in his own heritage.

There is no more use trying to persuade the white Southerner that he is a black man with a white skin than there is trying to persuade the Negro that he is a white man with a black skin—or trying to persuade both of them that they are undifferentiated and indistinguishable Americans with a slight accent. They are the oldest, the largest, and the most incorrigible of the hyphenate American minorities. "Negroes and white Southerners do, in fact, want to be Americans," as Robert Penn Warren remarks, "but by and large, they want to be themselves too; and the fact that both belong to minorities means that both may cling defensively to what they are, or what they take themselves to be.

They may refuse to be totally devalued, gutted and scraped before being flung into the melting pot." There is, of course, a Southern counterpart of the transplanted Yankee who seeks to outdo the natives in being Southern—just as there is a white counterpart of the Negro who tries abjectly to be a white man. But none of these performances, however expert, really commands respect or encourages self-respect. And none of them rings true psychologically as a solution to problems of identity—racial, regional, or national. In each of them there is a large ingredient of self-hatred. And self-hatred is hardly the healthiest foundation for identity or the soundest foundation for the new order that is now struggling to be born in the South.

CHAPTER 4

The Social Sciences and Recent Interpretations of Slavery

Most Americans began the twentieth century with profound reservations about "the lesser breeds" of men "within our gates." Did the "barbarous" (or "decadent") Orientals really belong in the United States? Most importantly, could the "intrinsically inferior" Negro ever really be assimilated? The answers to these questions were generally negative. Between 1883 and 1924 the United States excluded Asian and African immigration and in 1924 sharply curtailed the admission of "the inferior stocks" of Eastern and Southern Europe. Around the world Europeans carried "the white man's burden" and ruled black, brown, and red men. Citizens, politicians, and diplomats shared common ideas with most social scientists; and anthropologists, social psychologists, and sociologists confidently classified the "superior" and the "primitive" peoples and carried on a sustained debate using terms such as "racial characteristics" and "Caucasian civilization."

It is hardly surprising that historians belonged to this broadly based consensus; that a scholar like Ulrich B. Phillips charted the wastes of African "savagery" with the help of anthropologists; and that they in turn learned from him. While Phillips, the son of a Louisiana planter and a warm admirer of the antebellum South, may have had special reasons for his racial beliefs, he found them supported in academies throughout the country. His two books on slavery, published in 1918 and 1928, served for a generation as the almost universally accepted authoritative accounts and are still used in some colleges and universities. Phillips, despite many fine qualities such as erudition, an ample knowledge of plantation sources, and an eminently "reasonable" tone, worked from a racist context of assumption and argument which is totally unacceptable today. Phillips' Negroes, some of whom "resembled the orang-utan," moved from savagery into "the civilizing agency" of "Caucasian" culture. Although he granted his "abolitionist" opponents several points—he admitted that the slave trade was destructive and that the plantation had its harsher aspects—he nevertheless insisted that "the wrench from Africa" affected the Negro "temperament" little more than "his complexion." The white master merely replaced the African chief, and those Africans exempted from "happier futures" were left to the fate of "the African jungle with its bloody spectacle of human sacrifice and cannibalism." Even the descendants of abolitionists had come to recognize "the inherited inequality of the races and the unfitness of negroes to conduct white men's government."

The attribution of personality, individual conduct, and group behavior to "racial traits" lost credibility over a generation ago, and for years men have recognized the arbitrary nature of the old racial definitions and the total inadequacy of such concepts as African "savagery" and "Nordic" or "Caucasian" civilization. Melville Herskovits and Franz Boas might be cited as intellectual pioneers of the 1920s who did much to alter dominant notions of race and culture. The old patterns of thought which did not recognize the existence of a Negro past and cultural heritage were attacked by Herskovits in 1928 and again in 1941. If he exaggerated the extent of African "cultural survivals" in America, his mistakes were more than balanced by his presentation of a wealth of evidence on the vitality, diversity, creativity, and the history of the West African lands from whence so many Negroes had come. Boas led the scientific campaign to disassociate culture from race. His numerous books, articles, and lectures were followed by major studies of other scholars culminating in Gunnar Myrdal's famous report of 1944 on the tensions in a society which harbors both democratic values and racial oppression. While *The American Dilemma* has been made partly obsolete by the thousands of social science investigations of the past decades, it continues to be useful in many ways, and particularly as a summary of the 20 years of scholarship prior to 1944. To illustrate the trends of an entire generation two monographic studies can be cited. In 1937 John Dollard, a Yale social psychologist, published a book on the social structure of a Southern town controlled by the iron hand of a ruling white caste which dominated and demoralized the Negroes as an "inferior" caste. Fourteen years later, two psychiatrists, Abram Kardiner and Lionel Ovesey dealt with the psychological havoc wreaked by caste in a study which presented both individual case histories and group findings. A carefully analyzed series of Rohrschach tests revealed powerful mutilation fantasies and intense fears of the social environment; the same responses among white patients would have indicated homicidal tendencies, but the fears of many Negroes seemed to be "realistic," a "normal" adjustment to life in a hostile white world. Kardiner and Ovesey used the title *Mark of Oppression*, and a comparable sociological monograph bore the title *Children of Bondage*. If modern life could be so painful for black citizens, could slavery have actually been the mild and useful institution that Phillips and others had described? And if not, why did historians continue to use Phillips' ideas and propagate his opinions? If racial explanations were no longer considered valid, why did not all historians abandon them? Why did historians fail to use the new information, ideas, and insights of the social sciences? Ultimately many historians did move with the times, and the question is in large part one of cultural lag and the lack of communication between disciplines.

Even before the new ideas of the social sciences became generally known, some scholars began to develop new explanations from within the discipline and to move away from the timeworn stereotypes. In 1931 Frederic Bancroft produced a meticulously documented study which revealed the extent to which the domestic slave trade had disorganized and brutalized Negro life, the dependency of the Southeastern economy on the sale of slaves westward, and the role played by men from the highest social strata in the business of slave trading. Undoubtedly the continuing efforts of Carter G. Woodson and other Negro scholars had some influence, and popular books such as Henrietta Buckmaster's dramatic story of 1941 on the Underground Railroad gained the attention of many readers. The once neglected *Journal of Negro History* came into its own with dozens of articles such as Raymond A. and Alice H. Bauer's account in 1942 of "Day to Day Resistance to Slavery" and Harvey Wish's report of 1937 on slave disloyalty. The most sweeping attack on the stereotype of the inferior and contented slaves was provided in 1943 by Herbert Aptheker who presented a slave society almost constantly seething with plots, conspiracies, and rebellions. Although Aptheker's book relied little upon Marxist doctrine and was carefully based on extensive newspaper files, it was often dismissed for its "dogma" or its "exaggerations." Yet if only a fraction of the incidents were true he had made his case, and the fact of the slave master's belief in all of these rebellious acts is an important psychological clue which has still not been fully explored.

Meanwhile Phillips came under indirect attack by Richard Hofstadter in 1944 for relying on sources from the large plantations rather than the more representative smaller ones. (In 1962 Phillips was again taken to task by Ruben F. Kugler for willing and frequent distortion of evidence.) Hofstadter also suggested that another scholar with the same evidence and different presuppositions would reach far different conclusions. He called for a study oriented toward the slave himself and written by a scholar with both a knowledge of modern cultural anthropology and a comprehensive grasp of the concepts and procedures of modern social psychology.

The book called for by Hofstadter appeared in 1956 under the authorship of Kenneth M. Stampp. In the first few pages Stampp deftly and convincingly laid to rest the old racial and social myths which described white men as biologically unsuited for labor in the cotton fields and insisted upon the absolute need for slavery in the settlement of the country. After reading Stampp one was left with the conclusion that slavery did not represent the movement from "savagery to civilization" but an oppressive social institution for economic exploitation which ripped the captive violently from an organic position in a viable society and placed him "between two cultures." Ironically, it was the relatively high achievement of African agriculture which made the successful use of African slaves possible, and to compound the irony slave masters argued that the Negro was more "enslavable" than the nomadic Indian because Africans were more "barbarous" and "primitive." Stampp gained a wide hearing because he had mastered more plantation records than Phillips or any other scholar, but it was his familiarity with the best of modern social sciences and his ability to interpret psychological and social data so keenly which gave his work special distinction.

Stampp's book did not, however, end the scholarly debate over slavery. Other approaches were clearly possible. Eight years before the appearance of Stampp's work, Frank Tannenbaum had issued a slender volume on slavery in North and South America based on a standard approach (used by the social sciences) of comparing institutions across cultural lines. Borrowing insights and techniques from Tannenbaum and Stampp, Stanley M. Elkins in 1959 attempted to extend the comparison between slavery in "the liberal, Protestant, secularized, capitalist culture of the North" and "the conservative, paternalistic, Catholic, quasi-medieval culture of Spain and Portugal." The "conservative and quasi-medieval" factors tended to create in the New World an elaborate hierarchy of status groups in which color was only one feature among many, in contrast to the ruthless Northern dichotomy of black or white, slave or free, which produced in the United States a more oppressive system and "the most implacable race consciousness ever studied." The English law did not recognize slavery, and thus the system was allowed to grow in the direction of total power; whereas Spain and Portugal with long experience of regulated slavery and a code going back to Roman times tended to develop more limited forms of enslavement in their colonies. The Anglican establishment, a national "consensus" church based on a very broad religious settlement, lacked the fervor and the institutions for dynamic missionary work and in fact did not play a large role in the fate of the slave. However, the militant Counter-Reformation Catholic Church of Spain and Portugal did have both a great missionary drive and the institutions necessary to influence the life of the slave. Almost from the beginning Anglican parishes in Virginia exercised a substantial amount of home rule and were subjected only to loose supervision by the English hierarchy. Conversely the slave in South America tended to have more access to baptism, marriage, property ownership, and better prospects after emancipation, because institutions such as the crown, the church, the legal code, and Hispanic social patterns mediated between master and slave in contrast to the North where very little stood between the master and totalitarian power.

In an even more dramatic comparison Elkins used psychological data on the survivors of the Nazi death camps to draw an analogy between the prisoners' experience and that of the slaves. The Nazi camp data revealed instances in which the shock and trauma of midnight arrests, transportation under inhuman conditions, discovery of the sinister purpose of the camps, and the desperate marginal survival of a few in the midst of the constant "production of corpses" in "the death factory" led to a collapse of personality and the infantilization of the survivors. Personality patterns were reshaped under the sinister power of camp guards who as the masters of food, life, and death functioned as "perverse father figures" in the restructuring of personality. Elkins then compared this process with the experience of the slave passing through the shock of capture, abrupt removal to alien cultural circumstances, the long and painful march to the sea, the dehumanization of inspection and sale in the coastal barracoons, the oppressive and death-ridden middle passage across the Atlantic, and the usual "seasoning" through brutal adaptation to slave plantation "training" in the West Indies, and ultimate arrival in North America. After the first generation of enslavement, the process was largely a question of rearing children in a framework of slavery. To many scholars the analogy seemed strained or offensive, and the irreducible minimum of slave resistance seemed to belie the theory. Elkins also advanced some dubious speculations about the abolitionists and attempted without success to remove the slavery debate from the realm of moral judgments where it had flourished under scholars from Phillips to Stampp. Moreover, Tannenbaum and Stampp had preceded him in the comparison of institutions and the question of psychological damage. Even so, if Elkins' analogy is taken merely as a very broad statement used to express a tendency in the slave system rather than a comprehensive "realistic" description, the analogy has significant value.

The whole controversy emphasizes the difficulty of summarizing exactly the nature of slavery, and suggests the ultimate inaccessibility of the mind and thought of the slave. The slave narratives are very useful but leave much to be desired. In 1963 Wayman B. McLaughlin suggested one of the few roads which seemed to lead directly into the slave experience itself. McLaughlin, taking his cue from Eric Fromm's psychoanalytic study of religious symbolism, probed Negro spirituals for the psychological symbols of alienation, oppression, and the intense yearning for escape from slavery into a transcendent freedom. To assume, however, that these songs and Elkins' analogy tell the whole story would be to fall into the old fallacies which made the Negro as slave *and* citizen "the invisible man" to most Americans. The evidence on slavery clearly points to remnants of independence and moments of pleasure, and reminds the modern scholar that some slaves took the road of flight, rebellion, or "day to day resistance." The defenders of caste and slavery believed that the slave existed only as child, brute, and victim. Yet slavery did not render incompetent the 150,000 soldiers whose service was so vital to Union victory. Kenneth W. Porter in 1964 revealed the extent to which the long and bloody "Seminole" wars were also the struggles of fugitive slaves. It is difficult to exaggerate the destructive nature of slavery, but the balanced account will also note that great numbers escaped from slavery to function successfully as rebels, sailors, soldiers, cowboys, skilled workers, and masters of that most difficult art of human survival in a militantly hostile environment.

BIBLIOGRAPHY

Books and Articles Referred to in the Chapter Introduction

Ulrich B. Phillips, *American Negro Slavery* (1918), and *Life and Labor in the Old South* (1929).

Melville Herskovits, *The Myth of the Negro Past* (1941) and *The American Negro* (1928).

Gunnar Myrdal, *An American Dilemma* (1944).

John Dollard, *Caste and Class in a Southern Town* (1937).

Abram Kardiner and Lionel Ovesey, *The Mark of Oppression: A Psychosocial Study of the American Negro* (1951).

Allison Davis and John Dollard, *Children of Bondage* (1940).

Frederic Bancroft, *Slave-Trading in the Old South* (1931).

Carter G. Woodson and Charles H. Wesley, *The Negro in Our History* (10th ed., 1962).

Henrietta Buckmaster, *Let My People Go: The Story of the Underground Railroad and the Growth of the Abolition Movement* (1941).

Raymond A. and Alice H. Bauer, "Day to Day Resistance to Slavery," *Journal of Negro History* (1942).

Harvey Wish, "American Slave Insurrections Before 1861," *Journal of Negro History* (1937).

Herbert Aptheker, *American Negro Slave Revolts* (1943).

Richard Hofstadter, "U. B. Phillips and the Plantation Legend," *Journal of Negro History* (1944).

Ruben F. Kugler, "U. B. Phillips' Use of Sources," *Journal of Negro History* (1962).

Frank Tannenbaum, *Slave and Citizen: The Negro in the Americas* (1947).

Suggested Reading

For a list of nearly 500 articles and books in the social sciences dealing with the American Negro, see the footnotes to Thomas F. Pettigrew, *A Profile of the Negro American* (1964). For reminiscences of former slaves see B. A. Botkin, *Lay My Burden Down* (1945). On the changing attitudes toward color by Negroes themselves and the relations of these changes to international and domestic politics, see Harold R. Isaacs, *The New World of Negro Americans* (1963). On racism in most areas of American life and thought, see Thomas F. Gossett, *Race: The History of an Idea in America* (1963) and I. A. Newby, *Jim Crow's Defense, Anti-Negro Thought in America: 1900–1930* (1965). Some interesting comparisons of slavery and of color status differences can be found in M. G. Smith, "Slavery and Emancipation in Two Societies," *Social and Economic Studies* (1954); Stanley M. Elkins, "Culture Contacts and Negro Slavery," *Proceedings of the American Philosophical Society* (1963). On the question of "totalitarian" rule vs. slave resistance, Richard C. Wade argued that the Denmark Vesey affair was not an authentic conspiracy to revolt: see "The Vesey Plot," *Journal of Southern History* (1964). This conclusion was denied by John Lofton; *Insurrection in South Carolina* (1964). Wade discussed an environment in which the slaves were at least one step closer to freedom in *Slavery in the Cities* (1964), and Clement Eaton gave new evidence on a practice which provided the slaves with a small measure of freedom in "Slave-Hiring in the Upper South," *Mississippi Valley Historical Review* (1960). On the question of whether slavery was a declining and unprofitable institution, see Stampp and Elkins. For a partial summary of the controversy see Harold D. Woodman, "The Profitability of Slavery: A Historical Perennial," *Journal of Southern History* (1963). Much of the modern discussion revolves around the work of Alfred H. Conrad and John R. Meyer, "The Economics of Slavery in the Ante Bellum South," *Journal of Political Economy* (1958). Evidence on this point and others is given in Eugene D. Genovese, *The Political Economy of Slavery* (1965). See also Genovese, "The Significance of the Slave Plantation for Southern Economic Development," *Journal of Southern History* (1962). For other comparative points of view on slavery see Arnold A. Sio, "Interpretations of slavery: the Slave Status in the Americas," *Comparative Studies in Society and History* (1965); William L. Westermann, *Slave Systems of Greek and Roman Antiquity* (1955); Clarence Martin Wilbur, *Slavery in China During the Former Han Dynasty* (1943); and Moses I. Finley, *Slavery in Classical Antiquity* (1961). Roderick M. Nash gave an example of Negro resistance to Southern slave kidnappers operating in Pennsylvania; see *"William Parker and the*

Christiana Riot," Journal of Negro History (1961). For some former slaves who violated all the stereotypes, see Ralph A. Smith, "The Mamelukes of West Texas and Mexico," *West Texas History Year Book* (1963), and Philip Durham and Everett L. Jones, *The Negro Cowboys* (1965). The early chapters in *The Negro Family in the United States* by E. Franklin Frazier are very useful, as is *The Negro Church in America* (1964) by the same author. For an example of more freedom than one supposes was generally possible in slavery, see John H. Moore, "Simon Gray, Riverman: A Slave Who Was Almost Free," *Mississippi Valley Historical Review* (1962). On the interpretation of symbols, see Erwin R. Goodenough, "Symbols as Historical Evidence," *Diogenes* (1963).

1956

The Travail of Slavery*

KENNETH M. STAMPP

... A wise master did not take seriously the belief that Negroes were natural-born slaves. He knew better. He knew that Negroes freshly imported from Africa had to be broken in to bondage; that each succeeding generation had to be carefully trained. This was no easy task, for the bondsman rarely submitted willingly. Moreover, he rarely submitted completely. In most cases there was no end to the need for control—at least not until old age reduced the slave to a condition of helplessness.

Masters revealed the qualities they sought to develop in slaves when they singled out certain ones for special commendation. A small Mississippi planter mourned the death of his "faithful and dearly beloved servant" Jack: "Since I have owned him he has been true to me in all respects. He was an obedient trusty servant. . . . I never knew him to steal nor lie and he ever set a moral and industrious example to those around him. . . . I shall ever cherish his memory." A Louisiana

sugar planter lost a "very valuable Boy" through an accident: "His life was a very great one. I have always found him willing and obedient and never knew him to fail to do anything he was put to do."[1] These were "ideal" slaves, the models slaveholders had in mind as they trained and governed their workers.

How might this ideal be approached? The first step, advised those who wrote discourses on the management of slaves, was to establish and maintain strict discipline. An Arkansas master suggested the adoption of the "Army Regulations as to the discipline in Forts." "They must obey at all times, and under all circumstances, cheerfully and with alacrity," affirmed a Virginia slaveholder. "It greatly impairs the happiness of a negro, to be allowed to cultivate an insubordinate temper. Unconditional submission is the only footing upon which slavery should be placed. It is precisely similar to the attitude of a minor to his parent, or a soldier

[1] Baker Diary, entry for July 1, 1854; Alexander Franklin Pugh MS Plantation Diary, entry for June 21, 1860.

to his general." A South Carolinian . . . [de-scribed] a perfect relationship between a slave and his master: . . . "the slave should know that his master is to govern absolutely, and he is to obey implicitly. . . . He is never for a moment to exercise either his will or judgment in opposition to a positive order."[2]

The second step was to implant in the bondsmen themselves a consciousness of personal inferiority. They had "to know and keep their places," to "feel the difference be-tween master and slave," to understand that bondage was their natural status. They had to feel that African ancestry tainted them, that their color was a badge of degradation. In the country they were to show respect for even their master's nonslaveholding neigh-bors; in the towns they were to give way on the streets to the most wretched white man. The line between the races must never be crossed, for familiarity caused slaves to for get their lowly station and to become "impu-dent."[3]

Frederick Douglass explained that a slave might commit the offense of impudence in various ways: "in the tone of an answer; in answering at all; in not answering; in the expression of countenance; in the motion of the head; in the gait, manner and bear-ing of the slave." Any of these acts, in some subtle way, might indicate the absence of proper subordination. "In a well regulated community," wrote a Texan, "a Negro takes off his hat in addressing a white man. . . . Where this is not enforced, we may always look for impudent and rebellious Ne-groes."[4]

The third step in the training of slaves was to awe them with a sense of their mas-ter's enormous power. The only principle upon which slavery could be maintained, reported a group of Charlestonians, was the "principle of fear." In his defense of slavery

James H. Hammond admitted that this, un-fortunately, was true but put the responsi-bility upon the abolitionists. Anti-slavery agitation had forced masters to strengthen their authority: "We have to rely more and more on the power of fear. . . . We are de-termined to continue masters, and to do so we have to draw the reign tighter and tighter day by day to be assured that we hold them in complete check." A North Carolina mis-tress, after subduing a troublesome domes-tic, realized that it was essential "to make them stand in fear"![5]

In this the slaveholders had considerable success. Frederick Douglass believed that most slaves stood "in awe" of white men; few could free themselves altogether from the notion that their masters were "invested with a sort of sacredness." Olmsted saw a small white girl stop a slave on the road and boldly order him to return to his plantation. The slave fearfully obeyed her command. A visitor in Mississippi claimed that a master, armed only with a whip or cane, could throw himself among a score of bondsmen and cause them to "flee in terror." He accom-plished this by the "peculiar tone of author-ity" with which he spoke. "Fear, awe, and obedience . . . are interwoven into the very nature of the slave."[6]

The fourth step was to persuade the bondsmen to take an interest in the mas-ter's enterprise and to accept his standards of good conduct. A South Carolina planter explained: "The master should make it his business to show his slaves, that the ad-vancement of his individual interests is at the same time an advancement of theirs. Once they feel this, it will require but little compulsion to make them act as it becomes them."[7] Though slaveholders induced only a few chattels to respond to this appeal, these few were useful examples for others.

---

[2] *Southern Cultivator*, IV (1846), pp. 43–44; XVIII (1860), pp. 304–5; *Farmers' Register*, V (1837), p. 32.

[3] *Southern Planter*, XII (1852), pp. 376–79; *Southern Cultivator*, VIII (1850), p. 163; *Farm-ers' Register*, I (1834), pp. 564–65.

[4] Douglass, *My Bondage*, p. 92; Austin *Texas State Gazette*, October 10, 1857.

[5] Phillips (ed.), *Plantation and Frontier*, II, pp. 108–11; *De Bow's Review*, VII (1849), p. 498; Mary W. Bryan to Ebenezer Pettigrew, October 20, 1835, Pettigrew Family Papers.

[6] Douglass, *My Bondage*, pp. 250–51; Olmsted, *Back Country*, pp. 444–45; [Ingraham], *South-West*, II, pp. 260–61.

[7] *Farmers' Register*, IV (1837), p. 574.

The final step was to impress Negroes with their helplessness, to create in them "a habit of perfect dependence" upon their masters.[8] Many believed it dangerous to train slaves to be skilled artisans in the towns, because they tended to become self-reliant. Some thought it equally dangerous to hire them to factory owners. In the Richmond tobacco factories they were alarmingly independent and "insolent." A Virginian was dismayed to find that his bondsmen, while working at an iron furnace, "got a habit of roaming about and *taking care of themselves.*" Permitting them to hire their own time produced even worse results. "No higher evidence can be furnished of its baneful effects," wrote a Charlestonian, "than the unwillingness it produces in the slave, to return to the regular life and domestic control of the master."[9]

A spirit of independence was less likely to develop among slaves kept on the land, where most of them became accustomed to having their master provide their basic needs, and where they might be taught that they were unfit to look out for themselves. Slaves then directed their energies to the attainment of mere "temporary ease and enjoyment." "The masters," Olmsted believed, "calculated on it in them—do not wish to cure it—and by constant practice encourage it."[10]

Here, then, was the way to produce the perfect slave: accustom him to rigid discipline, demand from him unconditional submission, impress upon him his innate inferiority, develop in him a paralyzing fear of white men, train him to adopt the master's code of good behavior, and instill in him a sense of complete dependence. This, at least, was the goal.

But the goal was seldom reached. Every master knew that the average slave was only an imperfect copy of the model. He knew that some bondsmen yielded only to

superior power—and yielded reluctantly. This complicated his problem of control.

* * * * *

"Never be induced by a course of good behavior on the part of the Negroes, to relax the strictness of your discipline. . . . The only way to keep a Negro honest is not to trust him. This seems a harsh assertion; but it is unfortunately, too true." So wrote a Southerner who was giving advice to overseers. To a former slave it sometimes appeared that masters, "with skilled and practiced eyes," probed into the chattel's mind and heart to detect his changing moods. A slave, Olmsted observed, "is trusted as little as possible to use his own discretion, and it is taken for granted that he will never do anything desired of him that he dares avoid."[11]

Although cruelty was endemic in all slaveholding communities, it was always most common in newly settled regions. Along the rough southern frontier thousands of ambitious men were trying swiftly to make their fortunes. They operated in a frantically competitive society which provided few rewards for the virtues of gentility and almost put a premium upon ruthlessness. In the eastern tobacco and rice districts brutality was unquestionably less prevalent in the nineteenth century than it had been during the colonial period. But in the Southwest only limited areas had developed a mellowed gentry as late as 1860. In the Alabama-Mississippi Black Belt, in the cotton and sugar parishes of Louisiana, along the Arkansas River, and in eastern Texas the master class included the "parvenus," the "cotton snobs," and the "Southern Yankees." If these planters failed to observe the code of the patrician, they apparently thought none the less of each other for it.

The hired slave stood the greatest chance of subjection to cruel punishments as well

[8] *Southern Cultivator*, IV (1846), p. 44.
[9] *Southern Planter*, XII (1852), pp. 376–79; Olmsted, *Seaboard*, pp. 58–59; Charleston *Courier*, September 12, 1850.
[10] Olmsted, *Seaboard*, pp. 128–29.

[11] Printed instructions in Affleck, *Cotton Plantation Record and Account Book;* Douglass, *My Bondage*, pp. 276–77; Olmsted, *Seaboard*, pp. 478–79.

as to overwork. His employer, a Kentucky judge confessed, had no incentive to treat him kindly "except the mere feelings of humanity, which we have too much reason to believe in many instances . . . are too weak to stimulate the active virtue."[12] This was no exaggeration.

Southerners who were concerned about the welfare of slaves found it difficult to draw a sharp line between acts of cruelty and such measures of physical force as were an inextricable part of slavery. Since the line was necessarily arbitrary, slaveholders themselves disagreed about where it should be drawn. Was it barbarous to "correct" a slave by putting him in the stocks, or by forcing him to wear chains or an iron collar? How severely might a slave be flogged before the punishment became brutal? These were matters of personal taste.

But no master denied the propriety of giving a moderate whipping to a disobedient bondsman. During the seventeenth and eighteenth centuries the lash was used to punish free men as well as slaves. By mid-nineteenth century, however, it was seldom used upon any but slaves, because public opinion now considered it to be cruel. Why it was less cruel to whip a bondsman was a problem that troubled many sensitive masters. That they often had no choice as long as they owned slaves made their problem no easier to resolve.

Bennet H. Barrow, a Louisiana planter, kept an unusually full record of punishments—a record which illustrates the difficulty of distinguishing between cruelty and reasonable "correction." A substantial and respected man in his community, Barrow inherited lands and slaves from his father; he was in no sense a crude parvenu. Yet he flogged his chattels freely, sometimes severely. On various occasions he had a "general whipping frollick," whipped "every hand in the field . . . comencing with the driver," or gave "a number of them a good flogging." He broke his sword cane on the head of one offending slave, "beat" another

"very much" and "cut him with a club in 3 places verry bad." Barrow was one of the few large planters who refused to employ overseers, because of their bad reputation.[13]

If it was cruel to flog slaves so frequently and severely that their backs were permanently scarred, southern newspapers provided evidence of an abundance of this variety of inhumanity. The following illustrations are from antebellum fugitive-slave advertisements and from sheriffs' committal notices: Charles, "an old sinner" who escaped from a Louisiana plantation, had "many stripes of the lash"; a Mississippi slave had "large raised scars or whelks in the small of his back and on his abdomen nearly as large as a person's finger"; Nancy, a Georgia slave, was "considerably marked by the whip"; Esther, an Alabama slave, was "marked about the shoulders from whipping"; a Missouri fugitive had "many scars on his back"; Gid, according to his North Carolina master, had a "remarkably bad temper" and had in consequence "marks of the lash upon his back"; Tom, who was held by the jailer of Augusta County, Virginia, had "the appearance of frequent and severe flogging"; Anaca, who escaped from her Kentucky master, had "a large scar immediately on her chest from the cut of a whip."

After northern abolitionists began scanning the southern press for atrocities, specific references to slaves who were "marked by the whip" declined. The number of slaves identified more vaguely as having "scars" or "burns" increased.

Beyond this were cases of pure brutality —cases of flogging that resulted in the crippling, maiming, or killing of slaves. An early nineteenth-century Charleston grand jury presented "as a serious evil the many instances of Negro Homicide" and condemned those who indulged their passions "in the barbarous treatment of slaves."[14] "Salting—washing the cuts received from

---

[12] Catterall (ed.), *Judicial Cases*, I, p. 284.

[13] Davis (ed.), *Diary of Bennet H. Barrow*, *passim*.

[14] Henry, *Police Control*, pp. 67–68.

the whip with brine—was a harsh punishment inflicted upon the most obstinate bondsmen. Though all but a few deplored such brutality, slaveholders found themselves in a dilemma when nothing else could subdue a rebel.

If a master was too squeamish to undertake the rugged task of humbling a refractory bondsman, he might send him to a more calloused neighbor or to a professional "slave breaker." John Nevitt, a Mississippi planter not averse to the application of heroic remedies, received from another master a young chattel "for the purpose of punishing him for bad conduct." Frederick Douglass remembered a ruthless man in Maryland who had a reputation for being "a first rate hand at breaking young Negroes"; some slaveholders found it beneficial to send their beginning hands to him for training.[15]

The branding of slaves was a widespread custom in colonial days; it was less common in the nineteenth century. But as late as 1838, a North Carolinian advertised that Betty, a fugitive, was recently "burnt . . . with a hot iron on the left side of her face; I tried to make the letter M." In 1848, a Kentuckian identified his runaway Jane by a brand mark "on the breast something like L blotched."[16] Mutilation as a form of punishment also declined without disappearing entirely. A Louisiana jailer, in 1831, gave notice that he had a runaway in his custody: "He has been lately gelded, and is not yet well." Another Louisianian recorded his disgust for a neighbor who had "castrated 3 men of his."[17]

Some masters who were otherwise as humane as the peculiar institution would permit tolerated almost anything that might "cure" habitual runaways. Andrew Jackson once offered fifty dollars reward for the capture of a fugitive, "and ten dollars extra for every hundred lashes any person will give him to the amount of three hundred." A Georgian punished his runaways by pulling out one of their toenails with a pair of pincers. Others hunted them with shotguns. A North Carolinian advertised for an escaped slave who had "some marks of shot about his hips, thighs, neck and face." Bennet H. Barrow caught Jerry "in the Bayou behind the Quarter, [and] shot him in the thigh"; when Jerry absconded again, Barrow vowed he would this time "shoot to kill." A Mississippian, apparently wishing to give his slaves a stern warning, promised to compensate whoever captured his fugitive "dead or alive."[18]

The tracking of runaways with dogs was no figment of abolitionist imaginations; it was a common practice in all slave states, defended and justified in the courts. Groups of slaveholders sometimes rode through the swamps with their dogs and made the search for fugitives a sport comparable to fox hunting. Others preferred to hire professional slave catchers who provided their own "Negro dogs." A Mississippi master described the talents of a slave catcher he employed: "He follows a Negro with his dogs 36 hours after he has passed and never fails to overtake him. It is his profession and he makes some $600 per annum by it."[19] Southern newspapers carried the advertisements of professionals who solicited the patronage of slaveholders, and of those who trained "Negro dogs" for sale.

The dogs could give a fugitive a severe mauling if the owner was willing to permit it. After a Mississippi master caught an escaped slave he allowed his dogs to "bite him very severely." A Louisiana planter "treed" a runaway and then "made the dogs pull him out of the tree, Bit him very badly, think he

---

[15] Nevitt Plantation Journal, entry for June 5, 1828; Douglass, *My Bondage*, p. 203; Sydnor, *Slavery in Mississippi*, pp. 69–70.

[16] Johnson, *Ante-Bellum North Carolina*, pp. 493–94; Coleman, *Slavery Times in Kentucky*, pp. 248–49.

[17] Taylor, "Slavery in Louisiana," p. 236; Davis (ed.), *Diary of Bennet H. Barrow*, pp. 173–74.

[18] Phillips (ed.), *Plantation and Frontier*, II, pp. 85–88; Olmsted, *Texas*, pp. 104–5; Davis (ed.), *Diary of Bennet H. Barrow*, pp. 239, 242; Jackson *Mississippian*, July 11, 1834.

[19] Gustavus A. Henry to his wife, November 23, 1849, Henry Papers; Coleman, *Slavery Times in Kentucky*, pp. 61–62; Olmsted, *Back Country*, pp. 214–15.

will stay home for a while." On another occasion his dogs tore a slave naked; he then "took him Home before the other negro[es] . . . and made the dogs give him another over hauling."[20]

The angry mobs who dealt extra-legal justice to slaves accused of serious crimes committed barbarities seldom matched by the most brutal masters. "They call it Lintch's Law," wrote a frightened Louisiana plantation mistress during a local insurrection panic. "If they continue hanging, as they have done for some time past, we should be careful of the children, otherwise the World might be left without people."[21] Fear turned groups of decent white men into ferocious mobs—fear and the knowledge that the law was not strong enough to touch them.

After the Nat Turner rebellion a Richmond newspaper declared that the reprisals of the whites were "hardly inferior in barbarity to the atrocities of the insurgents." During the insurrection panic of 1856, a Texas editor affirmed that at such a time "the popular vengeance may be meted out to the criminal with as much necessity as we would strike down an enemy in self-defence, or shoot a mad dog in our path." A Mississippian was ready for the "fagot and the flame" and to "let every tree in the country bend with Negro meat." Four years later a Georgia editor urged the oldest and best citizens in each community to examine persons suspected of encouraging slave rebellions; if they were adjudged guilty, "swing the vagabonds from the nearest tree, and say nothing about it."[22]

Mobs all too frequently dealt with slaves accused of murder or rape. They conducted their own trials or broke into jails or court rooms to seize prisoners for summary execution. Their more fortunate victims were

hanged; the others were burned to death, sometimes in the presence of hundreds of bondsmen who were forced to attend the ceremony. Thus, wrote a Mississippian after one such incident, "justice was satisfied; the law of retaliation was inflicted . . . while the example made of this wretch had, no doubt, a salutary effect upon the two thousand slaves who witnessed his execution." An Alabama editor justified the burning of a slave at the stake by the "law of self-protection, which abrogates all other law. . . . There was no passionate conduct here. The whole subject was disposed of with the coolest deliberation and with regard only to the interest of the public."[23]

The abolition of slavery, of course, did not bring to a close the record of brutality in the South any more than it did elsewhere. But it did make less tenable the arguments that brutality was sometimes in the public interest. And it did rescue many a master from the dilemma he faced when his desire to be humane was compromised by the demands of proper discipline.

Surely there is room for comparison for a profoundly disturbed North Carolinian who owned several plantations in Mississippi. "My great desire is to have my blacks taken proper care of," he wrote. "I would be content with much less . . . cotton if less cruelty was exercised. I fear I am near an abolition[i]st. But I should consider myself an unjust and unfeeling man if I did not have a proper regard for those who are making me so much money[.]"[24] . . .

* * * * *

In Africa the Negroes had been accustomed to a strictly regulated family life and a rigidly enforced moral code. But in America the disintegration of their social organization removed the traditional sanctions which had encouraged them to respect their old customs. Here they found the whites organized into families having great social

[20] William Read to Samuel S. Downey, August 8, 1848, Downey Papers; Davis (ed.), *Diary of Bennet H. Barrow*, pp. 369–70, 376.

[21] Rachel O'Conner to Frances S. Weeks, September 7, 1835, Weeks Collection.

[22] Richmond *Whig*, quoted in Alexandria (Va.) *Phenix Gazette*, September 1, 1831; Austin *Texas State Gazette*, November 15, 1856; Jackson *Mississippian*, December 19, 1856; *Augusta Daily Chronicle and Sentinel*, September 9, 1860.

[23] Vicksburg *Weekly Sentinel*, June 13, 1855; Huntsville *Democrat*, quoted in Sellers, *Slavery in Alabama*, pp. 262–63.

[24] William Boylan to [George W. Mordecai], December 20, 1850, Cameron Family Papers.

and economic importance but regulated by different laws. In the quarters they were usually more or less encouraged to live as families and to accept white standards of morality.

But it was only outwardly that the family life of the mass of southern slaves resembled that of their masters. Inwardly, in many crucial ways, the domestic regimes of the slave cabin and of the "big house" were quite different. Because the slaves failed to conform to the white pattern, the master class found the explanation, as usual, in the Negro's innate racial traits. Actually, the differences resulted from the fact that slavery inevitably made much of the white caste's family pattern meaningless and unintelligible—and in some ways impossible—for the average bondsman. Here, as at so many other points, the slaves had lost their native culture without being able to find a workable substitute and therefore lived in a kind of cultural chaos.

The most obvious difference between the slave family and the white family was in the legal foundation upon which each rested. In every state white marriages were recognized as civil contracts which imposed obligations on both parties and provided penalties for their violation. Slave marriages had no such recognition in the state codes; instead, they were regulated by whatever laws the owners saw fit to enforce.

A few masters arbitrarily assigned husbands to women who had reached the "breeding age"; but ordinarily they permitted slaves to pick their own mates and only required them to ask permission to marry. On the plantations most owners refused to allow slaves to marry away from home and preferred to make additional purchases when the sexes were out of balance. Thus an Alabama overseer informed his employer that one slave was without a wife and that he had promised to "indever to git you to Bey a nother woman sow he might have a wife at home."[25] Still, it did frequently happen on both large and small estates that husbands and wives were owned by different masters. Sometimes, when a slave wished to marry the slave of another owner, a sale was made in order to unite them.

Having obtained their master's consent, the couple might begin living together without further formality; or their master might hastily pronounce them man and wife in a perfunctory ceremony. But more solemn ceremonies, conducted by slave preachers or white clergymen, were not uncommon even for the fieldhands, and they were customary for the domestics. The importance of the occasion was sometimes emphasized by a wedding feast and gifts to the bride.

After a marriage many masters ignored the behavior of the couple so long as neither husband nor wife caused any loud or violent disturbances. Others insisted that they not only live together but respect their obligations to each other. A Louisianian made it a rule that adultery was to be "invariably punished." On a Mississippi plantation, the husband was required to provide firewood for his family and "wait on his wife"; the wife was to do the family's cooking, washing, and mending. Failure to perform these duties was "corrected by words first but if not reformed . . . by the whip." According to a Georgian, "I never permit a husband to abuse, strike or whip his wife. . . . If the wife teases and provokes him . . . she is punished, but it sometimes happens that the husband petitions for her pardon, which I make it a rule not to refuse, as it imposes a strong obligation on the wife to . . . be more conciliating in her behavior."[26] Some masters apparently ran domestic relations courts and served as family counselors.

Divorce, like marriage, was within the master's jurisdiction. He might permit his slaves to change spouses as often and whenever they wished, or he might establish more or less severe rules. A Louisiana master granted a divorce only after a month's notice and prohibited remarriage unless a divorcee agreed to receive 25 lashes. James H.

25 J. B. Grace to Charles Tait, April 25, 1835, Charles Tait and Family Papers.

26 De Bow's Review, XXII (1857), pp. 376–79; Plantation Rules in William Erwin Ms. Diary and Account Book; Southern Agriculturist, IV (1831), p. 351.

Hammond inflicted 100 lashes upon partners who dissolved their marriage and forced them to live singly for three years. One day in 1840, Hammond noted in his diary: Had a trial of Divorce and Adultery cases. Flogged Joe Goodwyn and ordered him to go back to his wife. Dito Gabriel and Molly and ordered them to come together again. Separated Moses and Anny finally. And flogged Tom Kollock . . . [for] interferring with Maggy Campbell, Sullivan's wife."[27] While one master might enforce divorce laws as rigid as these, his neighbor might tolerate a veritable regime of free love—of casual alliances and easy separation. Inevitably the rules on a given estate affected the family life of its slaves.

Not only did the slave family lack the protection and the external pressure of state law, it also lacked most of the centripetal forces that gave the white family cohesiveness. In the life of the slave, the family had nothing like the social significance that it had in the life of the white man. The slave woman was first a full-time worker for her owner, and only incidentally a wife, mother, and homemaker. She spent a small fraction of her time in the house; she often did no cooking or clothes making; and she was not usually nurse to her husband or children during illness. Parents frequently had little to do with the raising of their children; and children soon learned that their parents were neither the fount of wisdom nor the seat of authority. Thus a child on a Louisiana farm saw his mother receive 25 lashes for countermanding an order his mistress had given him.[28] Lacking autonomy, the slave family could not offer the child shelter or security from the frightening creatures in the outside world.

The family had no greater importance as an economic unit. Parents and children might spend some spare hours together in their garden plots, but, unlike rural whites, slaves labored most of the time for their mas-

ters in groups that had no relationship to the family. The husband was not the director of an agricultural enterprise; he was not the head of the family, the holder of property, the provider, or the protector. If his wife or child was disrobed and whipped by master or overseer, he stood by in helpless humiliation. In an age of patriarchal families, the male slave's only crucial function within the family was that of siring offspring.

Indeed, the typical slave family was matriarchal in form, for the mother's role was far more important than the father's. Insofar as the family did have significance it involved responsibilities which traditionally belonged to women, such as cleaning house, preparing food, making clothes, and raising children. The husband was at most his wife's assistant, her companion, and her sex partner. He was often thought of as her possession ("Mary's Tom"), as was the cabin in which they lived.[29] It was common for a mother to raise her children to be considered a family without reference to the father.

Given these conditions—the absence of legal marriages, the family's minor social and economic significance, and the father's limited role—it is hardly surprising to find that slave families were highly unstable. Lacking both outer pressures and inner pulls, they were also exposed to the threat of forced separations through sales. How dispersed a slave family could be as a result of one or more of these factors was indicated by an advertisement for a North Carolina fugitive who was presumed to be "lurking in the neighborhood of E. D. Walker's, at Moore's Creek, who owns most of his relations, or Nathan Bonham's who owns his mother; or, perhaps, near Fletcher Bell's, at Long Creek, who owns his father." A slave preacher in Kentucky united couples in wedlock "until death or *distance* do you part." When Joshua and Bush asked for permission to marry, their Virginia master read them a statement warning that he might be

---

[27] Sitterson, *Sugar Country*, p. 58; Hammond Plantation Manual; Hammond Diary, entry for December 26, 1840.

[28] Marston Diary, entry for June 12, 1829.

[29] Johnson, *Sea Islands*, pp. 135, 137–38; *id., Ante-Bellum North Carolina*, p. 535.

forced to separate them, "so Joshua must not then say I have taken his wife from him."[30] Thus every slave family had about it an air of impermanence, for no master could promise that his debts would not force sales, or guarantee that his death would not cause divisions.

If the state did not recognize slave marriages, the churches of the Protestant South might have supplied a salutary influence, since they emphasized the sanctity of the home and family. The churches did try to persuade their own slave members to respect the marriage sacrament and sometimes even disciplined those who did not. But they were quite tolerant of masters who were forced by "necessity" to separate husbands, wives, and children. For example, in 1856, a committee of the Charleston Baptist Association agreed that slave marriages had "certain limitations" and had to be "the subject of special rules." Hence, though calling these marriages "sacred and binding" and urging that they be solemnized by a religious ceremony, the committee raised no objection to the separation of couples against their wills. Apparently the only sinful separation was one initiated by the slaves themselves.[31]

The general instability of slave families had certain logical consequences. One was the casual attitude of many bondsmen toward marriage; another was the failure of any deep and enduring affection to develop between some husbands and wives. The South abounded in stories of slaves who elected to migrate with kind masters even when it meant separation from their spouses. "Ef you got a good marster, foller him," was the saying in Virginia, according to an ex-slave. An equally common story, which was often true, was that chattels were not severely disturbed by forced separation and soon found new husbands or wives in their new homes. All who were familiar with the Negro, wrote a South Carolinian, understood how difficult it was "to educate even

the best and most intelligently moral of the race to a true view and estimation of marriage."[32] Here, presumably, was proof that separation through the slave trade caused no real hardship.

Still another consequence was the indifference with which most fathers and even some mothers regarded their children. An angry Virginian attributed the death of a slave infant to "the unnatural neglect of his infamous mother"; he charged that another infant was "murdered right out by his mother's neglect and barbarous cruelty." Fanny Kemble observed the stolid reaction of slave parents to the death of their children. "I've lost a many; they all goes so," was the only comment of one mother when another child died; and the father, "without word or comment, went out to his enforced labor."[33] Many slaveholders complained that mothers could not be trusted to nurse their sick children, that some showed no affection for them and treated them cruelly. This, of course, was not a manifestation of Negro "character" as masters seemed to think. How these calloused mothers could have produced the affectionate slave "mammies" of tradition was never explained. But one master spoke volumes when he advocated separating children from their parents, because it was "far more humane not to cherish domestic ties among slaves."[34]

The final consequence of family instability was widespread sexual promiscuity among both men and women. The case of a Kentucky slave woman who had each of her seven children by a different father was by no means unique. This was a condition which some masters tried to control but which most of them accepted with resignation, or indifference, or amusement. As to the slave's moral habits, wrote one discouraged owner, "I know of no means whereby to regulate them, or to restrain them; I attempted it for many years by preaching vir-

---

30 Wilmington (N.C.) *Journal*, May 2, 1851; Coleman, *Slavery Times in Kentucky*, pp. 58–59; Massie Slave Book, entry for September 24, 1847.
31 Charleston *Courier*, August 5, 1857.

32 Smedes, *Memorials*, p. 48; Olmsted, *Seaboard*, pp. 556–57; Charleston *Courier*, September 15, 1857.
33 Massie Slave Book; Kemble, *Journal*, p. 95.
34 Lyell, *Travels*, I, p. 184.

tue and decency, . . . but it was all in vain." Olmsted cited numerous instances of masters who regarded the whole matter with complete unconcern; and masters themselves rarely gave any sign of displeasure when an unmarried slave woman became pregnant. A Virginia planter kept a record of the fathers of his slave children when he knew who the fathers were, but often he could only guess—and sometimes he suggested that the child was sired "by the Commonwealth," or "by the Universe," or "God knows who by." Overseers were generally even less concerned; as one overseer explained, the morals of the slaves were "no business of his, and he did not care what they did. Nor was the law concerned. In Mississippi, when a male slave was indicted for the rape of a female slave; the state Supreme Court dismissed the case on the ground that this was not an offense known to common or statute law.[35]

If most slaves regarded the white man's moral code as unduly severe, many whites did too. Indeed, the number of bastardy cases in southern court records seems to confirm the conclusion that women of the poor-white class "carried about the same reputation for easy virtue as their sable sisters." Marriage, insisted Frederick Douglass, had no existence among slaves, "except in such hearts as are purer and higher than the standard morality around them." His consolation was that at least some slaves "maintained their honor, where all around was corrupt."[36]

That numerous slaves did manage somehow to surmount the corrupting influences everywhere about them, their masters themselves freely admitted. A South Carolinian admired the slave mother's "natural and often ardent and endearing affection for her offspring"; and another declared that "sound

policy" as well as humanity required that everything be done "to reconcile these unhappy beings to their lot, by keeping mothers and children together." The majority of slave women were devoted to their children, regardless of whether they had been sired by one or several fathers. Nor was sexual promiscuity a universal trait of southern Negroes even in bondage. Many slave couples, affirmed a Georgian, displayed toward each other a high degree of "faithfulness, fidelity, and affection."[37]

Seldom, when slave families were broken to satisfy creditors or settle estates, was a distinction made between those who were indifferent to the matter and those who suffered deeply as a consequence. The "agony at parting," an ex-slave reminded skeptics, "must be seen and felt to be fully understood." A slave woman who had been taken from her children in Virginia and sent to the Southwest "cried many a night about it; and went 'bout mazin' sorry-like all day, a wishing I was dead and buried!" Sometimes the "derangement" or sudden rebelliousness of a slave mother was attributed to "grief at being separated from her children." Often mothers fought desperately to prevent traders from carrying off their children, and often husbands and wives struggled against separation when they were torn apart.[38]

But the most eloquent evidence of the affection and devotion that bound many slave families together appeared in the advertisements for fugitives. A Virginian sought a runaway whose wife had been transported to Mississippi, "and I understand from some of my servants, that he had been speaking of following her." A Maryland master was convinced that a female fugitive would attempt to get back to

[35] Brown, *Narrative*, p. 13; *De Bow's Review*, X (1851), p. 623; Olmsted, *Back Country*, pp. 89, 113, 154; Massie Slave Book; Catterall (ed.), *Judicial Cases*, II, pp. 544–45; III, p. 363.

[36] Avery O. Craven, "Poor Whites and Negroes in the Ante-Bellum South," *Journal of Negro History*, XV (1930), pp. 17–18; Douglass, *My Bondage*, p. 86.

[37] *De Bow's Review*, XVII (1854), pp. 425–26; Abbeville District, South Carolina, Judge of Probate Decree Book, 1839–1858, May term, 1841; Catterall (ed.), *Judicial Cases*, II, p. 314.

[38] Henson, *Story*, pp. 10–11; Ingraham (ed.), *Sunny South*, p. 439; Catterall (ed.), *Judicial Cases*, I, p. 298; III, p. 632; V, p. 229–30; Loguen, *Narrative*, pp. 112–20; Andrews, *Slavery and the Domestic Slave Trade*, pp. 128–33.

Georgia "where she came from, and left her husband and two children." Even when fugitives hoped to reach the free states, husbands often took their wives and parents, their children, though this obviously lessened their chance of a successful escape. Clearly, to many bondsmen the fellowship of the family, in spite of its instability, was exceedingly important.

Some of the problems that troubled slave families, of course, had nothing to do with slavery—they were the tragically human problems which have ever disturbed marital tranquillity. One such domestic dilemma involved a slave whose wife did not return his devotion. "He says he loves his wife and does not want to leave her," noted the master. "She says she does not love him and won't live with him. Yet he says he can over come her scruples and live happily with her."[39] For this slavery was not the cause nor freedom the cure.

But other kinds of family tragedies were uniquely a part of life in bondage. A poignant example was the scene that transpired when an overseer tied and whipped a slave mother in the presence of her children. The frightened children pelted the overseer with stones, and one of them ran up and bit him in the leg. During the ruction the cries of the mother were mingled with the screams of the children, *"Let my mammy go—let my mammy go."*[40] . . .

Other slaves exhibited toward whites no strong emotion either of affection or hatred, but rather an attitude of deep suspicion. Many contemporaries commented upon their "habitual distrust of the white race" and noted that they were "always suspicious." When this was the Negro's basic attitude, the resulting relationship was an amoral one which resembled an unending civil war; the slave then seemed to think that he was entitled to use every tactic of deception and chicanery he could devise. Many ex-slaves who spoke of their former

masters without bitterness still recalled with particular pleasure the times when they had outwitted or beguiled them (" 'cause us had to lie").[41]

To a few slaves this civil war was an intense and serious business, because they felt for their masters (sometimes for all whites) an abiding animosity. In speaking of the whites, such bondsmen used "the language of hatred and revenge"; on one plantation the slaves in their private conversations contemptuously called their master "Old Hogjaw." Externally these slaves wore an air of sullenness. "You need only to look in their faces to see they are not happy," exclaimed a traveler; instead, they were "depressed" or "gloomy." Fieldhands often gave no sign of pleasure when their master approached; some made clumsy bows, but others ignored him entirely.[42]

The poor whites were the one group in the superior caste for whom the slaves dared openly express their contempt, and the slaves did so in picturesque terms. Masters often tolerated this and were even amused by it. However, it is likely that some slaves were thereby expressing their opinion of the whole white race. A transparent example of the malice that a portion of the slaves bore the whites occurred in St. Louis when a mob tarred and feathered a white man. "One feature of the scene I could not help remarking," wrote a witness: "the negroes all appeared in high glee, and many of them actually danced with joy."[43]

But the predominant and overpowering emotion that whites aroused in the majority of slaves was neither love nor hate but fear. "We were always uneasy," an ex-slave recalled; when "a white man spoke to me, I would feel frightened," another confessed. In Alabama, a visitor who lost his pocket-

---

[39] Gustavus A. Henry to his wife, December 11, 1839, Henry Papers.
[40] Douglass, *My Bondage*, pp. 92–95.

[41] Olmsted, *Back Country*, p. 114; Bremer, *Homes of the New World*, I, p. 292; Botkin, *Lay My Burden Down, passim.*
[42] Northup, *Twelve Years a Slave*, pp. 62–63, 197; Russell, *Diary*, pp. 133, 146–47, 258, 262; Stirling, *Letters*, p. 49; Buckingham, *Slave States*, I, pp. 62–63.
[43] Drew, *The Refugee*, pp. 156–57; Benwell, *Travels*, p. 99.

book noted that the slave who found it "was afraid of being whipped for theft and had given it to the first white man he saw, and at first was afraid to pick it up." A fugitive who was taken into the home of an Ohio Quaker found it impossible to overcome his timidity and apprehension. "I had never had a white man to treat me as an equal, and the idea of a white lady waiting on me at the table was still worse! . . . I thought if I could only be allowed the privilege of eating in the kitchen, I should be more than satisfied."[44]

The masters themselves provided the most vivid evidence of the frightening image that white men assumed in the minds of many slaves. When they advertised for runaways, the owners frequently revealed a distressing relationship between the two races, a relationship that must have been for these slaves an emotional nightmare. In their advertisements no descriptive phrases were more common than these: "stutters very much when spoken to"; "speaks softly and has a downcast look"; "has an uneasy appearance when spoken to"; "speaks quickly, and with an anxious expression of countenance"; "a very down look, and easily confused when spoken to"; "stammers very much so as to be scarcely understood."

"I feel lighter—the dread is gone," affirmed a Negro woman who had escaped to Canada. "It is a great heaviness on a person's mind to be a slave."[45] . . .

*   *   *   *   *

Critics of slavery, certain white men think, err, when they assume that Negroes suffered as much in bondage as white men would have suffered. One must remember, argue the critics of the critics, that to the Negroes slavery seemed natural; knowing no other life, they accepted it without giving the matter much thought. Not that slavery was a good thing, mind you—but, still, it probably hurt the Negro less than it did the whites. Indeed, the whites were really more enslaved by Negro slavery than were the Negro slaves. This postslavery argument, like the antebellum proslavery argument, is based upon some obscure and baffling logic. It is not unlike James H. Hammond's confident assertion that "our slaves are the happiest . . . human beings on whom the sun shines"; or his complaint that "into their Eden is coming Satan in the guise of an abolitionist."[46]

A former slave once pronounced a simple and chastening truth for those who would try to understand the meaning of bondage: "Tisn't he who has stood and looked on, that can tell you what slavery is—'tis he who has endured." "I was black," he added, "but I had the feelings of a man as well as any man."[47] One can feel compassion for the antebellum Southern white man; one can understand the moral dilemma in which he was trapped. But one must remember that the Negro, not the white man, was the slave, and the Negro gained the most from emancipation. When freedom came—even the quasi-freedom of "second-class citizenship" —the Negro, in literal truth, lost nothing but his chains.

---

[44] Drew, *The Refugee*, pp. 30, 86; Watson Diary, entry for January 1, 1831; Brown, *Narrative*, pp. 102–3.

[45] Drew, *The Refugee*, p. 179.

---

[46] *De Bow's Review*, VIII (1850), p. 123.

[47] Drew, *The Refugee*, pp. 201–2.

1959

Nazi Camp Survival and Slavery Compared*

STANLEY M. ELKINS

. . . We may suppose that every African who became a slave underwent an experience whose crude psychic impact must have been staggering and whose consequences superseded anything that had ever previously happened to him. Some effort should therefore be made to picture the series of shocks which must have accompanied the principal events of that enslavement.

The majority of slaves appear to have been taken in native wars,[1] which meant that no one—neither persons of high rank nor warriors of prowess—was guaranteed against capture and enslavement.[2] Great

numbers were caught in surprise attacks upon their villages, and since the tribes acting as middlemen for the trade had come to depend on regular supplies of captives in order to maintain that function, the distinction between wars and raiding expeditions tended to be very dim.[3] The first shock, in an experience destined to endure many months and to leave its survivors irrevocably changed, was thus the shock of capture. It is an effort to remember that while enslavement occurred in Africa every

---

* Reprinted from *Slavery* by Stanley M. Elkins by permission of the University of Chicago Press. Copyright 1959 by University of Chicago Press.

[1] There were other pretexts, such as crime or debt, but war was probably the most frequent mode of procurement. Snelgrave, *New Account*, p. 158; "John Barbot's Description," in Donnan, *Documents*, I, 284, 289, 294, 298; "Observations on the Slave Trade, 1789" [C. B. Wadström] in *ibid.*, II, 599; Matthews, *Voyage to Sierra-Leone*, pp. 145–46, 163. See also below, n. 34.

[2] As to "character types," one might be tempted to suppose that as a rule it would be only the weaker and more submissive who allowed themselves to be taken into slavery. Yet it appears that a heavy proportion of the slaves were in fact drawn from among the most warlike. "In a country divided into a thousand petty states, mostly independent and jealous of each other; where every freeman is accustomed to arms, and fond of military achievements; where the youth who has practised the bow and spear from his infancy, longs for nothing so much as an opportunity to display his valour; it is natural to imagine that wars frequently originate from very frivolous provocation." Park, *Travels*, p. 328. "The most potent

negroe," wrote William Bosman, "can't pretend to be insured from slavery; for if he ever ventures himself in the wars it may easily become his lot." *New and Accurate Description*, p. 183. It has often been pointed out that slavery already existed among the tribes themselves and that a considerable proportion of Africans were used to it and had in fact been born into it. It may be doubted, however, if substantial numbers of *these* slaves came to America, for apparently the native chiefs tended to sell only their war captives to the Europeans and to keep their hereditary and customary slaves—together with their most docile captives —for themselves. Park, *Travels*, p. 332. It has even been asserted that in many places the tribal laws themselves forbade the selling of domestic slaves, except for crimes, though apparently it was simple enough to trump up an accusation if one wanted to get rid of a slave. Matthews, *Voyage to Sierra-Leone*, p. 153; Edwards, *History*, II, 312.

[3] "The Wars which the inhabitants of the interior parts of the country, beyond Senegal, Gambia, and Sierra Leona, carry on with each other, are chiefly of a predatory nature, and owe their origin to the yearly number of slaves, which the Mandingoes, or the inland traders suppose will be wanted by the vessels that will arrive on the coast." "Observations" [Wadström], in Donnan, *Documents*, II, 599.

day, to the individual it occurred just once.[4]

The second shock—the long march to the sea—drew out the nightmare for many weeks. Under the glaring sun, through the steaming jungle, they were driven along like beasts tied together by their necks; day after day, eight or more hours at a time, they would stagger barefoot over thorny underbrush, dried reeds, and stones. Hardship, thirst, brutalities, and near starvation penetrated the experience of each exhausted man and woman who reached the coast.[5] One traveler tells of seeing hundreds of bleaching skeletons strewn along one of the slave caravan routes.[6] But then the man who must interest us is the man who survived—he who underwent the entire experience, of which this was only the beginning.

The next shock, aside from the fresh physical torments which accompanied it, was the sale to the European slavers. After being crowded into pens near the trading stations and kept there overnight, sometimes for days, the slaves were brought out for examination. Those rejected would be abandoned to starvation; the remaining ones —those who had been bought—were branded, given numbers inscribed on leaden tags, and herded on shipboard.[7]

The episode that followed—almost too protracted and stupefying to be called mere "shock"—was the dread Middle Passage, brutalizing to any man, black or white, ever to be involved with it. The holds, packed with squirming and suffocating humanity, became stinking infernos of filth and pestilence. Stories of disease, death, and cruelty on the terrible two-month voyage abound in the testimony which did much toward ending the British slave trade forever.[8]

The final shock in the process of enslavement came with the Negro's introduction to the West Indies. Bryan Edwards, describing the arrival of a slave ship, writes of how in times of labor scarcity crowds of people would come scrambling aboard, manhandling the slaves and throwing them into panic. The Jamaica legislature eventually "corrected the enormity" by enacting that the sales had to be held on shore. Edwards felt a certain mortification at seeing the Negroes exposed naked in public, similar to that felt by the trader Degrandpré at seeing them examined back at the African factories.[9] Yet here they did not seem to care. "They display . . . very few signs of lamentation for their past or of apprehension for their future condition; but . . . commonly express great eagerness to be sold."[10] The

---

[4] A number of excerpts describing these raids are cited in Thomas Fowell Buxton, *Letter on the Slave Trade to the Lord Viscount Melbourne* (London, 1838), pp. 34–38.

[5] Descriptions of the march may be found in Park, *Travels*, pp. 371 ff.; Buxton, *Letter*, pp. 41–44; Rinchon, *La traite et l'esclavage*, pp. 174–75; L. Degrandpré, *Voyage à la côte occidentale d'Afrique, fait dans les années 1786 et 1787* (Paris, 1801), II, 48–50.

[6] Buxton, *Letter*, p. 43.

[7] "When these slaves come to fida, they are put in prison all together, and when we treat concerning buying them, they are all brought out together in a large plain; where, by our Chirurgeons, whose province it is, they are thoroughly examined, even to the smallest member, and that naked too both men and women, without the least distinction and modesty. Those which are approved as good are set on one side; and the lame or faulty are set by as *invalides*, which are here called *mackrons*. These are such as are above five and thirty years old, or are maimed in the arms, legs, hands or feet, have lost a tooth, are grey-haired, or have films over their eyes; as well

as all those which are affected by any venereal distemper, or with several other diseases." Bosman, *New and Accurate Description*, p. 364. See also Degrandpré, *Voyage*, II, 53–56; Buxton, *Letter*, pp. 47–49; Rinchon, *La traite et l'esclavage*, pp. 188–89; "John Barbot's Description," in Donnan, *Documents*, I, 289, 295; Park, *Travels*, p. 360.

[8] Descriptions of the Middle Passage may be found in *An Abstract of the Evidence Delivered before a Select Committee of the House of Commons in the Years 1790, and 1791; on the Part of the Petitioners for the Abolition of the Slave Trade* (London, 1791); Alexander Falconbridge, *An Account of the Slave Trade on the Coast of Africa* (London: J. Phillips, 1788); Rinchon, *La traite et l'esclavage*, pp. 196–209; Edwards, *History*, II; Brantz Mayer, *Captain Canot* (New York: D. Appleton, 1854); Averil Mackenzie-Grieve, *The Last Years of the English Slave Trade, Liverpool 1750–1807* (London: Putnam, 1941).

[9] Degrandpré, *Voyage*, II, 55–56.

[10] Edwards, *History*, II, 340. See also *Abstract of Evidence*, pp. 46–47, and Falconbridge, *Account*, pp. 33–36.

"seasoning" process which followed completed the series of steps whereby the African Negro became a slave.

The mortality had been very high. One-third of the numbers first taken, out of a total of perhaps 15 million, had died on the march and at the trading stations; another third died during the Middle Passage and the seasoning.[11] Since a majority of the African-born slaves who came to the North American plantations did not come directly but were imported through the British West Indies, one may assume that the typical slave underwent an experience something like that just outlined. This was the man—one in three—who had come through it all and lived and was about to enter our "closed system." What would he be like if he survived and adjusted to that?

Actually, a great deal had happened to him already. Much of his past had been annihilated; nearly every prior connection had been severed. Not that he had really "forgotten" all these things—his family and kinship arrangements, his language, the tribal religion, the taboos, the name he had once borne, and so on—but none of it any longer carried much meaning. The old values, the sanctions, the standards, already unreal, could no longer furnish him guides for conduct, for adjusting to the expectations of a complete new life. Where then was he to look for new standards, new cues—who furnish them now? He could now look to none but his master, the one man to whom the system had committed his entire being: the man upon whose will depended his food, his shelter, his sexual connections, whatever moral instruction he might be offered, whatever "success" was possible within the system, his very security—in short, everything.

The thoroughness with which African Negroes coming to America were detached from prior cultural sanctions should thus be partly explainable by the very shock sequence inherent in the technique of procurement. But it took something more than this to produce "Sambo," and it is possible to overrate—or at least to overgeneralize—this shock sequence in the effort to explain what followed.[12] A comparable experience was also undergone by slaves coming into Latin America, where very little that resembled our "Sambo" tradition would ever develop. We should also remember that, in either case, it was only the first generation that actually experiences these shocks. It could even be argued that the shock sequence is not an absolute necessity for explaining "Sambo" at all.

So whereas the Middle Passage and all that went with it must have been psychologically numbing, and should probably be regarded as a long thrust, at least, toward the end product, it has little meaning considered apart from what came later. It may be assumed that the process of detachment was completed—and, as it were, guaranteed—by the kind of "closed" authority system into which the slave was introduced and to which he would have to adjust.[13] At any rate, a test of this detachment and its thoroughness is virtually ready-made. Everyone who has looked into the problem of African cultural features surviving among New World Negroes agrees that the contrast between North America and Latin America is immense. In Brazil, survivals from African religion are not only to be encountered everywhere but such carry-overs are so dis-

---

[11] Tannenbaum, *Slave and Citizen*, p. 28. As for the total exports of slaves from Africa throughout the entire period of the trade, estimates run as high as 20 million. "Even a conservative estimate," notes Mr. Tannenbaum, "would hardly cut this figure in half." *Ibid.*, p. 32.

[12] Its rigors, at least prior to the sea passage, were clearly not experienced with uniform intensity by all. For example, Onwuka Dike claims that among the tribes east of the Niger, nearly as many, and perhaps even more, of the slaves sold to Europeans were procured by nonviolent means, through the judgment of the Oracle, as were taken in wars. See Dike, *Trade and Politics*, pp. 40–41. It might also be added that the "long march" was probably not a universal experience either, since there was in West Africa a network of navigable rivers down which cargoes of slaves could be transported in canoes. On this point see *ibid.*, pp. 19–20.

[13] See above, pp. 37–63.

tinct that they may even be identified with particular tribal groups. "The Negro religions and cults," Arthur Ramos adds, "were not the only form of cultural expression which survived in Brazil. The number of folklore survivals is extremely large, the prolongation of social institutions, habits, practices and events from Africa."[14] Fernando Ortiz, writing of Cuba in 1905, saw the African witchcraft cults flourishing on the island as a formidable social problem.[15] One of our own anthropologists, on the other hand, despite much dedicated field work, has been put to great effort to prove that in North American Negro society any African cultural vestiges have survived at all.[16]

ADJUSTMENT TO ABSOLUTE POWER IN THE CONCENTRATION CAMP

A certain amount of the mellowness in Ulrich Phillips' picture of antebellum plantation life has of necessity been discredited by recent efforts not only to refocus attention upon the brutalities of the slave system but also to dispose once and for all of Phillips' assumptions about the slave as a racially inferior being. And yet it is important—par-

---

[14] Arthur Ramos, *The Negro in Brazil* (Washington: Associated Publishers, 1939), p. 94. Ramos devotes two full chapters to "The Cultural Heritage of the Brazilian Negro." Donald Pierson, in his *Negroes in Brazil* (Chicago: University of Chicago Press, 1942), likewise devotes two chapters to African influences in the customs of the Negroes of Bahia.

[15] Fernando Ortiz, *Los Negroes Brujos* (Madrid: Libería de F. Fé, 1906). This entire book is devoted to occult African practices in Cuba, including a chapter called "The Future of Witchcraft."

[16] Herskovits, *Myth of the Negro Past.* The real aim of this study seems more often than not to be that of "promoting" African culture in the United States by insisting on its values instead of describing its actual survivals—which the author himself admits are decidedly on the scanty side compared with those to be found in Latin America. Such "Africanisms" do not seem to go much beyond esoteric vestiges of a suspiciously circumstantial nature, in speech rhythms, certain symbols in folktales, habits of "temporary mating," etc. Professor Herskovits reveals, perhaps unwittingly, that efforts to convince American Negro audiences that they do, in fact, have an African cultural heritage, have met with hostility and tension.

ticularly in view of the analogy about to be presented—to keep in mind that for all the system's cruelties there were still clear standards of patriarchal benevolence inherent in its human side, and that such standards were recognized as those of the best Southern families. This aspect, despite the most drastic changes of emphasis, should continue to guarantee for Phillips' view more than just a modicum of legitimacy; the patriarchal quality, whatever measure of benevolence or lack of it one wants to impute to the regime, still holds a major key to its nature as a social system.

Introducing, therefore, certain elements of the German concentration-camp experience involves the risky business of trying to balance two necessities—emphasizing both the vast dissimilarities of the two regimes and the essentially *limited purpose* for which they are being brought together, and at the same time justifying the use of the analogy in the first place. The point is perhaps best made by insisting on an order of classification. The American plantation was not even in the metaphorical sense a "concentration camp"; nor was it even "like" a concentration camp, to the extent that any standards comparable to those governing the camps might be imputed to any sector of American society, at any time; but it should at least be permissible to turn the thing around —to speak of the concentration camp as a special and highly perverted instance of human slavery. Doing so, moreover, should actually be of some assistance in the strategy, now universally sanctioned, of demonstrating how little the products and consequences of slavery ever had to do with race. The only mass experience that Western people have had within recorded history comparable in any way with Negro slavery was undergone in the nether world of Nazism. The concentration camp was not only a perverted slave system; it was also—what is less obvious but even more to the point—a perverted patriarchy.

The system of the concentration camp was expressly devised in the 1930s by high officials of the German government to function as an instrument of terror. The first groups detained in the camps consisted of prominent enemies of the Nazi regime; later, when these had mostly been eliminated, it was still felt necessary that the system be institutionalized and made into a standing weapon of intimidation—which required a continuing flow of incoming prisoners. The categories of eligible persons were greatly widened to include all real, fancied, or "potential" opposition to the state. They were often selected on capricious and random grounds, and together they formed a cross-section of society which was virtually complete: criminals, workers, businessmen, professional people, middle-class Jews, even members of the aristocracy. The teeming camps thus held all kinds—not only the scum of the underworld but also countless men and women of culture and refinement. During the war a specialized objective was added, that of exterminating the Jewish populations of subject countries, which required special mass-production methods of which the gas chambers and crematories of Auschwitz-Birkenau were outstanding examples. Yet the basic technique was everywhere and at all times the same: the deliberate inflicttion of various forms of torture upon the incoming prisoners in such a way as to break their resistance and make way for their degradation as individuals. These brutalities were not merely "permitted" or "encouraged"; they were prescribed. Duty in the camps was a mandatory phase in the training of SS guards, and it was here that particular efforts were made to overcome their scruples and to develop in them a capacity for relishing spectacles of pain and anguish.

The concentration camps and everything that took place in them were veiled in the utmost isolation and secrecy. Of course complete secrecy was impossible, and a continuing stream of rumors circulated among the population. At the same time so repellent was the nature of these stories that in their enormity they transcended the experience of nearly everyone who had heard them; in self-protection it was somehow necessary to persuade oneself that they could not really be true. The results, therefore, contained elements of the diabolical. The undenied existence of the camps cast a shadow of nameless dread over the entire population; on the other hand the *individual* who actually became a prisoner in one of them was in most cases devastated with fright and utterly demoralized to discover that what was happening to *him* was not less, but rather far more terrible than anything he had imagined. The shock sequence of "procurement," therefore, together with the initial phases of the prisoner's introduction to camp life, is not without significance in assessing some of the psychic effects upon those who survived as long-term inmates.

The arrest was typically made at night, preferably late; this was standing Gestapo policy, designed to heighten the element of shock, terror, and unreality surrounding the arrest. After a day or so in the police jail came the next major shock, that of being transported to the camp itself. "This transportation into the camp, and the 'initiation' into it," writes Bruno Bettelheim (an ex-inmate of Dachau and Buchenwald), "is often the first torture which the prisoner has ever experienced and is, as a rule, physically and psychologically the worst torture to which he will ever be exposed."[17] It involved a planned series of brutalities inflicted by guards making repeated rounds through the train over a 12 to 36-hour period during which the prisoner was prevented from resting. If transported in cattle cars instead of passenger cars, the prisoners were sealed in under conditions not dissimilar to those of the Middle Passage.[18] Upon their arrival—if the camp was one in which mass exterminations were carried out—there might be sham ceremonies designed to reassure tem-

---

[17] Bruno Bettelheim, "Individual and Mass Behavior in Extreme Situations," *Journal of Abnormal Psychology*, XXXVIII (October, 1943), 424.

[18] A description of such a trip may be found in Olga Lengyel, *Five Chimneys: The Story of Auschwitz* (Chicago, 1947), pp. 7–10. See also Eugen Kogon, *The Theory and Practice of Hell* (New York: Farrar, Straus, 1946), p. 67.

porarily the exhausted prisoners, which meant that the fresh terrors in the offing would then strike them with redoubled impact. An SS officer might deliver an address, or a band might be playing popular tunes, and it would be in such a setting that the initial "selection" was made. The newcomers would file past an SS doctor who indicated with a motion of the forefinger, whether they were to go to the left or to the right. To one side went those considered capable of heavy labor; to the other would go wide categories of "undesirables"; those in the latter groups were being condemned to the gas chambers.[19] Those who remained would undergo the formalities of "registration," full of indignities, which culminated in the marking of each prisoner with a number.[20]

There were certain physical and psychological strains of camp life, especially debilitating in the early stage, which should be classed with the introductory shock sequence. There was a state of chronic hunger whose pressures were usually effective in detaching prior scruples of all kinds; even the

sexual instincts no longer functioned in the face of the drive for food.[21] The man who at his pleasure could bestow or withhold food thus wielded, for that reason alone, abnormal power. Another strain at first was the demand for absolute obedience, the slightest deviation from which brought savage punishments.[22] The prisoner had to ask permission—by no means granted as a matter of course—even to defecate.[23] The power of the SS guard, as the prisoner was hourly reminded, was that of life and death over his body. A more exquisite form of pressure lay in the fact that the prisoner had never a moment of solitude: he no longer had a private existence; it was no longer possible, in any imaginable sense, for him to be an "individual."[24]

Another factor having deep disintegrative effects upon the prisoner was the prospect of a limitless future in the camp. In the immediate sense this meant that he could no longer make plans for the future. But there would eventually be a subtler meaning: it made the break with the outside world a *real* break; in time the "real" life would become the life of the camp, the outside world an abstraction. Had it been a limited detention, whose end could be calculated, one's outside relationships—one's roles, one's very "personality"—might temporarily have been laid aside, to be reclaimed more or less intact at the end of the term. Here, however, the prisoner was faced with the apparent impossibility of his old roles or even his old personality ever having any future at all; it became more and more difficult to imagine himself resuming them.[25] It was this that un-

---

[19] Elie Cohen, *Human Behavior in the Concentration Camp* (New York: Norton, 1953), pp. 118–22; Kogon, *Theory and Practice*, pp. 66–76; Lengyel, *Five Chimneys*, pp. 12–22.

[20] One aspect of this registration ceremony involved a sham "inspection" of the body, whose effect on the women prisoners in particular was apparently very profound. See Lengyel, *Five Chimneys*, p. 19; Ella Lingens-Reiner, *Prisoners of Fear* (London: Victor Gollancz, 1948), p. 26. This may be compared with Degrandpré's description of a similar "inspection" on the African slave coast in the 1780s; see his *Voyage*, II, 55–56. "Apart from the fact that for every newcomer his transformation into a 'prisoner' meant a degradation," writes an ex-prisoner of Auschwitz and Mauthausen, "there was also the *loss of his name*. That this was no trifling circumstance should be apparent from the great importance which, according to Freud, a man attaches to his name. This is, in Freud's view, sufficiently proven by 'the fact that savages regard a name as an essential part of a man's personality. . . .' Anyhow, whether one agrees with Freud or not, the loss of one's name is not without significance, for the name is a personal attribute. Because he no longer had a name, but had become a number, the prisoner belonged to the huge army of the nameless who peopled the concentration camp." Cohen, *Human Behavior*, pp. 145–46.

[21] *Ibid.*, pp. 134–35, 140–43.

[22] These punishments are discussed most vividly in Kogon, *Theory and Practice*, pp. 102–8, 207–11.

[23] Bettelheim, "Individual and Mass Behavior," p. 445.

[24] The effects of never being alone are noted in Cohen, *Human Behavior*, pp. 130–31, and David Rousset, *The Other Kingdom* (New York: Reynal & Hitchcock, 1947), p. 133.

[25] "When the author [Bettelheim] expressed to some of the old prisoners his astonishment that they seemed not interested in discussing their future life outside the camp, they frequently

derlay the "egalitarianism" of the camps; old statuses had lost their meaning.[26] A final strain, which must have been particularly acute for the newcomer, was the omnipresent threat of death and the very unpredictable suddenness with which death might strike. Quite aside from the periodic gas-chamber selections, the guards in their sports and caprices were at liberty to kill any prisoner any time.[27]

In the face of all this, one might suppose that the very notion of an "adjustment" would be grotesque. The majority of those who entered the camps never came out again, but our concern here has to be with those who survived—an estimated 700,000 out of nearly eight million.[28] For them, the regime must be considered not as a system of death but as a way of life. These survivors did make an adjustment of some sort to the system; it is they themselves who report it. After the initial shocks, what was the nature of the "normality" that emerged?

A dramatic species of psychic displacement seems to have occurred at the very outset. This experience, described as a kind of "splitting of personality," has been noted by most of the inmates who later wrote of their imprisonment. The very extremity of the initial tortures produced in the prisoner what actually amounted to a sense of detachment; these brutalities went so beyond his own experience that they became somehow incredi-

ble—they seemed to be happening no longer to him but almost to someone else. "[The author] has no doubt," writes Bruno Bettelheim, "that he was able to endure the transportation, and all that followed, because right from the beginning he became convinced that these horrible and degrading experiences somehow did not happen to 'him' as a subject, but only to 'him' as an object."[29] This subject-object "split" appears to have served a double function: not only was it an immediate psychic defense mechanism against shock,[30] but it also acted as the first thrust toward a new adjustment. This splitting-off of a special "self"—a self which endured the tortures but which was not the "real" self—also provided the first glimpse of a new personality which, being not "real," would not need to feel bound by the values which guided the individual in his former life. "The prisoners' feelings," according to Mr. Bettelheim, "could be summed up by the following sentence: 'What I am doing here, or what is happening to me, does not count at all; here everything is permissible as long and insofar as it contributes to helping me survive in the camp.' "[31]

One part of the prisoner's being was thus, under sharp stress, brought to the crude realization that he must thenceforth be governed by an entire new set of standards in order to live. Mrs. Lingens-Reiner puts it bluntly: "Will you survive, or shall I? As soon as one sensed that this was at stake everyone turned egotist."[32] ". . . I think it of

---

admitted that they could no longer visualize themselves living outside the camp, making free decisions, taking care of themselves and their families." Bettelheim, "Individual and Mass Behavior," p. 439.

[26] M. Rousset tells of how, on one of the death marches, a prisoner came to him bringing a French compatriot and begging his protection for the wretched man. "He told me that he was a lawyer from Toulouse, and it was only with the greatest difficulty that I kept from laughing aloud. For this social designation, *lawyer*, no longer fitted the poor wretch in the slightest. The incongruity of the thought was irresistibly comic. And it was the same with all of us." Rousset, *Other Kingdom*, p. 77.

[27] Kogon, *Theory and Pratice*, p. 274; Cohen, *Human Behavior*, p. 155; Hilde O. Bluhm, "How Did They Survive?" *American Journal of Psychotherapy*, II (January, 1948), 5.

[28] Kogon, *Theory and Practice*, p. 277.

[29] Bettelheim, "Individual and Mass Behavior," p. 431. See also Cohen, *Human Behavior*, pp. 116–17, 172.

[30] "Many kept their bearings only by a kind of split personality. They surrendered their bodies resistlessly to the terror, while their inner being withdrew and held aloof." Kogon, *Theory and Practice*, p. 71. "I arrived at that state of numbness where I was no longer sensitive to either club or whip. I lived through the rest of that scene almost as a spectator." Lengyel, *Five Chimneys*, p. 20.

[31] Bettelheim, "Individual and Mass Behavior," p. 432. "We camp prisoners," writes Mrs. Lingens-Reiner, "had only one yardstick: whatever helped our survival was good, and whatever threatened our survival was bad, and to be avoided." *Prisoners of Fear*, p. 142.

[32] Lingens-Reiner, *Prisoners of Fear*, p. 23.

primary importance," writes Dr. Cohen, "to take into account that the superego acquired new values in a concentration camp, so much at variance with those which the prisoner bore with him into camp that the latter faded."[33] But then this acquisition of "new values" did not all take place immediately; it was not until some time after the most acute period of stress was over that the new, "unreal" self would become at last the "real" one.

"If you survive the first three months you will survive the next three years." Such was the formula transmitted from the old prisoners to the new ones,[34] and its meaning lay in the fact that the first three months would generally determine a prisoner's capacity for survival and adaptation. "Be inconspicuous": this was the golden rule.[35] The prisoner who called attention to himself, even in such trivial matters as the wearing of glasses, risked doom. Any show of bravado, any heroics, any kind of resistance condemned a man instantly. There were no rewards for martyrdom: not only did the martyr himself suffer, but mass punishments were wreaked upon his fellow inmates. To "be inconspicuous" required a special kind of alertness— almost an animal instinct[36] against the apathy which tended to follow the initial shocks.[37] To give up the struggle for survival was to commit "passive suicide"; a careless mistake meant death. There were those, however, who did come through this phase and who managed an adjustment to the life of the camp. It was the striking contrasts between this group of two- and three-year veterans and the perpetual stream of newcomers which made it possible for men like Bettelheim and Cohen to speak of the "old prisoner" as a specific type.

The most immediate aspect of the old inmates' behavior which struck these observers was its *childlike* quality. "The prisoners developed types of behavior which are characteristic of infancy or early youth. Some of these behaviors developed slowly, others were immediately imposed on the prisoners and developed only in intensity as time went on."[38] Such infantile behavior took innumerable forms. The inmates' sexual impotence brought about a disappearance of sexuality in their talk;[39] instead, excretory functions occupied them endlessly. They lost many of the customary inhibitions as to soiling their beds and their persons.[40] Their humor was shot with silliness and they giggled like children when one of them would expel wind. Their relationships were highly unstable. "Prisoners would, like early adolescents, fight one another tooth and nail . . . only to become close friends within a few minutes."[41] Dishonesty became chronic.

---

[33] *Human Behavior*, p. 136. The "superego," Freud's term for the "conscience," is discussed below, pp. 116–18.

[34] Bettelheim, "Individual and Mass Behavior," p. 438.

[35] Cohen, *Human Behavior*, p. 169.

[36] This should in no sense be considered as a calculating, "rational" alertness, but rather as something quite primitive. "Of myself," writes Dr. Cohen, "I know that I was not continuously occupied by the reflection: I am going to win through. The actions which contributed to my survival were performed instinctively rather than consciously. . . . Like animals warned by their instinct that danger is imminent, we would act instinctively at critical moments. These instinctive acts must, I think, be considered as manifestations of the life instinct. If the life instinct is not strong enough, the instinct will desert the individual, and instead of rising to the emergency, the individual will succumb, whereas a stronger life instinct would have seen him through." *Human Behavior*, p. 163.

[37] Those who had in fact succumbed to this apathy—who had given up the struggle, and for whom death would be a mere matter of time— were known as "Moslems." See above, n. 17.

[38] Bettelheim, "Individual and Mass Behavior," p. 141.

[39] Says Dr. Cohen, "I am not asserting that sex was never discussed; it was, though not often. Frankl also states 'that in contrast to mass existence in other military communities . . . here (in the concentration camp) there is *no smut talk.*'" *Human Behavior*, p. 141.

[40] "With reference to this phenomenon Miss Bluhm has pointed out that it is not at all unusual that people in extraordinary circumstances, for example soldiers in wartime, 'are able to give up their habitual standards of cleanliness without deeper disturbance; yet only up to certain limits.' The rules of anal cleanliness, she adds, are not disregarded. 'Their neglect means return to instinctual behavior of childhood.'" *Ibid.*, p. 175.

[41] Bettelheim, "Individual and Mass Behavior," p. 445.

"Now they suddenly appeared to be pathological liars, to be unable to restrain themselves, to be unable to make objective evaluation, etc."[42] "In hundreds of ways," writes Colaço Belmonte, "the soldier, and to an even greater extent the prisoner of war, is given to understand that he is a child. . . . Then dishonesty, mendacity, egotistic actions in order to obtain more food or to get out of scrapes reach full development, and theft becomes a veritable affliction of camp life."[43] This was all true according to Elie Cohen, in the concentration camp as well.[44] Benedikt Kautsky observed such things in his own behavior: "I myself can declare that often I saw myself as I used to be in my school days, when by sly dodges and clever pretexts we avoided being found out, or could 'organize' something."[45] Bruno Bettelheim remarks on the extravagance of the stories told by the prisoners to one another. "They were boastful, telling tales about what they had accomplished in their former lives, or how they succeeded in cheating foremen or guards, and how they sabotaged the work. Like children they felt not at all set back or ashamed when it became known that they had lied about their prowess."[46]

This development of childlike behavior in the old inmates was the counterpart of something even more striking that was happening to them: *Only very few of the prisoners escaped a more or less intensive identification with the SS.*[47] As Mr. Bettelheim puts it: "A prisoner had reached the final stage of adjustment to the camp situation when he had changed his personality so as to accept as his own the values of the Gestapo."[48] The

Bettelheim study furnishes a catalog of examples. The old prisoners came to share the attitude of the SS toward the "unfit" prisoners; newcomers who behaved badly in the labor groups or who could not withstand the strain became a liability for the others, who were often instrumental in getting rid of them. Many old prisoners actually imitated the SS; they would sew and mend their uniforms in such a way as to make them look more like those of the SS— even though they risked punishment for it. "When asked why they did it, they admitted that they loved to look like . . . the guards." Some took great enjoyment in the fact that during roll call "they really had stood well at attention." There were cases of nonsensical rules, made by the guards, which the older prisoners would continue to observe and try to force on the others long after the SS had forgotten them.[49] Even the most abstract ideals of the SS, such as their intense German nationalism and anti-Semitism, were often absorbed by the old inmates—a phenomenon observed among the politically well educated and even among the Jews themselves.[50] The final quintessence of all this was seen in the "Kapo"—the prisoner who had been placed in a supervisory position over his fellow inmates. These creatures, many of them professional criminals, not only behaved with slavish servility to the SS, but the way in which they often outdid the SS in sheer brutality became one of the most

---

[42] *Ibid.,* p. 421.

[43] Quoted in Cohen, *Human Behavior,* p. 176.

[44] *Ibid.*

[45] *Ibid.,* p. 174.

[46] Bettelheim, "Individual and Mass Behavior," pp. 445–46. This same phenomenon is noted by Curt Bondy: "They tell great stories about what they have been before and what they have performed." "Problems of Interment Camps," *Journal of Abnormal and Social Psychology,* XXXVIII (October, 1943), 453–75.

[47] Cohen, *Human Behavior,* p. 177. Italics in original.

[48] Bettelheim, "Individual and Mass Behavior," p. 447.

[49] *Ibid.,* pp. 448–50. "Once, for instance, a guard on inspecting the prisoners' apparel found that the shoes of some of them were dirty on the inside. He ordered all prisoners to wash their shoes inside and out with water and soap. The heavy shoes treated this way became hard as stone. The order was never repeated, and many prisoners did not execute it when given. Nevertheless there were some old prisoners who not only continued to wash the inside of their shoes every day but cursed all others who did not do so as negligent and dirty. These prisoners firmly believed that the rules set down by the Gestapo were desirable standards of human behavior, at least in the camp situation." *Ibid.,* p. 450.

[50] *Ibid.* See also Cohen, *Human Behavior,* pp. 189–93, for a discussion of anti-Semitism among the Jews.

durable features of the concentration-camp legend.

To all these men, reduced to complete and childish dependence upon their masters, the SS had actually become a father symbol. "The SS man was all-powerful in the camp, he was the lord and master of the prisoner's life. As a cruel father he could, without fear of punishment, even kill the prisoner and as a gentle father he could scatter largesse and afford the prisoner his protection."[51] The result, admits Dr. Cohen, was that "for all of us the SS was a father image. . . ."[52] The closed system, in short, had become a kind of grotesque patriarchy.

The literature provides us with three remarkable tests of the profundity of the experience which these prisoners had undergone and the thoroughness of the changes which had been brought about in them. One is the fact that few cases of real resistance were ever recorded, even among prisoners going to their death.

With a few altogether insignificant exceptions, the prisoners, no matter in what form they were led to execution, whether singly, in groups, or in masses, never fought back! . . . there were thousands who had by no means relapsed into fatal apathy. Nevertheless, in mass liquidations they went to their death with open eyes, without assaulting the enemy in a final paroxysm, without a sign of fight. Is this not in conflict with human nature, as we know it?[53]

Even upon liberation, when revenge against their tormentors at last became possible, mass uprisings very rarely occurred. "Even when the whole system was overthrown by the Allies," says David Rousset writing of

Buchenwald, "nothing happened. . . . The American officer appointed to command of the camp was never called upon to cope with any inclination toward a popular movement. No such disposition existed."[54]

A second test of the system's effectiveness was the relative scarcity of suicides in the camps.[55] Though there were suicides, they tended to occur during the first days of internment, and only one mass suicide is known; it took place among a group of Jews at Mauthausen who leaped into a rock pit three days after their arrival.[56] For the majority of prisoners the simplicity of the urge to survive made suicide, a complex matter of personal initiative and decision, out of the question. Yet they could, when commanded by their masters, go to their death without resistance.

The third test lies in the very absence, among the prisoners, of hatred toward the SS. This is probably the hardest of all to understand. Yet the burning spirit of rebellion which many of their liberators expected to find would have had to be supported by fierce and smoldering emotions; such emotions were not there. "It is remarkable," one observer notes, "how little hatred of their wardens is revealed in their stories."[57]

* * * * *

It is hoped that the very hideousness of

---

[51] Cohen, *Human Behavior*, pp. 176–77.

[52] *Ibid.*, p. 179. On this and other points I must also acknowledge my indebtedness to Mr. Ies Spetter, a former Dutch journalist now living in this country, who was imprisoned for a time at Auschwitz during World War II. Mr. Spetter permitted me to see an unpublished paper, "Some Thoughts on Victims and Criminals in the German Concentration Camps," which he wrote in 1954 at the New School for Social Research; and this, together with a number of conversations I had with him, added much to my understanding of concentration-camp psychology.

[53] Kogon, *Theory and Practice*, p. 284.

[54] *The Other Kingdom*, p. 137.

[55] "In the preference camp Bergen Belsen, only four cases of attempted suicide were witnessed by Tas, three of which were saved with great effort, while in the Stammlager Auschwitz only one successful attempt came to my knowledge. This does not mean that there were not more, but their number was certainly small. Kaas, on the other hand, witnessed several attempted suicides in Buchenwald. He has remembered three that were successful (two by hanging, one by rushing into the electric fence). He also knows of prisoners who were known to be depressive cases, and who were shot down when during the night they had deliberately gone out of bounds. As compared with the large number of prisoners, the number of suicides, however, was very small." Cohen, *Human Behavior*, p. 158.

[56] Kogon, *Theory and Practice*, pp. 166–67. This occurred during fearful tortures at the quarry, where the Jews knew they were about to be killed anyway.

[57] A. Hottinger, *Hungerkrankheit, Hungerö-*

a special example of slavery has not disqualified it as a test for certain features of a far milder and more benevolent form of slavery. But it should still be possible to say, with regard to the individuals who lived as slaves within the respective systems, that just as on one level there is every difference between a wretched childhood and a carefree one, there are, for other purposes, limited features which the one may be said to have shared with the other.

Both were closed systems from which all standards based on prior connections had been effectively detached. A working adjustment to either system required a childlike conformity, a limited choice of "significant others." Cruelty per se cannot be considered the primary key to this; of far greater importance was the simple "closedness" of the system, in which all lines of authority descended from the master and in which alternative social bases that might have supported alternative standards were systematically suppressed.[58] The individual, consequently, for his very psychic security, had to picture his master in

some way as the "good father,"[59] even when, as in the concentration camp, it made no sense at all.[60] But why should it not have

_____

dem, *Hungertuberkulose*, p. 32, quoted in Cohen, *Human Behavior*, p. 197. "After the liberation many writers were struck by the callousness of the onetime prisoners, and particularly by their apathy when relating their experiences, even the most horrible." *Ibid.*, p. 144.

[58] The experience of American prisoners taken by the Chinese during the Korean War seems to indicate that profound changes in behavior and values, if not in basic personality itself, can be effected without the use of physical torture or extreme deprivation. The Chinese were able to get large numbers of Americans to act as informers and to cooperate in numerous ways in the effort to indoctrinate all the prisoners with Communist propaganda. The technique contained two key elements. One was that all formal and informal authority structures within the group were systematically destroyed; this was done by isolating officers, noncommissioned officers, and any enlisted men who gave indications of leadership capacities. The other element involved the continual emphasizing of the captors' power and influence by judicious manipulation of petty rewards and punishments and by subtle hints of the greater rewards and more severe punishments (repatriation or nonrepatriation) that rested with the pleasure of those in authority. See Edgar H. Schein, "Some Observations on Chinese Methods of Handling Prisoners of War," *Public Opinion Quarterly*, XX (Spring, 1956), 321–27.

[59] In a system as tightly closed as the plantation or the concentration camp, the slave's or prisoner's position of absolute dependency virtually compels him to see the authority figure as somehow really "good." Indeed, all the evil in his life may flow from this man—but then so also must everything of any value. Here is the seat of the only "good" he knows, and to maintain his psychic balance he must persuade himself that the good is in some way dominant. A threat to this illusion is thus in a real sense a threat to his very existence. It is a common experience among social workers dealing with neglected and maltreated children to have a child desperately insist on his love for a cruel and brutal parent and beg that he be allowed to remain with that parent. The most dramatic feature of this situation is the cruelty which it involves, but the mechanism which inspires the devotion is not the cruelty of the parent but rather the abnormal dependency of the child. A classic example of this mechanism in operation may be seen in the case of Varvara Petrovna, mother of Ivan Turgenev. Mme Turgenev "ruled over her serfs with a rod of iron." She demanded utter obedience and total submission. The slightest infraction of her rules brought the most severe punishment: "A maid who did not offer her a cup of tea in the proper manner was sent off to some remote village and perhaps separated from her family forever; gardeners who failed to prevent the plucking of a tulip in one of the flower beds before the house were ordered to be flogged; a servant whom she suspected of a mutinous disposition was sent off to Siberia." Her family and her most devoted servants were treated in much the same manner. "Indeed," wrote Varvara Zhitova, the adopted daughter of Mme Turgenev, "those who loved her and were most devoted to her suffered most of all." Yet in spite of her brutality she was adored by the very people she tyrannized. David Magarshack describes how once when thrashing her eldest son she nearly fainted with sadistic excitement, whereupon "little Nicholas, forgetting his punishment, bawled at the top of his voice: 'Water! Water for mummy!'" Mme Zhitova, who knew Mme Turgenev's cruelty intimately and was herself the constant victim of her tyranny, wrote: "In spite of this, I loved her passionately, and when I was, though rarely, separated from her, I felt lonely and unhappy." Even Mme Turgenev's maid Agatha, whose children were sent to another village, when still infants so that Agatha might devote all her time to her mistress, could say years later, "Yes, she caused me much grief. I suffered much from her, but all the same I loved her! She was a real lady!" V. Zhitova, *The Turgenev Family*, trans. A. S. Mills (London: Havill Press, 1954), p. 25; David Magarshack, *Turgenev: A Life* (New York: Grove, 1954), pp. 14, 16, 22.

[60] Bruno Bettelheim tells us of the fantastic efforts of the old prisoners to believe in the be-

made sense for many a simple plantation Negro whose master did exhibit, in all the ways that could be expected, the features of the good father who was really "good"? If the concentration camp could produce in two or three years the results that it did, one wonders how much more pervasive must have been those attitudes, expectations, and values which had, certainly, their benevolent side and which were accepted and transmitted over generations.

For the Negro child, in particular, the plantation offered no really satisfactory father image other than the master. The "real" father was virtually without authority over his child, since discipline, parental responsibility, and control of rewards and punishments all rested in other hands; the slave father could not even protect the mother of his children except by appealing directly to the master. Indeed, the mother's own role loomed far larger for the slave child than did that of the father. She controlled those few activities—household care, preparation of food, and rearing of children—that were left to the slave family. For that matter, the very etiquette of plantation life removed even the honorific attributes of fatherhood from the Negro male, who was addressed as "boy"—until, when the vigorous years of his prime were past, he was allowed to assume the title of "uncle."

From the master's viewpoint, slaves had been defined in law as property, and the

master's power over his property must be absolute. But then this property was still human property. These slaves might never be quite as human as *he* was, but still there were certain standards that could be laid down for their behavior: obedience, fidelity, humility, docility, cheerfulness, and so on. Industry and diligence would of course be demanded, but a final element in the master's situation would undoubtedly qualify that expectation. Absolute power for him meant absolute dependency for the slave— the dependency not of the developing child but of the perpetual child. For the master, the role must aptly fitting such a relationship would naturally be that of the father. As a father he could be either harsh or kind, as he chose, but as a *wise* father he would have, we may suspect, a sense of the limits of his situation. He must be ready to cope with *all* the qualities of the child, exasperating as well as ingratiating. He might conceivably have to expect in this child—besides his loyalty, docility, humility, cheerfulness, and (under supervision) his diligence—such additional qualities as irresponsibility, playfulness, silliness, laziness, and (quite possibly) tendencies to lying and stealing. Should the entire prediction prove accurate, the result would be something resembling "Sambo."

The social and psychological sanctions of role-playing may in the last analysis prove to be the most satisfactory of the several approaches to Sambo, for, without doubt, of all the roles in American life that of Sambo was by far the most pervasive. The outlines of the role might be sketched in by crude necessity, but what of the finer shades? The sanctions against overstepping it were bleak enough,[61] but the rewards— the sweet applause, as it were, for performing it with sincerity and feeling—were something to be appreciated on quite another level. The law, untuned to the deeper harmonies, could command the player to

---

nevolence of the officers of the SS. "They insisted that these officers [hid] behind their rough surface of feeling of justice and propriety; he, or they, were supposed to be genuinely interested in the prisoners and even trying, in a small way, to help them. Since nothing of these supposed feelings and efforts ever became apparent, it was explained that he hid them so effectively because otherwise he would not be able to help the prisoners. The eagerness of these prisoners to find reasons for their claims was pitiful. A whole legend was woven around the fact that of two officers inspecting a barrack one had cleaned his shoes from mud before entering. He probably did it automatically, but it was interpreted as a rebuff of the other officer and a clear demonstration of how he felt about the concentration camp." Bettelheim, "Individual and Mass Behavior," p. 451.

[61] Professor Stampp, in a chapter called "To Make Them Stand in Fear," describes the planter's resources for dealing with a recalcitrant slave. *Peculiar Institution*, pp. 141–91.

be present for the occasion, and the whip might even warn against his missing the grosser cues, but could those things really insure the performance that melted all hearts? Yet there was many and many a performance, and the audiences (whose standards were high) appear to have been for the most part well pleased. They were actually viewing their own masterpiece. Much labor had been lavished upon this chef d'oeuvre, the most genial resources of Southern society had been available for the work; touch after touch had been applied throughout the years, and the result —embodied not in the unfeeling law but in the richest layers of Southern lore— had been the product of an exquisitely rounded collective creativity. And indeed, in a sense that somehow transcended the merely ironic, it was a labor of love. "I love the simple and unadulterated slave, with his geniality, his mirth, his swagger, and his nonsense," wrote Edward Pollard. "I love to look upon his countenance shining with content and grease; I love to study his affectionate heart; I love to mark that peculiarity in him, which beneath all his buffoonery exhibits him as a creature of the tenderest sensibilities, mingling his joys and his sorrows with those of his master's home."[62] Love, even on those terms, was surely no inconsequential reward.

But what were the terms? The Negro was to be a child forever. "The Negro . . . in his true nature, is always a boy, let him be ever so old. . . ."[63] "He is . . . a dependent upon the white race; dependent for guidance and direction even to the procurement of his most indispensable necessaries. Apart from this protection he has the helplessness of a child—without foresight, without faculty of contrivance, without thrift of any kind."[64] Not only was he a child; he was a happy child. Few Southern

writers failed to describe with obvious fondness the bubbling gaiety of a plantation holiday or the perpetual good humor that seemed to mark the Negro character, the good humor of an everlasting childhood.

The role, of course, must have been rather harder for the earliest generations of slaves to learn. "Accommodation," according to John Dollard, "involves the renunciation of protest or aggression against undesirable conditions of life and the organization of the character so that protest does not appear, but acceptance does. It may come to pass in the end that the unwelcome force is idealized, that one identifies with it and takes it into the personality; it sometimes even happens that what is at first resented and feared is finally loved."[65]

Might the process, on the other hand,

---

[62] Edward A. Pollard, *Black Diamonds Gathered in the Darkey Homes of the South* (New York: Pudney & Russel, 1859), p. 58.

[63] *Ibid.*, p. viii.

[64] John Pendleton Kennedy, *Swallow Barn* (Philadelphia: Carey & Lea, 1832).

[65] John Dollard, *Caste and Class in a Southern Town* (2d ed.; New York: Harper, 1949), p. 255. The lore of "accommodation," taken just in itself, is very rich and is, needless to say, morally very complex. It suggests a delicate psychological balance. On the one hand, as the Dollard citation above implies, accommodation is fraught with dangers for the personalities of those who engage in it. On the other hand, as Bruno Bettelheim has reminded me, this involves a principle that goes well beyond American Negro society and is to be found deeply imbedded in European traditions: the principle of how the powerless can manipulate the powerful through aggressive stupidity, literal-mindedness, servile fawning, and irresponsibility. In this sense the immovably stupid "Good Soldier Schweik" and the fawning Negro in Richard Wright's *Black Boy* who allowed the white man to kick him for a quarter partake of the same tradition. Each has a technique whereby he can in a real sense exploit his powerful superiors, feel contempt for them, and suffer in the process no great damage to his own pride. Jewish lore, as is well known, teems with this sort of thing. There was much of it also in the traditional relationships between peasants and nobles in central Europe.

Still, all this required the existence of some sort of alternative forces for moral and psychological orientation. The problem of the Negro in slavery times involved the virtual absence of such forces. It was with the end of slavery, presumably, that they would first begin to present themselves in generally usable form—a man's neighbors, the Loyal Leagues, white politicians, and so on. It would be in these circumstances that the essentially intermediate technique of accommodation could be used as a protective device beneath which a more independent personality might develop.

be reversed? It is hard to imagine its being reversed overnight. The same role might still be played in the years after slavery— we are told that it was[66]—and yet it was played to more vulgar audiences with cruder standards, who paid much less for

what they saw. The lines might be repeated more and more mechanically, with less and less conviction; the incentives to perfection could become hazy and blurred, and the excellent old piece could degenerate over time into low farce. There could come a point, conceivably, with the old zest gone, that it was no longer worth the candle. The day might come at last when it dawned on a man's full waking consciousness that he had really grown up, that he was, after all, only playing a part. . . .

---

[66] Even Negro officeholders during Reconstruction, according to Francis B. Simkins, "were known to observe carefully the etiquette of the Southern caste system." "New Viewpoints of Southern Reconstruction," *Journal of Southern History*, V (February, 1939), 52.

1963

Spirituals and the Far Side of Jordan*

WAYMAN B. McLAUGHLIN

The concrete problem of the present paper is to explore some basic aspects of symbolism and mysticism in the spirituals.[1] The spirituals are sacred folk music born out of the aches, pains, and joys of existence. The soul-life of a people is here woven into a testament of mystery and holiness. Nymph-like, amid shadows and echoes, the singers of this music weaved out of the matrix of economic, social, and religious circumstances a web of being

which was ultimate and personal. Thus, these songs reflect light and darkness in the heave and flow of a personal reality.

In pursuing this problem there is the need at the outset to define two terms: "symbolism" and "mysticism." Symbolism is simply the art of representing something by symbols. But what is a symbol? In general terms a symbol is an outward sign of an inward meaning. In the book, *The Forgotten Language*, Erich Fromm says this concerning the role of symbolical thinking in life:

Symbolical thinking represents the very substance of the psychic life. . . . Symbolical language is language in which the world outside is a symbol of the world inside, a symbol for our souls and minds.[2]

If this statement of Fromm be true, perhaps one of the most fruitful ways of thinking

---

* Wayman B. McLaughlin, "Symbolism and Mysticism in the Spirituals," *Phylon* (1963).

[1] Richard Wright, *White Man, Listen!* (New York, 1937), p. 128. Wright expresses the opposite point of view in the following words: "It was through the door of religion that the American Negro first walked into the house of Western culture, and it was through religious symbols that he has given voice to his most poignant yearnings. And yet, instead of his songs being mystical or metaphysical, they are simply and directly wish fulfillments, projections of his longings to escape his chains and blows." The view of this paper is that Wright's psychological factor is one among many others in the spirituals.

[2] Erich Fromm, *The Forgotten Language* (New York, 1951), p. 12.

about spirituals may be in terms of symbolical language and mystical meaning.

The term "mysticism" is an interesting word in our modern world. In many areas the word is considered to mean a kind of sixth sense. But the term is derived from the mystery religion of Greece. It meant a person who had entered into a hidden truth by a secret way. With the influence of Neoplatonism and Christian tradition, mysticism makes the claim of being an intuitive experience, that is, in direct communion with God.[3] Accordingly, mysticism may be defined as the experience of direct communion of the soul with God. Bergson's *The Two Sources of Morality and Religion* reveals the fragile beauty of the mystical criterion of truth in the following words:

What a shock to the soul is the passing from the static to the dynamic, from the closed to the open, from everyday life to mystic life. When the darkest depths of the soul are stirred, what rises to the surface and attains consciousness takes on there an image or an emotion. . . . The image becomes symbolic of what is about to happen. . . . The soul ceases to revolve around itself. It feels an indefinable presence, or divines through a symbolic vision. Then comes an enthralling rapture. God is there, and the soul is God.[4]

Specifically, Bergson is saying with Fromm that the outward symbol is the representation of inward experience. But Bergson reasons further the point of view of this paper, that in the mystical temper this inner experience witnesses through the symbol to a concrete event of man's relation to God.

It is clear, in the light of the foregoing, that the spirituals represent predominantly personal mysticism of the Christian tradition. They personalize in the concrete the individual's "I-Thou" encounter with God. They have dramatic intensification, extemporaneous creations, and spontaneous dialogues between man and God. We are

struck in these religious songs by the exceptional awareness of reality. In the floodlight of this reality it appears that the slaves stood with flaming souls in the somewhat Psalm-like beauty of the Hebrews.

The method of procedure in this paper will be a comparative-objective analysis of the symbolical and mystical thinking in the spirituals in light of some main principles of mysticism.

The mystic insight begins with the view of the unveiling of a mystery. Closely related to this view is the emphasis upon revelation rather than reason. The soul appears in utter loneliness to bring forth out of its own depths a within that is a beyond. Similarly, many of the spirituals issue out of a fourth dimension of personality, that is, the faith situation. Existentially, they whisper of hope, grief, affection, loneliness, regret, toil, struggle, death and faith. They have Apollonian and Dionysian qualities of Greek tragedy. The former implies an element of repose and peace; the latter refers to the element of passion and vitality. Like Dante's *Divine Comedy*, the intuitions of these songs were made into an insight concerning the panorama of life and destiny.

In the following spiritual the individual begins with the experience of cosmic exile from world and God that ends in an exclamatory faith:

I feel like a motherless child;
I feel like a motherless child;
Glory Hallelujah!
Sometimes my way is sad and lone,
When far away and lost from home;
Glory Hallelujah!

The dominant symbol, "motherless child," reveals the homesickness of the individual's soul. "Far away" and "lost from home" point to the feeling of destitution without any protective care. At this moment with mystic insight the singer experiences the deep consciousness of the presence of God. It is as if the soul has caught a glimpse of the divine spark. The singer realizes for a

---

[3] Bertrand Russell, *Mysticism and Logic* (London, 1917), p. 3.

[4] Henri Bergson, *The Two Sources of Morality and Religion* (New York, 1954), p. 230.

luminous moment that he is at home within the Absolute. This moment of certainty is to be found in his joyous epithet, "Glory Hallelujah!" This spiritual has the same motif of Augustine's *Confessions:* "Thou hast made us for Thyself, our heart is restless until it finds its rest in Thee."[5]

Another variation of the mystic sense of certainty is found in these words:

Oh, I know, I know, my Lord,
I know, and I know that my Redeemer lives.
Oh, Daniel in the lion's den, I know
That my Redeemer lives.
Oh, none but Jesus is Daniel's friend,
I know that my Redeemer lives.

In the symbol-characters of Shadrack, Moses, Samson, and others, the slave singers found men of voices like their own. Daniel's experiences illustrate his lively faith in the reality of God in the world.

Or take this beautiful folk song; here the singer's firm certainty of fulfillment in God is demonstrated:

I've just come from the fountain,
I've just come from the fountain,
Lord! I've just come from the fountain,
His name's so sweet.

This spiritual is like the morning star, full of splendor, light, and joy. It is one of the noblest spirituals in terms of mystical intuition. Its soul-poet points out that he has been to the "All-Source" of life with the beauty of sensuousness, "His name's so sweet." Free imagination, warmth, freshness, abandonment, majestic flashes, and depth of spiritual insight are at work here. Mystically, God is being symbolized without incredulity, somewhat as in Longfellow's *Tales of a Wayside Inn:*

That God at their fountain
Far off hath been raining.[6]

There is inherent within the mystical tradition the will to believe in a calling or task:

---

[5] Augustine, *Confessions*, Book I, 1.
[6] Longfellow, *Tales of a Wayside Inn.*

O, I know the Lord,
I know the Lord,
I know the Lord laid his hands on me.

Did you ever see the like before,
I know the Lord laid his hands on me;

King Jesus preaching to the poor,
I know the Lord laid his hands on me.

The thought-symbol of this song is found in the scene of Christ beginning his ministry (Luke 4:17-19). Graphic description is given by the gifted singers of these songs to Jesus' concept of being called to preach to the poor. "Did ever you see the like before . . . King Jesus preaching to the poor." As Rembrandt and Degas sought in their paintings to take some things in their immediacy and ugliness and turn them into a beautiful peace, so these chanters of songs felt called to justify in a higher realm of intuition the grubby facts. But this was not necessarily flight from reality; rather, it became an intenser apprehension of life in terms of some ultimate, central vision: "I know the Lord laid his hands on me."

This certainty of life is not a closed, static, frozen belief, but open, moving, and alive. In fact, there is always the need of more of it:

Did you ever see such a man as God?
A little more faith in Jesus,
A preaching the Gospel to the poor,
A little more faith in Jesus.

Another notable aspect of mysticism is its belief in unity. According to Heraclitus, "Good and ill are one." With this belief in unity there is the view of infinite peace in God. Allied with this idea is the mystical awareness that all humanity is a part of the great ocean of life which has its source in God.

The spirituals center around man's search for unity. The spiritual "Ezekiel Saw the Wheel" is a vision of beauty and the song of mankind. The words are:

Ezekiel saw the wheel,
Way up in the middle of the air,
Ezekiel saw the wheel,
Way up in the middle of the air.

Ezekiel saw the wheel of time,
Ev'ry spoke was of the humankind,
A wheel in a wheel,
Way in the middle of the air.

O, the big wheel runs by faith
And the little wheel runs by the grace of God,
A wheel in a wheel,
Way in the middle of the air.

Ezekiel's vision in the Old Testament is used to bring out the key symbols. "Ev'ry spoke was of the humankind." "The big wheel runs by faith," and "the little wheel runs by the grace of God." These symbols reveal that the real grandeur of mankind is seen as a moral elevation held by the grace of God. The strong, significant symbol, "Wheel in a wheel," expresses the universal harmony of the human family in God.

"He Has the Whole World in His Hands" has in it the echo of the world. It comes out of the heartsearch of experience, like Pushkin's poetry and Shakespeare's plays. Its symbols are concrete and universal. The charm and significance of this song lie in the intermingling of themes. It is enumerative of the universal in the particular. It starts with the "wind and rain." "He's got the wind and the rain in His hands, He's got the whole world in His hands." It states: "He's got the lying man," "He's got the gambling man," "He's got the crap shooting man in His hands." Then, it adds a tender touch, "He's got the little bits-a-baby in His hands." Next: "He's got you and me, sister, in His hands. He's got everybody in His hands. He's got the whole world in His hands."

The curious apprehension of this song is like the mind of a child, beautiful and rare. God, as it were, has the world like a globe in His hands. Generally, there is a mystical approach to God in which one can say with Sandburg's "Prologue" in *The Family of Man:*

There is only one man in the world
And his name is All Men.
There is only one woman in the world
And her name is All Women.

There is only one child in the world
And the child's name is All Children.[7]

A similar pitch with a sadder key can be seen in this spiritual. It is expressive of Heraclitus' view that the way up and the way down are one and the same in the totality of God's being.

Sometimes, I'm up, sometimes I'm down,
Oh, yes, Lord,

Sometimes, I'm almost to the ground,
Oh, yes, Lord,

Oh, nobody knows the trouble I've seen,
Glory Hallelujah!

Here the "Hallelujah" is very important. It is the symbol of the mystic moment of unity amid the dual functions of the "ups" and "downs" of life. The introduction of the word "Hallelujah" points to the fact that the singer has come in contact with the luminous reality of God. The term means "God be praised!"

Another dominant factor of mysticism is the denial of temporal time. The trinity of clock time, past, present, and future, is an illusion. The true being of time is one-future oriented event. Accordingly, time is viewed in terms of its eternalism.

Again and again, the spirituals strike this eternal note of time. For instance:

Soon I will be done with the
    troubles of the world,
Troubles of the world, troubles
    of the world;
Soon I will be done with the
    troubles of the world
Going home to live with God.

The view of time as being a future event of the "promised land" can be seen in the following:

I am a po' pilgrim of sorrow,—
I'm in this wide worl' alone.
No hope in this worl' for to-morrow,
I'm strivin'—for heav'n my home—

_____
[7] Edward Steichen, *The Family of Man* (New York, 1955).

Sometimes I'm both tossed and driven,
Sometimes I know not where to roam
I've heard of a city called heav'n
I've started to make it my home.

In their eternal view of time there is the affirmation of life in terms of an ideal end. Time is telescoped into the symbol of heaven. "Heavenly shoes," "long white robes," "starry crowns," "golden slippers," "golden street," "golden harp" are not mystic-mild, but mystic-potent symbols. This eternal world for them is the true time. Heaven and the royal gifts of shoes are symbols of the fact that they are a part of the true world of goodness, truth, and beauty. These are the riches of the kingdom of ends. Here will be found the priceless treasure of worth and dignity.

Thus, these bards of the spiritual life sang of it in all its mystic beauty:

I got shoes,
You got shoes,
All God's children got shoes.
When we get to Heaven
We're going to put on our shoes
And shout all over God's Heaven.
Heaven! Heaven!

According to John Lovell, "I Got Shoes" symbolizes that the slaves had latent abilities and talents that they could not realize in this world of man's time, but in the world of God's time their possibilities for good would be fulfilled. "Shout all over God's Heaven" implies that when the singers got a chance, they would make their influence felt in all areas of the heavenly community.[8]

In their Prometheus' struggle toward the light, the singers saw death as a necessary prerequisite in order to enter into the real world. Often the singers' symbol of death was a boat or ship crossing the river of Jor-

dan. Here original symbols were preserved to denote death:

Tis the old ship of Zion,
Get on board, get on board.

However, a new concept was retained by a vital symbolism in the slave's everyday experience. Death was emphasized as the "same train." This train carried off his mother, father, sister, and brother. The continuation of this process of death can be seen in the repetition of the term "same train" three times. The train will be back tomorrow for him.

Same train, same train, same train
Carry my mother,
Same train be back to-morrer.

Death was not an end, but the means of entering into God's eternity. As heaven was the true home, eternity was the true time. This view has many elements of the utopianism of Voltaire's *Candide*.

The growth of the spiritual life is envisioned often in mystical language as a voyage, a journey, a flight, a river, or the climbing of a ladder. According to this view, the Spirit of God is a continuing reality.

For instance:

Deep River, my home is over Jordan:
Deep River, my home is over Jordan.
O don't you want to go to that Gospel
        Feast
That Promised Land where all is peace?
Deep River, I want to cross over into
        camp ground.

The ultimate effect of this contact with the deep river of life is the sense of belonging, "My home is over Jordan." The symbols of "camp ground" and "promised land" represent the kingdom of ends where each moment a person will be a participant in the feast of the good, noble, and true.

The sheer joy and ecstasy of mystic yearning expressed with a superb poetic skill can be seen in the following:

---

[8] John Lovell, "The Social Implication of the Negro Spirituals," *Journal of Negro Education* (October, 1939), 636–43. Lovell emphasizes the social aspect of the spirituals. It is the point of this paper that the social aspect is one among other factors. One of the main other factors is the mystical and religious insight.

Lord, I want two wings to veil my face;
Lord, I want two wings to fly away.
Lord, I want two wings to veil my face;
So the world can't do me no harm.

Meet me Jesus meet me,
Meet me in the middle of the air,
And if my two wings fail me,
Meet me with another pair.

These folk songs are a spiritual *Iliad* of the soul in union with God. There is the progress toward moral idealism, that is, the engagement of the imagination, the passion, and the intellect within a willing of and striving toward moral values. The basic problem of the singers of the spirituals was similar to that of Shakespeare's Hamlet: "To be or not to be, that is the question." The symbol of wings points to the striving of the soul toward union with God. It has all of the ingredients of the ancient maxim, "When me they fly, I am the wings."

Another striking mystical symbol used in the spirituals is that of a ladder. The Christian life is the passing from darkness into light, from partiality to completeness. Each "round" is a growth stage until the individual reaches his creative maker and destiny. With a note that has the ring of reality, the singers cry out:

We are climbing Jacob's ladder
We are climbing Jacob's ladder
Soldier of the Cross.

Every round goes higher and higher
Every round goes higher and higher
Soldier of the Cross.

Jacob's ladder is really of mystic import. It is a signification of the communion of the soul with the Ultimate Other. With vibrant insight this spiritual reveals the constant process of growth toward the reality of the Divine.

Another remarkable aspect of mysticism is its concept of God. In Christian mysticism, the revelation of the character of God is considered basically revealed in the life of Jesus Christ.

Christ, in the spirituals, means God. As the slave singer saw it, Christ is a continuing consummation of the reality of God. There seemed to be, for them, no basic distinction between God and Christ. Although these slave bards used the basic symbols of the Old and New Testaments in their contemplation of the birth, life, and death of Christ, they gave fresh interpretation of these experiences by fusing them with their own experiences. In their songs an old issue was dealt with afresh.

As those on the mountain top first see the coming beams of the sun, the advent of Christ is symbolized in these words:

Go tell it on de mountain
Over the hills and everywhere,
Go tell it on de mountain
That Jesus Christ is born.

When I was a seeker,
I sought both night and day,
I asked de Lord to help me,
And he show'd me de way.

The universal significance of the birth of Jesus is symbolized in this statement, "Go tell it on de mountain/Over the hills and everywhere." However, there is also a clear personal symbol, "When I was a seeker." The word "seeker" must be understood in terms of the background of Quaker mysticism. It implies the searching for the inner light, finding the right path, and entering into a new truth. This spiritual connects the birth of Jesus with His coming into the life of the individual.

Another illustration within this same framework is as follows:

Mary, what you goin' to name that Pretty
Little Baby? I think I call Him Emmanuel.

The vivid image of Emmanuel means that God is with us, and these chanters of the good saw this as implying hope for their situation. The motif of the inspiring power of God appears to be emphasized.

"Were You There?" trembles with throbbing reality of the vital life. This spiritual brings together all ethnic groups in one all-important question, "Were You There?" According to Roland Hayes, the singer is saying, "Are you there?"[9]

The ontological solitude of Jesus, that is, the serenity of His spirit amid overwhelming odds, was seen by the slaves in the following words:

> They crucified my Lord, and He never said
>   a mumblin' word,
> Not a word, not a word.
> The blood came twinklin' down, but He
>   never said a mumblin' word,
> Not a word, not a word.

The soul singers meant to say "trinklin," implying that His blood was trickling down. But they said "twinklin." If this be a true image, it signalizes that like a sparkling,

[9] Roland Hayes, *My Songs* (Boston, 1948), p. 127.

shimmering star, the blood of Jesus was bejeweled. Here, if anywhere, shines forth the poetic essence of these remarkable souls. Mystically, it is no wonder that songs poured from their hearts like rain from Shelley's "Cloud."

"He Arose" is an instance in which the singers saw in the resurrection of Jesus a new hope for man's creativity, progress, and renewal. In the woof and warp of experience they saw a rhyme and reason stronger than the back of the mythological Greek figure, Atlas, able to "bear my spirit on."

This paper has maintained that the spirituals are high art spiritually motivated. In them there is the working of the Eternal Spirit. The symbolical and mystical insights are in fruitful interplay.

1964

Negroes in Rebellion, 1835-1842[*]

KENNETH W. PORTER

The second Seminole War lasted from December, 1835, to August, 1842, and cost over $40 million and the lives of approximately 1,500 members of the armed forces of the United States,[1] in addition to those

[*] Kenneth W. Porter, "Negroes and the Seminole War, 1835–1842," *Journal of Southern History*, XXX (November 1964), 427–40. Copyright 1964 by the Southern Historical Association. Reprinted by permission of the Managing Editor.

[1] George Catlin, *Letters and Notes on the Manners, Customs, and Condition of the North American Indians* (2 vols.; New York, 1841), II, 219*n*; John T. Sprague, *The Origin, Progress, and Conclusion of the Florida War* . . . (New York, 1848), 526–50; Joshua R. Giddings, *The Exiles of Florida* (Columbus, O., 1858), 315.

of white settlers and militiamen. It is usually referred to as the country's most protracted and expensive Indian war,[2] but Major General Thomas Sidney Jesup, who was in command in Florida during its most crucial period, announced emphatically late in 1836, "This . . . is a negro, not an Indian war." The General, of course, was employing hyperbole to emphasize his belief that if the war were "not speedily put down, the south will feel the effects of it on their slave population before the end of the next

[2] See, for example, Ethan Allen Hitchcock, *Fifty Years in Camp and Field* (New York, 1909), 81.

season"[3]—in other words, that a general slave insurrection might ensue. Actually the war, which was undoubtedly an Indian war, was just as certainly a Negro war during its most critical years. There is abundant evidence that Negroes were more important than Indians in bringing it about and keeping it up, as well as largely influential in bringing it to a conclusion.

Of the Negroes in the Florida Indian country the most important group were those with a recognized position in the Seminole tribe. A few of these were admittedly the lawful slaves of the Indians and an even smaller number were legally free; the great majority, perhaps four-fifths, were runaway or "captured" Negroes and their descendants, all of whom were thus legally the property of white citizens.[4] White observers, however, were inclined to regard all these Negroes—except for very recent runaways or captives—as in some sense the Indians' slaves. Nearly all, regardless of legal status, received almost identical treatment from the Indians, which differed so much from the treatment of slaves by whites that it was a difference of kind rather than of degree. Indian agent Gad Humphreys in 1827 declared, "The negroes of the Seminole Indians are wholly independent . . . and are Slaves but in name; they work only when it suits their inclination"; while brevet Major General Edmund P. Gaines, a decade or so later, referred to them not as the Indians' slaves but as "their black vassals and allies."[5]

Although the Seminole Indians were of all the so-called civilized tribes the least influenced by European-American civilization, some of their chiefs, for reasons of prestige, had purchased Negro slaves; and as traditional allies of the British the Seminole also had no scruples about capturing slaves or receiving fugitive Negroes from the rebellious Americans or the Spaniards. The Indians, however, had no intention of spending their lives in supervising Negroes; so, save for a very few employed in personal service, the Negroes were furnished with axes, hoes, and seed corn and left to take care of themselves.

A system of relationships between the Seminole Indians and their Negroes developed which was the admiration or horror of all beholders. The Negroes lived in separate villages of well-built houses, raised crops of corn, sweet potatoes, other vegetables, and even cotton, and possessed herds of livestock; their masters, or rather protectors, never presumed to meddle with any of this property so long as they received a reasonable "tribute" at harvest and butchering time.[6] The Negroes also had plenty of time for hunting and fishing, and under this almost idyllic regime they throve amazingly. Dressed in the easy Indian costume, they were, according to one observer, "stout and even gigantic in their persons . . . the finest looking people I have ever seen." They were known, moreover, as well-armed and brave warriors; a major of Georgia militia in 1812 declared of the Seminole that the Negroes were "their best soldiers."[7]

---

[3] Court of Inquiry—Operations in Florida, &c.: Letter from the Secretary of War . . . , House Docs., 25th Cong., 2d sess., No. 78 (Serial 323), 52; American State Papers, Military Affairs (7 vols.; Washington, 1832–61), VII, 820–21.

[4] Negroes, &c., Captured from Indians in Florida, &c.: Letter from the Secretary of War . . . , House Docs., 25th Cong., 3rd sess., No. 225 (Serial 348), 119–20, 57–65; American State Papers, Military Affairs, VI, 461, 465.

[5] Clarence Edwin Carter (ed.), The Territorial Papers of the United States (Washington, 1934–   ), XXIII, 911, XXIV, 669; American State Papers, Military Affairs, VI, 470–71, 533–34, VII, 427.

[6] Sources cited in note 5, and [Woodburne Potter] The War in Florida (Baltimore, 1836), 45–46; John Lee Williams, The Territory of Florida . . . (New York, 1837), 240; William Kennedy, Texas: The Rise, Progress, and Prospects of the Republic of Texas (2 vols.; London, 1841), I, 350. See also, however, George A. McCall, Letters from the Frontiers . . . (Philadelphia, 1868), 160; and Jedidiah Morse, A Report to the Secretary of War of the United States on Indian Affairs . . . (New Haven, 1822), 309–11.

[7] See the author's "Negroes and the East Florida Annexation Plot, 1811–1813," Journal of Negro History, XXX (January, 1945), esp. 22–23, and "Negroes and the Seminole War, 1817–1818," ibid., XXXVI (July, 1951), esp. 255–56, 273–75.

The Seminole Negroes' prestige and influence among the Indians were what impressed observers most forcibly. The Negroes speedily acquired the Muskogee or Hitchiti tongue of their protectors without forgetting the English or Spanish they had learned among the whites, which made them valuable interpreters. From interpreting it was an easy step to advising and counseling. Some observers believed they governed the Indians, and one with a taste for classical comparisons said that the Seminole nation approached a doulocracy.[8] A few groups of fugitive Negroes established villages which were not under Seminole control, and the Indians sometimes found it convenient to assert that all Negro settlements in their country were of this character.[9]

For obvious reasons it is impossible to determine how many Seminole Negroes there were on the eve of the Seminole War. Estimates ranged from 300 or 400 to as many as 1,100; the estimate of "more than five hundred" made in 1834 is perhaps the best.[10] The Negro population in Florida, however, consisted mostly of plantation slaves. In East Florida, the principal arena of the Seminole War, about half the population was colored; there were 4,095 slaves, 343 free colored, and 4,515 whites. In the counties bordering on the Indian country the Negroes considerably outnumbered the whites.[11] The slaves in East Florida were

looked upon as potentially more dangerous than those in other slaveholding regions. According to an old settler, most of the male slaves in the Mosquito region near the St. Johns River owned guns for hunting to save their masters the expense of supplying them with the usual salt-pork ration. Both slaves and free Negroes were well acquainted with the Seminole Indians and Negroes, their way of life, and their language. Many of the slaves had "wives among the Indian negroes, and the Indian negroes had wives among them."[12] Ownership of firearms and acquaintance with the Indians were doubtless most extensive among those Negroes owned by whites whose traditions went back to "Spanish days"; but Governor William P. DuVal is quoted as saying in 1828 that "many of the slaves taken to Florida are the very worst in the Union,"[13] and the need for labor on a newly opened frontier may indeed have resulted in an unusually large proportion of slaves who had been "sold down the river" for bad conduct.

Although the attempt to remove the Seminole from Florida—the spark which set off the seven-year war—was ostensibly part of the general program for Indian removal, the presence and peculiar position of the Negroes among them was a decisive factor. The Seminole, who did not lie directly in the path of white settlement, might have been permitted to remain on the peninsula had it not been for the Negroes; in fact, the hardier and more obdurate of the Florida Seminole were in the end allowed to stay.

Sentiment for the removal of the Seminole Negroes preceded that for Indian removal. As early as 1821 the Florida Indian

[8] For additional sources on the generally idyllic situation of the Seminole Negroes see: [William Hayne Simmons] *Notices of East Florida* (Charleston, S.C., 1822), 44–45, 50, 76; Mark F. Boyd, "Horatio S. Dexter and Events Leading to the Treaty of Moultrie Creek with the Seminole Indians," *Florida Anthropologist*, XI (September, 1958), 84; [W. W. Smith] *Sketch of the Seminole War and Sketches During a Campaign* (Charleston, S.C., 1836), 21–22.

[9] Boyd, "Horatio S. Dexter," 91–92; David Y. Thomas, "Report on the Public Archives of Florida," American Historical Association, *Annual Report*, 1906 (2 vols.; Washington, 1908), II, 152.

[10] Carter (ed.), *Territorial Papers*, XXIV, 668, 643–45; *American State Papers, Military Affairs*, VI, 465.

[11] *Memorial of the People of the Territory of Florida for Admission into the Union, House Docs.*, 25th Cong., 3rd sess., No. 208 (Serial 347), 25; Carter (ed.), *Territorial Papers*, XXIV, 505–6, 643–45.

[12] *Reminiscences of James Ormond Concerning the Early Days of the Halifax Country* (n.p.: Ormond Village Improvement Association, 1941), 5–6; Thomas Douglas, *Autobiography of Thomas Douglas, Late Judge of the Supreme Court of Florida* (New York, 1856), 120–23.

[13] Carter (ed.), *Territorial Papers*, XXIII, 1059.

agent said of "the maroon negroes, who live among the Indians" that it would "be necessary to remove from the Floridas this group of lawless freebooters, among whom runaway negroes will always find a refuge," although he admitted that if force were employed the Indians would probably take the Negroes' part.[14] It was soon recognized that it was impossible to persuade the Indians to rid Florida of a "Serious nusance" [sic] by selling their Negroes, because of the Indians' attachment to them. The bodily removal of the Indians themselves was increasingly regarded as the only solution to the Negro problem.[15]

The citizens of Florida, however, would not have been content with the removal of the Seminole Indians if it meant that the Indians would take their Negroes west with them. Planters who had lost slaves through flight to the Indian country were determined to repossess them. Official circles in Florida argued strongly that the baneful influence which the alleged indolence of the Negroes exerted on the Indians made their separation necessary,[16] but earlier attempts through pressure and fraud to gain possession of the Indians' Negroes[17] suggest that the desire of white men for cheap slaves was a more important motive for the proposed separation of the Negroes from the Indians.

The program for Seminole removal reached a climax on March 28, 1833, when a Seminole delegation inspecting the Indian Territory was wheedled and bullied into expressing satisfaction with the region of Creek country set aside for the Seminole and with the plan of uniting them with the powerful Creeks as one people. The government then asserted that this so-called treaty of Fort Gibson committed the entire tribe to move west within three years. The Seminole, insisting that the delegation was without power to bind the Nation, strongly objected to removal in general and in particular to the prospect that they would become a despised minority in the powerful half-breed-dominated Creek confederacy. One of their objections was that the Creeks claimed the Negro "property" of the Seminole because of slaves who had escaped to the Seminole when the latter were still considered Lower Creeks and for whom the Creek Nation had been forced to pay; they feared that the Creeks would attempt to seize their Negroes, either in satisfaction of the claim or merely by force majeure. For the Seminole Negroes, seizure by the Creeks would mean at best substitution of a stricter control in place of slavery in name only; at worst, sale into real servitude among the whites.

The Seminole Negroes' greatest dread was that they would never reach the Creek country. All, regardless of legal status, belonged to a race the members of which normally occupied the position of chattels; the Negro without a recognized owner or without the clearest evidence of freedom was liable to seizure, no matter how long he had been in effect his own master or how dubious the claimant's title might be. Since the Seminole were to be assembled at a central point for transportation west under military supervision, this would give opportunity both for the white owners of fugitive Seminole Negroes to present their legal claims and for the unscrupulous to urge illegitimate claims or even simply to kidnap likely Negroes. Whites, indeed, had already seized or fraudulently acquired numerous Negroes claimed by Indians. John Hicks, onetime principal Seminole chief who was friendly to the whites, complained in 1829, "A white man sells us a Negro, and then turns around and claims him again, and our big father orders us to give him up."[18] If this could happen when the Seminole were more or less secure in

14 Morse, *Report to the Secretary of War*, 149–50.

15 Carter (ed.), *Territorial Papers*, XXIII, 434, 454, XXIV, 668, 679.

16 *Ibid.*, XXIII, 414, 1003, XXIV, 668.

17 *Ibid.*, XXIII, 472–75, 483–84; Sprague, *Origin of the Florida War*, 34, 65–67.

18 Carter (ed.), *Territorial Papers*, XXIII, 472–75, 483–84, 549–50; Potter, *War in Florida*, 24–26; Sprague, *Origin of the Florida War*, 51, 57, 66.

their own country, what would be their fate when surrounded by white men and in their power? An outrage committed shortly after the outbreak of the Seminole War demonstrates that their fears were not groundless. A band of whites raided the village of the friendly old chief Econchat-temicco, rounded up the Negroes, including the chief's half-Negro granddaughter, and carried them off to slavery in Georgia.[19]

The Negroes, described in April, 1835, by the officer commanding in East Florida as "bold, active, and armed," were determined not to submit to removal and to do all in their power to persuade their Indian protectors not to remove.[20] They possessed able leaders in Abraham, head chief Mica-nopy's principal Negro, a middle-aged runaway slave of fluent speech and polished manners from Pensacola, and John Caesar, a shrewd, fierce old man who had been brought up among the Indians and was the "chief Negro" of King Philip (Emathla) of the St. Johns Indians, the second chief in the Nation.[21] During the three years of grace Abraham and Caesar, Osceola and Yaha Hajo, and other Negro and Indian militants were busy preparing for resistance. The plantation slaves, well aware of the idyllic existence of even the "slaves" of the Seminole, were in many cases receptive to urgings that, when war broke out, they should rise with axe and torch, wreak havoc on the plantations, and then, laden with plunder, escape into the swamps and hammocks to a life of freedom and plenty.[22]

Abraham, Caesar, and their associates did not neglect the 300 or 400 free colored people of East Florida, nearly half of whom were residents of St. Augustine and vicinity. These free blacks had much more to lose and less to gain by supporting Seminole resistance than did the plantation slaves, but they were disgruntled at having recently been deprived of the privileges they had enjoyed under Spanish law and at being put under a territorial code so severe that it had inspired protests even from prominent white citizens.[23] Abraham and the others did not call on those comparatively few free Negroes to rise in arms but rather to furnish supplies and information. With their help, and with that of the Spanish, Indian, and Negro fishermen, lumbermen, and smugglers of the Southern coast, Abraham proceeded to build up a reserve of ammunition. After the war had been going on for a year he reportedly was still receiving consignments of powder, disguised as barrels of flour, from a free St. Augustine Negro.[24]

Near the end of December, 1835, the long-smoldering conflict broke out. The Seminole did not wait for brevet Brigadier General Duncan L. Clinch to attempt to carry out his threat that if they were not at Tampa Bay by January 8, 1836, he would remove them forcibly. Instead they took the initiative. On December 26–27 King Philip's Indians and Indian Negroes, with the assistance of many cane-field slaves, fell on the sugar plantations of the St. Johns valley. On December 28 Micanopy's Indian and Negro warriors

---

[19] R. H. Stewart to Richard K. Call, May 25, 1836, in Caroline M. Brevard, *A History of Florida from the Treaty of 1763 to Our Own Times* (2 vols.; Deland, Fla., 1924), I, 278–79; Potter, *War in Florida*, 15–16.

[20] Carter (ed.), *Territorial Papers*, XXV, 133; Sprague, *Origin of the Florida War*, 100, 81; *American State Papers, Military Affairs*, VI, 454, 458.

[21] See the author's "The Negro Abraham," *Florida Historical Quarterly*, XXV (July, 1946), 1–43, and "John Caesar: Seminole Negro Partisan," *Journal of Negro History*, XXXI (April, 1946), 190–207.

[22] Charleston, S.C., *Courier*, April 30, 1836;

Douglas, *Autobiography*, 120–23; Myer M. Cohen, *Notices of Florida and the Campaigns* (Charleston, S.C., 1836), 81, 86–89; John C. Casey to Lt. F. Searle, August 25, 1837, in Thomas Sidney Jesup Papers (War Department Files, National Archives), No. 2; and the author's "Florida Slaves and Free Negroes in the Seminole War, 1835–1842," *Journal of Negro History*, XXVIII (October, 1943), 393.

[23] Carter (ed.), *Territorial Papers*, XXIV, 800–802.

[24] Thomas Sidney Jesup to Brig. Gen. J. M. Hernandez, January 21, 1837, in Jesup Papers, box 14.

ambushed and annihilated brevet Major Francis L. Dade's command of over a hundred men near the Wahoo Swamp; an intelligent and literate slave named Luis Pacheco, who had been hired as guide and interpreter to Dade's command, is said to have assisted the hostiles in laying their fatal ambush.[25] Two days later Micanopy's band—numbering from 200 to 250 warriors, of whom from 30 to 50 were Negroes—repulsed 600 regulars and militiamen from the Withlacoochee. Of the three Seminole killed and five wounded in this action, two of the slain and three of the wounded were Negroes.[26]

For many of the whites on the St. Johns, the destruction of Dade's command was less horrifying than the enthusiasm with which plantation slaves rallied to the hostiles. Although the young South Carolina volunteer and writer W. W. Smith insisted that with very few exceptions the slaves preferred to remain in their "happy and secure state of servitude," Florida planters and militia officers in closer contact with the situation were under no such illusions. Nearly 400 Negroes, it was reported, "have joined the Indians and are more desperate than the Indians." That most of them were not captives but volunteers was evidenced by the numbers seen under arms and in war paint. With their support the Seminole swept through the region east of the St. Johns and south of St. Augustine with torch and tomahawk, driving the population to take refuge in St. Augustine and other places of comparative safety.[27] Slave

recruitment did not end with the early weeks of the uprising but continued into the spring and summer.

The slave uprising on the St. Johns spread alarm, indeed almost hysteria, throughout Florida and even into adjacent states.[28] The situation in St. Augustine, where displaced planters had taken refuge with such of their Negroes as had not "moved off" with the Seminole, was particularly critical. With several hundred Negroes who were well acquainted with the Indians and their language concentrated within the city walls, "strong apprehensions were felt . . . that they would fire the town, and that, during the confusion," the Indians, "influenced by revenge, cupidity, and the advice of their black counsellors," might attempt to rush the city itself. The St. Augustine whites also had to guard against attempts by Seminole emissaries to enter the town in order to stir up the Negroes and to obtain information, and at the same time forestall attempts by local Negroes to escape to the hostiles with information and supplies. Despite the vigilance of all the available dismounted force, Negroes did escape, meet with the hostiles, and return. Florida passed a bill providing that free Negroes aiding the Seminole should be sold into slavery, and Major Benjamin A. Putnam of the Florida militia urged Governor Richard K. Call on July 26, 1836, to see to the strict enforcement of this law, suggesting a standing court-martial to deal summarily with captured Negroes. A few days later the Major wrote to Secretary of War Lewis Cass that "if strong measures were not taken to restrain our slaves, there is but little doubt that we should soon be assailed with a servile as well as Indian

---

25 *Niles' Weekly Register*, XLIX (January 30, 1836), 365–70; Smith, *Sketch of the Seminole War*, 36–37; Cohen, *Notices of Florida*, 72; Sprague, *Origin of the Florida War*, 91. See also the author's "Louis Pacheco: The Man and the Myth," *Journal of Negro History*, XXVIII (January, 1943), 65–72, and "The Early Life of Luis Pacheco *né* Fatio," *Negro History Bulletin*, VII (December, 1943), 52, 54, 62, 64.

26 Sprague, *Origin of the Florida War*, 92–93.

27 For the participation of plantation slaves in depredations during the early days of the war, see Porter, "Florida Slaves and Free Negroes," 393–95. See also Mrs. Jane Murray Sheldon, "Seminole Attacks near New Smyrna, 1835–1856 [*sic*]," *Florida Historical Quarterly*, VIII (April, 1930),

188–96; Earl C. Tanner (ed.), "The Early Career of Edwin T. Jenckes: A Florida Pioneer of the 1830's," *Florida Historical Quarterly*, XXX (January, 1952), 270–75; *American State Papers, Military Affairs*, VII, 259; Sprague, *Origin of the Florida War*, 106; Smith, *Sketch of the Seminole War*, 20–23.

28 Porter, "Florida Slaves and Free Negroes," 395–98; Carter (ed.), *Territorial Papers*, XXV, 283.

war."[29] The Major was still unwilling to admit that the war was already what he said he feared it would become.

Sporadic but frequently heavy fighting meanwhile continued in the Withlacoochee region. The Negroes, their ranks swelled by recent runaways, bore at least their full share of the "burden and heat of the day." Two authorities agreed on an estimated total of 250 Negro fighting men (a figure which one divided into 100 "Indian slaves" and 150 runaways) as compared to 1,450–1,650 Indian warriors; but when General Edmund P. Gaines was besieged on the Withlacoochee early in March by a force estimated at about 1,500 warriors, one observer said "there might have been four or five hundred negroes among them." Of three Seminole killed during the siege one was a Negro.[30] The principal action of an October expedition was an attack on a Negro town protected by a stream, but the Negro warriors, posted in and behind trees and assisted by Indian comrades, gave the troops such a warm reception that they were unable to cross.[31] An expedition of the following month drove a body of hostiles into the Wahoo Swamp, where—outnumbered more than three to one—they turned at bay. The force consisted of an estimated 420 Indian warriors and 200 Negro fighting men, "one of the most distinguished leaders" of whom was "a negro, the property of a Florida planter." The whites claimed a victory but on November 21 withdrew.[32]

The first year of the war had ended in complete failure to repress Seminole resistance. Early in December, 1836, however, Major General Thomas Sidney Jesup

assumed command in Florida. Jesup, recognizing the importance of the Negroes, immediately set about ascertaining their number and location. "Micanopy, Philip, and Cooper [Osoochee] . . . each with from one hundred and twenty to two hundred Indian and Negro warriors—the latter, perhaps, the more numerous"—were reported not far from Jesup's encampment. Osceola, Jumper, and Little Alligator also had numerous Negro followers. It was at this point that the General delivered his famous judgment that this was a Negro and not an Indian war.[33]

Shifting from the attempt to crush Seminole resistance in the field, Jesup instituted a policy of hunting down and capturing the Seminole in their camps, particularly the women and children, who could be used to exert powerful pressure for surrender upon the hostiles. He put special emphasis on raiding Negro villages, a device not original with him[34] but which under his command was made effective for the first time. Jesup was greatly assisted in his program by a regiment of Creek scouts who had been promised "such plunder as they may take from the Seminoles"—"plunder" being understood to mean primarily captured Negroes. From early December, 1836, to late January, 1837, Jesup's troops were engaged in combing the swamps, destroying villages, and driving to the east such Indians and Negroes as they failed to kill or capture. Their captives numbered 131, nearly all Negroes and mostly women and children. Their greatest triumph was breaking up Osceola's headquarters, a Negro village in the Panosufkee Swamp, and capturing 52 of his Negro followers and three Indians.[35]

[29] Porter, "Florida Slaves and Free Negroes," 396–98; Carter (ed.), *Territorial Papers*, XXV, 265, 327–28.

[30] Sprague, *Origin of the Florida War*, 97, 112–13; *Army and Navy Chronicle*, VIII (March 7, 1839), 154; II (1836), 151; *American State Papers, Military Affairs*, VII, 369.

[31] *American State Papers, Military Affairs*, VI, 998; *Niles' Weekly Register*, LI (November 5, 1836), 148–49.

[32] Sprague, *Origin of the Florida War*, 162–66; *Court of Inquiry—Operations in Florida*, 52.

[33] Porter, "Florida Slaves and Free Negroes," 400.

[34] *Niles' Weekly Register*, L (May 14, 1836), 188, and LII (April 1, 1837), 71; *American State Papers, Military Affairs*, VII, 277.

[35] *American State Papers, Military Affairs*, VII, 820, 825–28; *Army and Navy Chronicle*, IV (January 5, 1837), 12, and (February 2, 1837), 79, 111; "Major Childs, U.S.A.: Extracts from His Correspondence with His Family," *Historical Magazine*, s. 3, II (December, 1873), 371–72; Sprague, *Origin of the Florida War*, 167, 170–71.

The "principal Indian and negro force . . . retired from the Ocklawaha . . . towards the head of the Caloosahatchee," and on January 27 the army was close on its heels. A captured Negro said "a large number of negroes were in advance, and from forty to fifty Indians, with Abraham . . . in our rear." A sudden dash resulted in the seizure of the Negro baggage train of over 100 ponies and in the capture of something over 20 prisoners, mostly Negro women and children. The main body of the Seminole plunged into the Great Cypress Swamp and in a running fight killed two Marines and wounded four others. The bodies of two Negroes and an Indian were found on the field, and several more Negroes were captured.[36]

Jesup then conceived the idea of using a Negro captive named Ben, one of Micanopy's principal "slaves," to negotiate with Abraham and through him with the head chief and his circle. The Seminole had been roughly handled and might therefore be in a receptive mood, but no important warrior had surrendered or been captured. "The warriors," Jesup commented, "have fought as long as they had life, and such seems to me to be the determination of those who influence their councils—I mean the leading negroes."[37] Conciliation of the Negroes was seen as essential to successful negotiations.

Recent developments near St. Augustine had made Jesup particularly anxious to terminate the war. His campaign had driven Osceola's and Micanopy's people toward King Philip's territory. Philip himself, old and weary, hesitated to act, but his chief Negro, John Caesar, recognized the necessity of a diversion and organized a guerrilla campaign, employing principally runaway slaves. His campaign, however, was brief. Interrupted on January 17, 1837, in a horse-stealing raid on a plantation only two miles west of St. Augustine, his band was trailed to their camp; Caesar and two others, including a young free Negro named Joe Merritt, were killed and the rest fled in confusion. One would have expected such a coup to produce general satisfaction among the white population of St. Augustine, but actually it caused more alarm than relief. That a band composed almost entirely of Negroes—and plantation slaves at that—should have dared a raid so close to the city, and that their abandoned packs should have contained articles recently purchased in local shops, revived something of the panic of a year before. The city council, declaring that "we know not how soon firebrands may be thrown amongst us," demanded that the militia company responsible for the disruption of Caesar's band be kept near home and "employed to scour the country in the neighborhood."[38]

The most important and far-reaching effect of Caesar's abortive raid, however, was on Jesup. This raid was doubtless in his mind when on January 21 he wrote to General J. M. Hernandez of the Florida militia—one of whose slaves had been in Caesar's band—denouncing the father of the slain Joe Merritt as an agent of Abraham and reiterating, "This war . . . is a negro, not an Indian war."[39] Doubtless, too, it was in his mind a few days later when he sent out the Indian Negro Ben to arrange for a meeting with Abraham.

On January 31 the Seminole Negroes, and Abraham in particular, undertook a new and important role. An army officer has described them as "a most cruel and malignant enemy . . . active . . . bloodthirsty and cruel"; but the Seminole Negro leaders, even fierce old John Caesar, although opposed to a surrender which would expose them to servitude had never been

[36] "Major Childs," 372–73; *American State Papers, Military Affairs,* VII, 828–30; *Court of Inquiry—Operations in Florida,* 69–70; *Niles' Weekly Register,* LII (March 11, 1837), 30–31; Sprague, *Origin of the Florida War,* 170–72.

[37] *American State Papers, Military Affairs,* VII, 828–30, 832; "Major Childs," 373; *Army and Navy Chronicle,* IV (February 2, 1837), 80, and VIII (March 7, 1839), 154–55.

[38] Porter, "John Caesar," 197–201, and "Florida Slaves and Free Negroes," 401–4.

[39] Jesup Papers, box 14.

averse to negotiations.[40] Abraham now had the responsibility both of interpreting the talks between the General and the chiefs and of seeing to it that any peace terms should be acceptable to the Negroes.

Jesup's *sine qua non* for peace was immediate emigration. "There would be no difficulty in making peace . . . were it not for that condition. . . . The negroes . . . who rule the Indians, are all averse to removing to so cold a climate."[41] The Negro Abraham, however, an intelligent and widely traveled man who had been on a mission to Washington, D.C., and another to the Indian Territory, recognized the impossibility of achieving a decent life in Florida in the face of the government's determined attitude. His objective had been to put up a strong resistance until the Negroes were given satisfactory assurances. Now he felt that the time was ripe for negotiations.

The negotiations went on for over a month. On March 6, 1837, representatives of Micanopy and of Alligator—among the latter the subsequently famous Indian-Negro subchief John Ca-Wy-Ya (Cavallo)—signed an agreement to suspend hostilities and for the entire Nation to move to the west, for the performance of which the Indians gave hostages. The provisions affecting the Negroes were necessarily in cryptic language: "Major General Jesup, in behalf of the United States, agrees that the Seminoles and their allies who come in, and emigrate to the West, shall be secure in their lives and property; that their negroes, their *bona fide* property, shall accompany them to the West. . . ." By "their allies" the Seminole understood the Negroes living among them, and since before the war an estimated four-fifths of the Seminole Negroes, including Abraham, were runaway slaves—and during the war the Seminole had been joined by several hundred more runaways—the Seminole "allies" numbered far more Negroes than the Seminole

"slaves." But at this point no United States army officer could explicitly provide for the transportation west of Negroes on whom United States citizens might have a claim; brevet Major General Winfield Scott, one of Jesup's predecessors, had been specifically directed to "allow no pacification with the Indians while a living slave, belonging to a white man, remained in their possession."[42]

Jesup, nevertheless, at first intended to carry out his agreement in good faith. "The negroes," he wrote on March 26, "rule the Indians, and it is important that they should feel themselves secure; if they should become alarmed and hold out, the war will be renewed." But by the end of the month so many Seminole had assembled at Tampa Bay that the General became overconfident and, under pressure from Florida planters, decided to change his interpretation of the agreement. On April 8 he entered into a clandestine arrangement with Coi Hajo and other chiefs "to surrender the Negroes taken during the war." It was easier, however, to make such an agreement than carry it out. Some of the "captured Negroes," to be sure, had been taken against their will and were glad to be returned to their masters, but others, when they heard of the new arrangement, banded together for defense whether against white men or Indians. They were supported by more militant Indians like Osceola, who, when Coi Hajo announced in council that the runaways were to be returned, rose in a rage, declaring that so long as he was in the Nation it should never be done.[43]

Apparently Jesup had not sufficiently considered that legally most of the influential Seminole Negroes were as much the slaves of white men as were the recent runaways. When several Floridians arrived in the emigration camp to search for slaves

---

[40] Sprague, *Origin of the Florida War*, 100, 81; Porter, "John Caesar," 194–96.

[41] *American State Papers, Military Affairs*, VII, 827.

[42] Porter, "Florida Slaves and Free Negroes," 404–5; *American State Papers, Military Affairs*, VII, 834; *Message from the President . . . Relative to Indiana Hostilities in Florida*, Senate Docs., 24th Cong., 1st sess., No. 152 (Serial 281), 5.

[43] Porter, "Florida Slaves and Free Negroes," 404–7.

the Negroes and many Indians fled.[44] On June 2 the young militants, Osceola, Philip's son Wild Cat, and John Cavallo, seized and carried away the Seminole hostages given under the terms of the truce. "All is lost," Jesup despairingly announced, "and principally . . . by the influence of the Negroes."[45] The Seminole force was still largely intact, although an estimate that the warriors in East Florida numbered 2,500, not including Negroes, "who fight as well as the best of them,"[46] was probably an exaggeration.

Jesup was reduced to drafting plans for the future—the confusion of which indicated his own confused state of mind—and putting the best face possible on an admittedly bad situation. He was principally concerned with preventing the war from developing any further slave unrest. "The two races, the negro and the Indian," he declared, "are rapidly approximating; they are identified in interests and feelings." Plantation slaves had been prominent in depredations and one had occupied a position of leadership. "Should the Indians remain in this territory," Jesup continued, "the negroes among them will form a rallying point for runaway negroes from the adjacent states; and if they remove, the fastnesses of the country will be immediately occupied by negroes." But, somewhat inconsistently, he believed that the Indians would agree to "surrender all runaway slaves" if permitted to remain in "a small district near Florida Point."[47]

He also pointed out that he had been able to turn over about 90 captured Negroes to their legal owners and, much more important, had seized over a hundred Indian Negroes, among them a score of warriors including Abraham and three other chiefs. "The negro portion of the hostile force of the Seminole nation not taken," the General optimistically declared, "is entirely without a head."[48] More significantly, the capitulation had committed to emigration, on conditions, the most powerful East Florida group, the Alachua, or "original" Seminole, under Micanopy. And with Micanopy's chief Negro, Abraham, still in his hands, Jesup was well equipped to reopen negotiations with the Micanopy group and, through them, with other groups.[49]

The 1837 summer season was, as usual, uneventful, but early in September a serious break appeared within the Seminole ranks. It involved the Seminole Negroes, previously regarded as the strongest element of the hostiles. It came at a point where the Negroes in the Indian country had been quantitatively strengthened but qualitatively weakened by the mass recruitment of plantation slaves. Twenty months of fighting and hardship since the revolt of the St. Johns plantation slaves had operated to separate the strong, determined, freedom-loving Negroes from those who had been merely caught up in the enthusiasm of the December days and were now ready to exchange freedom to go hungry in the swamps for the regular rations of servitude. Early in September plantation Negroes, half-naked, "haggard and emaciated," began to straggle into forts and camps with pitiable tales of ill-treatment by the Indians. By mid-November over 50 had surrendered. Far more important, John Philip, a "slave" of King Philip and a former member of Caesar's daring guerrilla band, was per-

44 *Ibid.*, 408–9.

45 Jesup to Brig. Gen. R. Jones, October 21, 1837, in War Department, AGO Files (National Archives), 207; *Seminole Indians–Prisoners of War: Letter from the Secretary of War . . . , House Docs.*, 25th Cong., 2d sess., No. 327 (Serial 329), 10–11; *Negroes, &c., Captured from Indians*, 18; *Niles' Weekly Register*, LIII (December 23, 1837), 263.

46 Lt. Col. W. S. Harney to Jesup, May 4, 1837 (photostat, Florida Historical Society); *American State Papers, Military Affairs*, VII, 871; *Army and Navy Chronicle*, IV (1837), 329.

47 Porter, "Florida Slaves and Free Negroes," 409–11.

48 *American State Papers, Military Affairs*, VII, 842, 851–52; *Negroes, &c., Captured from Indians*, 18, 65–69.

49 Grant Foreman, *Indian Removal: The Emigration of the Five Civilized Tribes of Indians* (Norman, Okla., 1932), 349; "Letters of Samuel Forry, Surgeon, U.S. Army, 1837–1838," *Florida Historical Quarterly*, VI (January, 1928), 214.

suaded by his wife, a plantation Negro, to "come in" and surrender.

The surrender on September 8 of John Philip, whom Jesup now enthusiastically identified as "the only negro chief who had not been previously seized," was comparable to pushing over the first of a line of upright dominoes. The Indian Negro volunteered to guide a detachment to the camp of King Philip, who was captured with his entire party.[50] When King Philip's son Wild Cat learned of this, he rode to St. Augustine and offered, in exchange for his father's release, to bring in Philip's subordinate chiefs for a "talk" and to return all captured Negroes. Seventy-nine Negroes were shortly on their way, although probably under no compulsion since they were unescorted and said to be "in a starving condition." Later, however, the theory was advanced that Wild Cat and his followers had intended to rescue King Philip and that the Negroes had been sent to be on hand for the attack.[51]

Micanopy and his associates in the meantime had sent the young Negro-Indian subchief John Cavallo to confer with King Philip, Wild Cat, Osceola, and their associates and, if necessary, to interpret between them and white officers. A conference at the Indians' camp near St. Augustine between these chiefs and Hernan-

dez, who represented Jesup, was arranged, but Cavallo's part in carrying away the hostages in June caused Jesup, who had come to expect "foul play" wherever Cavallo was involved, to order Hernandez to have him and the other Seminole seized at once if they did not reply satisfactorily to a specified set of questions in regard to surrendering "captured Negroes." While the chiefs were discussing these and other questions they were surrounded and captured.[52]

Wild Cat and Cavallo remained prisoners less than six weeks. On the night of November 29–30 they with 18 others escaped from Fort Marion—with the help, Jesup was convinced, of local Negroes.[53] Their escape, however, had come too late to prevent a series of important surrenders. On November 30, Osceola's family and about 40 plantation slaves surrendered,[54] and a few days later all chiefs belonging to Micanopy's group except Alligator agreed to give themselves up.

By December, 1837, two opposing movements had set in among the Seminole Indians and Negroes still at large. One was toward the emigration camp. About 50 Indian Negroes proceeded to Tampa Bay, in response either to the orders of Micanopy and his group or to new appeals from Jesup promising them "something . . . GOOD" if they would "get away from the Indians."[55] The other current was toward

[50] Jacob Rhett Motte, *Journey into Wilderness: An Army Surgeon's Account of Life in Camp and Field During the Creek and Seminole Wars, 1836–1838,* James F. Sunderman (ed.) (Gainesville, Fla., 1953), 116–23, 132–33; *American State Papers, Military Affairs,* VII, 849–50, 882; *Army and Navy Chronicle,* V (September 28, 1837), 200, 203; Capt. Harvey Brown to Lt. J. A. Chambers, October 8, 1837, in Interior Department, Indian Office (Emigration) Files (National Archives), 1837 (196/447); *Court of Inquiry—Operations in Florida,* 181, 109–12; Capt. Nathan S. Jarvis, "An Army Surgeon's Notes of Frontier Service, 1833–1848," *Journal of the Military Service Institution of the United States,* XL (January-February, 1908), 277–78; *Niles' Weekly Register,* LIII (September 30, 1837), 66.

[51] Motte, *Journey into Wilderness,* 135–38; *Army and Navy Chronicle,* V (October 12, 1837), 236, and (October 26, 1837), 269–70; *Niles' Weekly Register,* LIII (October 14, 1837), 98, and (November 18, 1837), 178; "Letters of Samuel Forry," 88–105 *passim.*

[52] Motte, *Journey into Wilderness,* 138; Jarvis, "Army Surgeon's Notes," 278; *Army and Navy Chronicle,* V (November 2, 1837), 284–85, and (December 14, 1837), 377–78, and VII (July 26, 1838), 50; *Niles' Weekly Register,* LIII (November 4, 1837), 146, and (November 11, 1837), 165–66, and (December 23, 1837), 262–63; *Seminole Indians—Prisoners of War,* 2–8, 11; Hernandez to Jesup, October 22, 1837, and Jesup to Jones, October 21, 1837, both in War Department, AGO Files.

[53] See the author's "Seminole Flight from Fort Marion," *Florida Historical Quarterly,* XXII (January, 1944), 112–33, esp. 121.

[54] Jarvis, "Army Surgeon's Notes," 285; Frank L. White (ed), "The Journals of Lieutenant John Pickell, 1836–1837," *Florida Historical Quarterly,* XXXVIII (October, 1959), 159–60.

[55] Brig. Gen. W. K. Armistead to Lt. J. A. Chambers, December 20, 25, 1837, in Jesup Pa-

the lower Kissimmee and Lake Okeechobee where Wild Cat, Sam Jones, Alligator, and Cavallo were mustering die-hard Indians and Negroes for a last-ditch stand. Most of the Seminole Negroes still at large moved toward the camps of these stalwarts. In fact, some Negroes who had started out toward Tampa Bay turned back to join the resistance forces.[56]

During a period of about a month these diehards fought three of the most savage battles of the seven-year war. On Christmas, 1837, 380 Indians and Negroes, with Lake Okeechobee behind them and a swamp in front, met an attack by Colonel Zachary Taylor's thousand regulars and militia. Before the Indian-Negro force retreated they had killed 26 men and wounded over a hundred others. The bodies of eleven Indians and only one or two Negroes were found on the field, which suggests that Okeechobee was principally an Indian battle; probably most of the Negroes who had separated from Tampa-bound masters had not yet reached the camp of the holdouts. On January 15, 1838, however, a landing party of sailors and regulars near Jupiter Inlet was furiously attacked and badly routed, and nine days later Jesup himself encountered at the Locha Hatchee a force estimated at from 200 to 300 Indian warriors and "probably as many negroes." This was believed to be the same force which had defeated the whites at Jupiter Inlet. In both encounters the whites suffered heavy losses.[57]

After these costly engagements Jesup built a stockade called Fort Jupiter and considered his next move. His officers urged ending the war by a treaty which would permit the Seminole to remain in the southern part of the peninsula, a plan in accord with the General's own views and one which, when finally carried out over four years later, terminated the war. Negroes who had surrendered reported that if permitted to remain in Florida the Indians "would . . . sell and deliver up the plantation negroes." Jesup communicated his plan to Washington and sent out a Seminole Negro to invite the chiefs to a conference. By the end of February about 400 Indians and perhaps 150 Indian Negroes were encamped near the fort. The Negroes, according to a fascinated and repelled Southern officer, were "the most diabolical looking wretches I ever saw. . . . They had none of the servility of our northern blacks, but were constantly offering their dirty paws with as much hauteur and nonchalance as if they were conferring a vast deal of honor."

Jesup, however, was even more pleased with the presence of these Negroes, whatever their appearance, than he was with that of the larger number of Indians. Convinced that the Negroes would be a source of difficulty so long as they remained in Florida, that the Indians would not surrender so long as the Negroes held out, and that the Negroes would not give in until assured of their freedom, he appealed through Seminole Negro emissaries to "the negro chiefs August & John Cavallo" and to another named July, "to whom, and to their people, I promised freedom and protection on their separating from the Indians and surrendering." This was the vague "something . . . GOOD" hinted at the previous December.

The attraction of the offer was not, of course, "freedom" from Seminole "masters" but rather the "protection" of a United States general and United States troops against claims or kidnapping by whites. As Indian Negroes in Florida would be a constant encouragement to runaways, "it was stipulated that they should be sent to the west, as a part of the Seminole nation"

pers, box 5; Lt. R. W. Kirkham to Jesup, August 1, 1846, with statement by Tony Barnett, May 14, 1846, in War Department, QMGO Consolidated Files (National Archives).

[56] See, for example, White (ed.), "Journals of Lt. Pickell," 167.

[57] Sprague, *Origin of the Florida War*, 203–14, esp. 214; "The Battle of Okee Chobee," *United States Magazine* (February, 1857); *Niles' Weekly Register*, LIII (February 17, 1838), 388, and (February 10, 1838), 369–71; *Army and Navy Chronicle*, VII (July 26, 1838), 49–54; Motte, *Journey into Wilderness*, 195.

which had already migrated; Abraham, however, assured them that it was a fine country, though a bit chilly, and certainly preferable to the Everglades. During February and March the Negro chiefs August and July, reassured by these promises, voluntarily came in with about 150 Indian Negroes and five slaves of white citizens. Most of the Indian Negroes were promptly sent off "to join their masters," as an officer put it, "in their new homes west of the Mississippi."[58]

But how could Jesup justify granting freedom to Negroes four-fifths of whom were either runaways or their descendants and thus legally slaves? The answer is, of course, wartime necessity. In the first place, the Negroes were regarded as more dangerous than the Indians; persuading the Negroes to surrender would weaken the Indians "more than they would be weakened by the loss of the same number of their own people."[59] In the second place, it was imperative to remove from the slave-holding South all Negroes who had tasted freedom and knew the fortress of Florida. A well-informed officer commented,

The negroes, from the commencement of the Florida war, have, for their numbers, been the most formidable foe, more bloodthirsty, active, and revengeful, than the Indians. . . . The negro, returned to his original owner, might have remained a few days, when he again would have fled to the swamps, more vindictive than ever. . . . Ten resolute negroes, with a knowledge of the country, are sufficient

to desolate the frontier, from one extent to the other.[60]

The sort of thing Jesup feared was illustrated by a communication of February 10, 1839, from an officer at Fort Heileman, stating that the recalcitrant Creek Indians had "all left the Okefenokee & gone South," presumably to join the hostile Seminole. "There were seven runaway negroes from Georgia among them," the officer continued, "well armed & plenty of ammunition . . . the negroes have done most of the mischief in that quarter; the negroes also have left and on their way south burned the houses in the vicinity."[61]

Jesup had adopted the policy of shipping all Indian Negroes west as early as the preceding September, when he had revoked his promise to his Creek allies that they should have all the enemy property they could capture and offered instead to purchase their claims to 90 captured Indian Negroes for $8,000, since, as he wrote, "it is highly important to the slave-holding States that these negroes be sent out of the country." The Creeks declined this less than generous offer, but the army hung on to the Negroes claimed by the Creeks and succeeded in delivering them in the Indian Territory.[62]

To give his policy legal justification Jesup resorted to the fiction that *all* Indian Negroes, instead of a small minority, were legitimate Indian property. One statement of his order was that "all the property [sic] of the Seminole Indians . . . who separated themselves [sic] from the Indians, and delivered themselves up to the Commanding officer of the troops, should be free."[63] Technically, this order would apply only to

[58] Jesup to Wm. L. Marcy, April 5, 1848, in Jesup Papers, box 15; Kirkham to Jesup, August 1, 1846, with statement by Barnett, May 14, 1846, in War Department, QMGO Consolidated Files; Jesup to Wm. L. Marcy, July 1, 1848, in Interior Department, Indian Office, Seminole Files (National Archives), W-244, and M. Arbuckle to Brig. Gen. R. Jones, January 8, 1849, *ibid.*, J-143; *American State Papers, Military Affairs*, VII, 825–26; *Official Opinions of the Attorneys General of the United States* . . . (Washington, 1852–   ), IV, 720–29; *Army and Navy Chronicle*, VI (March 22, 1838), 177, 190; Motte, *Journey into Wilderness*, 207, 210–11; Sprague, *Origin of the Florida War*, 193–95.

[59] Jesup to Brig. Gen. R. Jones, February 28, 1838, in Seminole Files, W-244.

[60] Sprague, *Origin of the Florida War*, 309.

[61] Col. D. E. Twiggs to Gen. A. Macomb, February 10, 1839, in War Department, AGO Files, 66.

[62] *American State Papers, Military Affairs*, VII, 882; *Negroes, &c., Captured from Indians*, 20–22, 70–71; Foreman, *Indian Removal*, 347, 349, 365–66.

[63] Certificate from Bvt. Brig. Gen. Z. Taylor, April 30, 1840, in Interior Department, Indian Office Files.

that small minority to whom Indians had valid title and to only those in that small group who actually "separated themselves" from the Indians. As a practical matter, however, all Indian Negroes who came in were promptly marched to the emigration camp and embarked for the West.

Later, in 1841, the War Department decided that the 1832 treaty of Payne's Landing had canceled all claims against the Indians for any Negroes run away or captured prior to that treaty. "No demand can therefore be recognized for any negroes except those lost since the date of the treaty, unless the Indians are willing to give them up voluntarily. All except these must positively be removed with the Indians to the West. . . ." Still another legal fiction was developed in regard to those Negroes whose status as "Indian slaves" was most doubtful—who were, indeed, with little question the legal slaves of white citizens, captured or run away since the Payne's Landing treaty. The War Department order that these Negroes "should be surrendered" contained the all-important proviso, "unless the effect of this would be to prevent the Indians from coming in and removing." If so, "it will be better, rather than incur this danger that even the negroes to which the whites have a valid claim should also be removed."[64] On August 19, 1841, accordingly, Lieutenant Colonel W. J. Worth announced, "Indians have been solemnly guaranteed retention of slaves indifferently . . . to the mode or time . . . they obtained possession. . . ." That is, if an Indian claimed a Negro, his claim would be recognized without necessity of legal proof, while the citizen claiming such a Negro was, "upon identifying and proving property, paid a fair equivalent, determined upon by a board of officers." In defense of his policy Worth pointed out that "if . . . the swamps of Florida become . . . the resort of runaways, their intelligence, so superior to the Indian might impose upon the general government a contest quadruplicate in time and treasure than that now being waged."[65]

Although the policy of ignoring the legal status of even recent runaways was not publicly and explicitly announced until 1841, it had been applied several times by 1838. The classic example was that of the famous Luis Pacheco, who, despite his well-known status as slave to Mrs. Antonio Pacheco, had been shipped out of the country as a slave of Chief Jumper, because Jesup thought he was too dangerous to be left in Florida.[66]

Most of the slaves who during the war escaped from plantations or were captured by the Seminole probably were recovered by their owners, principally by voluntary surrender, but those recent runaways who were unwilling to return to plantation slavery and could induce Indians to claim them—no difficult task—could go west with the more legitimate "Indian slaves."

So far as the formidable Seminole Negroes were concerned, the war was practically over by the end of March, 1838. During the campaign of September, 1837–March, 1838, about 250 Seminole Negroes had surrendered or been captured; Operation Fort Jupiter alone had accounted for the taking of 167 Negroes, (including 15 slaves of whites) over 40 of whom were warriors, "nearly all armed with rifles." Over 500 Indians, too, had been made prisoners, for when the Secretary of War refused to approve Jesup's peace terms, the General on March 21 simply surrounded their camps near Fort Jupiter and scouring the country that night and the next two days succeeding in rounding up that number.[67]

---

[64] Carter (ed.), *Territorial Papers*, XXVI, 282–83.

[65] Sprague, *Origin of the Florida War*, 309–10; Porter, "Florida Slaves and Free Negroes," 419.

[66] *Negroes, &c., Captured from Indians*, 93–94; *Report . . .* [on] *the Petition of Joseph Elzaudi, House Reports*, 30th Cong., 1st sess., No. 187 (Serial 524), 1–6; Edwin C. McReynolds, *The Seminoles* (Norman, Okla., 1957), 240.

[67] *Negroes, &c., Captured from Indians*, 25, 81–89; *Army and Navy Chronicle*, VI (April 19, 1838), 248, and (April 26, 1838), 269; Jarvis, "Army Surgeon's Notes," 453–54.

Jesup was still confronted with the problem of the Negroes and Indians who, justifiably suspicious of all promises, had stayed away from Fort Jupiter. A large part of the Negroes still out were with Alligator and Cavallo, the last Negro chief still in the field. To them the General dispatched the Negro counselor Abraham and Holatoochee, said to have been Cavallo's brother-in-law. Their mission resulted in the surrender of Alligator, "with 88 of his people, among whom was John Cowaya and 27 blacks," and Alligator's capitulation led to the surrender during April of about 360 more Indians and Negroes, including 100 warriors.[68]

These captures and surrenders reduced any future actions to mere raids and skirmishes. They also marked the disappearance of Negroes as a major element in Seminole resistance. A few hostile Negroes, both "Indian Negroes" and recent runaways, continued as interpreters, counselors, and fighting men, and their influence with the hostile Indians was recognized in the government's decision of 1841 to abandon the idea of restoring "to their rightful owners" any slaves still among the Indians and instead remove them all to the west.[69] But we usually glimpse these Negroes fleetingly and singly[70]—in sharp contrast to the days when Negro warriors were numbered in the hundreds and on some occasions were reportedly as numerous as the Indians. Wild Cat's sadly shrunken band probably included the greatest number of remaining Negroes, some of whom he skillfully employed as spies, but when he was seized in May, 1841, his immediate fol-

lowing consisted of fifteen Indians and three Negroes. The company of 229 in which he was shipped west the following October included eighteen Negroes.[71]

The Seminole Negroes, having lost their importance as a factor in resistance, assumed the comparatively new role of government agents whose task it was to induce hostile Indians to surrender. Negro guides, interpreters, and negotiators—often in cooperation with Indian chiefs who had surrendered—were indispensable in establishing contact and communicating with the remaining hostile Indian leaders and, if they remained obdurate, in assisting the troops to locate their camps.

Several Negro guides and interpreters performed outstanding service. Sandy Perryman distinguished himself by locating and bringing in a number of chiefs to Fort King on May 17, 1839, for negotiations which resulted in an agreement that, in return for peace, the Indians should be permitted at least temporarily to remain in Southern Florida. Two months later, however, a band of Indians not parties to this agreement massacred on the Caloosahatchee a party for which Sandy was serving as interpreter and put him to death by torture.[72] Negro John, a "captured slave of Dr. H. B. Crews, served as guide to the aggressive Lieutenant Colonel W. S. Harney on an expedition of December, 1840, which resulted in the killing of the Spanish Indian chief Chekika, a leader in the Caloosahatchee and Indian Key massacres, and eight of his warriors, John himself was wounded in the encounter.[73] Sampson, who had been wounded and taken prisoner in

[68] Sprague, *Origin of the Florida War*, 195; *Niles' Weekly Register*, LIV (May 5, 1838), 145; Abraham to Jesup, April 25, 1838, in *Florida Historical Quarterly*, XXV (July, 1946), 38–39.

[69] Carter (ed.), *Territorial Papers*, XXVI, 276–77, 374–75.

[70] *Army and Navy Chronicle*, IX (August 8, 1839), 93, and XI (October 22, 1840), 268–69; *Niles' Weekly Register*, LIV (August 18, 1838), 386, and LVIII (May 23, 1840), 179–80, and (June 27, 1840), 260, and LX (April 10, 1841), 90; Hester Perrine Walker, "Massacre at Indian Key, Aug. 7, 1840, and the Death of Dr. Henry Perrine," *Florida Historical Quarterly*, V (July, 1926), 26–27.

[71] Sprague, *Origin of the Florida War*, 277, 280, 322.

[72] *Army and Navy Chronicle*, VIII (June 13, 1839), 379, and X (January 16, 1840), 39–40; *Niles' Weekly Register*, LVI (July 20, 1839), 321, and LVII (September 14, 1839), 44; Sprague, *Origin of the Florida War*, 233, 316.

[73] Logan Uriah Reavis, *The Life and Military Services of General William Selby Harney* (St. Louis, 1878), 144–45; *Niles' Weekly Register*, LX (April 3, 1841), 71–72; Lt. Col. W. S. Harney to Capt. W. W. Bliss, December 24, 1840, in War Department, AGO Files, A354, and "Old Book 3, Dept. of Florida, Bound as 1, Dept. of New Mexico, Feb. 1, 1842–Aug. 17, 1842," *ibid.*, 30.

the Caloosahatchee massacre, escaped after two years and in December, 1841, served with distinction as guide on an expedition into the Big Cypress which drove the hostiles out of their fastnesses and so softened them up that in the following summer the chiefs in southern Florida accepted the peace agreement which they had flouted three years earlier, thus bringing the long war to an end.[74]

Most important of these Negro agents was John Cavallo, or Gopher John as he was called by the officers. He had been the last Negro chief to surrender, and it was he who was responsible for the suggestion that delegations of prominent chiefs should be brought from the Indian Territory as proof positive to the hostiles that those who had surrendered had not been put to death but had been both spared and well treated. This move, which utilized Cavallo's old commander Alligator and his brother-in-law Holatoochee, proved highly effective. Cavallo was declared to have personally participated in bringing in 535 Indians and during the last two years of the war was very nearly the "indispensable man" in the army's relations both with the Indians who were still "out" and those who had finally consented to "come in."[75]

The decision to remove the Seminole from Florida was strongly influenced by the presence and position of the Negroes, and the Seminole Negroes also strongly influenced the general decision to resist removal. These Negroes were shrewd and farsighted in their plans for resistance and active and aggressive in carrying them out. Once convinced, however, that the government was inflexibly determined on Seminole removal, and persuaded, too, that if they and the Indians surrendered, their own freedom and the lives of both would be respected, they were almost as influential in persuading the more recalcitrant Indians to surrender as they had previously been in rallying Seminole resistance. Prolonged as the war was, the promise of freedom to the Negroes "tended very materially towards affecting the main object": the emigration of the great majority of the tribe.[76] It also made possible the termination in August, 1842, of a struggle which, having already lasted seven years, might otherwise have dragged on for another decade or more with the loss of millions of dollars to the government and hundreds of lives to both whites and Seminole.

---

[74] Sprague, *Origin of the Florida War*, 315–16, 357, 362, 364, 368, 370; White (ed.), "Journals of Lt. Pickell," 160.

[75] Kenneth W. Porter, "Davy Crockett and John Horse: A Possible Origin of the Coonskin Story," *American Literature*, XV (March, 1943), 10–15; Brig. Gen. W. K. Armistead to the Adju-

tant General, June 15, 1840, in War Department, AGO Files, 1840–146. See also Letter Book of Officer Commanding 8th Infantry (1840–1842), 95, 100–101, 103, 113–14, and "Head Quarters 9th M Department: Letters, from June 2d. 1841 to February 1st. 1842," I, 95–96, 223, both in War Department, AGO Files.

[76] Capt. J. T. Sprague to Jesup, July 25, 184?, in War Department, QMGO Consolidated Files, "Seminoles."

CHAPTER 5

The Abolitionists Reconsidered

As the Civil War receded into the past the number of Northerners who thought of themselves as heroes in the old antislavery movement increased sharply. Every schoolboy was free to draw upon what Robert Penn Warren in 1961 called "The Northern Treasury of Virtue" and to explain the war as a conflict begun for the single purpose of ending slavery. The ranks of alleged participants in the underground railroad grew with phenomenal speed after 1865, and time joined by fading memories strengthened the notion that virtually the entire Union army had risen in abolitionist wrath and marched off to war to strike the shackles from the slave. Larry Gara, who in 1961 attacked these claims as pretentiously inflated, was commended the following year by C. Vann Woodward and other scholars for his efforts. It now seems probable that much of the lore of elaborate secret signals and extensive networks of underground tunnels was largely mythical, that slaves actually fled in more modest numbers, and that the fugitives themselves and their Negro friends took the larger share of risks and did most of the work.

Earlier in 1956 David Donald approached the subject from another vantage point and proposed to analyze the abolitionists in terms of status politics. The reform leaders, descendants of old Federalist families, were a "displaced elite" without a function, men for whom "agitation allowed the only chance for personal and social fulfillment." The traditional twentieth-century charge of perverse motives was continued by Donald, who ascribed some of the abolitionist hostility toward Lincoln to the fact that he was "the killer of the dream" whose emancipation policies robbed the abolitionists "of the great crusade that had brought purpose and joy." The implication, one supposes, is that liberation played second fiddle to the reformers' quest for meaning and a social role. It is difficult to see what forces other than ideology would "displace" the reformers when thousands of men with very similar backgrounds rose to actual leadership in politics, in the professions, and in business. Nevertheless in 1960 Donald continued his probe of the antislavery mind in a brilliantly written prize study of Senator Charles Sumner which left strewn on the psychological battlefield damaging images of emotional impotence, latent homosexuality, and the escapism of a man who fled from his personal neuroses into reform politics.

"This holy blissful martyr," a "specimen of prolonged and morbid juvenility," went armed in the political world with "unvarnished egotism" and the weapons of "moral terrorism."

In many ways Donald's work sprang quite naturally from a long dominant historical trend. Although Negro scholars, Marxist writers, and scattered biographers such as Irving H. Bartlett, Martin Duberman, Richard Hofstadter, and Russel B. Nye wrote on antislavery without particular animus, the great majority of scholars have approached the subject with attitudes which have ranged from cool skepticism to aggressive hostility. Avery O. Craven in 1939 described the abolitionists as "violent demagogues" who saw that "false propaganda took the place of truth" and made Southern masters do "scapegoat service for all aristocrats and sinners." Craven assured his readers that Garrison could have profited a great deal from psychiatric help. More recently in 1948 William B. Hesseltine dismissed the whole complex web of commitment and moral action as "mere humanitarian gabble," and one of his students, Hazel C. Wolf, wrote a book in 1952 to show that the abolitionist pioneers were essentially sick men suffering from "a martyr complex." Garrison, it seemed, "had a mania for uniqueness and attention," his Middle Western colleague Theodore Weld "gloried in persecution," and all the leaders competed with great vigor in "bidding for a martyr's crown." The abolitionists have been described by various scholars as gullible, naïve, mistaken, dangerous, ignorant, self-righteous, fanatical, inflexible, dogmatic, vituperative, humorless, violent, and aggressive men who succeeded only in arousing Southerners to militant counter-responses. The radical reformers initiated an escalating attack which along with the responses of the hot-blooded Southern "counterparts" led directly to the mass slaughter of a "needless" Civil War. More than a few scholars have argued that the "worst" of the abolitionists, men such as John Brown, really belonged in insane asylums.

How can this remarkable stance of nearly unparalleled hostility by so many American scholars be explained? First of all, historians who accepted as "normal" a subordinate status for Negroes in modern times were apt to regard the abolitionists with puzzlement or hostility. Some scholars have been put off by what was really a leading antebellum style of speech and thought among many conservatives as well as among antislavery radicals—the emotional and declamatory rhetoric, the intense concern with human sin and divine retribution, the abstraction and idealization of issues, and the militant tones of self-righteousness. The abolitionists have also been condemned to enhance the reputations of their opponents. For example, conflicts both real and imaginary between Lincoln and the radical reformers have been "resolved" by denouncing the "incendiary emotionalism" of the abolitionists and exalting Lincoln's statesmanship of "moderation." If the great failure of the era is defined as the failure to resolve the crisis of slavery without war, it seems foolish to attribute to antislavery advocates so much power and responsibility. If blame must be distributed, surely the slaveowners, or the entire generation, or even the makers of the Republic, must accept a large share. Staughton Lynd suggested in 1965 that "the Abolitionists were right in seeing the Revolution as a Revolution betrayed"; this failure of the Founding Fathers to act at a time when the issue of slavery "was recognized, was manageable, and was shirked" made a future Civil War very probable. To take the antislavery spokesmen firmly to task for "causing" the Civil War is to deny both the oppressiveness of slavery and the reality of abolitionist ideology. The whole question was not nearly so simple as Craven implied. Although the North went to war "to save the Union" and the abolitionists had something to do with polarizing ante-bellum opinions, the radicals lacked the power to "cause" war or revolution, and for a time their work served largely to make some Northerners feel more noble about defending the immediate national self-interest. Moreover, the reform movement was not restricted to "fanatical" and "neurotic" recruits but rather, as Duberman indicated in 1962 and 1965, attracted a great variety of personality types from the mild-mannered and thoughtful James Russell Lowell to the militant and unbending John Brown.

The basic categories of thought which Americans used from the beginning simply were not adequate to comprehend the tragic issues of slavery and anti-slavery. Neither citizens nor scholars steeped in the politics of progress and amelioration, trained in compromise and consensus, and accustomed to think-ing in terms of "give-and-take" debate over tractable issues, could account for that "implacable consciousness of race" or measure the potential violence of caste and slavery. Certainly the admission of guilt and oppression would have seriously compromised the national optimism. When Southerners expressed a bitter intractability over slavery, when Northerners would not seriously con-sider admitting members of "a grossly inferior" race to the national consensus, how could the issues of oppression and freedom be translated into "reason-able" and "tolerant" compromise politics? If—as the abolitionists believed—slavery was a moral enormity almost beyond expression, were not drastic and militant means of opposition appropriate? Isolated, small in numbers, often ostracized, and sometimes threatened by violence, how could they have gained a hearing without intense concern and a militancy which might be described as "fanatical"?

The abolitionists have often been judged by special standards which were not applied to other cases. One may select a single aspect of mind or an un-representative mental tendency and ignore the total pattern of personality. For example, Lincoln, who was capable of lapsing into the deepest melancholy, might be dealt with as a manic depressive. One may also find a "neurotic" trait and ascribe a given political action to it: thus the discovery of a tendency to-ward claustrophobia in Benjamin Franklin could be used to explain his struggle for a large continental Republic. It should be noted that this line of reasoning was seldom if ever used with a Lincoln or a Franklin and nearly always applied to a Garrison or a Sumner. Many psychologists reject the conclusion that the proponents of substantial social change are necessarily "neurotic" and suggest that the capacity to involve oneself in affairs remote from the individual self may be a sign of a larger maturity than most men ever achieve.

In 1964 a Princeton psychologist, Sylvan S. Tomkins, argued very per-suasively for "the constructive role of violence and suffering for the individual and for his society." Tomkins reasoned that in a democratic society most men recognize a taboo on arbitrarily hurting another person but at the same time are capable of identifying with the aggressor. Thus, the reaction pattern to the mob which murdered the abolitionist Elijah Lovejoy might be: (1) anger at the mob, (2) a fleeting identification with the mob, (3) guilt reactions for this identification. A more powerful response would be anger against the aggressor who threatened the values and the persons of all (including oneself), followed by a crystallization of guilt over "base" feelings toward the man who fought the common battle of all. In this fashion men were brought to antislavery by the lynching of Lovejoy, the mobbing of Garrison, the burning of the Philadelphia antislavery hall, or the forced return of Anthony Burns from Boston to slavery. Most Northerners were profoundly ambivalent about slavery; they would have preferred not to think about the issue, but the persistent abolitionists would not allow them the luxury of escape. By the process of provoking opposition and offering themselves as victims in the defense of democratic values, the abolitionists gained an increasing commitment to their cause. The greatest provocation and sacrifice was made by John Brown. In 1964 Louis Ruchames insisted that we could not allow ourselves the luxury of dismissing Brown as "insane." Howard Zinn, also writing in 1965, added that we should not confine the case to subjective motives. What about objective consequences? If slavery was the great social evil in America, and if the abolitionists played an important role in the death of that institution, why did scholars fail to appreciate this fact? Zinn argued that many of the charges were arbitrary: "Emotionalism" was a very weak charge since "emotion" is a neutral instrument which may be attached to the worst or to the best of human activities. "Extremism" fares little better as an accusation since it is also relative to the context, and everyone is an "extremist" to someone at some point in changing time. Negro suffrage was too "extreme" for Garrison in 1830 but not in 1865.

The abolitionists were not so "doctrinaire, inflexible, uncompromising and impractical" as their critics have supposed. Considering their modest numbers and enormous tasks, they did an extraordinary work during the antebellum period in organizing the fight against slavery. When the first South Carolina areas fell into Union hands in 1861, the abolitionists did a very creditable job in sending teachers, ministers, and agents to organize the Port Royal experiment which Willie Lee Rose described so vividly in 1964. During the same year James M. McPherson, tracing antislavery activities in the Civil War and Reconstruction period, presented a very impressive portrait of abolitionists in the thick of politics, particularly during the critical time of emancipation and the passage of the Fourteenth Amendment. According to the needs of the cause, they attacked Lincoln or rushed to defend him, cooperated with the Republican leaders or defied them, and beyond the arena of national politics they organized Freedman's aid societies, directed help to the South, and in general conducted a vigorous fight for the freedom and equality of the American Negro. Not many men had been willing to follow John Brown into revolutionary action in 1859, but when the conflict began and the possibility arose for converting a war for the Union into a social revolution, the abolitionists played an important role in bringing these events to pass.

BIBLIOGRAPHY

Books and Articles Referred to in the Chapter Introduction

Robert Penn Warren, *The Legacy of the Civil War: Meditations on the Centennial* (1961).

Larry Gara, *The Liberty Line: The Legend of the Underground Railroad* (1961).

C. Vann Woodward, "The Antislavery Myth," *American Scholar* (1962).

David Donald, "Toward a Reconsideration of the Abolitionists," *Lincoln Reconsidered* (1956). For criticism of the Donald thesis see Robert A. Skotheim, "A Note on Historical Method," *Journal of Southern History* (1959); Louis Ruchames' review of Donald's biography of Sumner, *Massachusetts Quarterly* (1961); and Paul Goodman's review essay, "David Donald's *Charles Sumner* Reconsidered," *New England Quarterly* (1964). See also Louis Ruchames, "Charles Sumner and American Historiography," *Journal of Negro History* (1953).

David Donald, *Charles Sumner and the Coming of the Civil War* (1960).

Irving H. Bartlett, *Wendell Phillips, Brahmin Radical* (1961).

Richard Hofstadter, "Wendell Phillips, The Patrician as Agitator," *The American Political Tradition* (1948).

John L. Thomas, *The Liberator: A Biography of William Lloyd Garrison* (1963).

Russel B. Nye, *William Lloyd Garrison and the Humanitarian Reformers* (1955).

Martin B. Duberman, *Charles Francis Adams, 1807–1886* (1961).

Avery O. Craven, *The Repressible Conflict*, (1939).

William B. Hesseltine, *Lincoln and the War Governors* (1948).

Hazel C. Wolf, *On Freedom's Altar: The Martyr Complex in the Abolition Movement* (1952).

Staughton Lynd, "The Abolition Critique of the U.S. Constitution;" Sylvan S. Tomkins, "The Psychology of Commitment; The Constructive Role of Violence and Suffering for the Individual and for his Society;" and Fawn M. Brodie, "Who Defends the Abolitionist" all in Martin B. Duberman (ed.), *The Antislavery Vanguard* (1965).

Willie Lee Rose, *Rehearsal for Reconstruction: The Port Royal Experiment* (1964).

Suggested Reading

The indispensable book for ideas, interpretations, and new insights is *The Antislavery Vanguard* (1965), edited by Martin B. Duberman, containing an essay by Duberman on "The Northern Response to Slavery." A widely used narrative history of the movement is Louis Filler, *The Crusade Against Slavery* (1960). For a discussion of the great variety of persons involved in the antislavery movement, see Betty Fladeland, "Who Were the Abolitionists" *Journal of Negro History* (1964). See also her book *James Gillespie Birney: Slaveholder to Abolitionist* (1955); Benjamin P. Thomas, *Theodore Weld* (1950); and the biographies listed earlier by Bartlett, Hofstadter, J. L. Thomas, Nye, Duberman, and Donald. William and Jane Pease have put together an excellent anthology of sources in *The Antislavery Argument* (1965). Several briefer collections are Louis Ruchames (ed.), *The Abolitionists* (1963); and Richard O. Curry (ed.), *The Abolitionists: Reformers or Fanatics?* (1965). The most useful bibliographies are in McPherson and Filler, both cited earlier. On the Negro in antislavery, see the essays by Leon F. Litwack and James M. McPherson in the Duberman anthology cited earlier; Litwack, *North of Slavery* (1961); Howard H. Bell, "National Negro Convention of the Middle 1840's: Moral Suasion vs. Political Action," *Journal of Negro History* (1957), and "Expressions of Negro Militancy in the North, 1840–1860," *Journal of Negro History* (1960). For several recent and important accounts of developments within the antislavery movement, see David B. Davis, "The Emergence of Immediatism in British and American Antislavery Thought," *Mississippi Valley Historical Review* (1962); and John Demos, "The Antislavery Movement and the Problem of Violent Means," *New England Quarterly* (1964). David A. Williams provided an interesting account of changing scholarly opinion on Garrison; see "William Lloyd Garrison, the Historians, and the Abolition Movement," *Essex Institute Historical Collections* (1962). For information on the attempt of abolitionists to gain greater consistency by extending the freedom struggle to the North, see Leonard W. Levy and Harlan B. Phillips, "The Roberts Case: Source of the 'Separate but Equal' Doctrine," *American Historical Review* (1951); and Louis Ruchames, "Race and Education in Massachusetts," *Negro History Bulletin* (1949). On the last remnants of antislavery activity in the South, see Fletcher M. Green, "Northern Missionary Activities in the South, 1846–1861," *Journal of Southern History* (1955). Maryland was a microcosm of the divided and changing nation as Charles L. Wagandt indicated in *The Mighty Revolution: Negro Emancipation in Maryland* (1964). On abolition and civil rights in a Northern state, see Stanley I. Kutler, "Pennsylvania Courts, The Abolition Act, and Negro Rights," *Pennsylvania History* (1963). The decline of antislavery in the South was charted by Kenneth M. Stampp in "The Fate of the Southern Antislavery Movement," *Journal of Negro History* (1943). For a general discussion of the emancipation question in the North and the South, see Edgar A. Toppin, "Negro Emancipation in Historical Retrospective: Ohio," *Journal of Human Relations* (1963). Gilman M. Ostrander wrote a good summary of the dramatic response of New England intellectuals to John Brown, See "Emerson, Thoreau, and John Brown," *Mississippi Valley Historical Review* (1953). For a rare example of mass emancipation and resettlement see Ralph L. Ketcham, "The Dictates of Conscience: Edward Coles and Slavery," *Virginia Quarterly Review* (1960). See also David B. Davis, *The Problem of Slavery in Western Culture* (1966).

1962

Abolitionist Motives and Personalities*

MARTIN B. DUBERMAN

Out of their heightened concern with the pressing question of Negro rights, a number of historians, especially the younger ones, have begun to take a new look at the abolitionists, men who in their own day were involved in a similar movement of social change. About both them and ourselves we are asking anew such questions as the proper role of agitation, the underlying motives of both reformers and resistants, and the useful limits of outside interference. From this questioning a general tendency has developed to view

* Martin Duberman, "The Abolitionists and Psychology," *Journal of Negro History* (1962). This is a slightly revised version of Duberman's "The Abolitionists and Psychology." Among the footnotes in the original article were references to Gordon W. Allport, *Becoming, Basic Considerations for a Psychology of Personality* (1960); Philip Rieff, *Freud: the Mind of the Moralist* (1959); O. Hobart Mowrer, "Psychiatry and Religion," *Atlantic Monthly* (1961); Erich Fromm, *Psychoanalysis and Religion* (1959).

the abolitionists in a more favorable light than previously. As yet, however, it is a tendency only, and hostility to the abolitionists continues to be strong among historians.

Perhaps one reason why no fuller reevaluation has taken place is that historians have been made cautious by the fate of previous "revisionist" scholarship. We have seen how current preoccupations can prompt dubious historical re-evaluations. But this need not always be the case. Contemporary pressures, if recognized and contained, can prove fruitful in stimulating the historical imagination. This may lead us to uncover (not invent) aspects of the past to which we were previously blind.

If historians need more courage in their reconsideration of the abolitionists, they also need more information. Particularly do they need to employ some of the insights and raise some of the questions which developments in related fields of knowledge have made possible. Recent trends in psychology seem especially pertinent, though historians have not paid them sufficient attention. It is my hope in this paper to make some beginning in that direction.

It might be well to start by referring to one of psychology's older principles, the uniqueness of personality. Each individual, with his own genetic composition and his own life experience, will develop into a distinctive organism. There are, of course, certain drives and reflexes which are more or less "instinctive." There are also a variety of common responses conditioned by our membership in a particular group, be it family, class, church, or nation. These similarities among human beings make possible the disciplines of sociology, anthropology, and social psychology, which concern themselves with patterns of behavior, and demonstrate that no man is *sui generis*. But it does not follow that the qualities which are uniquely individual are mere irrelevancies. As Gordon Allport has said, ". . . all of the animals in the world are psychologically less distinct from one another than one man is from other men."

This is not to question, of course, the validity of attempts, whether they be by sociologists, psychologists, or historians, to find meaningful similarities in the behavioral patterns of various human groups. The point is to make certain that such similarities genuinely exist, and further, to be aware that in describing them we do not pretend to be saying everything about the individuals involved. Historians, it seems, are prone to ignore both cautions—their treatment of the abolitionists being the immediate case in point.

With barely a redeeming hint of uncertainty, many historians list a group of "similar traits" which are said to characterize all abolitionists: "impractical," "self-righteous," "fanatical," "humorless," "vituperative," and,—if they are very modern in their terminology—"disturbed." The list varies, but usually only to include adjectives equally hostile and denunciatory. The stereotype of the "abolitionist personality," though fluid in details, is clear enough in its general outlines.

But did most abolitionists really share these personality traits? The fact is, we know much less about the individuals involved in the movement than has been implied. Some of the major figures, such as Joshua Leavitt, have never received biographical treatment; others—the Tappans, Edmund Quincy, and Benjamin Lundy, for example—badly need modern appraisal. And the careers and personalities of the vast majority of significant secondary figures—people like Lydia Maria Child, Sidney Gay, Maria Weston Chapman, Henry B. Stanton, and Abby Kelley Foster—have been almost totally unexplored. Whence comes the confidence, then, that allows historians to talk of "the abolitionist personality," as if this had been microscopically examined and painstakingly reconstructed?

Certainly the evidence which we do have does not support such confident theorizing. In order to adhere to this conceptual straitjacket, it is necessary to ignore or discount much that conflicts with it—the modesty of Theodore Weld, the wit of James Russell Lowell, the tender humanity of Whittier, the worldly charm of Edmund Quincy. This does not mean that we need leap to the opposite extreme and claim all abolitionists were saints and seraphs. But if some of them were disagreeable or disturbed, we want, instead of a blanket indictment, to know which ones and in what ways; we want some recognition of the variety of human beings who entered the movement.

It seems to me that what too many historians have done is to take William Lloyd Garrison as a personality symbol for the entire movement (at the same time, ironically, that they deny him the commanding leadership which he was once assumed to have had). Fixing on some of the undeniably "neurotic" aspects of his personality (and bolstered, it should be said, by the eccentric psychographs of other abolitionists —a Gerrit Smith say, or a Stephen Foster), they equate these with the personality structures of all the abolitionists, and conclude that the movement was composed solely of "quacks." In doing so, they fail to do justice to the wide spectrum of personality involved; in fact, they do not even do justice to Garrison, for to speak exclusively of *his* oracular and abusive qualities is to ignore the considerable evidence of personal warmth and kindliness.

It may be that when we know more of other abolitionists, we may with equal certainty be able to single out qualities in them which seem palpable symptoms of "disturbance." But let the evidence at least precede the judgment. And let us also show a decent timidity in applying the label "neurotic." Psychiatrists, dealing with a multitude of evidence and bringing to it professional insights, demonstrate more caution in this regard than do untrained historians working with mere traces of personality. If the disposition to be hostile exists, "neurosis" can almost always be established. Under the Freudian microscope, it would be a rare man indeed whose life showed no evidence of pathological behavior. (Think, for one, of the admirable William

James, who, as his devoted biographer, Ralph Barton Perry, has shown, was subject to hypochondria, hallucinations, and intense oscillations of mood.) I am not suggesting that all men's lives, if sufficiently investigated, would show equally severe evidence of disturbance. I mean only to warn that, given the double jeopardy of a hostile commentator and the weight of a hostile historical tradition, we must take special precaution not to be too easily convinced by the "evidence" of neurosis in the abolitionists.

And even were we to establish the neurotic component of behavior, the story would certainly not be complete. To know the pathological elements in an individual's behavior is not to know everything about his behavior. To say that Garrison, in his fantasy world, longed to be punished and thus deliberately courted martyrdom, or that Wendell Phillips, alienated from the "new order," sought to work out his private grievances against the industrial system by indirectly attacking it through slavery is hardly to exhaust their range of possible motives. We know far too little about why men do anything—let alone why they do something as specific as joining a reform movement—to assert as confidently as historians have, the motives of whole groups of men. We may never know enough about the human psyche to achieve a comprehensive analysis of motivation; how much greater the difficulty when the subject is dead and we are attempting the analysis on the basis of partial and fragmentary remains.

Our best hope for increased understanding in this area—aside from the artist's tool of intuition—is in the researches of psychology. But at present there is no agreed-upon theory of motivation among psychologists. Gordon Allport, however, summarizing current opinion, suggests that behavior does not result solely from the need to reduce tension, but may also aim (especially in a "healthy" person) at distant goals, the achievement of which can be gained only by maintaining tension. Allport does not press his views, realizing the complexity of the problems at issue. But his hypotheses are at least suggestive as regards the abolitionists, for their motives, rather than being solely the primitive ones of eliminating personal tension (under the guise of ethical commitment), may also have included a healthy willingness to bear tension (in the form of ostracism, personal danger and material sacrifice) in order to persevere in pursuit of long-range ideals.

Acceptance of these suggestions runs into the massive resistance of neo-Freudian cynicism. How old-fashioned, it will be said, to talk in terms of "ideals" or "conscience," since these are only unconscious rationalizations for "darker" drives which we are unable to face. How old-fashioned, too, to talk as if men could exercise choice in their conduct, since all our behavior is determined by our antecedents.

But the surprising fact is that such views are not old-fashioned. On the contrary, they have recently returned to favor in psychoanalytical circles. Increasing dissatisfaction with the ability of behaviorist theory fully to explain human action has led to a reconsideration of the role of reason and the possibilities of purposive, deliberate behavior. The result is the influential new school of "ego psychology," which views man as endowed with a considerable margin of freedom and responsibility, and which has restored to the vocabulary such "old fashioned" terminology as character, willpower, and conscience. Moral earnestness, moreover, is no longer equated with self-deception. As Allport has said, the very mark of maturity "seems to be the range and extent of one's feeling of self-involvement in abstract ideals." Some of these new emphases had been prefigured in the work of such philosophers as Sartre, who have long stressed social action as a sign of "authenticity" in man.

But although all of this makes a re-evaluation of the abolitionists possible, it does not make one necessary. Men may now be thought capable of impersonal

devotion to ideals, but this does not mean that the abolitionists were such men. Maturity may now be defined as the ability to commit ourselves objectively to ethical values, but it does not follow that every man who makes such a commitment does so out of mature motives.

Yet at least some doubts should be raised in our minds as to whether we have been fair in regarding the abolitionists as psychologically homogeneous, and at that, homogeneous in the sense of being self-deceived. My own feeling goes beyond doubt, into conviction. I do not claim, to repeat, that because the abolitionists fought in a noble cause, their motives were necessarily noble—i.e., "pure" and "unselfish," unrelated in any way to their own inner turmoil and conflicts. A connection between inner problems and outer convictions probably always exists to some degree. But an individual's public involvement is never completely explained by discussing his private pathology. Yet it is just this that historians have frequently done, and to that degree, they have distorted and devalued the abolitionist commitment.

To provide a concrete example, by way of summary, consider the case of James Russell Lowell, whose biography I am writing, and about whom I can talk with more assurance than I might some other figure.

His history seems to me convincing proof that at least some people became abolitionists not primarily out of an unconscious need or deliberate, rational commitment to certain ethical values—recognizing, as I have said, that the two are never wholly unrelated. Lowell's active life as a reformer came during the period of his greatest contentment—secure in a supremely happy marriage, and confident of his talents and his future. His contemporaries agree in describing him as a gay, witty, warm man, without serious tensions or disabling anxieties. I have come across so little evidence of "pathology" in the Lowell of these years that when the standard picture of the abolitionist as a warped eccentric is applied to him, it becomes absurd.

And he *was* an abolitionist, though various arguments have been used to deny this. Lowell, it has been said, came to the movement late—and only at the instigation of his bride, Maria White, who was a confirmed reformer; he never fully committed himself to abolition, and finally left the ranks in the early 1850s. There may be some justice to these charges, but on the whole the argument is not persuasive. Given Lowell's youth (he was born in 1819) he could not have joined the movement much earlier than he did (which was around 1840), and there is evidence that he was involved in the cause before he met Maria White. The important point is that for roughly ten years he was unquestionably a serious abolitionist, both as an active member of the Massachusetts Anti-Slavery Society, and as a frequent contributor to abolitionist periodicals. The reasons for his drifting out of the movement are complex, but turn largely on the fact that his wife's death in 1853 destroyed the structure of his life and left him apathetic to public issues. (Might not this give added weight to the argument that it takes a reasonably contented man to interest himself in the problems of others?)

Even when it is admitted that Lowell was an abolitionist, he is dismissed as not having been a "typical" one. But who was the typical abolitionist? Is the standard of measurement meant to be some outstanding individual—Garrison, say, or Theodore Weld—and is everyone else to be considered more or less of an abolitionist depending on how closely he approximated the personality structure of the model? But a man may be prominent in a movement without necessarily typifying it. And which of several leading—and very different—figures should be chosen as the model? The decision is likely to be arbitrary (and unconscious), varying with each historian.

Or is the standard of measurement meant to be some composite group of traits which accurately describe the large number of abolitionists, so that when any single individual fails to exhibit these traits, he may justifiably be dismissed as "the exception which proves the rule? This approach is more reasonable, but here again we run up against the old difficulty of drawing a genuinely valid group portrait. We know so little about the individual personalities and careers of the majority of abolitionists that it seems like putting the cart before the horse to even talk about a composite portrait. Certainly the one which is now commonly accepted ("impractical"; "self-righteous," etc.) fails adequately to describe many of the abolitionists about whom we do have information. I mean here not only Lowell, but a number of others. What I have seen in my researches into papers of people like Edmund Quincy, Lydia Maria Child, or Maria Weston Chapman (to name only a few of the more prominent), has created the strong suspicion in my mind that if their personalities were to be investigated in depth, they too would be found to deviate from the accepted portrait in so many significant ways as further to undermine its reliability.

A conceptual scheme may yet be devised which adequately describes the motives and actions of most of the abolitionists. But if so, it will not be of the primitive kind thus far suggested. There is no reason why historians cannot legitimately investigate group patterns, but to do so meaningfully, they must become skilled in the techniques of sociology and other related disciplines. This takes time and inclination, and the historian, busy with his special interests and orientated toward the particular, rarely his either. Unfortunately this does not always prevent him from trying his hand, though the result has too often been the kind of elementary categorizing used to describe the abolitionists.

Opinions will continue to differ as to the best way of achieving desired social change. Our own generation's confrontation with segregation has made this clear. Many of us feel as strongly about the evil of that practice as the abolitionists did about the institution of slavery. Like them, too, we have scant faith in Southern voluntarism or the benevolent workings of time; patience and inactivity have not done their work. Naturally we would like to believe that our sense of urgency comes from concern for the Negro rather than from a need to escape from some private torment of our own. Because of this we are admittedly prone to credit our historical counterparts with the kind of good motives we would like to impute to ourselves. Our wish to think well of them may account for our doing so. But as Erich Fromm has said, "the fact that an idea satisfies a wish does not mean necessarily that the idea is false." There is much in the new psychology to encourage the belief that the idea is not false. At any rate, if we are to find out, we need less dogma, more research, and a chastening sense of wonder at the complexities of human nature.

1959

John Brown and the American Tradition*

LOUIS RUCHAMES

It is a hundred years since John Brown was hanged at Charlestown, Virginia, on December 2, 1859, for his attack on Harpers Ferry. Perry Miller, in his study of Jonathan Edwards, refers to Harpers Ferry as part of "the symbolism of America." As a symbol, Brown's desperate attack upon Harpers Ferry on Sunday night, October 16, 1859, has had different and frequently contradictory meanings for different groups. To the slaveholder and his sympathizers, both North and South, it was a criminal and murderous attack upon an institution sanctioned by law and justified by an ideology which regarded slavery as part of the very nature of things, with the white man born to rule and the Negro to serve. Brown was therefore a murderer and criminal who sought "to incite slaves to murder helpless women and children." His courageous behavior at his trial and execution was no more worthy of veneration than the similiar behavior of any criminal. "Pirates have died as resolutely as martyrs," said the Baltimore *American*. "If the firmness displayed by John Brown proves anything, the composure of a Thug, dying by the cord with which he had strangled so many victims, proves just as much."

To many Southerners, the attack was an earnest of what could and would happen, multiplied tenfold, under a government not totally commited to a defense of slavery. The thought of a possible Republican victory in the forthcoming election of

* Reprinted from *A John Brown Reader* by Louis Ruchames (ed.), by permission of Abelard-Schuman Ltd. All rights reserved. Copyright 1959.

November, 1860, when seen by Southerners in the context of Harpers Ferry, caused almost hysterical alarm. In the Senate, during the following January, Robert Toombs counseled his people, "Never permit this Federal government to pass into the hands of the black Republican party. It has already declared war against you and your institutions. It every day commits acts of war against you: it has already compelled you to arm for your defence. . . . Defend yourselves! The enemy is at your door, wait not to meet him at your hearthstone; meet him at the doorsill, and drive him from the Temple of Liberty, or pull down its pillars and involve him in a common ruin."

On the other hand, in Northern antislavery circles, Brown represented the highest idealism: the willingness to sacrifice one's life and possessions for the freedom and welfare of one's fellow men. In a lecture on November 8, 1859, in Boston, Emerson referred to Brown as "The Saint, whose fate yet hangs in suspense, but whose martyrdom, if it shall be perfected, will make the gallows as glorious as the Cross." In an address delivered in Concord almost two weeks after Harpers Ferry, Thoreau remarked that "when I think of him, and his six sons, and his son-in-law, not to enumerate the others, enlisted for this fight, proceeding coolly, reverently, humanely to work, for months, if not years . . . without expecting any reward but a good conscience, while almost all America stood ranked on the other side,— I say again, that it affects me as a sublime spectacle." Thoreau indeed anticipated his friend Emerson in comparing Brown to Jesus. "Some eighteen hundred years ago Christ was crucified; this morning, perchance, Captain Brown was hung. These are the two ends of a chain which is not without its links. He is not Old Brown any longer; he is an angel of light." Wendell Phillips, who had devoted the previous 25 years to the antislavery movement, went so far as to regard Harpers Ferry as the beginning of emancipation. Invoking

Brown as "marvellous old man," he said: "History will date Virginia Emancipation from Harpers Ferry. True, the slave is still there. So, when the tempest uproots a pine on your hills, it looks green for months, a year or two. Still, it is timber, not a tree. John Brown has loosened the roots of the slave system; it only breathes—it does not live—hereafter."

Few events in American history provide so vivid an illustration of the thesis that the historian's evaluations of men and events are dependent not upon facts alone but upon the basic premises from which he views those facts. It is his "inarticulate major premises," as Oliver Wendell Holmes accurately put it, that determine his judgments. In the case of Brown, the determining factor in all judgments, whether of the ordinary citizen or the scholar, was one's attitude toward slavery. To those who regarded slavery as "the sum of all villainies," as legalized kidnapping maintained by jails, the lash, and, ultimately, the death penalty for those who sought to secure their freedom or to help others do so, Brown's action was one of great idealism and placed him in the company of the great liberators of mankind. Theodore Parker, the great Unitarian clergyman and abolitionist, expressed this point of view as ably and frankly as anyone, in a letter to Francis Jackson, an outstanding antislavery leader in Boston. "A man held against his will as a slave," he wrote, "has a natural right to kill every one who seeks to prevent his employment of liberty. The freeman has a natural right to help the slaves recover their liberty, and in that enterprise to do for them all which they have a right to do for themselves." After asserting the duty of one man to help another get rid of a wolf or murderer in case of an attack, he asks: "Suppose it is not a murderer who would kill you, but a kidnapper who would enslave, does that make it less my duty to help you out of the hands of your enemy? Suppose it is not a kidnapper who would make you a bondman, but a slaveholder who would keep you one, does that remove my obligation to help you?" In the light of these opinions one can well appreciate Parker's final judgment that "there have been few spirits more pure and devoted than John Brown's, and none that gave up their breath in a nobler cause. Let the American State hang his body, and the American Church damn his soul; still, the blessing of such as are ready to perish will fall on him, and the universal justice of the Infinitely Perfect God will take him welcome home. The road to heaven is as short from the gallows as from a throne; perhaps, also, as easy." Even men like Garrison, who were non-resistants, and did not themselves wish to use force to achieve freedom for the slave, cheered Brown's effort as a valid alternative to continued slavery. "Rather than see men wearing their chains in a cowardly and servile spirit," he said at a meeting memorializing Brown, "I would, as an advocate of peace, much rather see them breaking the head of the tyrant with their chains. Give me, as a non-resistant, Bunker Hill, and Lexington, and Concord, rather than the cowardice and servility of a Southern slave-plantation."

Those whose opposition to slavery was only lukewarm, whose dislike of the institution led them to oppose its extension but was not sufficiently strong to cause them to strive for its elimination in the South, condemned Brown's attack and accepted his execution as justified. But they too saw a certain element of nobility in his character and behavior. Samuel J. Kirkwood, Governor of Iowa, expressed this point of view, which was shared by many, when he said: "While the mass of our people utterly condemn the act of John Brown, they feel and they express admiration and sympathy for the disinterestedness of purpose by which they believe he was governed, and for the unflinching courage and calm cheerfulness with which he met the consequences of his failure."

The conflict of ideologies has continued to our own day. The grandson of William Lloyd Garrison, Oswald Garrison Villard, a man of broad humanitarian sympathies, who has written the definitive biography of Brown, concludes his study with this observation, "The story of John Brown will ever confront the spirit of despotism, when men are struggling to throw off the shackles of social or political or physical slavery. His own country, while admitting his mistakes without undue palliation or excuse, will forever acknowledge the divine that was in him by the side of what was human and faulty, and blind and wrong. It will cherish the memory of the prisoner of Charlestown in 1859 as at once a sacred, a solemn and an inspiring American heritage."

In opposition to this point of view stands James Malin,[1] the foremost anti-Brown historian, who seems unable to forgive the North for having used force against Southern secession, or the abolitionists for having taught that the abolition of slavery would be a step forward for American society, or the Negro for having believed that his welfare would be furthered by the forceful elimination of slavery. To Malin, minor errors of date or place committed by writers who have a high regard for Brown are frequently labeled deliberate falsehoods, while the errors of Brown haters are simply unintentional blunders. Very few antislavery leaders and writers emerge unscathed under Malin's furious onslaught. Typical of his method are his comments on Emerson, Thoreau, Parker and the other leaders of New England opinion, whom he contemptuously refers to as the "New England Transcendental Hierarchy, the self-appointed keepers not only of New England culture, but, according to their own estimates, of national civilization." Following in the footsteps of earlier anti-Brown biographers, such as Hill Peebles Wilson and Robert Penn Warren, Malin refers to the sympathetic evaluation of Brown as "the John Brown legend," a "hoax" created largely by the above-

---

[1] James C. Malin, *John Brown and the Legend of Fifty-Six* (Philadelphia: American Philosophical Society, 1942).

mentioned "hierarchy." To expose the "hoax," he concludes, would result in breaking "the spell of its authority" and deflating "other fakes and fakers" as well. Malin has accumulated a wealth of facts in his volume and thereby has induced many historians to accept his point of view, but a closer examination of the book reveals many errors of fact,[2] and an approach which, though it claims to be scientific, is notably lacking in the dispassionate objectivity of the true scientist.

The purpose of this volume is not, however, the examination of all that has been written about John Brown, whether pro or con, or its evaluation from the point of view of historical accuracy. It is intended, rather, to present the positive impact of John Brown upon American thought, viewing his life and death as events which evoked great idealism as well as some of the noblest and most memorable writing in the history of American letters.

We approach this task from the point of view of those who believe that the struggle against slavery and its elimination during the Civil War was one of the great positive achievements in American history; that the abolitionists and other antislavery leaders, who devoted their lives to the achievement of freedom for the slave and equality of opportunity for Negro and white alike, seeking through their writings and lectures to educate the American public to the evils of slavery, were not paranoiacs or narrow-minded fanatics, but men

and women who were devoted to the highest ideals of equality and democracy, influenced by the best in the Judeo-Christian tradition and all that was good and noble in the thoughts and actions of the Founding Fathers. John Brown was one of this company of antislavery men. This anthology, by presenting the John Brown tradition, seeks to contribute to a firmer understanding of one of the vital aspects of American history, as well as to help our own generation in a small way, toward a greater appreciation of those very ideals which motivated Brown and his friends.

* * * * *

[John Brown] was found guilty . . . of three crimes: conspiring with slaves to rebel, murder, and treason. Though his lawyers sought to enter a plea of insanity on the basis of affidavits received from residents of Ohio, he rejected the attempts and refused to permit any such plea. Concerning the trial itself, Richard B. Morris, the well-known historian notes that it was "flagrantly unfair."

The right of the accused to a reasonable time to prepare for trial was shockingly violated. Brown was forced to stand trial the very same day he was indicted. Scrupulous though the court was to provide the accused with competent trial counsel, it erroneously denied him the right to engage lawyers of his own choice. When, finally, his own counsel took over, they were given no time to familiarize themselves with the case against their client.

To this catalogue of judicial errors must be added a last one: John Brown was tried and sentenced for a crime of which he could not conceivably have been guilty. How the accused could have committed treason against Virginia when he was neither a citizen nor a resident of that state and owed it no allegiance was never clarified by the law-enforcement authorities. Objectivity and reason gave way to hysteria and vigilantism. This was no time for technicalities. It was enough that John

---

[2] For example, on pp. 4–5, one finds at least eight errors in the reproduction of a letter from John Brown to his father. In other parts of the book, names are misspelled and key phrases omitted from documents. It is important to note that in the reconstruction of the events leading to the Pottawatomie killings in Kansas, the reminiscences of members of the Brown family are arbitrarily excluded. Furthermore, the book is based almost exclusively on the materials available in the files of the Kansas State Historical Society. The important collections of John Brown material owned by other state historical societies, the Library of Congress, college libraries, and authorities on John Brown such as Boyd B. Stutler and Dr. Clarence S. Gee are either not used at all or only in a very limited way.

Brown be convicted of a crime carrying the capital penalty and that the sentence of the court be carried out with expedition.[3]

Morris also suggests that Brown had been examined by an alienist or psychiatrist, and implies that if he had been, he might never have been brought to trial. As has just been indicated, efforts were made during the trial to have him adjudged insane. On the second day of the trial, Brown's lawyer received a telegram from A. H. Lewis of Akron, Ohio, editor of the *Summit Beacon,* emphasizing that insanity was hereditary in Brown's family on his mother's side. After the trial, in a further attempt to secure clemency, 19 affidavits, gathered by one of Brown's lawyers from relatives and friends in Ohio, repeated the same information and added that Brown was insane on the subject of slavery. At one point, Governor Wise, issued an order to have Brown examined by an alienist, but then countermanded the order.

As to whether Brown was or was not insane, the best answer lies in an examination of his behavior at the trial and afterward. Certainly, his remarks and actions at the trial show no indication of insanity, nor has it even been alleged that they do. His speech to the court before sentence was pronounced is regarded by many as one of the finest utterances in American literature; Emerson, indeed, compared it in later years to Lincoln's Gettysburg address. His letters from prison are models of lucidity and breathe a rare nobility   thought and character. "No lunatic," writes Villard, ever penned such elevated and high-minded, and such consistent epistles Brown's concentration upon slavery and its evils throughout the latter part of his life, which is the usual reason given for alleging his insanity, was indeed intense and unusual for his day. But it was not unusual when compared to that of such men and women as William Lloyd Garrison, Wen-

dell Phillips, Lydia Maria Child, Theodore Parker, Charles Sumner, Maria Weston Chapman, and Parker Pillsbury, to name but a few, who devoted their lives to the antislavery cause, suffered hardships and privations for its sake, and on various occasions were also accused of being fanatics and insane on the subject of slavery. The lesson to be learned from their example is simply that to be deeply sensitive to injustice, to be willing to devote one's life to an unpopular cause, to give up the pursuit of one's own gain to alleviate the suffering of others involves running the risk of being called fanatic and even insane by the smug, the callous, and the well-placed members of society. "The prophet is a fool, the man of the spirit is mad!" has echoed through the ages, from the days of Hosea to our own.

Finally, perhaps the most important evidence as to the nature of John Brown's mind and character is to be found in the devotion to him of the 21 young men—intelligent, able, and high-minded—who lived with him and knew him as a leader and a friend, and who followed him even unto death.[5]

---

[3] Richard B. Morris, *Fair Trial* (New York: Alfred A. Knopf, 1953), pp. 259–60.

[4] *Op. cit.,* p. 509.

[5] Among recent historians, Professors C. Vann Woodward and Allan Nevins have emphasized the case for Brown's insanity. Professor Vann Woodward has made much of the 19 affidavits testifying to insanity in Brown's family, especially on his mother's side, and to Brown's own insanity or "monomania" on the question of slavery. Putting aside the basic question of whether one's insanity may be established by the presence or absence of insanity in one's family, it may be noted that the affidavits are highly suspect as valid evidence. Their primary purpose was to save Brown from execution by showing him to be insane. They must, therefore, be regarded not as objective reports but as partisan statements made to achieve a certain purpose, with every possibility that the material they present may be biased in the direction of proving insanity. Moreover, their reliability as evidence is weakened still further by the fact that they include significant sections which are based, quite explicitly, not on direct knowledge but on hearsay and secondhand information.

By accepting the affidavits at their face value, Professor Vann Woodward, though a very careful historian, is led into committing several errors. He states, for instance, that one of Brown's brothers was insane. This assertion is made in only one of the affidavits and is not substantiated

John Brown's end came on December 2, on a scaffold in Charlestown. His execution served as a visible demonstration by the state of Virginia of the condign punishment ultimately in store for those who sought to tamper with the institution of slavery; for the slave seeking to escape from bondage and for the free man, white or colored, who dared to aid him.

To the North, however, Brown's execution brought a far different lesson. For in John Brown, whose venture at Harpers Ferry it first saw as the desperate act of a demented old man oblivious to the realties of the world, the North came to see the embodiment of all that was noble, courageous, and self-sacrificing in man's love for his fellow man. It saw beyond the bloodshed and death into the heart of a man who had identified himself with the poorest, the lowliest, the most forsaken people of the land, had thrown in his lot with theirs, had given up his home, his possessions, his ambitions, his wife and children whom he loved, even life itself, to bring freedom and dignity to men, women, and children who had known only the bitterness and hopelessness of slavery. As they saw the state of Virginia, in all of its majesty, proceed in indecent haste to exact the life of the man who had threatened its power, the people of the North learned, as little else could have taught them, that the structure of slavery remained intact primarily through the power of the whip, the gun, and the gallows and that when these were gone there was little else left. They learned, too, that wealth and happiness derived from the sweat of slaves was not less easily relinquished than that gotten through more honorable means, and that the slaveholder would fight desperately, with all the means at his disposal, to maintain the foundation of his wealth and power. It was then that many in the North realized that the issue of slavery and freedom would be decided by the weapons that the South had chosen. The battle at Harpers Ferry demonstrated what those weapons were.

When the war came, almost two years later, the man who had been hanged rose, as it were, from his grave to march again with those who had finally taken up the cause for which he had fought, and, by proffering the example of his life and work, helped to achieve the victory which he had lost in life but gained in death.

by any evidence. The brother referred to was the editor of the New Orleans *Bee* and a prominent figure in New Orleans public affairs. All that we know of him indicates that he was quite sane. Professor Vann Woodward also asserts that Brown's mother, grandmother, sister, and sister's daughter were insane. Family letters and other records cast doubt upon that part of the assertion which refers to the grandmother and sister's daughter, while a careful reading of the affidavits themselves fails to reveal any reference to the insanity of Brown's mother. All available evidence affirms her sanity.

One may also question Professor Nevins' evidence, which he has assiduously gathered, in seeking to prove Brown's insanity. Since limitations of space prevent an extended analysis, the following will have to suffice. Professor Nevins writes that Brown "was subject to extravagant religious fixations. In 1852, worried because his son John did not exhibit piety, he spent an entire month writing a letter of pamphlet length to him, composed largely of scriptual quotations. We might question the sanity of a nearly penniless man with a large family who devotes a month to such an exhortation —which proved futile." A close reading of the letter in question, which is printed in full in F. B. Sanborn's *John Brown*, pp. 45–51, reveals the very opposite of what Professor Nevins believes it to prove. In the letter Brown as follows: "It is now nearly a month since I began on another page. . . . I did mean that my letter should go off at once, but I have not become very stout, and have a great deal to look after, and have had many interruptions. We have done part of our sowing, and expect to get all our corn (of which we have a good crop) secure from frost this day." Prof. Vann Woodward's discussion of Brown is in "John Brown's Private War," *America in Crisis*, ed. by Daniel Aaron (New York: Alfred A. Knopf, 1952), pp. 109–30. Professor Nevins evaluates Brown in *The Emergence of Lincoln* (New York and London: Charles Scribner's Sons, 1950), II, 5 ff.

The Tactics of Agitation*

HOWARD ZINN

Few groups in American history have taken as much abuse from professional historians as that mixed crew of editors, orators, runaway slaves, free Negro militants, and gun-toting preachers known as the abolitionists. Many laymen sympathetic to the Negro have been inspired by Garrison, Phillips, Douglass, and the rest. Scholars, on the other hand (with a few exceptions), have scolded the abolitionists for their immoderation, berated them for their emotionalism, denounced them for bringing on the Civil War, or psychoanalyzed them as emotional deviates in need of recognition.

It is tempting to join the psychological game and try to understand what it is about the lives of academic scholars which keeps them at arm's length from the moral fervor of one of history's most magnificent crusades. Instead, I want to examine in fact the actions of the abolitionists, to connect them with later agitators against racial exclusiveness, and try to assess the value of "extremists," "radicals," and "agitators" in the bringing of desired social change.

At issue are a number of claims advanced by liberal-minded people who profess purposes similar to the radical reformers, but urge more moderate methods. To argue a case too heatedly, they point out,

provokes the opponent to retaliation. To urge measures too extreme alienates possible allies. To ask for too much too soon results in getting nothing. To use vituperative language arouses emotions to a pitch which precludes rational consideration. To be dogmatic and inflexible prevents adjustment to rapidly changing situations. To set up a clash of extremes precipitates sharp conflict and violence.

All of these tactical sins, adding up to immoderation, extremism, impracticality, have been charged, at different times, by different people, to the American abolitionists. But the charges have not been carefully weighed or closely scrutinized as part of a discussion of preferable tactics for reform. I am claiming here only to initiate such a discussion.

Twentieth-century man is marking the transition from chaotic and quite spontaneous renovation of the social fabric to purposeful and planned social change. In this transition, the tactics of such change need much more careful consideration than they have been given.

THE ABOLITIONISTS

There is no denying the anger, the bitterness, the irascibility of the abolitionists. William Lloyd Garrison, dean of them all, wrote in blood in the columns of the *Liberator* and breathed fire from speakers' platforms all over New England. He shocked people: "I am ashamed of my country." He

* Howard Zinn, "Abolitionists, Freedom-Riders and the Tactics of Agitation," in Martin Duberman, *The Anti-Slavery Vanguard* (1965). Reprinted by permission of the Princeton University Press. Copyright 1965 by the Princeton University Press.

spoke abroad in brutal criticism of America: "I accuse the land of my nativity of insulting the majesty of Heaven with the greatest mockery that was ever exhibited to man." He burned the Constitution before several thousand witnesses on the lawn at Framingham, calling it "source and parent of all other atrocities—a covenant with death and an agreement with hell" and spurred the crowd to echo "Amen!"[1]

He provoked his opponents outrageously, and the South became apoplectic at the mention of his name. South Carolina offered $1,500 for conviction of any white person circulating the *Liberator*, and the Georgia legislature offered $500 for the arrest and conviction of Garrison. Garrison's wife feared constantly that reward-seekers would lie in wait for her husband on his way back from a meeting and snatch him off to Georgia.

Wendell Phillips, richer, and from a distinguished Boston family, was no softer. "Don't shilly-shally, Wendell," his wife whispered to him as he mounted the speakers' platform, and he never did. The anger that rose in him one day in 1835 as he watched Boston bluebloods drag Garrison through the streets never left him, and it remained focused on what he considered America's unbearable evil—slavery. "The South is one great brothel," he proclaimed.

Gradualism was not for Phillips. "No sir, we may not trifle or dally. . . . Revolution is the only thing, the only power, that ever worked out freedom for any people." The piety of New England did not intimidate him: "The American church—what is it? A synagogue of Satan." He scorned patriotic pride: "They sell a little image of us in the markets of Mexico, with a bowie knife in one side of the girdle, and a Colt's revolver in the other, a huge loaf of bread in the left hand, and a slave whip in the right. That is America!"

---

[1] I have not given citations for the more familiar of Garrison's and Phillips' statements, and a few other quotations which are easily found in the better-known studies of the leading abolitionists, in biographies of Lincoln, and in standard works on the pre-Civil War period.

Phillips did not use the language of non-resistance as did Garrison. On that same green where Garrison burned the Constitution, Phillips said: "We are very small in numbers; we have got no wealth; we have got no public opinion behind us; the only thing that we can do is, like the eagle, simply to fly at our enemy, and pick out his eyes." And: "I want no man for President of these States . . . who has not got his hand half clenched, and means to close it on the jugular vein of the slave system the moment he reaches it, and has a double-edged dagger in the other hand, in case there is any missing in the strangulation."

But even Garrison and Phillips seem moderate against the figure of John Brown, lean and lusty, with two wives and 20 children, filled with enough anger for a regiment of agitators, declaring personal war on the institution of slavery. Speeches and articles were for others. The old man studied military strategy, pored over maps of the Southern terrain, raised money for arms, and planned the forcible liberation of slaves through rebellion and guerrilla warfare. On Pottowattomie Creek in the bleeding Kansas of 1856, on the Sabbath, he had struck one night at an encampment of proslavery men, killing five with a cold ferocity. On his way to the gallows, after the raid on the Harpers Ferry arsenal in Virginia in the fall of 1859, he wrote: "I John Brown am now quite certain that the crimes of this guilty land will never be purged away; but with Blood."

The Negro abolitionist Frederick Douglass, newly freed from slavery himself and long a believer in "moral suasion" to free others, talked with John Brown at his home in 1847 and came away impressed by his arguments. Two years later, Douglass told a Boston audience: "I should welcome the intelligence tomorrow, should it come, that the slaves had risen in the South, and that the sable arms which had been engaged in beautifying and adorning the South, were engaged in spreading death and devastation." He thought the Harpers Ferry plan wild, and would not go along; yet, to the end, he maintained that John Brown at Harpers Ferry began the war that ended slavery. "Until this blow was struck, the prospect for freedom was dim, shadowy, and uncertain. . . . When John Brown stretched forth his arm the sky was cleared."

These are the extremists. Did they hurt or help the cause of freedom? Or did they, if helping this cause, destroy some other value, like human life, lost in huge numbers in the Civil War? To put it another way, were they a hindrance rather than a help in abolishing slavery? Did their activities bring a solution at too great a cost? If we answer these questions, and others, we may throw light on the uses or disuses of modern-day agitators and immoderates, whose cries, if not as shrill as Garrison's, are as unpleasant to some ears, and whose actions, if not as violent as John Brown's, are just as distasteful to those who urge caution and moderation.

WHAT IS EXTREMISM?

The first four pages of a well-known book on Civil War politics (T. Harry Williams, *Lincoln and the Radicals*) refers to abolitionists, individually and collectively, in the following terms: "radical . . . zealous . . . fiery . . . scornful . . . revolutionary . . . spirit of fanaticism . . . hasty . . . Jacobins . . . aggressive . . . vindictive . . . narrowly sectional . . . bitter . . . sputtering . . . fanatical . . . impractical . . . extreme."[2] Such words, in different degrees of concentration, are used by many historians in describing the abolitionists. Like other words of judgment frequently used in historical accounts, they have not been carefully dissected and analyzed, so that while they serve as useful approximations of a general attitude held by the writer (and transferred without question to the reader) they fail to make the kinds of distinctions necessary to move historical narrative closer to the area of social science. The word "extremist," used per-

haps more often than any other in connection with the abolitionists, might serve as subject for inspection.

"Extremist" carries a psychological burden when attached to political movements, which it does not bear in other situations. A woman who is extremely beautiful, a man who is extremely kind, a mechanic who is extremely skillful, a child who is extremely healthy—these represent laudable ideals. In politics, however, the label "extremist" carries unfavorable implications. It may mean that the person desires a change in the *status quo* which is more sweeping than that requested by most people. For instance, in a period when most people are willing to free the slaves, but not to enfranchise them, one wanting to give them equal rights would be considered an extremist. Or it may mean someone who urges a more drastic action to attain a goal shared by most people; that is, someone who advocates slave revolts (like John Brown) rather than compensated emancipation followed by colonization abroad (like Lincoln).

Yet, in any given political situation, there is a very large number of possible alternatives, both in desired goals and in the means of achieving them. The actual alternatives put forward in any one situation are usually much fewer than the total range of possibilities. And the most extreme suggestion put forward at the time will be labeled "extremist" even though it may be far less sweeping than other possible courses of action.

For instance, William Lloyd Garrison, looked upon both by his antagonists and by modern historians as an "extremist," did not seek goals as far reaching as he might have. He explained, around 1830, his stand for "immediate abolition" as follows: "Immediate abolition does not mean that the slaves shall immediately exercise the right of suffrage, or be eligible to any office, or be emancipated from law, or be free from the benevolent restraints of guardianship." Yet the ideas of suffrage and officeholding were not too much for Thaddeus Stevens

[2] T. Harry Williams, *Lincoln and the Radicals* (Madison, Wis., 1941), pp. 3–6.

and Charles Sumner—nor for Garrison—in 1865, when actual freedom had come for the slaves.

Wendell Phillips, another "extremist," opposed the use of violence to free the slaves. He said, in 1852: "On that point, I am willing to wait. I can be patient. . . . The cause of three millions of slaves, the destruction of a great national institution, must proceed slowly, and like every other change in public sentiment, we must wait patiently for it." John Brown was not as patient.

Charles Sumner, the "radical" Republican in the Senate, did not urge going beyond the Constitution, which gave Southern states the right to maintain slavery if they chose. Garrison, burning the Constitution, was less restrained. The Anti-Slavery Society announced that "we will not operate on the existing relations of society by other than peaceful and lawful means, and that we will give no countenance to violence or insurrection." Yet, the society was denounced as a hotbed of extremism, the public memory of Nat Turner's violent insurrection having been dimmed by just a few years of time.

The point is, that we are not precise in our standards for measuring "extremism." We do not take into account all possible alternatives, in either goal or method, which may be more extreme than the one we are so labeling. This leads writers to call "extreme" any proposal more drastic than that favored by the majority of articulate people at the time (or by the writer). In a society where the word "extreme" has a bad connotation, in a literate community enamored of the Aristotelian golden mean, we often hurl that word unjustifiably at some proposal which is extreme only in a context of limited alternatives.

Consider how movements denounced as radical begin to look moderate as soon as still more radical movements appear. The NAACP, denounced all over the South as virtually Communist, began to look respectable and legalistic when the sit-inners and Freedom Riders moved into mass, extra-legal action in 1960 and 1961. And the White Citizens Councils of the South could lay claim to being "moderate" segregationists so long as the KKK was around. (The *deliberate* creation of a new extremist group to make an old one more palatable is not yet a major tactic by either right or left; McCarthyism could have been, though it probably was not, the clever offspring of someone who wanted to make "normal" Communist-hunting in this country seem mild.)

With the criterion for extremism so flexible, with the limits constantly shifting, how can we decide the value or wrongness of a position by whether it is "extreme" or "moderate"? We accept these labels because they afford us a test simple enough to avoid mental strain. Also, it is easy and comfortable—especially for intellectuals who do not share the piercing problems of the hungry or helplessly diseased of the world (who, in other words, face no *extreme* problems)—to presume always that the "moderate" solution is the best.

To jump to the cry "extremism" at the first glimpse of the unfamiliar is like a boy with his little telescope peering into the heavens and announcing that the star he dimly perceives at his edge of vision is the farthest object in the universe. It was James Russell Lowell who said: ". . . there is no cant more foolish or more common than theirs who under the mask of discretion, moderation, statesmanship, and what not, would fain convict of fanaticism all that transcends their own limits. . . . From the zoophyte upward everything is *ultra* to something else. . . ."[3]

If the notion of "extremism" is too nebulous to sustain a firm judgment on a goal or a tactic, how do we judge? One point of reference might be the nature and severity of the problem. Even that moderate, Lao Tzu, said you use a boat for a stream and a litter for a mountain path; you adapt your means to your problem. While more modest evils might be dislodged by a few sharp words, the elimination of slavery clearly

---

[3] James Russell Lowell, *The Anti-Slavery Papers of James Russell Lowell* (Boston, 1902), II, 82–83.

required more drastic action. The abolitionists did not deceive themselves that they were gentle and temperate; they quite consciously measured their words to the enormity of the evil.

Garrison said in 1833: "How, then, ought I to feel and speak and write, in view of a system which is red with innocent blood drawn from the bodies of millions of my countrymen by the scourge of brutal drivers. . . . My soul should be, as it is, on fire. I should thunder, I should lighten, I should blow the trumpet of alarm long and loud. I should use just such language as is most descriptive of the crime."

How evil was slavery? It was a complex phenomenon, different in every individual instance, with the treatment of slaves varying widely. But the whole range of variation was in a general framework of unspeakable inhumanity. Even at its "best," slavery was a ferocious attack on man's dignity. It was described matter-of-factly by a supporter of the system, Judge Edmund Ruffin of North Carolina: "Such services can only be expected from one who has no will of his own; who surrenders his will in implicit obedience to another. Such obedience is the consequence only of uncontrolled authority over the body. There is no remedy. This discipline belongs to the state of slavery. . . . It constitutes the curse of slavery to both the bond and the free portion of our population. But it is inherent in the relation of master and slave."[4]

And at its worst, slavery was, as Allan Nevins has said: ". . . the greatest misery, the greatest wrong, the greatest curse to white and black alike that America has ever known."[5] Ads for fugitive slaves in the Southern press (5,400 advertisements a year) contained descriptions like the following to aid apprehension: ". . . Stamped N.E. on the breast and having both small toes cut off. . . . Has some scars on his back that show above the skin, caused by

the whip. . . . Has an iron band around his neck. . . . Has a ring of iron on his left foot. . . . Has on a large neck iron, with a huge pair of horns and a large bar or band of iron on his left leg. . . . Branded on the left cheek, thus 'R', and a piece is taken off her left ear on the same side; the same letter is branded on the inside of both legs." One plantation diary read: ". . . whipped every field hand this evening."[6] A Natchez slave who attacked a white man was chained to a tree and burned alive.

Against this, how mild Garrison's words seem.

EMOTIONALISM AND IRRATIONALITY

In the 1820s, G. F. Milton wrote, in *The Eve of Conflict*, "a new and rival spirit welled up from the West . . . an emotional democracy, bottoming itself on Rousseau's mystic claims of innate rights, looking on Liberty as a spontaneous creation and asserting rights unconnected with responsibilities, among these the universal manhood competence for self-government. . . . The Abolition movement . . . was a manifestation of emotional democracy." Milton talks further of "deep-seated passions" and "the emotional flood . . . psychic forces clamoring for expression . . . a drive for reform, change, agitation, which boded ill for any arbitrament of intelligence." Thoreau, Parker, and other reformers, he says, "showed a remarkably keen insight into latent mass emotions and did not hesitate to employ appropriate devices to mobilize the mob mind."[7]

Fanaticism, irrationality, emotionalism —these are the qualities attributed again and again, in a mood of sharp criticism, to the abolitionists; and, indeed, to radical reformers in general. How valid is the criticism?

If being "emotional" means creating a state of excitement, both for oneself and

4 Ralph Korngold, *Two Friends of Man* (Boston, 1950), p. 85.

5 Allan Nevins, *Ordeal of the Union* (New York, 1947), I, 461.

6 Korngold, *loc. cit.*

7 George F. Milton, *The Eve of Conflict* (Boston, 1934), p. 156.

for others, which intensifies the forms of already existent behavior, or creates new, more energetic behavior patterns, then we need not argue. The abolitionists were all, in varying degrees, emotional in their response to situations and in the stimuli they projected into the atmosphere. What *is* arguable is the notion that this "emotionalism" is to be deplored.

The intellectual is taken aback by emotional display. It appears to him an attack on that which he most reveres—reason. One of his favorite terms of praise is "dispassionate." The words "calm . . . judicious . . . reasonable" seem to belong together. He points to evil rousers of emotion: the Hitlers, the Southern demagogues of racism, the religious charlatans, and faith healers. And yet, sitting in a Negro Baptist church in the deep South during the desegregation movement of the 1960s, and listening to the crowd sing "We shall overcome . . . we shall overcome. . . ." and hearing it cry "Freedom! Freedom!" the intellectual may well feel a surge of joy and love, damped only slightly by a twinge of uneasiness at his spontaneous display of feeling.

He is uneasy, I would suggest, because of a failure to recognize several things: that emotion is a *morally neutral* instrument for a wide variety of ends; that it serves a positive purpose when linked to laudable goals; that it is not "irrational" but "nonrational" because, being merely an instrument, its rationality is derived only from the value with which it is linked.

When, at a high moment of tension in the battle over slavery, William Lloyd Garrison first heard the freed Negro Frederick Douglass speak, at a crowded meeting in Nantucket, he rose and cried out: "Have we been listening to a man—or a thing?" The audience stirred. In this flash of words and transferred emotion, a group of New England men and women, far removed from the plantation and its daily reminders of human debasement, were confronted with an experience from which they were normally separated by space and social status. By this confrontation, they became more ready to act against an evil which existed just as crassly before Garrison's words were spoken, but whose meaning now flooded in on them for the first time.

The Horst Wessel Song drove Nazi myrmidons forward, but the Battle Hymn of the Republic inspired antislavery fighters. Like music and poetry, whose essence is the enlargement of sensuous experience, and whose potency can be focused in any ethical direction—or in none—the agitation of emotions by words or actions is an art. And as such, it is an instrument of whatever moral camp employs it.

What needs to be said, finally, to assuage the embarrassment of the emotionally aroused intellectual, is that there is no necessary connection between emotionalism and irrationality. A lie may be calmly uttered, and a truth may be charged with emotion. Emotion can be used to make more rational decisions, if by that we mean decisions based on greater knowledge, for greater knowledge involves not only extension but intensity. Who "knows" more about slavery—the man who has in his head all the available information (how many Negroes are enslaved, how much money is spent by the plantation for their upkeep, how many run away, how many revolt, how many are whipped, and how many are given special privileges) and calmly goes about his business, or the man who has less data, but is moved by a book (Harriet Beecher Stowe's) or by an orator (Wendell Phillips) to *feel* the reality of slavery so intensely that he will set up a station on the underground railroad? Rationality is limited by time, space, and status, which intervene between the individual and the truth. Emotion can liberate it.

DOES THE AGITATOR DISTORT THE FACTS?

Abolitionist reformers, and those who supported them, historian Avery Craven wrote in *The Coming of the Civil War*, spread thousands of distortions about the South. The American people, he said, "permitted their shortsighted politicians, their overzealous editors, and their pious reformers to emotionalize real and potential differences and to conjure up distorted impressions of those who dwelt in other parts of the nation. For more than two decades, these molders of public opinion steadily created the fiction of two distinct peoples contending for the right to preserve and expand their sacred cultures. . . . In time, a people came to believe . . . that the issues were between right and wrong; good and evil."[8] Craven's thesis is that the war was repressible, but abolitionist (and slaveholder) exaggerations brought it about.

A similar charge is made by T. Harry Williams in *Lincoln and the Radicals:* "Thirty years of abolitionist preachings had instilled in the popular mind definite thought patterns and reactions regarding the Southern people and their social system. It was widely believed that slavery had brutalized the Southern character, that the owner of human chattels was a dour, repulsive fiend, animated by feelings of savage hatred toward Negroes and Northern whites."[9]

Because the reformist agitator is so often charged with distortion and exaggeration, and because thinkers with an abiding concern for the truth are often led by such charges to keep a safe distance from such agitators, it is essential to discuss this point.

Distinctions ought first to be made between outright misstatements of fact and personal slander on the one hand, and, on the other, exaggerations of the truth and the singling out of those aspects of a complex truth which support the viewpoint of the reformer. It needs to be acknowledged that false statements have at times been made by radical reformers, and this is unpardonable, for if the reformer speaks the truth, then material exists on all hands to support him, and he needs no falsification

of the evidence to back his case. As for character denigration, it is not only repugnant to truth-seekers, but makes explanation embarrassing when the attacked person is revealed as something different. Witness Phillips' angry assault on Lincoln: "Who is this huckster in politics? Who is this county court advocate?" And during the war: ". . . if he had been a traitor, he could not have worked better to strengthen one side, and hazard the success of the other." And again, in a *Liberator* article, Phillips' headline: "Abraham Lincoln, the Slave-Hound of Illinois."

More serious, and more frequent, however, are charges of exaggeration and distortion leveled at the radicals. At the root of this problem is that once we get past simple factual statements ("On March 3, 1851, field hand . . . . was whipped by his master") and begin to deal with general characterizations of social institutions (like Nevins' statement about slavery being "the greatest misery, the greatest curse. . . .") we are in a realm where words like "true" and "false" cannot be applied so simply. Slavery was a complex institution, and no one statement can describe it fully. Slave–master relationships varied from kindness to cruelty and also defy generalization. We are here in that philosophical realm dealing with the theory of knowledge, a field in which historians play all the time, without paying any attention to the rules, while the philosophers sit in their studies discussing the rules and rarely look out the window to see how the game is played.

There is an answer to the problem of how to state simply a complex truth—but this requires an activist outlook rare among scholars. It means deciding from a particular ethical base what is the action-need of the moment and concentrating on that aspect of the truth-complex which fulfills that need. If we start from the ethical assumption that it is fundamentally wrong to hold in bondage—whether kindly or cruelly—another human being, and that the freeing of such persons requires penetrating the

---

[8] Avery Craven, *The Coming of the Civil War* (N.Y., 1942), 2.

[9] Williams, *op. cit.*, p. 285.

moral sensibilities of a nation, then it is justifiable to focus on those aspects of the complexity which support this goal. When you teach a child to be careful crossing the street, and say, "You can be killed by an automobile," you are singling out of the totality of automobile behaviors that small percentage of incidents in which people are killed. You are not telling the whole truth about automobiles and traffic. But you are emphasizing that portion of the truth which supports a morally desirable action.

The complaint by T. Harry Williams that as a result of abolitionist agitation, "It was widely believed that slavery had brutalized the Southern character. . . ." takes note of an abolitionist emphasis which does not photographically depict total reality. Not every white Southerner was brutalized by slavery. And yet, some were, and many others were affected—by the simple fact of learning to accept such a system without protest. These effects are so various and complicated that the word "brutalized" does not exactly fit, nor does any other word. But the focusing on this fact of brutalization points to a crucial aspect of slavery, and the recognition of that aspect may be decisive in overthrowing a terrible system. The scholar who accepts no harsh judgment because it does not do justice to the entire complex truth, can really accept no judgments about society, because all are simplifications of the complex. The result is scholarly detachment from the profound ethical conflicts of society and from that human concern without which scholarship becomes a pretentious game.

HISTORICAL PERSPECTIVE AND THE RADICAL

It is paradoxical that the historian, who is presumably blessed with historical perspective, should judge the radical from within the narrow moral base of the radical's period of activity, while the radical assesses his immediate society from the vantage point of some future, better era. If progress is desirable, and if escape from the bonds of the immediate is healthy, whose perspective is more accurate—that of the agitator, or that of the scolding historian?

James Russell Lowell wrote in 1849: ". . . the simple fact undoubtedly is that were the Abolitionists to go back to the position from which they started, they would find themselves less fanatical than a very respectable minority of the people. The public follows them step by step, occupying the positions they have successively fortified and quitted, and it is necessary that they should keep in advance in order that people may not be shocked by waking up and finding themselves Abolitionists."[10]

Garrison himself took note of the profound change in the nation by 1860, 30 years from the time he had started his tiny, maligned newspaper. He spoke to the Massachusetts Anti-Slavery Society, shortly after John Brown's execution, which had brought shock and indignation throughout the North: "Whereas, ten years since, there were thousands who could not endure my lightest rebuke of the South, they can now swallow John Brown whole, and his rifle into the bargain."

The historian too often moves back a hundred years into a moral framework barbarian by modern standards and thinks inside it, while the radical shakes the rafters of this framework at the risk of his life. Wendell Phillips, speaking affectionately of the abolitionist leader Angelina Grimké, said: "Were I to single out the moral and intellectual trait which most won me, it was her serene indifference to the judgement of those about her." That kind of indifference (David Riesman calls it inner-directedness) is hard to find in contemporary scholarship.

COMPROMISE

The argument over the wisdom of radical agitation in the tactics of social reform was aptly expressed in Boston in pre-Civil

10 Lowell, *op. cit.*, p. 53.

War years by two leading figures. Samuel May, speaking of Garrison, said: ". . . he will shake our nation to its center, but he will shake slavery out of it." Reverend Lyman Beecher said: "True wisdom consists in advocating a cause only so far as the community will sustain the reformer." The agitator, declare the moderate reformers, shakes so hard that he makes compromise impossible, alienates friends, and delays rather than speeds the coming of reform.

Compromise was not disdained by the abolitionists; they were fully conscious of the fact that the outcome of any social struggle is almost always some form of compromise. But they were also aware of that which every intelligent radical knows: that to compromise in advance is to vitiate at the outset that power for progress which only the radical propels into the debate. Lowell put this most vividly, declaring that the abolitionists "are looked upon as peculiarly ungrateful and impracticable if they do not devote their entire energies to soliciting nothing, and express a thankfulness amounting almost to rapture when they get it."[11]

The abolitionist took an advanced position so that even if pushed back by compromise, substantial progress would result. Garrison wrote: "Urge immediate abolition as earnestly as we may, it will be gradual abolition in the end." And Phillips said: "If we would get half a loaf, we must demand the whole of it." The Emancipation Proclamation itself was a compromise, the tortured product of a long battle between radicals and moderates in and out of the Lincoln administration, and only the compelling force of the abolitionist intransigents made it come as soon as it did.

Two factors demand recognition by moderates who disdain "extreme" positions on the ground that compromise is necessary. One is the above-mentioned point that the early projection of an advanced position ensures a compromise on more favorable terms than would be the case where the

timorous reformer compromises at the start (in which case the result is a compromise upon a compromise, since he will be forced to retreat even from his retreat after all the forces are calculated at the social weighing-in). The other is that there is a huge difference between the passive wisher-for-change who quietly adds up the vectors and makes a decision as to which is the composite of all existing forces, and the active reformer who pushes so hard *in the course of adding-up* that the composite itself is changed. The latter—the radical—is viewing compromise as a dynamic process, in which his own actions are part of the total force being calculated. He bases his estimate of what is possible on a graph in which his own action and its consequences are calculated from the first.

MODERATION AS TACTIC

Does the agitator alienate potential allies by the extremism of his demands, or the harshness of his language? Lewis Tappan, the wealthy New Yorker who financed many abolitionist activities, wrote anxiously to George Thompson, the British abolitionist: "The fact need not be concealed from you that several emancipationists so disapprove of the harsh, and, as they think, the unchristian language of *The Liberator,* that they do not feel justified in upholding it." This, in general, was the feeling of the Executive Committee of the American Anti-Slavery Society in the early years of the movement. Undoubtedly, the society itself was not diverted from its aim of abolishing slavery because of Garrison's immoderation; they were concerned lest others be alienated.

But who? The slaveholder? The slave? The moderate reformer? The open-minded conservative? It needs to be acknowledged that different sections of the population will respond differently to the same appeal, and in judging the effect of bold words upon the population, this population must be broken up into parts, based on the varying degrees of receptivity to the ideas of

---

11 *Ibid.*, p. 80.

the reformer. Why should the radical soften his language or his program to please that element of the population which cannot possibly be pleased by anything short of total surrender of principle, whose self-interest in fact dictates rejection of any reform? Lowell wrote: "The slaveholder, when Mr. Greeley would politely request him to state what method would be most consonant to his feelings, would answer, as did the . . . boy whose mother asked him what he would like for breakfast, 'Just what you ain't gut!' "[12]

Only the hypothesis of common interest for the entire population can justify an appeal to the opponent on the basis of reason, asking him to perceive his interest more accurately. But if in fact there is a diversity of interest, then the lighting up of the truth can only bring out more sharply that conflict which stands in the way of agreement. The slaveholders themselves pointed to the impossibility of their being won over by moderate overtures. In 1854, the editor of the Richmond *Enquirer* wrote: "That man must be a veritable verdigreen who dreams of pleasing slaveholders, either in church or state, by any method but that of letting slavery alone."[13] William Ellery Channing tried such appeal and failed. One of his brochures against slavery was so mild that some described it as putting people to sleep, but he was abused so harshly it might as well have been one of Garrison's flame-breathing *Liberator* editorials.

With a population of diversified interests, tactics must be adapted and focused specially for each group, and for the group most inimical to reform, it is doubtful that moderation is effective. With the intransigents, it may be only the most powerful action that impels change. It was Nat Turner's violent slave revolt in Virginia in 1831 that led the Virginia legislature into its famous series of discussions about the abolition of slavery. "For a while indeed," Ralph Korngold writes, "it seemed that what years of propaganda by the Quakers had failed to accomplish could come as a result of Turner's bloodletting."[14]

When friends of the reformers rail against harsh words or strong action (as the American Anti-Slavery Society did against Garrison it is clear that they themselves will not be put off from reform because of it, but fear the effects on others. And if neither extreme opposition nor hard-and-fast friends can be moved by tactics of moderation, this leaves, as a decisive group, that large part of the population which is at neither end of the ideological spectrum, which moves back and forth across the center line, depending on circumstances.

Garrison was quite aware that most of the American population to which he was appealing was not sympathetic with his views, and he was completely conscious of how distant were his own fiery convictions from those of the average American. But he was persuaded, as were Phillips and other leading abolitionists (John Brown felt it, and acted it, if he did not express it intellectually) that only powerful surges of words and feelings could move white people from their complacency about the slave question. He said once in Philadelphia: "Sir, slavery will not be overthrown without excitement, a most tremendous excitement." He must lash with words, he felt, those Americans who had never felt the whip of a slaveowner. To his friend Samuel May, who urged him to keep more cool, saying: "Why, you are all on fire," Garrison replied: "Brother May, I have need to be all on fire, for I have mountains of ice about me to melt."

We have the historical record as a check on whether the vituperative language of Garrison, the intemperate appeals of Wendell Phillips, hurt or advanced the popular sentiment against slavery. In the 1830s a handful of men cried out against slavery and were beaten, stoned, and shot to death by their Northern compatriots. By 1849,

---

12 *Ibid.*, pp. 88–89.
13 Korngold, *op. cit.*, p. 89.

14 *Ibid.*, p. 54.

antislavery sentiment was clearly increasing, and some of the greatest minds and voices in America were speaking out for abolition. Lowell asked curtly of those who charged the abolitionists with retarding the movement: ". . . has there really been a change of public opinion for the worse, either at the North or the South, since the *Liberator* came into existence eighteen years ago?"[15] And by 1860, with millions of Americans convinced that slavery was an evil, open insurrection by John Brown brought more public support than had the mere words of Garrison 30 years before.

This is not to say that extremists may not drive possible allies from their movement. But this is generally not because of the ferocity of their attack on an institution which is the object of general dislike but because of their insertion of other issues which do not touch public sensibilities as much. Theodore Weld, an effective Mid-

---

15 Lowell, *op. cit.*, p. 50.

western abolitionist, who was marvelous at organizing abolitionist societies in Ohio, criticized Garrison for his violent attacks on the clergy, for his anarchist utterances against government in general, and for his insistence on bringing many other issues— women's rights, pacifism, etc.—into the antislavery fight. For marginal supporters, such side issues may bring alienation. Whether such estrangement would be significant enough to offset the general social value of having one important issue ride on the back of another, is another question. . . .

The politician is annoyed and angry at the pushing of the radical reformer, and the moderate observer thinks the radical unfair and injudicious in making extreme demands of the man in office, but both critics fail to distinguish between the social role of the politician and that of the agitator. In general, this distinction is perceived more clearly by reformers than by officeholders. . . .

1964

The Abolitionists Fight on in Civil War and Reconstruction*

JAMES M. McPHERSON

Most historians have paid little attention to the abolitionist movement after 1860. Yet it was in the 1860s that the abolitionist crusade reached the height of its power and

---

* James M. McPherson, *The Struggle for Equality: Abolitionists and the Negro in the Civil War and Reconstruction* (1964). Reprinted by permission of Princeton University Press. Copyright 1964 by Princeton University Press.

saw the achievement of most of its objectives. After the outbreak of the Civil War, abolitionists were transformed almost overnight from despised fanatics to influential and respected spokesmen for the radical wing of the Republican party. Early in the war, abolitionists outlined a broad program of emancipation, employment of Negro soldiers in the Union Army, creation of a

Freedmen's Bureau, government assistance for the education of the freedmen, civil and political equality for all black men, and grants of confiscated land to the freed slaves. Under the military pressures of war and the political pressures of reconstruction, the Republican party adopted all of these policies except the wholesale confiscation of southern plantations. True, the North retreated from radicalism after 1870 and failed to enforce the provisions of Reconstruction after 1877, but the equalitarian achievements of the Civil War and Reconstruction remained in the Constitution and the statute books, where they constitute today the legal basis for the "Second Reconstruction" of the South.

Despite the prominence of abolitionists during the war and reconstruction years, standard historical treatments of the antislavery movement virtually ignore the period after 1860. The implicit assumption is that abolitionism merged itself with the Republican party during the war and therefore no longer possessed a separate identity or purpose. Garrison's willingness to cease publication of his *Liberator* and to dissolve the antislavery societies in 1865 is deemed proof that abolitionists considered the Thirteenth Amendment the consummation of their crusade and were little concerned with the Negro after emancipation. Nothing could be more misleading. It is true that for the first time in their lives, abolitionists marched in step with a major political party after 1861. But they marched far in advance of the Republican party, and frequently the party refused to follow them as fast as they desired. At such times they would chastise the Republicans with old-time vigor and abandon. Throughout the 1860s most abolitionists preserved their separate identity and cooperated with the Republican party only when that party was marching in the direction they wanted to go. Abolitionists showed a greater concern for the plight of the Negro after 1865 than anyone else except the Negro himself. The American Anti-Slavery Society and its auxiliaries remained in existence after the war

to wage battle for the full civil and political equality of the Negro. Even Garrison, despite his withdrawal from the antislavery societies in 1865, did not consider his crusade ended when the slave was freed. Along with many other abolitionists, he was active in the movement to educate the freedmen, and his denunciations of racial discrimination were no less militant after 1865 than before.

* * * * *

By 1863 the Civil War had become a revolution of freedom for 4 million slaves. The antislavery crusade, however, envisaged not only a negative freedom—the absence of chattelism—but a positive guaranty of equal protection of the laws to all men. Once freedom was won, most abolitionists were ready to proceed with the next step in the revolution—equality.

"This is a war not of geographical sections, nor of political factions, but of principles and systems," declared Theodore Tilton in 1863. "Our war against this rebellion is . . . a war for social equality, for rights, for justice, for freedom." In 1863 Moncure Conway wrote that "the war raging in America must be referred to a higher plane than that of Liberty. It is a war for Equality. It is to decide whether the Liberty which each race claims for itself, and knows to be good, shall be given impartially to all, of whatever colour or degree."[1]

These statements were summaries of an idea expressed many times by abolitionists during the war. The most eloquent and persistent spokesman for this revolution of racial equality was Wendell Phillips. His program of reconstruction, said Phillips early in 1862, was the creation of a nation in which there was "no Yankee, no Buckeye, no Hoosier, no Sucker, no native, no foreigner, no black, no white, no German,

---

[1] *Independent*, June 25, 1863; Moncure D. Conway, *Testimonies Concerning Slavery* (2d ed.; London, 1865), 131–32. For a brilliant discussion of the evolution of equal rights as a northern war aim, see C. Vann Woodward, "Equality: the Deferred Commitment," in *The Burden of Southern History* (Vintage Books, New York, 1961), 69–87.

no Saxon . . . only American citizens, with one law impartial over all." Phillips wanted to destroy the aristocratic society of the Old South and replace it with a new social order based on equal rights, universal education, and the dignity of labor. He declared: "I hold that the South is to be annihilated. I do not mean the geographical South. . . . [I] mean the intellectual, social, aristocratic South—the thing that represented itself by slavery and the bowie-knife, by bullying and lynch law, by ignorance and idleness. . . . I mean a society which holds for its cardinal principle of faith, that one-third of the race is born booted and spurred, and the other two-thirds saddled for the first to ride. . . . That South is to be annihilated. (Loud applause)" This social revolution must be accomplished primarily by the freedmen. "I want the blacks as the very basis of the effort to regenerate the South," said Phillips. "We want the four millions of blacks—a people instinctively on our side, ready and skilled to work; the only element the South has that belongs to the nineteenth century."[2]

Most abolitionists realized that free Negroes were treated little better in the North than in the South. The revolution of equality, they knew, must embrace North as well as South. "No Abolitionist condemns our Northern oppression of negroes one whit less than he does Southern Slavery," declared Sydney Gay in 1862. "North as well as South, this outraged people encounter DENIAL everywhere," asserted Gerrit Smith in a ringing denunciation of racial discrimination in the North. "Even the noblest black is denied that which is free to the vilest white. The omnibus, the car, the ballot-box, the jury box, the halls of legislation, the army, the public lands, the school, the church, the lecture-room, the social circle, the table, are all either absolutely or virtually denied to him."[3]

Abolitionists could not hope to revolutionize the southern social order without first improving the status of northern Negroes. Gilbert Haven stated the problem succinctly. When southerners observed "no recognition of the unity of man" in the North, he said, "when they see these, our brethren, set apart in churches and schools, or, if allowed to enter our churches, driven into the lowest seats; when they behold every avenue of honorable effort shut against them,—that no clerk of this complexion is endured in our stores, no apprentice in our workshops, no teacher in our schools, no physician at our sick-beds, no minister in our pulpits,—how can we reproach them for their sins, or urge them to repentance?"[4]

When the militant phase of abolitionism began in 1831 the status of northern Negroes was deplorable. Shut out from white schools and churches, forced to live in city slums and ghettos, denied equal civil and political rights, subject to Jim Crow legislation and degrading "black laws" in many states, confined to menial occupations, almost universally despised as members of an inferior race, the northern Negroes' lot in 1830 was a harsh one. In some respects their status actually deteriorated in the next 30 years. The huge influx of immigrants in the 1840s and 1850s drove colored people out of many of their former occupations and subjected them to the mob fury of socially and economically insecure immigrants. Some of the western states made their black laws more severe between 1830 and 1860.

At the same time, however, northern Negroes made significant gains in other areas, especially in New England, the center of abolitionist influence. By a combination of moral suasion and political pressure, abolitionists and free Negroes helped to bring about the desegregation of most public schools in New England and the abolition of Jim Crow on New England

---

[2] Speeches by Phillips published in *Liberator*, Apr. 25, May 23, Nov. 28, 1862.

[3] *New York Tribune*, Mar. 21, 1862; Gerrit Smith to the editor of the *New York Tribune*, July 1, 1861, published in the *Tribune*, July 7.

[4] Gilbert Haven, *National Sermons, Speeches, and Letters on Slavery and Its War* (Boston, 1869), 139.

stagecoaches, horsecars, and railroads. Abolitionist efforts were partly responsible for
the defeat of the Rhode Island constitution
of 1842, which had established *white* manhood suffrage, and the substitution of a
new constitution which granted Negro suffrage. Abolitionists registered their protests
against "Negro pews" by withdrawing from
churches that practiced this form of segregation and by joining or founding congre-
gations which admitted Negroes on an
equal basis. Abolitionist and antislavery
lecturers almost singlehandedly ended segregated seating in many lecture halls by
refusing to speak before segregated audiences. The Hutchinson family refused to
sing before segregated groups. In many
ways abolitionists tried to bear witness
against the system of racial discrimination
which prevailed in the antebellum North.

In 1860 Negroes enjoyed equal political
rights in all the New England states except
Connecticut. In New York, Negroes possessing property worth $250 could vote.
In all other northern states colored men
were denied suffrage.[5] All but a handful of
public schools in New England were open
to both races. Public transportation in most
of the North was nonsegregated. But Jim
Crow still prevailed on the New York, Philadelphia, Cincinnati, and San Francisco
streetcars. Public schools in most of the
North outside of New England were segregated, and in some areas no public schools
at all were open to Negroes. In several
western states Negroes were subjected to
severe legal discrimination and denied equal
rights in the courts. In many parts of the
North, including New England, Negroes
were discriminated against in housing, employment, restaurants, hotels, and places of
recreation.[6]

With the outbreak of war, some abolitionists feared that the campaign for equal
rights in the North might be buried by the
confusion and excitement of armed conflict.
"The laws respecting the colored man, in
Iowa, Illinois, and other Western States,
notwithstanding the predominance of Republican majorities, are disgraceful and
proscriptive," wrote a western abolitionist.
"It seems to me that the work of the Anti-
slavery Society ought to be carried on un-
relaxingly. Legislation of a just character
needs to be inaugurated. It will not answer
to trust these reforms to this war." The
Essex County (Massachusetts) Anti-Slavery Society resolved at the end of 1861 that
"we still deem the mission of the Abolitionists *unaccomplished* so long as a . . .
nominally free colored man is subjected to
any proscription, political, educational, or
ecclesiastical."[7] Stephen S. Foster declared
in January 1862, that the object of the
American Anti-Slavery Society was "not
merely to destroy the *form* of slavery, but
to destroy the *spirit of oppression*, which
shows itself at the South, in the form of
slavery, and at the North, in the bitter and
relentless prejudice against color." Later in
the year a Boston Negro reminded abolitionists that there was still much work for
them to do right in Boston, where Negroes
suffered discrimination in housing, employment, and some restaurants.[8]

In 1861 Susan B. Anthony pronounced
a severe indictment of racial discrimination
in the North. The northern people were
horrified by tales of southern cruelty to
slaves, she said, "and yet, what better do
we? While the cruel slave-drive lacerates
the black man's mortal body, we, of the

Most histories of the abolitionist movement and
biographies of abolitionist leaders contain references to the attempts of abolitionists to secure
equal civil and political rights for Negroes in the
antebellum North. For additional descriptions of
the condition of northern Negroes on the eve of
the Civil War, see *Anglo-African*, Jan. 7, 1860;
and *Liberator*, Oct. 5, 26, Nov. 2, Dec. 7, 1860,
Jan. 4, Mar. 15, 1861.

[7] *N.A.S. Standard*, June 22, 1861; *Liberator*,
Dec. 27, 1861.

[8] *Liberator*, Jan. 31, 1862, Aug. 15, 1862.

[5] In Ohio, men with a greater visible admixture
of Caucasian than Negro genes could vote. In
some respects, of course, this was a greater insult
to the Negro than the denial of suffrage to all colored men.

[6] For the best discussion of the status of northern Negroes before the Civil War and of the efforts
of abolitionists to improve that status, see Leon
F. Litwack, *North of Slavery* (Chicago, 1961).

North, flay the spirit." Even when the northern Negro obtained an education, he found the doors to many vocations shut in his face. Miss Anthony declared that reconstruction of the nation on the basis of equality for all men must begin in the North. She concluded: "Let us open to the colored man all our schools, from the common District to the College. Let us admit him into all our mechanic shops, stores, offices, and lucrative business avocations, to work side by side with his white brother; let him rent such pew in the church, and occupy such seat in the theatre, and public lecture room, as he pleases; let him be admitted to all our entertainments, both public & private; let him share all the accommodations of our hotels, stages, railroads and steamboats. . . . Extend to him all the rights of Citizenship. Let him vote and be voted for; let him sit upon the judge's bench, and in the juror's box. . . . Let the North thus prove to the South, by her acts, that she fully recognizes the humanity of the black man."[9]

Individually and in small groups, by private persuasion, precept, or example, abolitionists did what they could during the war to lessen prejudice and mitigate discrimination in the North. A Michigan abolitionist who owned a large farm told Garrison that he employed several Negro farmhands, paying them the same wages, serving them at the same table, and sleeping them in the same bunkhouse as his white laborers. Henry Cheever organized a "Freedom Club" in Worcester, containing men of both races, whose object was to break down the barriers between white and colored workingmen.[10] William H. Channing, abolitionist chaplain of the U.S. House of Representatives, invited Negro minister Henry Highland Garnet to occupy his pulpit in the House chamber one Sunday morning in February, 1865. Channing

considered this event an important step in the campaign against discrimination in the nation's capital. At about the same time Charles Sumner presented Boston Negro lawyer John Rock as a candidate to argue cases before the Supreme Court. Chief Justice Chase accepted Rock and swore him in, making him the first Negro ever to be accredited as a Supreme Court lawyer. This affair was regarded by abolitionists as a symbol of the revolution in the Negro's status since 1857, when Chief Justice Taney had denied the citizenship of black men.[11]

Abolitionists tried also to cleanse northern churches of segregation. It was not always an easy task. In 1863 the Reverend Horace Hovey, abolitionist pastor of the Congregational church in Florence, Massachusetts, preached that "the negro has the same right that we have . . . to obtain a first-rate education and to rise in social position according as he rises in worth; the same right to vote and to sit in legislative and congressional halls." Fifteen or twenty of his parishioners took offense at these words and walked out of the church. But there were some encouraging signs of progress. Maria Weston Chapman rejoiced in 1863 that the Park Street Church in Boston had reversed its long-standing policy of refusing to rent pews to Negroes.[12] Gilbert Haven succeeded in desegregating many New England Methodist churches, in expunging the word "colored" from the minutes of the New England Methodist Conference, and in securing admission of a Negro minister to the Conference as pastor of an integrated church.[13]

Education was another area in which

9 MS of speech, marked "1861," in S. B. Anthony Papers, LC.

10 H. Willis to Garrison, June 20, 1861, Garrison Papers, BPL; Henry Cheever to Gerrit Smith, July 20, 1864, Smith Papers, SU.

11 Octavius B. Frothingham, *Memoir of William Henry Channing* (Boston, 1886), 316; Channing to L. M. Child, Mar. 8, 1865, published in *Commonwealth*, Mar. 25, 1865; *New York Tribune*, Feb. 9, 1865.

12 Horace C. Hovey to M. W. Chapman, July 15, 1864, Weston Papers, BPL; M. W. Chapman to Mary Estlin, Dec. 29, 1863, Estlin Papers, BPL.

13 William Haven Daniels, *Memorials of Gilbert Haven* (Boston, 1880), 151, 182; William G. Cochrane, "Freedom without Equality: A Study of Northern Opinion and the Negro Issue, 1861–1870," Ph.D. dissertation, University of Minnesota, 1957, 294–96.

abolitionists worked to promote desegregation wherever they were in a position to do so. Segregation had been abolished in Boston's public schools in 1855 largely through the efforts of abolitionists and antislavery Republicans. During the war abolitionists extended their school desegregation efforts to New York. In 1863 Andrew D. White, antislavery Republican and future president of Cornell University, was elected to the New York legislature to represent the Syracuse district. Because of his teaching experience, White was appointed chairman of the Education Committee and given the task of codifying New York's education laws. A statute of 1841 had authorized the establishment of segregated schools in any district that wished to maintain them. White wanted to repeal this statute and abolish school segregation in the state. One of his closest friends in Syracuse was Samuel J. May, the veteran abolitionist crusader. White asked May for information and arguments against segregation. May supplied him with abolitionist writings on the inherent equality of the Negro, reports of the success of integration in New England schools, and a long letter outlining the main arguments for desegregation. Separate schools for Negroes, wrote May, were "a perpetual imputation of fault, unworthiness or inferiority, which must tend to discourage and keep them depressed" even if the facilities were equal to those of white schools. Colored children should enjoy "not only equal educational privileges, but the same, as the white people enjoy." The common schools were the nursery of the Republic, argued May, and the fostering of caste distinctions in the schools would create class and racial divisions in the nation which could prove fatal to democracy. The mission of America was "to show the world that *all* men, not white men alone, but all, of every complexion, language and lineage have equal rights to life, liberty and the pursuit of happiness. . . . Let then our common schools, from the lowest to the highest grade, be equally open to the children of all the people." The efforts of May and White were unavailing, however, and New York did not prohibit segregation in its public schools until nearly 40 years later.[14]

In 1861 there were still five New England cities that maintained segregated public schools: Hartford and New Haven, Connecticut, and Providence, Newport, and Bristol, Rhode Island. Abolitionists and Negroes in Rhode Island kept up a steady antisegregation pressure on school officials, city councilmen, and state legislators. They petitioned these bodies repeatedly, arguing that segregation placed a stigma of inferiority on Negro children and that the colored schools were provided with inferior funds and equipment. In May, 1864, abolitionists won a preliminary victory when the General Assembly's committee on education recommended abolition of separate schools in Rhode Island. In 1865 the lower House passed a bill embodying this recommendation. But the Senate defeated the measure by a narrow margin, largely because of the determined opposition of Newport senators. Thomas Wentworth Higginson had moved to Newport after his discharge from the army in 1864 and was elected to the school board in 1865. As a result of Higginson's efforts, Newport abolished its separate schools in September, 1865. With the opposition of

[14] James M. Smith, "The 'Separate But Equal' Doctrine: An Abolitionist Discusses Racial Segregation and Educational Policy during the Civil War," *Journal of Negro History*, XLI (April, 1956), 138–47. This article publishes the letter from May to White, Mar. 11, 1864, which can be found in the Collection of Regional History, Cornell University. The public schools of Syracuse, a center of antislavery activity in upstate New York, had been desegregated for more than 20 years. In his report on the condition of Canadian Negroes, Samuel Gridley Howe observed that "the colored children in the mixed schools do not differ in their general appearance and behavior from their white comrades. They are usually clean and decently clad. They look quite as bright as the whites. . . . The association is manifestly beneficial to the colored children. . . . The appearance, and the acquirements of colored children in the separate schools, are less satisfactory." Howe made a strong plea for school desegregation in the United States. Howe, *The Refugees from Slavery in Canada West* (Boston, 1864), 78–79.

Newport legislators thus removed, the Rhode Island legislature in 1866 outlawed school segregation in the entire state. Abolitionists rejoiced in the removal of "this last relic of slavery" from Rhode Island. The Connecticut legislature followed the example of its neighbor and abolished segregated public education in the Nutmeg State in 1868.[15]

Normal schools in New England were open to both races, but many of the private academies and preparatory schools were not. Abolitionists played an important role in desegregating two prominent New England private schools in 1865. John G. Whittier and Theodore Weld were instrumental in securing the admission of colored girls to Dr. Dio Lewis' girls' school in Lexington, Massachusetts, where Weld and his wife Angelina taught from 1865 to 1867.[16] The energetic Rhode Island Quaker abolitionist, Elizabeth Buffum Chace, decided in 1865 that the refusal of the Friends' school in Providence to admit colored applicants was a disgrace that could no longer be tolerated. Through her friend Dr. Samuel Tobey, a wealthy New England Quaker who was one of the main financial supporters of the school, Mrs. Chace obtained a promise from the trustees to admit henceforth all qualified applicants, regardless of race. The action of these two private schools paved the way for the lowering of the color bar at several other New England academies.[17]

More widely publicized than these school desegregation measures were the efforts to remove discrimination in the courts, transportation, and other areas. Charles Sumner was a leader of antidiscrimination activity at the national level. In 1862 he guided to Senate passage a bill to repeal an 1825 law barring colored persons from carrying the mail. Democrats and conservative Republicans defeated the measure in the House, but it finally passed both Houses and became law on March 3, 1865. In 1862 Massachusetts abolitionists called on Congress to enact legislation granting Negroes equal rights in federal courts. Sumner introduced a bill providing that in all proceedings of District of Columbia courts there would be no exclusion of witnesses because of race. The measure passed both Houses. In 1864 Sumner finally secured enactment of a law prohibiting the exclusion of witnesses from federal courts on grounds of race or color. During the war, Congress admitted Negroes to its visitors' galleries for the first time. Many white persons in Washington complained that it was an insult to every white man in the land to admit "niggers" to the congressional galleries, and called down direful maledictions upon the heads of "Sumner and the nasty abolitionists" for perpetrating this vulgar act, but their complaints were of no avail.[18]

In 1863 Sumner and the abolitionists opened an attack on segregation and exclusion of Negroes from the horsecars and railroads of the District of Columbia. Supported by a series of militant editorials in the *New York Tribune* (probably written by Gay), Sumner introduced amendments to the charter renewal grants of several Washington companies prohibiting them from excluding or segregating passengers

[15] *Liberator*, Sept. 6, 1861, Mar. 11, 18, 1864, Sept. 29, 1865; *Commonwealth*, Mar. 4, 18, 1865; *N.A.S. Standard*, Oct. 7, 1865, May 26, 1866; Higginson to Anna and Louisa Higginson, Apr. 19, 1874, Higginson Papers, HU; Irving H. Bartlett, *From Slave to Citizen: The Story of the Negro in Rhode Island* (Providence, 1954), 52–59; *Special Report of the Commissioner of Education on the Condition and Improvement of Public Schools in the District of Columbia . . .* (Washington, 1871), 328, 334–35.

[16] Dio H. Lewis to Whittier, Sept. 11, 1865, Whittier Papers, Essex Institute; Benjamin Thomas, *Theodore Weld: Crusader for Freedom* (New Brunswick, N.J., 1950), 253–57.

[17] Albert K. Smiley to J. B. Smith, Sept. 5, 1865, E. B. Chace to Samuel Tobey, Sept. 15, 1865, Tobey to Mrs. Chace, Sept. 18, 1865, Smiley to J. B. Smith, Sept. 18, 1865, in Lillie B. C. Wyman

and Arthur C. Wyman, *Elizabeth Buffum Chace* (2 vols.; Boston, 1914), I, 276–78.

[18] McPherson, *History of the Rebellion*, 239–40, 242–43, 593; *U.S. Statutes at Large*, XII, 351, 407, XIII, 515; *New York Tribune*, Apr. 12, 1862, June 30, 1864; *Liberator*, June 27, 1862; *Commonwealth*, Sept. 27, 1862; *Boston Advertiser*, quoted in *Liberator*, Jan. 6, 1865; *Anglo-African*, Jan. 4, 1862.

on account of race. Finally in 1865 Sumner obtained passage of a bill prohibiting segregation on every streetcar line in the District.[19] Desiring to test the effectiveness of this statute, the venerable Sojourner Truth, ageless Negro abolitionist who was working among the freedmen at Arlington, rode on the horsecars of several Washington lines. One conductor tried to make her ride on the outside platform. She threatened to sue him if he persisted, and he gave in. Another conductor pushed her roughly against the door in an effort to eject her from the car, causing a painful injury to her shoulder. She had him arrested and caused him to lose his job. Soon after this a conductor was seen to stop his car unasked and beckon kindly to some colored women standing timidly in the street. The right of Washington Negroes to ride in the horsecars was henceforth unquestioned.[20]

Nowhere in the North were Negroes and abolitionists more hated than in New York City. Irish laborers feared economic and social competition from the black man and had little use for a war fought to free the slave. Sparked by the enforcement of the draft, New York's immigrant and lower-class population rioted during four days of bloody mob violence in July, 1863. The mob lynched Negroes in the streets and burned the Colored Orphan Asylum to the ground. The rioters attacked the offices of the *New York Tribune* and ransacked the homes of abolitionists and Republicans. New York police and federal troops finally brought the mobs under control.[21]

Abolitionists went immediately to work to get New York's stricken Negro population back on its feet after the riots. The American Missionary Association disbursed temporary relief and assistance. Gerrit Smith contributed $1,000 to help the work. Abolitionists were unexpectedly aided in their efforts by New York City merchants, who organized a relief society and raised thousands of dollars for assistance and for the rebuilding of the orphan asylum. In fact, despite the murders and suffering, the riots in the long run helped to improve the status of New York Negroes. Angelina Weld reported two weeks after the uprising that a reaction against the Irish and in favor of colored people was setting in among the city's middle and upper classes. Wealthy families discharged Irish servants and hired Negroes. The average middle-class New Yorker began to realize that he had been partly responsible for the murderous outrages against Negroes. All classes of white citizens had held Negroes in contempt, spoken disrespectfully of them, and refused to admit them to streetcars, schools, restaurants, and hotels. Little wonder then that the lower classes mobbed and lynched them. A more kindly spirit toward colored people began to manifest itself in New York in the weeks and months after the draft riots.[22]

Taking advantage of this shift in public opinion, the three abolitionist newspapers in New York City (*Independent, Anti-Slavery Standard*, and *Principia*) plus the *Tribune* and the *Evening Post* inaugurated a campaign to abolish Jim Crow on all of

[19] McPherson, *History of the Rebellion*, 241–42, 593–94; *U.S. Statutes at Large*, XII, 805, XIII, 537; *New York Tribune*, Feb. 4, 11, 17, Mar. 1, 18, 1864; *Liberator*, Mar. 20, 1863; *Commonwealth*, Mar. 11, 1864.

[20] Lillie B. C. Wyman, *American Chivalry* (Boston, 1913), 110–12.

[21] Albon P. Man, Jr., "Labor Competition and the New York Draft Riots of 1863," *Journal of Negro History*, XXXVI (1951), 375–405; *New York Tribune*, July 13–20, 1863; Angelina Weld to Gerrit Smith, July 28, 1863, Smith Papers, SU; Oliver Johnson to Garrison, July 16, 1863, Garrison to Johnson, July 25, 1863, Sarah Pugh to R. D. Webb, Aug. 11, 1863, Garrison Papers, BPL. In 1862 and 1863 there were anti-Negro riots in

many northern cities, caused by real and potential labor competition between white and Negro workingmen. Williston Lofton, "Northern Labor and the Negro during the Civil War," *Journal of Negro History*, XXXIV (July, 1949), 251–73.

[22] Mattie Griffith to Elizabeth Gay, Aug. 6, 1863, Gay Papers, CU; S. S. Jocelyn to Gerrit Smith, July 22, 1863, Gerrit Smith Papers, SU; Jocelyn to Lewis Tappan, July 30, 1863, Tappan Papers, LC; W. E. Whiting to Gerrit Smith, July 20, 1863, Angelina Weld to Smith, July 28, 1863, Smith Papers, SU; L. M. Child to Frank Shaw, July 27, 1863, Child Papers, Wayland Historical Society; *Principia*, Jan. 7, 1864.

the city's street railroads. Most streetcar companies allowed Negroes to ride in their cars, but the Fourth Avenue and Eighth Avenue roads permitted their conductors to exclude colored people, and the Sixth Avenue company segregated them in special cars. Abolitionists contended that the railroads were common carriers and were required by law to provide transportation equally to everyone. They threatened to take the matter to court. The Fourth Avenue road finally began admitting Negroes to its cars in February, 1864, but the other two companies still refused to change their policy. In June, 1864, the controversy came to a head when the conductor of an Eighth Avenue car, aided by an Irish policeman, forcibly ejected the widow of a Negro sergeant who had been recently killed in battle. The *Tribune* exploded in anger: "It is quite time to settle the question whether the wives and children of the men who are laying down their lives for their country . . . are to be treated like dogs." Public opinion was hostile to the railroad. The policeman who had helped eject the woman was reprimanded by his superiors. The city police commissioner prohibited his men from helping conductors eject Negroes from the cars. The Eighth Avenue road capitulated to the surge of public opinion and ended its exclusion of Negroes. A few days later the Sixth Avenue road likewise surrendered. All of New York City's public transportation was thenceforth integrated.[23]

Philadelphia in 1860 had a larger Negro population than any other northern city. Several Philadelphia Negroes had amassed considerable wealth and resided in com-fortable, even luxurious homes. Most colored residents of the City of Brotherly Love, however, lived in squalor and poverty in unsanitary slums. Philadelphia was a rigidly segregated city. Negro children attended separate schools when they attended any schools at all. Some of the city's 19 streetcar and suburban railroad companies refused to admit Negroes to their cars; those that did admit colored people forced them to ride on the front platform. Negroes seeking transportation in the city were often compelled to walk or hire an expensive carriage.[24]

This extreme Jim Crowism in transportation came under powerful attack by Philadelphia abolitionists. Garrisonian abolitionism was stronger in Philadelphia than anywhere outside New England. A large number of the city's colored people were Garrisonians. Philadelphia's Negroes also supported thriving organizations of their own, particularly the Social, Civil, and Statistical Association of Colored People, which sponsored lectures, provided legal assistance to Negroes, and served as a pressure group in behalf of the interests of all colored people. William Still, a prominent Philadelphia Negro, was leader of this Association and was also an official in the Pennsylvania Anti-Slavery Society.[25]

The Colored People's Association, the Pennsylvania Anti-Slavery Society, and the Philadelphia Female Anti-Slavery Society all maintained standing committees to work for the abolition of discrimination in Philadelphia's transportation system. William Still inaugurated the militant phase of the

---

[23] George Cheever to Elizabeth Washburn, Aug. 5, 1863, Cheever Papers, AAS; *New York Tribune*, Aug. 4, 5, 7, 1863, June 21, 24, 30, 1864; *Principia*, Aug. 13, 1863; *Independent*, Jan. 21, 1864; *Liberator*, Mar. 4, 1864; *Boston Commonwealth*, June 24, 1864; *N.A.S. Standard*, July 2, 9, 16, 1864. Quotation is from *New York Tribune*, June 21, 1864. Segregation on San Francisco's street railroads was abolished by a district court ruling in October, 1864. *Liberator*, Nov. 18, 1864, quoting *San Francisco Bulletin*, Oct. 3, 1864. In Cincinnati, however, Jim Crow in public transportation was not ended until after the war.

[24] Ira V. Brown, "Pennsylvania and the Rights of the Negro, 1865–1887," *Pennsylvania History*, XXVIII (January, 1961), 45–46; *Liberator*, Sept. 21, 1860; *Twenty-Seventh Annual Report of the Philadelphia Female Anti-Slavery Society* (Phila., 1861), 17.

[25] Brown, "Pennsylvania and the Rights of the Negro," *op. cit.*, 49–50; Alberta S. Norwood, "Negro Welfare Work in Philadelphia, Especially as Illustrated by the Career of William Still, 1775–1930," M.A. thesis, U. of Pennsylvania, 1931, 18–24; Larry Gara, "William Still and the Underground Railroad," *Pennsylvania History*, XXVIII (January, 1961), 33–39.

antisegregation campaign in 1859 with a long letter to the press detailing the insults and hardships suffered by Negroes on Philadelphia's street railroads. The letter was widely reprinted and focused national attention on the subject. In 1862 Still obtained the signatures of 360 prominent white Philadelphians, including all of the city's leading abolitionists, to a petition requesting the Board of Presidents of the City Railways to end segregation on their lines. The board took no action on the petition, but from this time forward the anti-Jim Crow campaign grew in scope and intensity. The three abolitionist committees kept up the pressure by means of petitions, speeches, letters to the press, and private interviews with railroad presidents. In 1863 Still wrote an eloquent letter to the city's leading newspaper, the *Philadelphia Press,* describing in detail the humiliation suffered by a Negro who tried to obtain transportation in the City of Brotherly Love. The letter was widely published. It appeared in the *London Times,* and was reported by Moncure Conway to have done more harm to the Union cause in England than a military defeat.[26]

The emergence of a national policy of arming Negroes to fight for the Union gave an important fillip to the antisegregation efforts. The antislavery press began to publish stories of wounded colored soldiers who had been ejected from Philadelphia horsecars. Sensing a change in public opinion, abolitionists and Negroes, now supported by the whole Republican press of Philadelphia, stepped up their struggle against segregation. In October, 1864, a National Colored Men's Convention met in Syracuse and urged the formation of state Equal Rights Leagues throughout the North to work for desegregation and Negro suffrage. The first (and strongest) such league was formed in Philadelphia, and its initial target was streetcar segregation. It joined in the growing outcry for an end to discrimination in Philadelphia transportation.[27]

William Still suggested to J. Miller McKim the idea of holding a mass meeting at Philadelphia's Concert Hall to demand the abolition of Jim Crow. McKim used his contacts with leading Philadelphia Republicans and businessmen to arrange a meeting for January 13, 1865, sponsored by prominent white Philadelphians. The meeting adopted resolutions calling on the railroads to end their Jim Crow policy, and appointed a committee to negotiate with the railroad presidents. McKim and James Mott, secretary and president respectively of the Pennsylvania Anti-Slavery Society, were two of the leading members of this committee. Their efforts obtained some immediate results. The Philadelphia and Darby Railroad, a suburban line, put an end to segregation on its trains. A few days later a streetcar company also abolished segregation, and another line began admitting Negroes to *some* of its cars. After a month the first company reported that because of integration it had lost white passengers and its revenue had declined; therefore it would henceforth allow Negroes only in special "Colored" cars. The Board of Railway Presidents took a public "poll" in the streetcars and announced that a majority of white Philadelphians still opposed integration. But McKim's committee did not give up. They made a direct appeal to the mayor, a Democrat, who rebuffed them with the statement that he did not wish "the ladies of his family to ride in the cars with colored people."[28]

26 Norwood, "William Still and Negro Welfare Work," 52–60; William Still, *A Brief Narrative of the Struggle for the Rights of the Colored People of Philadelphia in the City Railroad Cars* (Phila., 1867), 3–10; *Twenty-Seventh Annual Report of the Philadelphia Female Anti-Slavery Society,* 17; *Thirtieth Annual Report of the Philadelphia Female Anti-Slavery Society* (1864), 23–24.

27 *New York Tribune,* Nov. 19, 1864; *N.A.S. Standard,* Oct. 15, Nov. 19, 1864, Jan. 14, 21, 1865; *Liberator,* Dec. 23, 1864, Jan. 6, 27, Mar. 24, 1865; *Thirty-First Annual Report of the Philadelphia Female Anti-Slavery Society* (1865), 17–18.

28 Still, *Brief Narrative,* 11–13; [Benjamin C. Bacon], *Why Colored People in Philadelphia Are*

Defeated at the city level, advocates of equal rights turned hopefully to the state legislature. There they found a staunch ally, Senator Morrow B. Lowry from northwestern Pennsylvania, who for six years had been urging passage of a state law to prohibit segregation in public transportation. Described by Garrison as "a most radical abolitionist, and reminding me alike of Gerrit Smith and Charles Sumner," Lowry was a genuine crusader for equal rights.[29] The State Senate passed Lowry's bill by a close vote, but it was shelved in the House. Lowry persisted, and in March, 1867, his bill finally passed both houses and became law. It prohibited discrimination in every form of public transportation in the entire state of Pennsylvania. It was an impressive victory for equal rights, and to abolitionists and Negroes must go the main credit for the triumph. It was they who initiated the struggle and kept up the pressure; and it was an abolitionist who piloted the bill through the state legislature.[30]

Not content with the policy of arming Negroes in separate regiments, a few enthusiastic integrationists among the abolitionists called for the abolition of colored regiments and the complete integration of the army. "I want to sink the differences of race," wrote Samuel Gridley Howe. "I do not believe in black colonies, or black regiments." Gilbert Haven said, "We must abolish colored regiments. . . . A citizen, if he volunteers, should join what regiment he chooses; if he is drafted, those that most need his musket."[31] Such a policy, however, was too radical for the 1860s. The enlistment of Negroes on any basis was a revolutionary step forward; full-scale integration of the armed forces would not come until nearly a century later.

In addition to the antidiscrimination measures described above, northern Negroes made other advances in civil rights during and immediately after the war. California abolished its laws excluding Negro testimony against whites in the courts in 1863. Illinois did the same in 1865, and repealed all the rest of her infamous "black laws" except the exclusion of Negroes from the polls. Chicago's public schools were desegregated in 1865. In 1866 the Indiana Supreme Court declared unconstitutional the worst of that state's black laws. In 1865 Massachusetts enacted the first comprehensive public accommodations law in American history, forbidding the exclusion of any person because of race or color from restaurants, inns, theaters, and places of amusement. The *New York Tribune* and *Anti-Slavery Standard* called for passage of a federal law to prohibit discrimination in public transportation. Such a law, said Sydney Gay, would be "a fit corollary to the Amendment which abolishes slavery." Senator Henry Wilson introduced a bill in February, 1865, providing for a fine of $500 against any railroad or steamship in the United States which discriminated against Negroes.[32]

Excluded from the Street-Cars (Phila., 1866), 3–4; *Thirty-Third Annual Report of the Philadelphia Female Anti-Slavery Society* (1867), 26–27; *Liberator*, Jan. 27, 1865; *Boston Commonwealth*, Jan. 28, 1865; *N.A.S. Standard*, Jan. 28, Feb. 25, 1865; *New York Tribune*, Feb. 10, May 3, 1865; William Still to J. Miller McKim, Nov. 10, 1871, McKim Papers, NYPL.

29 Garrison to Helen Garrison, Nov. 5, 1865, Garrison Papers, BPL.

30 Brown, "Pennsylvania and the Rights of the Negro," *op. cit.*, 48–49; Lewis Tappan to Morrow B. Lowry, Jan. 18, 1865, Tappan letterbook, Tappan Papers, LC; *Liberator*, Feb. 3, Mar. 3, 1865; *N.A.S. Standard*, Apr. 1, June 3, 1865, Dec. 1, 1866, Feb. 23, Mar. 30, 1867; *Report of the Committee Appointed for the Purpose of Securing to Colored People in Philadelphia the Right to the Street-Cars* (Phila., 1867).

31 Howe to John Andrew, n.d., but sometime in spring of 1863, Andrew Papers, MHS; Haven, *National Sermons*, 405, 510. The United States Navy had always been integrated.

32 *Commonwealth*, Apr. 17, 1863, Nov. 10, 1866; Benjamin Quarles, *The Negro in the Civil War* (Boston, 1953), 313; *New York Tribune*, Feb. 6, 10, 1865; *Special Report of the Commissioner of Education* . . . (Washington, 1871), 343; Milton R. Konvitz, *A Century of Civil Rights, with a Study of State Law Against Discrimination*, by Theodore Leskes (New York, 1961), 155; *Independent*, Aug. 3, 1865; *N.A.S. Standard*, Feb. 11, 1865. Gay's statement from *New York Tribune*, Feb. 5, 1865.

The time was not yet ripe for such a sweeping national law, and Wilson's bill was buried in committee. But the very fact that such a bill could be introduced in 1865 was an indication of the revolution in the status of colored men since 1861. Under the pressure of military necessity the Negro had been freed and given an opportunity to fight for the Union. He fought courageously and well, winning the grudging respect of millions of northern whites. The Negro's contribution as a soldier combined with the patient, effective work of civil rights advocates won large gains for the northern Negro during the war. Black laws and discrimination in civil rights were slowly crumbling away and Jim Crow was gradually disappearing from many parts of the North. Race prejudice, however, remained powerful and discrimination continued to prevail in many walks of life. Negroes in 1865 could vote on equal terms with whites in only five states, and these states contained only 7 percent of the *northern* Negro population. Negro suffrage would soon become the main issue of southern reconstruction, and so long as most northern states refused the ballot to black men, the North was in a false and stultifying moral position. Abolitionists appreciated this fact and kept up their agitation for equal suffrage in the North. Despite the preeminence of the southern problem during Reconstruction, the status of the northern Negroes continued to occupy much of the attention of abolitionists. . . .

The abolitionists could look back with considerable satisfaction in 1870 upon the achievements of the past decade. Most of the measures they had originally advocated had been adopted: the immediate and universal abolition of slavery, the enlistment of Negro soldiers, government assistance for the education of freedmen, the creation of a Freedmen's Bureau, and the incorporation of the Negro's civil and political equality into the law of the land. Abolitionists themselves had been transformed by the crucible of war from troublesome

fanatics to prophets honored in their own country.

But the next decade was to prove that many of the equalitarian achievements of the Civil War and Reconstruction were built on a foundation of sand. The freedom and equality of the Negro were based in part on the idealistic traditions of the abolitionist movement, but in greater part on the military and political exigencies of war and reconstruction. The North's conversion to emancipation and equal rights was primarily a conversion of expediency rather than one of conviction. The South was converted only by force. A policy based on "military necessity" may be abandoned when the necessity disappears, and this is what happened in the 1870s. It became expedient for northern political and business interests to conciliate southern whites, and an end to federal enforcement of Negro equality in the South was the price of conciliation. The mass of northern people had never loved the Negro, were tired of the "everlasting negro question," and were glad to see the end of it.

A few abolitionists acquiesced in the northern abandonment of Reconstruction, but most of them protested strongly against it. Not many northerners, however, listened to their protests after 1875. Abolitionists were not slow to discern and deplore the North's return to apathy. It was startling "to realize how completely the antislavery struggle is forgotten by the people, and how even the terrible expenditure of blood and treasure, which followed it, is fast sinking into oblivion," wrote Lydia Maria Child in 1878. "The lamentable misfortune is that emancipation was not the result of a popular *moral sentiment*, but of a miserable 'military necessity.' It was not the 'fruit of righteousness,' and therefore it is not 'peace.' " Five years later Frederick Douglass declared that "as the war for the Union recedes into the misty shadows of the past, and the Negro is no longer needed to assault forts and stop rebel bullets, he is . . . of less importance. Peace with the old master class has been war to the Negro. As the one has risen, the other has fallen."[33]

Abolitionists had done their best to rally the conscience of the nation, but in the final analysis the nation refused to follow their leadership. Was this a "failure of the American abolitionists," as one historian has called it?[34] Perhaps. Such abolitionist techniques as incisive criticism, harsh language, and moral absolutism may have been ill-suited to the conversion of conscience. But in a larger sense, their failure was the failure of the American people, and the United States has yet to measure up to the ideals of the abolitionist crusade. The civil rights movement of today has a greater chance of permanent success than did its counterpart in the 1860s. But whatever success the contemporary movement finally does achieve will be built partly on the foundations laid down more than a century ago by the abolitionists. They were the first "freedom riders," and their spirit still pervades the struggle for racial justice. The victories of Martin Luther King and his followers are, in a very real sense, victories of the abolitionist crusade.

[33] Lydia Maria Child to George Julian, Sept. 28, 1878, Giddings-Julian Correspondence, LC; Philip S. Foner (ed.), *The Life and Writings of Frederick Douglass* (4 vols.; New York, 1950–55), IV, 355.

[34] Merton L. Dillon, "The Failure of the American Abolitionists," *Journal of Southern History*, XXV (May, 1959), 159–77.

CHAPTER **6**

Lincoln and Emancipation

For more than a century Abraham Lincoln has been commonly regarded as the symbol of emancipation, the saintly and suffering leader in the struggle to free the suffering millions from the house of bondage. School children are still instructed in the legend of the young man who, after witnessing a New Orleans slave auction, determined "to hit this thing hard" if ever he had the chance. The Lincoln image emerges again and again, in the Illinois legislator taking a stand for freedom after the murder of the abolitionist Elijah Lovejoy, in the Whig congressman introducing a bill to end slavery in the District of Columbia, and in the senatorial candidate who spoke so eloquently for liberty in his "house divided" speech of 1858. We are reminded also of the statesman who experienced "continual torment" from the memory of slaves shackled on an Ohio riverboat in 1841, and the President who fervently wished in 1862 that "all men everywhere should be free." In the Lincoln legend all these thoughts and emotions came to a dramatic culmination in the Emancipation Proclamation.

Yet the realities of history are often more complex and confused than legend would have us believe. The New Orleans story is most probably a fable, and the "crusading" Illinois legislator objected at least as much to abolitionists as to slavery. Lincoln in the Illinois legislature once proposed "admitting all *whites* to the . . . suffrage, who pay taxes or bear arms (by no means excluding females)," and the young emancipator in his practice of law was perfectly willing as late as the Matson case of 1847 to help a master recover his slave property for return to bondage. The sight of slaves being sent down the river, which was described as a "continual torment" in 1854, originally reminded Lincoln that fate makes tolerable even so low a condition as slavery. Lincoln's District of Columbia Bill for compensated and gradual emancipation rested on the impossible condition that the proslavery population of the District approve the measure in a general election. The cautious criticism of slavery in 1858 came wrapped in sympathetic words for the South and the emphatic rejection of "the social and political equality of the white and black races" along with the right of Negroes to hold office, vote, serve on juries, or marry white persons. Physical differences, he argued, "forever forbid the races living together upon terms of social and political equality," and if the races *must* live together "I, as much as any man, am in favor of the superior [status] being assigned to the white man." Finally, President Lincoln energetically enforced the Fugitive Slave Act and resisted antislavery pressures until the issuance of the Emancipation Proclamation, which was based largely on military and political necessities and actually freed few slaves.

The most telling criticism was made in 1876 by Frederick Douglass at the dedication of a monument to Lincoln. Douglass recalled that Lincoln was as willing as any of his proslavery predecessors to draw the sword in defense of the peculiar institution, to execute all the "supposed constitutional guarantees" including the pursuit, recapture, and return of fugitive slaves, and to "suppress a slave rising for liberty, though his guilty master were already in arms against the Government." Douglass concluded that "the race to which we belong were not the special objects of his consideration. Knowing this, I concede to you, my white fellow citizens, a pre-eminence in his worship at once full and supreme. First, midst, and last, you and yours were the objects of his deepest affection and his most earnest solicitude. You are the children of Abraham Lincoln. We are at best only his stepchildren, children by adoption, children by force of circumstances and necessity."

Whatever reality the Lincoln legend may contain belongs to the final period of the President's life. Lincoln's oft-stated belief that Negroes and white men could not live in peace and equality led him to urge again and again that Negroes be transported from America, and if General Ben Butler's word can be trusted he still had not surrendered the idea a few weeks before his assassination. Certainly a large number of abolitionists never fully trusted Lincoln. It is also clear that Lincoln lagged behind the Republican majority in Congress as well as a half dozen or more Union generals, and that the President failed to use forcefully the First and Second Confiscation Acts or the Presidential war power to secure emancipation at the earliest possible moment. Ralph Korngold even suggested in 1955 that Lincoln may have issued the Proclamation to forestall more forcible action by Congress. Obviously the President promulgated the Proclamation only after using every stratagem to secure the adoption of his own plan of gradual compensated emancipation which would have left a substantial number of slaves in bondage until 1900. Lincoln doubted the legality of his own Proclamation, and assumed during most of the war period that any sudden conclusion of the conflict would have left vast numbers still enslaved. Finally, even his defense of the Thirteenth Amendment appears to have had a large dash of expediency and a somewhat more modest measure of concern for the rights of American Negroes.

How shall we deal with the large gap between the legendary Lincoln and so many of his actions and words? One could save the legend of emancipation and transfer homage to Charles Sumner or Wendell Phillips, or one could explore the various strategies of reconciliation between Lincoln and the myth. Carl Sandburg, the most popular of the Lincoln biographers, seemed scarcely aware of the problem, and like so many fellow scholars had at best a faint sense of slavery as a pressing moral issue in the 1850s and '60s. Lincoln considered the possibility of deporting Negroes in 1862, but put the idea aside after Secretary of State William Seward proposed to amend the Proclamation to indicate that "Negroes were to be sent out of the country only as they were willing to go." Sandburg described Seward's proposal as a "minor suggestion"!

The most prominent Lincoln scholar, James G. Randall, in the four-volume study of 1945–55, displayed more awareness of the anti-legendary aspects of his subject. Discussing the racial remarks in the Lincoln-Douglas debates, he observed: "The truth is, he had shared some of the anti-Negro prejudices of the people among whom he lived in Kentucky and southern Indiana and Illinois. But in the White House, he outgrew his prejudices." As evidence, Randall cited the frequently quoted remark of Frederick Douglass about the President's personal amiability. Douglass, however, was not simply "a Negro," but an able and articulate man who had served the President well, and Lincoln had ample reasons for maintaining cordial relations. Moreover, a closer examination of all remarks about Lincoln in Douglass' collected works indicates clearly that Randall built his case on one or two isolated remarks taken out of context. The net impression gleaned from all of Douglass' comments about the President does not suggest a great equalitarian emancipator. One finds Randall on other occasions forgetting his own theory of Presidential "growth": in discussions of deportation and colonization he informed his readers that "Lincoln was closer to Southerners than to abolitionists." Repeatedly Randall made the defense that exacting constituitonal scruples kept Lincoln from making his mere "private opinion" on slavery into public policy, but the President was not a man to be hindered by fine constitutional scruples when the Union cause itself fell into grave danger, and he seems to have had few qualms about conscription, suspending the writ of habeas corpus, or the expenditure of vast sums without congressional authorization. After defending Lincoln against the charge of excessive reluctance to act on the slavery issue, Randall in his fullest account of emancipation portrayed a Lincoln driven almost entirely by military and political necessity. The initial proclamation of September, 1862, was "only a warning and a prediction," and the actual proclamation of January, 1863, "had no immediate consequences."

Again and again Randall praised Lincoln for "fairness to the South," "conservatism," a "sense of fair dealing," and a "lack of vindictiveness" toward Confederates. It seems improbable that a man so concerned with the sensibilities of Southern masters could be "continually tormented" by the plight of the slave. In 1959 Norman A. Graebner joined Randall in stressing constitutional scruples as an obstacle to action against slavery and in praising Lincoln as a sane and reasonable moderate. Presumably Lincoln had little or nothing in common with the Radicals. Unlike the "moralist" Horace Greeley he knew that "liberation was no panacea"; and as a good "conservative" he "condemned all disrespect for property" and "reminded Congress that the liberation of slaves was the destruction of property." Moreover, his refusal to follow Greeley into emancipation was a highly "moral" action because he considered consequences and problems, as the abolitionists did not. Here Graebner, Randall, and other scholars revealed a strange syllogism. To suggest that Lincoln followed the dictates of expediency is one thing, but to celebrate his path of action as grand morality and to ascribe a poor appreciation of high ethics to the abolitionists is quite another matter. The tendency to sacrifice antislavery radicals and the cause they represented by trying to demonstrate the total rightness of the President whenever he encountered abolitionist opposition has been characteristic of much modern scholarship. We have been exposed often to the little vignettes in which the more militant enemies of slavery are taken to task for "hounding" the President, and the context invites the reader to extend all sympathies to Lincoln for "enduring" this kind of "ordeal." T. Harry Williams' aggressive denunciation of the radicals in 1941 provides the most startling example of this tendency, but Randall could also be used as an illustration. Although Randall acknowledged "the foul spirit of caste" and noted that Lincoln urged Negroes to leave the country in 1862, he failed to draw the obvious conclusions and ended by defending Lincoln. In the case of the Negro who replied to Lincoln's "colonization" plan by asking the President, "Pray tell us is our right to a home in this country less than your own?" Randall even went so far as to add his own comment about the "impertinence" of the remark.

The most widely acclaimed one-volume study of Lincoln, written in 1952 by Benjamin P. Thomas, was a model of scholarship in many respects but the book contained the same flaws which had marred the work of Sandburg, Randall, and others. Lincoln was praised for his refusal in 1858 to criticize Southern slaveholders, an act which was described as the lack of "prejudice against the Southern people." The concept of Lincoln guiding a middle course between "pro-slavery and anti-slavery extremists" (a perverse version of "the middle way"!) was emphasized and sympathies were extended to the President in his conflict with radical Republicans who proposed to "force Negro suffrage on the vanquished population."

In 1962 another highly praised biography of Lincoln by Don E. Fehrenbacher entitled *Prelude to Greatness* focused on the 1850s. Instead of defining greatness in moral terms or with direct reference to emancipation, "greatness" was equated with "national leadership," the "response of inner strength to an extraordinary challenge." In a way Fehrenbacher simply ignored the problem; for example, he boldly announced that Lincoln was "always opposed to the institution of slavery" (an invalid generalization for several reasons and quite clearly so because of the Matson case). Fehrenbacher seems to have been trying to rescue his subject from scholars such as Reinhard H. Luthin, who in 1960 described the early Lincoln as a conservative opportunist and a failure in the pre-Sumter crisis. Nevertheless Fehrenbacher himself provides a modern illustration of the old failure to grasp slavery as a compelling moral issue. More than once he appeared to lend implicit approval to Lincoln's lapses in moral imagination: in one instance Lincoln feared "the progressive degradation of all white men who earned their living by toil" as "more monstrous" than the "mere expansion of Negro servitude." If, as Fehrenbacher seemed to believe, the chief issue in the Lincoln-Douglas debates was a moral one, and if Douglas was open to criticism for moral obtuseness, then Lincoln was vulnerable to the same charge. Despite an impressive display of scholarship, Fehrenbacher's book provided no solution to the paradox posed by the Lincoln legend and the contradictory evidence.

One possible tactic was explored by David Donald in 1956. Donald stressed the conception of Lincoln as "an astute and dexterous operator of the political machine," the man who characteristically avoided the pitfalls of "dogma" by observing that "my policy is to have no policy." Lincoln refused "to force reality to fit a formula," rejected the "doctrinaire approach," and occupied a commanding middle position between proslavery apologetics and "the anti-slavery man's idealization of the Negro as God's image in ebony." (Again a curious "middle ground.") In brief, the President was the greatest of America's pragmatic statesmen.

Nearly all scholars stressed Lincoln's nationalism and none more percep-tively than Edmund Wilson in his essay of 1954 on "Lincoln and the Union as Religious Mysticism." Probably the best single essay on Lincoln from any vantage point was Richard Hofstadter's candid and penetrating account of 1948 in *The American Political Tradition*. Hofstadter began by insisting that Lincoln was always, and particularly on the slavery issue, a follower rather than a molder of public opinion. Moreover, "so far as the Negro was concerned, Lincoln could not escape the moral insensitivity that is characteristic of the average white American." Not until October 4, 1854, did Lincoln take a clear public stand against slavery and then only in an appeal to keep the West as "an outlet for white men everywhere the world over—in which Hans, and Baptiste, and Patrick" (but not "Cuffee") might better their condition. Hof-stadter suggested that in opposing the expansion of slavery into the territories, Lincoln and the Republicans hit upon an issue which sounded mildly anti-slavery without providing a source of irritation to even the most violent Negro-phobes. ("We want . . . [Western lands] for homes of free white people.") The Emancipation Proclamation obviously came after all other major proposals failed and had "all the moral grandeur of a bill of lading." Lincoln's persistently advocated "fantastic" plan to send Negroes out of the country sprang from the "caste psychology" of white supremacy which did not propose to put black and white men together in a "competitive labor market."

In 1958 Richard N. Current, like Randall and others who had gone before him, rested his case for Lincoln the emancipator on the belief that the President "grew in office." Current provided the most plausible version of this idea, and while the evidence is somewhat slender one may still wonder if the theory and the evidence have been sufficiently pursued. Perhaps we shall have to surrender the attempt to define precisely Lincoln's political beliefs and settle for some-thing like Roy P. Basler's description in 1959 of the President as a symbol tragically ridden with historical ambiguity. A few remarkable passages from Lincoln's speeches and works make us particularly reluctant to close the case. Consider, for example, a Lincoln letter of 1864 on Negro suffrage which referred to: "These people, who have so heroically vindicated their manhood on the battlefield, where, in assisting to save the life of the Republic, they have demonstrated in blood their right to the ballot, which is but the humane protection of the flag they have so fearlessly defended." Yet later during the same year in a second letter he suggested "in a private way" and not for publication that Louisiana leaders consider the *possibility* of giving the suffrage to a few Negroes. Even in the case of the eloquent statement first quoted, we must ask if he meant all Negroes or just those who served in the Union army, and, even more perplexing, we must also ask if the letter is actually authentic. The date is uncertain, the original no longer exists, and the corroboration from either the sender or the recipient is inconclusive. (Ludwell H. Johnson argued in 1966 that the key passages had been added by a New York reporter.) A more important bit of evidence can be found in a passage from the Second Inaugural Address which suggests anything but a conservative opportunist. If these words were written by a once reluctant emancipator, that reluctance seems absent from this somber and moving indictment of slavery: "Fondly do we hope— fervently do we pray—that this mighty scourge of war may pass away. Yet if God wills that it continue until all the wealth piled up by the bondsman's two hundred and fifty years or unrequited toil shall be sunk, and until every drop of blood drawn with the lash shall be paid by another drawn with the sword, as was said three thousand years ago, so still it must be said 'The judgments of the Lord are true and righteous altogether.'"

Perhaps a solution will yet be found for the enigma of Lincoln, and perhaps not. In any event the rhetoric should be traced to solid content, and no scholar should continue the tradition of taking from the abolitionists and their cause in order to brighten Lincoln's glory.

BIBLIOGRAPHY

Books and Articles Referred to in the Chapter Introduction

Philip S. Foner (ed.), *The Life and Writings of Frederick Douglass* (4 vols.; 1950–55).
Carl Sandburg, *Abraham Lincoln: The Prairie Years and the War Years* (1954). A one-volume condensation of an earlier six-volume series.
James G. Randall, *Lincoln, the President* (4 vols.; 1945–55). See also Richard N. Current's one-volume condensation, *Mr. Lincoln* (1957).
Norman A. Graebner, "Abraham Lincoln: Conservative Statesman," in Graebner (ed.), *The Enduring Lincoln* (1959).
Benjamin P. Thomas, *Abraham Lincoln* (1952).
T. Harry Williams, *Lincoln and the Radicals* (1941).
Don E. Fehrenbacher, *Prelude to Greatness: Lincoln in the 1850's* (1962).
Reinhard H. Luthin, *The Real Abraham Lincoln* (1960).
David Donald, *Lincoln Reconsidered* (1956).
Edmund Wilson, "Lincoln and the Union as Religious Mysticism," *Eight Essays* (1954).
Richard Hofstadter, *The American Political Tradition* (1948).
Roy P. Basler, "An Immortal Sign," in Graebner (ed.), *The Enduring Lincoln* (1959).

Suggested Reading

All Lincoln students will wish to consult Roy P. Basler (ed.), *The Collected Works of Abraham Lincoln* (9 vols.; 1953–55). The most recent account, John Hope Franklin, *The Emancipation Proclamation* (1963), is particularly valuable for the world context and for the immediate circumstances. For the most recent and lucid exposition of the creative tension between Lincoln and the abolitionists, see James M. McPherson, *The Struggle for Equality* (1964). The ultimate book for praising the "moderate" Lincoln and dealing vituperation to the abolitionists is T. Harry Williams, *Lincoln and the Radicals* (1941). A great deal of information on Lincoln and emancipation was given by Benjamin Quarles, *The Negro in the Civil War* (1953), and *Lincoln and the Negro* (1962). The best book on the subject as seen through the eyes of a Lincoln subordinate was written by Benjamin P. Thomas and Harold M. Hyman. See *Stanton: The Life and Times of Lincoln's Secretary of War* (1962). Harry V. Jaffa in *Crisis of the House Divided* (1959) attempted without much success to refute Hofstadter's comments on Lincoln's equalitarianism. On the emancipation question in the 1864 election see William F. Zornow's *Lincoln and the Party Divided* (1954). Among the most recent works on Lincoln, Don E. Fehrenbacher presented the most sympathetic portrait; Reinhard Luthin portrayed Lincoln as a conservative opportunist, and Donald W. Riddle took a similar view in *Congressman Abraham Lincoln* (1957). In Grady McWhiney (ed.), *Grant, Lee, Lincoln and the Radicals* (1965), David Donald defended his thesis on the Radicals and T. Harry Williams defended a moderate version of his old assault on the Radicals, with Donald presenting the more plausible case. Dudley T. Cornish, *The Sable Arm; Negro Troops in the Union Army, 1861–1865* (1956), and James M. McPherson, *The Negro's Civil War* (1965), suggested the very large part that Negroes played in their own emancipation. For a notion of the bitter hostility in Lincoln's region, see Jacque Voegeli, "The Northwest and the Race Issue," *Mississippi Valley Historical Review* (1963). William H. and Jane H. Pease revealed the extent to which race prejudice prevailed even in Canada; see *Black Utopia: Negro Communal Experiments in America* (1963). On racial violence in New York City, see Lawrence Lader, "New York's Bloodiest Week," *American Heritage* (1959).

1955

A Very Reluctant Emancipator[*]

RALPH KORNGOLD

On September 17, 1862, the battle took place at Antietam. Lee's march through Maryland was halted, but McClellan's victory was inconclusive. The Confederate commander retreated in good order. His army remained intact and was destined to win important victories. Five days later, on September 22, 1862, Lincoln issued the famous preliminary Emancipation Proclamation. Secretary Chase tells us about it in his *Diary*. He quotes Lincoln as saying:

The action of the army against the rebels has not been quite what I should have best liked. But they have been driven out of Maryland, and Pennsylvania is no longer in danger of invasion. When the rebel army was at

---

* Ralph Korngold, *Thaddeus Stevens, A Being Darkly Wise and Rudely Great* (1965). Reprinted by permission of Mrs. Ralph Korngold. Copyright 1955 by Ralph Korngold.

Frederick, I determined, as soon as it should be driven out of Maryland, to issue a Proclamation of Emancipation such as I thought most likely to be useful. I said nothing to any one; but I made the promise to myself, and [hesitating a little]—to my Maker. The rebel army is now driven out, and I am going to fulfill that promise. I have got you together to hear what I have written down. I do not wish your advice about the main matter for that I have determined myself.[1]

There exists, however, a diary entry made by James C. Welling, editor of the *National Intelligencer*, concerning a statement made to him by Edward Stanly, military governor of North Carolina, to whom Lincoln gave an entirely different version about what prompted him to issue the proclamation. Since Welling and Stanly are reliable witnesses and since, as we have seen, Lincoln was in the habit of contradicting himself, it is the historian's duty to give both versions and to try to ascertain the truth in the matter.

Stanly had been a congressman from North Carolina. He was an avowed Unionist but was opposed to any interference with slavery. He had accepted the military governorship of his state at great personal sacrifice and only after Lincoln had given him the assurance that he had no intention of interfering with slavery. When the preliminary Emancipation Proclamation appeared he thought Lincoln had played him false. So he hastened to Washington with the intention of handing in his resignation. He had several interviews with Lincoln and decided to remain at his post. Having made that decision he went to the office of the *National Intelligencer* and talked to Welling, who made the following entry in his diary:

September 27th.—Had a call at the *Intelligencer* office from the Honorable Edward Stanly, Military Governor of North Carolina. In a long and interesting conversation Mr. Stanly related to me the substance of several interviews which he had had with the President respecting the Proclamation of Freedom.

Stanly said that the President had stated to him that the proclamation had become a civil necessity to prevent the Radicals from openly embarrassing the government in the conduct of the war. The President expressed the belief that, without the proclamation for which they had been clamoring, the Radicals would take the extreme step in Congress of withholding supplies for carrying on the war—leaving the whole land in anarchy. Mr. Lincoln said that he had prayed to the Almighty to save him from this necessity, adopting the very language of our Saviour, "If it be possible, let this cup pass from me," but the prayer had not been answered.[2]

The extreme reticence of Lincoln's biographers and Civil War historians in general concerning this and other contradictory statements made by Lincoln during this trying period makes it evident that they have found them embarrassing. They ill accord with the image of Lincoln they appear to have been determined to present to the public. To the author of this volume they make Lincoln more, not less, sympathetic, since they make him appear more human. He was not all-wise, he made mistakes, he often contradicted himself. Notwithstanding all this he went steadfastly toward his goal—the preservation of the Union. Emancipation and all else—even truth sometimes—were subordinated to this. He wished to preserve the Union without having to resort to general emancipation if at all possible because he feared the postwar consequences of that form of emancipation to the country and to the Negro. It does not appear unlikely that his persistence in this prolonged the war. Stevens and many others thought so, and they may have been right. Lincoln finally was to acknowledge that far from having the serious consequences he had so often predicted, the Emancipation Proclamation had the opposite effect.[3] Yet we shall see that after he issued the final document he continued trying to get the border states to adopt gradual emancipation. Had

[1] *Diary*, vol. II, pp. 87–88.

[2] Rice, *op. cit.*, pp. 532–33.
[3] See Lincoln's letter to James C. Conkling, Aug. 26, 1863.

he succeeded it would have made the ratification of the Thirteenth Amendment abolishing slavery impossible and have led to serious complications.

Lincoln's statement to Stanly harmonizes with what we know concerning his dislike of general emancipation. It likewise harmonizes with his words and actions both before and after he issued the proclamation. The statement he made at the cabinet meeting does not. In corroboration of the version he gave to Stanly there can be cited his statement in his letter to Cuthbert Bullitt, July 28, 1862, in which he also expressed fear of congressional displeasure unless a change of policy is adopted by the administration. He wrote: "It is a military necessity to have men and money; and we cannot get either in sufficient numbers or amounts if we keep from or drive from our lines slaves coming to them."

Welling, who as editor of the *National Intelligencer*, an old and influential publication, had considerable inside information, and whose relations with members of Lincoln's cabinet were, as Allen Thorndike Rice assures us, "intimate and often confidential," was of the opinion that what Lincoln told Stanly accurately reflected his state of mind. He has written: "The proximate and procuring cause of the proclamation, as I conceive, is not far to seek. It was issued primarily and chiefly as a political necessity, and took on the character of a military necessity only because the President had been brought to believe that if he did not keep the Radical portion of his party at his back he could not long be sure of keeping an army at the front."[4]

Congressman George W. Julian, who, although one of those whom Lincoln's young secretary Hay called "Jacobins," was on the best of terms with the President, was of the same opinion. He wrote: "Mr. Lincoln feared that enlistments would cease, and that Congress would even refuse the necessary supplies to carry on the war, if

he declined any longer to place it on a clearly defined antislavery basis."[5] Lincoln's friend and partner William H. Herndon must have received information of a similar nature, for he wrote: "When he freed the slaves there was not heart in it."[6]

That unless McClellan won a decisive victory he would have to do something to placate the Radicals or there would be the devil to pay as soon as Congress met must have become obvious to Lincoln on September 17, 1862, the day the battle took place. While the guns were booming at Antietam, Stevens was speaking at Lancaster and what he said must have sounded ominous to the President. The Commoner made it plain that as soon as Congress reassembled he meant to strike where Lincoln was most anxious for Congress not to interfere—at slavery in the border states. Here is what he said:

"I have protested against the present policy, not only to the people, but to the face of the President and his Cabinet, and on the floor of Congress; . . . told them that they were exercising too much lenity at the request of border statesmen—not one of whom, in my judgment, has loyalty in his heart. I have accused the prime minister [Seward] to his face of having gone back from the faith he taught us, and instead of arming every man, black or white, who could fight for the Union, withholding a well-meaning President from doing so. . . . I have told these things to the President and Cabinet, and they replied—'It may come to this'. *'Come to this!'* when 200,000 men have melted away, and $2,000,000,000 spent! *'Come to this!'* when another half million lives have been lost, and a billion dollars more laid upon you in taxation. *I cannot and will not stand this."* He then told his constituents that if they returned him to Congress he would introduce a bill providing *"that every man be armed, black and white, who can aid in crushing the rebellion; that every inch of*

---

[4] Rice, *op. cit.*, pp. 530–31.

[5] *Ibid.*, p. 62.
[6] *Life of Lincoln* (edition annotated by Paul Angle), p. 483.

rebel soil be taken and sold to pay the debt of this war."[7]

What did this mean?

It meant that Stevens intended to introduce a bill requiring the administration to draft into the armed forces not only white men but black men, *including all able-bodied slaves in the border states.* On June 16 of that year he had managed to have a bill adopted authorizing the President to employ persons of African descent in the armed forces and providing that "when any man or boy of African descent shall render any such service . . . he, his mother, and his wife and children, shall for ever thereafter be free, any law, usage, or custom whatsoever to the contrary notwithstanding." The bill had excluded slaves belonging to border state slaveholders, now the exclusion was to end. To draft able-bodied slaves in the border states, or even to permit them to enlist, meant the end of slavery in those states. Now Lincoln had pinned his hopes on the border states helping him to solve the slavery problem in the only way he considered practical—by the adoption of compensated gradual emancipation with federal aid. More than that! He believed that if they did so the war would be practically ended. If Stevens succeeded in getting his bill adopted all hope of reaching that solution would have disappeared. For if the President threatened to veto the bill, the powerful chairman of the Ways and Means Committee might answer with the threat of holding up appropriations for the Army. Now that McClellan's victory had proved indecisive there appeared to be only one way to head off Stevens—to issue a preliminary Emancipation Proclamation.

None of the calamities the President had predicted might happen if he issued an Emancipation Proclamation put in an appearance. Kentucky did *not* "go out to the South." Twenty thousand soldiers from that state did *not* "throw down their muskets." Half the officers did *not* "fling down their arms." Fifty thousand soldiers from the border states did *not* "go over to the rebels." The President's predictions—some of which were sufficiently publicized—added to assurances given by border state slaveholders led the Confederates to believe, however, that if they took advantage of the opportunity some of these things might come to pass. They promptly invaded Kentucky. But on October 12, 1862, the Confederate commander Braxton Bragg ruefully reported to Richmond: "The campaign here was predicated on the belief and the most positive assurances that the people of Kentucky would rise in mass and assert their independence. No people ever had so favorable an opportunity, but I am distressed to add there was little or no disposition to avail of it."[8] In the fall elections, when Lincoln's own state went over to the opposition, Kentucky and other loyal border states sent an almost solid delegation of Unionists to Congress.

Stevens had always claimed that the President's anxiety concerning Kentucky and other loyal border states was exaggerated. As early as December 16, 1861, he said on the floor of Congress: "I do not understand where the President gets the facts in this respect. I believe he has been misled. I believe he is laboring under a hallucination of mind upon the subject as fatal as that of Samson under the manipulation of Delilah." The fact that in the Kentucky state elections of August, 1861, three-fourths of those elected to the legislature were Unionists makes his skepticism understandable. Lincoln appears to have used the border state argument to delay issuing the proclamation in the hope that the slaveholders of those states would have the wisdom and the patriotism to adopt the solution he so greatly favored.

On December 1, 1862, he again presented to Congress—and in doing so to the slave states, rebel as well as loyal—his compensated gradual emancipation plan. It evoked no response from the slave states

---

[7] *Liberator*, Sept. 19, 1862. Italics in original.

[8] *Offic. Rec.*, 1 ser., vol. XVI, pt. 1, p. 1088.

and was coldly received by Congress. On January 1 of the new year, he issued the final proclamation. After the document had made its appearance, Adam Gurowski wrote in his *Diary:* "The patriots of both Houses, as the exponents of the noble and loftiest aspirations of the American people, whipped in—and this literally, not figuratively—whipped Mr. Lincoln into the glory of having issued the Emancipation Proclamation. The laws promulgated by this dying Congress initiated the Emancipation—generated the Proclamation of the 22d of September, and of January 1st. History will not allow one to wear borrowed plumage."[9]

Robert Mallory of Kentucky, in a speech in the House on February 24, 1863, charged that the President had yielded to pressure from Stevens. The Commoner did not reply, and no supporter of the President ventured to contradict the charge. Mallory said in part:

"Soon after the War broke out, the gentleman from Pennsylvania and his great allies Horace Greeley and Wendell Phillips, and all his little allies in the House, began their pressure on the President and the Republican Party. In vain the President from time to time besought his friends, and those who had not been his friends, to relieve him from this pressure.

"The gentleman from Pennsylvania and his allies persevered. They demanded of the President his proclamation of emancipation. He refused. Again they demanded

---

[9] *Diary*, vol. II, pp. 99–100.

it; he refused again, but more faintly and exhibited himself in his letter to his 'dear friend Greeley' in the most pitiable and humiliating attitude in which an American President was ever exhibited to the American people—But the gentleman from Pennsylvania still pressed him and educated him and the Republicans.

"The Committee of Divines from Chicago, armed with authority from the other but not the better world, was brought to aid in the pressure; but apparently in vain. Sir, do you remember the reply of the President to that committee? It was conclusive, unanswerable. The reasons given for refusing to proclaim the freedom of slaves in the rebel states are perfectly irrefutable. 'I have not the power to do it,' said the President, 'and if I had, the proclamation would be impotent; it would be like the Pope uttering his Bull against the comet.'

"We then supposed the matter had been settled. But scarcely had this confidence entered the great conservative heart of the nation, when feeble or false, or both, or yielding to the teachings of the gentleman from Pennsylvania, he suddenly without notice, issued his celebrated Emancipation Proclamation."

The Kentucky representative was seriously mistaken in believing that in issuing the final proclamation Lincoln had given up the struggle and had adopted Stevens's program. As has already been remarked the President had a way of yielding so the advantage remained with him.

1958

A Great Capacity for Moral Growth?*

RICHARD N. CURRENT

Lincoln is a paradoxical hero. His name has been lighted down from generation to generation as a synonym for liberty and equality. His name also has been made to symbolize the opposite doctrine of white supremacy and black oppression.

Lincoln the friend of freedom is well and widely known. For most liberals, he occupies a place beside that of Thomas Jefferson. For many Negroes, he long has held a lone position as a kind of folk god.

His exaltation dates back to January 1, 1863, when throughout the North and the conquered areas of the South the colored people held proclamation meetings to celebrate his deed in their behalf. At a Washington meeting, which began on New Year's Eve, a pastor told each member of his flock to "get down on *both knees* to thank Almighty God for his freedom and President Lincoln too." To people such as these the proclamation, whatever its inward meaning, was the outward sign of an answer to their prayers.

Most of the abolitionists joined in honoring Lincoln at the time of his emancipation edict, but some of them qualified their praise, still doubting his sincerity. At last, when he had won congressional approval for the Thirteenth Amendment, almost all the lingering doubts were dispelled and almost all the doubters satisfied. Even William Lloyd Garrison no longer could con-

tain himself. To a Boston meeting of celebrators Garrison said: "And to whom is the country more immediately indebted for this vital and saving amendment of the Constitution than, perhaps, to any other man? I believe I may confidently answer—to the humble rail splitter of Illinois—to the Presidential chainbreaker for millions of the oppressed—to Abraham Lincoln!"

Less well known than Lincoln the slaves' chainbreaker is Lincoln the hero of Negro-baiters and white supremacists. Yet he has been that kind of image also. Few Negroes or friends of the Negro ever admired him more or praised him oftener than did a certain Mississippi advocate of white supremacy, James K. Vardaman.

In the early 1900s this long-haired, dramatic Great White Chief of Mississippi stood out as the most rabid racialist in the most racist-dominated Southern state. When Theodore Roosevelt dined with the Negro educator Booker T. Washington in the White House, Vardaman sneered at the President as a "wild broncho buster and coon-flavored miscegenationist." In his campaign for the governorship Vardaman said that if he were in office, he would do what he could to protect a captured Negro "fiend" from a lynching mob. "But if I were a private citizen I would head the mob to string the brute up, and I haven't much respect for a white man who wouldn't." As governor, he opposed what he called "this policy of spoiling young Negroes by educating them." In the United States Senate

---

* From *The Lincoln Nobody Knows* by Richard Current. Copyright 1958 McGraw-Hill Book Company. Used by permission.

during World War I, he took every opportunity to expound his belief in a white man's country. Do not draft Negroes into the Army, he advised his fellow senators, for it is dangerous to give them a sense of citizenship and a training in the use of guns. Repeal the Fifteenth Amendment so that Negroes cannot even pretend to have the right to vote. Enforce segregation and do not let the races mix, for the Negro is by nature morally inferior and must never be allowed to corrupt the pure blood of the heaven-favored white. Such were the aims and the convictions to which Vardaman devoted his real eloquence.

This Mississippian once made a pilgrimage to his hero's home town, to Springfield, Illinois. The year was 1909, the centennial of Lincoln's birth. The previous year had been a disgraceful one for Springfield. Municipal leaders were looking ahead to anniversary celebrations when, on a summer night, thousands of the townspeople suddenly went wild with hate. They set out to lynch a Negro who (though innocent) was being held on the charge of raping a white woman, and when the sheriff frustrated them by spiriting the man away, they turned their vengeance upon the whole colored community. It took 4,000 state troopers all of a week to quiet the city and end the so called race riot. (This incident, by the way, and not some crisis in the South, gave rise to the National Association for the Advancement of Colored People.) When Vardaman visited Springfield the feeling among local Negrophobes still ran high, and a huge crowd came out to applaud his lecture on the inherent virtue of the white race.

Vardaman never tired of praising "the immortal Lincoln," never tired of quoting "the wise words of this wondrous man." He insisted that he and Lincoln saw eye to eye. "I have made a very careful study of Mr. Lincoln's ideas on this question," he declared in a Senate speech, "and I have said often, and I repeat here, that my views and his on the race question are substantially identical." Next to Thomas Jefferson,

he thought, Lincoln understood the Negro problem better than anyone else of former days. To prove his point, Vardaman cited Lincoln's advocacy of Negro colonization. He explained the Lincoln policy thus:

"Up to the very time of Mr. Lincoln's death he told the Negroes who came to see him here in Washington, 'You will not be permitted to share in the government of this country, and I am not prepared to say that you ought to be, if I had the power to give you that right.' "

"He said further: 'The shackles of slavery will be stricken from your arms. You, the educated and more fortunate members of your race, take the others and go to some country'—his idea was the same that Jefferson's was—'and there work out your own salvation.' I do not pretend to quote Mr. Lincoln literally. The great desire of his patriotic heart was that the friction might be avoided by deportation."

The words of Lincoln that Vardaman repeated oftenest, the words he knew almost by heart, came from the debate with Douglas at Charleston, Illinois, on September 18, 1858. These words formed for Vardaman a sort of golden text. Here they are, exactly as Lincoln uttered them:

"I will say then that I am not, nor ever have been in favor of bringing about in any way the social and political equality of the white and black races, [applause]—that I am not nor ever have been in favor of making voters or jurors of Negroes, nor of qualifying them to hold office, nor to intermarry with white people; and I will say in addition to this that there is a physical difference between the white and black races which I believe will forever forbid the two races living together on terms of social and political equality. And inasmuch as they cannot so live, while they do remain together there must be the position of superior and inferior, and I as much as any other man am in favor of having the superior position assigned to the white race."

Yet, despite these contradictions, Lincoln does deserve his reputation as emancipator. True, his claim to the honor is supported very uncertainly, if at all, by the proclamation itself. The honor has a better basis in the support he gave to the Thirteenth Amendment. It is well founded also in his greatness as the war leader, who carried the nation safely through the four-year struggle that brought freedom in its train. But the best reason for his reputation is, perhaps, to be discovered in something else. Consider the example he set his fellow Americans by treating all men as human beings, regardless of the pigment of their skin.

The real and final emancipation of the Negro may depend more upon attitudes than upon laws. The laws, the constitutional amendments, are important, even indispensable. But, as the abolitionist Henry Wilson observed, many of those who voted for the Thirteenth Amendment and other antislavery measures did so without conversion or conviction. Many acted from a desire to hurt the slaveholder rather than to help the slave. Within their hearts still lurked the "foul spirit of caste," the spirit of race prejudice. Until this prejudice was overcome, the Negroes, though no longer the slaves of individual masters, would continue to be in a sense the slaves of the community as a whole.

Now, Lincoln himself was one of those who veered to an actively antislavery line for reasons of wartime expediency. He did not pretend to do otherwise. And he was well aware of race prejudice as an existing fact in the United States. Hence his pathetic eagerness to find new homes for freedmen in foreign lands. Yet he had the capacity to rise above prejudice, and he grandly rose above it. Again and again, during the last two years of his life, he made the White House a scene of practical demonstrations of respect for human worth and dignity. He proved that whites and Negroes, without the master-servant tie, could get along together happily in his own official home, no matter what the antagonisms that might trouble the nation at large. A kindly, unself-conscious host, he greeted

Negro visitors as no President had done before.

The distinguished former slave Frederick Douglass called upon Lincoln several times at his summer cottage at the Soldiers' Home. Douglass made at least three visits to the White House. On the final occasion, when he tried to enter as an invited guest at the inaugural reception in 1865, policemen manhandled him and forced him out. Making his way in again, he managed to catch Lincoln's eye. "Here comes my friend Douglass," the President exclaimed, and, leaving the circle of guests he had been conversing with, he took Douglass by the hand and began to chat with him. Years later Douglass wrote: "In all my interviews with Mr. Lincoln I was impressed with his entire freedom from popular prejudice against the colored race. He was the first great man that I talked with in the United States freely, who in no single instance reminded me of the difference between himself and myself, of the difference of color, and I thought that all the more remarkable because he came from a state where there were black laws."

There were black laws in Illinois indeed —laws that denied the Negro the vote and deprived him of other rights. Illinois in those days was a Jim Crow state. That was where Lincoln had spent most of the years of his manhood, among people who had migrated from slave country farther south, as he himself had done. Naturally he had shared some of the Negrophobic feeling of his neighbors in Kentucky, in southern Indiana, in central Illinois. That was where, in geography and in sentiment, he came from.

But he did not stay there. The most remarkable thing about him was his tremendous power of growth. He grew in sympathy, in the breadth of his humaneness, as he grew in other aspects of the mind and spirit. In more ways than one he succeeded in breaking through the narrow bounds of his early environment.

This helps to explain and to reconcile those conflicting images of Lincoln—on the one hand, the racist; on the other, the champion of the common man, black as well as white. The one view reflects the position he started from, the other the position he was moving toward. There is confusion regarding particular phases of his presidential career because nobody knows for sure just what point he had reached at any given moment. But there should be little question as to which way he was going.

To see Lincoln in this light is to make him more than ever relevant, more than ever inspiring, for us in the stormy present, in the fiery trial through which we too must pass. Lincoln, as a symbol of man's ability to outgrow his prejudices, still serves the cause of human freedom. He will go on serving so long as boundaries of color hem in and hinder any man, any woman, any child.

BIBLIOGRAPHICAL NOTE

All the biographers, of course, treat with comparative fullness the subject of Lincoln and slavery. A basic work, by a wartime Illinois congressman who knew the President, and who stressed the antislavery theme in his career, is Isaac N. Arnold's *The History of Abraham Lincoln and the Overthrow of American Slavery* (1866). A later work by Arnold, again emphasizing this theme, is *The Life of Abraham Lincoln* (1885). Another useful work by a contemporary antislavery politician is Henry Wilson's *History of the Rise and Fall of the Slave Power in America* (3 vols., 1872–77). Probably the best exposition of Lincoln's own, preferred emancipation plan is to be found in the second volume of Randall's *Lincoln the President*.

A recent and forthright statement of the view that Lincoln used his famous proclamation as a dodge to delay actual freedom is presented by Ralph Korngold in *Thaddeus Stevens* (1955). See especially Chapter VII, "The Truth about the Emancipation Proclamation." Some contemporary impressions of Lincoln's slow and incomplete conversion to the antislavery cause are recorded in *Reminiscences of Abraham Lincoln*, edited by Allen T. Rice (1885). On Lincoln's relationships with Negroes, see Frederick Douglass's recollections in the Rice volume; Benjamin Quarles's *The Negro in the Civil War* (1953); and Warren A. Beck's "Lincoln and Negro Colonization in Central America," in the *Abraham Lincoln Quarterly* (1950).

James K. Vardaman's views on Lincoln and the Negro are repeated and elaborated in a number of his Senate speeches, two of which have been noted in particular, those of February 6, 1914, and August 16, 1917, in the *Congressional Record*. There is a sketch of Vardaman in the *Dictionary of American Biography*, and there are several contemporary magazine articles concerning him, but no full-length study of the man has yet been published.

1966

Lincoln and Equal Rights: The Authenticity of the Wadsworth Letter[*]

LUDWELL H. JOHNSON

In the current national debate on the race problem, the authority of the Great Emancipator has been claimed by both sides. Some have represented Lincoln as an archsegregationist by quoting from the 1858 debates, in which he opposed political and social equality for Negroes, and by alluding to his advocacy of various colonizationist schemes.[1] The task of capturing the President for the equalitarian cause has been more difficult; the evidence here consists mainly of general remarks by Lincoln about his dedication to the principles of the Declaration of Independence, his suggestions to Governor Michael Hahn in March, 1864, and a letter he is said to have written to Major General James S. Wadsworth in January, 1864.[2] The last item goes far toward putting Lincoln squarely in the equalitarian camp—if it is authentic. There are circumstances, however, that cast doubt on its genuineness.

The letter, as it appears in Basler's *Collected Works of Lincoln*, follows:

TO JAMES S. WADSWORTH

[January, 1864?]

You desire to know, in the event of our complete success in the field, the same being followed by a loyal and cheerful submission on the part of the South, if universal amnesty should not be accompanied with universal suffrage.

Now, since you know my private inclinations as to what terms should be granted to the South in the contingency mentioned, I will here add, that if our success should thus be realized, followed by such desired results, I cannot see, if universal amnesty is granted, how, under the circumstances, I can avoid exacting in return universal suffrage, or, at least, suffrage on the basis of intelligence and military service.

How to better the condition of the colored race has long been a study which has attracted my serious and careful attention; hence I think

* Ludwell H. Johnson, "Lincoln and Equal Rights: The Authenticity of the Wadsworth Letter," *Journal of Southern History*, XXXII (February 1966), 83–87. Copyright 1966 by the Southern Historical Association. Reprinted by permission of the Managing Editor.

1 For example, see the advertisement of the Citizens' Councils of America, Washington *Post*, February 10, 1964.

2 See the *New York Times*, February 11, 1964, for comments of various historians on the advertisement mentioned in note 1. None of them mentioned the Wadsworth letter. The Washington *Post*, February 10, 1964, cited it in an editorial rebutting the advertisement. In arguing for Lincoln's commitment to equal rights, Fawn M. Brodie, in "Who Won the Civil War, Anyway?" *New York Times Book Review*, August 5, 1962, stressed Lincoln's "generally forgotten" letter to Wadsworth. The letter is accepted by Eric McKitrick, "The Decision to Reconstruct the South, 1865–1867: A Question of Alternatives," in Leonard W. Levy and Merrill D. Peterson (eds.), *Major Crises in American History: Documentary Problems* (2 vols.; New York, 1962), II, 15; and by Marvin R. Cain, "Lincoln's Views on Slavery and the Negro: A Suggestion," *Historian*, XXVI (August, 1964), 512, 515. No attempt has been made to compile an exhaustive list of such instances.

I am clear and decided as to what course I shall pursue in the premises, regarding it a religious duty, as the nation's guardian of these people, who have so heroically vindicated their manhood on the battle-field, where, in assisting to save the life of the Republic, they have demonstrated in blood their right to the ballot, which is but the humane protection of the flag they have so fearlessly defended.

The restoration of the Rebel States to the Union must rest upon the principle of civil and political equality of both races; and it must be sealed by general amnesty.[3]

The first three paragraphs were published in the *New York Tribune*, September 26, 1865. As the source for its version, the *Tribune* cited the *Southern Advocate* of September 18, 1865. The editors of the *Collected Works* admit that they have not been able to find this newspaper (neither has the present writer), to say nothing of the original letter.[4] The fourth paragraph did not appear in the *Tribune*. It originated as a quotation appearing in the Marquis de Chambrun's "Personal Recollections of Mr. Lincoln," *Scribner's Magazine*, Vol. XIII, No. 1 (January, 1893), p. 36: "They [Lincoln's ideas] seem to me far better summed up in a letter he wrote in 1864 to General Wadsworth, one of the victims of the civil war, in which he said . . ." and then follows the fourth paragraph enclosed in quotation marks; no other part of the letter is quoted. The editors of the 1905 edition of Nicolay and Hay's *Complete Works* attached it to the three paragraphs originally published in the *Tribune*, while omitting to point out that the Marquis himself had not alluded to those paragraphs.[5] The editors of Bas-

ler's *Collected Works* likewise included the fourth paragraph, citing the *Scribner's* article as their source. They then go on to say: "The contents of the excerpt [meaning the entire letter] is [sic], however, closely in keeping with the views expressed by Lincoln elsewhere (see Fragment, August 26, 1863, *supra*), and seems to be genuine." But the "fragment" cited makes no statement whatever about Negro suffrage, nor does Lincoln's letter to James C. Conkling of the same date, of which the fragment may at one time have been a part.[6]

Internal inconsistencies alone cast serious doubt on the integrity of the Wadsworth letter. The first paragraph is merely introductory and may be ignored. In the second, universal amnesty is made conditional upon either (1) suffrage for all Negroes as well as whites or (2) suffrage for Negroes "on the basis of intelligence and military service."

In the third paragraph, suffrage is asserted to be the "right" of those Negroes who have served in the Union army. This contrasts with the previous statement, which by clear implication links amnesty for Southern whites with suffrage for Southern Negroes. Furthermore, the style of this paragraph (in comparison to that of the second) does not sound like Lincoln, who was not given to talking of his "religious duty" or to describing himself as the "nation's guardian" of the Negro.

It is the final paragraph, however, which is totally anomalous. Here Lincoln supposedly asserts that the restoration of the Southern states "must rest upon the principle of civil and political equality of both races; and it must be sealed by general amnesty." No other public or private statement by Lincoln even remotely approximates the substance of that sentence. As is well known, Lincoln was anything but an equalitarian. For years he was a proponent of colonization as the best solution to the race question. In both his first and second

[3] Roy P. Basler *et al.* (eds.), *The Collected Works of Abraham Lincoln* (8 vols. and index; New Brunswick, 1953–55), VII, 101–2.

[4] *Ibid.*, 102n. The letter is not in the Wadsworth Papers, which are now in the Library of Congress.

[5] John G. Nicolay and John Hay (eds.), *Complete Works of Abraham Lincoln* (Biographical Edition, 12 vols.; New York, 1905), XI, 130–31. The letter was included in an appendix devoted to items that did not appear in Nicolay and Hay's original edition of the *Works*. This appendix was compiled by "numerous collectors" and especially by Gilbert Tracy.

[6] Basler *et al.* (eds.), *Collected Works of Lincoln*, VII, 102n; VI, 406–11.

annual messages to Congress he asked for appropriations for that purpose. The day before the Emancipation Proclamation was promulgated, the President signed a contract with Bernard Kock, who undertook to settle Negroes on Île à Vache, Haiti, for $50 a head. The colony was actually established in 1863, but failed miserably, the survivors being brought back to the United States in March, 1864.[7] On July 1 of that year John Hay remarked in his diary that Lincoln had given up colonization, apparently because of the dishonesty of the speculators involved.[8] However, if Benjamin F. Butler can be believed, Lincoln was still looking for a practicable method of expatriation just before his death. According to Butler, in April, 1865, he had a conversation with the President in which the latter said: "But what shall we do with the negroes after they are free? I can hardly believe that the South and North can live in peace, unless we can get rid of the negroes." The Union now had a large navy, Lincoln continued. Would it not be possible to send the freedmen overseas? He asked Butler to think about it and give him the benefit of his advice.[9]

If Lincoln wanted Negroes out of the country so badly, it is scarcely possible that he would make their "civil and political equality" a condition of reconstruction. And there is direct as well as circumstantial evidence demonstrating that he intended no such thing. His proclamation of December 8, 1863, establishing conditions under which Union governments could be erected in the South, said nothing whatever about suffrage, other than to disqualify certain categories of high-ranking Confederates.[10]

Such a government was set up in Louisiana by General Nathaniel P. Banks under the President's careful supervision. The free Negroes of the state urged Lincoln to insure that they be enfranchised by the new constitution. The result was the most extreme position Lincoln ever took on Negro suffrage, the well-known confidential letter of March 13, 1864, to Louisiana's Union governor, Michael Hahn. In it he "barely" suggested for Hahn's "private consideration" that "very intelligent" Negroes and those who had served in the United States army be given the vote. "But," he concluded, "this is only a suggestion, not to the public, but to you alone."[11] The Wadsworth letter, it will be recalled, was supposedly written early in 1864; necessarily, it could not have been written later than May, when Wadsworth was killed. Lincoln's attitude remained unchanged to the very end, for in his last public address (April 11, 1865) he said: "It is also unsatisfactory to some that the elective franchise is not given to the colored man [by the new Louisiana constitution]. I would myself prefer that it were now conferred on the very intelligent, and on those who serve our cause as soldiers."[12]

These statements are consistent with the second paragraph of the Wadsworth letter. They are only partially in agreement with the third paragraph. And they are completely at variance with the final paragraph. Had that paragraph been available to the *Tribune*, it would most certainly have been printed. Horace Greeley's slogan for reconstruction in 1865 was "Universal Amnesty and Impartial Suffrage."[13]

What doubtless happened was that the quotation from the Marquis de Chambrun's *Scribner's* article was merely his inaccurate summary of the letter which appeared in

[7] Frederic Bancroft, "The Colonization of American Negroes," in Jacob E. Cooke, *Frederic Bancroft, Historian* (Norman, Okla., 1957), 203; William B. Hesseltine, *Lincoln's Plan of Reconstruction* (Tuscaloosa, 1960), 93–94.

[8] Tyler Dennett (ed.), *Lincoln and the Civil War in the Diaries and Letters of John Hay* (New York, 1939), 203.

[9] Benjamin F. Butler, *Autobiography and Personal Reminiscences of Major-General Benj. F. Butler* (Boston, 1892), 903.

[10] Basler *et al.* (eds.), *Collected Works of Lincoln*, VII, 53–56.

[11] *Ibid.*, 243.
[12] *Ibid.*, VIII, 403.
[13] Glyndon G. Van Deusen, *Horace Greeley, Nineteenth-Century Crusader* (Philadelphia, 1953), 324. The *Tribune* (September 26, 1865) claimed that the letters (without the fourth paragraph, of course) showed that Lincoln favored both universal amnesty and universal suffrage.

the *Tribune* and other newspapers. Either he or *Scribner's* added quotation marks, whereupon it was taken by the editors of Nicolay and Hay's *Complete Works* and Basler's *Collected Works* as an additional paragraph.

To conclude, then, the first two paragraphs of the Wadsworth letter are completely in agreement with Lincoln's public and private statements on Negro suffrage. The third paragraph does not ring true and quite possibly may have been added by some zealous member of the *Tribune* staff. The fourth paragraph is not authentic. It is, of course, the key one for purposes of the present dispute on the race question.

Lincoln has been dead for a century, and yet he is so little understood that his spirit continues to be invoked to sanctify some absolute political or moral principle. It must reveal something about the American character when the most consummate pragmatist in our history is transformed into a Moses with commandments.

CHAPTER 7

The Causes and the Nature of the Civil War

Today scholars object to all accounts which attribute the coming of the Civil War to overly simplified explanations involving a single cause. Obviously slavery was the great source of sectional conflict, but a precise analysis involves the exploration of a very complex web of factors. In a 1960 symposium on causation and the Civil War, Cushing Strout and Lee Benson discussed the intricate problems inherent in the process of explanation and reminded their readers of the enormous difficulty in shaping causal theories acceptable to all, or even most scholars. Nevertheless, historians must continue the effort to explain events or give up the task of writing history. The causal theory which emerged in the North and the West during the 1850s and ruled the postwar era described sectional struggle as "an irrepressible conflict" between free labor and slavery. The most vehement and sustained attack on this conception was made in the 1930s and '40s by James G. Randall and Avery O. Craven who spoke of "the needless war," "the repressible conflict" which could be traced to the "emotionalism," the "irrationality," the "uncontrolled fanaticism" of abolitionists and Southern "fire eaters," and the "irresponsibility" of politicians in "a blundering generation." Randall, appalled by the slaughter and waste of the conflict, gave vent to an understandable reaction against the glorification of war and the romanticized accounts of a grim, and bloody struggle. He was also influenced by changing interpretations concerning the origins of World War I. In 1940 he briefly noted an abrupt "about face" among American scholars "around 1935" which moved away from German "war guilt" and Wilsonian idealization of the war as a "defense of civilization." The conflict seemed rather to be a "needless" and "repressible" mass killing for which many forces and all major participants shared the blame. In describing the American Civil War, Randall stressed the "crisis psychosis," the "highly artificial, almost fabricated" issue of slavery, "the despairing plunge, the unmotivated drift," the "twisted argument," the "advocate of rule or ruin, and the reform-your-neighbor prophet." Avery O. Craven in 1942 issued an even sharper denial of irrepressibility in his insistence that slavery was not a real war issue or even more than a minor factor in Southern life.

The first telling critique of the "needless war" school was made in 1949 by Arthur M. Schlesinger, Jr., who stressed the indifference of his predecessors to the reality of slavery as a social evil and a moral dilemma. He complained that modern scholars, callously indifferent to the oppressiveness of slavery, had arbitrarily denounced the critics of "the peculiar institution" as "fanatics." In reality, leaders of the Civil War era had only two alternatives: to abolish slavery or to continue it. Schlesinger took the arguments for an end to slavery without a major social upheaval and refuted them one by one. Pieter Geyl joined the discussion in 1951 by attacking Randall's assumption that history was governed by the conscious will of the majority. Every age, it would seem, is "a blundering generation" and both masses and leaders are often moved by "irrational" impulses. History sometimes moves on the plane of violent political storms and great social cataclysms, and Randall and Craven were mistaken in supposing that all great issues could be resolved within the framework of "liberal" compromise politics. Geyl, like Schlesinger, charged the Randall school with failure to accept abolitionist convictions as "a profound historical reality."

Randall and Craven built upon the work of the two giants of the first generation of professional American historians, Frederick Jackson Turner and Charles Beard. In 1892 Turner announced his celebrated "frontier thesis" which based history largely on geographical and economic forces. The "frontier" was presumably the great national crucible which transformed European men, ideas, and institutions into American democratic society. As his critics have noted, Turner neglected the influence of the East and of Europe, and tended to ignore immigration, urbanism, and the harsh realities of ethnic, religious, and racial conflict. Turner never really tried to explain the Civil War, and indeed, the nature of his thesis would have made the construction of a plausible explanation nearly impossible. The frontier experience had always been a far more complex social event in the North than Turner supposed, and his theory was simply beside the point for the Southwestern settlement, achieved largely by masters and their slaves. As one scholar so aptly phrased it, "Simon Legree was a frontier farmer." Turner thought of America as populated largely by a democratic yeomanry living from the land, and for explanatory patterns he relied heavily upon the sectional disputes between long settled Eastern areas and the newer, Western and more "democratic" communities. Yet even as Turner wrote, the Republic was moving relentlessly into the industrial era.

Although Charles Beard appreciated Turner's geographical and economic "realism," he preferred to deal with the raw and "real" economic factors which were changing America into an urban society based on mass production. For both Beard and Turner, slavery and abolition were secondary forces of less consequence than the frontier and the power of emerging capitalism. In 1927 Beard saw the Civil War and Reconstruction as "the second American Revolution" which defeated the last strongholds of "agrarianism" and established the supremacy of "industrialism." The image created by Thomas Jefferson and others of the independent, democratic, and largely self-sufficient farmer caught the imagination of both Turner and Beard—this "agrarian" was the loser in the major struggles of American society between the Constitutional Convention and the collapse of the Populist revolt in the 1890s. So sharp and furious was Beard's attack on Northern capitalism that, as Thomas J. Pressly observed in 1954, he became at times an ally of Calhoun and the proslavery argument. The habit of describing opposition to the "capitalists" as "mechanics and farmers," "agricultural interests," or "agrarians" involved basic confusions and even contradictions (see Chapter 2).

Beard described the Hamiltonian Federalists, the Whigs, and the Republicans as the representatives of an emerging American capitalism which was opposed by "the planting leaders of Jefferson's agricultural party" in the defense of "agricultural values" against "the onslaught" of rapacious capitalism. The entire slavery controversy seemed to enter the political scene as "mere subterfuge" for "an economic policy that meant the exploitation of the South for the benefit of Northern capitalism." As Staughton Lynd suggested in 1963, Beard confused at least three distinct agricultural groups: frontier subsistence farmers of the West, Northern commercial farmers, and Southern slaveowners. Moreover, Beard dismissed Republican antislavery inclinations as mere political rhetoric, a shield for capitalist conspiracy. Finally Beard tended to support the Southern school of thought which saw Reconstruction as the conspiratorial plunder of the South under the cover of the bogus cause of Negro freedom. Presumably the triumphant Republicans after the victory of 1860 proceeded to enact a long list of pro-capitalist measures—railroad subsidies, greenback currency issues, high tariffs, immigrant labor contract laws, and many more. Reconstruction was a mere device to consolidate Civil War capitalist gains behind the mask of equalitarian ideology.

A group of historians led by Thomas C. Cochran, Irwin Unger, Robert P. Sharkey, and Stanley Coben have cast doubt on nearly every aspect of Beard's economic thesis. They found no monolithic set of capitalist interests, but rather a complicated jigsaw pattern of competing and conflicting economic interests. Sometimes clear concepts of public morality overrode confused or muffled notions of business goals. Bray Hammond in 1961 provided an interesting demonstration of the falsity of the old idea that Civil War currency policies represented the rush of triumphant capitalists to produce enough currency for an expanding industrial economy. The plan to issue paper "greenbacks" which would be secured largely by faith in the federal government rather than by gold deposits was not the scheme of an activistic business community but actually a desperate wartime necessity, an unusually "immoral" scheme deplored and regretted by most people. For a time Secretary Chase, along with many politicians and businessmen, was convinced of both the "immorality" and the total unconstitutionality of the plan.

Robert P. Sharkey revealed in 1959 that organized labor had favored greenbacks from "general hatred and distrust of banks, bankers, and banknotes." The allegedly distressed "agrarians," who were actually enjoying a general prosperity, showed little concern with either the expansion or the deflation of the currency. Western bankers loved the greenbacks but Eastern bankers "with a vested interest in deflation" opposed them along with high protective tariffs and the whole apparatus of national war banking. The major financiers of the Northeast wished above all else to return to specie payment. As Sharkey suggested, manufacturers were divided among themselves, with wealthy New England mill men supporting a contraction of the currency and iron and steel men of the middle states seeking soft money policies. The political parties were also badly divided. Before 1867 the Democrats opposed soft money and then bitterly split into conflicting factions. Although Radicals such as Stevens, Wade, Butler, and Phillips favored greenbacks, other Republicans took several opposing positions. One might argue that many radicals tended to embrace high protection and soft money, but this argument is rather remote from Beard's line of thought.

In 1964 Irwin Unger who complained about the practice of supporting Beard's thesis with the example of the return to specie payment during 1879, pointed to the fact that Western businessmen denounced the action. Support came from importers and international traders in opposition to fluctuating paper money as a constant threat to their profits. Unger rejected the whole conception of the years between 1860 and 1880 as an era which brought economic revolution and marked the transformation of rural America into an urban, industrial society. The continuity of ideas and events impressed him far more than the changes which took place.

Thomas C. Cochran had made in 1961 an even sharper thrust at the Beardian notion that "the so-called Civil War . . . was a social war . . . making vast changes in the arrangement of classes, in the accumulation and distribution of wealth, in the course of industrial development." Cochran insisted that the war retarded industrial growth: the construction business fell to a lower growth rate; the rate of increase in total commodity output was greater before and after than during the war; pig iron, bituminous coal, copper, and businesses dependent on immigration all experienced a slackening of expansion; and the financial community registered the adverse effects of the war in bank loans and net capital formation. By the late 1850s, Cochran concluded, the United States had become "a rapidly maturing industrial state" which probably would have matured even more quickly without the Civil War.

Stanley Coben in 1959 gave particular stress to the years just after the Civil War and insisted that Radical Reconstruction could not be traced to economic conspiracy in the dominant Northeast. Many parts of the complex and divided business world were at war with one another. Individual radical politicians supported some "pro-capitalist" bills and opposed others: Thaddeus Stevens was a fervent protectionist *and* an advocate of paper inflation, while Charles Sumner defended very low tariffs *and* strongly opposed the resumption of specie payment. The same was true of business leaders; and the New York bankers and merchants who had the most to gain were very critical of the Radicals. In the final analysis it was simply not possible to use the business interests of the Northeast to account for the motives and goals of the Radicals.

Thus, the most popular historical explanation for the war ever devised in America collapsed. Not only did the notion of the Civil War as a capitalist conspiracy fail, but comparable conceptualizations of Reconstruction also expired. It was no longer possible to describe Reconstruction as an attempt "by the masters of capital" to bribe the West with railroads and pensions, to distract the East by waving the "bloody shirt" of "war" issues, and to concentrate on the economic exploitation of the South. In the final analysis even Beard's terminology was suspect. "Agrarian" has no value as a term of explanation and "capitalism" must be used cautiously and carefully. In one sense the slave-owners were themselves "agricultural capitalists," and the Civil War might be described as a struggle between capitalist factions. Certainly, as Staughton Lynd indicated in 1963, no theory which ignored slavery could be satisfactory. The scholars did not throw away the tool of economic explanation, but they did insist that theories take into account the complex and pluralistic nature of American society. New economic explanations would have to be more precise *and* more flexible, and they should appear in patterns linked with other forces such as ethnic and racial conflict, ideology, and concrete historical conditions.

BIBLIOGRAPHY

Books and Articles Referred to in the Chapter Introduction

Lee Benson, "Causation and the American Civil War," *History and Theory* (1960).

James G. Randall, "The Blundering Generation," *Mississippi Valley Historical Review* (1940).

Avery O. Craven, *The Coming of the Civil War* (1942).

Pieter Geyl, "The American Civil War and the Problems of Inevitability," *New England Quarterly* (1951).

Frederick Jackson Turner, *The Frontier in American History* (1920).

Charles A. and Mary R. Beard, *The Rise of American Civilization* (2 vols.; 1927).

Thomas J. Pressly, *Americans Interpret Their Civil War* (1954).

Robert P. Sharkey, *Money, Class, and Party* (1959).

Irwin Unger, *The Greenback Era* (1964).

Bray Hammond, "The North's Empty Purse, 1861–62," *American Historical Review* (1961).

Irwin Unger, "Businessmen and Specie Resumption," *Political Science Quarterly* (1959).

Suggested Reading

Thomas J. Pressly's book (listed earlier) summarized the debate to 1954 very effectively. The student should also look at the introduction to the second edition of his book. On the subject see David M. Potter, "The Background of the Civil War," *Yearbook of the National Council for the Social Studies* (1961). Two useful anthologies on the subject are Edwin C. Rozwenc (ed.), *The Causes of the American Civil War* (1961) and Kenneth M. Stampp (ed.), *The Causes of the Civil War* (1959). For an account of Beard's interpretations see Bernard C. Borning, *The Political and Social Thought of Charles A. Beard* (1962). Paul W. Gates stressed the competition for Western land in "The Struggle for Land and the Irrepressible Conflict," *Political Science Quarterly* (1957). Allan Nevins more or less covered the narrative ground in his exhaustively detailed *Ordeal of the Union* (2 vols.; 1947); *The Emergence of Lincoln* (2 vols.; 1950); *The War for the Union* (2 vols.; 1960). Thomas P. Abernethy, *The South in the New Nation, 1789–1819* (1961), suggested a sharper sectional conflict before the war in stressing the role of slavery in the settlement of the old Southwest. David Donald in "The Radicals and Lincoln," *Lincoln Reconsidered* (1956) provided a different image of Civil War politics by arguing persuasively that there was no permanent and biting hostility between Lincoln and the Radicals. David Donald discussed the reasons why contemporary historians no longer argue so frequently and heatedly about the causes of the Civil War in "American Historians and the Causes of the Civil War," *South Atlantic Quarterly* (1960). See also Thomas N. Bonner, "Civil War Historians and the 'Needless War,'" *Journal of the History of Ideas* (1956). Wallace D. Farnham reasoned that the weakness of American institutions had much to do with the coming of the Civil War: see "The Weakened Spring of Government: A Study in Nineteenth Century American History," *American Historical Review* (1963). A. E. Campbell emphasized "isolation," see "An Excess of Isolation: Isolation and the American Civil War" *Journal of Southern History* (1965).

Gerald Runkle provided a perceptive summary of Marx's responses to Civil War politics in "Karl Marx and the American Civil War," *Comparative Studies in Society and History* (1964). Much has been done in reexamining the economic cliches about the Civil War and Reconstruction era aside from the work of Cochran, Sharkey, Coben, and Hammond. See Allen Solganick, "The Robber Baron Concept and the Revisionists," *Science and Society* (1965) and Hal Bridges, "The Robber Baron Concept in American History," *Business History Review* (1958). Pershing Vartanian sharply criticized "the Cochran thesis" in "The Cochran Thesis: A Critique in Statistical Analysis," *Journal of American History* (1964). C. Vann Woodward made some interesting comments on the nature of the Civil War in "Reflections on Two Centennials: The American Civil War," *Yale Review* (1961). Traditions of interpretations established by Roy F. Nichols, James G. Randall, and Avery O. Craven were continued in modified form in a symposium by Norman A. Graebner, *Politics and the Crisis of 1860* (1961). The Beardian tradition was probably best represented by the books and articles of Howard K. Beale. For some of the ground-breaking attacks on the Beardian explanation, see Bray Hammond, *Banks and Politics in America from the Revolution to the Civil War* (1957). George Dangerfield, in *The Awakening of American Nationalism, 1815–1828* (1965), argued that the Compromise of 1820 was probably a mistake which made the Civil War inevitable, and that slavery expension could have been checked if the North had held firm. Ralph A. Wooster attempted to demonstrate that secession was the will of the Southern white majority see *The Secession Conventions of the South* (1962). Hamilton Holman, probing the crisis of 1850 in *Prologue to Conflict: The Crisis and the Compromise of 1850* (1964), left the impression that the compromise was unwise, unstable, and possible only through the bribery of certain key Southern congressmen. The "abstract" defenders of slavery were presented as dangerously aggressive in Robert R. Russel, "The Issues in the Congressional Struggle over the Kansas-Nebraska Bill of 1854," *Journal of Southern History* (1963). Robert W. Johannsen was kinder with the "Douglas Democracy" but found flaws there as well as still larger faults among the aggressive defenders of slavery, in "The Douglas Democracy and the Crisis of Disunion," *Civil War History* (1963). Warren J. Donnelly summarized the long debate over "Conspiracy or Popular Support: The Historiography of Southern Support for Secession," *North Carolina Historical Review* (1965). Richard N. Current, in an attempt to pin down Lincoln's role in the coming of the war, followed the President's day-by-day activities during the few weeks before Sumter in *Lincoln and the First Shot* (1963). Pieter Geyl has presented an amended version of his earlier account of the Civil War in "Synopsis: The American Civil War Viewed from the Netherlands," *Proceedings of the American Philosophical Society* (1962). For a recent summary of major schools of interpretation, see Joel H. Silbey, "The Civil War Synthesis in American Political History," *Civil War History* (1964). On the responses of intellectuals to the war, see George M. Frederickson's interesting study, *The Inner Civil War, Northern Intellectuals and the War*.

Slavery a Most Pressing Moral Issue[*]

ARTHUR M. SCHLESINGER, JR.

The Civil War was our great national trauma. A savage fraternal conflict, it released deep sentiments of guilt and remorse—sentiments which have reverberated through our history and our literature ever since. Literature in the end came to terms with these sentiments by yielding to the South in fantasy the victory it had been denied in fact; this tendency culminated on the popular level in *Gone with the Wind* and on the highbrow level in the Nashville cult of agrarianism. But history, a less malleable medium, was constricted by the intractable fact that the war had taken place, and by the related assumption that it was, in William H. Seward's phrase, an "irrepressible conflict," and hence a justified one.

As short a time ago as 1937, for example, even Professor James G. Randall could describe himself as "unprepared to go to the point of denying that the great American tragedy could have been avoided." Yet in a few years the writing of history would succumb to the psychological imperatives which had produced *I'll Take my Stand* and *Gone with the Wind;* and Professor Randall would emerge as the leader of a triumphant new school of self-styled "revisionists." The publication of two vigorous books by Professor Avery Craven—*The Repressible Conflict* (1939) and *The Coming of the Civil War* (1942)—and the

appearance of Professor Randall's own notable volumes on Lincoln—*Lincoln the President: Springfield to Gettysburg* (1945), *Lincoln and the South* (1946), and *Lincoln the Liberal Statesman* (1947)—brought about a profound reversal of the professional historian's attitude toward the Civil War. Scholars now denied the traditional assumption of the inevitability of the war and boldly advanced the thesis that a "blundering generation" had transformed a "repressible conflict" into a "needless war."

The swift triumph of revisionism came about with very little resistance or even expressed reservations on the part of the profession. Indeed, the only adequate evaluation of the revisionist thesis that I know was made, not by an academic historian at all, but by that illustrious semi-pro, Mr. Bernard De Voto; and Mr. De Voto's two brilliant articles in *Harper's* in 1945 unfortunately had little influence within the guild. By 1947 Professor Allan Nevins, summing up the most recent scholarship in *Ordeal of the Union*, his able general history of the 1850s, could define the basic problem of the period in terms which indicated a measured but entire acceptance of revisionism. "The primary task of statesmanship in this era," Nevins wrote, "was to furnish a workable adjustment between the two sections, while offering strong inducements to the southern people to regard their labor system not as static but evolutionary, and equal persuasions to the northern people to

[*] Arthur M. Schlesinger, Jr., "The Causes of the Civil War," *Partisan Review*, XVI, 10 (October 1949), 969–81. By permission of the author.

assume a helpful rather than scolding attitude."

This new interpretation surely deserves at least as meticulous an examination as Professor Randall is prepared to give, for example, to such a question as whether or not Lincoln was playing fives when he received the news of his nomination in 1860. The following notes are presented in the interests of stimulating such an examination.

The revisionist case, as expounded by Professors Randall and Craven, has three main premises. First:

(1) that the Civil War was caused by the irresponsible emotionalization of politics far out of proportion to the real problems involved. The war, as Randall put it, was certainly not caused by cultural variations nor by economic rivalries nor by sectional differences; these all existed, but it was "stupid," as he declared, to think that they required war as a solution. "One of the most colossal of misconceptions" was the "theory" that "fundamental motives produce war. The glaring and obvious fact is the artificiality of war-marking agitation." After all, Randall pointed out, agrarian and industrial interests had been in conflict under Coolidge and Hoover; yet no war resulted. "In Illinois," he added, "major controversies (not mere transient differences) between downstate and metropolis have stopped short of war."

Nor was the slavery the cause. The issues arising over slavery were in Randall's judgment "highly artificial, almost fabricated. . . . They produced quarrels out of things that would have settled themselves were it not for political agitation." Slavery, Craven observed, was in any case a much overrated problem. It is "perfectly clear," he wrote, "that slavery played a rather minor part in the life of the South and of the Negro."

What then was the cause of war? "If one word or phrase were selected to account for the war," wrote Randall, ". . . it would have to be such a word as fanaticism (on both sides), misunderstanding, misrepresenta-

tion, or perhaps politics." Phrases like "whipped-up crisis" and "psychopathic case" adorned Randall's explanation. Craven similarly described the growing sense of sectional differences as "an artificial creation of inflamed minds." The "molders of public opinion steadily created the fiction of two distinct peoples." As a result, "distortion led a people into bloody war."

If uncontrolled emotionalism and fanaticism caused the war, how did they get out of hand? Who whipped up the "whipped-up crisis"? Thus the second revisionist thesis:

(2) that sectional friction was permitted to develop into needless war by the inexcusable failure of political leadership in the fifties. "It is difficult to achieve a full realization of how Lincoln's generation stumbled into a ghastly war," wrote Randall. ". . . If one questions the term 'blundering generation,' let him inquire how many measures of the time he would wish copied or repeated if the period were to be approached with a clean slate and to be lived again."

It was the politicians, charged Craven, who systematically sacrificed peace to their pursuit of power. Calhoun and Adams, "seeking political advantage," mixed up slavery and expansion; Wilmot introduced his "trouble-making Proviso as part of the political game"; the repeal clause in the Kansas-Nebraska Act was "the afterthought of a mere handful of politicians"; Chase's Appeal to the Independent Democrats was "false in its assertions and unfair in its purposes, but it was politically effective"; the "damaging" section in the Dred Scott decision was forced "by the political ambitions of dissenting judges." "These uncalled-for moves and this irresponsible leadership," concluded Craven, blew up a "crack-pot" crusade into a national conflict.

It is hard to tell which was under attack here—the performance of a particular generation or democratic politics in general. But, if the indictment "blundering generation" meant no more than a general complaint that democratic politics placed a premium on emotionalism, then the Civil War would have been no more nor less "needless" than any event in our blundering history. The phrase "blundering generation" must consequently imply that the generation in power in the fifties was *below* the human or historical or democratic average in its blundering. Hence the third revisionist thesis:

(3) that the slavery problem could have been solved without war. For, even if slavery were as unimportant as the revisionists have insisted, they would presumably admit that it constituted the real sticking point in the relations between the sections. They must show therefore that there were policies with which a non-blundering generation could have resolved the slavery crisis and averted war; and that these policies were so obvious that the failure to adopt them indicated blundering and stupidity of a peculiarly irresponsible nature. If no such policies could be produced even by hindsight, then it would seem excessive to condemn the politicians of the fifties for failing to discover them at the time.

The revisionists have shown only a most vague and sporadic awareness of this problem. "Any kind of sane policy in Washington in 1860 might have saved the day for nationalism," remarked Craven; but he did not vouchsafe the details of these sane policies; we would be satisfied to know about one.[1] Similarly Randall declared that there were few policies of the fifties he would wish repeated if the period were to be lived over again; but he was not communicative about the policies he would wish pursued. Nevins likewise blamed the war on the "collapse of American statesmanship," but restrained himself from suggesting how a non-collapsible statesmanship would have solved the hard problems of the fifties.

In view of this reticence on a point so crucial to the revisionist argument, it is necessary to reconstruct the possibilities that might lie in the back of revisionism.

---

[1] It is fair to say that Professor Craven seems in recent years to have modified his earlier extreme position; see his article "The Civil War and the Democratic Process," *Abraham Lincoln Quarterly*, June, 1947.

Clearly there could be only two "solutions" to the slavery problem: the preservation of slavery, or its abolition.

Presumably the revisionists would not regard the preservation of slavery as a possible solution. Craven, it is true, has argued that "most of the incentives to honest and sustained effort, to a contented, well-rounded life, might be found under slavery. . . . What owning and being owned added to the normal relationship of employer and employee is very hard to say." In describing incidents in which slaves beat up masters, he has even noted that "happenings and reactions like these were the rule [sic], not the exception." But Craven would doubtless admit that, however jolly this system might have been, its perpetuation would have been, to say the least, impracticable.

If, then, revisionism has rested on the assumption that the nonviolent abolition of slavery was possible, such abolition could conceivably have come about through internal reform in the South; through economic exhaustion of the slavery system in the South; or through some government project for gradual and compensated emancipation. Let us examine these possibilities.

(1) *The internal reform argument.* The South, the revisionists have suggested, might have ended the slavery system if left to its own devices; only the abolitionists spoiled everything by letting loose a hysteria which caused the southern ranks to close in self-defense.

This revisionist argument would have been more convincing if the decades of alleged antislavery feeling in the South had produced any concrete results. As one judicious southern historian, Professor Charles S. Sydnor, recently put it, "Although the abolition movement was followed by a decline of antislavery sentiment in the South, it must be remembered that in all the long years before that movement began no part of the South had made substantial progress toward ending slavery. . . . Southern liberalism had not ended slavery in any state."

In any case, it is difficult for historians seriously to suppose that northerners could have denied themselves feelings of disapproval over slavery. To say that there "should" have been no abolitionists in America before the Civil War is about as sensible as to say that there "should" have been no anti-Nazis in the 1930s or that there "should" be no anti-Communists today. People who indulge in criticism of remote evils may not be so pure of heart as they imagine; but that fact does not affect their inevitability as part of the historic situation.

Any theory, in short, which expects people to repress such spontaneous aversions is profoundly unhistorical. If revisionism has based itself on the conviction that things would have been different if only there had been no abolitionists, it has forgotten that abolitionism was as definite and irrevocable a factor in the historic situation as was slavery itself. And, just as abolitionism was inevitable, so too was the southern reaction against it—a reaction which, as Professor Clement Eaton has ably shown, steadily drove the free discussion of slavery out of the South. The extinction of free discussion meant, of course, the absolute extinction of any hope of abolition through internal reform.

(2) *The economic exhaustion argument.* Slavery, it has been pointed out, was on the skids economically. It was overcapitalized and inefficient; it immobilized both capital and labor; its one-crop system was draining the soil of fertility; it stood in the way of industrialization. As the South came to realize these facts, a revisionist might argue, it would have moved to abolish slavery for its own economic good. As Craven put it, slavery "may have been almost ready to break down of its own weight."

This argument assumed, of course, that southerners would have recognized the causes of their economic predicament and taken the appropriate measures. Yet such an assumption would be plainly contrary to history and to experience. From the beginning the South has always blamed its economic shortcomings, not on its own economic ruling class and its own inefficient

use of resources, but on northern exploitation. Hard times in the 1850s produced in the South, not a reconsideration of the slavery system, but blasts against the North for the high prices of manufactured goods. The overcapitalization of slavery led, not to criticisms of the system, but to increasingly insistent demands for the reopening of the slave trade. Advanced southern writers like George Fitzhugh and James D. B. DeBow were even arguing that slavery was adapted to industrialism. When Hinton R. Helper did advance before the Civil War an early version of Craven's argument, asserting that emancipation was necessary to save the southern economy, the South burned his book. Nothing in the historical record suggests that the southern ruling class was preparing to deviate from its traditional pattern of self-exculpation long enough to take such a drastic step as the abolition of slavery.

(3) *Compensated emancipation.* Abraham Lincoln made repeated proposals of compensated emancipation. In his annual message to Congress of December 1, 1862, he set forth a detailed plan by which states, on an agreement to abolish slavery by 1900, would receive government bonds in proportion to the number of slaves emancipated. Yet, even though Lincoln's proposals represented a solution of the problem conceivably gratifying to the slaveholder's purse as well as to his pride, they got nowhere. Two-thirds of the border representatives rejected the scheme, even when personally presented to them by Lincoln himself. And, of course, only the pressure of war brought compensated emancipation its limited hearing of 1862.

Still, granted these difficulties, does it not remain true that other countries abolished slavery without internal convulsion? If emotionalism had not aggravated the situation beyond hope, Craven has written, then slavery "might have been faced as a national question and dealt with as successfully as the South American countries dealt with the same problem." If Brazil could free its slaves and Russia its serfs in the middle of the nineteenth century without civil war, why could not the United States have done as well?

The analogies are appealing but not, I think, really persuasive. There are essential differences between the slavery question in the United States and the problems in Brazil or in Russia. In the first place, Brazil and Russia were able to face servitude "as a national question" because it was, in fact, a national question. Neither country had the American problem of the identification of compact sectional interests with the survival of the slavery system. In the second place, there was no race problem at all in Russia; and, though there was a race problem in Brazil, the more civilized folkways of that country relieved racial differences of the extreme tension which they breed in the South of the United States. In the third place, neither in Russia nor in Brazil did the abolition of servitude involve constitutional issues; and the existence of these issues played a great part in determining the form of the American struggle.

It is hard to draw much comfort, therefore, from the fact that other nations abolished servitude peaceably. The problem in America was peculiarly recalcitrant. The schemes for gradual emancipation got nowhere. Neither internal reform nor economic exhaustion contained much promise for a peaceful solution. The hard fact, indeed, is that the revisionists have not tried seriously to describe the policies by which the slavery problem could have been peacefully resolved. They have resorted instead to broad affirmations of faith: if only the conflict could have been staved off long enough, then somehow, somewhere, we could have worked something out. It is legitimate, I think, to ask how? where? what? —at least, if these affirmations of faith are to be used as the premise for castigating the unhappy men who had the practical responsibility for finding solutions and failed.

Where have the revisionists gone astray? In part, the popularity of revisionism obviously parallels that of *Gone with the Wind*— the victors paying for victory by pretending

literary defeat. But the essential problem is why history should be so vulnerable to this literary fashion; and this problem, I believe, raises basic questions about the whole modern view of history. It is perhaps stating the issue in too portentous terms. Yet I cannot escape the feeling that the vogue of revisionism is connected with the modern tendency to seek in optimistic sentimentalism as escape from the severe demands of moral decision; that it is the offspring of our modern sentimentality which at once evades the essential moral problems in the name of a superficial objectivity and asserts their unimportance in the name of an invincible progress.

The revisionists first glided over the implications of the fact that the slavery system was producing a closed society in the South. Yet that society increasingly had justified itself by a political and philosophical repudiation of free society; southern thinkers swiftly developed the anti-libertarian potentialities in a social system whose cornerstone, in Alexander H. Stephens's proud phrase, was human bondage. In theory and in practice, the South organized itself with mounting rigor against ideas of human dignity and freedom, because such ideas inevitably threatened the basis of their own system. Professor Frank L. Owsley, the southern agrarian, has described inadvertently but accurately the direction in which the slave South was moving. "The abolitionists and their political allies were threatening the existence of the South as seriously as the Nazis threaten the existence of England," wrote Owsley in 1940; ". . . Under such circumstances the surprising thing is that so little was done by the South to defend its existence."

There can be no question that many southerners in the fifties had similar sentiments; that they regarded their system of control as ridiculously inadequate; and that, with the book burning, the censorship of the mails, the gradual illegalization of dissent, the South was in process of creating a real machinery of repression in order more effectively "to defend its existence." No society, I suppose, encourages criticism of its basic institutions. Yet, when a democratic society acts in self-defense, it does so at least in the name of human dignity and freedom. When a society based on bond slavery acts to eliminate criticism of its peculiar institution, it outlaws what a believer in democracy can only regard as the abiding values of man. When the basic institutions are evil, in other words, the effect of attempts to defend their existence can only be the moral and intellectual stultification of the society.

A society closed in the defense of evil institutions thus creates moral differences far too profound to be solved by compromise. Such a society forces upon every one, both those living at the time and those writing about it later, the necessity for a moral judgment; and the moral judgment in such cases becomes an indispensable factor in the historical understanding.

The revisionists were commendably anxious to avoid the vulgar errors of the post-Civil War historians who pronounced smug individual judgments on the persons involuntarily involved in the tragedy of the slave system. Consequently they tried hard to pronounce no moral judgments at all on slavery. Slavery became important, in Craven's phrase, "only as a very ancient labor system, probably at this time rather near the end of its existence"; the attempt to charge this labor system with moral meanings was "a creation of inflamed imaginations." Randall, talking of the Kansas-Nebraska Act, could describe it as "a law intended to subordinate the slavery question and hold it in *proper proportion*" (my italics). I have quoted Randall's even more astonishing argument that, because major controversies between downstate and metropolis in Illinois stopped short of war, there was reason to believe that the Civil War could have been avoided. Are we to take it that the revisionists seriously believe that the downstate-metropolis fight in Illinois—or the agrarian-industrial fight in the Coolidge and Hoover administrations —were in any useful sense comparable to the difference between the North and South in 1861?

Because the revisionists felt no moral urgency themselves, they deplored as fanatics those who did feel it, or brushed aside their feelings as the artificial product of emotion and propaganda. The revisionist hero was Stephen A. Douglas, who always thought that the great moral problems could be solved by sleight of hand. The phrase "northern man of southern sentiments," Randall remarked, was "said opprobriously . . . as if it were a base thing for a northern man to work with his southern fellows."

By denying themselves insight into the moral dimension of the slavery crisis, in other words, the revisionists denied themselves a historical understanding of the intensities that caused the crisis. It was the moral issue of slavery, for example, that gave the struggles over slavery in the territories or over the enforcement of the fugitive slave laws their significance. These issues, as the revisionists have shown with cogency, were not in themselves basic. But they were the available issues; they were almost the only points within the existing constitutional framework where the moral conflict could be faced; as a consequence, they became charged with the moral and political dynamism of the central issue. To say that the Civil War was fought over the "unreal" issue of slavery in the territories is like saying that World War II was fought over the "unreal" issue of the invasion of Poland. The democracies could not challenge fascism inside Germany any more than opponents of slavery could challenge slavery inside the south; but the extension of slavery, like the extension of fascism, was an act of aggression which made a moral choice inescapable.

Let us be clear what the relationship of moral judgment to history is. Every historian, as we all know in an argument that surely does not have to be repeated in 1949, imports his own set of moral judgments into the writing of history by the very process of interpretation; and the phrase "every historian" includes the category "revisionist." Mr. De Voto in his paraphrases of the revisionist position has put admirably the contradictions on this point: as for "moral questions, God forbid. History will not put itself in the position of saying that any thesis may have been wrong, any cause evil. . . . History will not deal with moral values, though of course the Republican radicals were, well, culpable." The whole revisionist attitude toward abolitionists and radicals, repeatedly characterized by Randall as "unctuous" and "intolerant," overflows with the moral feeling which is so virtuously excluded from discussions of slavery.

An acceptance of the fact of moral responsibility does not license the historian to roam through the past ladling out individual praise and blame: such an attitude would ignore the fact that all individuals, including historians, are trapped in a web of circumstance which curtails their moral possibilities. But it does mean that there are certain essential issues on which it is necessary for the historian to have a position if he is to understand the great conflicts of history. These great conflicts are relatively few because there are few enough historical phenomena which we can confidently identify as evil. The essential issues appear, moreover, not in pure and absolute form, but incomplete and imperfect, compromised by the deep complexity of history. Their proponents may often be neurotics and fanatics, like the abolitionists. They may attain a social importance only when a configuration of nonmoral factors—economic, political, social, military—permit them to do so.

Yet neither the nature of the context nor the pretensions of the proponents alter the character of the issue. And human slavery is certainly one of the few issues of whose evil we can be sure. It is not just "a very ancient labor system"; it is also a betrayal of the basic values of our Christian and democratic tradition. No historian can understand the circumstances which led to its abolition until he writes about it in its fundamental moral context. "History is supposed to understand the difference between a decaying economy and an expanding one," as Mr. De Voto well said, "between solvency and bankruptcy, between a dying social idea and one coming to world acceptance. . . . It is even supposed to understand implications of the difference between a man who is legally a slave and one who is legally free."

"Revisionism in general has no position," De Voto continues, "but only a vague sentiment." Professor Randall well suggested the uncritical optimism of that sentiment when he remarked, "To suppose that the Union could not have been continued or slavery outmoded without the war and without the corrupt concomitants of war is hardly an enlightened assumption." We have here a touching afterglow of the admirable nineteenth-century faith in the full rationality and perfectibility of man; the faith that the errors of the world would all in time be "outmoded" (Professor Randall's use of this word is suggestive) by progress. Yet the experience of the twentieth century has made it clear that we gravely overrated man's capacity to solve the problems of existence within the terms of history.

This conclusion about man may disturb our complacencies about human nature. Yet it is certainly more in accord with history than Professor Randall's "enlightened" assumption that man can solve peaceably all the problems which overwhelm him. The unhappy fact is that man occasionally works himself into a logjam; and that the logjam must be burst by violence. We know that well enough from the experience of the last decade. Are we to suppose that some future historian will echo Professor Nevins' version of the "failure" of the 1850s and write: "The primary task of statesmanship in the 1930s was to furnish a workable adjustment between the United States and Germany, while offering strong inducements to the German people to abandon the police state and equal persuasions to the Americans to help the Nazis rather than scold them"? Will some future historian adapt Professor Randall's formula and write that the word "appeaser" was used "opprobriously" as if it were a "base" thing for an American to work with his Nazi fellow? Obviously this revisionism of the future (already foreshadowed in the work of Charles A. Beard) would represent, as we now see it, a fantastic evasion of the hard and unpleasant problems of the thirties. I doubt whether our present revisionism would make much more sense to the men of the 1850s.

The problem of the inevitability of the Civil War, of course, is in its essence a problem devoid of meaning. The revisionist attempt to argue that the war could have been avoided by "any kind of sane policy" is of interest less in its own right than as an expression of a characteristically sentimental conception of man and of history. And the great vogue of revisionism in the historical profession suggests, in my judgment, ominous weaknesses in the contemporary attitude toward history.

We delude ourselves when we think that history teaches us that evil will be "outmoded" by progress and that politics consequently does not impose on us the necessity for decision and for struggle. If historians are to understand the fullness of the social dilemma they seek to reconstruct, they must understand that sometimes there is no escape from the implacabilities of moral decision. When social conflicts embody great moral issues, these conflicts cannot be as-

signed for solution to the invincible march of progress; nor can they be bypassed with "objective" neutrality. Not many problems perhaps force this decision upon the historian. But, if any problem does in our history, it is the Civil War.

To reject the moral actuality of the Civil War is to foreclose the possibility of an adequate account of its causes. More than that, it is to misconceive and grotesquely to sentimentalize the nature of history. For history is not a redeemer, promising to solve all human problems in time; nor is man capable of transcending the limitations of his being. Man generally is entangled in insoluble problems; history is consequently a tragedy in which we are all involved, whose keynote is anxiety and frustration, not progress and fulfillment. Nothing exists in history to assure us that the great moral dilemmas can be resolved without pain; we cannot therefore be relieved from the duty of moral judgment on issues so appalling and inescapable as those involved in human slavery; nor can we be consoled by sentimental theories about the needlessness of the Civil War into regarding our own struggles against evil as equally needless.

One must emphasize, however, that this duty of judgment applies to issues. Because we are all implicated in the same tragedy, we must judge the men of the past with the same forbearance and charity which we hope the future will apply toward us.

Causation and the American Civil War[*]

CUSHING STROUT

A specter haunts American historians—the concept of causality. After nearly a hundred years of passionate and dispassionate inquiry into "the causes of the Civil War" the debate is still inconclusive. Even more discouraging, according to the editor of a recent anthology of historical writings on the problem, "twentieth-century historians often merely go back to interpretations advanced by partisans while the war was still in progress."[1] Despite the impasse, historians are not often discouraged. Some take refuge in professional patience or the firm confidence that their opponents have simply hardened their hearts to truth. Others are reconciled to skepticism by the historical relativism, defended by Carl Becker and Charles Beard, which characterizes all historical interpretations as determined products of a temporary, dominant "climate of opinion." A few, like Beard himself, have drastically tried to cut the knot by surgical removal of the causal category itself from history, though his own practice of economic determinism flatly contradicted this Draconian proposal. When the investigation of the answer to a question has led to such frustrating difficulties, it is necessary to reexamine the question, even if it leads the historian into philosophical territory where he naturally fears to tread.

Historians are often vulnerable to Henry Adams's charge that their causal assumptions, "hidden in the depths of dusty libraries, have been astounding, but commonly unconscious and childlike,"[2] yet they can find no real help from the eccentric results of his own search for a historical physics which would unify the course of events under one abstract formula, "a spool upon which to wind the thread of the past without breaking it."[3] For all his brilliance his speculative theory has quite rightly struck most historians as an exotic hybrid of history and science, spoiling the integrity of each. The "scientific school of history" ended either in fanciful speculation about historical laws or a naïve cult of fact-finding as the essence of scientific method. If even the scientist, at the level of subatomic particles, must substitute statistical probability for causal universals, the historian has always been embarrassed by the effort to discover conditions which invariably produce certain results not otherwise accounted for. He cannot discriminate with exactness constants and variables by experimentation on a past forever gone, nor can he always confidently turn to social scientists for causal rules when their findings, even when valid and relevant, are limited historically to particular times and places. Grateful as the historian may be for generalizations about, say, the voting behavior of Americans, he is ruefully aware that recurring evidence for the behavior of Americans in civil wars is fortunately not available.

[*] Cushing Strout, "Causation and the American Civil War," *History and Theory* (1961).

[1] Kenneth M. Stampp, *The Causes of the Civil War* (Englewood Cliffs, N.J., 1959), vi.

[2] *The Education of Henry Adams* (New York, 1931), 382.

[3] *Ibid.*, 472.

The historian conventionally speaks of "multiple causes" because he knows he has no monistic formula to explain the course of history and no single generalization to cover all the necessary and sufficient conditions for a civil war. This fashion of speech is, however, misleading because he cannot escape his difficulties by multiplying them. If he does not believe that each of the many "causes" could have produced the Civil War by itself, then he must assume that the whole collection of them acted together as one in bringing about that effect. He is then left with the familiar problem of accounting for this causal relationship by reference to confirmed generalizations. What he cannot do for one "cause," he cannot do for a set of them acting as one.

Historians sometimes seek to avoid the problem of generalized causal rules by talking of a necessary chain of events.[4] Yet the events which are put into the so-called chains clearly have more determinants than are recognized by so placing them, and the same event can be put into a number of possible chains. The election of Lincoln, produced by a large number of small events, might well appear in two alleged chains of events which suggest quite different interpretations of the coming of the war. The chains are not, furthermore, really "necessary" unless their linkage is explained by theories or generalizations which the makers of chains seldom make clear, even to themselves.[5]

A deeper difficulty of the causal query is that it may be defined so as to conflict with the historical attitude itself. If the historian were to deduce consequences from antecedents, there would be nothing in the former not found in the latter. How then could he speak of anything new happening at all?

The special sensitivity of the historian is to the novel elements, the discontinuities, emerging in a situation. He discovers the relevant antecedents retrospectively with the help of the illumination of the consequences, which call out for a past. Looking backward, he discerns a process that does not logically or inevitably follow from certain antecedents but takes its life and form only from its development. There is no point at which the historian can declare that the Civil War became inevitable, even though he might find it increasingly probable. Those who have said it was inevitable have either deduced it from a dogmatic general proposition about the "necessary" conflict of classes in society, according to the determinism of historical materialism, or they have pointed instead to the stubbornness of the slavery problem and the moral and ideological imperatives which made certain policies humanly "necessary" (granted their premises), rather than historically inevitable in terms of an impersonal process.[6] In studying the Civil War the historian must know about such antecedents as the origins and expansion of slavery, for example, but he cannot deduce the war from the existence of that institution. "American historians have been too clever by half," Carl Becker once said, "in finding other causes of the Civil War,"[7] but the cleverness has been stimulated by knowledge of the fact that slavery existed and was eliminated elsewhere without civil war.

The serious difficulties of exact causal

---

[4] Adams described his own history of the United States as an effort to state "such facts as seemed sure, in such order as seemed rigorously consequent," so as to "fix for a familiar moment a necessary sequence of human movement." *Ibid.*, 382.

[5] Mario Bunge, *Causality: the Place of the Causal Principle in Modern Science* (Cambridge, Mass., 1959), 126.

[6] Arthur M. Schlesinger, Jr., sees the Civil War as a "logjam" which had to be "burst by violence," a common feature of the "tragedy" of history; but surely only commitment to policy positions deemed necessary and worth the price of force explains the "logjam" he describes. See his "The Causes of the Civil War: a Note on Historical Sentimentalism," *Partisan Review*, 16 (1949), 969–81. Pieter Geyl, who also attacks the "revisionist" thesis of a "needless war," carefully avoids making the claim that it was inevitable, leaving the issue moot. See his "The American Civil War and the Problem of Inevitability," *New England Quarterly*, 24 (1951), 147–68.

[7] Letter to Louis Gottschalk, Sept. 3, 1944, in C. Becker, *Detachment and the Writing of History*, ed. Phil L. Snyder (Ithaca, 1958), 88.

determination have led some thinkers to suggest that the historian make reasonable estimates of causes, based upon his judgment of what *would* have taken place in the absence of a particular factor being tested for causal relevance.[8] If the course of events would have been much the same, the factor is assumed to have had no causal significance. Some critics have replied that history is, as Beard maintained, "a seamless web"; but surely it is not so seamless that historians must follow Beard in believing that there is no more reason to explain American intervention in World War I by reference to the German policy of unlimited submarine warfare than by reference to the Kaiser's moustaches.[9] This extreme position denies to the historian that realistic sense of relevance which the study of history and direct experience of human affairs have traditionally provided. Many explanations in history certainly do reflect and depend upon this trained sense of relevance.[10] Modern historians have stressed slavery rather than states' rights in explaining the crisis of 1860 because they know that the legal position of states' rights has often sheltered Northerners and Southerners alike, depending on the more substantial interests it has been designed to protect. Beard himself rejected Turner's stress on the importance of free land to American development on the ground that though slavery, capitalism, and free land were "woven in one national mesh," yet "slavery would have been slavery and capitalism capitalism in essence even had there been no free land

with its accompaniments."[11] He could only arrive at this conclusion by imaginatively breaking the web he considered "seamless." (Even so, this procedure does not convincingly support Beard's thesis of the Civil War as a necessary conflict between capitalism and agrarianism, not only because the economic issue of the tariff had been gradually composed since 1832, but because it was during the competition for and debate over the western territories that relations between the sections became embittered to a state of crisis out of which the war came.)

Sidney Hook has persuasively argued for the importance of hypotheticals contrary to fact in establishing the interrelation of events. Yet he admits that though we have the right to make such predictions when they rest upon valid generalizations about individual and social behavior, still "we have no logical guarantee that they will continue to hold or that something new and completely unforeseen will not crop up. . . ."[12] The difficulty is that in dealing from a hypothetical point of view with a particular series of events we are assuming that it will not be intersected by other seemingly unrelated series of events. For this reason our calculations, even at their best, may be "well grounded and reliable but not certain." Is the process sound enough to justify our saying that slavery was the cause of the Civil War if by assuming its absence we could reasonably demonstrate there would have been no armed conflict? We would then have to show that none of the other issues between the sections was intractable or explosive enough to generate war. The problem is that slavery was so entangled with the other grievances of a political, economic, and social character that it is artificial to separate it out, nor do we have at hand a confirmed set of generalizations about the causes of war to apply. Whatever our calculations might

---

[8] See Max Weber, "Critical Studies in the Logic of the Cultural Sciences," reprinted in English in *The Methodology of the Social Sciences*, ed. Edward A. Shils and Henry A. Finch (Glencoe, Ill., 1949), esp. 164–88.

[9] See his *The Discussion of Human Affairs* (New York, 1936), 79, where he characterizes causal judgments as subjective, arbitrary ruptures of the "seamless web" of history.

[10] The relevance of training to the use of "guarded generalizations," neither purely analytic nor purely synthetic, is argued convincingly by Michael Scriven, "Truisms as the Grounds for Historical Explanations," in *Theories of History*, ed. Patrick Gardiner (Glencoe, Ill., 1958), 463–68.

[11] Letter to Frederick Jackson Turner, May 14, 1921, Box 31, Turner Papers, The Huntington Library.

[12] *The Hero in History: a Study in Limitation and Possibility* (New York, 1943), 132.

be, we could not satisfy the unknowns in the formula "if *a* and *only a*, then *b* and *only b*." We might well grant that though the North fought for the Union, and the South for the right of secession, still it was slavery which menaced the Union and needed Southern independence to protect its growth; even so, we could only conclude that the war was essentially fought *about* slavery, not that it was *produced* by it.

The hypothetical method of discovering causal relevance has awkward difficulties whenever the issues become complex. The historian is trained to think with respect to documentary evidence, which exists only for what did happen, not for what would have happened. He can reflect upon what might have happened in order better to evaluate what actually did happen, but to speculate on what would have happened often puts him in the position of building his hypothesis on a nest of bottomless boxes of untestable hypotheses. It is clear that the historian may sensibly ask if slavery might have expanded into the newly acquired territories in the 1850s and after. Whether or not Americans were quarreling about "an imaginary Negro in an impossible place" has turned on a discussion of the relevance of a staple-crop system inappropriate to the arid lands of the West, the potential use of slavery in mining, the expansionist ambitions of Southerners, or the fears of some future technological invention as potent as the cotton gin in bolstering slavery.[13] The question serves to highlight the possibilities contained within the situation of crisis, and it has a bearing on the historian's appreciation of the Republicans' position of containment of slavery.

Doubt over the significance of an event tends to generate the conditional query as a way of resolving it. If the historian wonders why the South seceded after Lincoln's election, he might ask himself what would have happened if Senator Douglas had been elected. Since Southern Democrats had already rejected Douglas at the Charleston Convention, they *might* have found him intolerable as president. The historian cannot be sure, but the question points up the South's demands and highlights the importance to Southern eyes of Lincoln's being the leader of a sectional party committed to containment of slavery. Since men who act in history must calculate the possible consequences of various alternatives, the historian in trying to understand them is led to do the same. Questions of what would have happened can be answered, of course, only by judgments of probability based on knowledge of the actual situation. They emphasize the significance of certain happenings without pretending to an impossible certainty, specificity, or scope.

A merely utopian conditional question allows equally plausible but contradictory answers. It has, for example, been argued that if the North had let the South secede in peace, the two nations would have enjoyed future friendly relations, thus saving the terrible costs of war.[14] It is not surprising that a Southerner might find this assumption convincing, but it clearly includes too many imponderables to justify any firm judgment. To raise questions that cannot be reasonably answered is an exercise in futility unless they are treated only as the indirect means of drawing attention to elements of an actual situation. Asking what would have happened if the North had "let the erring sister go," only serves to force a weighing of Lincoln's policy reasons for holding a symbol of federal authority in the South, as well as of the nationalistic sentiments of the Northerners who supported him. Provided the historian maintains his primary interest in what actually did happen, he may with propriety, under certain conditions, ask what might have happened

---

[13] See Harry V. Jaffa, "Expediency and Morality in the Lincoln-Douglas Debates," *Anchor Review*, 2 (1957), 199–204.

[14] Richard H. Shyrock, "The Nationalistic Tradition of the Civil War: A Southern Analysis," *South Atlantic Quarterly*, 32 (1933), 294–305. There is a useful extract in Stampp, *op. cit.*, 45–49.

or what would have happened. Such questions are especially useful for evaluating policy.

The most frequent type of historical explanation usually appears in causal disguise, which helps account for the historian's reluctance to banish the idea of cause. *Cause* often functions as *reason* or *purpose*. Explanation in terms of purpose is the natural way participants in a situation account for what happens. Thus the interpretations of the Civil War that prevailed at the time were couched by the North in terms of the aims of a "conspiracy" of aggressive slaveholders and by the South in terms of the ambitions of a radical group of abolitionist "Black Republicans." These simple theses were too obviously partisan charges of blame to find acceptance by later historians, whose professional confidence is rightly based on the principle that those who come after an event can, with the help of emotional distance, awareness of consequences, and wider perspective, know more about it than any participants. But even later historians have extensively used the language of purpose. The "revisionist" thesis of a needless war produced by "blundering statesmanship" essentially interprets the war in that way, as the consequence of human judgments and passions, though it condemns them as "irrational."

The historian cannot dispense with "cause" in this sense because, as Becker put it, "men's actions have value and purpose; and if we write history in such a way as to give it meaning and significance we have to take account of these values and purposes, to explain *why* men behave as they do, what they aim to accomplish, and whether they succeeded or not."[15] The critic might well say that a man's purpose may not be the cause of his action—yet apart from this "humanistic" concern history threatens to become a merely impersonal process which "might have occurred at any time and in any place, given a sufficient number of persons to operate the

events."[16] It is this intense commitment to the purposive dimension of history which leads many historians to feel a strong sympathy with literature and a sullen suspicion of social science. The occasional philistinism and arrogance of some propagandists for the social sciences have made many historians understandably defensive.

Yet in cooler moments the humanistic historian must acknowledge that this purposive dimension does not exhaust history. Historians have also been keenly interested in the explanatory relevance to American history of such relatively impersonal factors as De Tocqueville's "equality of condition," Turner's "frontier hypothesis," Beard's "capitalism and agrarianism," Potter's "abundance," and Hartz's "atomistic social freedom." These explanations need not be antagonistic when they are formulated without monistic claims. Turner, despite the dogmatism of his famous essay, was committed in principle to a "multiple hypothesis" approach; Beard was increasingly led to modify the monistic and deterministic implications of his economic interpretation; and both Potter and Hartz have explicitly repudiated the sufficiency of a single-determinant explanation.[17] The force of these various theories lies in their capacity to illuminate structure and continuity in American history, as demonstrated by specific historical illustrations, numerous enough to give significance to the generalizations. As such, they are not so much "causes" of specific events as they are ways of segregating out long-term conditions and tendencies of American culture and development. They give contour and meaning to the stream of events insofar as the historical evidence supports the generalizations.

---

15 Letter (n. 22 above), 87.

16 Becker, "Harnessing History," *New Republic*, 22 (1920), 322.

17 For Turner and Beard see my *The Pragmatic Revolt in American History: Curl Becker and Charles Beard* (New Haven, 1958), 21–23, 105–6. For the others see David M. Potter, *People of Plenty: Economic Abundance and the American Character* (Chicago, 1954), 165; Louis Hartz, *The Liberal Tradition in America* (New York, 1955), 20–23.

The causal problem becomes acute when the historian faces the task of explaining a complex series of events which have the ideal unity of a single event, like the Civil War. The general causal question is then propounded: what was "the fundamental cause" of the event? The notorious disparity of opinion on the answer to this question should suggest that there is some fallacy in seeking to find a prime mover that can be abstracted from the process to account for it, like slavery, rival economic systems, or the "blundering statesmanship" of agitators and leaders. None of these alleged fundamental causes can be understood apart from their specific historical context, nor could any person be said to understand the Civil War who only knew that its fundamental cause was any or all of these things. Otherwise history would merely be a cookbook for those sworn to fasting. These judgments of fundamental causality are only retrospective assessments of a reconstructed story and never a substitute for it. Actually they should be taken only as clues to the story being told. The pragmatic meaning of the assertion that slavery was "the fundamental cause" is only that the institution was so deeply entangled in the issues that divided the sections that it provides a valuable focus for examining the skein of events which culminated in war.

The historian does his work in good conscience, despite the difficulties of causality, because so much of his labor does not depend upon causal judgment. Whatever some philosophers may say, he knows that explanation is broader than causal explication. He may tell his readers much about the issues between Lincoln and Douglas, the legal status of slavery, the structure of classes in society, the economic interests of the sections, the character of the abolitionist movement, the balance of power in the Senate, the social and ideological differences between North and South, and the chronology of events without venturing beyond descriptive analysis into causal judgment. Characteristically, the historian explains by showing how a certain process

took shape, answering the "why" with more of the "what" and "how." "The careful, thorough and accurate answer to the question *How*," writes the English historian C. V. Wedgwood, "should take the historian a long way towards answering the question *Why*. . . ."[18] The historian is inescapably committed to narrative.

The relativists may quickly point out that the stories historians have told clearly reflect the "climate of opinion" in which they were constructed. Beard's economic interpretation grew out of a Progressive milieu in which the critics of industrial America had been drawn increasingly to economic analysis of contemporary problems; the "revisionism" of J. G. Randall betrayed some of the liberals' disillusionment with World War I and the fear of involvement with World War II; Arthur M. Schlesinger, Jr.'s, criticism of the "revisionist" thesis of "a needless war" openly compares the Nazi and Southern threats to an "open society" and reflects the postwar "hard" policy toward Soviet imperialism; and Avery Craven's latest analysis, a modified "revisionist" view, strikes a Cassandra pose by comparing the Civil War crisis to the frightening "cold war" situation of today, where huge power blocs compete for "satellites" and are deeply estranged from mutual understanding.[19] Inevitably, the historian's experience of present history will suggest questions and hypotheses, and in the attempt to relate his story to his public he will naturally try to find terms appropriate to his own age. Yet he must always be on guard against the insidious tendency of analogy to blur the important nuances of difference between a past age and his own. His fundamental premise as a historian must be that human experience significantly changes in its form and mean-

[18] *Truth and Opinion: Historical Essays* (London, 1960), 14.

[19] Schlesinger specifically refers to the problem of dealing with a "closed society" in both periods in "The Causes of the Civil War: a Note on Historical Sentimentalism," *Partisan Review*, 16 (1949), 969–81; and the "cold war" analogy is extensively developed in Avery O. Craven, *Civil War in the Making, 1815–60* (Baton Rouge, La., 1959), esp. xiii–xiv.

ing, that his present is only a phase of a process which calls out for historical analysis precisely because it is not uniform and continuous. The historian may believe that while one generation passes away and another generation comes, the earth abides forever, but it is his special obligation to note that the sun also rises on a new day.

The relativism of Becker and Beard was a valuable attack on the pretensions of nineteenth-century historical positivism, but its force was blunted by remnants of the same determinism they challenged. Becker considered historical judgments transient and arbitrary because he saw the mind of the historian as a mere product of the social forces active in his setting, projecting onto the blank screen of the past his own image, shaped by the hopes and fears generated by his "climate of opinion." Beard was nostalgic for the dream of an omniscient grasp of the totality of all happenings. He knew the dream was utopian; therefore, he settled instead for an "act of faith" in historical progress toward a specific future as the basis for interpretation of the past, a prediction which future history would validate or refute. But one must reply: if involvement in present history gives the historian his need to know the past, it does not necessarily prevent him from having enough detachment to apply articulate and impersonal standards to the evidence he examines; if the historian cannot know everything, it does not follow that he cannot know anything of historical importance; if the future is opaque, the past cannot be illuminated from a source which, being still indeterminate, will not furnish any light; if the historian is truly honored, it is because of his power of hindsight, not his power of prophecy.

If historians seem to have rented out a large hotel of "rooms with a view" in order to tell their story of the Civil War, it should be remembered that the sign out front should often read, "philosophy, not history, spoken here." Much of the recent debate over the Civil War centers on philosophical issues about economic determinism or rationalist politics. The historical materialists reduce the political, ideological, and moral questions to the "inevitable" conflicts of classes in society; the "revisionists" assume that violence is abnormal and that an event as bloody and tragic as civil war must have been avoidable by "rational" men; their critics point to the intractability of moral issues and the normality of nonrational factors in history.[20] Historians cannot escape such philosophical questions, but they need not entail a skepticism about historical truth.

The philosophy of history in America, as Morton G. White has pointed out, has been a very poor relation indeed. (Not even the Pragmatists, who did much to stimulate interest in history, paid it the honor of systematic attention. It is therefore encouraging that Mr. White should seek to lead philosophers to consider the "special kind of discourse" which is narration.[21]) The causal problem would be greatly clarified if both historians and philosophers realized that in telling a story the historian is committed to the "logic" of drama. In explaining the Civil War he necessarily seeks to recreate the strife of opposing forces out of which the war came. The connective tissue of his account then has a dialectical form: a person or group takes a position and performs an action because of and in relation to the position or action of another person or group. The historian's story becomes a narrative of this reciprocal response. Thus, by a crude sketch, the explanation of the event would have this character: Lincoln saw in the South's proslavery position a threat to the democratic traditions of the American community; the South saw in his election the menace of future interference with their "peculiar institution" and growing domination by an industrial North; Lincoln and the North saw in Southern secession a challenge to federal authority and the prestige

---

[20] Illustrative examples of these three positions can be found in Stampp, op. cit., 56–65, 83–87, 113–22.

[21] "A Plea for an Analytic Philosophy of History," in Morton G. White, Religion, Politics, and the Higher Learning (Cambridge, Mass., 1959), 74.

of national union; the South saw in the provisioning of Fort Sumter an intolerable danger to independence of the Confederacy. . . . In such terms, but with much greater richness and concreteness, the historian tries to reconstruct the dramatic "logic" of a sequence of events which demands to be humanly understood rather than scientifically explained.

This dialectical method does not entail any Hegelian scheme or "bloodless dance of the categories"; on the contrary, it keeps the historian in touch with the familiar existential world of human action, too concrete and passionate for final abstract accounting. Like the action of a novel or play, it can be imaginatively experienced as a meaningful plot in which character, events, and circumstances are woven together in a process made intelligible in human terms of tradition, interest, passion, purpose, and policy. This kind of historical action is understood in the same way as a novel's plot is understood, though the former must be faithful to given evidence and the latter to aesthetic standards. To ask the question "why?" is then meaningful only as a demand for enlightenment on some particular passage of the story which does not "make sense." The general causal question remains at worst an irrelevant basis for interminable disagreement, at best a generator of hypotheses to stimulate research which may promote understanding by leading to a richer, more coherent story.

In reconstructing the dramatic "logic" of a situation which eventuated in civil war, historians cannot expect to achieve a flawless coherence in their stories. They have no warrant for making history neat and tidy when experience itself has ambiguities. Often there is uncertainty about motives, even for the actor himself, because the flaw lies not in the historian's impotence but in the documents of life itself. Even if historians cannot agree, to cite a classic controversy created by conflicting evidence, whether Lincoln sent a relief ship to Sumter in the cunning expectation that the

South would commit aggression by firing on the fort, or, on the contrary, discovered by the attack how inaccurately he had measured the secessionist temper, nevertheless, they can still reach a common understanding of his policy reasons for risking war in the first place, whatever he expected or hoped would happen, after he had done what he felt had to be done.[22] Historians will never escape the need for critical debate on their findings to help them move toward a consensus of understanding, but this fate is no ground for despair. It is rather the dogmatic insistence on scientific explanations, especially when they are beyond historical competence, that dooms historians to endless and fruitless contention.

Mr. White prophesies "a new era in the philosophy of history" when "the tools of linguistic philosophy" shall be brought to bear on "clarifying the logic of narration."[23] Sharp as these instruments are, however, they involve the risk that the operation may kill the patient. In explaining narration it may be forgotten that narration is a form of explanation, which aims not at logical rigor of implication but at dramatic comprehensibility, appropriate to the untidy, passionate, and value-charged activities of men. Historians may be said to be engaged in constantly teaching that lesson, yet, as much of the long inconclusive debate about "the causes of the Civil War" makes clear, without really knowing it. It is time they directly confronted the specter that haunts them.

---

[22] The best discussion of this controversy is in David M. Potter, *Lincoln and His Party in the Secession Crisis* (1962), xxiii–xxxii and 371–75. The author makes a strong case for Lincoln's pacific intentions, pointing out that those who argue for the deliberately provocative nature of the Sumter policy fail to indicate what nonprovocative course could have been followed, granted Lincoln's aim to preserve a symbol of federal authority in the South. The provocative theory mainly rests on the hindsight testimony of those who had partisan reasons for making a miscalculation look like a clever stroke. The debate is a good example of the usefulness of asking questions about alternatives.

[23] White, *op. cit.*, 74.

1961

Did the Civil War Retard Industrialism?*

THOMAS C. COCHRAN

In most textbook and interpretative histories of the United States the Civil War
has been assigned a major role in bringing
about the American Industrial Revolution.[1]
Colorful business developments in the
North—adoption of new machines, the
quick spread of war contracting, the boost
given to profits by inflation, and the creation of a group of war millionaires—make
the war years seem not only a period of
rapid economic change but also one that
created important forces for future growth.
The superficial qualitative evidence is so
persuasive that apparently few writers have
examined the available long-run statistical
series before adding their endorsement to
the conventional interpretation. The following quotations taken from the books of
two generations of leading scholars illustrate the popular view.[2]

"The so-called Civil War," wrote
Charles A. and Mary R. Beard in 1927,
". . . was a social war . . . making *vast
changes* in the arrangement of classes, in
the accumulation and distribution of wealth,
in the course of industrial development."[3]

Midway between 1927 and the present, Arthur M. Schlesinger, Sr., wrote: "On these
tender industrial growths the Civil War
had the effect of a hothouse. For reasons
already clear . . . nearly every branch of
industry grew lustily."[4] Harold U. Faulkner, whose textbook sales have ranked near
or at the top, said in 1954: "In the economic history of the United States the Civil
War was extremely important. . . . In the
North *it speeded the Industrial Revolution*
and the development of capitalism by the
prosperity which it brought to industry."[5]
The leading new text of 1957, by Richard
Hofstadter, William Miller, and Daniel
Aaron, showed no weakening of this interpretation: "The growing demand for farm
machinery as well as for the 'sinews of
war' led to American industrial expansion.
. . . Of necessity, *iron, coal, and copper*
production boomed during the war years."[6]
A sophisticated but still essentially misleading view is presented by Gilbert C. Fite
and Jim E. Reese in a text of 1959: "The
Civil War proved to be a boon to Northern
economic development. . . . Industry, for

---

* Thomas C. Cochran, "Did the Civil War Retard Industrialization?" *Mississippi Valley Historical Review*, XLVIII (September 1961), 197–210.

[1] This article is based on a paper presented by
the author at the annual meeting of the Mississippi
Valley Historical Association in Louisville in
April, 1960.

[2] These particular authors are cited merely as
examples of historical opinion, not because they
are more in error than others. The reader needs
only to take down other texts from his own shelf
to find similar statements.

[3] *The Rise of American Civilization* (2 vols.;

New York, 1927), II, 53. In this and the following quotations the italics are mine.

[4] Homer C. Hockett and Arthur M. Schlesinger, *Land of the Free: A Short History of the
American People* (New York, 1944), 355. Schlesinger wrote the section beginning with the Civil
War.

[5] *American Economic History* (7th ed.; New
York, 1954), 345. The same statement appears
in a later edition (New York, 1960), 345.

[6] *The United States: The History of a Republic*
(Englewood Cliffs, N.J., 1957), 381.

example, was not created by the war, but wartime demands *greatly stimulated and encouraged industrial development* which already had a good start."[7] In a reappraisal of the Civil War, in *Harper's Magazine* for April, 1960, Denis W. Brogan, a specialist in American institutions, wrote: "It may have been only a catalyst but the War *precipitated the entry* of the United States *into the modern industrial world*, made 'the take-off' (to use Professor W. W. Rostow's brilliant metaphor) come sooner."[8]

In all of these reiterations of the effect of the Civil War on industrialism, statistical series seem to have been largely neglected. None of the authors cited reinforce their interpretations by setting the war period in the context of important long-run indexes of industrial growth. Since 1949, series for the period 1840 to 1890 that would cast doubt on the conventional generalizations have been available in *Historical Statistics of the United States, 1789–1945*.[9] In 1960 a new edition of *Historical Statistics* and the report of the Conference on Research in Income and Wealth on *Trends in the American Economy in the Nineteenth Century* have provided additional material to support the argument that the Civil War retarded American industrial development.[10] These volumes give data for many growth curves for the two decades before and after the war decade— in other words, the long-run trends before and after the event in question. The pattern of these trends is a mixed one which shows no uniform type of change during the Civil War decade, but on balance for the more

important series the trend is toward retardation in *rates* of growth rather than toward acceleration. This fact is evident in many series which economists would regard as basic to economic growth, but in order to keep the discussion within reasonable limits only a few can be considered here.

Robert E. Gallman has compiled new and more accurate series for both "total commodity output," including agriculture, and "value added by manufacture," the two most general measures of economic growth available for this period. He writes: "Between 1839 and 1899 total commodity output increased elevenfold, or at an average decade rate of slightly less than 50 percent. . . . Actual rates varied fairly widely, high rates appearing during the decades ending with 1854 and 1884, and a very low rate during the decade ending with 1869."[11] From the overall standpoint this statement indicates the immediately retarding effect of the Civil War on American economic growth, but since most of the misleading statements are made in regard to industrial growth, or particular elements in industrial growth, it is necessary to look in more detail at "value added by manufacture" and some special series. Gallman's series for value added in constant dollars of the purchasing power of 1879 shows a rise of 157 percent from 1839 to 1849; 76 percent from 1849 to 1859; and only 25 percent from 1859 to 1869.[12] By the 1870s the more

---

[7] *An Economic History of the United States* (Boston, 1959), 284.

[8] "A Fresh Appraisal of the Civil War," *Harper's Magazine* (New York), CCXX (April, 1960), 140.

[9] U.S. Bureau of the Census, *Historical Statistics of the United States, 1789–1945* (Washington, D.C., 1949).

[10] U.S. Bureau of the Census, *Historical Statistics of the United States: Colonial Times to 1957* (Washington, D.C., 1960); *Trends in the American Economy in the Nineteenth Century* (Princeton, 1960), published by the National Bureau of Economic Research as Volume XXIV of its *Studies in Income and Wealth*.

[11] *Trends in the American Economy*, 15.

[12] *Historical Statistics* (1960 ed.), 402. "Constant" or "real" means dollars adjusted to eliminate price changes. It should be remembered that all series expressed in current dollars need to be corrected for rather violent price movements during these 50 years. Precise adjustments would vary with every series, and would involve many problems, but the movement of wholesale prices in general (Warren-Pearson Index) may be roughly summarized as follows. In 1850 prices were 12 percent lower than in 1840, but by 1860 they were 11 percent higher than in 1850. From 1860 to 1865 prices rose 99 percent, but by 1870 the increase for the decade was only 46 percent. By 1880 the decline for the decade was 26 percent, and for the decade ending in 1890 it was 18 percent. *Ibid.*, 115. In other words, current dollars are a very unreliable indicator, particularly as applied to wholesale prices.

favorable prewar rates were resumed, with an increase of 82 percent for 1869–79, and 112 percent for 1879–89. Thus two decades of very rapid advance, the 1840s and the 1880s, are separated by 30 years of slower growth which falls to the lowest level in the decade that embraces the Civil War.

Pig-iron production in tons, perhaps the most significant commodity index of nineteenth-century American industrial growth, is available year-by-year from 1854 on. Taking total production for five-year periods, output increased 9 percent between the block of years from 1856 to 1860 and the block from 1861 to 1865. That even this slight increase might not have been registered except for the fact that 1857 to 1860 were years of intermittent depression is indicated by an 81 percent increase over the war years in the block of years from 1866 to 1870.[13] If annual production is taken at five-year intervals, starting in 1850, the increase is 24 percent from 1850 to 1855; 17 percent from 1855 to 1860; 1 percent from 1860 to 1865; and 100 percent from 1865 to 1870. While there is no figure available for 1845, the period from 1840 to 1850 shows 97 percent increase in shipments, while for the period 1870 to 1880 the increase was 130 percent. To sum up, depression and war appear to have retarded a curve of production that was tending to rise at a high rate.

Bituminous coal production may be regarded as the next most essential commodity series. After a gain of 199 percent from 1840 to 1850 this series shows a rather steady pattern of increase at rates varying from 119 to 148 percent each decade from 1850 to 1890. The war does not appear to have markedly affected the rate of growth.[14]

In the mid-nineteenth century copper production was not a basic series for recording American growth, but since three distinguished authors have singled it out as one of the indexes of the effect of the

war on industry it is best to cite the statistics. Before 1845 production of domestic copper was negligible. By 1850 the "annual recoverable content" of copper from United States mines was 728 tons, by 1860 it was 8,065 tons, by 1865 it was 9,520 tons, and by 1870 it was 14,112 tons. In this series of very small quantities, therefore, the increase from 1850 to 1860 was just over 1,000 percent, from 1860 to 1865 it was 18 percent, and from 1865 to 1870 it was 48 percent.[15]

Railroad track, particularly in the United States, was an essential for industrialization. Here both the depression and the war retarded the rate of growth. From 1851 through 1855 a total of 11,627 miles of new track was laid, from 1856 through 1860, only 8,721 miles, and from 1861 through 1865, only 4,076 miles. After the war the rate of growth of the early 1850s was resumed, with 16,174 miles constructed from 1866 through 1870. Looked at by decades, a rate of over 200 percent increase per decade in the 20 years before the war was slowed to 70 percent for the period from 1860 to 1870, with only a 15 percent increase during the war years. In the next two decades the rate averaged about 75 percent.[16]

Next to food, cotton textiles may be taken as the most representative consumer-goods industry in the nineteenth century. Interference with the flow of southern cotton had a depressing effect. The number of bales of cotton consumed in United States manufacturing rose 143 percent from 1840 to 1850 and 47 percent from 1850 to 1860, but *fell* by 6 percent from 1860 to 1870. From then on consumption increased at a little higher rate than in the 1850s.[17]

While woolen textile production is not an important series in the overall picture of industrial growth, it should be noted that, helped by protection and military needs, consumption of wool for manufacturing

13 *Ibid.*, 365–66.
14 *Ibid.*, 357.

15 *Ibid.*, 368.
16 *Ibid.*, 427–28.
17 *Historical Statistics* (1949 ed.), 187. This table is not carried back to 1840 in the 1960 edition.

more than doubled during the war, and then *fell* somewhat from 1865 to 1870. But Arthur H. Cole, the historian of the woolen industry, characterizes the years from 1830 to 1870 as a period of growth "not so striking as in the decades before or afterwards."[18]

Immigration to a nation essentially short of labor was unquestionably a stimulant to economic growth. Another country had paid for the immigrant's unproductive youthful years, and he came to the United States ready to contribute his labor at a low cost. The pattern of the curve for annual immigration shows the retarding effect of both depression and war. In the first five years of the 1850s an average of 349,685 immigrants a year came to the United States. From 1856 through 1860 the annual average fell to 169,958, and for the war years of 1861 to 1865 it fell further to 160,345. In the first five postwar years the average rose to 302,620, but not until the first half of the 1870s did the rate equal that of the early 1850s. Had there been a return to prosperity instead of war in 1861, it seems reasonable to suppose that several hundred thousand additional immigrants would have arrived before 1865.[19]

In the case of farm mechanization the same type of errors occurs as in the annual series on copper production. "Random" statistics such as the manufacture of 90,000 reapers in 1864 are frequently cited without putting them in the proper perspective of the total number in use and the continuing trends. Reaper and mower sales started upward in the early 1850s and were large from 1856 on, in spite of the depression. William T. Hutchinson estimates that most of the 125,000 reapers and mowers in use in 1861 had been sold during the previous five years.[20] While the business, without regard to the accidental coming of the war, was obviously in a stage of very rapid

growth, the war years presented many difficulties and may actually have retarded the rate of increase.[21] Total sales of reapers for the period 1861–65 are estimated at 250,000—a quite ordinary increase for a young industry—but the 90,000 figure for 1864, if it is correct, reinforces the evidence from the McCormick correspondence that this was the one particularly good year of the period. During these years William S. McCormick was often of the opinion that the "uncertainties of the times" made advisable a suspension of manufacturing until the close of the war.[22]

For a broader view of agricultural mechanization the series "value of farm implements and machinery" has special interest. Here the census gives a picture which, if correct, is explicable only on the basis of wartime destruction. Based on constant dollars the average value of machinery per farm *fell* nearly 25 percent in the decade of the war and showed nearly a 90 percent gain in the 1870s.[23] Differing from these census figures is a series prepared by Marvin W. Towne and Wayne D. Rasmussen based on the production of farm machinery. While this obviously does not take account of destruction of existing equipment or the rapid increase in the number of farms, the record of new production is hard to reconcile with the census figures. The production of implements and machinery reckoned in constant dollars is a sharply rising curve from 1850 on, with increases of 110 percent from 1850 to 1860; 140 percent from 1860 to 1870; and 95 percent from 1870 to 1880.[24] Meanwhile the number of farms increased by about one-third in each of the decades of the 1850s and 1860s and by one-half in the 1870s.[25] Whatever interpretation is given to these

[18] Arthur H. Cole, *The American Wool Manufacture* (2 vols.; Cambridge, 1926), I, 392.

[19] *Historical Statistics* (1960 ed.), 57.

[20] William T. Hutchinson, *Cyrus Hall McCormick* (2 vols.; New York, 1930–35), II, 67.

[21] *Ibid.*, II, 67–95.

[22] *Ibid.*, II, 88.

[23] *Historical Statistics* (1960 ed.), 285. For price index see note 12, above.

[24] *Trends in the American Economy*, 276.

[25] The percentage increases were 41 percent (1860 over 1850); 30 percent (1870 over 1860); and 51 percent (1880 over 1870). *Historical Statistics* (1960 ed.), 278.

figures, it does not appear that the war greatly increased the trend of agricultural mechanization. The series for gross farm product in constant dollars shows wide variations in increase from decade to decade, with the 1860s in the low group. The gains were 23 percent, 1840 to 1850; 42 percent, 1850 to 1860; 21 percent, 1860 to 1870; 52 percent, 1870 to 1880; and 20 percent, 1880 to 1890.[26]

Much American business expansion was financed by short-term bank loans continuously renewed. Thus major increases in business activity should be mirrored in increases in bank loans, both for financing short-term transactions and for additions to plant and working capital that would, in fact, be paid off gradually. If there was a really great Civil War boom in business activity it should be indicated in the series "total loans" of all banks. But it is not. In constant dollars, bank loans fell slightly between 1840 and 1850 and rose nearly 50 percent by 1860. It should be noted that none of these three decadal years were periods of high prosperity. During the war Confederate banking statistics were not reported by the comptroller of the currency, but by 1866 there is a comparable figure for the nation as a whole, and in constant dollars it is some 35 percent below that of 1860. Even by 1870 the constant dollar value of all loans was more than 15 percent lower than just before the war. If instead of examining loans one looks at total assets of all banks the decline in constant dollars from 1860 to 1870 is reduced to 10 percent, the difference arising from a larger cash position and more investment in government bonds.[27]

Net capital formation would be a more proper index of economic growth than bank loans or assets. Unfortunately, neither the teams of the National Bureau of Economic Research nor those of the Census Bureau have been able to carry any reliable

series back of 1868. From colonial times to 1960, however, the chief single form of American capital formation has undoubtedly been building construction. Farmhouses, city homes, public buildings, stores, warehouses, and factories have year by year constituted, in monetary value, the leading type of capital growth. Gallman has drawn up series for such construction based on estimating the flow of construction materials and adding what appear to be appropriate markups.[28] Admittedly the process is inexact, but because of the importance of construction in reflecting general trends in capital formation it is interesting to see the results. The rate of change for the ten-year period ending in 1854 is about 140 percent; for the one ending in 1859 it is 90 percent; for 1869 it is 40 percent; and for 1879 it is 46 percent. Taking a long view, from 1839 to 1859 the average decennial rate of increase was about 70 percent, and from 1869 to 1899 it was about 40 percent.[29] The *rate* of advance in construction was declining and the war decade added a further dip to the decline.

Since the decline in rate is for the decade, the exact effect of the war years can only be estimated, but the logic of the situation, reinforced by the record of sharp cutbacks in railroad building, seems inescapable: the Civil War, like all modern wars, checked civilian construction. The first year of war was a period of depression and tight credit in the Middle West, which checked residential and farm construction in the area that grew most rapidly before and after the war. In both the East and the West the last two years of the war were a period of rapid inflation which was regarded by businessmen as a temporary wartime phenomenon. The logical result would be to postpone construction for longterm use until after the anticipated deflation. The decline in private railroad con-

---

[26] *Ibid.*, 284.

[27] *Ibid.*, 624. The reader is again warned that deflation of current dollar values for this early period is an inexact process.

[28] *Trends in the American Economy*, 60–64.

[29] *Ibid.*, 24. Gallman has two alternate series which I have averaged. For the purposes of this paper either series leads to the same conclusions.

struction to a small fraction of the normal rate exemplifies the situation.

Lavish expenditure and speculation by a small group of war contractors and market operators gambling on the inflation seem to have created a legend of high prosperity during the war years. But the general series on fluctuations in the volume of business do not bear this out. Leonard P. Ayres's estimates of business activity place the average for 1861 through 1865 below normal, and Norman J. Silberling's business index is below its normal line for all years of the war.[30] Silberling also has an intermediate trend line for business, which smooths out annual fluctuations. This line falls steadily from 1860 to 1869.[31] Much of Silberling's discussion in his chapter "Business Activity, Prices, and Wars" is in answer to his question: "Why does it seem to be true that despite a temporary stimulating effect of war upon some industries, wars are generally associated with a long-term retarding of business growth . . . ?"[32] He puts the Civil War in this general category.

Collectively these statistical estimates support a conclusion that the Civil War retarded American industrial growth. Presentation of this view has been the chief purpose of this article. To try to judge the nonmeasurable or indirect effects of the war is extremely difficult. But since further discussion of the conventional qualitative factors may help to explain the prevailing evaluation in American texts, it seems appropriate to add some conjectural obiter dicta.

Experience with the apparently stimulating effects of twentieth-century wars on production makes the conclusion that victorious war may retard the growth of an industrial state seem paradoxical, and no doubt accounts in part for the use of detached bits of quantitative data to empha-

size the Civil War's industrial importance.[33] The resolution of the paradox may be found in contemporary conditions in the United States and in the nature of the wartime demand. The essential wastefulness of war from the standpoint of economic growth was obscured by the accident that both of the great European wars of the twentieth century began when the United States had a high level of unemployment. The immediate effect of each, therefore, was to put men to work, to increase the national product, and to create an aura of prosperity. Presumably, the United States of the mid-nineteenth century tended to operate close enough to full employment in average years that any wasteful labor-consuming activities were a burden rather than a stimulant.

By modern standards the Civil War was still unmechanized. It was fought with rifles, bayonets, and sabers by men on foot or horseback. Artillery was more used than in previous wars, but was still a relatively minor consumer of iron and steel. The railroad was also brought into use, but the building of military lines offset only a small percentage of the overall drop from the prewar level of civilian railroad construction. Had all of these things not been true, the Confederacy with its small industrial development could never have fought through four years of increasingly effective blockade.

In spite of the failure of direct quantitative evidence to show accelerating effects of the war on rates of economic growth, there could be long-run effects of a qualitative type that would gradually foster a more rapid rate of economic growth. The most obvious place to look for such indirect effects would be in the results of freeing the slaves. Marxists contended that elimination of slavery was a necessary precursor

[30] Leonard P. Ayres, *Turning Points in Business Cycles* (New York, 1939), 14; Norman J. Silberling, *The Dynamics of Business* (New York, 1943), 50.

[31] Silberling, *Dynamics of Business*, 61.

[32] *Ibid.*, 66.

[33] Ayres, Silberling, and some other students of economic activity such as Herbert Hoover, however, blame the breakdown of the 1930's on the dislocations caused by World War I. *Ibid.*, 65–66. See also *The Memoirs of Herbert Hoover: The Great Depression, 1929–1941* (New York, 1952), 105.

of the bourgeois industrialism which would lead to the socialist revolution. The creation of a free Negro labor force was, of course, of great long-run importance. In the twentieth century it has led to readjustment of Negro population between the deep South and the northern industrial areas, and to changes in the use of southern land.

But economically the effects of war and emancipation over the period 1840 to 1880 were negative. Richard A. Easterlin writes: "In every southern state, the 1880 level of per capita income originating in commodity production and distribution was below, or at best only slightly above that of 1840. . . . [This] attests strikingly to the impact of that war and the subsequent disruption on the southern economy."[34] In general the Negroes became sharecroppers or wage laborers, often cultivating the same land and the same crops as before the war. In qualification of the argument that free Negro labor led to more rapid industrialization it should be noted that the South did not keep up with the national pace in the growth of non-agricultural wealth until after 1900.[35]

Two indirect effects of the war aided industrial growth to degrees that cannot accurately be measured. These were, first, a more satisfactory money market, and, second, more security for entrepreneurial activity than in the prewar period. The sharp wartime inflation had the usual effect of transferring income from wage, salary, and interest receivers to those making profits. This meant concentration on savings in the hands of entrepreneurs who would invest in new activities; and this no doubt helps to explain the speculative booms of the last half of the 1860s and first two years of the 1870s which have been treated as the prosperity resulting from the war. Inflation also eased the burdens of those railroads which had excessive mortgage debts. But a great deal of new research would be needed to establish causal connections between the inflationary reallocation of wealth, 1863 to 1865, and the high rate of industrial progress in the late 1870s and the 1880s.

The National Banking Act, providing a more reliable currency for interstate operations, has been hailed as a great aid to business expansion although it would be hard to demonstrate, aside from a few weeks during panics, that plentiful but occasionally unsound currency had seriously interfered with earlier industrial growth.[36] The existence of $2.5 billion in federal bonds also provided a basis for credit that was larger than before the war. This led to broader and more active security markets as well as to easier personal borrowing. But two qualifications must be kept in mind. First, local bank lending to favored borrowers had probably tended to be too liberal before the war and was now put on a somewhat firmer basis. In other words, since 1800 a multiplication of banks had made credit relatively easy to obtain in the United States, and in the North this continued to be the situation. Second, the southern banking system was largely destroyed by the war and had to be rebuilt in the subsequent decades. It should also be remembered that by 1875 some 40 percent of the banks were outside the national banking system.[37]

Because of a few colorful speculators like Jay Gould, Daniel Drew, and Jim Fisk, and the immortality conferred on them, initially by the literary ability of the Adams brothers, the New York stock exchange in the postwar decade appears to have mirrored a new era of predatory wealth. But one has only to study the scandals of the London and New York stock exchanges in 1854 to see that there was little growth in the sophistication or boldness of stock op-

---

[34] *Trends in the American Economy*, 85.

[35] Simon Kuznets (ed.), *Population Redistribution and Economic Growth: United States, 1870–1950* (2 vols.; Philadelphia, 1957–60), I (*Methodological Considerations and Reference Tables*), 729–32; II (*Analysis of Economic Change*), 109.

[36] See Bray Hammond, *Banks and Politics in America: From the Revolution to the Civil War* (Princeton, 1957), 663–67, 670.

[37] *Historical Statistics* (1960 ed.), 628, 638.

erators during these 15 years.[38] In any case, the exploits of market operators were seldom related in a positive way to economic growth. Even a record of new issues of securities, which is lacking for this period, would chiefly reflect the flow of capital into railroads, banks, and public utilities rather than into manufacturing. Very few "industrial" shares were publicly marketed before the decade of the 1880s; such enterprises grew chiefly from the reinvestment of earnings.

There was strong government encouragement to entrepreneurial activity during the Civil War, but to ascribe to it unusual importance for economic growth requires both analysis of the results and comparison with other periods. Government in the United States has almost always encouraged entrepreneurs. The federal and state administrations preceding the Civil War could certainly be regarded as friendly to business. They subsidized railroads by land grants, subscribed to corporate bond issues, and remitted taxes on new enterprise.[39] Tariffs were low, but railroad men and many bankers were happy with the situation. Whether or not American industrialism was significantly accelerated by the high protection that commenced with the war is a question that economists will probably never settle.

The building of a subsidized transcontinental railroad, held back by sectional controversies in the 1850s, was authorized along a northern route with the help of federal loans and land grants when the southerners excluded themselves from Congress. Putting more than a hundred million dollars into this project in the latter half of the 1860s, however, may have had an adverse effect on industrial growth. In general, the far western roads were built for speculative and strategic purposes uneconomically ahead of demand. They may for a decade, or even two, have consumed more capital than their transportation services were then worth to the economy.

To sum up this part of the obiter dictum, those who write of the war creating a national market tied together by railroads underestimate both the achievements of the two decades before the war and the ongoing trends of the economy. The nation's business in 1855 was nearly as intersectional as in 1870. Regional animosities did not interfere with trade, nor did these feelings diminish after the war. By the late 1850s the United States was a rapidly maturing industrial state with its major cities connected by rail, its major industries selling in a national market, and blessed or cursed with financiers, security flotations, stock markets, and all the other appurtenances of industrial capitalism.

But when all specific factors of change attributable to the war have been deflated, there is still the possibility that northern victory had enhanced the capitalist spirit, that as a consequence the atmosphere of government in Washington among members of both parties was more friendly to industrial enterprise and to northern-based national business operations than had formerly been the rule. It can be argued that in spite of Greenbackers and discontented farmers legislation presumably favorable to industry could be more readily enacted. The Fourteenth Amendment, for example, had as a by-product greater security for interstate business against state regulation, although it was to be almost two decades before the Supreme Court would give force to this protection. By 1876, a year of deep depression, the two major parties were trying to outdo each other in promises of stimulating economic growth. This highly generalized type of argument is difficult to evaluate, but in qualification of any theory of a sharp change in attitude we should remember that industrialism was growing rapidly from general causes and that by the

[38] See James K. Medbury, *Men and Mysteries of Wall Street* (Boston, 1870), 319 ff.; Margaret G. Myers, *The New York Money Market* (2 vols.; New York, 1931), I, 140.

[39] Myers, *New York Money Market*, I, 296; National Bureau of Economic Research, *Capital Formation and Economic Growth* (Princeton, 1955), 382. See also Carter Goodrich, *Government Promotion of American Canals and Railroads, 1800–1890* (New York, 1960).

1870s it was to be expected that major-party politics would be conforming to this change in American life.

Massive changes in physical environment such as those accompanying the rise of trade at the close of the Middle Ages or the gradual growth of industrialism from the seventeenth century on do not lend themselves readily to exact or brief periodization. If factory industry and mechanized transportation be taken as the chief indexes of early industrialism, its spread in the United States was continuous and rapid during the entire nineteenth century, but in general, advance was greater during periods of prosperity than in depressions. The first long period without a major depression, after railroads, canals, and steamboats had opened a national market, was from 1843 to 1857. Many economic historians interested in quantitative calculations would regard these years as marking the appearance of an integrated industrial society. Walter W. Rostow, incidentally, starts his "take-off" period in the 1840s and calls it completed by 1860.[40] Others might prefer to avoid any narrow span of years. Few, however, would see a major stimulation to

economic growth in the events of the Civil War.

Finally, one may speculate as to why this exaggerated conception of the role of the Civil War in industrialization gained so firm a place in American historiography. The idea fits, of course, into the Marxian frame of revolutionary changes, but it seems initially to have gained acceptance quite independently of Marxian influences. More concentrated study of the war years than of any other four-year span in the nineteenth century called attention to technological and business events usually overlooked. Isolated facts were seized upon without comparing them with similar data for other decades. The desire of teachers for neat periodization was probably a strong factor in quickly placing the interpretation in textbooks; thus, up to 1860 the nation was agricultural, after 1865 it was industrial. Recent study of American cultural themes suggests still another reason. From most standpoints the Civil War was a national disaster, but Americans like to see their history in terms of optimism and progress. Perhaps the war was put in a perspective suited to the culture by seeing it as good because in addition to achieving freedom for the Negro it brought about industrial progress.

[40] W. W. Rostow, *The Stages of Economic Growth* (Cambridge, Eng., 1960), 95.

1959

Economic Interests Do Not Explain Civil War and Reconstruction*

STANLEY COBEN

Historians have generally accepted the view that Radical Reconstruction "was a successful attempt by northeastern business, acting through the Republican party, to control the national government for its own economic ends: notably, the protective tariff, the national banks, [and] a 'sound' currency."[1] The Radical program is also said to have been "the method by which the 'Masters of Capital' . . . expected to exploit the resources of the southern states" behind federal protection.[2] Western hostility to these eastern business designs was avoided by large appropriations for rivers, harbors, railroads, free land, and pensions, and by use of the ever-potent "bloody shirt." Thus is supposed to have been prevented a union of western and southern agrarian opposition to the industrial and financial masters of the East.[3]

This thesis has met with little serious challenge and has been subjected to only occasional qualification. It continues to influence studies of the political and economic history of the post-Civil War era.[4] Yet a closer examination of the important economic legislation and congressional battles of the period, and of the attitudes of businessmen and influential business groups, reveals serious divisions on economic issues

---

* Stanley Coben, "Northeastern Business and Radical Reconstruction," *Mississippi Valley Historical Review*, XLVI (June 1959), 67–90.

[1] This is the conclusion of the most recent survey of historians' attitudes toward Radical Reconstruction. T. Harry Williams, "An Analysis of Some Reconstruction Attitudes," *Journal of Southern History*, XII (November, 1946), 470. Williams calls this the "Beale thesis," because it has been most completely developed by Howard K. Beale in his *The Critical Year: A Study of Andrew Johnson and Reconstruction* (New York, 1930), and his "On Rewriting Reconstruction History," *American Historical Review*, XLV (July, 1940), 807–27.

[2] William B. Hesseltine, "Economic Factors in the Abandonment of Reconstruction," *Mississippi Valley Historical Review*, XXII (September, 1935), 191.

[3] Helen J. and T. Harry Williams, "Wisconsin Republicans and Reconstruction, 1865–1870," *Wisconsin Magazine of History*, XXIII (September, 1939), 17–39.

[4] For recent expressions of the "Beale thesis," see C. Vann Woodward, *Origins of the New South, 1877–1913* (Baton Rouge, 1951), 23–24; George R. Bentley, *A History of the Freedmen's Bureau* (Philadelphia, 1955), 34–36; William B. Hesseltine, *Confederate Leaders in the New South* (Baton Rouge, 1950), 136; Arthur S. Link, *American Epoch: A History of the United States since the 1890's* (New York, 1955), 4–5; George R. Woolfolk, *The Cotton Regency: The Northern Merchants and Reconstruction, 1865–1880* (New York, 1958).

Earlier statements of the thesis may be found in Charles A. and Mary R. Beard, *The Rise of American Civilization* (2 vols.; New York, 1927), II, Chap. XX; Louis M. Hacker, *The Triumph of American Capitalism* (New York, 1940), Chap. 25; Richard N. Current, *Old Thad Stevens: A Story of Ambition* (Madison, 1942), Introduction, Chap. IV, and pp. 226, 249, 260; Matthew Josephson, *The Politicos, 1865–1896* (New York, 1938), Chap. I. James S. Allen, *Reconstruction: The Battle for Democracy, 1865–1867* (New York, 1937), is a Marxist version of the thesis.

among Radical legislators and northeastern businessmen alike. Certainly neither business leaders nor Radicals were united in support of any specific set of economic aims. Considerable evidence also suggests that the divisions among businessmen often cut across sectional as well as industrial lines. Furthermore, evidence indicates that few northeastern business groups were interested in southern investments in the early postwar years, and that these few were hostile to Radical Reconstruction.

The evident need for new interpretations of the motivation of northern Radicals and of the economic history of the entire period is demonstrated by a reexamination of the most important of the "economic ends" usually agreed upon as motives for Radical Reconstruction: the tariff and the currency issues, and the charge that northern business interests sought federal protection for the exploitation of the South.

The tariff split northeastern businessmen more than any other issue.[5] So fierce was business competition in this era, and so eager were the antagonists to use every possible means of winning an advantage, that almost all important tariff schedules became battlegrounds between industries, as well as between firms within the same industry. The copper, iron, linseed, and woolen textile industries, for example, were bitterly divided on crucial tariff schedules. The most significant split, however, was between certain high protectionist Pennsylvania interests on one side and influential low-tariff groups in New England and New York on the other. Pennsylvania coal mine operators feared the competition of rich Nova Scotia deposits, mined by low-wage labor, close to major American markets. Iron and steel manufacturers, the largest highly protected interest, were faced with the competition of long-established, technologically advanced English producers, whose wage scale was only a fraction of

that of the Americans. Pennsylvania carpet, glass, and wool industries demanded protection for similar reasons. The Keystone State was the largest extractor of iron ore and coal, the largest manufacturer of every form of iron and steel, of carpets, glass, and chemicals. On the other hand, powerful opposition to the tariff objectives of the Pennsylvanians came from the cotton and many of the woolen textile manufacturers of New England, and from the intertwined importing, financial, and railroad interests of New York.

New Englanders had become strong advocates of lower tariffs in the 1850s. The sharp tariff reductions of 1857 were accomplished chiefly by southern and New England votes.[6] New England manufacturers, especially textile producers, desired cheap imported raw materials in order to lower the price of their finished goods on the international market. Furthermore, they agreed to reduced rates on manufactured goods to discourage the growth of domestic competition.[7] Among American manufacturers, New England producers as a group were farthest from domestic sources of raw materials, closest to sources of cheap foreign commodities. Cheap supplies of coal, lumber, flaxseed, building stone, fine wool, and other commodities were available in nearby Canada and Nova Scotia. Scottish

---

[5] For a very different point of view, see Howard K. Beale, "The Tariff and Reconstruction," *American Historical Review*, XXXV (January, 1930), 276–94.

[6] Davis R. Dewey, *Financial History of the United States* (New York, 1903), 263. Dewey calculated the House vote for the 1857 tariff by section: New England 18 to 9 in favor, South 60 to 2 in favor, West 14 to 33 opposed, Middle States 24 to 28 opposed. There was no roll call on the final vote in the Senate, but see speeches by Senator Henry Wilson of Massachusetts, *Congressional Globe*, 34th Cong., 3rd sess., Appendix, 333–34 (February 26, 1857), and Senator Daniel Clark of New Hampshire, *ibid.*, 36th Cong., 2d sess., 1023 (February 19, 1861). See also Richard Hofstadter, "The Tariff Issue on the Eve of the Civil War," *American Historical Review*, XLIV (October, 1938), 50–55.

[7] George W. Bond and George Livermore, *Report of the Boston Board of Trade on Wool for 1859* (Boston, 1860), 2; Frank W. Taussig, *The Tariff History of the United States* (8th ed.; New York, 1931), 142; Melvin T. Copeland, *The Cotton Manufacturing Industry of the United States* (Cambridge, 1912), 14.

and British iron, Indian linseed, and Russian and Philippine hemp were imported into Boston in large quantities for the benefit of manufacturers.[8] Hardly any wool for the finer grades of cloth was produced in America, either before or after the war; nor were the rough, lowest grades, used in carpets and blankets, available at home.[9] By the end of the war, northeastern cotton manufacturers were importing the cheap Indian Surat cotton already widely used in England.[10]

English textile manufacturers, rivals of the New Englanders both in world markets and in America, obtained their raw materials free of duty.[11] There were good reasons for northeastern producers to believe that only the American system of imposts kept them from equaling the British in world trade. By the 1850s, many American mills had been in operation for three generations. They had experienced managers and weavers, cheap and abundant credit, modern machinery and production methods. In cotton cloth manufacturing, for which machinery could be used most extensively, New England labor was the most productive in the world. By 1860, the average number of looms per weaver was four in America, two in Great Britain. French and German manufacturers lagged even farther behind in methods and machinery.[12]

In addition to high productivity which made their goods competitive in the world markets, and the need to import cheap raw materials, many New England manufacturers preferred low tariffs from a fear that high textile duties would foster the growth of new competitors at home. New producers might bring cutthroat competition and periodic chaos to the industry by their poor judgment of market conditions. A special committee of the Boston Board of Trade acknowledged in 1858 that New England textile manufacturers had potentially dangerous rivals, especially in Pennsylvania; but the committee concluded that the tariff reduction of 1857 removed any immediate threat. "Under the impulse of a high protective tariff they accomplished so little, that now, under a change of policy, there seems no present cause of alarm."[13] When the higher Morrill duties came before the House in 1860, Representative Alexander H. Rice of Massachusetts, speaking for the manufacturers of his state, declared that "excessive protection" would stimulate "ruinous and irresponsible competition at home." In the Senate, textile manufacturer Henry Wilson proclaimed: "A high protective policy . . . is calculated to raise up rivals at home, and is more injurious to us than foreign competition."[14]

After the war, fear of the growth of protected competition continued to influence New England tariff sentiment. Edward Atkinson, president of the Cotton Spinners of New England, and a director of the Boston Board of Trade, wrote to Henry Wilson in 1866: "The strongest men in the trade are more afraid of the unskillful competi-

[8] See, for example, "Review of the Boston Market for the Year 1865," *Twelfth Annual Report of the Boston Board of Trade* (Boston, 1866), 72–95.

[9] Arthur H. Cole, *The American Wool Manufacture* (2 vols.; Cambridge, 1926), II, 310, 319, 330; John L. Hayes, *Statement of Fact Relative to Canada Wools and the Manufacture of Worsted* (Boston, 1866), 10, 19.

[10] "It may soon become imperatively necessary to us to be able to obtain foreign cotton on even terms with English manufacturers if we expect to compete with them in other markets." *Boston Board of Trade: Report of a Committee upon the Cotton Tax* (Boston, 1867); *Ninth Annual Report of the Boston Board of Trade* (Boston, 1863), Appendix, 99.

[11] Shepard B. Clough and Charles W. Cole, *Economic History of Europe* (3rd ed.; Boston, 1952), 472–76, 605–7.

[12] Copeland, *Cotton Manufacturing Industry*, 10. "What this country wants," Massachusetts cotton manufacturer Edwards Atkinson wrote

Senator Henry Wilson in 1866, "is cheap iron. Our cotton mills now cost to build $30 per spindle complete with looms, etc., etc., against $10 to $12 in England." Atkinson to Wilson, July 7, 1866, Harold F. Williamson, *Edward Atkinson: The Biography of an American Liberal* (Boston, 1934), 67.

[13] *Fifth Annual Report of the Boston Board of Trade* (Boston, 1859), 96–97.

[14] *Congressional Globe*, 36th Cong., 1st sess., 1867 (April 26, 1860); *ibid.*, 36th Cong., 2d sess., 1026 (February 19, 1861). Rice later became president of the Boston Board of Trade, then governor of Massachusetts.

tion built up at home by high duties than they are of foreign competition."[15] Enoch R. Mudge, one of the most influential New England textile men, told the organizing meeting of the National Association of Cotton Manufacturers and Planters in 1868: "When we speak of protection, I think it should be given only at the point where the cotton manufacturer requires it."[16] For well-established, efficient New England producers, of course, there were comparatively few points at which protection was necessary. They had seen evidence of the success of their low tariff theories in the few years the 1857 schedules were in force. "The operation of the tariff of 1857 has contributed largely to the prosperity of our woolen manufactures," one of Boston's largest wool dealers reported in 1859.[17] Exports of cotton cloth had risen steadily, from an average of $7 million in the years 1851 through 1856, to almost $11 million in 1860.[18]

The government's need for revenue allowed protectionists an almost unchallenged ascendancy during the Civil War,[19] but the battle between northeastern business groups over tariff schedules was resumed after Appomattox. For example, when a resolution for lower tariffs was placed before the National Board of Trade Convention in 1869, delegates from the Boston Board of Trade and Boston Corn Exchange voted 6 to 1 for the resolution; Philadelphia delegates voted 7 to 0 against it.[20]

The Boston Board of Trade also worked unsuccessfully to prevent abrogation of the reciprocity treaty with Canada; Philadelphia's board joined western agricultural interests in demanding an end to reciprocity.[21]

These divisions within the business community were likewise reflected in the congressional debates and voting on important tariff schedules. Cotton manufacturers resumed their prewar demands for lower schedules, even for cotton textiles. Senator William Sprague, whose sprawling Rhode Island mills were relatively inefficient, protested against the 25 percent cut in cotton textile duties proposed in 1867. He was answered by Senator William P. Fessenden of Maine, sponsor of the measure: "I am informed by the commissioner [Revenue Commissioner David A. Wells] that these duties were fixed at a rate perfectly satisfactory to those engaged in the manufacture of cottons, who appeared before him. . . . The cotton interest of this country has got so that it can stand of itself pretty much."[22]

Schedules on coal similarly came under attack. As power looms replaced hand looms, and steam power replaced water power, New England manufacturers became increasingly interested in lower coal duties.[23] Under reciprocity and the low tariff of 1857, imports of coal into Boston rose steadily from 88,531 tons in 1858, to 209,225 tons in 1865, most of this being cheap Nova Scotia fuel.[24] Representative George S. Boutwell and Senator Charles Sumner of Massachusetts tried in vain to

---

[15] Atkinson to Wilson, July 7, 1866, Williamson, *Atkinson*, 67–68.

[16] *Proceedings of a Convention for the Purpose of Organizing the National Association of Cotton Manufacturers and Planters* (Boston, 1868), 13.

[17] Bond and Livermore, *Report on Wool*, 2.

[18] Copeland, *Cotton Manufacturing Industry*, 14; Taussig, *Tariff History*, 142.

[19] Dewey, *Financial History*, 265–67, 272, 301–4; Taussig, *Tariff History*, 150, 159–62; Edward Stanwood, *American Tariff Controversies in the Nineteenth Century* (2 vols.; Boston, 1903), II, 130.

[20] *Proceedings of the Second Annual Meeting of the National Board of Trade* (Boston, 1870), 321.

[21] *Eleventh Annual Report of the Boston Board of Trade* (Boston, 1865), 42; *Thirteenth Annual Report of the Boston Board of Trade* (Boston, 1867), 2–3; *Thirty-first Annual Report of the Philadelphia Board of Trade* (Philadelphia, 1864), 17.

[22] *Congressional Globe*, 39th Cong., 2d sess., 709, 744 (January 24, 25, 1867).

[23] Copeland, *Cotton Manufacturing Industry*, 29; J. Herbert Burgy, *The New England Cotton Textile Industry: A Study in Industrial Geography* (Baltimore, 1932), 24, 30, 34, 100.

[24] *Twelfth Annual Report of the Boston Board of Trade* (Boston, 1866), 75.

prevent higher coal schedules from being placed in the proposed tariffs of 1866 and 1867. Sumner acknowledged that there was a lot of coal in Pennsylvania, West Virginia, and the West. "But why," he asked, "should New England, which has a natural resource comparatively near at home, be compelled at a great sacrifice to drag her coal from these distant supplies?" Sumner's amendment was defeated 11 to 25, with eight New Englanders, both New Yorkers, and one senator from Oregon comprising those favoring lower duties on coal.[25]

Many other schedules in the proposed bills of 1866 and 1867 were fought out by competing or conflicting business interests. Manufacturers, especially New Englanders, dependent upon cheap imported raw materials, were continually in opposition to the combined efforts of raw material producers and competing manufacturers closer to these native sources of supply. When Senator Benjamin F. Wade of Ohio moved to raise the duty on linseed, largely grown in the West, Fessenden of Maine accused him of asking the higher rate "for this simple, selfish reason: that the trade of crushing seed and manufacturing oil on the seacoast may be utterly destroyed for the benefit of crushers of seed and the manufacturers of oil in the West."[26]

Rolling mills, chiefly eastern, which controlled the American Iron and Steel Association,[27] almost forced through an extremely low duty on scrap iron. Such a duty would allow the mills to import huge quantities of cheap European used rails, and to re-roll them in lieu of using domestic pig iron for new rails. Senator Zachariah Chandler, from the iron producing state of Michigan, demanded that the proposed duty on wrought scrap iron be quadrupled and the duty on cast scrap be almost tripled. Lower schedules, he declared, would close the iron mines, put out every blast furnace, and mean "total ruin to the iron interests of the United States. . . . It is a bill gotten up to suit the railroad rolling-mills, and to sacrifice every other iron interest in the United States." The rolling mills won one Senate vote, but Chandler forced another, which was won by those sympathetic with the mine operators and pig iron producers. Almost all the western senators and both Pennsylvanians voted for higher duties on scrap metal. All but one senator from New England and New York voted for the low schedule.[28]

The only tariff adjustment besides the wool and woolens bill to become law in the early postwar years was a measure passed in 1869, greatly increasing the duties on copper. Eastern smelters, who used a combination of eastern and cheap South American ores, were forced out of business by this bill, passed for the benefit of Lake Superior mine operators, whose domestic ores did not require smelting. The Lake Superior mine owners, some of whom were eastern financiers, were thus given a monopoly of the American market. They were thereby enabled to charge much higher than world prices at home and to dump their surplus abroad at much lower prices.[29] Similar conflicts among business interests developed on tariff schedules for salt (used

---

[25] *Congressional Globe*, 39th Cong., 1st sess., 3569 (July 3, 1866); 39th Cong., 2d sess., 830, 857 (January 29, 30, 1867).

[26] *Ibid.*, 39th Cong., 2d sess., 705 (January 24, 1867). Linseed oil was important in the manufacture of paints, dyes, and varnishes.

[27] Pig iron producers, still the dominant segment of the iron and steel industry in the early 1870's, withdrew from the American Iron and Steel Association in 1871 and formed their own association, which by 1873 numbered 200 firms. For the sharp division which this association saw between itself and the American Iron and Steel Association, see *The American Pig Iron Manufacturing Association, Meeting Held in New York City, February 19, 1873* (Philadelphia, 1873), 32, 64.

[28] *Congressional Globe*, 39th Cong., 2d sess., 799–801 (January 28, 1867), 860–62 (January 30, 1867).

[29] Taussig, *Tariff History*, 219–21; *Letter of Henry Martin, Esq., President of the Baltimore Copper Company to the Senate of the United States in Opposition to the Bill Increasing the Duty on Imported Copper Ores* (Baltimore, 1869); Bliss Perry, *Life and Letters of Henry Lee Higginson* (Boston, 1921), 263–64; William B. Gates, *Michigan Copper and Boston Dollars* (Cambridge, 1951), 33–35, 45–47.

for scouring wool), zinc, lead, nickel, and building stones.[30]

The wool and woolens bill of 1867, which considerably raised most schedules, has been cited as a prime example of the cooperation of business interests, because it was devised in a conference between a committee of wool growers and representatives of the National Association of Wool Manufacturers. What has generally been overlooked is the fact that the manufacturers' association, like the American Iron and Steel Association, was dominated by a well-organized segment of the industry, in this case by worsted and carpet manufacturers, whose interests conflicted with those of other important groups within the woolen industry.

Most influential of the men who negotiated the agreement for the manufacturers were Erastus B. Bigelow, president and founder of the Association, and America's leading carpet manufacturer; John L. Hayes, permanent secretary of the Association; and J. Wiley Edmonds, treasurer of the giant Pacific Mills, a leading worsted producer. Hayes reported to the membership that "for six months Mr. Bigelow gave himself unremittingly to the great work . . . [and to him they] must attribute the happy results of the conference." Before this "happy" conclusion, Hayes conceded, most woolen manufacturers "were becoming more and more disposed to look abroad for the chief supply of raw material . . . and were inclined to advocate the British policy of free trade in raw materials, including wool."[31] Certainly the re-

sults of the conference were not so happy for manufacturers of woolen cloth, the largest item of domestic woolen output. These producers would be forced to pay much higher rates for imported raw wool than the worsted manufacturers with whom they competed. Carpet and blanket manufacturers would pay by far the lowest rates.[32]

The largest manufacturer of wool cloth taking part in the negotiations with the growers was Edward Harris of the Harris Manufacturing Company, Woonsocket, Rhode Island. Harris later declared that he had no part in deciding the schedules and that his name had been appended to the agreement without his knowledge or consent.[33] Senator Henry Wilson of Massachusetts, a manufacturer of fine woolen cloth, told the Senate Finance Committee that if the new schedules were put into effect, he would have to close his factory. He subsequently declared in the Senate: "Some of the very ablest men in Massachusetts and in New England earnestly believe that this bill, so far as it concerns two thirds of the woolen manufacturers of the country, is not so good as the present tariff. [Only] the carpet manufacturers are abundantly satisfied." Wilson's statement was reinforced by other New England senators. William Sprague of Rhode Island, William P. Fessenden of Maine, and Lot M. Morrill of Maine reported similar opinions of the wool and woolens bill among the cloth manufacturers in their constituencies.[34] Nevertheless, there was no organized opposition in Washington to the energetic Hayes or to the large number of western congressmen who were anxious to honor

---

[30] *Congressional Globe*, 39th Cong., 2d sess., 680, 765, 793, 798, 821 (January 23, 26, 28, 29, 1867).

[31] *Transactions of the National Association of Wool Manufacturers, Second Annual Report* (Boston, 1866), 12, 20. For interesting evidence of Edmonds' part in this agreement, see speech by Senator Jonathan P. Dolliver, *Congressional Record*, 61st Cong., 1st sess., 1717 (Many 4, 1909). For the protectionist ideas of Bigelow and Hayes, see Erastus B. Bigelow, *Objects and Plan of the National Association of Wool Manufacturers* (Boston, 1865), 3–4; John L. Hayes, *The Fleece and the Loom: An Address before the National Association of Wool Manufacturers at the First

Annual Meeting in Philadelphia, September 6, 1865 (Boston, 1866), 60.

[32] For more detailed discussion of the schedules, see Chester W. Wright, *Wool Growing and the Tariff* (Cambridge, 1910), 213–15; Haldor R. Mohat, *The Tariff on Wool* (Madison, 1935), 23–25; Taussig, *Tariff History*, 195–218.

[33] Edward Harris, *Memorial of Manufacturers of Woolen Goods to the Committee on Ways and Means* (Washington, 1872), 22.

[34] *Congressional Globe*, 39th Cong., 2d sess., 909–11 (January 31, 1867).

an agreement which gave protection to wool growers. The wool and woolens bill passed easily despite adverse votes from men like Wilson, Sumner, and Sprague who had close associations with the New England woolen industry.[35]

Northeastern opposition to the cloth schedules continued after the passage of the bill, and in the winter of 1869–70, Edward Harris and 43 other New England woolen manufacturers petitioned Congress to reduce the duties on wool for cloth as low as carpet wool duties, which were one-fifth as high. On reaching Washington with this petition, Harris was informed that the wool growers and John Hayes, who said he represented 300 companies and individuals associated with the woolen industry, had first claim on congressmen's votes.[36] In 1889, the woolen cloth manufacturers obtained 530 signatures from wool manufacturers and dealers asking the lower duties— and again failed. Finally, in 1909, the cloth manufacturers formed a separate organization to do permanent battle in Washington with the worsted and carpet interests.[37]

For somewhat different reasons a low-tariff sentiment similar to that in New England was also strong in New York City, by far the largest importing and financial center in the country. New York merchants, shippers, and those who financed their activities opposed tariffs which might restrict imports, while the railroad financiers protested that under the proposed tariff of 1866 the Erie and the New York Central systems alone would have to pay out an-

nually "about two million dollars by way of protection."[38] The New York Chamber of Commerce had opposed the Morrill bill of 1861 as "a radical change in the tariff policy of the country," but had patriotically refrained from strenuous protests as tariff rates steadily rose during the war.[39] In listing the organization's postwar objectives, however, Secretary John Austin Stevens declared: "The principles of free, unshackled trade, which it has ever upheld, must be reaffirmed."[40] A few months after the war's end, the *Commercial and Financial Chronicle* observed: "Signs are not wanting that the subject of Free Trade will be made the text of the next political agitation in this country." The *Journal of Commerce* also began agitating for lower tariffs soon after the war; and the introduction of the first postwar tariff bill, providing for generally increased rates, naturally brought a strong protest from the New York Chamber of Commerce.[41]

Clearly, then, New England cotton manufacturers and many wool and other manufacturers preferred and worked for lower

---

[35] *Ibid.*, 1958 (March 2, 1867). A relatively small but well-informed and organized group within the woolen industry was able to write schedules to suit itself because they had to be phrased in complicated, technical language. See Senator Dolliver's comments on this subject, *Congressional Record*, 61st Cong., 1st sess., 1715 (May 4, 1909). The major reason for passage, however, was the fact that the schedules pleased leading wool growers.

[36] Edward Harris, *The Tariff and How It Effects the Woolen Cloth Manufacture and Wool Growers* (Woonsocket, 1871), 14–15; *Carded Wool Bulletin* (Boston), I (May, 1910), 6; Edward Atkinson, *Reply to the Argument by Mr. John L. Hayes* (Woonsocket, 1872).

[37] Mohat, *Tariff on Wool*, 19; Taussig, *Tariff History*, 316–17.

[38] Statement of Representative Henry J. Raymond of New York, *Congressional Globe*, 39th Cong., 1st sess., 3516 (June 30, 1866).

[39] *Fourth Annual Report of the Chamber of Commerce of the State of New York* (New York, 1862), 2–3; *Fifth Annual Report of the Chamber of Commerce of the State of New York* (New York, 1863), 4–5. Senator Edwin D. Morgan, a member of the Chamber, voted for tariff increases during the war, then reverted to fighting high schedules in 1866. James A. Rawley, *Edwin D. Morgan, 1811–1883: Merchant in Politics* (New York, 1955), 207–9.

[40] *Centennial Celebration of the Chamber of Commerce of the State of New York . . . : Report of Proceedings* (New York, 1868), 21; also, *Ninth Annual Report of the Chamber of Commerce of the State of New York* (New York, 1867), Part I, p. 5.

[41] *Commercial and Financial Chronicle* (New York), I (July 8, 1865), 38; New York *Journal of Commerce*, May 23, 1865; *Ninth Annual Report of the Chamber of Commerce of the State of New York*, Part I, pp. 29, 30, 60, 61. The Chamber's protest could not be ignored. The organization's membership included many of the largest campaign contributors to both parties, including, in 1866, such merchants and importers as Moses Grinnell, Alexander T. Stewart, William E. Dodge, Horace Claflin, and Senator Edwin D. Morgan; and such financiers as Henry Clews, Levi P. Morton, John Austin Stevens, Moses Taylor, John J. Cisco, and J. Pierpont Morgan.

tariff schedules—as did most of New York's financial and mercantile community. This fact was obvious to contemporary protectionists, especially the fervent Pennsylvanians. They recognized the role New Yorkers and New Englanders played in reducing many schedules, and in defeating, by obstructionist tactics, bills of which they disapproved. A delegate from Philadelphia's Board of Trade complained to the National Board of Trade in 1869 that New England's industries had been built up behind tariff walls. "Now they are marked disciples of free trade. . . . They overlook the interests yet in their infancy. . . . Is this right? Is this just?"[42] Henry C. Carey, leading spokesman for Pennsylvania iron, coal, and other protected interests, charged in 1867 that for 20 years, on tariff questions, "It has pleased the representatives of Massachusetts to array themselves on the side of cotton planters, slave owners, railroad monopolists."[43]

Northeastern businessmen were thus far from united in support of high tariffs after the Civil War. Leading business interests of New England and New York believed that they lost more than they gained from high postwar tariffs. Had reconstruction politics allowed them a choice, it seems likely that these important groups would have preferred a return to the coalition which had produced the low tariff of 1857 —a coalition which included the South.

Certainly they would not have opposed the return of southern representatives in order to retain high imposts.

The business interests of the Northeast were divided into fiercely competing groups not only by the tariff issue, but by currency questions as well. These conflicts were brought into the open shortly after the Civil War by attempts to contract the swollen wartime currency. Secretary of the Treasury Hugh McCulloch's proposals for contraction, designed for quick resumption of specie payments, won a cordial response from many importers and financiers, who would gain materially from the elimination of the premium on gold and a consequent rise in the market value of government bonds.[44] Many businessmen longed for the currency stability they believed resumption would bring. But McCulloch met with warnings and protests from other important northeastern business groups. The Philadelphia Board of Trade immediately warned against hasty action, "lest by injudicious measures and rapid contraction," the people's interests should be sacrificed. A few weeks later, the *Commercial and Financial Chronicle*, a firm advocate of hard money, was forced to admit: "There is little doubt that the depression in public confidence, of which a proof will be found in our account of the week's fluctuation in the Stock Market, is closely connected with the anticipated effects of the contraction movement of the Secretary of the Treasury."[45]

Although only a moderate amount of currency was taken out of circulation,

[42] *Proceedings of the Second Annual Meeting of the National Board of Trade* (Boston, 1870), 312. For a justification of their low tariff policies, see the comments by New England textile men in *First Annual Meeting of the National Board of Trade* (Boston, 1869), 127–34.

[43] Henry C. Carey, *Reconstruction: Industrial, Financial and Political, Letters to the Hon. Henry Wilson, Senator from Massachusetts* (Philadelphia, 1867), 34. As Carey observed, votes on the complex tariff bills of 1866 and 1867 were not an accurate indication of tariff sentiment. Some additional insight into these bills is provided by Herbert R. Ferleger, *David A. Wells and the American Revenue System, 1865–1870* (New York, 1942), 22–168; Williamson, *Atkinson*, 64–71; Taussig, *Tariff History*, 175–77. Carey was especially hurt by what he considered the apostasy of his friend, Revenue Commissioner Wells, who went over to the camp of the low-tariff New Englanders in 1866–67.

[44] It should be noted that while immediate resumption would have raised the market value of federal bonds, it would also have reduced the value of interest payments, which were made in gold. Important dealers in government bonds, like Henry Clews and Jay Cooke, opposed contraction. Cooke wrote his brother in 1867, "As to getting back to specie payments, the least said about that the better, as it is the premium on gold that enables us to sell the 5-20's." Jay Cooke to Henry D. Cooke, September 20, 1867, Henrietta M. Larson, *Jay Cooke: Private Banker* (Cambridge, 1936), 204, 209–10.

[45] *Thirty-third Annual Report of the Philadelphia Board of Trade* (Philadelphia, 1866), 1. *Commercial and Financial Chronicle*, II (January 13, 1866), 31; *Iron Age* (New York), V (November 7, 1867), 2, 4.

businessmen continued to fear that goods bought at high prices with inflated greenbacks might have to be sold at much lower prices if McCulloch were allowed to proceed with contraction. Wholesale prices fell sharply after January, 1866, confirming their fears.[46] As general price depreciation continued through 1866 and 1867, businessmen's objections to contraction became increasingly loud and widespread. The Commercial Exchange of Philadelphia adopted a resolution in January, 1867, "That premature resumption will prove a curse and not a blessing." A vice-president of the New York Chamber of Commerce, who approved contraction, recalled "living in the midst of the clamor against that process, where almost every man I met was denouncing the Secretary and predicting ruin upon all the interests of the country unless the policy was discontinued."[47]

Opposition to McCulloch's policy spread to Congress, where Representative William D. Kelley of Pennsylvania called it the "road to bankruptcy."[48] Finally, in January, 1868, Senator John Sherman of Ohio introduced legislation to end contraction. "We hear the complaint from all parts of the country," he said, "from all branches of industry . . . that industry for some reason is paralyzed and that trade and enterprise are not so well rewarded as they were. Many, perhaps erroneously, attribute all this to the contraction of the currency."[49]

Passage of Sherman's measure, however,

did not end the conflict among northeastern businessmen over currency. Most seem to have favored a stable money supply, and to have opposed currency expansion and quick resumption alike. Many of the more conservative bankers, importers, and merchants, however, continued to support an early return to specie payments. There was also an influential and vocal group of businessmen which persistently called for currency inflation. This last group found adherents among those manufacturers and merchants who sought to take advantage of great postwar demand for their products, but who had difficulty obtaining capital for plant and inventory expansion, even at extremely high interest rates. Many of those who borrowed large sums for investments in factories, mines, and railroads were apt to favor currency expansion, which they believed would lower interest rates, raise prices, and make debts easier to pay. Radical Senator Sprague, for example, in control of a Rhode Island empire of factories, real estate, utilities, and banks, complained to the Senate that "The interest paid by the borrower today is just double what it was at the close of the War." He placed the blame on "the power centralized in New York."[50]

It is significant that Jay Cooke, once an ardent hard money man, became something of an inflationist after he borrowed millions to build the Northern Pacific, and saw his corporation become a huge land speculator through government grants. In a letter to his brother and partner, written in 1868, Cooke called for moderate currency expansion which would keep pace "with the new habits and enlarged area of Country." "Why," he asked, "should this Grand and Glorious Country be stunted and dwarfed—its activities chilled and its very life blood curdled by these miserable

---

[46] Wesley C. Mitchell, *Gold, Prices, and Wages under the Greenback Standard* (Berkeley, 1909), 26; "Review of the Boston Market for the Year 1866," *Thirteenth Annual Report of the Boston Board of Trade* (Boston, 1867), 43. Wholesale prices fell fastest, affecting manufacturers and the larger merchants and importers more than retailers. Both wholesale and retail prices fell faster than wages and farm prices.

[47] *Proceedings of the First Annual Meeting of the National Board of Trade* (Boston, 1869), 114, 173.

[48] "Contraction, the Road to Bankruptcy," reprinted in William D. Kelley, *Speeches, Addresses, and Letters on Industrial and Financial Questions* (Philadelphia, 1872), 210.

[49] *Congressional Globe*, 40th Cong., 2d sess., 407, 537, 674 (January 9, 15, 22, 1868).

[50] *Ibid.*, 40th Cong., 1st sess., 65, 361 (March 15, 30, 1867). Sprague's overextended empire went into bankruptcy in 1873 when his loans were called in. Zechariah Chafee, Jr., "Weathering the Panic of '73," *Dorr Pamphlets* (Providence), No. 4 (1942).

'hard coin' theories—the musty theories of a by gone age?"[51]

Pennsylvania iron and steel men, through their representatives and periodicals, led eastern demands for an increased supply of currency. Their industry was expanding rapidly behind high tariff walls, stimulated by the postwar spurt in railroad building. Iron manufacturer Thaddeus Stevens was a leader in congressional schemes to inflate the currency. Both Stevens and Kelley of Pennsylvania supported textile manufacturer Benjamin F. Butler's resolution to pay the wartime bonds in paper rather than gold.[52] Representative Daniel J. Morrell, a bank president as well as former general manager of the giant Cambria Iron Works in Pennsylvania, called for more circulation, and contended that under a program of inflation "Capital would be less valuable, and a larger share of the increase in wealth would go to the enterprise and labor which created it."[53] Pennsylvania iron and steel periodicals took up the fight against the bankers. "In the seaboard cities," said *Iron Age* in 1867, "the money power seeks to attain a position of irresistible control, and to subdue and subordinate to itself all the interests of industry."[54] The lines of battle were perhaps drawn most succinctly and cogently in a speech by Representative Kelley in January, 1867. "The contest," he said, "is between the creditor and the debtor class—the men of investments and the men of enterprise."[55]

The issue, however, was not as simple as Kelley put it. Most foreign goods were paid for with gold, not greenbacks. Customs duties were also payable in gold. As long as specie payments could be post-poned, the premium on gold would remain. In the early postwar years, the premium fluctuated between 30 and 40 percent. The effect was to raise the cost of foreign goods about one-third above what their cost would be if specie resumption should occur.[56] Monetary inflation would tend to raise the premium and consequently the price of imports even higher. This fact was not lost on the Pennsylvanians. As early as 1863, the Philadelphia Board of Trade noted that the "premium on foreign exchange adds greatly to tariff and transportation costs."[57] In 1864, Samuel J. Reeves, iron manufacturer and chairman of the executive committee of the American Iron and Steel Association, wrote the Commissioner of Internal Revenue: "The constant advance in the price of gold has acted as so much protection to the home manufacturer above the duty. . . . The iron manufacture now finds its safety only in the high cost of gold; what is to become of it when there will be no premium on gold?"[58] The answer, so far as many iron manufacturers were concerned, was to retain the premium on gold.

The significance of the Pennsylvanians' currency policies was obvious to importers, financiers, and many manufacturers in New York and New England. Most of these favored hard money and low tariffs. The Boston Board of Trade's "Wool Report" for 1863 noted the effect of the gold premium on the price of wool.[59] New York merchants protested that the high price of gold seriously discouraged imports, and the city's Chamber of Commerce adopted a resolution charging that "Powerful inter-

---

[51] Jay Cooke to Henry D. Cooke, November 23, 1869, Larson, *Jay Cooke*, 205.

[52] *Congressional Globe*, 40th Cong., 2d sess., 212–13 (December 16, 1867).

[53] *Ibid.*, 41st Cong., 2d sess., Appendix, 142 (March 10, 1870).

[54] *Iron Age*, V (October 24, 1867), 4; *ibid.* (November 7, 1867), 4; *Industrial Bulletin*, VIII (November, 1871), 4.

[55] Kelley, *Speeches, Addresses, and Letters*, 226.

[56] See statement of costs of English rails in *Bulletin of the American Iron and Steel Association* (Philadelphia), No. 2 Supplement (February 6, 1867), 186. The association's figures show the premium to have been a greater share of total cost than was the tariff duty.

[57] *Thirtieth Annual Report of the Philadelphia Board of Trade* (Philadelphia, 1863), 40.

[58] "Extracts from a letter to the Hon. Joseph J. Lewis . . . from Samuel J. Reeves," *Thirty-second Annual Report of the Philadelphia Board of Trade* (Philadelphia, 1865), 76.

[59] Bond and Livermore, *Report on Wool*, 3.

ests are striving to perpetuate the existing depreciation of the currency."[60]

When contraction was abruptly ended and tariff reform failed, in 1867–68, some businessmen in New York and New England felt that the government's policies were falling under the control of high tariff and paper money men. On the other hand, Henry C. Carey, spokesman for Pennsylvania protectionists, charged that New England, aided by New Yorkers, was attempting to create a monopoly in money and manufacturing. One instrument of the monopolists, said Carey, was a low tariff, which New England manufacturers could afford because of their low interest charges and modern machinery, and which they used to ruin domestic competition and to obtain cheap foreign raw materials to aid New England producers. A second instrument, he continued, was the banking system —"a great money monopoly for the especial benefit of the Trading States." Even with this monopoly, Carey complained, the traders wished to contract the currency, further reducing the pittance allowed Pennsylvania and further raising interest charges manufacturers would have to pay. Either the New Englanders would change their ways, he warned, or they would be compelled to do so by a combination of southern, western, and middle states, in which Pennsylvania would take the lead.[61] In reply, cotton manufacturer Edward Atkinson "rejoiced" at this analysis of New England's advantage, and assured Carey that henceforth the New England representatives would support the low tariff and hard money policies even more strongly.

Instead of fearing the threatened combination of sections under Pennsylvania's leadership against those policies, he prophesied that New England would join with the South and the West in promoting them.[62]

Both Carey and Atkinson overstated the unity of New England manufacturers, oversimplified the varied and conflicting interests in the West, and conjectured about the probable political and economic alignments of the postwar South. Nevertheless, both were more realistic than historians who have explained northeastern leadership of Radical Reconstruction in terms of a unified northeastern business interest anxious to keep the South out of the Union in order to protect high tariffs and hard money.

Nor can the direction and support which northeastern representatives gave to Radical Reconstruction be accurately explained as an attempt to "make easy the road for northern economic penetration and exploitation of the South."[63] Few important northeastern capitalists had any desire to place their money in a war-torn, unsettled region. Eventually, northerners invested huge sums in southern factories, mines, railroads, and real estate; but it is significant that only a small number did so as long as Radicals controlled southern state legislatures.

Many southern leaders and periodicals recognized the need for northern capital after the Civil War, and numerous cordial invitations were extended.[64] That such invitations were futile was obvious to business-

---

[60] *Eighth Annual Report of the Chamber of Commerce of the State of New York* (New York, 1866), Part II, p. 90; *Memorial to the Honorable the Senate and House of Representatives* (New York, 1869), signed by A. A. Low and Samuel Babcock for the New York City Chamber of Commerce; remarks by A. A. Low in *Eighth Annual Report of the New York Chamber of Commerce* (New York, 1866), Part I, p. 28; and *Ninth Annual Report of the New York Chamber of Commerce* (New York, 1867), Part I, pp. 74, 76.

[61] Carey, *Reconstruction*, 4, 8, 21, 24–26, 50, 53–58, 67–68.

[62] Atkinson to Carey, November 11, 1867, Williamson, *Atkinson*, 79–80. For further details of this controversy see Henry Wilson to Carey, September 21, 1867; Carey to Wilson, September 25, 1867; George L. Ward to Carey, October 16, 1867; Carey to Ward, October 18, 1867; David A. Wells to Carey, November 1, 6, 1867; Carey to Atkinson, November 18, 1867, Henry C. Carey Papers, Edward Carey Gardiner Collection (Historical Society of Pennsylvania, Philadelphia).

[63] Hesseltine, *Confederate Leaders in the New South*, 136.

[64] For example, see Petersburg (Va.) *News*, quoted in New York *Journal of Commerce*, May 20, 1865. A number of similar appeals for northern capital are cited in John F. Stover, *The Railroads of the South, 1865–1900: A Study in Fi-*

men, North and South. "We want capital attracted to the South," said the *Commercial and Financial Chronicle* of New York City, "and this cannot be, so long as the States are under semi-military rule." And from the South *De Bow's Review* echoed, "It is idle to ask capital to venture until order is restored." South Carolina exempted manufacturers from all state and local taxation, but failed to attract northern capital partly because of the uncertainties of Reconstruction.[65] Thomas W. Conway, a former Freedmen's Bureau official, who toured the North in 1866 trying to induce businessmen to make southern investments, reported to the New York Chamber of Commerce, which had encouraged his mission: "The substantial men met by me in all parts of the country are sick of the delay in regard to the settlement of our national political difficulties." Until such settlement occurred, he predicted, there would be continued uncertainty and violence in the South, and poor prospects for northern investment.[66]

Even Pennsylvania's Representative William D. Kelley, who was both a Radical leader and an enthusiastic advocate of northern investments in the postwar South, soon found that Radical Reconstruction interfered with southern industrial growth. In March, 1868, Kelley demanded immediate readmission of Alabama—a potential economic paradise, he said, whose wealth was "paralyzed" while Reconstruction ran its violent course. Thaddeus Stevens, less interested in southern industrial development than was Kelley, fought against his colleague's haste, insisting that Alabama must first guarantee the suffrage rights of Negroes.[67]

New England cotton manufacturers, dealers, and shippers feared that northerners' refusal to send their capital south would result in an insufficient cotton crop. Edward S. Tobey, Boston cotton merchant and manufacturer, recommended that the Freedmen's Bureau be authorized to take over the role of private capital in organizing Negro labor for cotton cultivation. The South's deficiency of capital, Tobey told the Boston Board of Trade in a famous speech in November, 1865, was proved by "frequent applications from Southern men to Northern capitalists to invest in cotton lands at low prices." It would be ideal if private investors could supply this want; but capital, Tobey observed, "is seldom placed by its possessors where society is disorganized and life and property comparatively unprotected by a stable and efficient government." The Board approved Tobey's suggestion.[68]

A few months after Tobey's speech, however, the New Englanders' plans were changed by a sudden shift in the cotton market. The southern cotton crop was larger than expected. Furthermore, the English, with new machinery and methods for manufacturing with cheap Indian Surat cotton, had become increasingly less dependent upon American producers. New England manufacturers and dealers were caught with large supplies of cotton as the price dropped almost 40 percent in the first four months of 1866.[69] The momentary interest New England businessmen had shown in reconstruction legislation dropped with the price of cotton. The Boston Board of Trade's "Review of the Boston Market for the Year

---

nance and Control (Chapel Hill, 1955), 54–55. See also Broadus Mitchell, *The Rise of Cotton Mills in the South* (Baltimore, 1921), 237.

[65] *Commercial and Financial Chronicle*, II (February 17, 1866), 198; *De Bow's Review*, After the War Series, Vol. IV (November, 1867), 451; Francis B. Simkins and Robert H. Woody, *South Carolina during Reconstruction* (Chapel Hill, 1932), 290–91.

[66] Thomas W. Conway, "Introduction of Capital and Men into the Southern States of the Union," *Ninth Annual Report of the Chamber of Commerce of the State of New York* (New York, 1867), Part II, pp. 8–13.

[67] *Congressional Globe*, 40th Cong., 2d sess., 2139–41 (March 26, 1868). For another significant conflict between Kelley and Stevens see *ibid.*, 39th Cong., 1st sess., 3687–88 (July 9, 1866).

[68] Edward S. Tobey, *The Industry of the South . . . : A Speech Delivered before the Boston Board of Trade, November 27, 1865* (Boston, 1878). See also *Twelfth Annual Report of the Boston Board of Trade* (Boston, 1866), 57.

[69] *Thirteenth Annual Report of the Boston Board of Trade* (Boston, 1867), 47.

1867," declared: "Business men, generally, are loud in their complaints against the course of legislation for two years past. Important interests have been neglected by Congress, and too much time has been wasted on questions which only led to discord and bad feeling in the different branches of the Government."[70]

Most large northern investors, instead of being concerned over the difficulties of investing in the South, turned their attention to the many lucrative opportunities elsewhere—in Minnesota timberlands, Michigan iron and copper mines, Pennsylvania coal and oil, and railroads in almost every state. Significantly, the Pennsylvania Railroad, with abundant capital and great influence in Congress, did not attempt to create its "Southern empire" until Radical Reconstruction was nearing its conclusion. Until 1871, the Pennsylvania preferred to take advantage of investment opportunities in the Northwest. When Thomas A. Scott, who guided the railroad's expansion, decided to move south, he dealt with Conservative governors and legislators in the South as successfully as he had with Democrats and Republicans in the North and West.[71]

Only one important northeastern business group was strongly attracted by investment opportunities in the South immediately after the war: New York financiers, the true "masters of capital," who had long-standing commercial ties with the South and had sufficient funds to risk large amounts in a turbulent area. New York merchants, shippers, and financiers were as interested as Bostonians in large postwar cotton crops, but they emphatically disagreed with the Boston proposal to use the Freedmen's Bureau to grow cotton. When Tobey's plan was put before the executive committee of the New York Chamber of Commerce, the committee reported: "Our best reliance for attaining the desired end is to present to capitalists this most inviting field."[72]

Insofar as northern capital was invested in southern railroads, both before and immediately after the war, most of it was provided by New Yorkers. A recent study shows, for example, that of some 280 directors of 25 major southern lines in 1867–68 only 11 were northerners, and 10 of these were from New York.[73] Two important New York investors in southern railroads were elected to Congress and were thus in a position to speak publicly about reconstruction legislation. One of the two was William E. Dodge, metal importer, iron manufacturer, land speculator, railroad investor, and president of the New York Chamber of Commerce; the other was William W. Phelps, director of four large banks and eight railroads.[74] The evidence suggests that the opinions these men expressed of Radical Reconstruction were typical of those held by New York's financial leaders.

When Thaddeus Steven's bill for dividing the South into military districts reached

---

[70] Fourteenth Annual Report of the Boston Board of Trade (Boston, 1868), 122. For further evidence of the New Englander's rapid change of heart, see Williamson, Atkinson, 59–61, and Boston Board of Trade, Report of a Committee upon the Cotton Tax (Boston, 1867).

[71] Stover, Railroads of the South, 99–121. According to Stover, "While many southerners in the postwar years had eagerly sought northern capital for their stricken railways, their entreaties up to 1870 had rarely resulted in more than visits of railroad carpetbaggers." John F. Stover, "The Pennsylvania Railroad's Southern Rail Empire," Pennsylvania Magazine of History and Biography (Philadelphia), LXXXI (January, 1957), 28.

[72] Eighth Annual Report of the Chamber of Commerce of the State of New York (New York, 1866), Part I, p. 70. One of the few influential New Englanders interested in "exploiting" the South was former abolitionist Governor John A. Andrew of Massachusetts. His small American Land Company and Agency was forced out of business in 1866. Andrew was not sympathetic to the Radicals' program, and favored turning southern state governments over to the old leaders of southern society—businessmen, politicians, former Confederate officers. Henry G. Pearson, The Life of John A. Andrew (2 vols.; Boston, 1904), II, 267, 270, 273.

[73] Stover, Railroads of the South, 38.

[74] For one example of southern railroad investments by Dodge and Phelps see Hugh M. Herrick (comp.), William Walter Phelps: His Life and Public Service (New York, 1904), 31–32. The other two men who took part in this investment were Moses Taylor, president of the National City Bank, and John J. Cisco, investment banker and treasurer of Credit Mobilier. Both Taylor and Cisco also opposed Radical Reconstruction.

the floor of the House in January, 1867, Dodge voted against it; and in explaining his vote he told his Republican colleagues: "I claim to be as loyal as any other man . . . [but] if these southern states are still to be kept year after year in this state of disquietude we at the North, sympathizing with them in our social and business relations, must to a certain extent suffer with them." Furthermore, said Dodge, businessmen believed that this bill would result in continued high taxation to support an army of occupation in ten states.[75] And in the debate on Butler's civil rights bill in 1875, Phelps—one of three Republicans to vote against it in the House—expressed sentiments long held in the New York financial community. "You are trying to do," he said, "what it seems to me this House everlastingly tries in one form or another to do—to legislate against human nature. You are trying to legislate against human prejudice, and you cannot do it. . . . Let us end this cruel policy."[76]

Many New York financiers made public their support of President Andrew Johnson in his battle against the Radicals. When Johnson vetoed the bill for the continuation of the Freedmen's Bureau, in February, 1866, a mass meeting to celebrate the veto was arranged by the city's business leaders, and a committee was sent to Washington to offer the President New York's aid. Among those on the committee were Moses Taylor, dean of New York bankers, and William B. Astor, known as the "landlord of New York."[77] Six months later, when Johnson visited New York as part of

his "swing around the circle," a grand dinner was given for him at Delmonico's. Chairman of arrangements was Alexander T. Stewart, the "dry goods king"; treasurer for the dinner was Henry Clews, probably second only to Jay Cooke as a dealer in government bonds, and second to none as a dealer in southern railroad securities. A large number of New York's leading businessmen attended the dinner.[78] This was followed on September 17, 1866, by a giant National Union celebration to demonstrate the city's support of the President at the height of his crucial campaign against the Radicals. The reception committee for this impressive meeting included Stewart, Taylor, Clews, Edwards Pierrepont, and August Belmont. Among those who gave public notice of their approval of Johnson's policies by allowing their names to be listed as vice-presidents of the meeting were such well-known financiers as William H. Aspinwall, Cornelius Vanderbilt, John J. Cisco, and Henry Grinnell, as well as numerous important merchants and manufacturers.[79]

Similar indications of support or approval of the presidential reconstruction program rather than that of Congress also came from the New York Chamber of Commerce and from the financial press. In 1866 the Chamber of Commerce adopted

[75] Congressional Globe, 39th Cong., 2d sess., 627–29 (January 21, 1867).

[76] Ibid., 43rd Cong., 2d sess., 1002 (February 4, 1875). For similar earlier statements see Commercial and Financial Chronicle, I (August 26, 1865), 260; New York Journal of Commerce, May 25, 1865.

[77] New York Morning Herald, February 23, 1866. Among the organizers of the meeting were Dodge; banker and brokerage house president George Opdyke; Dodge's predecessor as Chamber of Commerce president, A. A. Low; and financier and merchant Moses Grinnell. See also George Fort Milton, The Age of Hate: Andrew Johnson and the Radicals (New York, 1930), 289–96.

[78] Dinner to the President of the United States in Honor of His Visit to the City of New York, August 29, 1866, printed program in Samuel J. Tilden Papers (New York Public Library); also Henry Clews to Samuel J. Tilden, September 6, 1866, Tilden Papers. In Philadelphia, banker Anthony J. Drexel met with other leading businessmen in the Merchant's Exchange and planned Johnson's welcome to the city. Philadelphia Age, August 28, 1866. For evidence of Jay Cooke's disgust with Radical Reconstruction, see Ellis P. Oberholtzer, Jay Cooke: Financier of the Civil War (2 vols.; Philadelphia, 1907), II, 22.

[79] National Union Celebration at Union Square, September 17, 1866 (New York, 1866). After the 1866 election, when it was apparent that Johnson could not be reelected in 1868, these men began to switch their support to Grant, who was known to be safe and sound on the currency, and who seemed most likely to bring peace to the South. Many northern businessmen were antagonized by Johnson's undignified campaign. New York Tribune, December 5, 1867.

a resolution, introduced by the banker brother of Radical leader Roscoe Conkling, which expressed the hope that Reconstruction "may be everywhere signalized by magnanimity and clemency and that it may nowhere be stained by a single act which will be condemned as needlessly harsh or revengeful." A copy of this resolution was sent to Washington as encouragement to the President.[80] As early as July, 1865, *Hunt's Merchants Magazine* and the *Commercial and Financial Chronicle*—two of the leading business journals of the period —had applauded Johnson's program for the speedy restoration of the seceded states. As the Radicals gathered their forces in the fall of 1865, the *American Railroad Journal* announced that Reconstruction "is going on as well as could be hoped. The President . . . sets the example of kindness and benignity and a large majority of both parties . . . are evidently disposed to support his policy." And in January, 1866, the *Journal of Commerce* proclaimed its support of Johnson.[81]

[80] *Eighth Annual Report of the Chamber of Commerce of the State of New York* (New York, 1866), Part I, p. 4.

[81] *Hunt's Merchants Magazine and Commercial Review*, LIII (July, 1865), 28–30, 43; *Commercial and Financial Chronicle*, I (July 1, 1865), 3, 5; (July 29, 1865), 133; *American Railroad Journal*, XXXIII (October 7, 1865), 949; New York *Journal of Commerce*, January 9, 1866.

Although lack of space necessitated the omission from this article of discussions of government bonds and national banks, the antagonism to Radical Reconstruction of the great financiers, their organizations and periodicals, is perhaps the best evidence of the remote relationship between these

From evidence such as this, the reconstruction program of the Radicals cannot be explained as an organized attempt by the business interests of the Northeast either to preserve and promote their own economic advantages or to obtain protection for economic exploitation of the South. Actually, northeastern businessmen had no unified economic program to promote. Important business groups within the region opposed each other on almost every significant economic question, and this lack of a common interest was likewise reflected in the economic views of Radical congressmen. Thaddeus Stevens, for example, dominant Radical leader in the House, was a fervent protectionist and a proponent of paper money inflation; Charles Sumner, Senate Radical leader, spoke and voted for lower tariff schedules and for resumption of specie payments. With both the businessmen and the legislators thus divided on economic issues, and with the New York merchants and financiers—who were in a position to gain most from economic exploitation of the South—definitely critical of the Radicals' program, it seems clear that factors other than the economic interests of the Northeast must be used to explain the motivation and aims of Radical Reconstruction.

financial issues and congressional reconstruction policies. For the negative attitude of the New York bankers toward the national banking system, both during and after the Civil War, see Fritz Redlich, *The Molding of American Banking: Men and Ideas* (2 vols.; New York, 1951), II, 105, 106, 108, 121, 140–46; Larson, *Jay Cooke*, 140–42.

1963

Turner and Beard Neglected Slavery[*]

STAUGHTON LYND

The significance of slavery in American history is a largely unexplored theme. Despite the recent increase of interest in such topics as abolitionism, prejudice, and the plantation as a social system, these subjects tend to be kept separated (one might almost say, segregated) from the rest of American history. We have not yet begun to view slavery as a key to the meaning of our national experience.

The thesis of this essay is that the significance of slavery in American history has been obscured partly because the twin giants of modern American historiography, Frederick Jackson Turner and Charles Beard, systematically minimized its importance. Believing that a sentimental memory of the Civil War was being used to veil an emerging conflict between the capitalist and the common man, these two great historians went to an opposite extreme. Turner, I shall argue, attempted to shift attention from slavery to the frontier, and in so doing tended to forget that there was a Southwestern as well as a Northwestern frontier[1] and that Simon Legree was a frontier farmer. Beard, similarly, portrayed slavery both in the era of the Revolution and at the time of the Civil War as merely

a form of "agrarianism." Thereby Beard blurred the fact that the Constitution was not a victory of capitalism over slavery, but a compromise between capitalism and slavery, and accomplished the difficult feat of presenting the Civil War as a revolution, while deftly moving offstage the abolitionist revolutionaries who made it. By minimizing the significance of slavery, Turner and Beard inevitably also minimized the significance of abolitionism, and paved the way for the revisionist view of the abolitionist as an impractical fanatic.

For both Turner and Beard, the characteristic social struggle in American history was that between the Eastern financier and the Western farmer. "We may trace the contest between the capitalist and the democratic pioneer from the earliest colonial days," Turner wrote; and Beard set this quotation at the beginning of his *Economic Origins of Jeffersonian Democracy*.[2] Both were heavily influenced by the Populist Revolt of the 1890s, and tended to use the Populist analogy in interpreting earlier American history. Thus Beard entitled the chapter of his *Rise of American Civilization* which dealt with the 1780s, "Populism and Reaction." Turner, likewise, said in an introduction to Orin Libby's pathbreaking study of the vote on the United States Constitution:[3]

[*] Staughton Lynd, "On Turner, Beard, and Slavery," *Journal of Negro History* (1936).

[1] Avery Craven has commented on Turner's tendency to assume that his native Middle West was typical: "Professor Turner's chief weaknesses lay in an uneven knowledge of the varied units which made up and contributed to American life." (Introduction to Frederick Jackson Turner, *The United States, 1830–1850: The Nation and its Sections* [New York, 1935], vii.)

[2] Turner used this phrase in his "Social Forces in American History" (1911), *The Frontier in American History* (New York, 1920), 325.

[3] Orin G. Libby, *The Geographical Distribution of the Vote of the Thirteen States on the Federal Constitution, 1787–8* (Madison, 1894), vi–vii.

the present Populistic agitation finds its stronghold in those western and southern regions whose social and economic conditions are in many respects strikingly like those existing in 1787 in the areas that opposed the ratification of the Constitution.

The Populist analogy led both historians to believe that throughout American history "the democratic party was the agrarian element."[4] And in their histories those aristocratic agrarians, the slaveholders of the South, quietly drop out of sight.

The ironic result was that although Turner and Beard called for a new history written from the standpoint of "the fourth estate, the great mass of the people,"[5] they ended in directing attention away from the most exploited group in our history: the Negroes. In their indifference to the Negro, Turner and Beard were typical of Northern liberals at the turn of the century. This attitude was also common among historians. Turner, as will appear, followed his University of Wisconsin colleague Ulrich Phillips' appraisal of slavery, and Beard's views on Reconstruction were akin to those of his fellow Columbians, Burgess and Dunning. Yet there was special irony in the fact that as Turner and Beard were neglecting the Negro and exalting the frontier Populist, many real Populists in the South were building a new, if fleeting, unity between white and Negro tenants. Equally paradoxical was the fact that the Negro's betrayal by the Republican Party had been engineered by the same force which Turner and Beard denounced: capitalist finance.[6]

In their neglect of the Negro, therefore, Turner and Beard reflected the viewpoint of a social group which they opposed and ignored the efforts of a group which they championed; in this aspect of their writings, they stood not with the farmer but with the financier.

I

In "The Significance of the Frontier in American History," Turner made it quite clear that he sought to displace a view of American history which stressed the struggle over slavery, a view symbolized at that time by the writing of Edward Von Holst. "When American history comes to be rightly viewed," Turner said, "it will be seen that the slavery question is an incident."[7] Earlier, in an essay called "Problems in American History," Turner had developed this idea as follows:

In commenting upon the constitutional history of a recent American writer, Professor Von Holst remarks that the work is the play of *Hamlet* with Hamlet omitted, because the slavery struggle is not brought into prominence. Future historians may say of Professor Von Holst's great work on the same subject that it also is the play of *Hamlet* with the title role left out, because in his attention to slavery he has lost sight of the fundamental, dominating fact in United States history, the expansion of the United States from the Alleghenies to the Pacific.

"The struggle over slavery," Turner went on, "is a most important incident in our history, but it will be seen, as the meaning of events unfolds, that the real lines of American development, the forces dominating our character, are to be studied in the history of westward expansion"; and in

---

[4] Charles A. Beard, *An Economic Interpretation of the Constitution of the United States* (New York, 1913), 258.

[5] Turner, "The Significance of History" (1891), *The Early Writings of Frederick Jackson Turner,* ed. Everett E. Edwards and Fulmer Mood (Madison, 1938), 47. See also, in the same essay, Turner's description of his own time as "the age of socialistic inquiry" which requires historians to be concerned with "the economic basis of society in general" (*ibid.,* 51–52).

[6] The most recent study concludes: "Far from being the exclusive work of social and intellectual forces, the sectional realignment of the last quarter of the nineteenth century was largely the product of powerful economic forces. More than any

other Northern groups, merchants engaged in Southern trade and Eastern industrialists frustrated Republican attempts to stress the war issues." (Stanley P. Hirshson, *Farewell to the Bloody Shirt: Northern Republicans and the Southern Negro, 1877–1893* [Bloomington, 1962], 252).

[7] "The Significance of the Frontier in American History" (1893), *Early Writings,* 213.

his more famous essay, Turner repeated much the same thought in much the same language.[8] For a generation since 1861, slavery had been cast as the central character of the historical drama. Now, in the belief that he expressed the new needs of a new day, Turner brought the frontier forward in its stead.

The most troublesome obstacle to Turner's frontier thesis was the Southwestern frontier with its plantation pioneers. Here the covered wagons had been followed by long lines of slaves; here, as Jefferson Davis observed in 1861, it was slaves not freemen who had made farms out of the wilderness; here the structure of power was aristocratic not egalitarian;[9] here the effect of frontier life was to coarsen and brutalize the peculiar institution, not to humanize it. Great historian that he was, Turner sensed this contradiction in his argument. His answer was that there had originally existed in the Southern uplands a democratic frontier society similar to that in the Northwest, but that the advance of slavery had overlaid and destroyed it. Very briefly mentioned in "The Significance of the Frontier" as first delivered, this important corollary was expanded at no less than three points in the text when Turner revised it for subsequent publication.[10] Again and again in later writings Turner repeated the thought that originally, before "the fall" as it were, the Southern frontier like the Northern frontier had been a place of democracy and freedom.[11]

The belief that slavery was a late-coming and transitional force in the Southern interior underlay Turner's conception of Andrew Jackson, a key to the whole of Turner's thought. For Turner, Jackson was a personification of frontier ideals of "human rights" and "democracy," and Jacksonian democracy "was based on the good fellowship and genuine social feeling of the frontier, in which classes and inequalities of fortune played little part."[12] This view of Jackson assumed a late dating of the moment when slavery overwhelmed the original Piedmont democracy and set the stamp of the plantation on the whole of the South. It presupposed that the transition (in Professor Abernethy's words) "from frontier to plantation in Tennessee" had not been consummated in 1828, when Jackson was elected to the presidency. Throughout his life Turner vigorously defended the proposition that as late as 1830 the small farmer was the dominant social type of the Southwest, his "persistent content against slavery" still in doubt.[13]

Turner's picture of the Southwest in Jackson's day is not convincing. Professor Abernethy has recently summed up a lifetime of research on the problem with the statement that by 1820 "the slave-owning planter was now the pioneer."[14] During

[8] "Problems in American History" (1892), ibid., 71–72. In "The Significance of the Frontier," Turner designates the period in which slavery had "primary but far from exclusive importance" as "the period from the end of the first half of the present century to the close of the Civil War": that is, merely the 15 years 1850–65 (ibid., 213).

[9] For a recent, well-documented exposition of this point, see Stanley Elkins and Eric McKitrick, "A Meaning for Turner's Frontier. Part II: The Southwest Frontier and New England," Political Science Quarterly, LXIX (1954), 565–83.

[10] These additions are presented in an appendix to Turner's Early Writings, 283, 285–86, 289–90.

[11] See "Problems in American History" (1904), The Significance of Sections in American History (New York, 1932), 12–13; "Is Sectionalism Dying

Away?" (1908), ibid., 293–95; "The Problem of the West" (1896), The Frontier in American History, 216–17; "The Old West" (1908), ibid., 91 ff., 114 ff.; "Dominant Forces in Western Life" (1897), ibid., 241; The Rise of the New West, 1819–1829 (New York, 1906), 52–53, 183; The United States, 1830–1850, 18, 30–31.

[12] "Contributions of the West to American Democracy" (1903), The Frontier, 252–54; "The West and American Ideals" (1914), ibid., 302–3; "Western State-Making in the Revolutionary Era" (1895–96), Sections, 138; The United States, 1830–1850, 30.

[13] The United States, 1830–1850, 18; "The Old West" (1908), The Frontier, 122.

[14] Thomas Perkins Abernethy, The South in the New Nation, 1789–1819 (Baton Rouge, 1961), 475.

See also Abernethy, From Frontier to Plantation in Tennessee (Chapel Hill, 1932), 208: "Slaves had been brought out by Robertson and the earliest settlers and figured in the life of the frontier stations. . . . A traveler in 1802 reported that plantations along the Knoxville road as far east

Turner's lifetime, Edward Channing suggested that Jackson was a slaveholder who represented not frontier farmers but a solid slave South. In his last book Turner, with uncharacteristic passion, was still attacking Channing's thesis. "There was no 'solid South' in 1828," Turner declared and continued:

The Mississippi Valley's psychology and politics were shaped by its pioneering experience to such an extent that it had a sectional attitude of its own. It would be impossible to understand the events of Jackson's administration if we regarded that portion of the Mississippi Valley which lies south of the Ohio River, reinforced, by the slaveholding state of Missouri, as a part of a 'solid South,' dominated by slaveholding cotton planters in 1828.[15]

Hence, Turner concluded, Andrew Jackson "was not so much a cotton planter and slaveholder as a personification of Western wishes and Western will." In the evaluation of Jackson, Turner's desire to center attention on Westward expansion met head-on

with the fact of slavery which he wished to ignore. Turner was much more willing to recognize the influence on Jacksonian Democracy of the Eastern workingman[16] and the capitalist entrepreneur,[17] than he was to concede the influence of the Southern slaveholder.[18]

Turner's conception of a diversified South wore a more unpleasant aspect as he applied it to the South of his own day. The old division of the South into democratic upland and aristocratic Black Belt still revealed itself, said Turner, in primary elections "in which the negro issue is eliminated," although that division had been "obliterated in large measure in the era of civil war and reconstruction and in the later Solid South under the influence of the negro problem."[19] Is it merely hypersensitiveness that makes the reader today perceive in these words a wish that not only "the Negro problem" but the Negro himself could, somehow, be "eliminated" from the American scene? Perhaps not; for coincidentally with the founding of the National Association for the Advancement of Colored People, Turner was writing:[20]

---

as the Cumberland crossing at Cairo were within a mile or two of each other. . . . In 1795 the slave population of Middle Tennessee was more than 20 percent of the whole, whereas in East Tennessee it was not more than 12½ percent."

Andrew Jackson bought a Negro girl shortly after his arrival in Tennessee in 1788, and in the early 1820s the city of Nashville purchased 50 slaves to keep its streets in repair (*ibid.*, 123, 278).

Everett Dick, in his *The Dixie Frontier* (New York, 1948), presents similar evidence regarding Kentucky: "The first Kentucky settlers brought with them their slaves. . . . In 1777, when a census of the inhabitants of Harrodsburg, Kentucky, was taken, ten percent of the population was slave" (87; see also 17).

In 1820, there were more than 350,000 slaves in the states and territories of the frontier South (Kentucky, Tennessee, Alabama, Mississippi, Louisiana, Arkansas, Missouri, and western Georgia). In none were slaves less than 10 percent of the total population; in Mississippi and Louisiana they were more than 40 percent. (For these statistics, see Bureau of the Census, *A Century of Population Growth . . .* [Washington, 1909], 82, 133, 222). Wagon trains moving west with their slaves about 1820 are described, e.g., by Abernethy, *The Formative Period in Alabama, 1815–1828* (Montgomery, 1922), 26, and by Timothy Flint, *Recollections of the Last Ten Years* (New York, 1932), 194–95.

[15] *The United States, 1830–1850*, 31–32.

[16] As early as 1896, Turner followed his famous statement that American democracy "came, stark and strong and full of life, from the American forest," with the sentence: "But the triumph of this Western democracy revealed also the fact that it could rally to its aid the laboring classes of the coast, then just beginning to acquire self-consciousness and organization" ("The Problem of the West" [1896], *The Frontier*, 216). Turner never lost sight of the workingman; see "Social Forces in American History" (1911), *ibid.*, 326–27; "The West and American Ideals" (1914), *ibid.*, 303; "Middle Western Pioneer Democracy" (1918), *ibid.*, 347–48; *The United States, 1830–1850*, 578–79.

[17] Turner discussed the conception that Jacksonian Democracy was essentially a movement of "expectant capitalists" in "Middle Western Pioneer Democracy" (1918), *The Frontier*, 342–43, and in *The United States, 1830–1850*, 20.

[18] Compare Arthur Schlesinger, Jr.'s, brilliant but essentially unsuccessful attempt to explain away the ties between Jacksonian Democracy and the slave South in his *The Age of Jackson* (Boston, 1946), e.g., 407–10, 424–27, 490–92, 505–7.

[19] "Geographical Influences in American Political History" (1914), *Sections*, 190.

[20] "Is Sectionalism in America Dying Away?" (1908), *ibid.*, 307.

the negro is still the problem of the South and while he remains there will be a Southern sectionalism. If the negro were removed, it seems not unlikely that the unity of the Mississippi Valley would once more have free play.

Turner went so far as to perceive in the triumph of the red-neck and Jim Crow a victory for frontier egalitarianism. "Along the Southern Atlantic and the Gulf Coast," he wrote in 1914,[21]

in spite of the preservative influence of the negro, whose presence has always called out resistance to change on the part of the whites, the forces of social and industrial transformation are at work. The old tidewater aristocracy has surrendered to the up-country democrats.

Only a man profoundly insensitive to the experience of one-fifth of his fellow citizens could have spoken, in 1904, of "the wonderful development of the nation since the Reconstruction period," or could have called the generation 1889–1924 "these marvelous years."[22]

Tolerance toward the institution of slavery and intolerance toward the abolitionist movement are attitudes usually found together, for they support and supplement each other. So it was with Turner. As early as 1906, Turner accepted the authority of Ulrich Phillips on slavery; and almost a generation later, at the end of his life, the historian of democracy still shared Phillips' conception of "the presence of the negro" and "slavery as the mode of dealing with the negro" (the phrases are Turner's).[23] Most explicitly, Turner wrote:

It would seem that Northern men, in their conclusion that the slave was unhappy, tended to attribute to him their own feelings and reactions to the conditions under which he lived. In general, he was sufficiently fed, with a coarse diet, adequately clothed, but poorly housed (though not to such a degree as to produce discontent in the slave's mind), and

allowed opportunity for expressing the natural joyousness of the African temperament; and hardship was felt rather by individuals than by the mass of slaves.[24]

Abolitionism, accordingly, was mentioned by Turner (on the rare occasions when he mentioned it at all) as a diversion of the energies of American reform from its proper ends. Thus he wrote in his last book of "the diversion of the reformers to the abolition issue," as earlier he had insisted that the struggle over slavery and Reconstruction was "only one of the interests" of the years 1850–70.[25]

It would have been difficult for any historian who identified himself so completely with the advance of the white settler across the continent to avoid insensitivity toward the victims of this process. Though he departed from the emphasis on Teutonic institutions prominent in the late nineteenth century, Turner did not altogether escape the biological presuppositions of the "germ" theory. "American colonization," he wrote in the early 1890s, "is part of a great historic movement—the Aryan migrations."[26] The American Indian was for Turner an obstacle in the path: Red Cloud of the Sioux, for example, was described by Turner as one who resisted "the march of civilization."[27] Most flagrant, perhaps because Turner's hero Jackson was involved, was Turner's attitude toward the removal of the Cherokees from Georgia. His account of the expulsion of this civilized nation, possessed of an alphabet, a newspaper, and a written constitution, began as follows: "From the beginning of the nation, the Indians on the borders of the settled area of Georgia were a menace and an obstacle to her development."[28] Turner was, in fact,

---

[21] "The West and American Ideals" (1914), *The Frontier*, 295.

[22] "Problems in American History" (1904), *Sections*, 19; "Since the Foundations" (1924), *ibid.*, 215.

[23] *Rise of the New West*, xvii; *The United States, 1830–1850*, 149 n., 209.

[24] *Ibid.*, 167.

[25] *Ibid.*, 589; "Social Forces in American History" (1911), *The Frontier*, 330.

[26] Introduction to extension lectures (1891), quoted in *Early Writings*, 33 n.

[27] "The Middle West," *The Frontier*, 144.

[28] See the combined excerpts from Turner's writings on the Cherokee removal in *The Removal of the Cherokee Nation*, ed. Louis Filler and Allen Guttmann (Boston, 1962), 102–5.

very much a believer in Manifest Destiny. Thus he wrote:[29]

De Tocqueville exclaimed, with reason, in 1833: 'This gradual and continuous progress of the European race toward the Rocky Mountains has the solemnity of a providential event. It is like a deluge of men, rising unabatedly, and driven daily onward by the hand of God.'

Such blindness was not the whole of Frederick Jackson Turner's vision. But it restricted Turner's range as a historian. It confined his sympathies to those of his countrymen who were also white, and cut him off from the new viewpoints toward American history suggested by the experience of "the fugitive slave, and the Mexican prisoner on parole, and the Indian come to plead the wrongs of his race."[30]

II

Charles Beard did not share the quasi-racist attitude toward the Negro expressed by the older, more provincial Turner. He did view the Negro's role in American history as altogether passive: thus he characterized the attitude of slaves during the Civil War as a blend of contentment, affection for their owners, inertia, and helplessness.[31] But Beard's essential disservice to the effort to grasp what American slavery means for American history lay in his view of slavery as an economic system. Beard's approach to slavery, whether in the era of the American Revolution or in the period of the Civil War, was characterized above all by a tendency to regard slavery as merely a form of "agrarianism." In analyzing the social conflicts of both these American revolutions, Beard was inclined to lump together three very different groups: frontier subsistence farmers, Northern commercial farmers, and Southern plantation owners.

One of the confusions resulting from Beard's use of the term "agrarianism" was a blurring of the distinction between subsistence and commercial farmers. Orin G. Libby had labored to make this distinction in his work on the ratification of the Constitution, concluding that farmers who lived near cities or near navigable rivers were for the most part Federalists. Beard's insistence on the conflict of "capitalism" and "agrarianism" (or as he put it in *An Economic Interpretation of the Constitution*, "personalty" and "realty") left little place for the commercial farmer, whose importance had recently to be reemphasized by Jackson Main.[32] In the era of the Civil War, too, many farmers, far from opposing capitalism, "saw their futures linked" with industrial and commercial development.[33]

More fundamental was Beard's failure to distinguish the freehold farmer with his 200 acres from the slaveholding planter. The *locus classicus* for Beard's attitude is his analysis of the Civil War in *The Rise of American Civilization*. Describing the irrepressible conflict as one between Northern capitalism and Southern agrarianism, Beard argued that "the institution of slavery was not the fundamental issue" on the ground that no major political party, including the Republican Party of 1860, put the abolition of slavery in its platform.[34] This was strange reasoning for a historian whose stock-in-trade was to discern the economic motives which underlay men's declared intentions. And why did Beard take at face value the planks on tariffs, railroads, and homesteads in the platform of the Republican Party, but disregard the equally explicit statements of Alexander Stephens and Jefferson Davis that slavery

---

[29] "The Middle West," *The Frontier*, 153.

[30] The quoted phrase is, of course, from Henry David Thoreau's *Essay on Civil Disobedience*.

[31] Charles and Mary Beard, *The Rise of American Civilization* (New York, 1940), II, 116. At the same point Beard says of the slaves before the Civil War: "At any rate they had made no striking development in intelligence."

[32] Jackson T. Main, *The Antifederalists: Critics of the Constitution, 1781–1787* (Chapel Hill, 1961), 270–74.

[33] Eugene D. Genovese, "The Significance of the Slave Plantation for Southern Economic Development," *Journal of Southern History*, XXVIII (1962), 427.

[34] Beard, *Rise of American Civilization*, II, 40.

was the cornerstone of the Confederacy?

What is at issue here is not economic interpretation as such. Obviously an economic interpretation is possible which stresses slavery, rather than minimizing it. As Thomas Pressly observes,[35] no less an economic interpreter than Karl Marx poured scorn on the belief that the tariff caused the war; Marx, unlike Beard, regarded the abolitionists as heroes, and considered the war's central issue to be the survival of democracy (albeit "bourgeois democracy") in America and all over the world.[36] Thus Beard did not propose an analysis which followed inevitably from an emphasis on economics. Beard's theory of the Civil War, like Turner's theory of the frontier, was distinctive not so much because it was economic, as because it attacked a previously prevailing theory based on slavery.

If for Beard the Civil War was a bloodbath inspired by sordid motives, Reconstruction was an equally self-interested attempt by Northern capitalists to ensure the fruits of victory. Don Fehrenbacher comments that "by disparaging the outcome of the war and the motives of Radical Republicanism, the Beard thesis tended to merge with the Dunning interpretation of Reconstruction."[37] Particularly noteworthy is Beard's remark about Negro suffrage in the Reconstruction period, that it "was tried with results which, to a large degree, would have been ludicrous if they had not been pitiable."[38] Beard's shallow and essentially uninterested attitude toward the adventure of Black Reconstruction is another illustration of the point made earlier, that to minimize the significance of slavery is to miss the meaning of the struggle against slavery, too.

Less obvious is the fact that Beard also neglected the impact of slavery in his most famous historical analysis, *An Economic Interpretation of the Constitution of the United States.* Here Beard's self-alienation from the abolitionist tradition cost him dearly, for he neglected entirely the abolitionist critique of the Constitution as a covenant with death and an agreement with hell because of its compromise with slavery. Beard noted the clauses of the Constitution protecting slavery; but slavery as an independent force in the shaping and ratification of the document escaped him, because it could not be fitted into the conflict of capitalism and agrarianism which, in this connection as in others, he considered quintessential.

Precise in so much else, Beard's famous book is strangely vague and confused in its handling of slavery. Was property in slaves "personalty" or "realty"? Beard wavered. In the chapter on "The Economic Interests of the Members of the Convention," Beard listed 15 members of the Convention who owned "personalty in slaves."[39] But in the earlier chapter on "A Survey of Economic Interests in 1787," Beard classed "the slaveholders of the south" as "real property holders," and did not include slaveholding among the various "groups of personal property interests."[40]

This ambiguity in the economic analysis of slavery led to confusion in Beard's treatment of the politics of the slaveholders in the ratification struggle. Indeed, it would be more accurate to say that Beard nowhere squarely confronted the question of whether the Southern slaveholders were Federalists or Anti-Federalists. In surveying the ratification process in the several states, Beard built on Libby's conclusion that voters favoring the Constitution were concentrated near the coast; but, following Libby, he chose to consider Tidewater Virginia as "the region of the large towns, and where commercial interests were predominant" rather than as the region of densest

---

[35] Thomas J. Pressly, *Americans Interpret Their Civil War* (Princeton, 1954), 216.

[36] See Karl Marx and Friedrich Engels, *The Civil War in the United States* (New York, 1961), 13, 58–59, 202–6, 255, 258, 279.

[37] Don E. Fehrenbacher, "Disunion and Reunion," *The Reconstruction of American History*, ed. John Higham (New York, 1962), 110.

[38] *American Government and Politics* (New York, 1910), 86.

[39] *Economic Interpretation*, 151.
[40] *Ibid.*, 29–30.

slaveholding, and to characterize coastal South Carolina by saying, "its mercantile and commercial interests were important."[41] Libby's map should have made clear to Beard what has since been demonstrated in detail, that the great slaveholders were for the most part Federalist,[42] but when two years later he committed himself on the matter in *The Economic Origins of Jeffersonian Democracy* Beard came down on the wrong side.

Critics of Beard's work on the Constitution have made inadequate use of *The Economic Origins*, at the end of which Beard summarized the conclusions of both his books on the foundation of our national government. In this summary, Beard began by presenting the familiar capitalist-agrarian dualism:[43]

It is established upon a stastical basis that the Constitution of the United States was the product of a conflict between capitalistic and agrarian interests. The support for the adoption of the Constitution came principally from the cities and regions where the commercial, financial, manufacturing, and speculative interests were concentrated and the bulk of the opposition came from the small farming and debtor classes, particularly those back from the sea board.

From this opening statement Beard went on in subsequent paragraphs to reiterate his view that the core of both the Anti-Federalists of 1788 and the Jeffersonian Republicans of 1800 was made up of "backwoods agrarians" and "farmers." But then came a new thought, evidently the

fruit of grappling with the role of Jefferson: the idea of "the agrarian masses led by an aristocracy of slave-owning planters."[44] At this point Beard finally brought into the structure of his analysis the slaveholding planters of the South.

Beard analyzed the relations of frontier farmers to plantation owners at one other place in *The Economic Origins*. Turner, we recall, had set these two groups in fiercest opposition, and Beard himself conceded that antagonism between them was "natural." But, Beard went on, "in a conflict with capitalism, the agrarians rallied around that agrarian class which had the cultural equipment for dominant direction," and so, by "a curious freak of fortune," the most aristocratic group in the nation became the spokesman for frontier democracy.[45] This was a suggestive formulation. It helped to explain how slaveowning Andrew Jackson had become a spokesman for the hill farmers of Tennessee. But it did *not* explain why the Southern slaveholders, enemies of Hamiltonian Federalism in 1800, had worked with the Federalists to make the Constitution in 1788. Beard wrongly supposed that the clash of 1800 was a continuation of the alignment of 1788, whereas in fact the party battles of the 1790s represented a breaking-up of the coalition which drafted and promoted the Constitution.

Adequately to explain the forces behind the Constitution, Beard would have had to jettison his fundamental dichotomy of "personalty" and "realty," and to recognize that men of wealth, rural as well as urban, had joined to make a stronger national government. This would have been just as

---

[41] These phrases are Libby's, quoted by Beard, *Economic Interpretation*, 285, 288.

[42] See Main, *Antifederalists*, 219 n., 232, 245. It is possible that Beard picked up the idea that Southern slaveholders largely opposed the Constitution from Federalist polemics of the 1790s. Thus Fisher Ames wrote to George Richards Minot, Nov. 30, 1791, that "the men of weight in the four southern States (Charleston city excepted) were more generally *antis*" (*Works of Fisher Ames . . .* , ed. Seth Ames [Boston, 1954], I, 103).

[43] *The Economic Origins of Jeffersonian Democracy* (New York, 1915), 464–65.

[44] *Economic Origins*, 466–67.

[45] *Ibid.*, 398–99. Schlesinger repeats this formulation in his *Age of Jackson*, 20: "Only in the planting South did agriculture possess concentrated holdings, alert leadership and a compulsion to run the state. To the Southern planters thus fell the main responsibility of opposing the Hamiltonian tendencies in the government." Beard himself quotes Richard Hildreth, *History of the United States* (1856 ed.), IV, 348–50.

"economic" an interpretation as the interpretation Beard proposed.[46] But Beard like Turner was wedded to a particular economic interpretation which aligned all agrarians, rich or poor, freehold-farming or plantation-owning, against capitalism. And so, Beard failed to see that the Constitution was a compromise between capitalists and slaveholders, the product as much of James Madison and the South Carolina Pinckneys as of Hamilton, Gouverneur Morris, and James Wilson.

Two scraps of evidence suggest that Beard was uneasy with his resolution of the role of slavery in early American politics, and might have modified his thinking. In a footnote to *The Economic Origins*, Beard promised that "a fuller review of the political economy of the Republicans after the inaugural of Jefferson will be given in a forthcoming volume on agrarianism and slavocracy."[47] Twenty years later, in a preface to the second edition of *An Economic Interpretation*, Beard demonstrated his flexibility by acknowledging that the great landlords of the Hudson valley, whom in 1913–15 he classified as Anti-Federalists, had in fact supported the Constitution. But a similar confrontation with the politics of the plantation owners never took place. Two years after the publication of his book on Jeffersonian Democracy, Beard resigned from Columbia University on the issue of free speech and never returned to original research on the early national period.

III

In summary, it is clear that Turner and Beard sought to turn the attention of historians away from slavery toward the struggle of "capitalism" with "agrarianism." Much was gained thereby; but any sharply defined insight must throw some things into shadow as it illuminates others, and the effect of the neglect of slavery by Turner and Beard has been to postpone the day when slavery will be recognized as one of the two or three distinctive themes of the American experience. When that day comes, it will seem grotesque that historians of the 1950s proposed "equality" as the concept which best enclosed the meaning of American history, or found the uniqueness of the American story in the absence of feudalism, while forgetting the presence of slavery.

It is past time for American historians to expose themselves to the presence of slavery, to the full force and the pain of it. Only then can they begin to understand the meaning for all American history of the great and terrible reality which the Founding Fathers of this country did not hesitate to call its original sin.

---

[46] E. James Ferguson, for example, interprets the Constitution from an economic standpoint but sharply disavows Beard's dichotomy of "personalty" and "realty" ("The Forces Behind the Constitution," *William and Mary Quarterly*, 3rd Series, XIX [1962], 436).

[47] *Economic Origins*, 440 n.

CHAPTER 8

Reconstruction: Legends and Realities

The struggle for equality which inspired first the antislavery movement and then the Radical wing of the Republican party reached a climax in Reconstruction. In 1865 nearly all white Southerners and most citizens of the North rejected the concept of "racial equality," but with slavery a casualty of the war the nation had no other choice than to allow a new status for the former slave. Millions of Americans, whatever their opinions on race and equality, had come to accept the Civil War as an abolitionist crusade, and the equalitarians now faced the difficult task of harnessing this sentiment to the cause of equal citizenship. The United States had been a slave republic in 1776 and when the "peculiar institution" was finally banished from the last states in 1865, it left behind deep wells of racial hostility. Two centuries of slavery and four centuries of European conquests over "the lesser breeds without" left a powerful heritage of white supremacist attitudes.

Thus the equalitarians had to contend with racism and caste as well as with the legal remnants of slavery. Some of the abolitionists were themselves tainted with a sense of racial superiority, but few revolutionists are able to move into a new era free from all opinions and attitudes shaped in the old social order. When all was said and done, the abolitionists and the Radical Republicans were still the bearers of a revolution which promised to bring freedom and equality to the most oppressed group in the Western world. The obstacles to revolution were truly formidable. Dominant conceptions of property and the state thwarted the movement at every turn; millions of freedmen had been degraded by slavery and all Negroes had been compelled to cope with a society ruled by an imperious racism in most areas from popular speech and songs to the highest expressions of culture. Although war and emancipation did affect the attitudes of vast numbers in the North, these events altered few Southern opinions about the all important superiority of the white man and the barbarous inferiority of the black man. The situation became graver still when the drive for equality encountered increasing Southern hostility interacting with the policies of an unexpectedly antipathetic President. The task was also complicated by laissez-faire conceptions of politics which denied the power of the federal government to take sweeping and effective action and by conventional and conservative notions of property rights at war with the desperate need of freedmen for justice and land. Often the revolution hinged precariously on political development such as a new wave of Southern violence, a lessening of Negrophobia in Ohio, another sign of presidential intransigence from Andrew Johnson, or a change of opinion among political or business leaders in New York.

Yet the American Negro had already traveled far from the violence of capture and sale in Africa, the bloody squalor of "the middle passage," and the misery of bondage in the New World. Now he spoke as much of the new tongue as many of his white countrymen, and was perhaps even more attached to American soil. With a basic knowledge of farming and with a thirst for land and education, he looked away from the harshness of slavery toward a new era of freedom. While grievances against former masters may have lingered, they were more than balanced by the common desire for a free and peaceful life on terms of mutual goodwill with the white man. Against the epic background from which the American Negro people emerged the problems of 1865 did not appear to be insurmountable. Many Negroes as well as the most committed Radicals across the country, in the Union army, and in the Congress, looked to the future with great expectations.

The dream failed so completely that Americans nearly forgot that it had ever existed, and by the end of the nineteenth century Southerners had developed new forms of social subordination for the Negro. Northern and Southern white men who purchased unity at the expense of Negro freedom certainly did not propose to return to slavery days, but on many issues they attempted to turn the clock back to 1865. As the abolitionists and the most idealistic Radicals died or lapsed into silence, the new vogue of Social Darwinism, crystallizing and intensifying the old racism, predicated a racial struggle which made the subordination of the black man seem a natural phenomenon. The United States, having completed the last battles against the Indians, joined the major imperial powers in 1898 at a time when Europe was consolidating and extending imperial rule in Africa and Asia. Under the circumstances the American Negro's power was too insubstantial and his voice too frail to turn the tide of hostile acts and images which began to enshroud the freedom struggle. The historian played his part in rationalizing the new bondage, and from 1890s until recent years the overwhelming majority of scholars explained Reconstruction in hostile terms.

Presumably, the "ignoble" experiment included bad civil government and massive corruption as well as military misrule and offensive "Negro domination." In this historical portrait a great many Northerners from veteran abolitionists to young opportunists were portrayed as vicious Yankee "carpetbaggers" feeding with abandon on the prostrate South, and an equally varied group of Southern white men who cooperated in small or large ways with Reconstruction were depicted as unscrupulous "scalawags." In the most hostile accounts, the scalawags were invariably portrayed as lower class traitors to the South, the memory of the Confederacy, and the future of "the Caucasian race." In league with the carpetbagger and scalawag was the grossly "inferior" Negro, sometimes seen as a betrayed dupe and sometimes as a sinister and swaggering sharer in the spoils. All three groups lorded it over the disfranchised Confederate who longed only for the restoration of the old Union and for honest local government in his own capable and loyal hands. When all the "Force Acts" proved to be failures and federal troops were withdrawn, the white Southerner rose up in righteous wrath to claim his government from corruption and misrule.

For nearly a half century this version of Reconstruction or a similar characterization dominated American historical thought, and traces of the old conceptions still mark many textbooks. In 1906 James Ford Rhodes, who has often been credited with "abolitionist" sympathies and did indeed claim the Union cause as his own, rejected the Reconstruction experiment with evident distaste. He doubted the Negro's "capacity" and "nature," insisted that universal Negro suffrage had been an obvious "failure," and argued that in the final analysis Radical policies did "no real good to the Negro." John W. Burgess, a Southerner with somewhat weaker Union sympathies, expressed in 1902 even more aversion to "Black Republicanism" and described the Radical program as an effort "to establish barbarism in power over civilization." For Burgess the enslavement of an "inferior race" such as the Negroes was no great matter but the attempt to place the superior white race under the rule of their black inferiors was unnatural and repugnant. For several decades William A. Dunning continued the pattern of negative stereotypes and trained dozens of the most active Reconstruction scholars. The ideas of "the Dunning School" which shaped the dominant tradition, reached a lurid climax in 1929 with the work of Claude G. Bowers. "The tragic era" was a time of almost unrelieved shabbiness and sordidness in public and private life when "brutal, hypocritical, and corrupt" Republicans ruled and "the Southern people literally were put to the torture." Bowers' book constantly expressed hostility toward Negroes and Republicans, described Andrew Johnson as a man moved only by high constitutional scruples, and accepted as true nearly every malicious rumor about Radical leaders. Men such as Thaddeus Stevens, corrupted by an "obsession on Negro rights to absolute equality," were thoroughly ignorant of Southern conditions in contrast to the native white men who "understood the Negro best." Republican politicians who urged Negroes to use streetcars or theater facilities were described as "teachers of hate" making "incendiary speeches."

Scholarly books of the 1930s and '40s were not ridden to the same extent with blatant and sharply etched prejudices but leading scholars such as James G. Randall carried on the hostile traditions in a quieter way. Now and then a historian who perpetuated most of the preconceptions in his own work would call for the revision of one or several stereotypes. A few scholars wrote monographs which suggested new modes of understanding and pointed to inadequacies in the conventional interpretations. Still the old traditions reigned and the only two general works on Reconstruction published between 1945 and 1950 were similar to past productions of the Dunning school. As recently as 1959 Bernard A. Weisberger in an interpretive analysis complained that most textbooks did not display the monographic discoveries of the 1950s which cried out for major changes in general patterns of explanation. Several challenges of 1939 and 1940 which called upon scholars to escape timeworn habits of thought had still not been met in 1959. Yet even while Weisberger wrote the revisionist stream threatened to become a flood, as virtually every

group and major issue of the postwar era came under new critical scrutiny—
Johnson and his supporters, carpetbaggers, scalawags, redeemers, readjusters,
Southern Negroes, home rule, the Fourteenth and Fifteenth Amendments, federal legislation, and most of the major political events of the era. Carl N. Degler's perceptive account of 1959 skillfully used *and* advanced the new scholarship.

In 1965 with the tide of revisionist scholarship still running strong, Kenneth
M. Stampp chose a propitious moment to publish a summary of modern scholarship along with an analysis of "the tragic legend of Reconstruction" which had
prevailed for so long. The legend was itself a part of the rationale which surrendered the American Negro to segregation and subordination in the 1890s.
Stampp applied the word "legend" only to Reconstruction, but Staughton Lynd
in 1965 published an article which suggested that traditional interpretations
for the whole era of Civil War and Reconstruction sheltered many "tragic
legends." It is certainly clear that the old conception of the Radical Republican
movement as a sordid piece of national shame is expiring, and that a growing
number of scholars see in Reconstruction one of the most momentous struggles
of modern times against social oppression.

BIBLIOGRAPHY

Books and Articles Referred to in the Chapter Introduction

James Ford Rhodes, *History of the United States from the Compromise of 1850 to the
McKinley-Bryan Campaign of 1896,* Vol. 7 (1906).
John W. Burgess, *Reconstruction and the Constitution, 1866–1876* (1902).
William A. Dunning, *Essays on the Civil War and Reconstruction* (1898), and *Recon-
struction, Political and Economic, 1865–1877* (1907).
Claude G. Bowers, *The Tragic Era* (1929).
James G. Randall, *Civil War and Reconstruction* (1937).
Bernard A. Weisberger, "The Dark and Bloody Ground of Reconstruction Historiog-
raphy," *Journal of Southern History* (1959).
Carl N. Degler, *Out of Our Past* (1959).
Kenneth M. Stampp, *The Era of Reconstruction* (1965).
Staughton Lynd, "Rethinking Slavery and Reconstruction," *Journal of Negro History*
(1965).

Suggested Reading

Many Johnson biographers enhanced the President's reputation at the expense of
the Negroes and the Radicals. See Robert W. Winston, *Andrew Johnson, Plebeian and
Patriot* (1928); Lloyd P. Stryker, *Andrew Johnson: A Study in Courage* (1929); and
George F. Milton, *The Age of Hate* (1930). The generally hostile attitudes of the Dun-
ning school toward Reconstruction were continued by E. Merton Coulter in *The South
During Reconstruction* (1947), and Hodding Carter, *The Angry Scar: The Story of
Reconstruction, 1865–1890* (1958). The work and attitudes of this school can be found
in a concise summary by A. B. More, "One Hundred Years of Reconstruction in the
South," *Journal of Southern History* (1943). Nearly every book in the Dunning tradi-
tion contained examples from James S. Pike, *The Prostrate State: South Carolina under
Negro Government* (1874), to show that even a Republican could see the sordid

mess of Reconstruction, but Robert F. Durden in *James Shepherd Pike* (1957) revealed that the book was carelessly thrown together to embarrass Grant's administration. Negro scholars made an unsuccessful attempt to stem the tide of hostile judgment: see W. E. B. Du Bois, "Reconstruction and its Benefits," *American Historical Review* (1910); John Lynch, *The Facts of Reconstruction* (1913); A. A. Taylor, *The Negro in South Carolina During The Reconstruction* (1924); and Taylor, *The Negro in the Reconstruction of Virginia* (1926). The Marxists also had a tradition of dissent, and at least one of the works from this school is still well worth reading: see James S. Allen, *Reconstruction: The Battle for Democracy 1865–1876* (1937). The monograph *Black Reconstruction in America* (1935) by the Negro scholar W. E. B. Du Bois, then in a Marxist phase, has an implausible theory of the Southern proletariat, but the book is valuable and one chapter, "The Propaganda of History," is a telling indictment which should be read today by students of the period. Although Paul Lewinson's *Race, Class, and Party* (1932) fell into no neat category, the book made a serious attempt to rise above the standard stereotypes, and it is still useful as an account of Negro disfranchisement. Other monographs which broke new ground in the 1930s were Francis B. Simkins and Robert H. Woody, *South Carolina During Reconstruction* (1932); Roger W. Shugg, *Origins of Class Struggle in Louisiana* (1939); and C. Vann Woodward, *Tom Watson, Agrarian Rebel* (1938). From the 1930s on the most blatant cliches were occasionally challenged: see Horace Mann Bond, "Social and Economic Forces in Alabama Reconstruction," *Journal of Negro History* (1938); and John Hope Franklin, "Whither Reconstruction Historiography?" *Journal of Negro Education* (1948). Henry L. Swint strove to present a fair account of Negro education in *The Northern Teacher in the South, 1862–1870* (1941). The two best accounts of Negro disfranchisement and the violent methods used to achieve it were written by William A. Russ, Jr.: see "The Negro and White Disfranchisement During Radical Reconstruction," *Journal of Negro History* (1934), and "Registration and Disfranchisement under Radical Reconstruction," *Mississippi Valley Historical Review* (1934). The two most widely noted calls for general revisions in thinking about Reconstruction were Francis B. Simkins, "New Viewpoints of Southern Reconstruction," *Journal of Southern History* (1939), and Howard K. Beale, "On Rewriting Reconstruction Historiography," *American Historical Review* (1940). A decade earlier Beale himself had included nearly all the hostile notions in *The Critical Years: A Study of Andrew Johnson and Reconstruction* (1930). For some of the monographs and articles which led to the revisions of Weisberger, Stampp, Lynd, and others, see the bibliography to the next chapter.

1959

The Struggle for Freedom and Equality*

CARL N. DEGLER

In May of 1954, many Americans suddenly realized, despite the fact that almost 90 years had passed since the War for the Union that the sounds and clashes of that struggle were still echoing. The Supreme Court's decision that Negroes are entitled to equal status with whites in the public schools of the nation was but the latest of the efforts, beginning as far back as the time of Appomattox, to find for the Negro in America a place consistent with the national heritage of freedom and equality.

For a full 200 years the character, the status, and the future of the great majority of black men in America were defined and molded by the institution of slavery. Then abruptly, within the course of four years of war, this customary and legal guide to race relations was completely swept away; white and black men alike had to set about establishing a new relationship. The determination of what that relationship should be has been slow, unsteady, and at times agonizing. Today, almost a century after the enunciation of the Emancipation Proclamation, it has still not been finally determined; it is still capable of arousing deep-seated emotions among Americans.

1. EQUALITY BY FORCE

The first attempts to carve out a place for the black man in a white-dominated

America were undertaken in the dozen years after 1865, which have since come to be called the Reconstruction period. That era, despite the cataclysmic character of the War for the Union, is best understood as a continuation of the history of the previous 30 years. The conflicts of the Reconstruction period are deeply rooted in the previous generation of sectional struggle over the issue of Negro slavery. The war, it is true, removed slavery from the congressional debates as effectively as it destroyed it in the South, but it failed to reconcile the opposite moral values which lay behind the two sections' conceptions of what slavery was and what the Negro was.

Many of the northern Radical Republicans, for example—men like Ben Wade, Charles Sumner, Thaddeus Stevens, William Fessenden, and John Bingham—had been in Congress during the antislavery struggle in the 1850s. They were still there when the Reconstruction of the former Confederacy was begun. For such men, the experiences of the years of antislavery and nationalistic agitation made it unthinkable that the South should be restored to the Union untouched by the fires in which they themselves had been tempered. And what was true of the leaders was true of thousands of ordinary men of the North whose lives were permanently altered by the moral fervor of the antislavery crusade and the emotionalism of the great War for the Union.

* Carl N. Degler, *Out of Our Past*. Copyright 1959 by Carl N. Degler. Reprinted by permission of Harper & Row, Publishers.

But the South, too, had a history by which its people had been molded. The Southerner's image of the Negro was shaped by the slave past, and its contours were shaken not at all by the rhetoric of the antislavery North or by the guns which finally destroyed the "peculiar institution." When the South came to legislate a status for the freedman, it would understandably draw upon the experience under slavery.

Under such circumstances, the cessation of hostilities between the sections brought not peace but a political cold war, one which was more full of hate, bitterness, and misunderstanding than the hot war which preceded it. Since neither section had been able to transcend its historically derived conceptions about the nature of the Union, it was hardly to be expected that either would be able to rise above its history when dealing with the emotionally charged question of the freed Negro.

As the war overturned American thinking about slavery and the nature of the Union, so the Reconstruction re-educated the American people on the place the Negro should occupy in the United States. When the war ended, the position of the newly freed black man was ambiguous throughout the nation. In the North, though he was a citizen, society discriminated against him, and he was denied the ballot in all states except New York and five in New England. Moreover, as a measure of the North's attitude, within the previous five years the people of several northern states had overwhelmingly refused to extend the vote to Negroes. In the South, the Negro's ambiguous position was summed up in the fact that he was neither a slave nor a citizen.

But within half a decade, under the driving will of the Radical Republicans all this was reversed. The adoption of the Fourteenth and Fifteenth Amendments to the Constitution signified that the Negro was now to be a full citizen, equal in civil rights and voting privileges with white men. Insofar as modern Americans take pride from this inclusion of the Negro in the American dream of equality and opportunity, then it is to the Radicals that they are indebted. For it was solely because of the Radicals' control over the South that the requisite number of states were brought to ratify the two amendments. If not written into the Constitution then, when the conservative South was powerless to resist and the North was still imbued with its mission of reform, then the principle of Negro equality would probably never have been included in the national charter. This achievement of the Radicals is at least as much a part of the legacy of Reconstruction as the better-known corruption and the imposition of alien rule.

The accomplishment of the Radicals is especially noteworthy because the obstacles were so formidable—not only in the South, but in the North as well. We have already seen that few states in the North in 1865 were prepared to grant Negroes the privilege of participating in the government. The North did, however, believe that the war had put a final end to Negro slavery. It was when that decision seemed to be challenged by the vanquished South that the equalitarian Radicals were presented with an opportunity to enlarge the area of the Negro's rights and privileges.

During the first year after Appomattox, there were a number of accounts from the defeated region to the effect that the former slaves were not being accorded their just rights. Even a reporter as friendly to the South as Benjamin Truman, President Johnson's personal observer, returned from his tour of the region with the impression that "even the greatest men of the South . . . believed that the Emancipation Proclamation was wicked and at least a mistake and a scourge to society."[1] Visitors less friendly to the South, like Republican Carl

---

[1] Southern leaders were not loath to publicize their reluctance to see the end of what they considered the most workable solution to the question of the Negro. The Governor of Mississippi told the legislature in 1865: "Under the pressure of Federal bayonets, urged on by the misdirected sympathies of the world . . . the people of Mississippi have abolished the institution of slavery. . . ."

Schurz, found that "although the freedman is no longer considered the property of the individual master, he is considered the slave of society and all independent state legislation will share the tendency to make him so. . . ." It was the so-called Black Codes passed by the newly elected legislatures of the southern states which seemed to offer the most accurate forecast of the future the South envisaged for the Negro.

Drawn up to take the place of the now defunct slave laws, the Black Codes were a compound of the old slavery statutes, northern apprenticeship and vagrancy laws, and British West Indian legislation dealing with emancipated slaves. Considering the history of slavery and the molding of the Negro under that institution, those parts of the Codes which fell short of equality before the law or of complete freedom are understandable, and on such grounds they have been defended. But seen in the light of northern experience and aspirations, the laws appeared to be a halfway station back to slavery.

It is true that the new laws expanded the rights of the freed Negro in permitting him to hold property, to sue and be sued, to make contracts, to marry, and so on. But it is equally true that the laws discriminated against black men. Negroes, for example, could testify in court only when their own race was involved, they could not carry firearms, and in several states restrictions were placed on their renting or owning land. Even more important, perhaps, was the fact that the laws required the freedman to work and forbade him to leave his job, thereby denying to him an important, if not indispensable, ingredient of freedom, namely, economic mobility.[2]

When these provisions are coupled with the knowledge that servitude without pay was often the penalty for infraction of the Codes, it was only a short step to believing, as did many Northerners, that the laws were in effect re-establishing slavery. The people of the North were also aware that the Codes left the Negroes at the mercy of their white employers, since judges and juries were always white. Even under the slave regime, the self-interest of the master, at least, had assured a measure of justice for the black man in the white man's courtroom or in the sheriff's office.

If the Black Codes reflected the influence of slavery on southern thinking about the Negro, the northern reactions to the laws were the result of the emotions left over from the long antislavery crusade. For many Northerners the Codes seemed to demonstrate that the South was trying to do by subterfuge what it was unable to do on the battlefield—preserve slavery.

Those Northerners who could not be especially aroused against the South by stories of atrocities against Negroes were often moved by tales of outrages against southern white Unionists. Here, too, it seemed as if the South was refusing to accept the verdict of the war. "Hour after hour the democracy here are becoming more bold, more insolent, more proscriptive," wrote one Virginian Unionist in 1866. "Under democratic rule again," he warned, "hell would be a Garden of Eden compared to the Southern States. . . ."

Under the skillful management of the Radical leadership, the unsettling reports of conditions in the South, the Black Codes, and the pleas of southern Unionists appeared as insulting mockeries of the North's wartime sacrifices and the long years of antislavery activity. This was the first step in the Radicals' effort to convince

---

[2] It has been argued that such provisions were necessary in order that economic production might be gotten under way again; that the Negro would not work unless compelled to. This argument falls to the ground, however, when it is recognized that the Codes were never put into any extensive practice (the United States military authorities and the Freedmen's Bureau suspended them and the later Radical state governments repealed them); yet the Negro certainly went to work and production increased. Such a defense of the Codes only serves to underscore the fact that the laws were actually devices to use the power of the state in the securing of a cheap, tractable, and convenient labor supply and not for the purpose of introducing the Negro to freedom.

the people of the North that southern institutions needed federal renovation.

But before the Radicals could take advantage of the North's newly aroused concern and act against the South, it was necessary that Lincoln's plan for the rapid restoration of the Union be set aside. The President's plan, which his successor Andrew Johnson adopted, was deliberately lenient to the defeated South in order that the Union as it was in 1860 might be restored as speedily as possible. In pursuit of this aim, the presidential policy left the disposition of the status of the Negro in the hands of the southern states.

By the end of 1865, all of the former Confederate states had completed the requirements under this plan and awaited only the resumption of their seats in Congress to put the final seal upon their restoration to the Union. Since southern representation in Congress would have rendered impossible any further federal interference in the affairs of the South, the Radicals, who now controlled Congress, refused to seat the southern representatives.

By thus holding the southern states in a condition of constitutional suspended animation, the Radicals hoped to be able to work a social and political revolution upon the institutions of the region. Thaddeus Stevens, the leader of the Radicals in the House, made no secret of his aims. In January, 1866, he candidly told the House that he did not want the southern states returned to the Union until the Negro had been made a good citizen under the tutelage of northern missionaries. "I do not want them [the Southern states] to have the right of suffrage," he declared, "before this Congress has done the great work of regenerating the Constitution and the laws of this country according to the principles of the Declaration of Independence."

The goals of this revolution, as they unfolded in the next few years, included Negro equality, Negro suffrage, and a Negro-based Republican party in the South. Though only part of his ambitious program was apparent in 1865–66, there could be

no doubt even then of the Radicals' desire to protect the Negro in his rights as a free man. In the spring of 1866, the Congress passed the Civil Rights and Freedmen's Bureau bills, both of which employed the federal power to insure the Negro's equality before the law and his equality of treatment in public places. The President's veto of these bills and the South's adamant opposition to them were answered by a new demand upon the defeated region. The Radicals now demanded as the price of readmission to the Union—in line with Stevens' statement in January—the ratification of the newly written Fourteenth Amendment to the federal Constitution.

Aside from its remarkably nationalistic tone, which we have already noticed, the Fourteenth Amendment proclaimed the equality of all Americans, black and white. Beginning by declaring that all persons born in the United States are citizens (thereby including Negroes), it went on to forbid any state to "make . . . any law which shall abridge the privileges or immunities of citizens of the United States," or to "deprive any person of life, liberty, or property, without due process of law," or to "deny to any person within its jurisdiction the equal protection of the laws." The amendment was submitted to the states, both northern and southern, in June, 1866, but its sweeping affirmation of equality was obviously directed first of all against those states which had been lately in rebellion.

The categorical and peremptory refusal of ten of the former Confederate states to ratify the amendment was a turning point in the history of Reconstruction. One cannot be sure, of course, what would have happened if the southern states had acted differently. We do know, though, that in the case of one state, Tennessee, whose ratification Congress accepted, readmission to the Union followed immediately, and Tennessee was not molested by congressional Reconstruction thereafter. If the other ten states had similarly been restored to the Union, then, presumably, there could

have been no Radical Reconstruction as we
know it simply because southern representation in Congress in concert with President Johnson could have stopped any such
efforts. But even if the southern states were
not restored to the Union, ratification of
the amendment would have removed the
primary justification for the later imposition of military rule. For it was in order
to secure the necessary ratifying states that
Congress later moved to the military subordination of the South. By refusing to
ratify, the southern states gained little if
anything, since it should have been obvious, given the temper of the country as revealed in the election triumph of the Radicals in 1866, that some effort to realize the
equalitarian spirit of the times would succeed sooner or later.[3] By their intransigence, the southern states presented the
Radicals with a lever with which to overturn the social structure of the Southland.

Viewed from the perspective of almost
a century, the requirement that the southern states ratify the Fourteenth Amendment does not appear revengeful or vindictive,[4] but neither does it seem conciliatory;

[3] It is interesting to note that the governors of
Louisiana, Arkansas, and Virginia recommended
ratification of the Fourteenth Amendment to their
legislatures, but, of course, their advice was not
heeded.

[4] Many historians, led by J. G. Randall, have
come to refer to the Radicals as Vindictives. Such
a simplistic view of the Radical motivation, however, obscures the remarkable lack of revenge displayed by the victors. Virtually no reprisals were
taken against the South for the rebellion, despite
the fact that the President of the United States
was assassinated by a southern sympathizer. Probably never before in the history of any nation
which had just suppressed a great rebellion could
it be said, as was true of the United States, that
not a single leader of the rebels was executed, or
even tried for treason. Only one, Jefferson Davis,
was imprisoned for any length of time, and he
was released after two years. None of the military
leaders was held even momentarily, though a good
number of them, like Lee, had left the federal
service to join the Confederacy. The greatest economic blow levied against the South was the abolition of slave property without compensation, but
this was not the work of the Radical Reconstruction. The evidence which is usually brought against
the Radicals to show their vindictiveness does not
support the charge so much as it demonstrates
their interest in effecting a revolution in southern

few social revolutions, however, are easy
to swallow. The amendment struck at the
two most cherished canons of southern
thought: states' rights and the inferiority
of the Negro. The proud South was the
prisoner of its history, and once again, as
in the 1850s, it came up against the North's
equally historical sense of mission and reform. And once again the North possessed
the preponderance of power.

After the election of 1866 the North's
support of the Radical program could be
doubtful in no one's mind. The people of
the North seemed prepared to go along
with the social revolution which the Radicals were planning for the South. Moreover, they were apparently quite willing to
have it apply to themselves, too, for the
Fourteenth Amendment was ratified by
over three-quarters of the northern states
within the first year. The Radical election
victory was overwhelming, even though
President Johnson had embarked upon an
unprecedented campaign against the Radicals and their program. New York returned
a majority for the Republicans double what
it had given Lincoln in 1864; New Jersey,
traditionally Democratic, sent a majority
of Republican congressmen; Pennsylvania
elected eighteen Republicans and only six
Democrats to the Congress; Michigan and
Iowa returned solid Republican delegations. Only three border states, Delaware,
Kentucky, and Maryland, went Democratic. All told, the Republicans secured
143 seats in a House of 192, enough to
override any veto of the unfriendly President. The people of the North were solidly
behind the Radicals' assertion that restoration of the Union must wait upon the
South's acceptance of the equality of rights
for Negroes.

"They have deliberated, they have
acted," exclaimed Congressman James

thinking and mores. Such enforced changes are
admittedly painful, but hardly vindictive when
viewed dispassionately. To persist in forcing
through such changes is not any more vindictive
than to redistribute Japanese land after World
War II or to insist that anti-Semitism be prohibited in Germany.

Garfield in February, 1867, when the ten southern states refused to ratify the Fourteenth Amendment. "The last of the sinful ten has, with contempt and scorn, flung back into our teeth the magnanimous offer of a generous nation. It is now our turn to act." Armed with the victory at the polls, the Radicals now took their most extreme step. They placed the recalcitrant ten under military rule and, in addition to ratification of the Fourteenth Amendment, the southern states were required to extend the suffrage to the Negro and to revise their constitutions so as to grant equality to black men.

Since the northern states would soon be asked to grant suffrage to the Negro, it is instructive to set forth Thaddeus Stevens' justification for such a proposal. In placing his arguments before the Congress in January, 1867, Stevens candidly appealed to the three great principles for which the North had fought the war: the Negro, the Union, and the Republican party. "There are several good reasons for the passage of this bill," he began. "In the first place, it is just. . . . Have not loyal blacks quite as good a right to choose rulers and make laws as rebel whites? In the second place, it is a necessity in order to protect the loyal white men in the seceded States." With Negro suffrage, Stevens believed, pro-Union men in the southern states, both black and white, would constitute majorities, "control the States, and protect themselves." The final reason he offered was that "it would assure the ascendancy of the Union party. . . . I believe that on the continued ascendancy of that party depends the safety of this great nation."

To compel the South to accept Negro suffrage was to ask of that region more than the North at that time appeared willing to give.[5] But the North's opposition to Negro voting was deceptively weak, as the rapidity with which the Fifteenth Amendment was ratified demonstrated. In February, 1869, less than two years after Negro suffrage was imposed upon the South, the Fifteenth Amendment was on its way to the states. Ratification, with the assistance of the now Radicalized southern states, was achieved within 13 months thereafter. By a combination of persuasion and emotion in the North, and ruthless suppression in the South, the Radicals had completed their revolution. In the eyes of the national Constitution the former slave was now a full citizen, equal before the law and in possession of the ballot.

2. HOW BLACK WAS BLACK RECONSTRUCTION?

But, it will be said, the price the South and the nation paid for this ideal of equality was outrageously high. And because the history of Reconstruction in the South has been so overlaid with myth and emotion, it is necessary at this point to digress somewhat in an attempt to put that unhappy decade into some perspective.

There is a myth of Reconstruction history to which most Americans, Northerners and Southerners alike, give credence. In brief outline it goes something like this. In 1867, a vengeful Congress placed the southern states under a military despotism which supported by its bayonets an alien regime in each of the states, composed of white adventurers—the carpetbaggers and scalawags—and their ignorant Negro alliers. For a decade thereafter, the story continues, these regimes looted the treasuries of the southern states, impoverished the region with high taxes, denied the southern white people any say in their own governance, and spread terror throughout the Southland. Not until the withdrawal of federal troops in 1877, it is said, did this nightmare end and decency in government return to the South. As in most myths, there is some truth in this one; but a balanced picture of Reconstruction is quite different.

[5] As late as 1868, only four states outside of New England and New York granted the suffrage to Negroes: Nebraska, Iowa, Minnesota, and Wisconsin. Colorado and Connecticut had rejected Negro suffrage in 1865; Ohio and Kansas did so in 1867; Missouri and Michigan in 1868.

For one thing, though it is common to think of Reconstruction as lasting the ten years from 1867 to 1877, the actual duration of the military and Radical regimes varied considerably from state to state. Democratic or conservative governments came to power in Virginia and North Carolina as early as 1870 (in fact, Virginia never experienced a true Radical civilian government at all); in Georgia in 1871; in Texas, Arkansas, and Alabama in 1874; in Mississippi in 1876. Only South Carolina, Florida, and Louisiana depended upon the withdrawal of federal troops in 1877 for the overthrow of their Radical government. In brief, Radical Reconstruction, including the military phases as well as the civilian, lasted as short as three years in two states and as long as ten years in only three.

Because it is so often assumed that Radical Reconstruction was synonymous with military rule, the role of the Army in the South during this period must be precisely understood. Under the congressional plan of Reconstruction as set forth in the acts of 1867, the South was divided into five military districts, each under a major general. It was the responsibility of these generals to oversee the establishment of registration lists for voters for the constitutional conventions and the election of new governments in the states of their districts. Once this was accomplished, civil governments based on the new constitutions would assume power. Generally, the ending of military rule roughly coincided with the date at which Congress admitted the state to the Union. Thus military rule ended in 1868 in all of the southern states except Virginia, Texas, and Mississippi, and in those states it was over in 1869 or 1870. (Only in Georgia was military rule ever imposed again.) Often, it must be admitted, the Radical civil governments required or utilized the aid of militia and sometimes the federal troops to support their regimes, but this does not mean that an extraconstitutional government was in power. For the greater part of Radical Reconstruction, then, the southern states were under civil, not military, government, and, in most cases, these were governments which conservative white Southerners could influence with their votes. Indeed, it was by losing elections that many of the Radical governments fell into conservative hands before 1877.

But even when the southern states were under the military, it should not be assumed that the government was corrupt, oppressive, or unfair toward the whites. Contrary to the usual conception of the military occupation of the South, the number of troops actually stationed in the whole region was very small. No more than 20,000 men were involved in the whole "occupation," of whom fully 7,000 were concentrated in the two states of Louisiana and Texas. No garrison, except those in Richmond and New Orleans, which contained 1,000 each, numbered more than 500 men. The relative weakness of the military force, of course, is a measure of the southern acceptance of northern control.

Though weak in manpower, the military was supreme in law. In fact, the whole machinery of government and law was at the disposal of the Army; its authority was final. But the acquiescence in this on the part of the Southerners—for there was no organized opposition—is weighty testimony to the relative fairness of the administration. "It would be hard to deny that, so far as the ordinary civil administration was concerned," William A. Dunning, the authority on Reconstruction and no friend of the Radicals, has written, "the rule of the generals was as just and efficient as it was far-reaching. Criticism and denunciation of their acts were bitter and continuous; but no very profound research is necessary in order to discover that the animus of these attacks was chiefly political. . . ." There is good reason for believing, he continued, "that military government, pure and simple, unaccompanied by the measures for the institution of Negro suffrage, might have proved for a time a useful aid to social readjustment in the South, as preliminary to the final solution of political problems."

Even later, when the federal troops intervened in the South, it was with care and with a concern for fairness to the whites. President Grant in 1871, much disturbed by the attacks of the Ku Klux Klan upon Negroes, prevailed upon Congress to pass an act to aid in the suppression of the violence. Only once, however, did the President invoke the broad powers which Congress granted; this was in the famous incident of the nine counties of South Carolina in 1871. But even in this instance, Grant was careful enough to have the Attorney General investigate the situation in the area before he acted, and the President withdrew his order for one county when he found he was mistaken as to the disorders and conditions there.

In the prosecution of Southerners for infractions of the so-called enforcement acts, passed in 1870–71 to assist in the suppression of opposition to Negro suffrage, the federal courts tried hard to be fair. Out of the hundreds of cases against whites for infringements of these laws, there were relatively few convictions. One authority, William W. Davis, a Southerner, has estimated that only about 20 percent of the cases under the acts resulted in conviction; and about 70 percent of them were dismissed or nol-prossed. "The Federal courts," Davis has written, "insisted on reasonable testimony, and the judges, with some notorious exceptions, were generally fair in their rulings." Moreover, he added, "White judges were inclined toward leniency in judging the white man prosecuted under the force acts on the testimony of black men." In summary, then, it would seem that justice was obtainable for the white man even during the grimmest days of so-called Black Reconstruction.[6]

Perhaps the explanation most commonly offered for the ascendancy of the Radicals

and the Negroes in southern state governments is that the conservative whites were disfranchised at the same time the Negroes were enfranchised. As a literal and non-quantitative statement, this is true, but as an explanation it will not hold water. At no time were sufficient whites deprived of the ballot to permit the Negroes and Northerners to take over the governments of the southern states by default.

Before the numbers involved can be discussed, the two different kinds or phases of disfranchisement must be understood. The first was during military rule, when Congress stipulated that those who had deserted federal office for the Confederacy or had voluntarily given aid to that cause were to be denied the suffrage and office-holding. Though it is impossible to obtain a completely accurate record of the number disfranchised under this rule (thousands of whites, for example, refused to register as a form of protest, but they are sometimes counted as disfranchised), the figure usually accepted is 150,000 for the whole South. This is to be compared with a total registration for whites in 1868 of about 630,000. Regardless of the size of the figure, under this disfranchisement only two elections were held, that for the choosing of the delegates to the state constitution conventions and that for the selection of the officers of the new governments created under the constitutions. After that, the qualifications for voting would be those decided upon in the conventions and written into the new constitutions. And that was the second phase of disfranchisement.

Again, contrary to the usual opinion, the states, on the whole, in their Radical-dominated conventions were not as ruthless in disfranchisement as one might expect. And those which were, found that their disabling

[6] Even a work as critical and penetrating as W. J. Cash, *The Mind of the South*, published as recently as 1941, contains exaggerated presentations of what happened during Reconstruction. "For ten years the courts of the South were in such hands that no loyal white man could hope to find justice in them as against any Negro or any white creature of the Yankee policy; for twenty years and longer they continued, in many quarters, to be in such hands that such justice was at least doubtful."

clauses were removed before ratification. In the end, only Louisiana, Alabama, and Arkansas actually enforced suffrage and officeholding restrictions against whites; the other seven states placed no legal obstacle in the way of white voting. Finally, it should be noted that the number of southern leaders upon whom the disabilities of the Fourteenth Amendment were visited was greatly reduced as early as 1872. At that date no more than 750 Southerners, those who had occupied high office under the United States in 1860–61 and had deserted to the southern cause, were still barred from officeholding. The disabilities against these men were not removed until the time of the Spanish-American War.

In view of the foregoing, it is illusory to look to white disfranchisement for an explanation of the electoral successes of the Radicals in the southern states. Rather it has to be sought in the fact that many whites did not vote, either in protest or because of indifference, while many Negroes did, either from understanding of the issues or from compulsion from their white and Negro leaders. It should not be forgotten, in this regard, that the proportion of Negroes in the southern states was uniformly greater at that time than it is now. Three states, for example—Louisiana, South Carolina, and Mississippi—contained a majority of Negroes, and one would expect, everything being equal, to encounter a Negro-Radical majority in those states. Moreover, a comparison of the number of Negroes registered in 1868 in each of the southern states with the number of Negro males over 21 as listed in the Census of 1870 discloses that only in Alabama was the actual number of Negro registrants out of line with the potential number as counted in the census. In all the other states the registration figures are plausible and not the result of obvious padding or fraud.

This is not to suggest that fraud did not occur in Reconstruction elections any more than it is meant to convey the impression that New York City elections at this time were innocent of fraud; undoubtedly there was much in both places and on both sides of the political fence. The purpose here, rather, is to show that there is solid justification for the strong showing which the Radicals made at the polls and that it is not to be casually attributed to the "counting out" of the whites. As a matter of fact, even under military-run registration in 1868, white voters outnumbered Negro voters in Georgia, Virginia, Texas, and North Carolina, a fact which rather effectively demolishes the argument that military reconstruction disfranchised the white majorities. Yet, of the two phases of disfranchisement, this was the stricter.

Looming over all discussions of Reconstruction, whether by Southerners or Northerners, is always the question of Negro domination. Surely, in the fear-ridden mind of the South, the unforgettable evil of Reconstruction was the participation of the Negro in government. Actually, though, aside from the exercise of the suffrage, which will be left until later, the Negro played a relatively minor political role in the Reconstruction of the southern states. Indeed, so limited were the number of offices available to Negroes that some of the Negro leaders, one southern authority has written, complained to their white mentors that their race was getting too few plums of office. Often northern whites who came to the South did not look with favor upon Negroes in office, and Southerners who collaborated with the Radicals, retaining, at least in part, their Southern-born attitudes on race, were chary of permitting too many Negroes to hold office.

Negroes, of course, did hold some offices under Reconstruction; in fact, outside of the position of Governor, which no Negro held in any state, black men filled each executive office at one time or another. In only one state, however, was a Negro a member of the Supreme Court; that was in South Carolina. The vast majority of Negro officeholders, however, were local officials like county superintendents of education and justices of the peace.

Contrary to the legend, Negroes did not dominate the legislatures of the southern states. The popularity of James S. Pike's sensational and partisan book, *The Prostrate State*, a contemporary description of the South Carolina legislature, has fostered the erroneous conclusion that such a body was typical of Radical regimes. In truth, Negroes were a majority in the legislatures of South Carolina and Louisiana only, and even there not for all the sessions of the period. Negroes were also a minority in all of the constitutional conventions called under the military, except, again, in the instance of South Carolina, and in Louisiana, where the whites and Negroes were equally divided. (South Carolina and Louisiana stand out in this regard because each contained a large and old city in which lived numbers of free Negroes who had some education and experience outside of slavery.)

Perhaps if there had been Negro domination, Reconstruction in the southern states would have been milder, for in both the conventions and the legislatures of the states the Negro members were the opposite of vindictive toward the whites. "I have no desire to take away any rights of the white man," said Tom Lee, delegate to the Alabama Constitutional Convention in 1867, "all I want is equal rights in the court house and equal rights when I go to vote." Even in the Negro-dominated legislature of South Carolina, there was no disfranchisement of whites beyond that prescribed for officeholding in the Fourteenth Amendment. Whenever the question of amnesty for Confederates came up in the United States Congress, where several Negroes sat during Reconstruction, the Negroes were usually found on the side of leniency toward the white man.

The South Carolina convention was extreme and unrepresentative of its sister conventions when it sought to ban terms of opprobrium like "Nigger" and "Yankee." South Carolina was also out of line with the other states when it provided for racially integrated schools; only two other states followed that example. For the overwhelming majority of Southerners, Reconstruction did not involve the mixing of races in the public schools. Nor did it mean the legalization of intermarriage between the races; the antebellum statutes prohibiting such unions were retained by the Radical regimes. The Negroes, in the main, wanted equality, not dominance.

Among the advantages which Radical Reconstruction brought to the southern states were the new constitutions which the Negroes and Radical whites wrote in each of the states. These organic laws stand up well upon comparison with earlier and subsequent ones in the South. As E. M. Coulter of the University of Georgia, and no friend of Reconstruction Radicals, has written, "The Constitutions finally turned out were much better than the Southerners had ever hoped for: in fact, some of them were kept for many years after the whites again got control of the governments." Generally they were "more democratic than the documents they supplanted, made so by increasing the electorate through Negro suffrage, requiring the total population as the basis for representation, reducing the terms of office, and by adding such principles as homestead exemptions and non-imprisonment for debt." The constitutions also provided for "free education for all and favored the economic development of the South," Coulter concludes.

Unquestionably, the evil most often charged against Reconstruction was the extension of the suffrage to a people the overwhelming majority of whom had only recently emerged from the dependent status of slavery. It is true that Negro suffrage in the South, aside from the intense fears it stirred up in the whites, was conducive to fraud, deception, and, at the very least, thoughtless voting. But viewed through the glasses of hindsight and with the recognition that universal suffrage is fundamental to a democratic society, the enfranchisement of the Negro appears considerably less "radical" today. The insouciant manner in which the suffrage was proffered to former slaves and the universality of the extension are certainly open to question, but the elementary justice of some form of Negro suffrage cannot be denied by any sincere advocate of democratic government.[7]

Unfortunately, on the matter of the suffrage, neither white Southerners nor northern Radicals were prepared to adjust their conception of the Negro to reality. Though some free Negroes were obviously capable of voting intelligently in 1865, as Lincoln, for example, recognized, and most Negroes would be after the mentally crippling effects of slavery had had a chance to be outgrown, few Southerners could shed their blanket view of the Negro as an incompetent. "The fact is patent to all," a South Carolina convention of whites asserted in 1867, "that the Negro is utterly unfitted to exercise the highest functions of the citizen." The South would not change. "Left to itself," southern historian Francis Simkins has concluded, "the region would not have accorded the Negro the vote or other manifestations of equality. . . ."

On the other hand, the northern Radicals, fearful that the South, once back in the Union, would deny the vote to all Negroes, and especially desirous of creating a large number of new Republicans, went to the other extreme and decreed universal Negro suffrage. This solution, however, overlooked the obvious disabilities which slavery had temporarily stamped upon a majority of the Negroes and seriously underestimated the tenacity of the historically ingrained racial feeling of the whites. Today the only comfort which can be drawn from the thoughtless and opportunistic policy of the Radicals is that it did provide a means for the inclusion of the Negro in the electorate, even if the means almost smothered the ideal with disrepute.

Radical Reconstruction in the South left a more permanent monument than the Negro's transient experience in public office and a nobler one than the southern white's nightmares of racial amalgamation. This was the laying of the foundation of southern free public education. Almost all of the Reconstruction conventions and legislatures erected or revived systems of free public education—a not insignificant manifestation, it might be noted parenthetically, of the Radical propensity for making over Dixie in the image of the North. In most of the southern states, these Reconstruction efforts in behalf of public education remained after 1877 to become the bases upon which post-Radical governments built their school systems. Though the South had always had some free schools and even some local public-school systems, free education as it was known in the North by the 1850s began in the South only after the war for southern independence.

The other educational achievement of Radical Reconstruction in the South was the conversion of the whites to the view that Negro education was not only desirable but a necessity. This was largely the work of the Freedmen's Bureau. Prior to Radical Reconstruction in Georgia, for example, as Mildred Thompson has pointed out, the postwar government provided public education only for whites. Education for the Negroes was viewed as a waste of effort and perhaps even dangerous. All over the South in 1865–67, northern whites who attempted to instruct Negroes were subject

---

[7] It should not be thought that illiteracy was one of the legitimate arguments against Negro suffrage. Thousands of southern whites enjoyed the franchise even though they could neither read nor write. In 1880, for example, white illiterates averaged over a quarter of the population in Georgia, Alabama, and North Carolina. J. T. Trowbridge, the journalist, who made a tour of the South in 1865–66, concluded that the Negroes should be granted the suffrage. "They are," he wrote, "by all moral and intellectual qualifications, as well prepared for it as the mass of poor whites in the South." In a good number of states of the Union at this time, even immigrants were granted the vote prior to their acquisition of citizenship. The only valid argument against universal Negro suffrage, it would seem, was the lack of independent experience which was inherent in the Negro's former slave status.

to attack and violence. The blazing Negro schoolhouse of this period was the predecessor of the later burning cross.

Despite such opposition, the Freedmen's Bureau succeeded in establishing Negro schools before 1867. At its height, the Bureau operated over 4,000 primary schools, 74 normal schools, and 61 industrial schools for Negroes. George Bentley, a recent historian of the Bureau, concludes that by 1867 Negro and white alike in the South had come to accept the necessity for public education of the former slave. "Certainly in this respect," Bentley observes, "the Bureau had performed a commendable service for the Negroes, for the South and for the nation."

By the time the reader has gotten this far in the "other side" of Reconstruction, he is probably somewhat annoyed at the absence of references to the well-known corruption and fraud so much a part of the conventional picture of the period. He is convinced that this noisome aspect will be conveniently forgotten. There is no denying the disreputable character of all too many of the Radical state governments. Certainly the history of Louisiana, South Carolina, Florida, and Alabama during this period provides rather painful examples of what corruption can be and what government should not be.

But again it is necessary to emphasize that the total picture is not all dark. Mississippi, for example, under Radical Republican rule enjoyed a government as administratively honest as most Democratic ones, and in some ways decidedly more honest. "The only large case of embezzlement among the state officers during the post-bellum period," writes James Garner, the historian of Mississippi Reconstruction, "was that of the Democratic state Treasurer in 1866." Mildred Thompson, writing about her native states, says that in comparison with states like Alabama and South Carolina, Georgia under Radical Reconstruction "shows a marked moderation in her government, a lesser degree of reconstruction evils, less wanton corruption and extravagance in public office, less social disorder and upheaval. In Georgia," she concludes, "Negroes and carpet-baggers were not so conspicuous, and conservative white citizens were better represented."

Though Virginia escaped entirely the period of Radical Reconstruction which other southern states endured after the cessation of military rule, she did not escape extravagance. In 1869, the first and last election under military rule brought the defeat of the Radicals in a free polling. But under the conservatives who then took office, Virginia contracted as staggering a public debt as those run up in the Radical-dominated states. Even the usual stories of the high taxes imposed by the Radical governments in the various states are susceptible of a different interpretation when put into some perspective. In 1870, for instance, when the average tax rate for the southern states was 15 mills, that of Illinois was 45.

The fraudulent dealings of the Radical regimes appear less exceptional and noteworthy if they are placed within the context of the times. For instance, it is instructive to realize that after the end of Reconstruction, each of the conservative Democratic governments in Georgia, Alabama, Virginia, Mississippi, Louisiana, and Tennessee had treasurers or other officials who absconded with or embezzled state funds, the individual defalcations often running to half a million dollars. Then, of course, the years of Reconstruction also included the Tweed swindles in New York City, in which perhaps over $100 million was robbed from the public treasury. And on the national level, the frauds and stealings carried out under the unseeing eye of President Grant serve to round out the picture.

Though not at all excusing the Radical frauds, the corrupt climate of the times does make it clear that the Radical pilferings were little more than particular instances of a general postwar phenomenon.

And once this fact is grasped, it becomes apparent that it is not corruption which has fastened disrepute upon these short-lived regimes, but the fact that Negroes participated in them. "Corruption and extravagance increased the intolerance with which the Negro regimes were regarded," Southern historian Francis Simkins has written, "yet even if these regimes had shown exemplary statesmanship they would have been unacceptable to white Southerners as long as Negroes comprising any part of them were regarded as political equals."

3. CASTE WILL OUT

The tragedy of Reconstruction is that it failed. Rather than liberating the South from its fear of the Negro, Reconstruction exacerbated it; instead of reestablishing a two-party political system, it further fastened a benumbing single party upon a region which once had led the nation in political creativity. Yet neither that section nor the North was alone responsible for the failure; both have to bear the national failure — the South for its intransigent conservatism, the North for its bungling idealism.

As is apparent today, it was imperative in those first years after Appomattox that a way be found whereby the nation and the Negro might confidently look forward to the former slave's full and equal participation in American life. But the unique opportunity of those first years was squandered. Neither Southerners nor Northerners were capable of disenthralling themselves, as Lincoln had counseled; both continued to act within their historically determined attitudinal patterns. Lincoln himself, for that matter, failed to grasp the crucial nature of the postwar era, so far as the Negro was concerned. His plan for the rapid restoration of the southern states indicated that he was quite prepared to throw away the single opportunity for realizing the equalitarian precepts of the Declaration of Independence to which he so often referred. And though the Radicals succeeded in enshrining in the Constitution their vision of equality for all, thereby illuminating the path the nation was ultimately to follow, they were woefully unequal to the complicated and delicate task of implementing their vision. Having failed to meet the problem of the Negro at its inception, Americans have been compelled to grapple with it in each succeeding generation down to our own day. . . .

BIBLIOGRAPHICAL NOTE

The basic collection of sources on Reconstruction is Walter F. Fleming, ed., *Documentary History of Reconstruction* (2 vols.; Cleveland, 1906–7), upon which I have drawn often. Herbert Aptheker (ed.), *Documentary History of the Negro People in the United States* (New York, 1951), contains a section on the Reconstruction period in which the selections are designed to show the Negro's positive contributions. The view of a moderate Northerner in the years immediately after the war is J. T. Trowbridge, *The South: A Tour of Its Battlefields and Ruined Cities* (Hartford, 1866). The two contradictory reports of the South's reaction to defeat are Carl Schurz's, to be found in his *Speeches, Correspondence and Political Papers*, edited by Frederic Bancroft (6 vols.; New York, 1913), and Benjamin Truman's *Report* in Senate Executive Documents, 39th Cong., 1st sess., No. 2. The history of Reconstruction in Mississippi is told by a Negro Republican in John Lynch, *Facts of Reconstruction* (New York, 1913). It is highly suggestive in regard to the possibilities of Negro-white collaboration before the debacle of the Grant regime aborted them. For a long time the standard account of an "eyewitness" of South Carolina Reconstruction was James S. Pike's *Prostrate State* (New York, 1874), but recently Robert F. Durden, *James Shepard Pike* (Durham, N.C., 1957), has shown it to be superficially prepared and animated by a desire to embarrass the Grant regime. One carpetbagger of unquestioned liberal views has revealed his efforts in the South in Louis F. Post, "A Carpet-bagger in South Carolina," *Journal of Negro History*, X (January, 1925), 10–79. I have found John William de Forest, *Union Officer in the Reconstruction* (New Haven, 1948), invaluable for visualizing the day-to-day problems of a conscientious Northerner dealing with ignorant ex-slaves in a society trying to live under a new dispensation. Though reports of Georges Clemenceau, later Premier of France and then a Washington correspondent, in *American Reconstruction, 1865–1870* (New York, 1928), deal with events at the capital, they offer a European view of the Radicals' efforts to remold the South.

Though the writing on Reconstruction has been enormous and, since 1900, largely favorable to the southern point of view, Claude Bowers, *The Tragic Era* (Cambridge, Mass., 1929), has probably done more than any other book to delineate the view now so commonly accepted regarding the enormities of Reconstruction. William A. Dunning's *Reconstruction, Political and Economic 1865–1877* (New York, 1907) and *Essays on the Civil War and Reconstruction* (New York, 1898) are still important, but they are marred by the then prevalent attitude of seeing the Negro as incapable of taking a place as a full citizen. I am indebted to several of the works on Reconstruction which Dunning's students completed: C. Mildred Thompson, *Reconstruction in Georgia* (New York, 1915); James Garner, *Reconstruction in Mississippi* (New York, 1901); J. G. de R. Hamilton, "Southern Legislation in Respect to Freedmen, 1865–1866," and W. W. Davis, "Federal Enforcement Acts," both in *Studies in Southern History and Politics* (New York, 1914).

Soon after the students of Dunning completed their investigations of individual states, reevaluations of some of them began to appear; a pioneer in looking at Reconstruction from a positive point of view was Francis Simkins and Robert H. Woody, *South Carolina During Reconstruction* (Chapel Hill, N.C., 1932). R. W. Shugg, *Origins of Class Struggle in Louisiana* (University, La., 1939), covers the 1850s as well as the Reconstruction and sees the latter period as much more than a conflict between southern whites on the one hand and northern carpetbaggers and Negroes on the other. Vernon L. Wharton, *The Negro in Mississippi, 1865–1890* (Chapel Hill, N.C., 1947), stresses the achievements of Negroes in that state and plays down the so-called atrocities of the era. James S. Allen, *Reconstruction: The Battle for Democracy* (New York, 1937), though the work of a dedicated Marxist with an ax to grind, is important for its canvassing of the Negro's attempt to get land for himself after slavery. The role of the Negro school in early Reconstruction is carefully and fairly treated in Henry Swint, *Northern Teacher in the South, 1862–1870* (Nashville, 1941). The most recent treatment of Reconstruction as a whole, E. M. Coulter, *The South During Reconstruction, 1865–1877* (Baton Rouge, 1947), fails to build upon the new turn taken in Reconstruction studies and so continues the essentially biased attitude toward the Negro so common in earlier studies. I have relied for much of my information regarding disfranchisement on two articles by William A. Russ, "Negro and White Disfranchisement During Radical Reconstruction," *Journal of Negro History*, XIX (April, 1934), 171–92, and "Registration and Disfranchisement Under Radical Reconstruction," *Mississippi Valley Historical Review*, XXI (September, 1934), 163–80. The approach historians take toward Thaddeus Stevens seems to be dependent on things other than evidence: Richard N. Current's *Old Thad Stevens* (Madison, Wis., 1942) is a good example of one which puts the worst construction on many of the things Stevens did and said; Ralph Korngold, *Thaddeus Stevens* (New York, 1955), sees him as pure gold; there is still need for a critical but objective biography of the leader of Radical Reconstruction.

Understandably, the reinterpretation of Reconstruction has been led by Negro scholars, notably W. E. B. Du Bois. His "Reconstruction and its Benefits," *American Historical Review*, XV (July, 1910), 781–99, was followed by Alrutheus A. Taylor's pedestrian but informative volumes *Negro in South Carolina During Reconstruction* (Washington, 1924) and *Negro in the Reconstruction of Virginia* (Washington, 1926). By the time Du Bois wrote his overall study of the period, *Black Reconstruction* (New York, 1935), derived largely from his winnowing of the Dunning and other studies, he had become a Marxist, and this pathbreaking book is seriously marred by his attempt to fit Reconstruction history into the mold of the class struggle. Two of several articles on the reinterpretation of Reconstruction to which I am indebted are Francis B. Simkins, "New Viewpoints on Southern Reconstruction," *Journal of Southern History,* V (February, 1939), 49–61, and Howard K. Beale, "On Rewriting Reconstruction History," *American Historical Review,* XLV (July, 1940), 807–27. Simkins has offered concrete data for his view in Chapters 17–19 of his survey, *A History of the South* (New York, 1953). Two very good studies of the Freedmens' Bureau portray that much-maligned institution in a manner which highlights its immense aid in the rehabilitation of the South and the Negro: Paul Peirce, *The Freedmen's Bureau* (Iowa City, 1904); and George Bentley, *A History of the Freedmen's Bureau* (Philadelphia, 1955), the latter trying a little too hard to find economic motivation behind the Bureau's work. John and LaWanda Cox, "General O. O. Howard and the Misrepresented Bureau," *Journal of Southern History,* XIX (November, 1953), 427–56, also defends the Bureau. In *Lincoln and the Radicals* (Madison, Wis., 1941), T. Harry Williams portrayed the President as fighting against the extreme Radicals before his assassination; this view has been seriously disputed in David H. Donald, *Lincoln Reconsidered* (New York, 1956). The respectable nature of some so-called scalawags has been convincingly argued in Donald's "The Scalawags in Mississippi Reconstruction," *Journal of Southern History,* X (November, 1944), 447–60.

1965

The Tragic Legend of Reconstruction[*]

KENNETH M. STAMPP

In much serious history, as well as in a durable popular legend, two American epochs—the Civil War and the reconstruction that followed—bear an odd relationship to one another. The Civil War, though admittedly a tragedy, is nevertheless often described as a glorious time of gallantry, noble self-sacrifice, and high idealism. Even historians who have considered the war "needless" and have condemned the politicians of the 1850s for blundering into it, once they passed the firing on Fort Sumter, have usually written with reverence about Civil War heroes—the mar-

tyred Lincoln, the Christlike Lee, the intrepid Stonewall Jackson, and many others in this galaxy of demigods.

Few, of course, are so innocent as not to know that the Civil War has its seamy side. One can hardly ignore the political opportunism, the graft and profiteering in the filling of war contracts, the military blundering and needless loss of lives, the horrors of army hospitals and prison camps, and the ugly depths as well as the nobility of human nature that the war exposed with a fine impartiality. These things cannot be ignored, but they can be, and frequently are, dismissed as something alien to the essence of the war years. What was real and fundamental was the idealism

* Reprinted by permission of Alfred A. Knopf, Inc., from *The Era of Reconstruction* by Kenneth Stampp. Copyright 1965 by Kenneth Stampp.

and the nobility of the two contending forces: the Yankees struggling to save the Union, dying to make men free; the Confederates fighting for great constitutional principles, defending their homes from invasion. Here, indeed, is one of the secrets of the spell the Civil War has cast: it involved high-minded Americans on both sides, and there was glory enough to go around. This, in fact, is the supreme synthesis of Civil War historiography and the great balm that has healed the nation's wounds: Yankees and Confederates alike fought bravely for what they believed to be just causes. There were few villains in the drama.

But when the historian reaches the year 1865, he must take leave of the war and return to another epoch, reconstruction, when the task was, in Lincoln's words, "to bind up the nation's wounds" and "to do all which may achieve and cherish a just and lasting peace." How, until recently, reconstruction was portrayed in both history and legend, how sharply it was believed to contrast with the years of the Civil War, is evident in the terms that were used to identify it. Various historians have called this phase of American history "The Tragic Era," "The Dreadful Decade," "The Age of Hate," and "The Blackout of Honest Government." Reconstruction represented the ultimate shame of the American people —as one historian phrased it, "the nadir of national disgrace." It was the epoch that most Americans wanted to forget.

Claude Bowers, who divided his time between politics and history, has been the chief disseminator of the traditional picture of reconstruction, for his book, *The Tragic Era,* published in 1929, has attracted more readers than any other dealing with this period. For Bowers reconstruction was a time of almost unrelieved sordidness in public and private life; whole regiments of villains march through his pages: the corrupt politicians who dominated the administration of Ulysses S. Grant; the crafty, scheming northern carpetbaggers who invaded the South after the war for political and economic plunder; the degraded and depraved southern scalawags who betrayed their own people and collaborated with the enemy; and the ignorant, barbarous, sensual Negroes who threatened to Africanize the South and destroy its Caucasian civilization.

Most of Bowers' key generalizations can be found in his preface. The years of reconstruction, he wrote, "were years of revolutionary turmoil, with the elemental passions predominant. . . . The prevailing note was one of tragedy. . . . Never have American public men in responsible positions, directing the destiny of the nation, been so brutal, hypocritical, and corrupt. The constitution was treated as a doormat on which politicians and army officers wiped their feet after wading in the muck. . . . The southern people literally were put to the torture . . . [by] rugged conspirators . . . [who] assumed the pose of philanthropists and patriots." The popularity of Bowers' book stems in part from the simplicity of his characters. None are etched in shades of gray; none are confronted with complex moral decisions. Like characters in a Victorian romance, the Republican leaders of the reconstruction era were evil through and through, and the helpless, innocent white men of the South were totally noble and pure.

If Bowers' prose is more vivid and his anger more intense, his general interpretation of reconstruction is only a slight exaggeration of a point of view shared by most American historians from the late nineteenth century until very recently. Writing in the 1890s, James Ford Rhodes, author of a multi-volumed history of the United States since the Compromise of 1850, branded the Republican scheme of reconstruction as "repressive" and "uncivilized," one that "pandered to the ignorant negroes, the knavish white natives and the vulturous adventurers who flocked from the North." About the same time Professor John W. Burgess, of Columbia University, called reconstruction the "most soul-sickening spectacle that Americans

had ever been called upon to behold."[1]
Early in the twentieth century Professor
William A. Dunning, also of Columbia
University, and a group of talented grad-
uate students wrote a series of monographs
that presented a crushing indictment of the
Republican reconstruction program in the
South—a series that made a deep and lasting impression on American historians. In
the 1930s, Professor James G. Randall, of
the University of Illinois, still writing in the
spirit of the Dunningites, described the reconstruction era "as a time of party abuse,
of corruption, of vindictive bigotry." "To
use a modern phrase," wrote Randall,
"government under Radical Republican
rule in the South had become a kind of
'racket.' " As late as 1947, Professor E.
Merton Coulter, of the University of
Georgia, reminded critics of the traditional
interpretation that no "amount of revision
can write away the grievous mistakes made
in this abnormal period of American history."[2] Thus, from Rhodes and Burgess
and Dunning to Randall and Coulter the
central emphasis of most historical writing
about reconstruction has been upon sordid
motives and human depravity. Somehow,
during the summer of 1865, the nobility
and idealism of the war years had died.

A synopsis of the Dunning School's version of reconstruction would run something
like this: Abraham Lincoln, while the Civil
War was still in progress, turned his
thought to the great problem of reconciliation; and, "with malice toward none and
charity for all," this gentle and compas-
sionate man devised a plan that would
restore the South to the Union with minimum humiliation and maximum speed.
But there had already emerged in Congress a faction of radical Republicans,

sometimes called Jacobins or Vindictives,
who sought to defeat Lincoln's generous
program. Motivated by hatred of the
South, by selfish political ambitions, and
by crass economic interests, the radicals
tried to make the process of reconstruction
as humiliating, as difficult, and as prolonged as they possibly could. Until Lincoln's tragic death, they poured their scorn
upon him—and then used his coffin as a
political stump to arouse the passions of
the northern electorate.

The second chapter of the Dunning version begins with Andrew Johnson's succession to the presidency. Johnson, the old
Jacksonian Unionist from Tennessee, took
advantage of the adjournment of Congress
to put Lincoln's mild plan of reconstruction into operation, and it was a striking
success. In the summer and fall of 1865,
Southerners organized loyal state governments, showed a willingness to deal fairly
with their former slaves, and in general accepted the outcome of the Civil War in
good faith. In December, when Congress
assembled, President Johnson reported that
the process of reconstruction was nearly
completed and that the old Union had been
restored. But the radicals unfortunately
had their own sinister purposes: they repudiated the governments Johnson had
established in the South, refused to seat
southern Senators and Representatives,
and then directed their fury against the
new President. After a year of bitter controversy and political stalemate, the radicals, resorting to shamefully demagogic
tactics, won an overwhelming victory in the
congressional elections of 1866.

Now, the third chapter and the final
tragedy. Riding roughshod over presidential vetoes and federal courts, the radicals
put the South under military occupation,
gave the ballot to Negroes, and formed
new southern state governments dominated
by base and corrupt men, black and white.
Not satisfied with reducing the South to
political slavery and financial bankruptcy,
the radicals even laid their obscene hands
on the pure fabric of the federal Consti-

---

[1] James Ford Rhodes: *History of the United
States from the Compromise of 1850* . . . (7 vols.;
New York, 1893–1906), Vol. VII, p. 168; John
W. Burgess: *Reconstruction and the Constitution*
(New York, 1902), p. 263.

[2] James G. Randall: *Civil War and Reconstruction* (Boston, 1937), pp. 689, 852; E. Merton
Coulter: *The South during Reconstruction, 1865–
1877* (Baton Rouge, 1947), p. xi.

tution. They impeached President Johnson and came within one vote of removing him from office, though they had no legal grounds for such action. Next, they elected Ulysses S. Grant President, and during his two administrations they indulged in such an orgy of corruption and so prostituted the civil service as to make Grantism an enduring symbol of political immorality.

The last chapter is the story of ultimate redemption. Decent southern white Democrats, their patience exhausted, organized to drive the Negroes, carpetbaggers, and scalawags from power, peacefully if possible, forcefully if necessary. One by one the southern states were redeemed, honesty and virtue triumphed, and the South's natural leaders returned to power. In the spring of 1877, the Tragic Era finally came to an end when President Hayes withdrew the federal troops from the South and restored home rule. But the legacy of radical reconstruction remained in the form of a solidly Democratic South and embittered relations between the races.

This point of view was rarely challenged until the 1930s, when a small group of revisionist historians began to give new life and a new direction to the study of reconstruction. The revisionists are a curious lot who sometimes quarrel with each other as much as they quarrel with the disciples of Dunning. At various times they have counted in their ranks Marxists of various degrees of orthodoxy, Negroes seeking historical vindication, skeptical white Southerners, and latter-day northern abolitionists. But among them are numerous scholars who have the wisdom to know that the history of an age is seldom simple and clear-cut, seldom without its tragic aspects, seldom without its redeeming virtues.

Few revisionists would claim that the Dunning interpretation of reconstruction is a pure fabrication. They recognize the shabby aspects of this era: the corruption was real, the failures obvious, the tragedy undeniable. Grant is not their idea of a model President, nor were the southern

carpetbag governments worthy of their unqualified praise. They understand that the radical Republicans were not all selfless patriots, and that southern white men were not all Negro-hating rebels. In short, they have not turned history on its head, but rather, they recognize that much of what Dunning's disciples have said about reconstruction is true.

Revisionists, however, have discovered that the Dunningites overlooked a great deal, and they doubt that nobility and idealism suddenly died in 1865. They are neither surprised nor disillusioned to find that the Civil War, for all its nobility, revealed some of the ugliness of human nature as well. And they approach reconstruction with the confident expectation that here, too, every facet of human nature will be exposed. They are not satisfied with the two-dimensional characters that Dunning's disciples have painted.

What is perhaps more puzzling in the legend of reconstruction is the notion that the white people of the South were treated with unprecedented brutality, and that their conquerors, in Bowers' colorful phrase, literally put them to the torture. How, in fact, *were* they treated after the failure of their rebellion against the authority of the federal government? The great mass of ordinary Southerners who voluntarily took up arms, or in other ways supported the Confederacy, were required simply to take an oath of allegiance to obtain pardon and to regain their right to vote and hold public office. But what of the Confederate leaders—the men who held high offices, often after resigning similar federal offices; the military leaders who had graduated from West Point and had resigned commissions in the United States Army to take commissions in the Confederate Army? Were there mass arrests, indictments for treason or conspiracy, trials and convictions, executions or imprisonments? Nothing of the sort. Officers of the Confederate Army were paroled and sent home with their men. After surrendering at Appomattox, General Lee bid farewell to his troops and rode home to live his remaining years undisturbed. Only one officer, a Captain Henry Wirtz, was arrested; and he was tried, convicted, and executed, not for treason or conspiracy, but for "war crimes." Wirtz's alleged offense, for which the evidence was rather flimsy, was the mistreatment of prisoners of war in the military prison at Andersonville, Georgia.

Of the Confederate civil officers, a handful were arrested at the close of the war, and there was talk for a time of trying a few for treason. But none, actually, was ever brought to trial, and all but Jefferson Davis were released within a few months. The former Confederate President was held in prison for nearly two years, but in 1867 he too was released. With a few exceptions, even the property of Confederate leaders was untouched, save, of course, for the emancipation of their slaves. Indeed, the only penalty imposed on most Confederate leaders was a temporary political disability provided in the Fourteenth Amendment. But in 1872 Congress pardoned all but a handful of Southerners; and soon former Confederate civil and military leaders were serving as state governors, as members of Congress, and even as Cabinet advisers of Presidents.

What then, constituted the alleged brutality that white Southerners endured? First, the freeing of their slaves, second, the brief incarceration of a few Confederate leaders; third, a political disability imposed for a few years on most Confederate leaders; fourth, a relatively weak military occupation terminated in 1877; and, last, an attempt to extend the rights and privileges of citizenship to southern Negroes. Mistakes there were in the implementation of these measures—some of them serious—but brutality almost none. In fact, it can be said that rarely in history have the participants in an unsuccessful rebellion endured penalties as mild as those Congress imposed upon the people of the South, and particularly upon their leaders. After four years of bitter struggle costing hundreds of thousands of lives, the gener-

osity of the federal government's terms was quite remarkable.

If northern brutality is a myth, the scandals of the Grant administration and the peculations of some of the southern reconstruction governments are sordid facts. Yet even here the Dunningites are guilty of distortion by exaggeration, by superficial analysis, and by overemphasis. They make corruption a central theme of their narratives, but they overlook constructive accomplishments. They give insufficient attention to the men who transcended the greed of an age when, to be sure, self-serving politicians and irresponsible entrepreneurs were all too plentiful. Among these men were the humanitarians who organized Freedmen's Aid Societies to help 4 million southern Negroes make the difficult transition from slavery to freedom, and the missionaries and teachers who went into the South on slender budgets to build churches and schools for the freedmen. Under their auspices the Negroes first began to learn the responsibilities and obligations of freedom. Thus the training of Negroes for citizenship had its successful beginnings in the years of reconstruction.

In the nineteenth century most white Americans, North and South, had reservations about the Negro's potentialities—doubted that he had the innate intellectual capacity and moral fiber of the white man and assumed that after emancipation he would be relegated to an inferior caste. But some of the radical Republicans refused to believe that the Negroes were innately inferior and hoped passionately that they would confound their critics. The radicals then had little empirical evidence and no scientific evidence to support their belief—nothing, in fact, but faith. Their faith was derived mostly from their religion: all men, they said, are the sons of Adam and equal in the sight of God. And if Negroes are equal to white men in the sight of God, it is morally wrong for white men to withhold from Negroes the liberties and rights that white men enjoy. Here, surely, was a projection into the reconstruction era of the idealism of the abolitionist crusade and of the Civil War.

Radical idealism was in part responsible for two of the most momentous enactments of the reconstruction years: the Fourteenth Amendment to the federal Constitution which gave Negroes citizenship and promised them equal protection of the laws, and the Fifteenth Amendment which gave them the right to vote. The fact that these amendments could not have been adopted under any other circumstances, or at any other time, before or since, may suggest the crucial importance of the reconstruction era in American history. Indeed, without radical reconstruction, it would be impossible to this day for the federal government to protect Negroes from legal and political discrimination.

If all of this is true, or even part of it, why was the Dunning legend born, and why has it been so durable? Southerners, of course, have contributed much to the legend of reconstruction, but most Northerners have found the legend quite acceptable. Many of the historians who helped to create it were Northerners, among them James Ford Rhodes, William A. Dunning, Claude Bowers, and James G. Randall. Thus the legend cannot be explained simply in terms of a southern literary or historiographical conspiracy, satisfying as the legend has been to most white Southerners. What we need to know is why it also satisfies Northerners—how it became part of the intellectual baggage of so many northern historians. Why, in short, was there for so many years a kind of national, or intersectional, consensus that the Civil War was America's glory and reconstruction her disgrace?

The Civil War won its place in the hearts of the American people because, by the end of the nineteenth century, Northerners were willing to concede that Southerners had fought bravely for a cause that they believed to be just; whereas Southerners, with few exceptions, were willing to concede that the outcome of the war was probably best for all concerned. In an era of intense nationalism, both Northerners and Southerners agreed that the preservation of the federal Union was essential to the future power of the American people. Southerners could even say now that the abolition of slavery was one of the war's great blessings—not so much, they insisted, because slavery was an injustice to the Negroes but because it was a grievous burden upon the whites. By 1886, Henry W. Grady, the great Georgia editor and spokesman for a New South, could confess to a New York audience: "I am glad that the omniscient God held the balance of battle in His Almighty hand, and that human slavery was swept forever from American soil—the American Union saved from the wreck of war." Soon Union and Confederate veterans were holding joint reunions, exchanging anecdotes, and sharing their sentimental memories of those glorious war years. The Civil War thus took its position in the center of American folk mythology.

That the reconstruction era elicits neither pride nor sentimentality is due only in part to its moral delinquencies—remember, those of the Civil War years can be overlooked. It is also due to the white American's ambivalent attitude toward race and toward the steps that radical Republicans took to protect the Negroes. Southern white men accepted the Thirteenth Amendment to the Constitution, which abolished slavery, with a minimum of complaint, but they expected federal intervention to proceed no further than that. They assumed that the regulation of the freedmen would be left to the individual states; and clearly most of them intended to replace slavery with a caste system that would keep the Negroes perpetually subordinate to the whites. Negroes were to remain a dependent laboring class; they were to be governed by a separate code of laws; they were to play no active part in the South's political life; and they were to be segregated socially. When radical Republicans used federal power to interfere in these matters, the majority of southern white men formed a resistance movement to fight the radical-dominated state governments until they were overthrown, after which southern whites established a caste system in defiance of federal statutes and constitutional amendments. For many decades thereafter the federal government simply admitted defeat and acquiesced; but the South refused to forget or forgive those years of humiliation when Negroes came close to winning equality. In southern mythology, then, reconstruction was a horrid nightmare.

As for the majority of northern white men, it is hard to tell how deeply they were concerned about the welfare of the American Negro after the abolition of slavery. If one were to judge from the way they treated the small number of free Negroes who resided in the northern states, one might conclude that they were, at best, indifferent to the problem—and that a considerable number of them shared the racial attitudes of the South and preferred to keep Negroes in a subordinate caste. For a time after the Civil War the radical Republicans, who were always a minority group, persuaded the northern electorate that the ultimate purpose of southern white men was to rob the North of the fruits of victory and to re-establish slavery and that federal intervention was therefore essential. In this manner radicals won approval of, or acquiescence in, their program to give civil rights and the ballot to southern Negroes. Popular support for the radical program waned rapidly, however, and by the middle of the 1870s it had all but vanished. In 1875 a Republican politician confessed that northern voters were tired of the "worn-out cry of 'southern outrages,' " and they wished that "the 'nigger' the 'everlasting nigger' were in—Africa." As Northerners ceased to worry about the possibility of another southern rebellion, they became increasingly receptive to criticism of radical reconstruction.

The eventual disintegration of the radical phalanx, those root-and-branch men who, for a time, seemed bent on engineer-ing a sweeping reformation of southern society, was another important reason for the denigration of reconstruction in American historiography. To be sure, some of the radicals, especially those who had been abolitionists before the war, never lost faith in the Negro, and in the years after reconstruction they stood by him as he struggled to break the intellectual and psychological fetters he had brought with him out of slavery. Other radicals, however, lost interest in the cause—tired of reform and spent their declining years writing their memoirs. Still others retained their crusading zeal but became disenchanted with radical reconstruction and found other crusades more attractive: civil service reform, or tariff reform, or defense of the gold standard. In 1872 they repudiated Grant and joined the Liberal Republicans; in subsequent years they considered themselves to be political independents.

This latter group had been an important element in the original racial coalition. Most of them were respectable, middle-class people in comfortable economic circumstances, well educated and highly articulate, and acutely conscious of their obligation to perform disinterested public service. They had looked upon Senator Charles Sumner of Massachusetts as their political spokesman, and upon Edwin L. Godkin of the New York Nation as their editorial spokesman. Like most radicals they had believed that the Negro was what slavery had made him; give the Negro equal rights and he would be quickly transformed into an industrious and responsible citizen. With the radical reconstruction program fairly launched, they had looked forward to swift and dramatic results.

But reconstruction was not orderly and the Negro's progress was not nearly as swift and dramatic as these reformers had seemed to expect. The first signs of doubt came soon after the radicals won control of reconstruction policy, when the Nation warned the Negroes that the government had already done all it could for them. They were now, said the Nation, "on the dusty and rugged highway of competition"; henceforth "the removal of white prejudice against the Negro depends almost entirely on the Negro himself." By 1870 this bell-wether of the reformers viewed with alarm the disorders and irregularities in the states governed by Negroes and carpetbaggers; by 1871 it proclaimed: "The experiment has totally failed. . . . We owe it to human nature to say that worse governments have seldom been seen in a civilized country." And three years later, looking at South Carolina, the *Nation* pronounced the ulti-mate epithet: "This is . . . socialism." Among the former radicals associated with the *Nation* in these years of tragic disillu-sionment were three prewar abolitionists: Edmund Quincy of Massachusetts, James Miller McKim of Pennsylvania, and the Reverend O. B. Frothingham of New York.

Finally, in 1890, many years after the reconstruction governments had collapsed, the *Nation,* still accurately reflecting the state of mind of the disenchanted reform-ers, made a full confession of its past errors. "There is," said the *Nation,* "a rap-idly growing sympathy at the North with Southern perplexity over the negro prob-lem. . . . Even those who were not shocked by the carpet-bag experiment . . . are be-ginning to 'view with alarm' the political prospect created by the increase of the negro population, and by the continued in-ability of southern society to absorb or assimilate them in any sense, physical, social, or political. . . . The sudden admis-sion to the suffrage of a million of the recently emancipated slaves belonging to the least civilized race in the world . . . was a great leap in the dark, the ultimate con-sequences of which no man now living can foresee. No nation has ever done this, or anything like this for the benefit of aliens of any race or creed. Who or what is . . . [the Negro] that we should put the inter-ests of the 55,000,000 whites on this con-tinent in peril for his sake?" Editor Godkin answered his own question in a letter to another one-time radical: "I do not see . . . how the negro is ever to be worked into

a system of government for which you and I would have much respect."

Actually, neither the obvious shortcom-ings of reconstruction nor an objective view of the Negro's progress in the years after emancipation can wholly explain the dis-illusionment of so many former radicals. Rather, their changed attitude toward the Negro and the hostile historical interpre-tation of reconstruction that won their favor were in part the product of social trends that severely affected the old Amer-ican middle classes with whom most of them were identified. These trends had their origin in the industrial revolution; they were evident in the early nineteenth cen-tury but were enormously accelerated after the Civil War. Their institutional symbols were the giant manufacturing and railroad corporations.

In the new age of industrial enterprise there seemed to be no place for the old families with their genteel culture and strong traditions of disinterested public service. On the one hand, they were over-shadowed by new and powerful indus-trial capitalists whose economic strength brought with it vast political influence. Legislative bodies became arenas in which the political vassals of oil, steel, and rail-road barons struggled for special favors, while the interests of the public—and the old middle classes liked to think of them-selves as *the public*—counted for nothing. On the other hand, they were threatened by the immigrants who came to America to work in the mines and mills and on the railroads—Italians, Slavs, and Jews from Poland and Russia. The immigrants crowded into the tenements of eastern cities, responded to the friendly overtures of urban political bosses, and used their ballots to evict the old middle-class fam-ilies from power. Here was a threat to the traditional America that these families had loved—and dominated—to that once vig-orous American nationality that was Prot-estant, Anglo-Saxon, and pure. Henry James commented bitterly about the people he met on Boston Common during a stroll one Sunday afternoon: "No sound of English, in a single instance escaped their lips; the greater number spoke a rude form of Italian, the others some outland dialect unknown to me. . . . The types and faces bore them out; the people before me were gross aliens to a man, and they were in serene and triumphant possession."

Soon the new immigrant groups had become the victims of cruel racial stereotypes. Taken collectively, it would appear that they were, among other things, innately inferior to the Anglo-Saxons in their intellectual and physical traits, dirty and immoral in their habits, inclined toward criminality, receptive to dangerous political beliefs, and shiftless and irresponsible.

In due time, those who repeated these stereotypes awoke to the realization that what they were saying was not really very original—that, as a matter of fact, these generalizations were *precisely* the ones that southern white men had been making about Negroes for years. And, in their extremity, the old middle classes of the North looked with new understanding upon the problems of the beleaguered white men of the South. Perhaps all along Southerners had understood the problem better than they. Here, then, was a crucial part of the intellectual climate in which the Dunning interpretation of reconstruction was written. It was written at a time when xenophobia had become almost a national disease, when the immigration restriction movement was getting into high gear, when numerous northern cities (among them Philadelphia and Chicago) were seriously considering the establishment of racially segregated schools, and when Negroes and immigrants were being lumped together in the category of unassimilable aliens.

Several other attitudes, prevalent in the late nineteenth century, encouraged an interpretation of reconstruction that condemned radical Republicans for meddling in southern race relations. The vogue of social Darwinism discouraged governmental intervention in behalf of Negroes as well as other underprivileged groups; it encouraged the belief that a solution to the race problem could only evolve slowly as the Negroes gradually improved themselves. A rising spirit of nationalism stimulated a desire for sectional reconciliation, and part of the price was a virtual abdication of federal responsibility for the protection of the Negro's civil and political rights. An outburst of imperialism manifested in the Spanish-American War and the annexation of the Hawaiian Islands, found one of its principal justifications in the notion that Anglo-Saxons were superior to other peoples, especially when it came to politics. In the words of Senator Albert J. Beveridge of Indiana: "God has not been preparing the English-speaking and Teutonic people for a thousand years for nothing but vain and idle self-admiration. No! He has made us the master organizers of the world to establish system where chaos reigns. . . . He has made us adepts in government that we may administer government among savages and senile peoples." What folly, then, to expect Italians and Slavs to behave like Anglo-Saxons—or to accept the sentimental doctrine that Negroes deserve to be given the same political rights as white men!

Finally, at this critical juncture, sociologists, anthropologists, and psychologists presented what they regarded as convincing evidence of innate racial traits— evidence indicating that Negroes were intellectually inferior to whites and had distinctive emotional characteristics. The social scientists thus supplied the racists of the late nineteenth and early twentieth centuries with something that antebellum pro-slavery writers had always lacked: a respectable scientific argument. When, in 1916, Madison Grant, an amateur cultural anthropologist, published *The Passing of the Great Race*, his racism was only a mild caricature of a point of view shared by numerous social scientists. Examining the history of the United States, Grant easily detected her tragic blunder:

Race consciousness . . . in the United States, down to and including the Mexican War, seems to have been very strongly developed among native Americans, and it still remains in full vigor today in the South, where the presence of a large negro population forces this question upon the daily attention of the whites. . . . In New England, however . . . there appeared early in the last century a wave of sentimentalism, which at that time took up the cause of the negro, and in so doing apparently destroyed, to a large extent, pride and consciousness of race in the North. The agitation over slavery was inimical to the Nordic race, because it thrust aside all national opposition to the intrusion of hordes of immigrants of inferior racial value, and prevented the fixing of a definite American type. . . . The native American by the middle of the nineteenth century was rapidly becoming a distinct type. . . . The Civil War, however, put a severe, perhaps fatal, check to the development and expansion of this splendid type, by destroying great numbers of the best breeding stock on both sides, and by breaking up the home ties of many more. If the war had not occurred these same men with their descendants would have populated the Western States instead of the racial nondescripts who are now flocking there.[3]

In this social atmosphere, armed with the knowledge of race that the social scientists had given them, historians exposed the folly of radical reconstruction. At the turn of the century, James Ford Rhodes, that intimate friend of New England Brahmims, gave his verdict on Negro suffrage—one that the Dunningites would soon develop into the central assumption, the controlling generalization, of the reconstruction legend. "No large policy in our country," concluded Rhodes, "has ever been so conspicuous a failure as that of forcing universal negro suffrage upon the South. . . . From the Republican policy came no real good to the negroes. Most of them developed no political capacity, and the few who raised themselves above the mass did not reach a high order of intelligence. . . . The negro's political activity is rarely of a nature to identify him with any movement on a high plane. . . . [He] has been politically a failure and he could not have been otherwise."[4]

In the course of time the social scientists drastically revised their notions about race, and in recent years most of them have been striving to destroy the errors in whose creation their predecessors played so crucial a part. As ideas about race have changed, historians have become increasingly critical of the Dunning interpretation of reconstruction. These changes, together with a great deal of painstaking research, have produced the revisionist writing of the past generation. It is dangerous, of course, for a historian to label himself as a revisionist, for his ultimate and inevitable fate is one day to have his own revisions revised.

But that has never discouraged revisionists, and we may hope that it never will, especially those who have been rewriting the history of the reconstruction era. One need not be disturbed about the romantic nonsense that still fills the minds of many Americans about their Civil War. This folklore is essentially harmless. But the legend of reconstruction is another matter. It has had serious consequences, because it has exerted a powerful influence upon the political behavior of many white men, North and South.

---

[3] Madison Grant: *The Passing of the Great Race* (New York, 1916), pp. 77–9.

[4] Rhodes: *History of the United States*, Vol. VII, pp. 168–70.

BIBLIOGRAPHICAL NOTE

This bibliographical note is not an exhaustive compilation of reconstruction literature or of the books and articles that I have consulted. Rather, it is highly selective, containing only those items that I have drawn on for factual material, that have influenced my interpretations, or that represent significant points of view in reconstruction historiography. For a comprehensive critical bibliography and a list of relevant biographies, autobiographies, memoirs, and published diaries and letters, see James G. Randall and David Donald, *The Civil War and Reconstruction* (Boston, 1961). The best recent historiographical essay is Bernard Weisberger, "The Dark and Bloody Ground of Reconstruction Historiography," *Journal of Southern History*, XXV (1959), pp. 427–47.

The following general works illustrate the traditional anti-radical interpretation of reconstruction: James Ford Rhodes, *History of the United States from the Compromise of 1850* . . . (7 vols.; New York, 1893–1906), Vols. V–VII; John W. Burgess, *Reconstruction and the Constitution, 1866–1876* (New York, 1902); William A. Dunning, *Reconstruction, Political and Economic, 1865–1877* (New York, 1907); Walter L. Fleming, *The Sequel of Appomattox* (New Haven, 1919); Claude G. Bowers, *The Tragic Era* (Boston, 1929); James G. Randall, *The Civil War and Reconstruction* (Boston, 1937); Robert S. Henry, *The Story of Reconstruction* (Indianapolis, 1938); E. Merton Coulter, *The South during Reconstruction, 1865–1877* (Baton Rouge, 1947); and Hodding Carter, *The Angry Scar* (New York, 1959).

Much of the early protest against the anti-Negro, anti-radical biases of Rhodes and Dunning came from Negro and Marxist writers. A Negro historian, William E. B. Du Bois, in "Reconstruction and Its Benefits," *American Historical Review*, XV (1910), pp. 781–99, and an able Mississippi Negro politician, John R. Lynch, in *The Facts of Reconstruction* (New York, 1913), stress the positive achievements of the era. However, Du Bois's attempt at a full-scale revisionist study, *Black Reconstruction* (New York, 1935), is disappointing. Though rich in empirical data, the book presents a Marxian interpretation of southern reconstruction as a proletarian movement that is at best naïve. The Marxist historian James S. Allen, in *Reconstruction: The Battle for Democracy, 1865–1876* (New York, 1937) offers an interpretation that is more credible but equally schematic.

Recent non-Marxian revisionism began with a series of historiographical critiques of traditional interpretations. The most important of these is Howard K. Beale, "On Rewriting Reconstruction History," *American Historical Review*, XLV (1940), pp. 807–27. See also Alrutheus A. Taylor, "Historians of Reconstruction," *Journal of Negro History*, XXIII (1938), pp. 16–34; Francis B. Simkins, "New Viewpoints of Southern Reconstruction," *Journal of Southern History*, V (1939), pp. 49–61; T. Harry Williams, "An Analysis of Some Reconstruction Attitudes," *Journal of Southern History*; XII (1946), pp. 469–86; and John Hope Franklin, "Whither Reconstruction Historiography?" *Journal of Negro Education*, XVII (1948), pp. 446–61.

Most of the books and articles written by revisionists deal with some special aspect of reconstruction, but two syntheses are available: John Hope Franklin, *Reconstruction after the Civil War* (Chicago, 1961), and Randall and Donald, *Civil War and Reconstruction*, cited above. A comparison of the 1937 edition of Randall's book with Donald's 1961 revision will illustrate the points at which revisionists have modified the traditional interpretation of reconstruction. Revisionist interpretations are also incorporated in two valuable essays: Grady McWhiney, "Reconstruction: Index of Americanism," in Charles G. Sellers, Jr., ed., *The Southerner as American* (Chapel Hill, 1960), pp. 89–103; and C. Vann Woodward, "The Political Legacy of Reconstruction," in *The Burden of Southern History* (Baton Rouge, 1960), pp. 89–107. . . .

CHAPTER 9

Reconstruction: 1865-77

Any contemporary account of Reconstruction must begin by noting that most of the traditional interpretations have been abandoned. In 1944 David Donald published an essay on Mississippi "scalawags" which traced much of the white Republican leadership to very respectable Whig political and social origins. Donald's thesis has been criticized and it obviously cannot be extended to other areas without substantial amendment, but it is no longer possible to think of the scalawags after the old conception of unscrupulous and unsavory poor whites. In 1947 Vernon L. Wharton published an account of the Negro in postwar Mississippi which challenged nearly all the cliches about "Negro domination," massive corruption, shocking misrule, and the nature and extent of violence by white Southerners. These two studies have been multiplied many times and today we have fresh ideas and new research on nearly all the protagonists of the era. Thaddeus Stevens, Benjamin Wade, and other Radicals are no longer commonly associated with sinister fanaticism or buffoonery. Several scholars have portrayed General O. O. Howard as an astute administrator and his Freedman's Bureau as a useful institution engaged in badly needed work. If no historian has given us a fully satisfactory study of the Negro in Reconstruction, much useful research has been done, and the old tone of general hostility has been replaced by more judicious perspectives. Recent studies of abolitionists, missionaries, teachers, young businessmen, and adventurers who went South because of ideology, opportunity, adventure, or exploitation demonstrate how misleading it was to place so many types of men under the single label of "carpetbagger" and to describe the entire lot as a predatory and malicious band. In 1961 John Hope Franklin summarized the work of many colleagues in a book which stressed the substantial accomplishments of Reconstruction constitutional conventions and legislatures, and helped lay to rest the ancient ghost of pervasive and extraordinary corruption.

It would be erroneous to assume that the new conceptions emerged quickly and conquered all opposition at once. Political transformations may take place overnight but change comes to the general structure of American historical interpretation only by degrees and over a period of time. The point can be illustrated by examining three major works of scholarship printed between 1960 and 1963 on Andrew Johnson and the first year of his presidency. Although the authors all rejected the cliches describing Johnson as a courageous constitutionalist cast in the role of both hero and victim, each approached the topic from a somewhat different point of view. The first of the three books, written by Eric L. McKitrick and published in 1960, bore no traces of racial stereotypes or the cant which placed so heavy a burden of social evil on the Radicals. The book contained some sharp criticism of the President and presented new ideas, insights, and approaches, but the author perpetuated several traditional judgments and sympathies which many contemporary scholars reject. The central tragedy, according to McKitrick, sprang from the fact that the reunification of the North and the South came not in 1865 but slowly and painfully a generation later. Yet the chief movers of the times, the equalitarian Radicals, regarded citizenship for the Negro as a more important goal than the immediate reunification of Northerners and Southern white men. More recently, scholars have sympathized with Radicals and traced the major tragedy of Reconstruction to the ultimate surrender of the freedman into new forms of bondage.

In a perceptive account of different Northern and Southern psychological interpretations of victory and defeat, McKitrick argued convincingly that Northerners expected a recognition of error, or at least a symbolic expression of defeat and repentance. Southerners, who had no consciousness of wrongdoing, disappointed Northern expectations by acting as if defeat meant no more than the grudging surrender of secession and the right of individuals to hold slaves. A "total" surrender of the type Germany made in 1945, McKitrick asserted, would have been "grotesque" and a tragic barrier to sectional reunification. Skeptics may wish to question this conclusion after considering that a sense of wrongdoing could have been manipulated to create a more substantial local foundation for Negro citizenship. Southern "innocence" coupled with an intense devotion to white supremacy contributed much to the ultimate defeat of Reconstruction.

Despite a barrage of criticism directed against Johnson, McKitrick clearly preferred the President's initial impulse toward "moderation" over the "harsh" plans of the Radicals. This is a preference which many scholars do not share. Certainly one may ask if the evidence sustains the notion that the best hope for the Republic lay in the crystallization of common action between Northern "moderates" and Southern counterparts such as Wade Hampton of South Carolina. McKitrick regretted "the ruthless quality" of Reconstruction and confessed that "the North for three generations has had something on its conscience which will probably never be exorcised." Curiously enough, the notion of guilt seems to refer not to the abandonment of the Negro but to Reconstruction itself. The most militant of the Radicals proposed the revolutionary change of bringing Negroes to the freedom and equality of full citizenship in the face of bitter and determined opposition, and it is difficult to imagine how this could have been accomplished except by "harsh" methods.

A significant number of white Southerners cooperated with Reconstruction from a great variety of motives ranging from sheer opportunism and "the acceptance of the inevitable" to the wish for national unity and an authentic desire to help the freedman establish himself in a new life. In New Orleans even famous Confederate generals such as Longstreet and Beauregard supported integrated schools and Negro participation in politics. Much of the willingness to cooperate, however, sprang from the belief that the federal government meant to *insist* on making the former slave a citizen. When the federal presence was removed or when Republican leaders wavered, white Southern cooperation tended to melt away. In the long run Negroes stood to gain very little from Southern "moderates," and turned naturally enough to the more determined Radicals.

If McKitrick gave due consideration to Northern Negrophobia and the mixture of motives in the minds of many Radicals, he failed to take into account the intensity of Southern race consciousness or the fierce desire to keep Negroes in firm subordination. One may well ask if plans "milder" than the Radical program could have worked any major social changes at all. The "moderate" Wade Hampton came to power in South Carolina with a number of promises to Negroes, some of which he kept, but far more important to his political victory in 1876 was the prophetic wave of terror and coercion sponsored by his military bands of "Red Shirts." In brief, while McKitrick's theory of moderation seems dubious, his book opened new areas of debate and destroyed the myth of Andrew Johnson as the injured leader of high states' rights principles undone by the unscrupulous Radicals.

In 1963 an English scholars, William R. Brock, provided a more stringent analysis of Johnson and his policies. It seemed unlikely to Brock that any "centrist" or "moderate" policy led by Johnson and based on "moderate" Republicans and Democrats would have been feasible or desirable. Indeed, such a political coalition would have sounded the death knell of Reconstruction. Brock, even more critical than McKitrick of Johnson, described him as ignorant of Southern conditions and incapable of foreseeing or understanding Northern responses. Like McKitrick, Brock began with Northern and Southern psychological expectations at the end of the war, but he argued that without Northern demands for repentance and the substitution of national sentiment for provincial loyalty, Reconstruction would have been impossible. He also insisted that the Northern commitment to a higher status for the Negro, however vaguely defined or grudgingly granted, was a powerful force in the postwar era. Unlike nearly all the scholars before him, Brock understood the unity in the minds of many Republicans between their "materialistic" and their "idealistic" interests. The Radicals, who saw no conflict between assisting business prosperity and defending the cause of freedom, thought that moral progress joined to material advances would bring the Republic to a new pinnacle of human civilization. In the final analysis the Republican belief in the sanctity of property hindered considerably the effort to give Negro freedom an effective economic base, but the Radicals were still the best hope the freedman had. Brock answered an old complaint that the Radicals were a conspiratorial minority who came to power through devious means by explaining that the Radicals not only had the advantages of a dynamic ideology and Johnsonian blunders but that they also gained much from simply knowing the congressional ropes and the best uses of legislative rules and procedures.

LaWanda and John Cox joined the growing circle of Johnson critics in 1963. They too saw Johnson as an inept politician whose blunders hurt the nation grievously, and they outlined several of his faults with a new clarity. Johnson, it seemed, was motivated by suspicion and hostility toward Negroes, by the insecurities and the vanity of a man who had risen from the grinding poverty of Southern "poor white" origins to hold in his hands the fate of all Southern "aristocrats." The President, consumed by political ambition, worked incessantly to preserve his power and to gain renomination in 1868 by means of a new coalition of Democrats and conservative Republicans. Fortunately for the country Johnson lacked the ability to execute his own ill-conceived and dangerous plans.

The Coxes proved that the basic split between Congress and Johnson came over the issue of civil rights, and James M. McPherson in 1964 demonstrated more fully than anyone else the reality and force of equalitarian ideology as a fundamental cause of Reconstruction. Johnson, who opened hostilities with the initially well-disposed Radicals, staked his grand political design on the immediate "restoration" of the old Confederate states to the Union. Consequently Southerners had free rein to work out a system for replacing individual slave ownership with collective subordination. When Johnson vetoed the Civil Rights Act, he declared himself against "the Africanization of half the United States" and took a position fraught with racist concepts. Negro prospects for a higher status in the South were dim without federal help, and the passage of legislation over the executive veto owed much to equalitarian thought. If the conflict of the President and Congress involved several major issues, the chief one was the struggle of racist and equalitarian ideologies. The veto and the repassage of the Civil Rights Bill marked the real beginning of Reconstruction, and made the struggle for freedom and equality the central issue of the times.

After the scholarship of the past decade, the timeworn notions about Johnson's role as the heir to Lincolnian "moderation" seem extremely unlikely. On the face of the matter, one can see that "moderation" to most white Southerners meant harshness to the freedmen, and that sympathetic help to freedmen meant "harshness" to the great majority of Southern whites. The theory of Johnsonian and Lincolnian "moderation" was often spun around Lincoln's remark in the Second Inaugural Address which called for a peace with malice toward none and charity for all. In the sentence immediately prior to this much quoted remark, Lincoln suggested that the war might well be a terrible punishment sent to both North and South for the monstrous sin of slavery. He concluded the thought with the observation that if the conflict cost all of the wealth piled up by two-and-one-half centuries of bondage and if all the blood shed in slavery had to be repaid on the field of battle, then Americans could only say that God was just. After this thought the "charity" remark certainly seems poor evidence for a hypothetical postwar toleration of Southern intransigence by Lincoln. Much evidence points to the possibility that Lincoln considered a "sterner" policy for the South just before his death, but the nature of his "Pragmatic" bent, the ability to act with the Radicals today and the "moderates" tomorrow while keeping on good terms with all factions, makes any speculation about Lincoln's postwar conduct hazardous. Still it is difficult to imagine that Lincoln would have been as dogmatic, inflexible, and politically unwise as Johnson. Whatever the correct judgment on Lincoln may be, scholars are inconsistent and unconvincing when they present the image of the Great Emancipator and then suggest that the President would have eagerly destroyed many results of his own emancipation policies during the Reconstruction era.

Although both Lincoln and Johnson were tossed on the tide of turbulent times which carried them beyond their expectations, Lincoln could ride with the tide while Johnson fell prey to the illusion that he could stem the surge of events. After Johnson tried to oppose the Freedmen's Bureau and the implementation of the Civil Rights Act by inattention, obstruction, and the appointment of hostile officials, both he and Congress carried their respective cases to the country and in the fall of 1866 the Radicals won a smashing victory at the polls. Obviously not all the Republican voters were equalitarians—far from it—but Johnson and the Southerners appeared to many Northerners as men who would undo the results of victory and challenge the peace. When the South resisted the Civil Rights Act, Radical leaders decided to commit its substance to the Constitution in the form of the Fourteenth Amendment. After the Southern states rejected the amendment and met the drive for Negro citizenship with the kind of violence described in 1962 by John A. Carpenter, it became clear that only military reconstruction would be effective.

Harold M. Hyman in 1960 demonstrated that Southern violence and harassment seriously affected the Union army, and actually helped to bring about a powerful alliance between the Radicals and the military. It was Johnson's determination to remove from the South the military commanders sympathetic to Reconstruction and to replace Secretary Stanton in the War Department with a man hostile to the Radicals which persuaded Congressional leaders to attempt the impeachment of the President. If Johnson prevailed, the Republican program was undone. In retrospect it seems probable that the impeachment trial represented the high-water mark of Reconstruction, and that both the Radicals and the struggle for Negro citizenship suffered a major defeat in Johnson's acquittal. In 1958 Jack B. Scroggs made very clear the desperate need of Southern Radicals for the federal presence and a sympathetic president.

While Northern racial hostilities receded in the postwar era, they nonetheless remained strong enough to deny Negroes many basic civil rights. In the face of continuing Southern resistance and national racial animosities, the election of Grant by a narrow margin in 1868 did not dispel the fear of a Democratic resurgence which would waste the fruits of victory, threaten moral and material progress, and destroy the Republican majority upon which all else depended. To protect the rights of Negroes in the North and in the South *and* to preserve the Republican majority Congress produced the Fifteenth Amendment and a series of Enforcement Acts passed between 1870 and 1873. As Everette Swinney indicated in 1962, the effectiveness of the amendment depended upon the quantity of energy and sustained enforcement allocated to the task by the federal government. Grant was alternately rigorous and slack in enforcement, but his presidency did see the notable addition to earlier measures of the Civil Rights Bill of 1875 which spelled out the freedman's right to equal use of public accommodations. It may well be that the seeds of defeat were sown long before 1875, but many Americans could look with satisfaction at the decade past as a time when the constitutional amendments, the civil rights bills, and the enforcement acts fulfilled the promise of emancipation and created a solid foundation for freedom and equality. New churches and schools for the freedman dotted the Southern countryside and a Negro middle class of modest proportions began to take shape. If the churches had begun to withdraw with undue haste as early as 1868, leaders in every major Northern denomination continued to express serious concern with the task of Reconstruction, and while the Freedman's Bureau had ceased to exist many years before 1875, there was still hope that the federal government might grant new forms of aid. Above all, the new state constitutions, the Southern units of the Republican party, and the active presence of the federal government seemed to give some substance to the hope that the task of Reconstruction would be completed.

BIBLIOGRAPHY

Books and Articles Referred to in the Chapter Introduction

David Donald, "The Scalawag in Mississippi Reconstruction," *Journal of Southern History* (1944). See Allen W. Trelease for criticism of Donald, "Who Were the Scalawags?" *Journal of Southern History* (1963); and a reply by Donald and a rejoinder by Trelease in *Journal of Southern History* (1964).
Vernon L. Wharton, *The Negro in Mississippi, 1865–1890* (1947).
John Hope Franklin, *Reconstruction After the Civil War* (1961).
William R. Brock, *An American Crisis: Congress and Reconstruction, 1865–1867* (1963).

Suggested Reading

The best general introductions to Reconstruction are Kenneth M. Stampp, *The Era of Reconstruction* (1965) and Franklin, cited earlier. Two recent and brief anthologies can be consulted: Richard N. Current (ed.), *Reconstruction, 1865–1877* (1965); and James P. Shenton (ed.), *The Reconstruction: A Documentary History of the South After the War* (1963). Perhaps the best recent account of the Radicals is in Harold M. Hyman (ed.), *The Radical Republicans and Reconstruction* (1966), which has an excellent introductory essay on Radical thought. James G. Randall and David Donald, *The Civil War and Reconstruction* (2d ed.; 1961) is a detailed general survey. The bibliography, which is indispensable contains titles issued as late as 1961, but the listings are most comprehensive for the period prior to 1955. Brock, cited earlier, has the best account of Congress; and the Coxes, cited earlier, bring much new information on Johnson, Seward, and the conflict with Congress which developed between December, 1865, and April, 1866. For an attack on one of the chief myths about Johnson's impeachment trial, see Ralph J. Roske, "The Seven Martyrs?" *American Historical Review* (1959). McKitrick, cited earlier, is useful in several areas. For attacks on the notion of Reconstruction as a capitalist conspiracy, see Chapter VII, and for books on Lincoln and Reconstruction see Chapter VIII. On the idealism which motivated many Radicals, see Hyman, the Coxes, and McPherson, all cited earlier. Ralph E. Morrow has given a fine account of idealism and its limits in Northern Protestantism. See *Northern Methodism and Reconstruction* (1956). For some of the biographies which attempted to give more balanced accounts of leaders much maligned in earlier days, see Ralph Korngold, *Thaddeus Stevens: A Being Darkly Wise and Rudely Great* (1955); Fawn M. Brodie, *Thaddeus Stevens: Scourge of the South* (1959); Benjamin P. Thomas and Harold M. Hyman, *Stanton: The Life and Times of Lincoln's Secretary of War* (1962); Hans L. Trefousse, *Benjamin F. Wade: Radical Republican from Ohio* (1963); Robert Kirkwood, "Horace Greeley and Reconstruction in 1865," *New York History* (1959); Ira V. Brown, "William D. Kelley and Radical Reconstruction," *Pennsylvania Magazine of History and Biography* (1961); David Montgomery, "Radical Republicanism in Pennsylvania, 1866–1883," *Pennsylvania Magazine of History and Biography* (1961); Edward F. Sweat, "Francis L. Cardozo—Profile of Integrity in Reconstruction Politics," *Journal of Negro History* (1961); James M. McPherson, "Grant or Greeley? The Abolitionist Dilemma in the Election of 1872," *American Historical Review* (1965). Several scholars have explored the earliest experiments in Reconstruction. See Martha M. Bigelow's "Freedman of the Mississippi Valley, 1862–1865," *Civil War History* (1962); "Plantation Lessee Problems in 1864," *Journal of Southern History* (1961), and Willie Lee Rose's dramatic and illuminating *Rehearsal for Reconstruction: The Port Royal Experiment* (1964). On the origins of Reconstruction, see McPherson's account of abolitionist thought during the war and postwar periods. John G. Sproat in "Blueprint for Radical Reconstruction," *Journal of Southern History* (1957) wrote an excellent account of the part played by Sumner's brainchild, the American Freedman's Inquiry Commission, in wartime planning for Reconstruction. John G. Clark provided a brief survey of one large segment of historiography which deals with origins. See "Historians and the Joint Committee on Reconstruction," *The Historian* (1961). For other forces and factors which helped bring about Reconstruction see LaWanda Cox, "The Promise of Land for the Freedman," *Mississippi Valley Historical Review* (1958); Richard B. Drake, "Freedman's Aid Societies and Sectional Compromise," *Journal of Southern History* (1963); Hans L. Trefousse, "The Joint Committee on the Conduct of the War, A Reassessment," *Civil War History* (1964); John G. Clark, "Radicals and Moderates on the Joint Committee on Reconstruction," *Mid-America* (1963). More information on resistance and violence in the South can be found in William P. Randel, *The Ku Klux Klan: A Century of Infamy* (1965), which, despite the organizational flaws of the final chapters, is still the best book on the subject. See also Grady McWhiney and Francis B. Simkins, "The Ghostly Legend of the Ku Klux Klan," *Negro History Bulletin* (1951); Herbert Shapiro, "The Ku Klux Klan During Reconstruction: The South Carolina Episode," *Journal of Negro History* (1964); Jack D. L. Holmes, "The Effects of the Memphis Race Riots of 1866," *West Texas Historical Society Papers* (1958); Jerrell H. Shofner, "Fraud and Intimidation in the Florida Election of 1876," *Florida Historical Quarterly* (1964). See also David M. Chalmers' several works on Reconstruction politics and the Klan in Florida. The best account of the three Reconstruction amendments are as follows: the Coxes for the Thirteenth Amendment; Jacobus tenBroek, *The Antislavery Origins of the Fourteenth Amendment* (1951), and Joseph B. James, *The Framing of the Fourteenth Amendment* (1965); and for the Fifteenth Amendment, William Gillette, *The Right to Vote: Politics and Passage of the Fifteenth Amendment* (1965). See also Alfred H. Kelly, "The Fourteenth Amendment Reconsidered: The Segregation Question," *Michigan Law Review* (1956); Robert Harris *The Quest for Equality* (1960). On the Civil Rights Act of 1866, see LaWanda and John Cox; for the Civil Rights Act of 1875, see James M. McPherson, "The Abolitionists and the Civil Rights Act of 1875," *Journal of American History* (1965). On the neutralization and destruction of the Negro militias, see Otis A. Singletary, *The Negro Militia and Reconstruction*

(1957). For Negro activities during and after the Civil War which contributed to the coming of Reconstruction see Dudley T. Cornish, *The Sable Arm: Negro Troops in the Union Army, 1861–1865* (1956); James M. McPherson, *The Negro's Civil War* (1965); Martin Abbott, "Freedom's Cry: Negroes and their Meetings in South Carolina, 1865–1869," *Phylon* (1959); Benjamin Quarles, "The Abduction of the 'Planter,'" *Civil War History* (1958); Alan F. Westin, "Ride-In!" *American Heritage* (1962); Elsie M. Lewis, "The Political Mind of the Negro, 1865–1900," *Journal of Southern History* (1955); August Meier, *Negro Thought in America, 1880–1915* (1963). Louis R. Harlan wrote an interesting account of "Desegregation in the New Orleans Public Schools During Reconstruction," *American Historical Review* (1962). For discussions of "scalawags" and "carpetbaggers," see Donald, Trelease, and Wharton, listed earlier: Sarah Van Woolfolk, "Five Men Called Scalawags," *Journal of Negro History* (1964); Thomas B. Alexander, "Persistent Whiggery in the Confederate South, 1860–1877," *Journal of Southern History* (1961); other articles on the same theme by Alexander; John Hope Franklin's Introduction to the new edition of Albion W. Tourgee's *A Fool's Errand* (1961); Otto H. Olson, *Carpetbagger's Crusade: The Life of Albion W. Tourgee* (1965); Joel Williamson, *After Slavery* (1965); and Guion G. Johnson, "Southern Paternalism Toward Negroes After Emancipation," *Journal of Southern History* (1957). In 1965 David Donald in *The Politics of Reconstruction, 1863–1867* provided an analysis of congressional voting patterns on Reconstruction.

1960

Johnson Fumbles Away Power and Opportunity*

ERIC L. McKITRICK

What had happened? Besides leading the South into realms of fantasy regarding the true location of Northern authority, the nature of majority sentiment, and the support which he himself could command for whatever policies he deemed proper, the President had at the same time thrown away most of the vast bargaining power with which he had started out. Having placed an extraordinary amount of faith

* Reprinted from *Andrew Johnson and Reconstruction* by Eric L. McKitrick by permission of The University of Chicago Press. Copyright 1960 The University of Chicago Press.

in the non-coercive side of his role—a side which by definition put extra stress upon techniques of persuasion and negotiation— he had then proceeded to breach all the most basic principles of advocacy, diplomacy, and bargaining. As advocate for the plaintiff, he had in effect conspired with the defendant; as representative of a sovereign nation, he had cut himself off from the power of his government; as bargaining agent, he had kept shifting the terms of the bargain so that nobody could be sure what he was asking for. Even as judge, as mediator, as go-between—to whatever extent his role partook of those functions—he had got himself and his emotions openly involved in the claims of the one side, at the expense of those of the other. Such behavior would certainly have sabotaged the business of any courtroom, chancellery, or bargaining table; as for the affairs of an entire nation, the disruption which may have been effected there, and the extent of its consequences, can only invite speculation. That the primary victim of those consequences—the defeated South—should have been in any position to point out the President's errors, to resist them, or to aid him in repairing them, is a likelihood that cannot be taken with very great seriousness. For once the President's attitude had been fully revealed, the South, by the very nature of its position, could not for a minute afford to see things through eyes other than his.

But if the President had done disservice to Southern claims—to say nothing of Northern—in his negotiating character, it is just as conceivable in a curious way that from the coercive side of his role he may have done them even deeper mischief. To say that the problem had its negotiating aspects is most important, but it should never carry us too far from the primary thing, which was that the South had been defeated in war; no amount of words could talk away the fact that the South was being confronted by its conquerer. Nor was there any use pretending that the South was not in some sense being asked to pay; no fact, for the South, could have been more immediate. Thus no matter what the beaten enemy might be asked to do, no matter how little, it would be idle to imagine that he should derive the least pleasure from it—except for the relief, once it was done, of having it cleanly and honorably over with. Moreover, it is much to be doubted that there was any real mercy in telling the enemy that his punishment, especially if never made fully clear, must be undergone voluntarily—or much realism in expecting, on that basis, that he would go about it in any but a confused and afflicted

state of mind. In those areas in which the South was, indeed, without choice, it was conceivably better to say so, and to order that the thing be done—coolly, sparing the Southern gentlemen those words about "forgiveness" and "fraternal love" which could not sound in their ears without some ring of mockery until a later, happier day. Some things are easiest to do when there is no choice at all.

On those rare occasions when President Johnson, in his dealings with the South, did come in any way close to laying down the law, those concerned responded immediately, almost with alacrity. Contrasted with the oddly inhibited character of most of the President's dispatches, there is something of the coiled spring in his message to Holden on the North Carolina debt:

> Every dollar of the debt created to aid the rebellion against the United States should be repudiated finally and forever. The great mass of the people should not be taxed to pay a debt to aid in carrying on a rebellion which they in fact, if left to themselves, were opposed to. Let those who have given their means for the obligations of the State look to that power they tried to establish in violation of law, constitution, and the will of the people. They must meet their fate. . . . I repeat [etc.]. . . .

He spoke to Georgia in similar language, and in both cases the thing was done.[1] In Alabama, the relative case with which the Executive wishes were carried out was doubtless due in some measure to the fact that there happened to be in Washington men of influence communicating those wishes to Governor Parsons in terms stronger and more precise than those used by the President himself.[2] In South Carolina, at the same time, Governor Perry's success in convincing the convention delegates that he could be counted on to represent reliably to them what the President would and would not stand for was what gave him such extraordinary influence. Sid-

---

[1] "Provisional Governors," pp. 226, 236.
[2] Thomas Sykes *et al.* to L. E. Parsons, Sept. 19, 1865, Johnson MSS.

ney Andrews, who was present at the time of the convention, wrote of Perry that

his position, in the peculiar circumstances of the hour, makes his word and wish of very unusual significance. . . . it is an almost every-hour occurrence, in the debates, that the question is asked, "Is that view approved by the Provisional Governer?" or that the remark is made, "I think we had better consult the Governor first." So it may be said that he is the leader of the Convention.[3]

Indeed, there were repeated occasions on which the Southerners themselves had to beg Johnson to make himself clear on a thing if he really wanted them to do it. A member of the South Carolina legislature wrote, regarding the unrepudiated debt: "Make the *requirement absolute*, the state will meet it." Indeed, Johnson's strong words to North Carolina and Georgia on that same subject were not forthcoming until the governors themselves, in each case, urged the President by telegraph to declare himself. Even in Tennessee, when difficulty arose in November over the enactment of a Negro testimony bill, the Tennessee secretary of state, recognizing that the bill would not pass unless the legislature were convinced that its failure to do so would have a bad effect on Tennessee's chances of readmission, implored the President to telegraph an "opinion" for his use in the matter. A question of some delicacy in Georgia was the election of United States senators. The preference in the legislature was for such men, prominent in the Confederacy, as Alexander Stephens and Herschel Johnson, and the election of a Unionist like Joshua Hill would only be possible through the express influence, unmistakably exerted, of the administration. Hill himself informed the President to this effect. "I tell you," a prominent man of Richmond said to Whitelaw Reid, "President Johnson can name his Senators and they will be straightway elected. He can say what he wants, the Virginia legislature,

so-called, will register his edicts in legislative enactments."[4]

There was much evidence that men of influence in the South initially understood their own position a good deal more clearly than did the President. There was much quibbling in the early sessions of the Mississippi convention over abolishing slavery in the state constitution, and a series of resolutions was introduced by one of the ablest delegates, casting doubts upon the validity of emancipation. Three prominent judges, men of conservative views, thereupon took the occasion, one by one, to lay things on the line and remind the convention exactly where it stood, and in terms Johnson himself would never have dreamed of using. J. W. C. Watson reminded the delegates that they were a conquered people, that their freedom of action was impaired by the very circumstances under which they met, and that they had no right to dictate to Congress the terms of their readmission. "Gentlemen talk as if we had a choice," Judge Amos Johnston then declared, "but we have no choice, and it is no humiliation to admit it. The only course we can pursue is that dictated to us by the powers at Washington." Judge William Yerger spoke of the Northern people's determination not to be "trifled with." "As men of sense," he admonished them, "let us endeavor to remedy what we cannot alter, and gather together whatever may tend to palliate our misfortunes." The speeches made quite an impression on the convention, and by a large majority the resolutions were tabled forthwith.[5]

The "men of sense" whom Judge Yerger invoked had declined in influence by November, but there were enough of them, even then, who were appalled at the passage of the black code. The laws were denounced by some of the foremost news-

---

[3] Andrews, *The South since the War*, pp. 49–50.

[4] A. S. Wallace to Seward, Dec. 25, 1865, Johnson MSS; "Provisional Governors," pp. 81, 226, 236; A. J. Fletcher to Johnson, Nov. 20, 1865; Joshua Hill to Johnson, Dec. 20, 1865, Johnson MSS; Reid, *After the War*, p. 321.

[5] Garner, *Reconstruction in Mississippi*, pp. 87–90.

papers of the state, including the leading one, the Jackson *Clarion*. The Columbus *Sentinel* said that the legislature had been controlled by

a hard and shallow-headed majority, that were far more anxious to make capital at home than to propitiate the powers at Washington. They were as complete a set of political Goths as were ever turned loose to work destruction upon a State. The fortunes of the whole South have been injured by their folly.[6]

Nowhere in the South, any time, could more than a tiny minority have been assembled to enact of its own free will even a qualified Negro suffrage. But it is important to note that things were still open enough in the summer of 1865, all through the South, that men of standing could discuss with surprising freedom even this subject as a possibility. Professor Fleming, writing in 1905, said that in Alabama political leaders talked a great deal about suffrage in 1865, and that even before the Reconstruction Acts, Negroes were allowed to vote in a few local elections.[7] General James L. Alcorn of Mississippi, one of the two senators elected by that state in 1865, was convinced that if the whites did not make the Negroes their friends through the franchise, their path would be "red with blood and damp with tears."[8] A few of the leading men in South Carolina felt that it would be wise and proper to enact a limited Negro suffrage; among them were A.

Toomer Porter, Wade Hampton and his brother Christopher, Joseph LeConte, and Judge Edward Frost (who had headed the delegation that visited the President on June 25). "I insisted," wrote LeConte, "that the convention should adopt a franchise *without distinction of color*, but with a small educational and property qualification. My friends admitted the wisdom of the suggestion but said that it was impossible, as the leaders had not 'backbone' enough to propose it, and the people were not ready to indorse it."[9]

Here we may revert once more to the early aftermath of the surrender, with the themes it contained, and make a final effort to appreciate the crushing effects of defeat, the ruin which lay in all hearts and minds, the South's apprehension of unnamable penalties, and the mute petition of the South for any kind of settlement. "The months of May and June," wrote Whitelaw Reid, "were the chaotic period of the returning Rebel States. All men were overwhelmed and prostrated under the sudden stroke of calamity which the fewest number had anticipated." The theme of irreconcilability—of rage, bitterness, and hate—was mingled and balanced with that of submission, and of exposed sensitivity, and readiness to do what had to be done.

The first feelings were those of baffled rage. . . . Then followed a sense of bewilderment and helplessness. Where they were, what rights they had left, what position they occupied before the law, what claim they had to their property, what hope they had for an improvement of their condition in the future—all these were subjects of complete uncertainty.

. . . They expected nothing; were prepared for the worst; would have been thankful for anything.

In North and South Carolina, Georgia, and

---

[6] *Ibid.*, p. 116; Vernon L. Wharton, *The Negro in Mississippi* (Chapel Hill: University of North Carolina Press, 1947), pp. 89–90. J. H. Jones, a Confederate colonel and later a legislator and lieutenant-governor, wrote: "Looking back upon the methods by which that Legislature undertook to deal with the negro problem, one is amazed at such stupidity. . . ." "Reconstruction in Wilkinson County," *Publications of the Mississippi Historical Society*, VIII (1904), 156. There was similar sentiment in South Carolina; see Simkins and Woody, *South Carolina during Reconstruction*, p. 52.

[7] Walter L. Fleming, *Civil War and Reconstruction in Alabama*, pp. 386–90.

[8] Wharton, *Negro in Mississippi*, p. 140. Alexander Stephens of Georgia was also an early exponent of qualified Negro suffrage; see C. Mildred Thompson, *Reconstruction in Georgia* (New York: Columbia University Press, 1915), p. 160.

[9] *Autobiography of Joseph LeConte*, ed. W. D. Armes (New York: D. Appleton, 1903), pp. 235–36; A. Toomer Porter, *Led On! Step by Step* . . . (New York: G. P. Putnam's Sons, 1898), p. 224; Simkins and Woody, *South Carolina during Reconstruction*, p. 41; Reid, *After the War*, pp. 288–89; *Nation*, I (August 17, 1865), 208; *ibid.*, I (Aug. 24, 1865), 238.

Florida, we found this state of feeling universally prevalent. The people wanted civil government and a settlement. They asked no terms, made no conditions. They were defeated and helpless—they submitted. Would the victor be pleased to tell them what was to be done?[10]

But things had apparently begun to happen when the President started imposing himself on Southern feelings. J. R. Dennett, much impressed by the orderly state of sentiment in South Carolina in midsummer (the people of that state having gone into the rebellion "more earnestly and honestly" than anywhere else, had acquiesced in their defeat "more honestly and promptly than any others"), thought it just possible by late August that a "reaction" may have occurred, "caused by the premature establishment of civil government, unsettling their minds, and interrupting a healthy progress of opinion."[11] Reid, who had been in the South from early May to midsummer, took another trip in November and found the people's temper much changed. "Yesterday they cringed for pardon at the feet of 'the boorish and drunken tailor' they had denounced; today they are harder to satisfy than ninety and nine just men who have no need of repentance."[12] About this time Johnson's own provisional governor in North Carolina, William W. Holden, wrote to the President in rather pathetic words that betrayed something close to a failure of nerve:

I regret to say that there is much of a rebellion spirit still in this state. In this respect I admit I have been deceived. In May and June last these rebellious spirits would not have dared to show their heads even for the office of constable; but leniency has emboldened them, and the Copperhead now shows his fangs. . . .

I communicate these corrections with regret. It may be that the policy of the government has been too lenient; or it may be that

I have seriously erred in the discharge of duty, or that I was not the proper person for Provisional Governor. . . . I am ready and willing at any moment to retire from this position; and if you have the shadow of a wish that I should do so, I pray you as a friend to let me know it.[13]

Johnson had encouraged the Southern people to think of him as their protector against the Black Republicans of the North. He himself had so defined the picture for them, and such were the illusions he had given them of his power, that even a year later, when any remnants of that power had all but collapsed, they could still look forward to the fall elections of 1866— which would actually bring Republican landslides—expecting a triumphant vindication for the President and themselves. Their shock may well have been all the worse, since they had come to know that the President would not use his power to coerce *them*. Meanwhile the President, all unwittingly, may have worked a still subtler mischief with the feelings of two whole peoples as they emerged from conflict. Standing in the ambiguous position which he had taken up between them, he had with the best of intentions cut himself off from the deepest needs of both. It may be supposed that these enemies, when the fight was over, wanted at least to respect each other, so that they might the more respect themselves for the exertions they had made, and to put aside their arms at least in the honorable knowledge of pride well served. This may be the point at which the "balm of time" idea is actually most relevant. A certain decent punctilio of reserve was needed, a due season of correctness and repose not to be interrupted by too many exhortations to "fraternal love" from a man whose title to the place he held could never be quite above doubt—a man whom neither North nor South, with all good will, could quite help regarding as an outsider. In such a setting as this, and with John-

---

[10] Reid, *After the War*, pp. 295–96.
[11] *Nation*, I (Aug. 24, 1865), 238.
[12] Reid, *After the War*, p. 317.

[13] Holden to Johnson, Dec. 6, 1865, Johnson MSS.

son's special position vulnerable just on general principles, one can imagine that the President's resources might have been much augmented by a greater willingness to share his authority.

In the interests of the South's own pride, it might possibly have been as well that the basic terms of the settlement, if there was going to be one, should initially be concluded with a minimum of reference to the people—though for maximum success the parties to it would have had to be men whom the people trusted, men fully identified with the cause. The possibilities of secret diplomacy, if such it might be called, were about at an end by December, 1865. One of the reasons was that the presidential power, to which Southerners had been so ready to adjust earlier, was not being put to coercive uses. Since by winter this was more or less clear to all, the new power to which Southern political leaders were now having to adjust, in ever increasing degree, was the power of their own constituencies—that is, the will of the people. Democracy in such circumstances is of course the enemy of diplomacy. All this placed ever greater limits on these men's freedom of action, so limited already —a kind of freedom indispensable for com-

plying with demands bound to be distasteful no matter what. Moreover, they needed sanctions of coercion at their backs, for their own protection, so that they might tell the people, as Judge Johnston told the Mississippi convention, "we have no choice, and it is no humiliation to admit it." Every "political Goth" (as the Columbus *Sentinel* might have put it) that came down from the Mississippi hills to sit in the legislature spelled that much less influence for the likes of Judge Johnston, Judge Yerger, and General Alcorn. And, finally, the President might denounce the secessionists of South Carolina and the abolitionists of Massachusetts as much as he chose,[14] but for all his talk, no real peace could be made until South Carolina and Massachusetts were, in some sense, brought face to face.

------

[14] "As a Tennessee politician, it had been necessary for him to denounce the 'Abolitionists and fanatics of the North;' to declare, in the stereotyped phrase of the stump, that he had equal hatred for the Secessionists of South Carolina and the Abolitionists of Massachusetts. They [pardon-seeking Southerners] asked him if he was going to let Massachusetts Abolitionists lead him now and control his Administration, while his own native South lay repentant and bleeding at his feet. He was ambitious, proud of his elevation, but stung by the sneer that after all he was only an accidental President." Reid, *After the War*, 305.

1963

Civil Rights Was the Issue[*]

LaWANDA AND JOHN H. COX

Even the Republican papers that remained friendly in their attitude toward the President made clear their own support for some form of national guarantee of the freedmen's rights. A few reconciled their own attitude with that of the President by pointing to his concluding promise, the one Johnson had incorporated from Seward's draft, and insisting that the President was not opposed to federal protection. Most of the Republican press, however, saw the veto as drawing a sharp line between the position of the President and that of their party.[1]

What had been taking place in the Republican party since the close of the civil conflict was a gradual metamorphosis, similar to the one that had taken place during the war. The war years transformed the Republicans, a political amalgam originally united on the principle of opposition to the extension of slavery, into a party committed to the destruction of slavery. This objective had been formally embodied in the party platform of 1864. The platform, however, had not included a plank supporting equal legal status for the freed slaves, despite the fact that such a plank was offered and considered. By the winter of 1865, Republicans generally had expanded their repudiation of slavery into a condemnation of legal discriminations which by then seemed to them the last vestiges of slavery. Important elements within the party held that the freedmen's rights must include an equality of suffrage, but on this more advanced position, Republicans were not yet agreed. They had, however, come to identify Republicanism with a defense of basic civil rights for the freed slave.[2] Sometimes this identification of Republicanism with the principle of equal status before the law was stated explicitly; sometimes it was expressed through generalizations that invoked liberty, freedom, or humanity. A characteristic argument, advanced by one Republican paper, was that if the position on equal civil rights embodied in Johnson's veto message were correct, then "all the principles of democracy and freedom upon which our creed of Republicanism rests are false and we must recant them."[3] When Republicans accused Johnson of treachery to the Republican

---

[*] Reprinted with permission from *Politics, Principles and Prejudices, 1865–1866* by John and LaWanda Cox. Copyright 1963 by The Free Press of Glencoe, a division of The Macmillan Company.

[1] These generalizations are based primarily upon the extensive press clippings on the Civil Rights veto.

[2] Before the opening of Congress in December, 1865, Schuyler Colfax, Speaker of the House, made a speech which was widely regarded as a statement of majority Republican opinion. He abjured any inflexibility of policy, spoke warmly of what the President had already accomplished in securing commitments from the Southern states, but made clear that some additional assurances were considered necessary. The first of these, and indeed the only one that was substantive, was that "the Declaration of Independence be recognized as the law of the land" by the protection of the freedmen in their rights of person and property including the right to testify. He made no mention of suffrage for the Negro nor of any punitive action against the South. For text of speech, see *New York Times*, Nov. 19, 1865.

[3] Clipping from a Buffalo paper, March 29, 1866, Scrapbook, Johnson MSS.

party and Republican principles, or with greater forbearance simply asked that he give them some unmistakable evidence so that they might "continue to confide in him as a *Republican*,"[4] they were identifying their party with the principle of equality in legal status for all freedmen.

Thus what had once been an advanced, or "Radical," position within Republican ranks, by 1866 had become accepted and moderate. To most opponents of equal civil status, however, the principle still appeared "Radical." Herein lies one clue to the confusion in the use of the term "Radical" which plagues any serious student of the period. The term is inescapable; yet a man labeled a "Radical" by one set of contemporaries or historians is often found designated a "moderate" by another group of contemporaries or historians. All would agree that Charles Sumner, Thaddeus Stevens, and Wendell Phillips, extreme men though not of one mind, were the prototypes of Radicalism. The term *radical,* however, has often been used to identify, and castigate, all Republican opponents of Andrew Johnson. Many of these men were almost as critical of Sumner, Stevens, and Phillips as were their Conservative adversaries. Few fellowed Stevens in his demand for confiscation; most were ready to abandon or drastically compromise Sumner's aim of Negro suffrage. Though they wished to proceed with caution, there was no strong desire among them for an indefinite postponement of restoration by reducing the South to the status of "territories" or "conquered provinces." In other words, many Radicals were moderate men. The Radical opponents of President Johnson were united in one demand—that of national protection for the freedmen. On other issues of Reconstruction they held widely divergent views.

It has sometimes been assumed that a common economic attitude united Radicals and marked them off from pro-Johnson men. This assumption is demonstrably false. Some were protariff men, some antitariff men; some advocated cheap money, some upheld a sound gold standard; some were spoilsmen, others were among the spoilsmen's bitterest critics.[5] In 1865 and 1866 substantial members of the business community were as often found in the ranks of the President's supporters as in those of the opposition.[6] John A. Dix, a key figure in the Johnson movement, was president of the Union Pacific. A $20,000 reception and dinner at the famed Delmonico's, at the opening of Johnson's ill-fated Swing-around-the-Circle, was attended by many of the most powerful figures of New York business and finance.[7] As late as September, 1866, the *New York Times*, in an editorial entitled "Business and Politics—the Conservatism of Commerce"—spoke of the "great unanimity of the commercial and business classes in supporting the conservative policy of the Administration, and in opposing with their

---

[4] Chicago *Evening Journal*, March 28, 1866, *ibid*.

[5] *See* Stanley Coben, "Northeastern Business and Radical Reconstruction: A Re-examination," *Mississippi Valley Historical Review*, XLVI (June, 1959), pp. 67–90; Robert P. Sharkey, *Money, Class and Party: An Economic Study of Civil War and Reconstruction* (Baltimore, 1959); Irwin Unger, "Business Men and Specie Resumption," *Political Science Quarterly*, LXXIV (March, 1959), pp. 46–70. Howard K. Beale's study made much of economic issues, but his findings showed that they had not been central to the political campaign of 1866. Johnson's failure to make them such, Beale considered "a fatal error in political judgment." *The Critical Year*, p. 299.

[6] Letters in the Johnson MSS indicate this support, see those of August Belmont, March 24, 1866, A. J. Drexel, May 3, 1866, Alexander T. Stewart, June 18, 1866; also reports of business support in the letters of W. G. Smith, March 2, 1866 (Buffalo), J. B. Hussey, March 3, 1866 (New York), W. J. Hilton, March 7, 1866 (Albany), R. B. Carnahan, March 16, 1866 (Pittsburgh), G. W. Morgan, July 14, 1866 (Ohio), D. S. Seymour, Nov. 8, 1866 (Troy).

[7] In the Tilden MSS there are printed letters outlining the arrangements, including a seating chart for the dinner and itemizing the expenses with assessments. Tilden's share of the cost was $145.38. Smythe, Johnson's appointee as Collector of the Port, feared the plans for Johnson's New York visit would give the impression that "a *few* are to get hold of you" and advised the President to stop at the Fifth Avenue Hotel, rather than Delmonico's to "give *'the people'*" a better opportunity to see him. Smythe to Johnson, Aug. 25, 1866, Johnson MSS.

might the schemes of the Radical Destructives."[8]

Nor were the Radicals distinguishable from the general run of Union men, as is often claimed, by vindictiveness toward the South or clamor for the heads of "traitors." Indeed, New York's outstanding Radical leader, Horace Greeley, was a leading figure in the movement for amnesty and forgiveness. Henry Wilson, Radical senator from Massachusetts, wrote to Johnson in support of a plea for the parole of Clement C. Clay of Alabama.[9] Even Thaddeus Stevens offered his services in the defense both of Clay and of Jefferson Davis.[10] The feeling against Southern leaders of the rebellion, which found expression both in a stubborn indignation at the prospect of their speedy return to the halls of Congress and in an emotional demand for Jefferson Davis' trial and conviction, cut across the division between pro-Johnson and anti-Johnson men. Thus in December, 1865, the House passed a resolution supporting the stringent Test Oath of July, 1862, as binding without exception upon all branches of government. Only one Republican registered opposition.[11] A few days earlier, without a single dissenting voice, the House had declared treason a crime that should be punished; 34 Democrats joined the Republicans in voting "yea."[12] In June, after the break with the President, a resolution calling for the trial of Jefferson Davis passed by a vote of 105 to 19, with no Republican voting against it. Six of the seven Conservatives who had broken with the majority of their party to support Johnson in the Civil Rights veto registered their approval of this demand.[13]

The only common denominator that united the Radicals of 1866, and the only characteristic they shared which could logically justify the term *radical*, was their determination that the rebel South should not be reinstated into the Union until there were adequate guarantees that the slaves liberated by the nation should enjoy the rights of free men.[14] It is true that Johnson's opponents believed Congress should have some voice in Reconstruction and that they were profoundly disturbed by the prospect of a restored South, united with the Northern Democracy, immediately controlling the destinies of the nation. They were also extremely sensitive to any patronage moves that might seem to indicate Johnson's support of the Democracy or an intent to punish Republicans for failure to agree completely with the President's position. These attitudes, however, can hardly be termed radical; and they were not decisive factors with most of the men who broke with the President after the veto messages. Possibly, without the civil rights issue, one of these points of friction might have generated warfare and become the dividing line between Johnson's opponents and his supporters; but this is extremely doubtful. The testimony of such men as Samuel Bowles, Thurlow Weed, Jacob D. Cox, and John Cochrane must be given weight. They believed that the President could achieve his goal of speedy restoration and renewed fellowship between North and South if only he endorsed some effective

---

[8] *New York Times,* Sept. 2, 1866.

[9] Wilson to Johnson, March 3, 1866, Johnson MSS.

[10] McKitrick, *Andrew Johnson and Reconstruction,* p. 19, footnote 2.

[11] The roll call came on a motion to table the resolution. McPherson, *Political Manual for 1866,* pp. 110–11.

[12] *Ibid.,* p. 109.

[13] *Ibid.,* p. 113; compare the vote p. 81.

[14] On the meaning of "Radical," compare McKitrick, *Andrew Johnson and Reconstruction,* pp. 53–67. The *Chicago Tribune,* the leading Radical newspaper, had some revealing comments. Before the Republican convention of 1860, it identified the "more radical" wing of the party as a body of men "somewhat in advance of the party's creed," zealous, honest, and possibly impractical, who recognized that they had no power to interfere with slavery in the states but still hoped "that the election of a Republican President will in some way tend to the crippling of the institution they hate." In 1866, the *Tribune* defined as the vestige of slavery "all discrimination against freedmen." Until these be removed, it held that the South would not be at peace with itself or with the North. *Chicago Tribune,* Feb. 6, 1860, Feb. 16, 1860, and clipping on Freedmen's Bureau veto, Scrapbook, Johnson MSS.

national guarantee of the freedmen's civil rights as citizens.[15] One of the most distinguished students of congressional Reconstruction, thoroughly sympathetic to Johnson, concluded that the moderate leadership in Congress desired just three conditions and would have settled for two: a guarantee of "the negroes' civil rights" and recognition of "the prerogative of Congress."[16] Since executive action alone could not guarantee the South's permanent acquiescence in the freedmen's newly gained rights, such security could be had only by way of the second condition, acceptance of some congressional action in the matter. In other words, the two conditions were inseparable; Johnson's consent to the first would have automatically fulfilled the second. Had Johnson come to terms with the moderates on the civil rights issue, the truly radical men of the party would have been clearly distinguishable from Republicans generally; and the true "Radical" would have faced the choice of compromise or defeat. Instead, except for a handful of Conservatives who totally accepted Johnson's leadership, "Republican" tended to become synonymous with "Radical."

The Democracy had a major responsibility for the blurring of distinction between the terms *Radical* and *Republican*. Even before the vetoes, they had tended to stigmatize the entire Republican leadership in Congress as "Radical"; after the vetoes, they delighted in maligning the Freedmen's Bureau Bill and the Civil Rights Act as parts of a sinister Radical design to defeat Johnson's plan for speedy restoration. This was good political strategy. Political expediency and propaganda, however, are not a complete explanation. In the eyes of Democrats, North and South, the claim of "equality," in any form, for the newly freed Negro was indeed radical, an outrageous postwar version of prewar

abolitionism. Both before and after the vetoes, one finds expressions in the Democratic press and in private letters of the period which indicate an unmistakable identification of "Radical" with "Abolitionist." Thus, a Tennessee judge, complaining about the interference of the military, started to write that this was "just what the abominable Abolitionis [*sic*]" desired, then crossed out "Abolitionis" and substituted the word "Radicals."[17] It is true that Northern Democratic spokesmen and responsible Southerners at times urged upon the Southern states full equality in civil proceedings; but they did so because this appeared to them not only an inescapable concession to Republican opinion but a necessary condition for Presidential support as well. Moreover, so long as exclusive state authority was maintained, concessions made by state action before restoration could be undone by state action after restoration.

There is a certain validity in the Democratic equation that denied the historical differences between old-time abolitionists, postwar extremists, and those moderate Republicans of 1866 who upheld equal civil rights for the Negro. Between pro-Johnson Conservatives and anti-Johnson Radicals—whether the latter was moderate or extreme—the dividing line was marked by a distinction in race attitude. Wide differences existed on each side of the line, and there were those who took their places in each camp for reasons primarily of political expediency and advantage. Yet by 1866 all Radicals accepted, indeed most held as an article of faith, a nationally enforceable equality of civil status, even though their attitudes might differ in respect to equality of suffrage and equality of social status for the Negro. The position of Johnson supporters varied from extreme racism to an uncomfortable accommodation to the probability that legal discrimination and inequitable treatment for the freed slave would follow upon an

---

[15] *See* the quotations cited above, footnotes 5, 6, 32, 43.

[16] Kendrick, *Journal of the Joint Committee on Reconstruction*, 251–52.

[17] T. Barry to Grider, March 8, 1866, Johnson MSS.

unrestrained local autonomy in race relations. The anti-Johnson side attracted men with a deep sense of concern and responsibility for the freed slave; the pro-Johnson ranks drew men who thought national responsibility had ended with the destruction of property rights in human beings. The latter preferred to base formal argument upon aversion to centralized government, a defense of states' rights, respect for the Constitution, and devotion to a reunited Union. But behind such arguments there most often lay some shade of that prejudice of race which still divides the nation.

The racist tendency among Northern Democrats hardly needs further demonstration. If evidence is desired, it can be found among the editorials with which the veto messages were greeted. Johnson does not believe, wrote one New England Democratic editor, "in compounding our race with niggers, gipsies and baboons, neither do we . . . [or] our whole Democratic people."[18] A Washington paper editorialized:

The negro is to have full and perfect equality with the white man. He is to mix up with the white gentlemen and ladies all over the land . . . at all public meetings and public places he is to be your equal and your associate. . . . How long will it be if Congress can do all this before it will say the negro shall vote, sit in the jury box, and intermarry with your families? Such are the questions put by the President.[19]

The *Ohio Statesman* declared it was no crime for the President to "esteem his race as superior to an inferior race. In this hour of severe trial, when the President is endeavoring so to administer the government that the white man shall not be subordinated to the negro race, will not the white man stand by him."[20] The Radicals, commented a Pennsylvania paper with satisfaction, "now find that President Johnson regards this government as the White man's."[21] One set of huge headlines read:[22]

ALL HAIL!
GRAND AND GLORIOUS!
GREAT VICTORY FOR THE WHITE MAN
REJOICE, WHITE MAN REJOICE!
THE HOUR OF YOUR DELIVERANCE HAS
   COME
SATAN IS BOUND
RADICALISM REBUKED
TAXPAYERS RELIEVED
PRESIDENT JOHNSON TURNS OUT TO BE
   A FULL BLOODED WHITE MAN
HAS VETOED THE FREEDMEN'S BUREAU
   BILL
'THE NEGROES HAVE TO WORK'

The limitations of Andrew Johnson's own benevolence toward the freedmen have already been explored.[23] A word more should be added as to the overtones of race prejudice apparent in his veto message. These may have been unintended expressions of his own bias or, more probably, deliberate appeals to the race prejudice of others. The first veto offended much less overtly than the second, although it called forth at least one protest against its appeal to "a low prejudice against color."[24] The offending passage was the argument that Congress could hardly appropriate moneys for relief, lands, and schools for the freedmen when it had never considered itself authorized "to expend the public money for the rent or purchase of homes for the thousands, not to say millions of the white race who are honestly toiling from day to day for their subsistence." The Civil Rights veto claimed that "the distinction of race and color is, by the bill, made to operate in favor of the colored and against the white race." It also raised the emotion-laden subject of intermarriage between whites and blacks, although the matter had little relevance to the President's argument. And in a passage clearly not intended as a

[18] *State and Union*, April 5, 1866, Scrapbook, *ibid.*
[19] *Constitutional Union*, March 28, 1866, *ibid.*
[20] Clipping on Civil Rights veto, *ibid.*

[21] Boylestown *Democrat*, Feb. 27, 1866, *ibid.*
[22] Wayne County [Ohio] *Democrat, ibid.*
[23] See Chapter 8 in the Coxes' book.
[24] Portland *Press*, Scrapbook, Johnson MSS.

compliment, it equated 'the entire race designated as blacks, people of color, negroes, mullattoes, and persons of African blood" with Chinese, Indians, and "the people called Gipsies."[25]

The racist attitudes of the Blairs and of James Gordon Bennett, men whose influence with Johnson was very considerable, have already been sufficiently established.[26] The attitude of Conservative Republicans who stood with the President is less evident and requires examination.

Though not without criticism of the President, Gideon Welles agreed more completely with him than did any other member of the original Cabinet. Welles alone thoroughly approved of the Civil Rights veto. What he criticized in Johnson's conduct of affairs was *too little* of the very qualities most other critics have thought the Tennessean had in excess— inflexibility and boldness. The fact is that Welles at one end of the Republican spectrum was at least as dogmatic and extreme as was Charles Sumner at the other. An old Jacksonian Democrat, Welles's narrow views of national power and states' rights were unaffected by his adherence to the Republican party. Qualified only by fading personal loyalties and a stout defense of the war effort, his sympathies throughout the postwar period were with the Democrats. A sanctimonious curmudgeon, whom history has largely taken at his own self-evaluation, Welles had kind words for few men. Even so, the sustained animus and distortion that he directed against the Radicals in his famed diary are particularly malicious.

With a record of having broken with the Democratic party over slavery and of having ordered the wartime Navy to protect runaway slaves and to enlist Negroes, Welles's hostility toward the Radicals might be thought to have arisen entirely from his states'-rights views. This, however, was not the sole explanation. In the diary, Welles revealed a marked distaste for the "ingrained Abolitionism"[27] which he thought motivated Johnson's opponents. He was also frank in stating that he was "no advocate for social equality, nor do I labor for political or civil equality for the negro. I do not want him at my table, nor do I care to have him in the jury-box, or in the legislative hall, or on the bench."[28] The Washington correspondent of the Springfield *Republican*, while unconvinced by rumors that Welles had told his Democratic friends in Connecticut that he was opposed to Negro suffrage just before the state was to vote upon the question, thought it quite likely that Welles, who "never was very radical on the slavery question . . . retains many of his prejudices against the colored people."[29] Welles agreed with Sumner that there was "a dreadful state of things South" and that "the colored people were suffering"; but his own concern was for the whites who had also passed through a terrible ordeal and had hardship enough without "any oppressive acts from abroad."[30] Sumner told Welles that he, New England's representative in the Cabinet, misrepresented New England sentiment,[31] in this judgment, Sumner was most certainly correct.

Senator Doolittle of Wisconsin, the strongest pro-Johnson Republican in Congress, was not without compassion for the Negro, but his view of future race relations precluded any possibility of equality. Before and during the civil conflict, Doolittle had been acutely aware of the race problem and the difficulty of its solution. In his opposition to the extension of slavery, a key consideration was the desire to save the western lands for white settlers. He had been willing that the North should join in paying the expense of colonizing Southern

---

25 For the texts of the messages we have used McPherson, *Political Manual for 1866.*

26 See Chapter 3, footnotes 29, 30, 31; Chapter 5, footnotes 18, 21, 22, 25; Chapter 10, footnote 3 in the Coxes' book.

27 *Diary of Gideon Welles*, II, p. 369.
28 *Ibid.*, p. 374.
29 Springfield *Republican*, Sept. 30, 1865.
30 *Diary of Gideon Welles*, II, p. 431.
31 *Ibid.*, p. 394.

Negroes in Latin America, and he had developed a strong feeling of resentment against the abolitionists.[32]

In the fall of 1865, Doolittle proposed as a solution of the Negro problem that a part of Texas, and perhaps of Florida as well, be ceded to the federal government for a segregated freedmen's territory. His object was to attract the entire Negro population of the South to these exclusively Negro territories by the offer of free homesteads. Only thus, in his view, could they "save themselves from being trodden under foot by the advancing tide of Caucasian emigration from Europe and from all the North."[33] Short of such a territorial haven, Doolittle apparently thought that the problem would be resolved only by the passing away of the Negro due to his excessively high death rate in freedom.[34] He believed that rather than the comprehensive freedom given by the Thirteenth Amendment, it would have been far better for the slaves had their emancipation been gradual, with those born after a certain date made free at 21 or even 30 years of age.[35] After the veto of the Civil Rights Bill, the Wisconsin legislature instructed Doolittle, who had not voted on its original passage, to support the measure. When he refused to do so, the legislature called for his resignation.[36]

The draft argument of Senator Edgar Cowan of Pennsylvania for Johnson's veto of the Freedmen's Bureau Bill is revealing. In it there is no kind word for the freedmen or for the Bureau. Cowan viewed with distaste not only the military jurisdiction which the bill authorized but also the fact that it went "the whole length of putting the negroes upon the same footing precisely as the whites as to all *civil rights and immunities*." He not only argued a want of power on the part of the federal government to purchase lands for the relief of destitute freedmen or to establish school buildings for their benefit, but added:

> The people were willing to emancipate the slave in order that he might have a chance to take care of himself—but they will be very unwilling to pay for his maintenance and support out of the public purse—and they say justly that if he is unable to cope with his neighbors, in the battle for life—he must be content with the fate which awaits him and not expect them to feed him at the nation's expense.[37]

After the first veto, it is clear that Cowan recognized that general opinion in the North was not altogether in accord with his own. He urged Johnson to veto the Civil Rights Bill, but warned that the President's public opposition to the measure should not include an attack upon its principle of equal status.[38]

Cowan had been one of the three Republican senators voting against the Civil Rights Bill on its passage in early February, before the first veto; the other thirty-three Republicans who voted supported the measure.[39] On the Freedmen's Bureau Bill a few days earlier he had registered no vote, but in the course of discussion, when he had referred to himself as a friend of the Negro, Senator Henry Wilson had sharply attacked his record. "Why, Sir, there has hardly been a proposition before the Senate of the United States for the last five years leading to the emancipation of the negro and the protection of his rights that the Senator from Pennsylvania has not sturdily opposed. . . . He has made himself the champion of 'how not to do it.' "[40] A sympathetic student of Cowan's

[32] James L. Sellers, "James R. Doolittle," *Wisconsin Magazine of History*, XVII (Dec., 1933), 176; (March, 1934), pp. 287–88, 293, 302–3.

[33] Doolittle to Johnson, Sept. 9, 1865, Johnson MSS.

[34] J. C. G. Kennedy to Doolittle, March 9, 1866; notes for speech, March or April 1866, Doolittle MSS.

[35] Doolittle to wife, Mary, Nov. 11, 1866, *ibid.*

[36] Sellers, "James R. Doolittle," *Wisconsin Magazine of History*, XVIII (September, 1934), pp. 26–27.

[37] Messages, Johnson MSS. See Cox, "Andrew Johnson and His Ghost Writers," p. 463.

[38] Cowan to Johnson, March 23, 1866, Johnson MSS.

[39] McPherson, *Political Manual for 1866*, p. 80.

[40] Quoted in B. J. Pershing, "Senator Edgar A.

public career quotes Wilson's speech at length, and then comments, "These were strong words yet underneath them there was much truth."[41] The following May, Cowan was arguing that the men who were repudiating the Union-Republican platforms of Chicago (1860) and Baltimore (1864) were not those who stood by the President, but those "who go away after false lights, who wander in dangerous places, who cook up Freedmen's Bureau and civil rights bills."[42]

About James Dixon of Connecticut, the third of Johnson's Republican supporters in the Senate, we have little evidence. In October, 1865, he wrote the President that "the People desire justice to the Negro but they are tired of the perpetual reiteration of his claims upon their attention to the exclusion of all other interests. Moreover, as you will see by the recent vote of Connecticut on the question of extending suffrage to the colored population, there are grave doubts as to his fitness to govern the country, even *here*."[43] These words do not sound like those of a man with a deep concern for the Negro and his status. The same implication appears in an attack upon Senator Dixon by a fellow Connecticut Republican, who publicly accused him in 1863 of caring only for power. "I was forced to the conclusion that his [Dixon's] sympathies were not with his own section, but were with the Southern oligarchy. . . . That he hated republicanism for its humanity, and its self-sacrificing devotion to principle."[44]

The Thomas Ewings were among the

most influential of Johnson's political counselors. Both father and son had a staunchly antislavery prewar record; yet the elder Ewing was known as a conservative Whig and Republican, not "as one of the 'earnest' or 'progressive' men of his time."[45] That the want of "earnestness" characterized his view of the Negro would seem evident from Ewing's notes for a public statement in 1867. In arguing against Negro suffrage in the South, he maintained that in the North "the popular mind cannot be excited to enthusiasm in favor of negro equality, social or political." Neither laborers, mechanics, nor professional men would admit a Negro man or woman on terms of equality to their parties, dinners, or dances, for the consequence would be mixed marriages. The feeling might be "vulgar prejudice, but if so, I am content to acknowledge myself therein essentially vulgar—I would be most unwilling to have a black daughter in law." According to Ewing, some Republicans thought that Providence would interfere and bring about Negro suffrage because it was founded on eternal justice, but God knew when he created man what was good for his creatures. "It is not probable that he will by a special miracle suddenly change his nature—his instincts, his prejudices and his passions in order to adapt him to any man's or any party's purposes."[46]

Two intimate associates of Ewing's were brought into Johnson's Cabinet in 1866 on his recommendation, Henry Stanbery as Attorney General and Orville H. Browning as Secretary of the Interior. Though a Republican, Stanbery described himself to Democrats in 1868 as having been an "old guard" Whig who ceased to be one only when that party ceased to exist. Apparently he had not voted for Lincoln: "My last vote was given to that party [Whig] in the Presidential contest of 1860."[47] He was the

Cowan, 1861–1867," *Western Pennsylvania Historical Magazine*, IV (October, 1921), pp. 229–30.

[41] *Ibid.*

[42] *Speech of Hon. Edgar Cowan of Pennsylvania on Executive Appointments and Removals, Delivered in the Senate of the United States, May 9, 1866* (pamphlet, Washington, D.C., 1866), p. 13.

[43] Dixon to Johnson, Oct. 8, 1865, Johnson MSS.

[44] Mark Howard, *Despotic Doctrines Declared by the United States Senate Exposed; and Senator Dixon Unmasked* (pamphlet, Hartford, 1863), p. 8.

[45] From the Toledo *Commercial*, in Ellen Ewing Sherman, comp., *Memorial of Thomas Ewing of Ohio* (New York, 1873), p. 123.

[46] Ewing MSS.

[47] Speech in rely to a toast, published in *An*

author of those passages in Johnson's Civil Rights veto which appealed to race prejudice by interjecting the question of mixed marriages.[48] According to Gideon Welles, Stanbery told Cabinet members in 1867 that as a member of the Ohio legislature he had voted against Negro suffrage, and that he would do so again were he in Ohio.[49] Before the Supreme Court in 1875, it was Stanbery who argued the famous case of U.S. *vs.* Reese, thereby helping to set aside the Civil Rights Enforcement Act of 1870.[50]

Stanbery's colleague in the Cabinet, Orville Browning, had been an antislavery man, but one of the most conservative variety, an outspoken opponent of abolitionists.[51] During the war he deplored Lincoln's action in issuing the Emancipation Proclamation.[52] The Thirteenth Amendment, in Browning's opinion, merely gave the slaves personal freedom and did not confer other rights "not necessary incidents of personal liberty, and not necessary for its enjoyment"; and he was opposed to further legislation or constitutional amendment to secure additional liberties. "If the general government will take its hands off, and let the thing alone, it will soon adjust itself upon a better and more satisfactory basis for all parties, than it can ever be forced to do by Federal interference."[53] Even after

the ratification of the Fifteenth Amendment, Browning was numbered among those who opposed suffrage and nonsegregation for the Negroes in the conviction that, as an "inferior" race, their legal equality would threaten Anglo-Saxon institutions.[54]

Alexander W. Randall, who came into the Cabinet along with Stanbery and Browning, had been a vigorous war governor of Wisconsin, and then as Assistant Postmaster under Lincoln had assisted effectively in mending the President's political fences in preparation for his reelection in 1864.[55] Retaining that politically strategic post under Johnson, Randall was soon recognized as an active political lieutenant of the new President. In the Cabinet reorganization of 1866, he was raised to the rank of Postmaster General. While a young man in Wisconsin politics, Randall had helped prepare a proposal for Negro suffrage to be submitted for referendum in connection with the revision of the state constitution, an action which made him highly unpopular and kept him out of politics for some time.[56] Although associated with the Free Soil Democracy, he is said to have taken little part in its activities because of his opposition to the radical ideas of its leaders.[57] There is little evidence of his racial attitudes during the Johnson period. To judge from his position as reported by Gideon Welles, Randall was equivocal and politically minded rather than either prejudiced or deeply concerned in respect to matters touching equality for the freedmen.[58]

Hugh McCulloch, Secretary of the Trea-

Appeal to the Senate to Modify its Policy and Save from Africanization and Military Despotism the States of the South, printed by order of the National Democratic Resident Committee (pamphlet, Washington, D.C., 1868).

[48] Messages, Johnson MSS. See Cox, "Andrew Johnson and His Ghost Writers," pp. 475, 477–79.

[49] Diary of Gideon Welles, III, p. 4.

[50] Charles Warren, The Supreme Court in United States History (rev. ed., 3 vols.; Boston, 1937), II, p. 603.

[51] J. G. Randall and David Donald, The Civil War and Reconstruction (Boston, 1961), p. 24. Maurice G. Baxter, Orville H. Browning: Lincoln's Friend and Critic (Bloomington, Indiana, 1957), pp. 19–20, 67–69.

[52] For Browning's wartime position, see Baxter, Orville H. Browning, pp. 119–20, 141–43, 148.

[53] National Union Club Documents, Speeches of Hon. Edgar Cowan, Hon. Jas. R. Doolittle, Hon. Hugh McCulloch, Letter of Hon. O. H. Browning and an Address by a Member of the Club; also the Condition of the South: A Report

of Special Commissioner B. F. Truman (pamphlet, Washington, 1866), pp. 21–22; Diary of Gideon Welles, II, pp. 534, 638.

[54] Baxter, Orville H. Browning, pp. 228, 246–56.

[55] Joseph Schafer, "Alexander W. Randall," Dictionary of American Biography, XV, pp. 344–45.

[56] Ibid.; H. A. Tenney and David Atwood, Memorial Record of the Fathers of Wisconsin (Madison, 1880), pp. 134–35.

[57] Clark S. Matteson, The History of Wisconsin (Milwaukee, 1892), p. 303.

[58] Diary of Gideon Welles, II, pp. 534, 608–9, 617–18, 628, III, pp. 64, 83.

sury under both Lincoln and Johnson, believed firmly in the superior intelligence and energy of the white race.[59] He was reported to have said that "so far as the pretended equality of races was concerned," history showed that the Anglo-Saxon race in contact with an inferior one must "dominate or exterminate."[60] Like many another resident of Indiana, he was opposed to granting the vote to the Negroes even in the Northern states.[61] Charles Sumner, who found it difficult to condone the position of Seward and Welles on the question of Negro suffrage in the South, was inclined to more charity toward McCulloch as one "imbued with the pernicious folly of Indiana."[62] McCulloch was aware that Johnson's veto of the Civil Rights Bill, together with his February 22 speech, had "turned not only the Republican party but the general public sentiment of the northern states against him"; yet he had wanted the Administration forces to make an open attack upon the proposed Fourteenth Amendment.[63] In his reminiscences written more than two decades after the struggle between Johnson and Congress, when the Reconstruction amendments were the law of the land, McCulloch characterized the Negroes as "an alien race" and held that the federal government should abstain "from all interference with local affairs" on their behalf. Once outside "interference" was discontinued and "colored people understand that the government, by their emancipation, had done for them all it can do, and that hereafter their welfare and elevation must depend upon their own efforts, the great problem of what is to be the political future of these states must be worked out by the joint action of the two races."[64]

Lewis D. Campbell, perhaps Johnson's most active personal political emissary in the West, was a man who had only scorn for the prewar Oberlin antislavery movement and its underground railroad activities.[65] An ardent opponent of Negro suffrage in Ohio as well as in the South, he held that in crushing secession, slavery had been only an *incidental* casualty and that there was no basis for the idea being promulgated by "wild one-idea fanatics" that the mission of the Union party was "to advance the interests of the *black* man and disregard those of the *white* man."[66] Campbell's perception was so limited that when Sumner, during a private interview with the President at which Campbell was present, expressed concern for the freedmen, the Ohioan saw in Sumner's attitude only the shedding of "crocodile tears."[67]

The support given to the President by Seward and by Raymond is of special interest. Neither man was a party to that prejudice of race so common among adherents of Johnson's cause. Raymond broke with the pro-Johnson movement during the campaign of 1866; Seward remained loyal to the President until the bitter end. A definitive historical understanding and evaluation of Seward, if ever one can be reached, must wait upon a comprehensive modern study of the man. His prewar national repute was based upon his public identification with the opposition to slavery as a moral wrong; he had rallied devotion to himself and to the Republican party by his appeal to "the higher law" and the "irrepressible conflict." Whatever part the pull of oratory or of political ambition may have played in calling forth Seward's ringing phrases, there is no reason to think that they cloaked hypocrisy or an antislavery stand concerned only with the interest of white men. Seward's ardor may have weakened since the days when his words stirred the nation. There had been the cruel defeat of his presidential aspirations, due in considerable part to the very effectiveness of his phrases; there was the death of his wife,

[59] Hugh McCulloch, *Men and Measures of Half a Century: Sketches and Comment* (New York, 1889), p. 518.

[60] Mobile *Times*, Oct. 24, 1865, reprinted in New York *Herald*, Nov. 2, 1865.

[61] *Diary of Gideon Welles*, III, p. 4.

[62] *Ibid.*, II, p. 394.

[63] McCulloch, *Men and Measures*, p. 381; *Diary of Gideon Welles*, II, pp. 531, 534.

[64] McCulloch, *Men and Measures*, pp. 515–18.

[65] Campbell to Johnson, Aug. 21, 1865, Johnson MSS.

[66] Campbell to Johnson, Jan. 22, 1866, *ibid.*

[67] Campbell to Johnson, May 1, 1866, *ibid.*

which severed a close personal tie between Seward and the moral intensity of anti-slavery sentiment.[68] The uncertainty of conjecture is compounded because in the postwar years, as we have noted,[69] Seward did not wish to reveal even in private his innermost convictions and intentions. Yet he retained more than compassion for the former slaves. He believed in their right to citizenship and equal status before the law—even equality of suffrage—though for the attainment of the latter, in his characteristically sanguine way, Seward would rely upon some vague development of the future rather than upon federal authority.[70] It was Seward's adamant opposition that prevented an open attack upon the proposed Fourteenth Amendment, a position favored by the President, in issuing the call for the Philadelphia Convention to mobilize the pro-Johnson forces for the election battle of 1866.[71] After the Radical

victory, the paper which Seward submitted as a basis for the President's message to Congress was conciliatory, leaving open an avenue for accommodation to congressional policy.[72] It was this draft message, its authorship unknown, which has been interpreted, erroneously, as evidence that Johnson in November, 1866, first decided not to oppose the Amendment further, then changed his mind, revived the quarrel with Congress and urged Southern states not to reconsider their refusal to ratify.[73] Not Johnson, but Seward, sought conciliation; and there is nothing to suggest a change of mind on the part of the Secretary of State.[74]

With these attitudes, why did Seward defer to Johnson? Why did he not like other moderates of similar sympathies break with the President? Why did he open himself to bitter repudiation by old friends and to political isolation, a fate which must at least have loomed as an ominous possibility by late spring of 1866?[75] Again, we cannot say with certainty; but a number of considerations come readily to mind. Seward believed that he had already made a major contribution to the cause of freedom by his part in the abolition of slavery and

[68] The possible importance of the death of his wife was suggested to us by Professor Glyndon G. Van Deusen, who has a very special knowledge of the Seward MSS.

[69] See Chapter 2, footnote 28 in the Coxes' book.

[70] *Diary of Gideon Welles*, III, p. 4.

[71] *Ibid.*, II, pp. 534–35, 608–10. In the Seward MSS are two documents, one of which suggests that between the overriding of the Civil Rights veto and the call for the Philadelphia Convention, Seward was trying to obtain a reasonable compromise on an amendment; the other indicates an unyielding position on the part of the President during the same period. The first is a copy of House Bill No. 543, for restoring the states lately in insurrection, submitted by Stevens for the Committee on Reconstruction April 30, 1866. In his own hand, Seward made changes and additions that would have softened the proposal but left intact the provisions for protecting civil rights. The second is a copy dated May 28, 1866, of the constitutional amendment suggested the previous January by the President that provided only for representation according to voters and direct taxation based on the value of property. On its reverse side is noted the following:

"No amendment to the Constitution, or laws passed by Congress, as conditions precedent to the admission by Congress of loyal Representatives.

"Representation from the several States should be left where the Constitution now places it.

"No committals to any plan or proposition which may be made, while incomplete, and before thorough consideration by the President." Note particularly the first statement. It is in marked

contrast to Seward's proposal on the April bill that when any state should ratify the amendment, its senators and representatives would be admitted (after taking the required oaths of office.)

[72] Messages, Johnson MSS. See Cox, "Andrew Johnson and His Ghost Writers," p. 461.

[73] Beale, *The Critical Year*, pp. 400–2.

[74] Welles says that Seward's endorsement of the message in cabinet meeting was "formal not from the heart, but yet not against it." *Diary of Gideon Welles*, II, p. 628.

[75] Letters of criticism from old friends, some written in anger, more in sorrow, are preserved in the Seward MSS. See letters to Seward from J. Warren, Feb. 24, 1866, C. C. Royce, March 10, 1866, I. A. Gates, April 16, 1866, July 17, 1866, E. G. Cook, April 20, 1866, A. Conkling, May 4, 1866, L. M. Bond, May 24, 1866, R. Balcom, July 13, 1866, W. G. Bacon, July 16, 1866, D. C. Gamble, July 18, 1866, G. Hall, July 19, 1866, S. M. Hopkins, July 22, 1866, J. Henderson, July 27, 1866, C. L. Wood, July 29, 1866, and G. Dawson to F. W. Seward, July 14, 1866, July 18, 1866, Seward to Ryerson, April 30, 1866, Seward to Conkling, May 7, 1866, Seward to Balcom, July 14, 1866, Seward to Hopkins, July 25, 1866. The coldness of lifelong friends broke Weed. Sarah Pellet to Seward, March 6, 1869, Seward MSS.

the treaty with Britain to suppress the slave traffic. With these great ends accomplished, and his always hopeful view of the future, perhaps he felt, as Weed had implied in explanation to an English friend's concern for the freedmen, that what "the Freedmen must suffer while the relationships arising between capital and labour are being adjusted" was a minor evil, to be borne with rather than publicly fought.[76] And the consequences of an open fight, the surrender of his post as Secretary of State without assurance of some other major position in national affairs, would have been a hard and selfless decision.

Since the days of the battle for the Thirteenth Amendment, Seward had been committed to a reorganization of parties that would attract the support of Southerners and of Northern Democrats by a speedy and generous restoration of the secession states. He had undoubtedly been influential in directing Johnson toward that objective. Indeed, opinion in Congress in 1866 viewed him as the "head and front of the new party movement," though by the end of July he was thought to have given it up for "reconciliation between the President's particular friends and the body of the Union party."[77] And the President, while withholding full support for Seward's strategy as to both practical politics and basic policy, nevertheless deferred to him to an extent that would naturally have evoked Seward's loyalty and also his hope for a political victory that would renew his national influence and prestige. Then there was the Secretary's concern with the record and the achievement of his stewardship of foreign affairs. These were delicately balanced in 1865 and 1866, and he may well have felt that his departure from the Cabinet would lead to a dangerous adventuristic policy toward Mexico such as the Blairs had been urging. Or he may have been concerned lest any recognition on his part of basic disunity in the country weaken the nation's position abroad. In addition, Seward together with Stanton had become the symbol of Johnson's refusal to embrace the Democracy unconditionally.[78] To the Secretary, this role may have appeared not mere symbol but substance. What other man in the Cabinet could offset the full pressure of the Democracy? And if they were not kept at arm's length what might not be the consequences? The possible result was a matter of patronage and party power, but not that alone. There were extreme programs of action in the air, defiance of Congress with a denial of its legitimacy, recognition of a national legislature with Southern representatives seated by force if necessary. Contemporaries feared another civil war, more fratricidal

---

[76] A. F. Kinnaird to Weed, Dec. 30, 1865, Weed MS.

[77] Unidentified member of the House of Representatives, quoted in C. L. Wood to Seward, July 29, 1866, Seward MSS. For Seward's public position in May, see his Corning Hall, Auburn, speech, draft, and printed copy, *ibid*.

The failure of the Philadelphia Convention to organize a third party did not indicate that this goal was abandoned. One reason for postponement was the desire to win support from Republican ranks, which was essential to victory and also to the creation of a new party that would be more than a rejuvenation of the Democratic party under another label. Republicans were saying that no idea could be "more crazy than that of getting up a new Union party. There was nothing to be furnished from the Republican side but leaders, and the Democrats are not such d——d fools as to supply all the rank and file" without demanding leadership also. Unidentified member of the House of Representatives, quoted in C. L. Wood to Seward, July 29, 1866, *ibid*.

Raymond's curiously contradictory account of his interview with Johnson prior to the Philadel- phia Convention is of interest in this connection. While Raymond opposed a third party and the President agreed that the convention should not attempt to organize one, Raymond yet reported his impression that the President was eager to gain a foothold in the South and to lay the foundation for a *"National"* party that would absorb the Democratic party of the North and West and all of the Union party except the Radicals. Raymond commented that this seemed to him a desirable object! "Extracts from the Journal of Henry J. Raymond (edited by his son), Fourth Paper: The Philadelphia Convention of 1866," *Scribner's Monthly*, XX (June, 1880), pp. 276-77; *see also* John A. Krout, "Henry J. Raymond on the Republican Caucuses of July, 1866," *American Historical Review*, XXXIII (July, 1928), p. 839.

[78] This fact is clearly evident from the correspondence in the Barlow MSS.

than the first.[79] The possibility of such dire consequences may have stirred Seward's very real sense of devotion and responsibility to the nation.

Which considerations weighed with Seward, whether he viewed them as politician or statesman or something of both, we cannot know. But in his papers for 1868 there is an interesting passage, not revealing, but suggesting much. It appears in the draft of a response to an affectionate letter from a friend, a reply that was a far from modest affirmation of his historic role as "first secretary to the President." The passage reads: "The Government has been seriously endangered first by ambition on one side and the reckless passions on the other. I have been *felt* if not always *seen* in saving it from both. Only four months of trial remain, before the Government and the Constitution thus saved are in a constitutional way to be delivered into the keeping of a new administration when I shall be entitled to my discharge."[80]

Although Raymond voted to uphold Johnson's veto of the Civil Rights Bill, his entire course shows a consistent concern to protect the basic rights of the freedmen. In the summer and fall of 1865, the *New York Times* editorials made this objective abundantly clear and identified it with the President's policy. Raymond's paper even found no difficulty in accepting the principle that color should not be a basis for exclusion from the voting franchise, although it did not favor the national government's forcing Negro suffrage upon the South.[81] It had hoped that the President might sign the Civil Rights Bill. The critical first section, with its "absolute equality of civil rights," was, according to the *Times,*

"unquestionably just and right"; the objection was to the arbitrary enforcement provisions of the second section.[82] This position was very close to Senator Morgan's.[83]

Raymond was the Administration leader in the House, Chairman of the Union (Republican) National Executive Committee, and a close ally of Seward. These political commitments constituted a very formidable restraint upon his championship of equality for the freedmen. Yet in the House of Representatives, the *Times* editor voted "yea" on the roll call for the Fourteenth Amendment. The fact that no enabling legislation accompanied the passage of the Amendment, which would have made clear that its ratification was a condition for readmission of the rebellious states, helped Raymond reconcile his vote for the Amendment with his support of the President, who publicly opposed any prerequisite to the return of Southern representatives.[84] Raymond had considered the object of the Freedmen's Bureau Bill of "utmost importance" and explained that he had not supported the Civil Rights Bill because he, along with Bingham and others, thought that it was not warranted by the Constitution. He had introduced an alternate proposal to declare all persons born in the United States citizens, entitled to all the privileges and immunities of citizenship. All the main principles of the Fourteenth Amendment he considered "eminently wise and proper."[85]

It was the desire to placate Raymond and to insure the support of the *Times* for the pro-Johnson movement which broke down the intent of Welles, Cowan, Doolittle, Browning, and McCulloch to include

---

[79] Even so restrained a man as John Sherman wrote in early July, 1866: "I almost fear he [Johnson] contemplates civil war." J. Sherman to W. T. Sherman, July 8, 1866, *The Sherman Letters, Correspondence Between General and Senator Sherman from 1837–1891* (Rachel Sherman Thorndike (ed.), New York, 1894), p. 276.

[80] Italics added. Draft, Seward to Seymour, Oct. 14, 1868, Seward MSS.

[81] See Chapter 4, fn. 49, and Chapter 8, fn. 47–56 in the Coxes' book.

[82] *New York Times*, March 26, 1866.

[83] See fn. 22 and 23 in the Coxes' book.

[84] *New York Times*, July 30, 1866, June 15, 1866, and McKitrick, *Andrew Johnson and Reconstruction*, p. 358.

[85] Raymond's letter to the committee requesting him to run again for Congress, Sept. 15, 1866, in Augustus Maverick, *Henry J. Raymond and the New York Press* Hartford, 1870), pp. 175–84. See also Raymond's address of February, 1866, at Cooper Institute, in *ibid.*, pp. 175–84.

an open attack upon the proposed Fourteenth Amendment in their call for the Philadelphia Convention.[86] For that meeting, Raymond prepared an address which recognized the need for the enlargement of Federal powers in respect to the freedmen's rights, and also the power of Congress and the states to make such amendments; but this part of his statement evoked sharp opposition and was deleted.[87] The resolutions adopted by the convention stated that it was the desire and purpose of the Southern states that all inhabitants should receive "equal protection in every right of person and property," but omitted any statement that might be interpreted as acquiescence in federal authority over civil rights unless by amendment after the admission of the Southern states and with their free consent.[88] This was the most that Raymond could achieve in his effort to gain Southern agreement to the principle of "equal protection by law, and by equal access to courts of law, of all the citizens of all the states, without distinction of race or color.[89] He himself was ready to accept the provisions of the Fourteenth Amendment as the platform of the party, and he felt that the President had "made a great mistake in taking ground against those amendments."[90] Johnson's defeat in the fall elections of 1866 was interpreted by Raymond as a popular decision in favor of the

principles of the Amendment, particularly "the absolute equality of civil rights to all the people of the United States."[91]

Although Raymond's break with Johnson did not come over the civil rights issue, his defection to the opposition was consonant with his basic convictions in respect to equality of citizenship for the Negro. Most other key Republican moderates who took their stand against Johnson shared those convictions. Senator John Sherman had long been troubled by the probability that freedmen would be oppressed if they had no share of political power. As for the Civil Rights Bill, he wrote, "I felt it so clearly right that I was prepared for the very general acquiescence in its provisions both North and South. To have refused the negroes the simplest rights granted to every other inhabitant, native or foreigner, would be outrageous."[92] The veto was a major factor in Sherman's repudiation of Johnson, whom he had hitherto defended. "The President's course on the Civil Rights Bill and constitutional amendment was so unwise that I could not for a moment allow anyone to suppose that I meant with him to join a coalition with the rebels and Copperheads."[93] Senators Lyman Trumbull of Illinois, James Grimes of Iowa, and William Fessenden of Maine were all men of moderation and principle, able to withstand terrific pressures, as their votes against Johnson's conviction on impeachment charges later made amply clear; their principles included a commitment to basic civil rights for the freedmen. All three wished to work with the President rather than against him, but, to use Welles's characterization of the latter two men, "their natural tendency would I knew in-

[86] Diary of Gideon Welles, II, pp. 534, 618; III, p. 251.
[87] "Extracts from the Journal of Henry J. Raymond: The Philadelphia Convention," pp. 278–79; McKitrick, Andrew Johnson and Reconstruction, p. 411.
[88] Edward McPherson, Handbook of Politics for 1868 (Washington, 1869), p. 241. Raymond drafted the resolutions after hearing those proposed by William B. Reed of Pennsylvania, Governor Sharkey of Mississippi, and Senator Cowan, all of which he considered too pro-Southern. "Extracts from the Journal of Henry J. Raymond: The Philadelphia Convention," p. 278.
[89] Maverick, Henry J. Raymond, p. 189. See also Raymond's address to the convention in The Proceedings of the National Union Convention Held at Philadelphia, August 14, 1866 (pamphlet, n.p., n.d.), pp. 12–13.
[90] Raymond to R. Balcom, July 17, 1866, in Maverick, Henry J. Raymond, pp. 173–74.

[91] New York Times, Oct. 11, 1866, Nov. 12, 1866.
[92] J. Sherman to W. T. Sherman, May 16, 1865, April 23, 1866, The Sherman Letters, pp. 251, 270; see also John Sherman, Recollections of Forty Years in the House, Senate and Cabinet: an Autobiography (2 vols.; Chicago, 1895), I, pp. 364, 366–67, 369.
[93] J. Sherman to W. T. Sherman, Oct. 26, 1866, The Sherman Letters, p. 278.

cline them to the opposition. They are both intense on the negro."[94] The same might be said for other moderates, for Governor John Andrew of Massachusetts, for Henry Ward Beecher, for Samuel Bowles of the Springfield *Republican,* for John Bingham of Ohio, for Henry Dawes of Massachusetts, for James Hawley of Connecticut, and for General O. O. Howard of the Freedmen's Bureau.

The case of the two influential Midwestern governors, Oliver P. Morton of Indiana and Jacob D. Cox of Ohio, is not so clear. Both were chief executives of a citizenry much given to discrimination against the Negro and closely divided between Republicans and Democrats. Although Cox had strong convictions in respect to the evil of slavery and took great satisfaction as a military officer in freeing refugee "contrabands," he disappointed antislavery men who had hoped that his early Oberlin training and his close relationship to Charles G. Finney would bring support for Negro suffrage. Such support Cox refused, and

instead issued a public statement proposing separation of the races in the Southern states, with schools, homesteads, and full political privileges for the Negroes.[95] Later in advising Johnson to accept the Civil Rights Bill, Cox stressed political expediency; but he also assumed that the President as well as himself and "all true Union men" believed in the principle of equality before the law—that it was right."[96] While still supporting Johnson, he accepted the Fourteenth Amendment, expressing privately his approval of all parts of the Amendment except the disqualifying clause of the third section.[97] In the campaign of 1867 to amend the Ohio constitution, he argued for Negro suffrage since it had already been forced upon the South.[98]

Governor Morton was a political enemy of Radicals in Indiana; and his public opposition in September, 1865, to making Negro suffrage a condition for Southern restoration was widely publicized and enthusiastically received by pro-Johnson men. An examination of his speech discloses not an opposition to Negro suffrage as such but the argument that Indiana was in no condition to urge voting privileges for Negroes in the South when the state itself discriminated so grossly against the "many very intelligent and well qualified" colored people within its own borders. Morton pointed out the restriction not only upon their political power but also upon their testimony in court, their access to public schools, and, if they had come into the

---

[94] *Diary of Gideon Welles,* II, p. 448. For Trumbull's repudiation of the President after the Civil Rights veto see footnote 24.

For Grimes, see William Salter, *The Life of James W. Grimes, Governor of Iowa, 1854–1858 and Senator of the United States, 1859–1869* (New York, 1876), pp. 75, 392; F. I. Herriott, "James W. Grimes versus the Southrons," *Annals of Iowa,* XV (July, 1926), pp. 325–27; Fred B. Lewellen, "Political Ideas of James W. Grimes," *Iowa Journal of History and Politics,* XLII (October, 1944), pp. 383–95.

For Fessenden, *see* Francis Fessenden, *Life and Public Services of William Pitt Fessenden* (2 vols.; Boston and New York, 1907), I, pp. 283–87, II, pp. 29–32, 34–35, 65–66, 314–15; and William A. Robinson, "William Pitt Fessenden," *Dictionary of American Biography,* VI, pp. 348–50.

For Trumbull, *see* Horace White, *The Life of Lyman Trumbull* (Boston, 1913), p. 277; *also* Arthur H. Robertson, *The Political Career of Lyman Trumbull* (M.A. thesis, University of Chicago, 1910), pp. 37–39, 56, 59, 75. Robertson's study indicates that Trumbull's prewar view of the race problem included colonization and the conviction that Negroes could not be placed upon an equal social or political position with whites. However, by the winter of 1865–66, there can be no doubt of Trumbull's deep sense of national responsibility for the freedmen nor of his sincerity in fighting to secure for them equal rights, short of suffrage and officeholding.

[95] George H. Porter, *Ohio Politics During the Civil War Period* (New York, 1911), pp. 210–13; Homer C. Hockett, "Jacob Dolson Cox," *Dictionary of American Biography,* IV, pp. 476–78; Jacob Dolson Cox, *Military Reminiscences of the Civil War* (2 vols.; New York, 1900), I, pp. 157–63; James Rees Ewing, *Public Services of Jacob Dolson Cox* (Ph.D. dissertation, Johns Hopkins University, 1902), pp. 8, 14–15; William C. Cochran, *General Jacob Dolson Cox: Early Life and Military Services* (pamphlet, Oberlin, Ohio, 1901), pp. 10–13.

[96] Cox to Johnson, March 22, 1866, Johnson MSS.

[97] Cox to Johnson, June 21, 1866, *ibid.*

[98] Ewing, *Public Services of Jacob Dolson Cox,* p. 15.

state since 1850, their legal right to make valid contracts. He spoke highly of the fighting record of the Indiana colored regiment and pointed to the ironic fact that half the men who composed it could not legally come back into the state. The tone of the address was not one of defending discrimination but one of gently criticizing his fellow Hoosiers. As for Southern freedmen, Morton believed that they should have time to acquire property and obtain a little education, and then "at the end of 10, 15, or 20 years, let them come into the enjoyment of their political rights."[99] The governor was clearly in advance of state sentiment in advocating for Negroes the benefit of schooling and the right to testify in court. His sponsorship of the repeal of the state statute which excluded their testimony finally resulted in the elimination of that discrimination.[100] It was Morton who warned Johnson that a veto of the Civil Rights Bill would separate the President and the Union-Republican party, that if he did not sign the measure the two men could not again meet in political friendship.[101] Morton's decision to oppose Johnson was no doubt essentially a political one, but his attitude toward the Negro was not identical with that of the President.[102]

Behind conciliatory Republican leaders whose personal attitudes might in other circumstances have enabled them to accept a solution which would leave the future status of the freedmen in the hands of Southern whites, there was the pressure of mass Republican opinion. The overwhelming preponderance of Republican sentiment was behind a national guarantee for basic civil equality, short of suffrage, for the freedmen. This sentiment is unmistakable in newspaper editorials and private correspondence;[103] it was also reflected in the congressional vote on what was to become the Fourteenth Amendment. In the Senate, Republicans divided thirty-three to four in its favor. The "nays" were those of Senators Cowan, Doolittle, Norton of Minnesota and Van Winkle of West Virginia. Senator Dixon was absent and not voting. In the House, 138 Republican votes were cast for the Amendment; not a single Republican voted against it.[104] This vote was taken *before* Johnson made clear his political intentions by issuance of the call for the Philadelphia Convention.

After the Civil Rights veto, Republican opinion had crystallized in a determination to set further conditions before accepting Southern representatives back into the counsels of the nation, but not just any conditions.[105] The matters dealt with in sections two and three of the Fourteenth Amendment, namely the basis of future Southern representation, the granting of suffrage to the Negro, and the degree of proscription of Confederate leaders were negotiable; the question of equality before the law, federally enforceable, was no longer open to compromise. The issue of civil rights and national protection for the freedmen was not, as has sometimes been implied, the product of campaign propaganda and exaggeration, nor even of the shocking impact of the Memphis and New Orleans riots. The civil rights issue predated those developments.

Although in deference to Seward and Raymond the pro-Johnson leaders had attempted to evade discussion of the Fourteenth Amendment, it was generally recognized as being at stake in the ensuing campaign. After Radical victories in the

---

[99] Printed in William Dudley Foulke, *Life of Oliver P. Morton* (2 vols.; Indianapolis, 1899), I, p. 449.

[100] *Ibid.*, pp. 434, 455; James, *Framing of the Fourteenth Amendment*, pp. 29, 200. *See also* Governor Morton's message of November, 1865, in W. H. Schlater (of the President's staff) to Johnson, Nov. 12, 1865, Johnson MSS.

[101] Foulke, *Life of Oliver P. Morton*, I, pp. 466–67; McKitrick, *Andrew Johnson and Reconstruction*, pp. 309–10.

[102] Compare Beale, *The Critical Year*, pp. 106–7, 121–22, 178, 180, 184–86.

[103] See footnotes 4–9, 20–23, 27, 31–49 in the Coxes' book.

[104] McPherson, *Handbook of Politics for 1868*, p. 102.

[105] Compare McKitrick, *Andrew Johnson and Reconstruction*, p. 443.

states that voted in September and early October, pressure was put upon the President to accept the Amendment. As early as September 19, Bennett in the *Herald* foresaw defeat unless the President would "take up" the proposed Fourteenth Amendment and "push it through all the still excluded Southern States as rapidly as possible" with the kind of pressure he had used in behalf of the Thirteenth Amendment. Bennett at last deplored the condition he had done so much to provoke, "the widening of his [Johnson's] conflict with the radicals to a conflict with Congress." He now viewed the Amendment as "not a radical measure, but a measure of the republican conservatives of Congress."[106] When Samuel S. Cox asked the President about the rumors that he would modify his opposition to the amendment in keeping with "the poplar [*sic*] current," Johnson "got as ugly as the Devil. He was regularly mad. . . . There's no budge in him. Browning's letter is his view."[107]

S. L. M. Barlow's attitude toward the Amendment's role in campaign strategy is pertinent. He was much opposed to the President's yielding unless the Johnson forces should suffer defeat in New York. In that event, he thought the President might be "compelled to yield on the Constitutional amendment, but to yield to the pressure now, before our election, would destroy him & be in gross bad faith . . . as we are making a good fight & cannot now change our course."[108] If faced with defeat in November, however, Barlow thought Johnson could say to the South, "While I have not thought the ratification of the amendment necessary . . . the Northern people have decided otherwise—You must be represented. . . . Ratify the amendment therefore." Barlow explained that Johnson could "be supported in this, if necessary,

after November, not only here but by the ablest presses of the South in New Orleans, Mobile, Charleston & Richmond — To change *now* would deprive him, practically of every paper and every voter—The Radicals would not be won back to him and he would lose the whole power of the democratic party."[109]

Browning's letter, to which Representative Cox referred, is additional proof of the importance of the Amendment as a campaign issue. It is also, and more importantly, added evidence that the opposition of the pro-Johnson forces to the Amendment was not merely limited to a distaste for section three, which denied Southern leaders state and national office. The heart of Browning's argument, approved by the President, was that section one, the civil rights guarantee, would restrict the states in functions properly their own. It would subject the "authority and control of the States over matters of purely domestic and local concern . . . to criticism, interpretation and adjudication by the Federal tribunals, whose judgments and decrees will be supreme."[110]

Johnson's refusal, despite great pressure and much advice, to capitulate on the Fourteenth Amendment after his election defeat cannot be attributed alone to his stubborn nature. The explanation that he decided for reconciliation, then reversed course on the basis of the Radicals' behavior, is exploded by the identification of the early conciliatory draft message as the work of Seward.[111] Another factor entered into policy considerations, the hope

---

[106] New York *Herald*, Sept. 19, 1866.

[107] Cox to Marble, Oct. 9, 1866, Marble MSS. See also Barlow to R. Taylor, Oct. 26, 1866, Barlow MSS.

[108] Barlow to R. Johnson, Oct. 24, 1866, Barlow MSS.

[109] Barlow to T. J. Barnett, Sept. 27, 1866, *ibid.*

[110] Browning to W. H. Benneson and H. V. Sullivan, Oct. 13, 1866, printed in *New York Times*, Oct. 24, 1866. See also the earlier public statement of Democratic and Conservative members of Congress to the effect that the "dignity and equality of the States" must be preserved, including "the exclusive right of each State to control its own domestic concerns"; published in the New York *Herald*, July 4, 1866.

[111] Professor Beale erroneously assumed that Seward's unidentified draft message had been prepared by Johnson and had reflected his views. *The Critical Year*, pp. 400–3.

of ultimate victory and the tactical advantage to be gained by encouraging extreme action on the part of the opposition with a view to ultimate popular reaction against it. Doolittle wrote Browning on November 8: "The elections are over and we are beaten for the present. But our cause will live. If all the states not represented refuse to ratify the amendment . . . the extreme Rads will go . . . for reorganizing the southern states on negro suffrage. . . . That will present the issue squarely of forcing negro suffrage upon the South and upon that we can beat them at the next Presidential election."[112] A short time later, Weed was writing Seward that he had rebuffed Senator Morgan's suggestion of an organization in Congress against "extreme men." Weed explained, "I think that if the pressure should be withdrawn the Radicals would hang *themselves*."[113] From Ohio the prediction reached the President that "If Congress resorts to rash and violent means to carry out the destructive purposes of the radicals, their own party will break to pieces."[114] From New York came more positive advice: "Are those proposed amendments to be adopted, changing the whole nature of our government? I trust not. I think a year or two of Radicalism more, will satisfy the country that the principles contained in that old instrument are too dear to us to be frittered away. . . . I believe that with you standing firmly on the ground you have assumed and each state organizing her conservative men on the Philadelphia platform, two years more will have seen the end of the Radical race."[115] Analysts of the 1866 election returns pointed out to the President that if the potential vote of the unrepresented South were added to the Conservative vote in the North, a large majority of the nation supported the President and opposed the amendment, and that ultimately the President must triumph.[116]

Raymond's editorials in the *Times* had urged the President to accept the decision of the people in favor of the Amendment, and either to recommend its ratification by the Southern states or to stand aside while they made a settlement with Congress upon the basis of its principles. By the end of December, however, Raymond had come to the conclusion that Johnson's opposition to the Amendment was unyielding. The President, he explained, intended to hold to his earlier position in the conviction that his policy would ultimately prevail. Johnson believed that the Supreme Court would set aside any conditions Congress might impose upon the South or, failing such a resolution of the conflict, that the use of military power to enforce congressional policy would become so "expensive, odious and intolerable" that the voters would expel from power the party responsible for such a policy.[117]

The losses which the Radicals sustained in the state elections of 1867 seemed to justify the President's hope of victory and the strategy of no compromise. News of the defeat of the Radicals in Connecticut's April election of that year was received by Johnson as "the turn of the current" and by Welles as "the first loud knock, which admonishes the Radicals of their inevitable doom."[118] Welles believed that the returns from Pennsylvania and Ohio in October "indicates the total overthrow of the Radicals and the downfall of that party."[119] In November, 1867, Johnson celebrated the election results by a victory speech before

---

112 Doolittle to Browning, Nov. 8, 1866, Doolittle MSS; see also James, *Framing of the Fourteenth Amendment*, p. 178, and McKitrick, *Andrew Johnson and Reconstruction*, pp. 464–65, especially footnote 38.

113 Weed to Seward, Nov. 24, 1866, Seward MSS. By the end of February, Weed was apprehensive of congressional reconstruction proposals and uncertain of the best presidential tactics; Weed to Seward, Feb. 21, 1867, *ibid.*

114 P. W. Bartley to Johnson, Nov. 9, 1866, Johnson MSS.

115 S. Smith to Johnson, Nov. 10, 1866, *ibid.*

116 T. S. Seybolt to Johnson, Nov. 8, 1866, F. A. Aiken to Johnson, Nov. 26, 1866, *ibid.*

117 *New York Times*, Oct. 31, 1866, Nov. 3, 9, 12, 17, 19, 1866, Dec. 4, 27, 31, 1866.

118 *Diary of Gideon Welles*, III, p. 78.

119 *Ibid.*, p. 232.

a group of serenaders in which he held that "the people have spoken in a manner not to be misunderstood."[120] The President's "stubbornness" of the previous November seemed to have prepared the way for success in the presidential election of 1868. The hope proved an illusion; but the hope was present, and died hard.[121]

In refusing to accept the equal rights provisions of the Civil Rights Act or of the Fourteenth Amendment, Johnson won lasting gratitude from white Southerners to whom the concept of equality between the races was anathema,[122] and this despite the ordeal of military government and immediate universal Negro suffrage which they in all likelihood would have been spared had Johnson's course been different. But with this decision, the President lost the confidence and respect of moderate Republicans. Lyman Trumbull and John Sherman both felt a sense of betrayal in Johnson's veto of the Civil Rights Bill. "Besides," confided Sherman to his brother, "he [Johnson] is insincere; he has deceived and misled his best friends."[123] The confidence in John-

son's assurances of justice for the freed people, which characterized Republican opinion, except that of extreme Radicals, in December, 1865, turned to mistrust. No longer were misgivings directed toward Presidential policy alone; they came to embrace the President's intention and integrity, and corroded his public influence. "The truth is," Senator Fessenden wrote to Senator Morgan in mid-1867, "Mr. Johnson has continued to excite so much distrust that the public mind is easily played upon by those who are seeking only the accomplishment of their own purposes."[124] By standing adamant against a federally enforceable pledge of minimum civil equality for the Negro as a prerequisite to restoration of the secession states, Johnson precipitated a great issue of moral principle central to the battle over Reconstruction; and he brought upon himself an unparalleled humiliation.

---

[120] *New York Times*, Nov. 14, 1867; McKitrick, *Andrew Johnson and Reconstruction*, p. 498.

[121] See pp. 95–106 in the Coxes' book.

[122] Of the 65 votes which Johnson obtained on the first ballot for the presidential nomination of the Democratic party in 1868, all but four were from Southern delegates. Charles H. Coleman, *The Election of 1868: The Democratic Effort to Regain Control* (New York, 1933), pp. 164, 208.

[123] J. Sherman to W. T. Sherman, July 8, 1866,

The Sherman Letters, p. 276. For Trumbull's reaction see *Congressional Globe*, 39th Cong., 1st sess., p. 1761 (April 4, 1866); and C. H. Ray to M. Blair, April 10, 1866, enclosure in Blair to Johnson, April 15, 1866, Johnson MSS. A digest and explanation of the bill, unsigned, but in Trumbull's handwriting, is in the Johnson MSS; see Cox, "Andrew Johnson and His Ghost Writers," p. 473.

[124] Fessenden to Morgan, June 26, 1867, Morgan MSS. The distrust, of course, involved party as well as principle. By mid-1866, it was widely believed that Johnson intended to bring the Democracy back into national power and ascendancy, and that he had deliberately sought to wreck the party that had elected him.

1962

Southern Violence and Reconstruction[*]

JOHN A. CARPENTER

One of the most controversial subjects of the history of Reconstruction is that of atrocities against Negroes, carpetbaggers, and scalawags. The dispute is over the degree of intensity and seriousness of the atrocities. If they were as bad as the Radical Republicans maintained in the years up to the time that the Ku Klux Klan became active in 1868,[1] then there was greater justification for the refusal to recognize the work of Reconstruction completed under the Johnson plan in the last six months of 1865, for the framing of the Fourteenth Amendment, and for the enactment of the Reconstruction Acts of 1867. For the principal reason advanced to justify these actions was the assertion, in Congress and in the North generally, that Southerners could not be trusted to deal fairly with the freedmen and Unionists and furthermore were actively engaged in a program of oppression and violence against these groups.

On the other hand, if the reports of atrocities were either largely untrue or so grossly exaggerated that they deserved to be ignored, then the Radical Republicans perpetrated a terrible fraud upon the Southern states and the best that can be said for these Radicals is that they were deceived. If the conditions in the South immediately following the war were as bad as has been alleged, it is hard to see how the Congress could have done other than it did; and the argument that congressional interference only made matters worse is not an indictment of Congress but of the white people of the South who took part in and condoned the atrocities and outrages. But if the interference was unnecessary, if physical violence was not invoked in the South, to any excessive degree, against freedmen and loyalists then there remained to the Radicals as reason for intervention the argument that the freedman was not accorded civil and political equality, an argument which probably would not have carried enough weight in 1865 and 1866 to have justified the actions which the Congress eventually adopted.

Most accounts of Reconstruction tend to minimize the amount of atrocity and either imply or directly state that the cases were greatly exaggerated or even completely fabricated. Another device frequently used is to attribute what atrocities there were to the poor whites and state that the better element deplored this sort of things. Throughout these accounts is the intimation that because there was ex-

[*] John A. Carpenter, "Atrocities in the Reconstruction Period," *Journal of Negro History* (1962).

[1] There appears to be little doubt about the fact that the Klan was responsible for numerous outrages against Negroes, carpetbaggers, and scalawags in the Reconstruction period. See, e.g., Stanley F. Horn, *Invisible Empire: The Story of the Ku Klux Klan 1866–1871* (Boston, 1939), pp. 361–62.

aggeration then somehow those atrocities that did occur were really not so bad after all. For example, James Ford Rhodes wrote in his *History of the United States from the Compromise of 1850,* "That affairs of the sort ["cruelties practised upon the negroes"] occurred as one of the results of the social revolution was undoubted but on the other hand exaggerated accounts of them were readily believed by those who desired to use them as an argument for a severe policy towards the South."[2] Or take what Robert S. Henry says in *The Story of Reconstruction.* "There can be no doubt," he writes, "that injustices and cruelties were practiced on the freed Negroes, as there have been in all times and all societies on the weak and defenseless. Equally without doubt, there were innumerable instances of kindly and friendly relations between the races. For political purposes, these must be ignored or minimized, which was not difficult to do; the 'atrocities' [note the quotation marks] must be multiplied and exaggerated."[3] After noting that "No atrocity story was too extraordinary to find credence," he goes on to cite examples of trumped-up atrocity stories, or at least stories which he intimates are trumped up because no names were ever given by the reporting officer.[4]

One more example will perhaps be enough even though the number could be more or less indefinitely extended. The most recent history of the Freedmen's Bureau, that by George R. Bentley, contains a few passages which intimate that there was not really much to the atrocity reports. For instance, he refers to atrocity "tales." Bentley does admit, though, that "Unfortunately, there was considerable truth in the postwar reports of violence and cruelty." He attributes this to the abnormal times. But, he hastens to add, Bureau agents "were frequently prone to exaggerate the violence they encountered and to report rumors without determining their authen-

ticity."[5] Then for the next four pages he cites examples of unfounded atrocity reports.[6] In one sentence he admits that there was "considerable truth in the . . . reports" and in four pages he shows how such reports were exaggerated!

That there was inadequate reason for interference seems, without much doubt, to be the generally accepted view. The attemped renewal of the Freedmen's Bureau in February, 1866, was, it has been maintained, an unnecessary continuation of a temporary institution whose powers were too extensive and whose agents were desperately trying to hold on to their jobs by sending in imaginary or exaggerated atrocity stories.[7] The various provisions of the Fourteenth Amendment, especially the disfranchising section, were merely devices to punish the South unnecessarily.[8] The Reconstruction Acts of 1867 were largely intended to establish, through Negro voting, Republican domination of the South.

In other words, there was little valid excuse for doing all this. The motive was not anything other than desire to punish the South and to enable the Republican Party to remain indefinitely in office. Such is the argument of those who believed that Radical Reconstruction was indefensible.

What of the other side of the argument? Were the Negroes in such danger that only federal intervention could protect them? Reports coming to the Commissioner of the Freedmen's Bureau, Major General Oliver Otis Howard, from the assistant commissioners and Bureau agents in many parts of the South seemed to indicate that this truly was the case. These reports, the testimony given to the Joint Committee on Reconstruction, and occasional accounts appearing in the Northern press (especially reports of several large-scale race riots in Memphis, New Orleans, and other places in the South) constituted the bulk of the

---

[2] N.Y., 1904, V, 563.
[3] N.Y., 1938, pp. 84–85.
[4] *Ibid.,* p. 85.

[5] George R. Bentley, *A History of the Freedmen's Bureau* (Philadelphi, 1955), p. 110.
[6] *Ibid.,* pp. 111–14.
[7] E.g., *ibid.,* pp. 110–11.
[8] Henry, *Story of Reconstruction,* pp. 167–68.

evidence to support the Radical contention that the Southern state governments as established under President Johnson's plan of reconstruction could not be depended upon to give the Negro protection and fair treatment. To write these off as exaggerations and fabrications is to ignore some rather substantial evidence.

The agents and assistant commissioners of the Freedmen's Bureau submitted reports which indicated that the Negroes were frequently subjected to violent attack, including murder. Other reports simply stated that the freedmen were not receiving equal treatment. These reports, tempered it is true by others which asserted the opposite, came so incessantly and in such volume that the only way one can gain a true appreciation of their impact is by seeing them in their entirety. A fair sampling, however, can convey the impression in part.

One of the earliest complaints was that of Capt. D. W. Whittle who had been on General Howard's staff during the Georgia campaign. At the time he wrote, June 8, 1865, he was on garrison duty at Union Springs, Alabama. He stated that the white people found it difficult to grasp the idea that slavery was dead. ". . . there has got to be a constant pressure brought to bear upon the former slave-holders,'" Whittle continued, "to make them deal fairly with the negroes. . . . they were very well as slaves, but in any other relation they hate them, and will place every possible obstacle in the way of their elevation. . . ."[9]

Howard's assistant adjutant general, Joseph S. Fullerton, on an inspection trip to South Carolina in July, 1865, stated that only a few had any hope that slavery would be re-established, but he was of the opinion that "the result of the war [had] not changed the *animus* of the former slave owner."[10]

The assistant commissioner for Tennessee, Clinton B. Fisk, reported in September, 1865, that while things in general were progressing favorably, there were, however, too many "who [would] not accept the conclusions of the strife. . . . There is nothing the matter down this way," Fisk said, "'but *injustice to the negro*. . . . It is lamentable and astonishing with what tenacity the unsubjugated cling to the old barbarism."[11]

Davis Tillson, assistant commissioner for Georgia, and one of the more conservative men in the Bureau organization, late in November, 1865, wrote to Howard urging the retention of a military force in Georgia. "If we really mean to keep sacred the solemn promises made the freed people to protect them in their rights," Tillson said, ". . . the army must not be withdrawn."[12] About three months later Tillson again wrote to Howard reporting the favorable news that plantation owners on the Sea Islands were entering into satisfactory labor arrangements with the freedmen. Yet in another part of the same letter, which was written immediately following receipt of news of President Johnson's veto of the Freedmen's Bureau bill, Tillson expressed fear lest Johnson disturb the system of Bureau courts which he [Tillson] had established. If Johnson should do this, wrote Tillson, ". . . all hope of justice to the freedpeople, for the present, will be lost. I shall decline to act in my present position when no longer able to protect the freedpeople— it would be too mortifying to be endured."[13]

In October of the same year Tillson sent to Bureau headquarters the copy of a letter he had written to the leading citizens of Henry County in Georgia. It seems that these citizens had complained to Tillson of the continued presence of troops in their country. The assistant commissioner replied that it was necessary to retain troops there because the civil authorities had done nothing to protect the Negroes, nothing to investigate crimes against Negroes or to

9 D. W. Whittle to Howard, June 8, 1865, National Archives, hereafter referred to as NA.

10 J. S. Fullerton to Howard, July 28, 1865, NA.

11 C. B. Fisk to Howard, Sept. 2, 1865, NA.

12 D. Tillson to Howard, Nov. 28, 1865, NA.

13 D. Tillson to Howard, Feb. 24, 1866, Howard Papers, Bowdoin College.

prosecute criminals, nothing to protect the person or the office of the Bureau agent. Tillson went on to explain how ". . . on many . . . occasions the rightful authority of the Government of the United States had been insulted, defied and treated with contempt by the citizens and civil authorities of Henry County." He told them that the Bureau agent had reported to him personally, ". . . that he called upon the Sheriff of Henry County and asked him to arrest certain parties charged with committing outrages on freed people. The sheriff replied that 'it would be unpopular to punish white men for anything done to a negro—it might be unsafe—that he was not going to obey the orders of any damned Yankee—and that the rebellion was not over yet in Henry County.'" It would be his duty, said Tillson, to retain troops in that county until the conduct of the people there should convince him that the freedmen would receive protection. "Longer to trust mere profession," he concluded, "in the presence of facts in my possession, would be to indulge in criminal credulity."[14]

Other assistant commissioners shared the same views. Major General Joseph B. Kiddoo in Texas faced a most difficult problem. Distances were great, the population much dispersed, and the number of troops small. In August, 1866, he reported an increase in the amount of violence and murder committed against freedmen. He had become, he said, ". . . so powerless to give proper protection, for want of troops to sustain my agents and make arrests, that I grow *sick at heart*. . . .The only remedy I can suggest is Army officers for Agents, and troops to sustain them. If in your judgment it is the *settled policy* of the Executive to leave the Bureau without adequate military protection, I will desist making these official appeals, but until I am thus informed, I must continue to plead for such force as will make my duties here a *reality* instead of a *farce*."[15] In an earlier letter

Kiddoo had complained that he was unable to obtain justice for the freedmen from the civil courts in criminal cases. Trial of such cases in civil courts is, he said ". . . *worse than a farce*."[16]

The assistant commissioner for South Carolina, Robert K. Scott, reported at the end of 1866 that whenever garrisons had been removed, crimes against the freedmen had increased. Included in his letter to Howard was this expression of concern: ". . . even under the most favorable circumstances that can be anticipated under the present system of laws the freed people will fail to receive from the civil authorities that protection to which they are entitled both by right and by law, and without which they cannot but gradually revert back to a condition differing little from their former slavery—save in name."[17]

Major General E. O. C. Ord, who held the two positions of district commander and assistant commissioner in Arkansas, was so convinced that the Negroes could not expect equal treatment from the whites that he advocated physical separation of the two races. Until this could be done (and it is doubtful whether he seriously believed his suggestion would be implemented), he urged the retention of troops in Arkansas.[18]

The district commander and assistant commissioner for North Carolina, Major General Nelson A. Miles, urged in December, 1867, that the Bureau's life be extended at least another year until the new state government could have the opportunity of becoming well established. The freedmen, he noted, were ". . . almost as much within the grasp of their former owners as in the days of slavery."[19]

Not only the assistant commissioners but lesser officials, the agents of the Bureau, frequently reported the same general conditions. They were really in the best posi-

---

14 D. Tillson to Elijah Foster and A. M. Campbell, Oct. 16, 1866, NA.
15 J. B. Kiddoo to Howard, Aug. 8, 1866, NA.
16 J. B. Kiddoo to Howard, June 26, 1866, NA.
17 R. K. Scott to Howard, Dec. 18, 1866, NA.
18 E. O. C. Ord to Howard, Feb. 19, 1867, NA.
19 N. A. Miles to Howard, Dec. 4, 1867, NA.

tion to know at first hand the true conditions which prevailed in the South.

The agent at Lunenburg Court House in Virginia addressed a letter to the Bureau authorities in Richmond in April, 1866, telling of an increase in outrages on Negroes. There was no assurance that the civil courts would aid in punishing the guilty parties and he concluded by saying, "Unless I have power given to give these poor people protection, self respect will compel me to resign."[20]

From Greenville Court House, South Carolina, the Bureau agent, Major A. E. Niles, told of the unfavorable conditions existing in his district. "Toward the Government," Niles wrote, "the feeling is very unfriendly, with no prospect of a change for the better. . . . Toward the Freedmen, there is much bad feeling, and but for the presence of one small garrison I can hardly see how he would manage to live. The men that understand the Freedmen to have, or that they are entitled to any more rights than a horse are exceptions to the general rule."[21]

In his regular report in June, 1867, Lieutenant J. C. De Gress, Bureau agent in New Orleans, complained that civil officials were too prejudiced to grant the freedmen equal justice. ". . . whenever they can grind a poor Black man down, they do it to gain popularity, 'as it is nothing but a cursed nigger,' (using their own language)."[22]

Examples such as these could be continued indefinitely. Surely the agents on the local level were aware of a tendency on the part of white southerners to deal unjustly with the freedmen.[23]

Violence has been common to the South throughout its history.[24] Is it any wonder that violence characterized the Reconstruction years? Why should historians assume that stories of violence to Negroes were either fabricated or exaggerated when everyone knows what has been happening to Negroes in the South ever since Negroes first were there?[25] It would have been singularly amazing had there not been an excessive amount of murders (the word lynching seems to belong to a later period) and other atrocities committed against Negroes in the South during the first years after liberation. And what is the evidence? The evidence is that murder and atrocity were as common as one would expect them to be.

In the atmosphere of hostility toward freedmen reported by the assistant commissioners and other agents of the Freedmen's Bureau and described above, specific acts of violence occurred far more frequently than has been generally conceded by the historians of this period. And the extent of this violence made interference by the national government excusable if not justified; in fact interference became obligatory in the light of the responsibility of the national authority toward those whom it had so recently liberated.

In response to an order from Commissioner Howard the various assistant commissioners reported the instances of outrages and murders committed against Negroes in the various Southern states.[25a] From these reports which came in during October and November, 1866, it is pos-

---

[20] Lt. J. Arnold Yeckley to Capt. James A. Bates, April 19, 1866, NA.

[21] A. E. Niles to Major H. W. Smith, May 2, 1866, NA.

[22] Report of Lt. J. C. De Gress, June 24, 1867, NA.

[23] Not just officials of the Freedmen's Bureau but civilians from the North also reported on the unhappy lot of the Negro in the South. One of these, owner of a plantation near Augusta, Georgia, wrote to Secretary of War E. M. Stanton, "The white people about here openly declare that

when the Bureau is removed, they will show the Yankees how the Negro should be treated. . . . If the Bureau continues to protect them all will be well, but if it is removed, I tremble for the consequences." C. Stearns to Stanton, Aug. 30, 1866, NA.

[24] See, e.g., John H. Franklin, *The Militant South* (Cambridge, Mass., 1956); C. Vann Woodward, *Origins of the New South* ([Baton Rouge], 1951), pp. 158–60.

[25] See, e.g., Otis A. Singletary, *Negro Militia and Reconstruction* (Austin, Texas, 1957), pp. 3–6.

[25a] A. P. Ketchum to Assistant Commissioners, Sept. 24, 1866, NA.

sible to gain some idea of the extent of the problem.

Most of these reports were specific rather than general, naming names, time, and place. In some instances the reports did make general charges without details and it is possible that some were fabrications, as is so frequently charged. Yet even these reports came from responsible army officers of high rank and ought not to be airily dismissed. An example of this type of report would be that of Brigadier General John R. Lewis, assistant commissioner for Tennessee, who in October, 1866, reported the murder of 33 freedmen by white persons since April, 1865. It was Lewis' belief that many more unreported murders had occurred.[26]

The assistant commissioners for Arkansas and South Carolina sent in lists of 29 and 24 murders respectively.[27] Here in most instances are names, dates, and places.[28]

General Joseph B. Kiddoo in Texas not only made an overall report but he also enclosed excerpts from the reports of his subordinates in the various parts of the state who had firsthand acquaintance with the individual murders. There is a genuine frankness about these that makes it highly unlikely that these outrages were dreamed up for any ulterior purpose. One extract is from a letter written by the Bureau agent in Victoria, Victoria County, on May 30, 1866. "Again it is my painful duty," wrote the agent, "to report the wilful murder of a freedman, Martin Cromwell, formerly a slave of Mr. Alex. Cromwell, and a man over 50 years of age, was wantonly shot, and killed by Alex. Cromwell Jr. a young man of about 21 yrs on Sunday evening the 27th inst. on the plantation of his father." In the list of some 70 other cases are with few exceptions the name of the murdered

person, the name of the murderer (though some have simply "unknown" in this column), the date, and remarks. Some of the remarks are enlightening as, for example, "Killed because he did not take off his hat to Murphy," or "shot him as he was passing in the street to 'see him kick' as Bullock remarked."[29]

One of the most conservative assistant commissioners was General Jefferson C. Davis whose views frequently were at variance with those of the Bureau. Davis' list of murders should be viewed by the skeptical, then, as being somewhat more authentic than those of some of the other, more radical, assistant commissioners. Davis' territory was Kentucky, a particularly troublesome state. He named 19 freedmen who had been killed, giving exact dates and the names of the counties where the crimes had been committed. In addition, he said that 233 freedmen had been badly maltreated and in none of these cases of outrage had any action toward punishing the offenders been reported by the state civil authorities.[30]

Major General Joseph A. Mower, Sheridan's successor in Louisiana, in March, 1867, sent in a very complete report on outrages in that state from the beginning of the Bureau until February 20, 1867. He gave a detailed account of 70 murders of freedmen by whites and stated that the number might have been twice that. He also told of 210 cases of whipping, beating, and stabbing and noted that in almost every instance the persons guilty of these offenses had not been apprehended. Mower's report is 30 pages long and much of it is detailed information concerning the individual murders. One, for instance, tells of the murder of Abraham Allen by Jules Guidry, constable of Donaldsonville, Louisiana. The grand jury several months later failed to find a true bill against Guidry. Another case was that of Martin Day at Lake Providence on May 27, 1866. Day, it seems,

---

[26] J. R. Lewis to Howard, Oct. 3, 1866, NA.
[27] R. K. Scott's list from South Carolina covered only the period since he took office, i.e., from January, 1866.
[28] J. W. Sprague to Howard, Oct. 1, 1866, NA; R. K. Scott to Howard, Oct. 5, 1866, NA.

[29] J. B. Kiddoo to Howard, Oct. 25, 1866, NA.
[30] J. C. Davis to Howard, Nov. 27, 1866, NA.

answered a white boy "quickly," and was knocked down by a white man by the name of Kingsley. The Bureau agent told how the freedman was "taken thro' the town and across the Levee, and there stripped and terribly beaten, with raw-hides by Kingsley, and some 6 or 8 other men, who put a rope around his neck, nearly choked him, jumped upon him etc." The civil authorities, according to the agent, "took no notice of the affair."[31]

The Bureau agent in Atlanta, Georgia, reported to his immediate superior, Brigadier General Davis Tillson, the murder of a colored soldier on the very day it occurred. He named the murderer, P. Perry, who escaped. "Citizens with whom I have talked," wrote the agent, "seem to justify Berry [sic] in his cowardly act, and with but little reason, other than the soldier was a 'd——d nigger.' "[32]

These examples are only a small fraction of the total to be found in the records of the Freedmen's Bureau. They extend over a considerable span of years and seem to demonstrate beyond a reasonable doubt a high degree of lawlessness in almost all sections of the South. That some of the reports were exaggerated or fabricated does not alter the basic fact: that the freedmen were grossly mistreated by Southern whites during the Reconstruction era. The record of lynchings and other forms of brutality toward the Negro which has disgraced the South in the years since Reconstruction rather puts the burden of proof upon those who question the authenticity of the reports of outrages.

Now it would be quite inaccurate to convey the idea of total lawlessness in the South during the Reconstruction. There is abundant evidence that in some places at some times the treatment of freedmen was at least nonviolent. Colonel T. W. Osborn, assistant commissioner for Florida, stated in November, 1865, that cases of violence

toward freedmen were of "rare occurrence."[33] The assistant commissioner in Mississippi, Colonel Samuel Thomas, admitted that without the Bureau there would be no hesitancy on the part of the white people to oppress and defraud the freedmen but that the "foolish stories of terrible outrages [that] find their way to the press of the North . . . are nearly always greatly exaggerated or entirely without foundation."[34]

That same month General Ord in Arkansas reported "a better feeling prevailing in all the richest cotton counties, to satisfy and protect freedmen . . ."[35] and soon after General Lewis remarked that there was a general disposition to do what was just by the freedmen in his state of Tennessee.[36]

Obviously the treatment of freedmen varied considerably as is borne out by an inspection report of General Eliphalet Whittlesey, one-time assistant commissioner and, at the time of the report, assistant adjutant general of the Bureau. Whittlesey toured Louisiana and Arkansas early in 1867 and observed that treatment of freedmen was spotty. This would, he said, account for the conflicting stories appearing in the Northern press. Yet he passed along to General Howard reports of numerous outrages against freedmen, their inability to gain justice, their being cheated of wages, and the breaking up of Negro schools. Many agents told Whittlesey that they could not carry out their duties without troops.[37]

Over two years later, Howard, in his annual report to the Secretary of War, admitted that atrocity reports seemed to convey the impression that every white person in the South was engaged in a deliberate policy of extermination of the freedmen.

---

[31] Joseph A. Mower to Brig. Gen. Samuel Thomas, March 9, 1867, NA.
[32] Lt. Col. George Curkendall to Davis Tillson, Dec. 26, 1865, NA.

[33] Col. Thomas W. Osborn to Howard, Nov. 1, 1865, NA.
[34] Col. Samuel Thomas to Howard, April 12, 1866, NA.
[35] E. O. C. Ord to Howard, Nov. 7, 1866, NA.
[36] J. R. Lewis to Howard, Dec. 17, 1866, NA.
[37] Bvt. Brig. Gen. E. Whittlesey to Howard, Feb. 25, 1867, NA.

But, he went on to say, "careful investigation has proved that the worst outrages were generally committed by small bands of lawless men, organized under various names, whose principal objects were robbery and plunder. There was no civil government with strength enough to arrest them, and they overawed and held in terror the more quiet citizens who were disposed to treat the freedmen with fairness and humanity." It was the bureau, according to Howard, together with the federal troops in the South which gave the freedmen, "these victims of cruelty and wrong," some means of protection. "And the evils remedied have probably been far less than the evils prevented. No one can tell what scenes of violence and strife and insurrection the whole South might have presented without the presence of this agency of the government to preserve order and to enforce justice."[38]

Whittlesey's and Howard's admissions serve to correct the false impression which might be conveyed by a simple catalog of atrocity reports turned in by the Bureau assistant commissioners and agents, and of accounts of race riots in Memphis and other Southern towns reported in the Northern press; they do not, on the other hand, wipe out the record of those reports. The years of Reconstruction in the South were filled with an unusual amount of atrocities, deprivations of rights, and other forms of illegal treatment of Negroes so much so that the federal government, which had assumed a moral responsibility in its emancipation measures to do more than merely liberate the slaves, had little choice but to intervene. This it did do in successive acts creating and then continuing the Freedmen's Bureau, in the Civil Rights Act, the Fourteenth and Fifteenth Amendments, the Reconstruction Acts, and finally, the Ku Klux Klan Acts of 1870 and 1871. The fate of the freedmen was a decisive factor in the adoption of all this legislation

and of the two amendments.[39] The contention of President Johnson and of the Southern whites that the Negro did not need any assistance from the federal government flew in the face of the obvious fact that he was receiving anything but equal, fair, and humane treatment. The policy of intervention, unfortunately, led up a blind alley; there was no way out except to abandon the policy, for it could not be continued indefinitely. Instead of the situation which the policy was supposed to produce—a tranquillity and a harmonious relationship between the races—there resulted an even greater determination on the part of the Southern whites to end all semblance of federal control, all vestiges of carpetbag rule, and any attempt to allow the Negro civil and political equality. That this would be the result might have been anticipated before any intervention began but even if it had been, the obligation to intervene would still have been there.

The failure of intervention meant abandonment of the policy of the Grant administration, and this in turn meant abandonment of the Negro. In the last years of the nineteenth century the growing number of lynchings proved what a hostile white population could do to the Negro when left alone to deal with him as it pleased.[40] In the light of these events and those which have continued to take place in ensuing years, is it being credulous to believe the reports of the assistant commissioners and agents of the Freedmen's Bureau in the first years of transition from slavery to freedom that an unreasonable hostility existed in the South toward the freedmen which made necessary a policy of intervention and control? The solid evidence of these reports seems to lead to but one answer.

_____

[38] Report of Gen. O. O. Howard, Oct. 20, 1869, NA.

[39] See, e.g., Eric L. McKitrick, *Andrew Johnson and Reconstruction* (Chicago, 1960), p. 478.

[40] More than 2,500 lynchings occurred in the last 16 years of the nineteenth century, mostly of Negroes, and mostly in the South. John H. Franklin, *From Slavery to Freedom* (N.Y., 1947), p. 431.

The Army as a Force in Reconstruction*

HAROLD M. HYMAN

Seventy years ago William A. Dunning saw the involvement of Ulysses Grant and other army officers in the political developments that resulted in Andrew Johnson's impeachment as a ". . . mere accidental feature of the general issue . . . throwing over the situation a sort of martial glamour."[1] Accepting this premise without questioning its validity, historians have understated if not altogether ignored the army's role, desires, and needs during the first three years after Appomattox. Studies of the Reconstruction period have stressed political and economic approaches to the impeachment theme, and in the process some writers have created a sentimental and incorrect image of Johnson as a vigorous defender of constitutional rights and presidential prerogatives.[2]

A growing interest in civil-military relations has recently led some investigators into fresh pathways. Lloyd Lewis, for example, while on the trail of Grant's actions during the confused months after Lee surrendered, had by 1947 come to the tentative conclusion that ". . . Grant . . . and the [other] Generals were convinced that Andrew Johnson was going so fast in readmitting 'Rebels' to power, that the nation was endangered." The "modern" view, Lewis continued in a private letter, "that Johnson was merely restoring Lincoln's merciful [Reconstruction] policy and that was all there was to it overlooks a hell of a lot of unreconstructed things the old Bourbons . . . were doing at the time."[3]

Untimely death cut short Lewis' work on Grant in which this judgment might have appeared as a firm conclusion. Lewis was on the right track. The period from early 1865 through 1867 still requires reexamination in order to ascertain what Grant and other generals felt and did about events, and to clarify the ultimately conflicting purposes and policies of Presi-

---

* Harold M. Hyman, "Johnson, Stanton and Grant: A Reconsideration of the Army's Role in the Events Leading to Impeachment," *American Historical Review*, Vol. 66 (1960), pp. 85–100. Mr. Hyman, associate professor at the University of California, Los Angeles, and author of *To Try Men's Souls: Loyalty Tests in American History* (Berkeley, Calif., 1959), read portions of this article as a paper at the 1959 meeting of the Pacific Coast Branch, American Historical Association.

[1] William A. Dunning, "The Impeachment and Trial of President Johnson," American Historical Association, *Papers* (5 vols.; New York, 1886–91), IV, 479–80.

[2] Bernard A. Weisberger, "The Dark and Bloody Ground of Reconstruction Historiography," *Journal of Southern History*, XXV (November, 1959), 427–47, and Thomas J. Pressly, *Americans Interpret Their Civil War* (Princeton, N.J., 1954), 302–33, offer useful surveys of extant bibliography. The major studies of Johnson are devoted to sustaining his conduct; see George F.

Milton, *The Age of Hate: Andrew Johnson and the Radicals* (New York, 1930), Lloyd P. Stryker, *Andrew Johnson: A Study in Courage* (New York, 1929), and Claude G. Bowers, *The Tragic Era: The Revolution after Lincoln* (Boston, 1929). Eric L. McKitrick, *Andrew Johnson and Reconstruction* (Chicago, 1960), was unfortunately not available during the preparation of this article. It offers a valuable and provocative revision of its subject's role, in essential harmony with the theme of this article, but McKitrick does not include consideration of the military institution.

[3] *Letters from Lloyd Lewis* (Boston, 1950), 52.

dent Johnson and his holdover war secretary, Edwin M. Stanton, the army's civilian overlords. When viewed from the perspective of the professional army officer of this time, these controversial personalities and complex problems gain new illumination.

With the surrender of the last real forces, the hurriedly reorganized regulars of the United States Army faced four primary responsibilities. In order to meet them, Stanton and Grant grouped the troops into what in effect were two separate "armies." The first "army" was assigned to relatively traditional duties. It patrolled the Mexican border to impress the French adventurers at the Halls of Montezuma, sought to suppress the Indian tribesmen who had grown bold from wartime incitements, and in smaller detachments garrisoned posts along the unquiet Canadian border and performed training and ceremonial chores in eastern cities. This "army" never became a political issue. Its commanders remained within the traditional pattern of civilian direction from the White House and War Department; Congress was content to let Johnson control it.[4]

In defeated Dixie, however, the warborn military galaxy faced a task unique in American history—the military government of large numbers of their countrymen after hostilities had ceased. Here the second "army" came into being. Its commanders had at hand only the lessons in occupation administration learned since 1861 to guide them. No one in the early months of 1865 knew if these precedents were adequate for peacetime. A new and untried President was in the White House. Marking time until Johnson indicated what he wished the army to do in the South, Stanton and Grant sanctioned the police

and welfare activities which local commanders undertook, and devoted their energies to solving demobilization and reorganization problems.

In April, 1865, Stanton, Grant, and the senior army officers were prepared to offer Johnson the same cordial support that they had tendered to Lincoln.[5] They assumed that Johnson would give the army the same firm executive backing that Lincoln had done. In the soldiers' terms, this meant that the new President would use the troops in the South to make worthwhile the wartime sacrifices of a hundred thousand Billy Yanks, and that he would employ the powers of his office to protect military personnel who were performing duties to which he had assigned them. Three years later Congress impeached Johnson for attempting to exercise commander in chief powers over the second "army," and in this the legislators had the soldiers' cordial acquiescence. By early 1868 the United States Army units on southern occupation duty were under Congress' command rather than the President's. It had become a separate "army" in law as well as in fact.

Divorce between the White House and the War Department was an improbable eventuality when Johnson announced his Reconstruction and pardon program for the South in May, 1865. The President was confident that he was carrying out the spirit of Lincoln's plans, and, to be sure,

---

[4] Sensing this, William Tecumseh Sherman, who usually tried to stay clear of the political jungle, saw to it that he was assigned to western duties, and except for intervals when he dabbled in the Grant-Stanton-Johnson imbroglio, Sherman escaped serious involvement in the army crisis. See Lloyd Lewis, *Sherman: Fighting Prophet* (New York, 1958), 581–94.

[5] On army reorganization, see Secretary of War, *Annual Report, 1865* (Washington, D.C., 1866); *Army and Navy Journal* (May 13, 1865), 600. Wartime precedents for occupation of the South are discussed in A. H. Carpenter, "Military Government of Southern Territory, 1861–1865," *Annual Report, American Historical Association, 1900* (2 vols.; Washington, D.C., 1901), I, 465–98, and Wilton P. Moore, "The Provost Marshal Goes to War," *Civil War History*, V (March, 1959), 62–71. The tendency of Stanton and the army commanders to support Johnson is evident in "Original Letters of General Grant," *Colorado Magazine*, XIV (March, 1937), 65; Charles A. Dana to James S. Pike, May 10, 1865, Calais Free Library; and the numerous memoranda in the Stanton MSS, Manuscript Division, Library of Congress, detailing the war secretary's accord with the new President.

his pronouncements concerning the former rebel states had the ring of his predecessor's. Like Lincoln, Johnson based his Reconstruction proclamation on a broad view of executive power, adequate to employ the army to build new and ostensibly loyal state governments in the South. To this end and for their own protection, the soldiers were to use martial law to expedite the process. True, Johnson ignored the tendency Lincoln had exhibited shortly before the war ended for including some substantial portion of southern Negroes in the electorates of the new states. But the significance of this omission was not immediately apparent.

It soon became obvious, however, to most of the officers on southern duty and to Stanton and Grant who read their reports that fundamental differences existed between the Reconstruction plans of the two Presidents. Lincoln had used the December, 1863, proclamation primarily as a war weapon to seduce southern whites away from their allegiance to the Confederacy. Thus conceived and successfully employed by the Union army, Lincoln's plan and his exercise of presidential powers sustained the northern soldier. As Johnson's program developed through 1865, Union officers became convinced that it strengthened only former rebels and returned to positions of official power in the South men who had brought the nation to civil war, but who had since received Johnson's pardons for their rebellious pasts. General Philip Sheridan was later to term Johnson's southern policy "a broad macadamized road for perjury to travel on," by which unrepentant southern whites were encouraged to harass federal soldiers and Unionists, and through vicious legalisms to escape punishment for these transgressions.[6]

Consider one aspect of Reconstruction

in 1865 that outraged most soldiers. In southern state courts reborn under Johnson's auspices and through the efforts of the army, former rebels initiated scores of suits against federal military personnel. These claimants asked damages for soldiers' actions made under martial law during and after the war. Army officers on southern duty confessed to the War Department that they were now fearful of exercising their assigned functions, for if these suits succeeded, they would be ruined. In these state courts judges, jurors, and claimants were white men, and almost all were former rebels. What soldier or white or Negro Unionist, officers inquired, could expect fair hearings from such assemblages?

Then, late in 1865, Stanton was sued for damages arising from the wartime arrest of a disloyal northern civilian, Joseph E. Maddox. If Maddox won against the mighty Mars, then similar verdicts would inevitably follow against hundreds of lesser officers.

Maddox's counsel, Caleb Cushing, soon realized that he was involved in something more than a damage claim. Cushing learned that the men who were now the President's chief advisers, the Blair trio (Francis P., Sr., Jr., and Montgomery) and Manton Marble of the New York *World,* had inspired Maddox to sue in order to break Stanton. Marble and the Blairs also wanted to frighten off army officers in the South from enforcing property confiscation and Freedmen's Bureau legislation. Perhaps with Cushing's connivance, Grant and Stanton learned what was afoot. Neither the war secretary nor the commanding general assumed that the President was privy to the plot. But they were outraged that men close to the White House should involve the Army in this combination of personal vendetta and policy struggle. They were bitter that they could not convince Johnson to order the southern state courts to hold off the many damage suits pending against military personnel. The realization sank home at the War Department that the White House was not

<hr />

[6] Harold M. Hyman, *To Try Men's Souls: Loyalty Tests in American History* (Berkeley, Calif., 1959), 139–218; Jonathan T. Dorris, *Pardon and Amnesty under Lincoln and Johnson* (Chapel Hill, N.C., 1953), chap. viii; Fawn M. Brodie, "A Lincoln Who Never Was," *Reporter,* XX (June 25, 1959), 25–27.

going to exert itself to protect soldiers from the legal consequences of wartime actions or postwar activities in the South. If something was to be done, army headquarters would have to do it.

Grant arranged a compromise with Cushing so that Maddox dropped the suit against Stanton. Moving to protect Army personnel at least so far as suits originating in the South were concerned, Grant and Stanton took advantage of the fact that Johnson's Reconstruction proclamations sanctioned the use of martial law in the former Confederacy. On January 3, 1866, Grant issued General Order 3 to all southern commands. It was designed "To protect loyal persons against improper civil suits and penalties in the late rebellious States." By its terms, soldiers and civilians, including Negroes, who asserted that justice was unobtainable in southern state courts could transfer any suits pending against them to the Freedmen's Bureau paramilitary tribunals or to federal civil courts. In the former, martial law prevailed. In the latter, Congress had prescribed that all federal court personnel, jurors, attorneys, and claimants, had to swear an ironclad oath of past loyalty to the Union.

As a solution to the damage suit problem, General Order 3 was satisfactory if the situation remained static. But a perverse genius for instability seemed to afflict the leading actors and institutions on the political stage. After a nine-year abstention from significant policy pronouncements, the United States Supreme Court introduced a new and unsettling element.

In April, 1866, the Court issued a preliminary judgment in the Milligan case. This involved the Army's right to employ martial law in noncombat areas. Although the full opinion in this case was not to be issued until the Court's forthcoming December term, it was obvious in April that the jurists did not look kindly upon martial law's being employed anywhere except in the vicinity of battle. Would the Court in December bring forth a decision condemning all martial law in the postwar South? As the War Depart-

ment saw the situation, the White House and the Supreme Court seemed determined to hamstring the Army.

Stanton and Grant turned toward Congress in hope that the Army might find friends on Capitol Hill. They knew that General Order 3 dealt only with damage suits from the South, but not with those like Maddox's claim, lodged by northern residents over whom the Army now claimed no control. The Secretary and the general, therefore, pressured friendly congressmen to amend the 1863 Habeas Corpus Act to provide greater protection for officers who had acted under its provisions anywhere in the nation during the war. Republicans in Congress cooperated.[7] The Army was finding its bulwark in Congress, not in the President.

This explains why Stanton and Grant chose to support the Freedmen's Bureau court system in its jurisdictional feud with the provost courts of the army field commands, a carry-over from war organization. Congress had given the Freedmen's Bureau special legislative support lacking in the provost units, which operated only on the wartime executive authority now questioned at the White House and in the Supreme Court as well as in lower federal courts.

But the War Department was still only disturbed, not wrenched away from support of the President. When Congress had convened in December, 1865, Stanton and Grant cooperated with Johnson in suppressing the unsavory Smith-Brady report, which indicated that the state governments set up by Lincoln in the Mississippi Valley were centers of vast corruption rather than of renascent Unionism. Johnson wanted the report suppressed because he believed that he was following Lincoln's policies and did not want his own state creations in the South

---

[7] Brief and correspondence on *Maddox* v. *Stanton* in Caleb Cushing Papers, Manuscript Division, Library of Congress. For General Order 3, see Adjutant General's Office, *Index of General Orders, 1866* (Washington, D.C., 1867), and *Army and Navy Journal* (June 16, 1866), 687. Details on the Milligan suit are in *The Milligan Case*, ed. Samuel Klaus (New York, 1929), 43–47.

tarred by the Smith-Brady brush. Grant wanted it hushed up because the report indicated that hundreds of Army officers were involved in the sordid peculations discovered in Louisiana, Arkansas, and in parts of Missouri.[8] But it is the fact of the cooperation more than the reasons for it which is significant here.

The Republicans of Congress, like the Army officer corps, were not under Radical control in the early months of 1866, but they clearly distrusted Johnson's accomplishments in state making in the South. Congress prevented the "Confederate brigadiers"— the delegates-elect from the former rebel states—from taking seats at the national legislature, and the President and Congress commenced their joust for power. Meanwhile the evidence of southerners' attacks on northern test oath requirements, the inequities of the Black Codes, and the tragic race riot at Memphis gave added weight to Radical arguments that the South was unrepentant and untrustworthy.

As the debate raged, Johnson proved rigid and doctrinaire in his convictions concerning federal-state relations and the power and influence he had at hand to wield. He deceived himself into thinking that he was emulating Lincoln not only in the form of Reconstruction policy but also in the exercise of executive leadership. He failed to see that Lincoln had never sought perfection, but only realizable goals, had never been willing to battle Congress but instead compromised with or circumvented its leaders, and had never dared lose the support of the Union soldiers.

To be sure the war was now over, and the last mass armies were replaced by volunteer professionals. But that, to many Republican legislators and apolitical generals,

was the point. It was well enough for Lincoln to have proclaimed emancipation and Reconstruction policies on the basis of war powers, but he had always agreed that these were extraordinary wartime acts, subject to postwar judicial or legislative amendment, and even during the war Congress had protested against Lincoln's assumptions of leadership. Now Johnson insisted that the war was finished, and that no one, therefore, could legitimately limit the revived southern states. Yet he simultaneously claimed a monopoly on pardoning and state-making power for the executive on which Congress might not infringe. He wanted presidential power and at the same time professed a doctrine of weakness for the entire national government, used the Army to get the South on its feet, but refused soldiers the right to shackle the spurred boots of the former rebels so that they might not kick out again. This, at least, was the way many saw the situation.[9]

As if to prove the accuracy of this contention, Johnson on April 2, 1866, almost coincident with the preliminary Milligan decision, proclaimed that the rebellion was ended everywhere and that the southern states were restored to the Union. Army headquarters in Washington soon learned of the intense confusion into which military commanders in the South were cast by this statement and by the Court's pronouncement. Was martial law operating? Did the Freedmen's Bureau, under Congress' authority rather than the President's, now lose its power to hold special military tribunals if civil courts failed to provide justice? Did Army personnel, insulted and assaulted by jubilant southern whites, now become defenseless?

A week later, on April 9, Grant sent out a confidential circular to military commanders stationed in the former Confederacy. He cautioned them to exercise discreet restraint

[8] The intra-army court dispute is best described in "Final Reports of Provost Marshals," MSS, Army Commands, Record Group 98, National Archives. Smith-Brady Commission Report and evidence, MSS, Record Group 94, *ibid.*, largely unexploited, offer rich rewards to investigators. See, too, *Investigations at New Orleans* (*House Executive Document*, 39th Cong., 1st sess., No. 96.).

[9] These attitudes are best described in John L. Motley, *Four Questions for the People* (Boston, 1868), 31–32, and Laurence Oliphant, *On the Present State of Political Parties in America* (London, 1866), 9, 12–13.

in dealing with the "reconstructed" state governments and with southern civilians. But he also authorized them to employ martial law whenever they felt it necessary, despite Johnson's clear statement that peace was at hand and in defiance of the Court's inference that martial law was inapplicable in a peacetime situation. In addition, Grant advised his subordinates that the Freedmen's Bureau was exempt from the President's jurisdiction, although it was part of the Army, for the general concluded that the Bureau was Congress' creation. Where southern civil authorities failed to provide or obstructed justice to soldiers or to southern Unionists, the Army might still step in.

Clearly Grant was moving toward a sharp break in tradition so far as his view of civil-military relationships was concerned. Events had pushed him and Stanton so far by the spring of 1866 that the two men were willing to use their immense prestige and popularity within the Army and with the public to counter what they felt to be error on Johnson's part. They were beginning to align the Army with Congress because they felt that the President was leaving the soldiers helplessly adrift.

Neither Grant nor Stanton, however, desired an outright clash with Johnson. Both men still hoped to win him to their views, which at this point approximated those of moderate Republican congressmen. Thus, on May 1, Grant issued through normal Army channels General Order 26, specifying compliance with Johnson's April peace proclamation. The general knew that his earlier secret circular had forewarned army commanders to ignore the President's peace policy if necessary. They could be confident that Grant would block any retaliation from the White House.[10]

More evidence accumulated, meanwhile, of outrages in the South directed against soldiers and Negroes. Feeling that they had acted correctly in checking the President's policy, Stanton and Grant were convinced that the Army still had work to do in Dixie. They now shared the view of most army commanders assigned to southern stations that former rebels were incapable of true reformation. Grant went a step further to strengthen his subordinates' positions. On July 6 he issued General Order 44, supplementing General Order 3 of the past January. The July order empowered all army commanders in the South down to the post or company level to arrest civilians charged with crimes against federal civil or military personnel, or against "inhabitants of the United States, regardless of color, in cases where the civil authorities have failed, neglected, or are unable to arrest and bring such parties to trial." Those arrested were to stay in confinement "until such time as a proper judicial tribunal may be ready and willing to try them."

This curious document neither imposed martial law nor obeyed the President's clear statement of April that civil authority must take precedence over military power in the South. In substance, it openly informed Johnson, as many persons including Jonathan Worth of North Carolina complained to him, that Stanton, Grant, and most commanders of the Army disagreed with his position and thought the April peace proclamation hasty, ill advised, unfair to military personnel, and an unreal estimate of southern conditions. [11]

Later that month the President prepared to retaliate by reading a proclamation not only that the rebellion had ended but spelling out that martial law was inoperative everywhere in the country. Thus encouraged, the "reconstructed" governor of Virginia on July 21 informed Stanton that he was reactivating the state militia and requested surplus army weapons for the members, all of whom, Grant learned, were whites, and most of whom were former

[10] *A Compilation of the Messages and Papers of the Presidents, 1789–1902,* ed. James D. Richardson (10 vols.; New York, 1903), VI, 429–32; the Apr. 9 circular is in Box 102, Record Group 108, National Archives; and General Order 26 in Adjutant General's Office, *General Orders, 1866* (Washington, D.C., 1867).

[11] *Ibid.*; Jonathan Worth to Stanton, July 30, 1866, Secretary of War Correspondence File, Box 317, Record Group 107, National Archives.

rebels and holders of the President's pardons. Informed of this by Grant, Johnson refused to cancel the governor's request. To Grant this seemed equivalent to putting arms back in the hands of men still capable of using them against the victors, and the general delayed in complying.[12]

No open rupture yet existed between the White House and the Army, but the President's southern policy was forcing individual Army officials to make choices concerning their political allegiance. Stanton, Grant, Sheridan, Daniel Sickles, John Pope, M. C. Meigs, and Edward Ord were clearly in sympathy with the Republicans of Congress; William Tecumseh Sherman and Winfield Scott favored Johnson; E. D. Townsend remained determinedly neutral. But to attach traditional political party labels to these officers seems irrelevant and inaccurate. To be sure, Congress' supporters in the Army were becoming "radicals" in the sense that they had come to believe that Negro suffrage must be imposed upon the South as the only means to insure the subordination of the old secessionist class. If Congress was willing to see to it that Negroes voted, then these men were going to favor Congress.

The New Orleans riot seemed to prove the acuity of the "radical" officers' analysis. Soon after that event, General Pope made a speech after first securing Stanton's and Grant's approval for its text. He argued that if the "military power is suspended" in the South, "at once the old political & personal influences will resume their activity," and the Copperheads of the North and the Bourbons of the South would seek again to sunder the Republic. It may be, of course, that Pope was merely spouting Republican propaganda. Yet the man was no politician, and he was risking his professional career by assuming his public position. In openly defying the President's orders, Grant was chancing the political laurels he secretly

coveted, and Stanton, who wanted more than all else to get out of politics, was only making it impossible for himself to quit the War Department. These men wanted Pope's words to be clarion calls of warning, to alert a somnolent North to what they feared was a clear and present danger. Aging General Ethan Allen Hitchcock wondered, "Have we run our race as a Republic? I hope not —but fear it. Grant and Stanton were determined to use military influence to prevent the civilian President from keeping the nation on a disastrous course.[13]

Realizing that so long as Stanton and Grant were working together the Army in the South was out of his control, Johnson decided to split the team, replace Grant with a more cooperative commanding general, and then to oust Stanton in turn. He brought the nation's third most popular man, General Sherman, to Washington to be at hand offered Grant a trumped-up diplomatic assignment to Mexico, intending then to put Sherman in first as commanding general, and once Grant was away to slip either him or Montgomery Blair in as Secretary of War in place of Stanton. But Grant refused to play, Sherman would not take issue with his beloved commander, and the scheme foundered.[14]

---

[12] The proclamation was issued Aug. 20, 1866; *Messages and Papers of the Presidents*, ed. Richardson, VI, 434–38; Grant to Stanton, July 21, 1866, Headquarters of the Army, Box 97, Record Group 108, National Archives.

[13] Pope to Grant, July 24, 1867, including pamphlet copy of Pope's 1866 speech initialed by Stanton and Grant, in Secretary of War Correspondence File, Box 327, Record Group 107, National Archives. Hitchcock's comment is on the margin of an article on Johnson in the *Atlantic Monthly*, in the Hitchcock Papers, Manuscript Division, Library of Congress.

[14] William B. Hesseltine, *Ulysses S. Grant, Politician* (New York, 1935), 77–79; Stanton to W. P. Fessenden, Oct. 25, 1866, Huntington Library. Including Stanton as a popular figure may surprise some, but see a contemporary attestation to Stanton's general prominence in *Miscellaneous Writings of the Late Honorable Joseph P. Bradley*, ed. Charles Bradley (Newark, N.J., 1901), 57. Such evidence is strikingly different from recent commentaries on Stanton in Otto Eisenschiml, *Why Was Lincoln Murdered?* (Boston, 1937), and Theodore Roscoe, *The Web of Conspiracy* (Englewood Cliffs, N.J., 1959), which should be measured against James G. Randall's plea for a realistic appraisal of Stanton, in "Civil War Restudied," *Journal of Southern History*, VI (November, 1940), 455–56.

Deciding to exploit Grant at home in the 1866 congressional elections if he could not employ him abroad, Johnson swung around the circle with the disgusted general in tow. The results of that "critical" election gave the Republicans a thumping victory and a working majority in Congress adequate to override any veto. Now the question was: Would Johnson acquiesce in the verdict of the ballot boxes? "Things have changed here somewhat since the last election," Grant advised in a confidential note to his protégé, General Phil Sheridan, but he could not predict the nature of the change.

Johnson had no intention of signaling surrender by suggesting that the southern states ratify the pending Fourteenth Amendment. His secretary, Colonel William G. Moore, realized that the President was convinced that the white men of the South would be submerged under a sable sea if the freedmen exercised the ballot. This concern merged with Johnson's views of the nature of the federal system and the purposes of the Civil War, and it combined with his combative personality to help create the critical situation in which the nation found itself. "He seemed never to be happy unless he had some one to strike at or to denounce," recalled Hugh McCulloch, Johnson's personal friend, treasury secretary, and political supporter. As 1866 closed, Andrew Johnson should have been a very happy man.[15]

Somehow Johnson missed the significance of the 1866 election results, for they were barely counted when he "suggested" to Grant, bypassing Stanton completely, that the Army issue 10,000 tons of arms to the revived Virginia state militia. Grant replied properly through Stanton's office that "I would not recommend the issue of arms for the use of the militia of any of the states lately in rebellion in advance of their full

restoration and the admission of their representatives by Congress."[16]

The Republicans, now dominating Congress, prepared Reconstruction legislation for the South which included much of what the Army had wanted since Appomattox: the continued use of martial law, legal protection for army personnel, and the disfranchisement of most former rebels. Then in the first weeks of 1867, the Supreme Court threw three bombshells into the legislators' works. In the Milligan, Garland, and Cummings decisions, the jurists denounced military trials of civilians and federal and state test oath laws as unconstitutional excesses. This at least was the way excited and indignant Republican spokesmen portrayed the decisions, while Democrats lauded them as noble defenses of civil liberties and individual rights.[17] President Johnson was naturally delighted that his constitutional views now had had judicial support. To the Army, however, the Court's pronouncements spelled disaster, and to Radical Republican congressmen, they were reactionary obstructions that must be overcome or ignored.

Now Stanton and Grant leaped fully over the wall into the Radical camp, Stanton openly and Grant still secretly. The two men arranged for Congress to provide for the Army's needs. By the military appropriations bill of 1867, Grant was made autonomous of the President so far as the location of his headquarters was concerned and the funnel through which Johnson had to transmit orders to subordinate army

---

15 Grant to Sheridan, Nov. 15, 1866, Sheridan Papers, Manuscript Division, Library of Congress; Hugh McCulloch, *Addresses, Speeches, Lectures, and Letters Upon Various Subjects* (Washington, D.C., 1891), 144; entry, Apr. 9, 1868, W. G. Moore MSS diary, Manuscript Division, Library of Congress.

16 Grant to Johnson, Nov. 9, 1866, Secretary of War Correspondence File, Box 323, Record Group 107, National Archives.

17 Henry Steele Commager's conviction, expressed in *Majority Rule and Minority Rights* (New York, 1943), 49, that the test oath and Milligan cases were ". . . perhaps the best example of judicial protection of personal rights in the whole of our history" seems valid only when considering these decisions from the viewpoint of the 1940s. In their contemporary context, however, they meant the continued subordination of freedmen and of white Unionists in the South. On Republican reaction, see my *Era of the Oath: Northern Loyalty Tests during the Civil War and Reconstruction* (Philadelphia, 1954), 113–20.

commanders. Congress, in brief, determined that Grant, whom the legislators trusted, be the commander in chief as well as the commanding general of the southern section of the Army. It would no longer be possible legally for Johnson to replace him, as the President had recently tried to do by sending him to Mexico, or to bypass him and Stanton as Johnson had done with fateful results with General Absalom Baird at New Orleans just before the tragic riot there. And by protecting Stanton in the war secretary's position through the Tenure of Office Act, the Republican majority in Congress felt that it had effectively blocked the President's power to control the Army in the South. To the surprise of many persons, Johnson at last seemed willing to acquiesce in the legislative will, although he did helplessly veto these laws as they emerged from Congress, in what Grant privately described as "the most ridiculous veto message[s] that ever issued from any President."[18]

Buoyed up by the Court's decisions, Johnson now had a new scheme. He intended to water down the effects of the Reconstruction law that Congress passed on March 2, 1867, by having Attorney General Henry Stanbery issue interpretations that would in effect let the President take the teeth from the disfranchising and Negro suffrage provisions. Again the army commanders found themselves at issue with the White House, for most of the senior officers felt that the Reconstruction law was a moderate and necessary enactment.

On March 27, 1867, Sheridan removed from their offices in the Louisiana state government men Johnson had pardoned for rebellion. This was the first test of a military commander's powers under the new law of Congress, and Grant secretly applauded the action. "It is just the thing," Grant confidentially wrote Sheridan, "and merits the approbation of the loyal people

at least. I have no doubt but that it will also meet with like approval from the reconstructed." Johnson ordered that no more removals occur until the Attorney General's opinion was available. On April 3 Grant obediently transmitted this order, but also sent Sheridan a private message, warning him that "there is a decided hostility to the whole Congressional plan of reconstruction at the 'White House,' and a disposition to remove you from the command you now have. Both the Secretary of War and myself will oppose any such move, as will the mass of the people." They would oppose it by claiming that in the southern army commands Congress had made officers independent of the President, of the Secretary of War, and of the commanding general. Thus, if the President somehow managed to evade, transfer, or replace Stanton and/or Grant, the Reconstruction acts could still be enforced by local commanders.

Grant assured Sheridan that in the Reconstruction law, Congress "intended to give District Commanders entire control over the civil governments of these [southern] districts." The army commanders in the South ". . . shall be their own judges of the meaning of its provisions." By this analysis, any opinion of the Attorney General, the President's legal representative, would merely be advisory rather than binding on the military officers assigned to Reconstruction duty. The Army in the South, Grant inferred, was Congress' army, no longer under the White House or under the War Department except for routine administrative purposes.[19]

To his friend, Congressman Elihu Washburne, Grant wrote ". . . all will be well if Administration and Copperhead influences do not defeat the objects of that reconstruction measure." He advised Sheridan, his favored subordinate: "Go on giving your own interpretation to the law." No wonder that after informing Grant that he intended

---

[18] Grant to E. B. Washburne, Mar. 4, 1867, Illinois State Historical Library. It has seemed unnecessary to document these familiar political events.

[19] Adam Badeau, *Grant in Peace* (Hartford, Conn., 1887), 70–71, 102; exchange between Stanton, Grant, Sheridan, and Johnson, Mar. 27–Apr. 13, 1867, Sheridan Papers.

to remove more of Johnson's state officials, Sheridan boasted to him that "The Attorney General should not hamper me too much; no one can conceive or estimate, at so great a distance, the precautions necessary to be taken . . . here." When General Pope wrote Grant from Georgia that the Milligan decision would have no effect in his command, Grant replied: "My views are that District Commanders are responsible for the faithful execution of the Reconstruction Act of Congress, and that in civil matters I cannot give them an order. I can give them my views, however . . . and above all, I can advise them of views and opinions here which may serve to put them on their guard." Grant comforted Sheridan with the assurance that "I think your head is safe above your shoulders at least so that it can not be taken off to produce pain."[20] In midsummer the President told Grant that he was thinking of dismissing Sheridan. Warning the younger man, Grant again assured him of his and Stanton's support. "Removal cannot hurt you if it does take place, and I do not believe it will," he wrote. "You have carried out the Acts of Congress, and it will be difficult [for Johnson] to get a general officer who will not."

Then the Attorney General issued his opinion. As expected, it watered down the significant aspects of the Reconstruction law and put the military commanders back into almost the same untenable position they had held before Congress enacted this law. Grant and Stanton moved swiftly on two fronts. They had cooperating Congressmen prepare supplements to the Reconstruction law, countering Stanbery's restrictive opinion. And while this was in the works, Grant bolstered sagging army morale by writing to Sheridan and to General Ord in Virginia that "the Attorney General or myself can do no more than

give our opinions as to the meaning of the law." Responsibility and autonomy were still where Congress had vested them, in the district commanders, Grant insisted, and he advised them that "Congress may [soon] give an interpretation of their own acts, differing possibly from those given by the Attorney General."[21]

Johnson finally acted, but against Stanton rather than Sheridan. Striking now hard and swiftly, if belatedly, the President in early August suspended Stanton. Giving the slow-thinking Grant little time to ponder, Johnson swept him into the cabinet as combined war secretary ad interim and commanding general. The President thought he had won the campaign now that Grant was in a frankly Democratic cabinet. Surely the general would benefit from exposure to proper constitutional and political views, and at the same time would become unacceptable as Republican presidential timber in 1868, thereby increasing Johnson's own chances for a Democratic bid, which he greatly desired. But Johnson was to find that Grant, while cooperative enough as Secretary of War in matters of administrative detail, was still acting against the White House when he put on his second hat, the peaked cap of the commanding general of the Army.

On the day he took over the war office, Grant had a trusted friend, General James Forsyth, secretly warn Sheridan of the impending changes, so that "in case the President insists upon your removal, that whoever may be assigned to your command, can be directed by General Grant to carry out the Military Reconstruction Acts as interpreted by you, and foreshadowed by your orders—in fact General Grant wants things in such a condition in Louisiana that your successor (in case you are relieved) will have to carry out the [Reconstruction] Law as you have viewed it; and without the opportunity to change your programme."

[20] Badeau, *Grant in Peace*, 62, 65–68; Grant to Sheridan, Apr. 7, 1867, Andrew Johnson Papers, Manuscript Division, Library of Congress; Sheridan to Grant, Apr. 21, 1867, Sheridan Papers.

[21] Badeau, *Grant in Peace*, 66, 83, 102; Grant to Sheridan, June 24, 1867, Sheridan Papers.

Over Grant's vigorous protests in the cabinet, Johnson decided to remove Sheridan from the Louisiana command. Flashing off a secret warning to the younger man, Grant advised him to ". . . go on your course exactly as if this communication had not been sent to you, and without fear of consequences. That so long as you pursue the same line of duty that you have followed thus far in the service you will receive the entire support of these Headquarters." By "these Headquarters" Grant meant himself as commanding general. In this capacity he considered himself autonomous of the President by virtue of Congress' enactments, far more independent than as interim war secretary. Like Stanton he had learned that the power of this cabinet post was questionable and its tenure uncertain.[22] Grant could not as war secretary, for example, prevent Johnson from suspending Sheridan, Sickles, Pope, or Ord. As commanding general, however, he saw to it that all the army commanders in the South knew they had a friend in the cabinet and at army headquarters. Until Congress reassembled in December, 1867, when the Senate would judge whether Johnson had acted rightly in suspending Stanton, Grant held the War portfolio in a defensive, caretaker, rearguard action. Johnson had trapped himself. Thinking that once Stanton was out of the way he could easily overawe Grant, whom he, Gideon Welles, and the Blairs mistook for a simple, malleable soul, the President learned that Grant definitely had a mind of his own.

But he learned it too late. In January, 1868, Grant let Stanton return to the war office. When Johnson again sought to oust the sticky war secretary in favor of General Lorenzo Thomas, Congress impeached the President. During the long weeks from February to May, 1868, as Congress tried Johnson for seeking to be commander in chief of the army units stationed in the

South, the nation teetered on the brink of renewed violence. Johnson escaped conviction by one vote. Cowed at last, he accepted General John Schofield as a compromise Secretary of War. A total breakdown of the national government was narrowly avoided. For the rest of 1868 Grant remained as commanding general, then he took over the presidency. During that year he saw to it that Johnson kept out of internal army administration. The President, at last brought to caution by the narrowness of the Senate vote on his conviction, accepted what he could not prevent. The Supreme Court sustained Congress' actions in the South, for the jurists had been frightened by the legislators' attacks on them.[23]

Schofield served as a dignified clerk, bearing messages from White House to army headquarters and back, in the manner of prewar Secretaries of War. The military had won. Reconstruction proceeded henceforth in the manner that the soldiers had felt necessary since 1865, and with their own status and safety assured by Congress' laws and sympathy.

Until the complex interaction of the military institution with the civilian political branches of the national government is thoroughly reported, the full story of the background of impeachment will remain partially untold. Thus far the study of this

---

[22] Badeau, *Grant in Peace*, 104; Forsyth to Sheridan, Aug. 12, 14, 1867, Sheridan Papers.

[23] William A. Russ, Jr., "Was There Danger of a Second Civil War during Reconstruction?" *Mississippi Valley Historical Review*, XXV (June, 1938), 39–58. On the Court, see *Mississippi* v. *Johnson*, 4 Wallace, 465 (1867), and *Georgia* v. *Stanton*, 6 *ibid.*, 50 (1867). Leonard D. White, *The Republican Era, 1869–1901* (New York, 1958), 23–24, makes the point that in 1869 Grant took with him to the White House the conviction that the Congress should lead the President, derived from his participation in these events. The theory that impeachment was the result of the Radical leaders' interest in removing Johnson so that the industrial development of the North might continue unchecked is most recently criticized in Stanley Coben, "Northeastern Business and Radical Reconstruction: A Re-examination," *Mississippi Valley Historical Review*, XLVI (June, 1959), 67–90.

period has suffered from the one-sided nature of the sources most widely utilized. The great *Diary* kept by Gideon Welles, for example, indispensable as it is, in the words of the man who edited it for publication, offers a view of events ". . . too much like sitting at the prize-ring and see-

ing only one pugilist."[24] The Army was another contender, crouched in a posture of self-defense in a ring full of aggressive combatants. It should be invisible no longer.

[24] *The Diary of Gideon Welles*, ed. John T. Morse, Jr. (3 vols.; Boston, 1911), I, xxxi–xxxii.

1964

Abolitionist Idealogy and the Fourteenth Amendment*

JAMES M. McPHERSON

In his first annual message to Congress on December 2, 1865, President Johnson restated his belief that he had no right to prescribe suffrage qualifications in the southern states and declared that the reconstructed state governments provided ample protection and security for all citizens. Radical abolitionists derided the message. They noted again the President's inconsistency in appointing provisional governors and prescribing certain conditions for reconstruction but denying the right to fix suffrage requirements. As for the protection and security of citizens, one needed only to read the black codes or scan the daily reports of atrocities against freedmen to perceive the falsity of Johnson's assertion.[1] A good example of the

southern attitude, said abolitionists, was a box received by Charles Sumner in the mail containing the severed finger of a Negro and a note: "You old son of a bitch, I send you a piece of one of your friends, and if that bill of yours passes I will have a piece of you."[2]

Abolitionists were gratified when Congress, in effect, repudiated Johnson's annual message by refusing to admit southern congressmen and by creating the Joint Committee of Fifteen to formulate a reconstruction policy.[3] A few days later the American Freedmen's Aid Commission, a union of the secular freedmen's aid societies, memorialized Congress for a continuation and enlargement of the Freedmen's Bureau. In an address written by McKim, the societies noted that freedmen could not get justice in the civil courts of the South, where they were excluded as jurors and sometimes as witnesses. McKim urged Congress to create military courts for the

* James M. McPherson, *The Struggle for Equality*. Reprinted by permission of the Princeton University Press. Copyright 1964 by Princeton University Press.

[1] James D. Richardson (ed.), *Messages and Papers of the Presidents* (20 vols.; Washington, 1897–1913), VIII, 3551–60; *N.A.S. Standard*, Dec. 9, 30, 1865, Jan 6, 27, 1866; *Commonwealth*, Dec. 9, 23, 30, 1865, Jan. 20, 1866; *Liberator*, Dec. 15, 1865; *Independent*, Jan. 4, Feb. 8, 1866.

[2] *Right Way*, Jan. 27, 1866.
[3] Tilton to Thaddeus Stevens, Dec. 6, 1865, Stevens Papers, LC.

Negroes under the auspices of the Freedmen's Bureau.[4] Soon after this Senator Lyman Trumbull introduced two bills intended to clarify and protect the status of southern freedmen. One bill enlarged the scope of the Freedmen's Bureau; the second defined the civil rights of freedmen and empowered federal district courts to enforce these rights.[5]

While Congress debated these measures, abolitionists continued to urge Negro suffrage as a minimum condition of restoration. The first test of the suffrage question came on a bill to grant the ballot to colored men in the District of Columbia. Petitions for enactment of this bill poured in from abolitionists and Negroes all over the North. The House passed the bill on January 18, 1866, to the thundering applause of 300 Negroes in the galleries. Abolitionists hailed the event as the greatest victory for the Negro since the Thirteenth Amendment.[6]

While the District of Columbia suffrage bill rested in Senate committee, the full Senate took up an enabling act to admit Colorado as the newest state of the Union. Republicans backed the Colorado bill in order to gain two additional Republican senators to help override Johnson's vetoes. But Sumner and the abolitionists opposed admission because Colorado's constitution limited the franchise to white men. They appreciated the partisan advantages of two more Republican senators, but they were trying to make Negro suffrage the main issue of reconstruction, and admission of a new northern state without equal suffrage would stultify their efforts and create a disastrous precedent. Senator Henry Wilson took the lead in urging Colorado's admission, and abolitionists denounced him unmercifully for his action. Despite the

efforts of Sumner and the abolitionists, Congress passed the enabling act. But Johnson vetoed it on the ground that Colorado's population was insufficient for statehood, and Congress could not muster enough votes to override the veto. It was the only Johnson veto of which abolitionists ever approved.[7]

Meanwhile the tension between President Johnson and the Republican congressional majority was mounting. At the beginning of the session Horace Greeley, George Stearns, and John Andrew made several attempts to preserve harmony between the President and Congress. Greeley journeyed to Washington in an effort to prevent a breach between Johnson and Republican leaders. Stearns made a personal appeal to his old friend Johnson for reconstruction on the basis of equal rights. In his valedictory address to the Massachusetts legislature on January 5, 1866, Andrew pleaded for the goodwill and cooperation of all classes, North and South, in solving the complex problem of reconstruction.[8]

Many abolitionists disapproved of these efforts to reconcile President Johnson and the Congress. Phillips thought that Republicans had carried conciliation far enough and that it was time for them to strike boldly against Johnson's policy. In reply to the moderate Republican argument that precipitate action would drive the President into the Democratic party, Phillips said: "If he is capable of being there, he ought to be. If he means to betray his party, the sooner the better." In January Senator

[4] Liberator, Dec. 22, 1865.

[5] Eric McKitrick, Andrew Johnson and Reconstruction (Chicago, 1960), 277–79.

[6] Liberator, Dec. 15, 1865; N.A.S. Standard, Dec. 16, 80, 1865, Jan. 27, Feb. 8, 1866; Commonwealth, Jan. 20, 1866; Right Way, Dec. 23, 1865, Jan. 20, 27, 1866; Independent, Jan. 25, 1866.

[7] Edward McPherson, Political History of the United States of America during the Period of Reconstruction (Washington, D.C., 1871), 81–83; Edward L. Pierce, Memoir and Letters of Charles Sumner (4 vols.; Boston, 1877–94), IV, 284–86; Independent, Feb. 8, Mar. 15, May 8, 1866; N.A.S. Standard, May 12, 19, 1866; Right Way, Apr. 28, 1866; Commonwealth, Jan. 27, Apr. 21, 28, May 5, 19, 1866.

[8] Glyndon G. Van Deusen, Horace Greeley, Nineteenth Century Crusader (Phila., 1953), 342–43; Right Way, Dec. 16, 1865; Stearns to Johnson, Dec. 14, 1865, Johnson Papers, LC; Henry G. Pearson, The Life of John A. Andrew (2 vols.; Boston, 1904), II, 276–87.

Fessenden, chairman of the Joint Committee of Fifteen, publicly stated that there was no breach between the President and the Republican congressional majority. A special meeting of the American Anti-Slavery Society in Boston on January 24, denounced Fessenden's attempt to harmonize Johnson and Congress. "Those who bestow general approval of the President take off the edge of public vigilance," said Phillips. If Fessenden and his associates really thought there was no major difference of opinion between themselves and Johnson, "the leaders of the Republican party are to be watched, not trusted. . . . We need outside pressure and remorseless criticism upon Congress and the President."[9]

During the congressional session a delegation of Negro abolitionists, headed by George Downing, came to Washington to lobby for Negro suffrage. On February 7 Downing, Frederick Douglass, and three other Negroes held an important interview with President Johnson. In short introductory speeches Downing and Douglass assured the President that they came in a spirit of respect and friendship. They urged Johnson to enfranchise the Negro as a measure of justice and necessity. In his reply, the President declared that he had always been a friend of the colored race. "If I know myself, and the feelings of my own heart, they have been for the colored man. I have owned slaves and bought slaves, but I never sold one." Warming to his subject, Johnson declared that Negro suffrage in the South could cause a war of races. If enfranchised the freedmen would become mere political pawns of the planter class, who would use them to grind down further the small white farmers. The President could see no solution of the race problem except emigration of the Negroes from the South. Stunned by Johnson's remarks, Douglass tried to reply, but was cut

off by the President before he could utter more than a few sentences. The delegation was ushered out of Johnson's office.[10]

After consultation with radical congressional leaders, Douglass penned a reply to the President's statement and published it in the *Washington Chronicle*. Douglass denied that Negro suffrage would create a race war or that the Negro voter would become the pawn of the planter class. Enmity between Negro and poor white grew out of slavery. In freedom the Negroes and the small white farmers would have similar interests and would vote accordingly. Even if hostility between poor white and Negro did continue in freedom, said Douglass, how was the freedman to protect himself without equal rights? Experience proved that "Men are whipped oftenest who are whipped easiest." To keep the Negro politically powerless would only invite abuse and oppression of the defenseless freedmen. "Peace between races is not to be secured by degrading one race and exalting another," concluded Douglass, "but by maintaining a state of equal justice between all classes."[11]

The interview and Douglass' reply attracted widespread attention. The Republican press was almost unanimously critical of Johnson's behavior toward the Negroes. Abolitionists exploded in anger at this new evidence of Johnson's race prejudice. In an editorial entitled "Our Poor White President" the *Anti-Slavery Standard* assailed Johnson's address to the colored delegation as "one of the most brutal and insolent

---

[9] *N.A.S. Standard*, Jan. 20, Feb. 3, 1866. See also Phillips to Sumner, Dec. 25, 1865, Sumner Papers, HU; *Principia*, Jan. 11, 1866; and *Commonwealth*, Jan. 27, 1866.

[10] *Washington Chronicle*, Feb. 8, 1866. One of Johnson's private secretaries reported to a friend that after the "darkey delegation" had left his office, the President "uttered the following terse Saxon: 'Those d----d sons of b----s thought they had me in a trap! I know that d----d Douglass; he's just like any nigger, and he would sooner cut a white man's throat than not.' " P. Ripley to Manton Marble, Feb. 8, 1866, quoted by LaWanda Cox and John H. Cox, *Politics, Principle, and Prejudice, 1865–1866: Dilemma of Reconstruction America* (New York, 1963), 163.

[11] *Washington Chronicle*, Feb. 8, 1866. An account of the interview and a copy of Douglass' reply are in McPherson, *History of Reconstruction*, 52–56. See also *New York Tribune*, Feb. 12, 1866.

speeches anywhere on record." Elizabeth Cady Stanton commented that the interview showed "how much better Douglass understands the philosophy of social life and republican institutions than the President." The Worcester Freedom Club resolved that the interview had revealed the real attitude of the President toward the Negro: there was no longer any doubt that Johnson's policy was based on the belief that the country belonged to white men alone.[12]

Most abolitionists had given up hope of securing Johnson's cooperation for a just reconstruction program, but there were still many Republicans seeking a basis of accommodation with the President. In mid-February their hopes centered on Trumbull's Freedmen's Bureau bill, recently passed by large majorities in both houses of Congress. Senators Trumbull and Fessenden fully expected Johnson to approve the act. Speaker of the House Schuyler Colfax wagered a box of Havana cigars that the President would sign. J. Miller McKim scouted Democratic rumors that the President would veto the bill. "I can hardly think he will be so unwise as to do so," wrote McKim. "That bill . . . is a growth of the loyal and virtuous public sentiment of the land. To veto it . . . would be to fly in the face of the whole people."[13]

But on February 19 Johnson shocked Republicans by vetoing the act. The *Anti-Slavery Standard* was not surprised. Phillips tossed an "I told you so" editorial at the Republicans who had labored to reconcile President Johnson and the Congress. Two days after the veto Theodore Tilton told his friend Greeley that "it is a crime henceforth to deceive the Nation by the pretence that Andrew Johnson is the head of the Republican Party. . . . All disguise is now taken off. The way to victory is no longer by going *with* him but *against* him." Greeley was stunned by the veto and expressed his grief in a series of *Tribune* editorials. He did not yet take Tilton's advice to break completely with the President, but his editorials were henceforth much more critical of the administration.[14]

Among abolitionists there was hardly one who ever again said a good word for Johnson. Stearns, Oliver Johnson, McKim, Garrison, and others who had been hoping against hope that the President could be dissuaded from his wrongheaded course were completely disillusioned by the veto. "What is to be done with Andrew Johnson?" asked Samuel May, Jr., dejectedly. "It looks to me now that he has *betrayed his friends,* when he might have easily prevented any rupture if he chose." General Howard, head of the Freedmen's Bureau, told McKim that the veto had emboldened white southerners to increase their attacks on the Bureau and had made freedmen's aid efforts in the South more difficult. "I have talked hopefully of the President," reported McKim from Washington. "We have kept our fears to ourselves. But it is no use. Loyal and virtuous men here, who are well informed, as a general thing have no confidence in & no sanguine hope of much good from President Johnson."[15]

Johnson followed his veto with one of the most remarkable public speeches ever uttered by an American president. On February 22 a group of Democrats held a Washington's Birthday celebration at Grover's Theatre in the capital. They adopted resolutions endorsing Johnson's reconstruction policy and affirming that "the grand

[12] *N.A.S. Standard,* Feb. 17, 1866. See also *ibid.,* Feb. 24, 1866; *Commonwealth,* Feb. 17, 1866; *Independent,* Feb. 15, Mar. 1, 1866; *Right Way,* Feb. 24, Mar. 3, 1866.

[13] McKitrick, *Andrew Johnson and Reconstruction,* 284; *New York Tribue,* Feb. 14, 15, 1864; *N.A.S. Standard,* Feb. 24, 1866; McKim to Joseph Simpson, Feb. 16, 1866, McKim letterbook, I, 273, McKim Papers, Cornell.

[14] *N.A.S. Standard,* Feb. 24, 1866; Tilton to Greeley, Feb. 21, 1866, Tilton Papers, Misc. Mss, NYPL; *New York Tribune,* Feb. 20, 21, 23, 1866.

[15] Samuel May, Jr., to McKim, Feb. 20, 1866, McKim Papers, NYPL; McKim to Joseph Simpson, Feb. 28, 1866, McKim letterbook, I, 398–400, McKim Papers, Cornell. See also *Right Way,* Mar. 3, 1866; Oliver Johnson to Garrison, Feb. 20, 1866, Garrison Papers, BPL; George Thompson to Oliver Johnson, Feb. 22, 1866, Dickinson Papers, LC.

old declaration that 'all men are created equal' was never intended by its authors . . . [to place] the African race in this country on a civil, social, or political level with the Caucasian."[16] In a festive mood the revelers trooped to the White House to serenade President Johnson, who responded with a long speech full of diatribes against radical leaders. Johnson compared himself to Christ; he denounced the radicals as traitors and disunionists, and when asked to name his tormentors, he called out the names of Thaddeus Stevens, Charles Sumner, and Wendell Phillips. These plotters were planning to assassinate him, charged Johnson. "If my blood is to be shed because I vindicate the Union and the preservation of this government in its original purity and character," he proclaimed, "let it be shed; let an altar to the Union be erected, and then, if it is necessary, take me and lay me upon it, and the blood that now warms and animates my existence shall be poured out as a fit libation to the Union of these States."[17]

The nation was mortified by the President's speech. Some of his best friends were appalled. Even abolitionists who believed Johnson capable of any villainy were taken aback. "Has the [presidential] office *ever* been so degraded before?" asked Samuel May, Jr. J. Miller McKim, usually restrained of speech, was moved by Johnson's behavior to call the President "an obstinate, pigheaded, ill-conditioned, border-state, 'poor white,' and loco-foco Democrat." Garrison delivered a few well-publicized speeches and wrote several articles for the *Independent* denouncing Johnson and calling for his impeachment.[18]

Radical abolitionists who had long urged an unremitting war against the President

were delighted by the public reaction to his Freedmen's Bureau veto and his February 22 speech. Many moderate Republicans turned against the President. Eight state legislatures passed resolutions rebuking Johnson.[19] The disillusionment with the President raised the stock of abolitionists who had been declaiming against him for months. Republican newspapers that had previously criticized the abolitionists for inciting ill will between President Johnson and the Congress now printed their speeches with editorial endorsement. Abolitionists spoke to cheering crowds on the lecture circuit. Radical congressional leaders encouraged their work of agitation. "Every school district in the country should be canvassed in the cause of justice and equality," Congressman William D. Kelley told Phillips. In March, 1866, Sumner urged Phillips to hold the antislavery societies together. "You and they are doing indispensable work; in this I express the conviction of every Senator and every Representative on our side of the pending questions."[20]

One of the pending questions was Trumbull's Civil Rights bill. This measure was passed by Congress in March. Again there was much speculation about whether Johnson would veto or sign it. Recovered somewhat from the debacle of February, moderate Republicans were negotiating for a reconciliation with Johnson on the basis of the Civil Rights bill. But again the President spurned their overtures and vetoed the bill. For most Republicans this was the last straw. From that time forward there was a virtually irreparable breach between the President and the party that had elected him. On April 9 Congress passed the Civil Rights bill over Johnson's veto. Abolitionists were overjoyed. At last

---

[16] Garrison to W. P. Garrison, Feb. 22, 1866, Garrison Papers, BPL; *Independent*, Mar. 1, 1866.

[17] The speech is reprinted in McPherson, *History of Reconstruction*, 58–63.

[18] Samuel May, Jr., to McKim, Mar. 5, 1866, McKim Papers, NYPL; McKim to Arthur Albright, Mar. 23, 1866, McKim Papers, BPL; *New York Tribune*, Feb. 28, 1866; *N.A.S. Standard*, Mar. 10, 1866; *Independent*, Mar. 29, April 26, 1866. See also McKitrick, *Andrew Johnson and Reconstruction*, 295.

[19] *Commonwealth*, Feb. 24, 1866; *New York Tribune*, Mar. 5, 1866; *N.A.S. Standard*, Mar. 3, 10, 24, 1866; *Philadelphia Press*, Feb. 27, 1866; *Right Way*, Mar. 17, 1866.

[20] Kelley quoted in *N.A.S. Standard*, May 12, 1866; Sumner to Phillips, Mar. 17, 1866, quoted by Carlos Martyn, *Wendell Phillips: The Agitator* (New York, 1890), 353. See also *N.A.S. Standard*, Mar. 10, 17, 1866.

the Republicans had shown a bold and united front against the perfidious President. "Things begin to look a little brighter," commented young Frank Garrison, "and if we can only keep the two-thirds majority obtained for the bill, we can snap our fingers at the wretched occupant of the White House." Abolitionist David Plumb praised Congress for its defiance of the executive. "Now for the *'Main Question'*—the Suffrage of the Negro," wrote Plumb. "I do not expect great things from the 'Civil Rights Bill,' unless backed by Negro Suffrage. . . . Since half-measures cannot win the President, now, why not go for a whole one?"[21]

Plumb expressed the sentiments of many abolitionists. Despite their happiness with the passage of the Civil Rights bill, they were far from satisfied. The Civil Rights bill, said Tilton, was all right as far as it went, "but the negro will never be thoroughly protected, even in person and property, until he has the ballot." Gerrit Smith wrote an open letter to Senator Henry Wilson declaring that "the Civil Rights Bill cannot serve the black man in place of the ballot." "What is suffrage, if it be not a civil right?" asked the *Anti-Slavery Standard*. "What are civil rights worth that do not include suffrage?" The *Standard* welcomed Congress' display of backbone in passing the bill over Johnson's veto, but nevertheless considered the measure only "half the loaf. And if this be, as many fear, *the substitute for suffrage,* it may prove far worse than no bread."[22]

Abolitionists looked hopefully but not confidently to the Joint Committee of Fifteen for favorable action on the suffrage question. Since the beginning of January the committee had been deliberating the problem of reconstruction. One of the first questions to come before it was the increase in southern representation occasioned by the abolition of slavery. Before emancipation the slave had counted for three-fifths of a man in determining congressional representation; the freed Negro now counted as a whole man. Without a constitutional amendment the South could return to the Union stronger than ever in Congress, her Negro population disfranchised but counted for representation purposes. In January the Joint Committee sent to Congress a constitutional amendment which would reduce the size of a state's congressional delegation if that state denied or abridged the franchise on account of race or color. Believing that northern public opinion would not sanction a direct grant of Negro suffrage, moderate Republicans rallied behind the apportionment amendment as the best attainable substitute.[23]

Abolitionists denounced the amendment. In a public letter Gerrit Smith asserted that if the South were readmitted under such a plan she would gladly accept reduced representation in order to keep her Negro population disfranchised. Tilton assailed the proposed amendment because it "puts the Negro into the hands of the Rebel. . . . It proves that a Republic is ungrateful." The American Anti-Slavery Society resolved that the amendment was "only fitted to protect the North and the white race, while it leaves the Negro to his fate. . . . In times of revolution the decisions, the mistakes, of a single hour may settle the opinions of a nation and its forms of civil life for cenutries." Therefore it would be better to defeat this half measure than to accept it and run the risk of its becoming the final basis of settlement.[24]

21 McKitrick, *Andrew Johnson and Reconstruction,* 298–324; *Independent,* Mar. 22, 29, Apr. 5, 12, 1866; *New York Tribune,* Mar. 28, Apr. 9, 10, 1866; Francis Jackson Garrison to Fanny Garrison Villard, Apr. 8, 1866, F. G. Villard Papers, HU; David Plumb to Sumner, Apr. 12, 1866, Sumner Papers, HU.

22 *Independent,* Feb. 8, 1866; *Gerrit Smith's Reply to Henry Wilson,* Mar. 26, 1866, broadside (Peterboro, 1866); *N.A.S. Standard,* Apr. 7, 14, 1866.

23 Joseph James, *The Framing of the Fourteenth Amendment* (Urbana, Ill., 1956), 55–56; McKitrick, *Andrew Johnson and Reconstruction,* 336–37.

24 *Gerrit Smith to Senator Sumner,* Feb. 5, 1866, published letter (Peterboro, 1866); Tilton to Sumner, Feb. 2, 1866, Sumner Papers, HU; *N.A.S. Standard,* Feb. 3, 1866. See also *Commonwealth,* Jan. 27, 1866; *Principia,* Feb. 8, 1866; *Independent,* Feb. 1, 8, 15, 1866.

Sumner was in complete accord with abolitionists on this question. The amendment was passed by the House at the end of January, but in the Senate it ran into the opposition of the powerful senator from Massachusetts. In a marathon Senate speech occupying two days (February 5 and 6), Sumner uttered an exhaustive excoriation of the amendment and pleaded for congressional enactment of Negro suffrage. Abolitionists and northern Negroes praised Sumner's speech as the greatest effort of his life. They moved quickly to back up his efforts with petitions and memorials against the proposed amendment.[25] Democrats as well as radical Republicans opposed the amendment, and by the middle of February Sumner claimed to have enough Senate votes to defeat it. When the vote was taken on March 9 it fell short of the two-thirds majority necessary for passage. Abolitionists rejoiced in its failure and heaped renewed praise on Sumner.[26]

Victory in the battle of the ballot, however, still seemed remote. Convinced that northern public opinion opposed Negro suffrage, moderate Republican leaders continued to seek a less radical solution to the reconstruction puzzle. Abolitionists denounced these Republicans for their willingness to sacrifice the Negro on the altar of political expediency. "They have sought only to tinker, not to *change* 'the President's plans'; to merely prune, not to uproot and destroy," charged the *Anti-Slavery Standard* in April. "Were the Democrats in power, they could not possibly be worse."[27] In an effort to improve the

climate of public opinion and exert pressure on Congress, the Boston Emancipation League reorganized in March, 1866, as the Impartial Suffrage Association. The association sponsored lectures and aided George Stearns in the circulation of newspapers and pamphlets throughout the nation.[28]

Disturbed by Congress' failure to propose an effective reconstruction program, Robert Dale Owen came to Washington at the end of March and laid before Thaddeus Stevens a comprehensive plan. Owen proposed a constitutional amendment that would prohibit discrimination in civil rights, enact impartial suffrage in every state after July 4, 1876, and provide for proportional reduction of the representation of any states that denied Negro suffrage before that date. Stevens professed enthusiasm for the plan, but Sumner and the abolitionists disliked the postponement of equal suffrage until 1876. Even this modest Negro suffrage proposal, however, was too strong for the Joint Committee. With the congressional elections of 1866 looming on the horizon, they were extremely sensive to political considerations. The committee rewrote Owen's amendment. On April 30 Fessenden and Stevens reported to Congress a constitutional amendment that prohibited states from abridging the civil rights of citizens or denying any person the equal protection of the laws; provided for the proportional reduction of the congressional representation of any state that abridged or denied suffrage to any of its male citizens; disfranchised until 1870 all persons who had voluntarily supported the rebellion; and forbade payment of the Confederate debt. Congress struck out the section disfranchising all rebels and substituted a provision to disqualify from political office certain classes of leading Confederates. Otherwise the proposal submitted on April 30 was substantially the same as the mea-

[25] Pierce, *Sumner*, IV, 277–81; "Memorial of a Delegation Representing the Colored People," *House Miscellaneous Documents*, #109, 39th Cong., 1st sess.; *Commonwealth*, Feb. 10, 17, 1866; *N.A.S. Standard*, Feb. 17, Mar. 24, Apr. 21, 1866. There are nearly a dozen letters from abolitionists to Sumner praising his speech against the proposed Fourteenth Amendment in the Summer Papers, HU.

[26] *Congressional Globe*, 39th Cong., 1st sess., 1,224–35, 1,275–89; *Commonwealth*, Mar. 17, 1866; *N.A.S. Standard*, Mar. 17, 1866.

[27] *N.A.S. Standard*, Apr. 14, 1866. See also *ibid.*, Apr. 21, June 23, 1866; *Independent*, Apr. 19, 1866.

[28] Loring Moody to Gerrit Smith, Mar. 20, 1866, Smith Papers, SU; *Right Way*, Mar. 17, 31, Apr. 14, May 5, 1866.

sure eventually adopted as the Fourteenth Amendment.[29]

The *Anti-Slavery Standard* denounced the Joint Committee's proposed amendment as a "fraud." On the central issue of Negro suffrage it was no better than the amendment defeated in March. "It is a substitute for suffrage and citizenship," said the *Standard*. "It is the blighted harvest of the bloodiest sowing the fields of the world ever saw." Phillips told Thaddeus Stevens that the report of the Joint Committee was "a fatal & total surrender. The South carries off enough of the victory to enable her to control the Nation, mould its policy & shape its legislation for a dozen years to come." Tilton vigorously criticized the amendment in the columns of the *Independent*.[30]

Not all abolitionists reacted so sharply to the action of the Joint Committee. George Stearns expressed unwillingness "to accept as a finality any thing less than Impartial Suffrage," but thought that Congress should pass the amendment "rather than have 'no policy.'" Adoption of the amendment would not preclude radicals "from asking all we need at a future time. . . . Our support of Congress would be more efficient and direct, if, without denouncing this scheme we claim all we ought to have." The *Boston Commonwealth* regretted that Negro suffrage had not been incorporated into the proposed Fourteenth Amendment. But with an eye to the 1866 elections, the editor commended the amendment as the best that could be obtained at this time. The *Right Way* considered it "criminal and idiotic" to enfranchise rebels and withhold the ballot from black loyalists. Nevertheless adoption of the Fourteenth Amendment would be "of great value for national security and national justice." Meanwhile, declared the

Right Way, abolitionists should urge the inclusion of Negro suffrage in the enabling acts admitting southern states and the adoption of a Fifteenth Amendment incorporating equal manhood suffrage into the Constitution.[31]

Abolitionists therefore were divided into two camps in their attitudes toward the proposed Fourteenth Amendment. Neither group approved the measure as the final condition of reconstruction. One faction, led by Phillips, condemned the amendment unequivocally and hoped for its defeat, fearing that adoption would lead to the admission of southern states when they had ratified the amendment. The other faction, led by George Stearns, approved the amendment as far as it went, urged its passage, and hoped by an enabling act or a Fifteenth Amendment to secure Negro suffrage.

The House passed the Fourteenth Amendment in its original form on May 10. While the Senate deliberated, Phillips and his followers stepped up their attacks. In *Anti-Slavery Standard* editorials Phillips charged that by failing to enact Negro suffrage Congress had, in effect, surrendered to President Johnson and the South. The vaunted "practical statesmanship" of Fessenden, Trumbull, and other Republican leaders who had formulated the Fourteenth Amendment was nothing but "hypocrisy, fear, and a compromise." In a series of powerful sermons and discourses, several of which were published in pamphlet form, George Cheever excoriated the amendment as a fraud, a sham, a political trick, and a "robbery of the colored race." Frederick Douglass considered the measure a personal insult to every Negro. "For to tell me that I am an equal American citizen, and, in the same breath, tell me that my right to vote may be constitutionally taken from me by some other equal citizen or citizens, is to tell me that my citizenship

---

[29] James, *Framing of Fourteenth Amendment,* 100–02, 109–16; McKitrick, *Andrew Johnson and Reconstruction,* 343–49.

[30] *N.A.S. Standard,* May 5, 1866; Phillips to Stevens, Apr. 30, 1866, Stevens Papers, LC; *Independent,* May 3, June 14, 1866.

[31] Stearns to Sumner, May 1, 1866, Sumner Papers, HU; *Commonwealth,* May 5, 19, 26, June 2, 1866; *Right Way,* May 12, June 9, 1866.

is but an empty name," declared Douglass. "To say that I am a citizen to pay taxes . . . obey the laws, support the government, and fight the battles of the country, but, in all that respects voting and representation, I am but as so much inert matter, is to insult my manhood."[32] The New England Anti-Slavery Society resolved that admission of rebel states under the proposed Fourteenth Amendment would be "total surrender" and "an unworthy trick to mislead the nation." In a speech at the Society's annual convention Phillips expressed hope for defeat of the Republican party if it fought the 1866 elections on the basis of the Fourteenth Amendment. "The Republicans are occupied chiefly in keeping up their own organization," charged Phillips. "Let that party be broken that sacrifices principle to preserve its own existence."[33]

Garrison, Oliver Johnson, and McKim condemned Phillips' anti-Republican speeches and called for support of Congress and the Fourteenth Amendment. They professed to be no less ardent in their desire for Negro suffrage than Phillips, but declared that this objective would sooner be reached by cooperating with the Republican majority than by defying it. Stearns organized a mass meeting at Faneuil Hall on May 31 under the auspices of the Impartial Suffrage Association. The meeting adopted resolutions endorsing the Fourteenth Amendment and urging Congress to pass enabling acts requiring southern states to enact impartial suffrage being returning to the Union.[34]

Meanwhile a Senate Republican caucus bound all Republicans to vote for the Fourteenth Amendment on the Senate floor. Sumner and a few other radicals were opposed to the amendment. But they were bound by the caucus decision and voted for the measure when it passed the Senate on June 8. The battle line for radicals now became the enabling act setting forth the conditions under which former Confederate states would be admitted. Sumner introduced a bill drafted by abolitionist lawyer Samuel Sewall requiring equal suffrage as a condition of readmission. Congressional radicals rallied behind this measure, and Tilton gave it the support of the powerful *Independent.* But moderate Republicans considered Negro suffrage in an enabling act just as much a political liability as in a constitutional amendment. A majority of Republicans were reluctant to commit themselves to any final conditions of readmission. They preferred to go to the country on the basis of the Fourteenth Amendment as it stood, leaving the final terms of reconstruction to the next session of Congress after the 1866 elections. Congress adjourned in July without passing any enabling legislation.[35]

Most abolitionists were not reluctant to see this issue postponed until the next session, hoping that time, circumstances, and an improved state of public opinion would make Congress more radical in December. But in the last weeks of the 1865–66 ses-

---

[32] *N.A.S. Standard,* May 27, June 2, June 30, 1866; George B. Cheever, *Impartial Suffrage a Right; and the Infamy of the Revolution Against It in the Proposed Amendment of the Constitution* (New York, 1866), *Protest Against the Robbery of the Colored Race by the Proposed Amendment of the Constitution* (New York, 1866), *The Republic or the Oligarchy? Which? An Appeal Against the Proposal Transfer of the Right to Vote from the People to the State* (New York, 1866); Douglass' statement quoted in *N.A.S. Standard,* July 7, 1866.

[33] *N.A.S. Standard,* June 9, 1866.

[34] Oliver Johnson to Garrison, June 16, 1866, Garrison Papers, BPL; McKim to John Bingham,

July 20, 1866; McKim letterbook, II, 144; McKim Papers, Cornell; *N.A.S. Standard,* June 23, 1866; *Commonwealth,* June 2, 1866; *Right Way,* June 9, 1866.

[35] James, *Framing of Fourteenth Amendment,* 142–52, 169–70; S. E. Sewall to Sumner, June 1, 1866, Sumner Papers, HU; Sumner to Tilton, June 27, 1866, Tilton Papers, NYHS; *Independent,* June 7, 21, 1866; *Commonwealth,* June 16, July 14, 1866. In line with the decision of the Republican majority to play down the suffrage issue, the Senate quietly shelved the House bill granting the ballot to colored men in the District of Columbia. The *Anti-Slavery Standard* could hardly find words to express its disgust with Republicans for this new act of cowardice. *N.A.S. Standard,* June 23, July 28, 1866.

sion Tennessee, having ratified the Fourteenth Amendment, knocked on the congressional door for readmission. Moderate Republicans seized upon Tennessee's application as an opportunity to display the good faith of Congress and the success of its reconstruction policy by admitting the state with no other conditions than those contained in the Fourteenth Amendment. Sumner in the Senate and Boutwell in the House tried to incorporate an equal suffrage provision in the act of admission, but their motions were defeated. Tennessee was restored to the Union by joint resolution on July 23. Sumner was deeply discouraged and many abolitionists were sullen. Tilton feared that Tennessee's restoration would create a precedent for the admission of other southern states without Negro suffrage. "Tennessee is permitted to deny to her blacks a voice in the state, while she herself is permitted to resume her place in the nation," he wrote in the *Independent*. "The spectacle is a national humiliation."[36]

Meanwhile Phillips had been thinking over his statement of May 31 that a Republican defeat in the 1866 elections would be better than a victory on the platform of the Fourteenth Amendment. Phillips' radical friends warned him that expression of such opinions could destroy his influence in the Republican party. At a Fourth of July celebration in Framingham, Massachusetts, Phillips renewed his attacks on the Fourteenth Amendment. But this time instead of calling for the defeat of the Republican party, he proclaimed his belief that the amendment would not be ratified. He predicted that the South would reject it. Phillips announced that his radical Republican friends did not want the amendment ratified; they considered it nothing more than

a platform for the fall elections, and hoped to enact a more thorough reconstruction program at the next session of Congress. Phillips therefore hoped the Republican party would succeed. "I know no other channel, this summer, in which to work. I cannot tell you to desert the Republican party; I know nowhere else for you to go."

This advice was not entirely welcome to some abolitionists. Gerrit Smith said that he could never support a party that campaigned on the basis of the infamous Fourteenth Amendment. Stephen S. Foster introduced a resolution declaring that abolitionists would support no party that did not recognize the absolute equality of all men before the law. Phillips hastily replied that he had not meant that abolitionists should give unqualified support to the party. They should condemn Republican shortcomings, as they had always done, but "let us support any one in that organization who does maintain, and promises to support, the true ideas of freedom." In the end Foster's resolution was adopted unanimously, with the understanding that it did not preclude abolitionist support of individual radical Republicans who were true to the idea of equality.[37]

As election day approached, abolitionists toned down their criticism of Republicans and concentrated their fire on President Johnson and his supporters, who were making a determined bid for electoral endorsement of Johnson's reconstruction policy. In June, conservatives issued a call for a National Union convention on August 14 in Philadelphia to rally all of Johnson's supporters in a new party. Republicans and abolitionists directed their main attacks on this new conservative threat. The *Anti-Slavery Standard* described the National Union movement as a bid for power by those who "agree that this is a white man's government. . . . It is virtually a move-

36 James, *Framing of Fourteenth Amendment*, 171–72; Pierce, *Sumner*, IV, 286–87; Sumner to Moncure Conway, July 30, 1866, Conway Papers, CU; *Right Way*, July 28, 1866; *N.A.S. Standard*, July 28, Aug. 11, 1866; *Commonwealth*, July 28, 1866; *Independent*, July 26, 1866.

37 *N.A.S. Standard*, July 14, 1866. See also *New York Tribune*, July 6, 1866; *Commonwealth*, July 7, 14, 1866; and *N.A.S. Standard*, July 28, Aug. 4, 11, 18, 1866.

ment for the re-establishment of slavery."[38]

One of the major issues of the 1866 campaign was in the increasing oppression of freedom in the South. In May a mob of white men in Memphis, aided by part of the police force, went on a drunken, murderous rampage against the city's Negro population, burning, raping, and pillaging in the colored section of town and killing 46 Negroes. Northerners were appalled. Republicans charged that the riot was the inevitable result of Johnson's reconstruction policy. With Memphis as an example, observed the *New York Tribune* sarcastically, "who doubts that the Freedman's Bureau ought to be abolished forthwith, and the blacks remitted to the paternal care of their old masters, who 'understand the nigger, you know, a great deal better than the Yankees can?' "[39] The Republican and abolitionist press continued to publish reports of outrages against freedmen all through the summer. Despite conservative charges that the Republican press exaggerated these reports for political purposes, the atrocity stories had some basis in fact. In September, 1866, the assistant commissioner of the Freedman's Bureau in Arkansas reported officially that crimes against freedmen had increased sharply since March. He stated that southern whites felt that "any effort to secure justice for the Freedmen is simply the work of abolitionists . . . and [was] in direct opposition to the wishes of the President of the United States."[40]

The most spectacular anti-Negro violence occurred in New Orleans on July 30. A convention of radical whites and Negroes which had been called to consider a Negro suffrage amendment to Louisiana's Constitution was attacked by a mob of New Orleans whites containing many po-

licemen and former Confederate soldiers. Scores of Negroes and their white allies were killed or wounded by the cold-blooded assault. In the North the affair redounded with great discredit to President Johnson and his policy. Republicans were quick to depict the riot as the inevitable consequence of Johnson's reconstruction program. Some abolitionists went even further and blamed the affray partly on the conservative policy of Congress. Gerrit Smith hoped that the New Orleans murders had "opened the eyes of Congress to its folly in restoring Tennessee, & to the folly of restoring any other Rebel State whilst such State was continuing to oppress the negro." Most radicals joined Elizur Wright in hoping that the riots would prove a blessing in disguise by rousing the people to the necessity of a thorough reconstruction.[41]

Abolitionists unleashed a volley of ridicule and denunciation of the National Union convention when it met in Philadelphia on August 14. The convention adopted a resolution stating that "there is no section of the country where the Constitution and the laws of the United States find more prompt and entire obedience than in [the former Confederate] States." Gerrit Smith was appalled by the mendacious effrontery of this resolution. "This is said of that half of our country in every part of which it is unsafe to be a black man or the friend of a black man," wrote Smith. "Can the people respect the men who so trifle with truth?" Another radical described the Philadelphia convention as "a meeting of marvelous odds and ends, the reconstructed shreds and patches of rebellion; cunning men from down East . . . gangs of rough and ready men from New York, freebooters in politics; several sol-

[38] *New York Tribune,* July 6, 1866; *Independent,* July 12, 19, 1866; *Commonwealth,* July 7, 1866; *N.A.S. Standard,* July 7, 1866.

[39] *Independent,* May 17, 1866; *New York Tribune,* May 22, 1866.

[40] Quoted in George R. Bentley, *A History of the Freedmen's Bureau* (Phila., 1955), 158.

[41] Gerrit Smith to Garrison, Aug. 5, 1866, Garrison Papers, BPL; article by Wright in *Independent,* Aug. 16, 1866. McKitrick, *Andrew Johnson and Reconstruction,* 422–27, is the best brief discussion of the New Orleans riot and its political consequences.

emn old men from Pennsylvania, who will stand by the Constitution as it ought to have been two thousand years ago . . . old pro-Slavery fossils from North Carolina; South Carolina implacables, with the whip-hand itching; . . . Mississippi gentlemen, who are determined to reconstruct by burying the negro." These men had come together "to stand by the Union, and the Constitution, and Andrew Johnson, to defend the New-Orleans massacre, and indorse the policy which gave us the murders at Memphis."[42]

To counter the National Union movement, a convention of Southern Loyalists met in Philadelphia in early September. Hundreds of northern Republicans attended as observers and as "honorary" delegates. The issues of Negro suffrage and the Republican party's relation to the Negro nearly broke up the convention. Trouble began when Rochester Republicans elected Frederick Douglass as a delegate. Many Republicans feared that Douglass' attendance would hurt the party in parts of the North where "social equality" was anathema. One Republican urged Thaddeus Stevens to use his influence to keep Douglass away from Philadelphia. "If he goes it will certainly injure our cause and we may lose some Congressmen in doubtful districts."[43]

Douglass was not deterred by the fears of white Republicans. He told Governor Oliver Morton of Indiana that if he was prevented from attending the convention the Republican party would gain a reputation for "hypocrisy and cowardice." Failing to persuade Douglass to stay away from Philadelphia, Republican leaders decided to ignore him as much as possible at the convention. When the delegates assembled at Independence Hall for a grand procession to National Hall where the con-

vention was to be held, all Republicans but General Butler shied away from Douglass. The delegates were supposed to march two abreast, but it appeared that Douglass would have to walk alone until Theodore Tilton came up, locked arms with Douglass, and marched proudly with him down streets lined with cheering onlookers.[44] Despite the cheers, many Republicans were alarmed by the incident. "A good many people here are disturbed by the practical exhibition of racial equality in the arm-in-arm performance of Douglass and Tilton," wrote Thaddeus Stevens to Congressman William D. Kelley. "It does not become radicals like us particularly to object, but it was certainly unfortunate at this time. The old prejudice, now revived, will lose us some votes."[45]

At the convention itself there was some reluctance to seat Douglass as a delegate, and a motion to invite him to sit on the platform was ignored. But Douglass and a Negro delegate from Louisiana were finally seated. The significance of their presence, however, was soon overshadowed by the mighty struggle over Negro suffrage. Without Negro votes, Republicans from the deep South would be politically powerless. Most of the delegates from former Confederate states, therefore, wanted a declaration by the convention in favor of Negro suffrage. They were encouraged in this direction by a number of abolitionists at the convention. Under the leadership of Tilton the New York delegation passed a Negro suffrage resolution. But the "practical politicians" of the Republican party exerted all their influence to prevent any statement on the suffrage question. A caucus of northern Republican governors resolved that the question of Negro suffrage must be kept

42 Article by Gerrit Smith in *N.A.S. Standard,* Sept. 1, 1866; *New York Tribune,* Aug. 14, 1866. See also *Independent,* Aug. 23, 30, 1866.

43 Samuel Shock to Thaddeus Stevens, Aug. 27, 1866, Stevens Papers, LC.

44 Philip S. Foner, *The Life and Writings of Frederick Douglass* (4 vols.; New York, 1950–55), IV, 25–26; Benjamin Quarles, *Frederick Douglass* (Washington, D.C., 1948), 229–31.

45 Stevens to Kelley, Sept. 6, 1866, Stevens Papers, LC.

out of the campaign. Governor Samuel Cony of Maine said that he favored equal suffrage as much as any man in the country, "but I don't believe in making negro suffrage an issue now. Our great object now is to secure the next Congress. If we don't get that, then all is lost; if we do get it, then all is safe."[46]

In this temper the convention spent three days attacking Andrew Johnson and the Democrats. But on the fourth day the Committee on Unreconstructed States submitted a report that included an endorsement of Negro suffrage. Border-state delegates tried to force an adjournment, and failing that, most of them withdrew, leaving an unorganized and confused mass of delegates from former Confederate states. Seizing the opportunity, Theodore Tilton, Frederick Douglass, and Anna Dickinson marched to the platform and proposed a reorganization of the convention into a popular mass meeting. The enthusiastic southerners agreed, and selected Tilton as chairman. Douglass, Dickinson, and Tilton made rousing speeches that evoked thunderous cheers from the crowd. The southerners, most of whom had never before heard a woman speak in public, were absolutely entranced by Anna Dickinson. After several hours of oratory the meeting broke up in high spirits. The next morning the Southern Loyalists met again formally and the Committee on Unreconstructed States again submitted its Negro suffrage resolutions. At the climax of the debate which followed, reported Tilton, Dr. Randolph, the Negro delegate from New Orleans, "leaped to the stage, and made an electric speech, picturing the wrongs of his race, demanding redress, claiming the ballot, and, suddenly turning to a colossal portrait of Mr. Lincoln behind the platform, exclaimed, 'We are coming, Father Abraham, three hundred

thousand more!' The effect was irresistible. The house sprang to its feet, and gave cheer after cheer." The Negro suffrage resolution was adopted by an overwhelming majority. Moderate northern Republicans were chagrined, but abolitionists were jubilant. The endorsement of Negro suffrage by southern Republicans was an important victory for the radical cause. Many observers agreed that had it not been for the prompt action and persuasive eloquence of Tilton, Douglass, and Dickinson the Southern Loyalists would have adjourned in confusion without declaring for Negro suffrage.[47]

In a campaign speech at Cleveland on September 3, President Johnson repeated his familiar argument that northern radicals who opposed restoration of the Union under his reconstruction policy were traitors. "He who is opposed to the restoration of this Government and the reunion of the States is as great a traitor as Jeff Davis or Wendell Phillips," shouted Johnson. "I would ask you, Why not hang Thad Stevens and Wendell Phillips?"[48] Phillips laughed off the president's bloodthirsty question. But Johnson's designation of Phillips and Stevens as his greatest enemies pointed up an important fact: despite his strictures of the Republican party, Phillips was an influential leader of the party's radical wing. It ws an era highly charged with excitement; Phillips was a bold, exciting, uncompromising spokesman for radicalism, and every word he uttered attracted attention. He might have been elected to Congress in 1866. He was nominated for Congress by a workingmen's party in Boston, and a word from Phillips

[46] *New York Herald*, Sept. 5, 6, 1866; *Independent*, Sept. 13, 1866; Foner, *Douglass*, IV, 26–27; Howard K. Beale, *The Critical Year: A Study of Andrew Johnson and Reconstruction* (2d ed.; New York, 1958), 185–86.

[47] *Independent*, Sept. 13, 1866. See also *New York Herald*, Sept. 7, 8, 1866; *N.A.S. Standard*, Sept. 15, 22, 1866; *Commonwealth*, Sept. 15, 1866; Frederick Douglass to E. C. Stanton, Feb. 6, 1882, Douglass Papers, Anacostia; Douglass to Anna Dickinson, Sept. 10, 1866, Ben Butler to Anna Dickinson, Sept. 8, 1866, Whitelaw Reid to Anna Dickinson, Nov. 11, 1866, Dickinson Papers, LC. Miss Dickinson received many letters of praise and thanks from Southern Loyalists for her part in the convention.

[48] McPherson, *History of Reconstruction*, 135.

probably would have given him the Republican nomination also. But the great orator declined, believing that he could be more influential as an independent, unfettered spokesman of radicalism than as a member of Congress where he would be hampered by party responsibilities and the exigencies of party politics.[49]

Phillips was not the only abolitionist held in high regard by radical Republicans. The party recruited an army of abolitionist speakers for the 1866 campaign, headed by Anna Dickinson. But despite the participation of abolitionists in the campaign, Republican strategy in most parts of the North was to avoid the Negro question and concentrate on excoriating Johnson and extolling the Fourteenth Amendment. The Amendment was praised not so much as a benefit to the Negro but as a defense of the North from the renewed ascendancy of the South in national politics. The *Anti-Slavery Standard* complained in September that "most Republicans on the stump, and most Republicans in the press, are alike in this: they denounce the President unsparingly, praise the Congress and its proposed Amendment unmeasuredly, and threaten the rebels unfearingly. But *the negro* is, with them, nowhere remembered: 'The South Carolina rebel shall not have two votes to the New York loyalist's one;' but whether the loyalist of South Carolina shall have one or not, our halting Republican friends do not say. Northern Unionists —being all white—are to be protected; Southern Unionists—being nineteen-twentieths black—are to be left to rebel discretion."[50]

The question whether the Fourteenth Amendment constituted Congress's final terms of reconstruction emerged as a major campaign issue. Moderate Republicans insisted in stump speeches and newspaper editorials that Congress would readmit southern states when they had ratified the Amendment. They pointed to Tennessee as an example. "There can be no question that the amendment was proposed with the distinct intention of submitting it as the final condition of restoration," declared the influential *Boston Advertiser*. The *Nation* stated that enough Republican candidates had committed themselves on the issue to insure southern readmission in return for ratification. Even the *New York Tribune*, while continuing to plead for impartial suffrage and universal amnesty, conceded that readmission on the basis of the Fourteenth Amendment was favored by a majority of the party. In September the Republican National Committee issued an official address which proclaimed the Amendment to be "a just and safe plan of reconstruction" upon acceptance of which the southern states would be readmitted.[51]

Abolitionists and radical Republicans were alarmed by this renewed evidence of Republican perfidy to the Negro. They hastened to denounce the moderates and to deny that the Fourteenth Amendment constituted the final terms of reconstruction. Congress had made no formal commitment, argued the *Right Way*, and the admission of Tennessee was in no way a binding precedent. "We know personally

---

[49] *Commonwealth*, Aug. 18, 1866; *Independent*, Sept. 13, Oct. 4, 1866; *New York Times*, Aug. 28, 1866; *N.A.S. Standard*, Sept. 15, 29, Oct. 6, 1866; *New York Herald*, quoted in *N.A.S. Standard*, Oct. 6, 1866.

[50] *N.A.S. Standard*, Sept. 8, 1866. Republican speakers tailored their remarks to the temper of the area in which they were speaking. In the middle states and the Old Northwest they carefully avoided any mention of Negro suffrage. In New England and parts of upstate New York, northern Ohio, etc., where antislavery sentiment had always been strong, Republican orators frequently advo-

cated equal suffrage. As one Ohio correspondent of Chief Justice Chase explained: "In the Reserve counties, some of our speakers have openly advocated impartial suffrage, while in other places it was thought necessary, not only to repudiate it but to oppose it." D. R. Cowan to Chase, Oct. 12, 1866, Chase Papers, LC.

[51] *Boston Advertiser*, Sept. 29, 1866; *Nation*, III (Oct. 4, 1866), 270; *New York Tribune*, Sept. 26, 1866; address of the Republican National Committee reprinted in *Right Way*, Sept. 29, 1866. For a discussion of the part this issue played in the 1866 election, see James, *Framing of Fourteenth Amendment*, 169–73.

every prominent member of Congress, and we know that the leaders do not mean to admit the unadmitted States on the mere adoption of the amendment," asserted Theodore Tilton emphatically. "In the name of the radical party, whose heart we know, and whose voice we speak, we repudiate the Committee's pledge to the rebels as wholly unauthorized, invalid, and void. . . . The radical party . . . can assent to no reconstruction short of Impartial Suffrage."[52]

In a rousing New York speech on October 25, Phillips unleashed another broadside against the Fourteenth Amendment. "The Constitutional amendment, so far as the negro is concerned, is a swindle," he said. "The absent, the unheard, the disfranchised race is sacrificed between the upper and nether millstones of Rebeldom, while the Republican party knowingly, systematically and persistently sacrifice it to preserve their political supremacy."[53] But despite their anger with the Republicans, abolitionists were gratified by the overwhelming Republican victory in the 1866 congressional elections. "The House of Representatives can send a dozen members off to a picnic," exulted Tilton, "and yet leave a majority large enough to pass a radical measure over the President's veto." Both Tilton and Phillips interpreted the election results as a thumping repudiation of Johnson but not necessarily a popular endorsement of the Fourteenth Amendment as the final condition of reconstruction. "The Radical men of the North are neither to be conquered by the Democratic, nor trifled with by the Republican, party," wrote Tilton. Phillips declared that Congress, "which abdicated leadership and postponed action till they were 'certain sure' what the elections would be, can now resume their places. Let them go back and, throwing this chaff of Reconstruction out of one window and swindling amendments out of the other," enact a thorough reconstruction program granting the ballot to the freedmen.[54]

The New York Daily News affirmed that "where Mr. Phillips stood a few months ago the Radicals stand to-day; where he stands to-day they will doubtless be a few months hence." But despite this comment, most of the evidence in November, 1866, indicated that if southern states ratified the Amendment, the moderate Republican majority would admit them to the Union with few if any additional conditions. If this happened the future of Negro suffrage would be dark. Abolitionists and radicals looked hopefully to the South for negative action on the Fourteenth Amendment and girded themselves for a sharp struggle in Congress.[55]

---

[52] Right Way, Sept. 29, 1866; Independent, Sept. 27, 1866. See also Commonwealth, Sept. 29, Oct. 6, 13, 1866; N.A.S. Standard, Sept. 22, Oct. 6, 13, 1866.

[53] New York Tribune, Oct. 26, 1866.

[54] Independent, Nov. 15, 1866; N.A.S. Standard, Nov. 17, 1866.

[55] New York Daily News, quoted in N.A.S. Standard, Nov. 24, 1866; James, Framing of Fourteenth Amendment, 174–77; McKitrick, Andrew Johnson and Reconstruction, 449–54.

Southern Radicals Fight for Reconstruction

JACK B. SCROGGS

The advent of Radical Republican leadership in the reconstruction of the recently rebellious states of the South in early 1867 resulted in sweeping changes in both the form and substance of government in this conquered area. Of revolutionary political significance, this shift brought to the fore a new group of leaders gathered from Negroes, the heretofore politically submerged class of native whites, and recently arrived Northerners. The fortunes of this unusual alliance, especially during the early phase of Reconstruction, depended largely upon the success of the Radical party in Congress, a circumstance which led to widespread efforts by state leaders to establish a close liaison with the national party. Correspondence from the Southern Republicans to congressional Radicals discloses many of the problems which they encountered and presents Reconstruction from a point of view frequently ignored by many historians. Here is found an intimate record of local political leaders striving to revamp Southern political institutions despite the determined opposition of Southern spokesmen trained in the school of conservatism. This task, ambitious at best, was made increasingly difficult by intraparty factionalism on the state and local level

and by the failure to maintain close cooperation between the national Republican leadership and the Radical party in the South. A cross section of regional Radicalism, based on the voluminous correspondence from the South Atlantic states—Virginia, North and South Carolina, Georgia, and Florida—clearly reveals these difficulties inherent in the organization of state parties dedicated to radical reform within the framework of a national party rapidly evolving as the agent of conservative interests.

The return to power of traditional political leaders in 1865 and 1866 touched off an initial storm of protest from Southern Radicals. Union men vigorously charged that these former rebels continued to be hostile toward the government and could not be trusted with the job of reconstructing the economy, politics, and society of the South. From North Carolina and Virginia came complaints that rebels held the offices of "trust, honor, or emolument" to the exclusion and proscription of men loyal to the Union.[1] An observer in North Carolina asserted that "the feelings of by far the larger proportion of the people of this State are disloyal to the Govt—and enamored by the bitterest hatred towards the North." He expressed the view that the

* Jack B. Scroggs, "Southern Reconstruction: A Radical View," *Journal of Southern History,* XXIV (November 1958), 407–29. Copyright 1958 by the Southern Historical Association. Reprinted by permission of the Managing Editor.

[1] John Robinson to Thaddeus Stevens, February 22, 1866; Augustus Watson to Stevens, May 3, 1866, in Thaddeus Stevens Papers (Manuscripts Division, Library of Congress).

duplicity of Southern leaders led observers like General Grant to form hasty and erroneous opinions of their loyalty.[2] Thaddeus Stevens, Radical leader in the House, received a report from Georgia that the rebellious spirit in that state was greater than when the state seceded from the Union.[3] Former rebels were accused of tampering with the mails and practicing discrimination in the courts; one North Carolinian expressed fear of mob violence should the rebels discover that he had written to Charles Sumner.[4]

Initially this proscriptive attitude was displayed most prominently toward Southerners who had resisted the Confederacy,[5] but Northerners and freedmen complained of similar treatment. The assistant superintendent of the Freedmen's Bureau at Harpers Ferry declared that "to be an Officer of the U S is to subject one to continual insult, without the power of redress."[6] Protesting against the action of the Georgia convention of 1865 in requiring two years prior residence for voting, a recent immigrant to that state wrote to Thaddeus Stevens: "The loyal men thousands in number now residing in Georgia appeal to you to save them from this rebel act which has been passed to disfranchise them because they are loyal."[7] The former rebels were accused not only of being unwilling to extend any considerable rights and privileges to the Negroes but also of subjecting them to abuse and refusing to encourage them to labor for themselves.[8] A Georgia correspondent, refuting the claim that the Negro was indolent, maintained that "the Southern people as a whole, are not faithful or true exponents of the negroe's [sic] character or his ability."[9] Negro testimony in a similar vein came from freedmen at Halifax, North Carolina, who requested aid from Elihu B. Washburne in collecting a fund to allow them to emigrate to Liberia. They complained that landowners would not let land to black men and they were unable to collect their wages, in arrears for two years. Seeing no hope for freedom in the South, they lamented: "There is nothing in this country for a blackman that has comon sence but cruelty starvation & bloodshed."[10] Also from North Carolina came the warning that the "protection afforded on account of property interest, and the social attachments of Master & Slave are destroyed, and now God have mercy on the blacks, if they are turned over to the government of their old masters, who seem determined to prove emancipation a curse."[11] Southern Radicals argued that Congress should remove the ex-Confederates from office and place Reconstruction in the hands of loyal Union men.[12] Although not wholly responsible for the changing attitude of Congress, these pleas undoubtedly exerted considerable influence

[2] G. F. Granger to Stevens, January 11, 1866, *ibid.* In November, 1865, General Grant had made a hurried trip through some of the Southern states and had made a report highly favorable to the former rebellious citizens.

[3] L. Black to Stevens, December 18, 1865, *ibid.*

[4] Marion Roberts to Stevens, May 15, 1866, *ibid.*; W. T. Laflin to Charles Sumner, February 25, 1867, in Charles Sumner Papers (Houghton Library, Harvard University). From a lower stratum of society came a more fervent plea: "I ask is thar no protection to union men my god how long shall I be prosacuted by Secessions." J. W. Ragland to Stevens, February 8, 1866, in Stevens Papers.

[5] See Roberts to Stevens, May 15, 1866, in Stevens Papers, for an account of Southern reaction to returning western North Carolina veterans of the Union army.

[6] A. [F.] Higgs to Elihu B. Washburne, December 27, 1866, in Elihu B. Washburne Papers (Manuscripts Division, Library of Congress).

[7] Frank S. Hesseltine to Stevens, April 26, 1866, in Stevens Papers.

[8] Granger to Stevens, January 11, 1866, *ibid.* See also Dexter E. Clapp to Benjamin F. Butler, November 9, 1865, in James A. Padgett (ed.), "Reconstruction Letters from North Carolina," in *North Carolina Historical Review* (Raleigh, 1924–), XIX (October, 1942), 398–99.

[9] William Strother to Stevens, April 28, 1866, in Stevens Papers.

[10] Charles Snyder *et al.* to Washburne, February 1, 1868, in Washburne Papers.

[11] Clapp to Butler, November 9, 1865, in Padgett, "Reconstruction Letters from North Carolina," in *North Carolina Historical Review,* XIX (October, 1942), 398–99.

[12] Watson to Stevens, May 3, 1866, in Stevens Papers. Watson wrote: "The true and simple *policy* is to declare every citizen (irrespective of color) a *voter,* and disfranchise every rebel both in the state and National Governments."

in crystallizing congressional action against the relatively lenient policies of President Johnson.

With the overthrow of the Johnson-supported state governments by the Reconstruction Acts of 1867, the three factions of Southern Republicans saw no further impediment in the path toward reform and personal aggrandizement.[13] The exuberant Radicals suggested that the incumbent state officers be immediately dismissed and replaced by loyal Republicans.[14] Although congressional Radicals refused to aid Southern Republicans to this extent, the influence of Radicals in the South began to show a remarkable growth. Negro meetings called by Southern Conservatives tended to evolve into Radical rallies. The freedmen, safely under the control of carpetbag leadership, refused to respond to Conservative overtures, preferring to remain with the party which promised to preserve their political and civil rights.[15]

Armed with the twin weapons of Negro enfranchisement and partial white disfranchisement, Southern Radicals faced the convention elections of the autumn of 1867 with unbounded confidence. From Augusta, Georgia, a local Republican wrote: "We are going to carry Ga for a Convention and frame a Radical Constitution with a *Liberal disfranchising* clause for rebels."[16] John T. Deweese, a leading carpetbagger in North Carolina, anticipated carrying the convention election by 20,000 or 30,000

votes and declared that the Republicans could carry the state for either Grant or Salmon P. Chase in the 1868 presidential election.[17] From Florida carpetbaggers came optimistic predictions along with requests for campaign funds.[18] Only from Georgia were there complaints of bitter opposition by the Conservatives. One Radical in Augusta wrote that the Conservatives "talk confidently of the 'near approach of the day when all the Yanks & white niggers will have to leave the South' "; another reported from Savannah: "Our enemies *here*, are as *Savage as rattlesnakes.*"[19]

True to pre-election predictions, the people of the South voted for conventions and returned large Republican majorities in each of the South Atlantic states, but exultant reports of victory from Southern Radicals were intermingled with their charges of fraud by the Conservative opposition. A carpetbagger in Florida announced that "God is good and the 'radical team' has triumphed . . . in opposition to all the rings Cliques and Statemakers in the State." Declaring that the convention would be "extremely radical," he boasted: "We have secured the confidence of the masses so that we do not much fear opposition."[20] From Georgia came complaints of Conservative fraud; one writer maintained that "Disloyalty was as rampant here during said election in *spirit* as I have seen it at any time during the Rebellion."[21] Forecasting future difficulties for the Republicans, a Georgia carpetbagger wrote: "The white people of Georgia have thrown off their 'masterly inactivity', of which they boasted so much during the canvass and election for delegates . . . and

---

[13] Joseph H. Williams to Sumner, March 15, 1867; J. B. Hall to Sumner, March 17, 1867, in Sumner Papers; S. A. Daniel, Jr., to John Sherman, March 13, 1867, in John Sherman Papers (Manuscripts Division, Library of Congress); W. F. Henderson *et al.* to Stevens, March 4, 1867, in Stevens Papers.

[14] Henderson *et al.* to Stevens, March 4, 1867, in Stevens Papers; J. Bowles to Saul Shellabarger, October 11, 1867, in Washburne Papers.

[15] Thomas W. Conway to Salmon P. Chase, April 23, 1867, in Padgett (ed.), "Reconstruction Letters from North Carolina," in *North Carolina Historical Review,* XXI (July, 1944), 233–35; Daniel Richards to Washburne, November 13, 1867, in Washburne Papers.

[16] Bowles to Shellabarger, October 11, 1867, in Washburne Papers.

[17] John T. Deweese to Washburn, October 30, 1867, *ibid.*

[18] Richards to Washburne, November 11, 13, 1867, *ibid.*

[19] Bowles to Shellabarger, October 11, 1867, *ibid.;* C. H. Hopkins to William E. Chandler, November 16, 1867, in William E. Chandler Papers (Manuscripts Division, Library of Congress).

[20] Richards to Washburne, November 19, 1867, in Washburne Papers.

[21] Benjamin F. Bigelow to Sherman, November 18, 1867, in Sherman Papers.

are going to work in earnest to *defeat the constitution, whatever it may be!*"[22] John C. Underwood, carpetbag leader in Virginia, complained that the state judiciary was "most unrelenting in the persecution of every white or colored voter who is favorable to the Republican party." He further alleged that "thousands have been discharged for the avowed reason that they voted the Republican ticket in October."[23]

Faced with heightening Conservative opposition, Southern Radicals became more insistent upon assurances from Congress of continued support during this inchoate period of their new governments. In Virginia, Underwood wrote of threats "that if the colored and poor laboring people continued to vote against the land holders . . . they would find themselves between the upper & nether mill stones & would be ground to powder." A Conservative member of the Virginia constitutional convention was charged with declaring that no such voter could live upon his land and that he "would sooner see it all grow up in broom sedge & scrub pine." Underwood declared: "These threats are made boldly & defiantly by those who hold all the offices with very rare exceptions & who are at heart just as rebellious as when they were in arms against us." Faced with these threats to the rising power of the Radicals, Underwood asked, "Can Congress save us from annihilation?"[24] From Georgia John Sherman received urgent pleas for firm action by Congress with the prophecy that if the South were to go Democratic "the poor negroes will have no rights and I may truthfully say will not be allowed even to exist except as the nominal slaves of the landed aristocracy of this section."[25]

A member of the Georgia convention told of being "grossly insulted . . . for being a member of a 'Yankee and negro Convention,' " and warned that if Congress should take a backward step the cause would be lost.[26] A Florida carpetbagger expressed fear that the Supreme Court might declare the Reconstruction Acts unconstitutional and precipitate another struggle in which "hopes for the 'lost Cause' would be revived and the hot breath of these infernal fiends would make this Southern country anything but comfortable."[27]

Despite such warnings of tightening opposition, the constitutional conventions which met to reform the state governments were safely in the control of the Radicals, and reports received by congressional leaders were optimistic of the ultimate success of the Republican party in the South. Although the South Carolina group contained a Negro majority, congressional Radicals were assured by a leading white member that "we have now a convention composed of better material than any other Southern state."[28] Urged by Elihu B. Washburne to finish the Florida constitution in time to get it ratified before the Chicago Republican convention, a Radical leader from that state predicted early agreement on the new frame of government.[29] Virginia Radicals wrote for advice on the further disfranchisement of rebels; many Virginia Republicans favored disfranchisement but hoped to avoid anything that would injure the Republican party or "impede its glorious march toward human freedom."[30] North Carolina leaders were optimistic, but Albion W. Tourgée, outstanding carpetbag leader in that state, advised congressional Radicals to defer action on Sherman's Alabama Bill until after all the state elections in order to

[22] A. L. Harris to Sherman, November 29, 1867, *ibid.*

[23] John C. Underwood to Washburne, December 16, 1867, in Washburne Papers. This charge was bolstered by similar complaints against officials of the Petersburg area. James H. Platt, Jr., to George F. Edmunds, December 28, 1867, in Sherman Papers.

[24] Underwood to Washburne, December 9, 16, 1867, in Washburne Papers.

[25] Blodgett to Sherman, December 30, 1867, in Sherman Papers.

[26] Hopkins to Stevens, January 3, 1868, in Stevens Papers.

[27] Richards to G. W. Atwood, January 13, 1868, in Washburne Papers.

[28] J. P. M. Epping to Washburne, February 22, 1868, *ibid.*

[29] Richards to Washburne, January 27, 1868, *ibid.*

[30] J. W. D. Bland to Washburne, March 15, 1868, *ibid.*

lull the Conservatives into a continuation of their policy of inaction.[31]

Relative harmony attended the deliberations in all the constitutional conventions except that of Florida. In that state the Republican organization, much to the delight of the Conservatives, broke into three factions, each of which was led by carpetbaggers. The regular Republicans, under the leadership of Daniel Richards, Liberty Billings, and William U. Saunders, reflected the opinions of the Republican national committee, and their power rested upon the political potentialities of the Union Leagues, which they controlled. A more moderate group, led by Harrison Reed, from Wisconsin, and O. B. Hart, a local Union man, possessed some capital and was supported by the businessmen in the party. The third faction, of lesser power and significance, was led by T. W. Osborn, formerly of Massachusetts.[32] A vivid, partisan description of this dissension is to be found in the regular reports forwarded to Washburne by Daniel Richards.

In the struggle for control of the convention, scheduled to meet in Tallahassee on January 20, 1868, the Billings-Richards wing of the party made the initial move. A week before the assembling of the convention, Richards reported that the regular Republicans had rented a house and spent $400 or $500 converting it into a "mess" for 15 to 20 delegates in order to keep them from being subjected to corrupting influences.[33] This action was countered by similar activity on the part of the Reed forces, whereupon Richards claimed that the Johnson officeholders were behind the move and accused them of "running a hotel free of expense and . . . pouring out money and whiskey most profusely to try and break up the organization of the Convention." He further asserted that Reed, who was the administration mail agent for Florida and Georgia, had authority to draw upon Postmaster General A. W. Randall for $13,500 for campaign expenses. The affluence of the Reed forces constituted a threat to the other factions in their struggle for delegates. Richards reported: "Probably ¾ of them [delegates] had to borrow money to come with and of course all those of easy virtue soon fall a prey to these minions of the devil and A. Johnson who have plenty of money."[34]

On February 11 Richards reported that Johnson men had continued to ply members with money, whiskey, and offers of office until a test vote on eligibility revealed that the Radical wing of the party controlled a majority of one. With all hope of controlling the convention gone, the minority left the city, adjourned to a meeting place 25 miles away, and set up a rival constitutional convention. The rump convention in Tallahassee, in perfect harmony, then adopted a constitution extremely Radical in character. In spite of the fact that the seceding delegates returned in mass, broke into the convention hall around midnight of February 10, organized, and requested recognition as the lawful convention, Richards maintained: "We feel quite certain that our Constitution will be popular with our people and acceptable to Congress."[35]

Richards' optimism was premature. With the support of General George G. Meade, military commander of the district, the seceders did gain recognition as the legal constitutional assembly and drafted a more restrictive document than that proposed by the ousted rump convention. Even with the solid support of the Negroes, the Radicals in Florida were defeated, and their constitution was never presented to the people for ratification.[36]

The campaign for ratification of the new

[31] A. W. Tourgée to Benjamin Wade, February 1, 1868, in Benjamin F. Wade Papers (Manuscripts Division, Library of Congress).

[32] William W. Davis, *The Civil War and Reconstruction in Florida* (New York, 1913), 470–73.

[33] Richards to Washburne, January 13, 1868, in Washburne Papers.

[34] Richards to Washburne, February 2, 11, 1868, *ibid.*

[35] Richards to Washburne, February 11, 1868, *ibid.*

[36] John Wallace, *Carpetbag Rule in Florida* . . . (Jacksonville, 1888), 63–65; Davis, *Civil War and Reconstruction in Florida*, 509–15.

state constitutions revealed a growing Conservative opposition which gave rise to another flurry of protests from Southern Republicans. A Savannah resident wrote that organized clubs of Conservatives were using all sorts of spurious promises to win Negro support and by the use of threats were making freedom of speech impossible. Merchants in Savannah were reportedly advertising that they did not want any further trade from Radicals.[37] Another Georgia observer declared: "These are parties of rebels now going about through the state murdering loyal citizens in their houses at night and shooting them from bushes during the day. . . . These murdering parties are said to be chiefly composed of slave holders sons."[38] Virginia Republicans complained of social ostracism of Yankees and animosity toward further settlement of Northerners; a Richmond Republican informed Stevens that "the Southern white man has become so demoralised in the late rebellion that very few can be trusted politically or in honorable business transactions."[39] A North Carolinian reported that Conservatives in his state bitterly opposed the new constitution because it required the payment of the interest on the state debt, thus increasing taxation.[40] Thaddeus Stevens was urgently requested to curb further the power of President Johnson as a requisite to victory in South Carolina.[41]

The ratification contest also brought a renewal of party strife in Florida, and both factions of Republicans sought congressional support. An adherent of the "Johnson" Republicans wrote: "The rebel element is powerless in Florida before a *united* Republican party, but in the event of disaffection among ourselves and a consequent division of our strength, a Conservative (rebel) ticket will *inevitably* be put in the field and the hazard of our success would be very great."[42] Washburne's faithful reporter, the carpetbagger Richards, warned that "a perfect reign of terror is most imminent." He pointed out that Klan outrages were applauded in Florida and that "threats of violence against all those who dare oppose the adoption of the Rebel Constitution come from high quarters so that we are not permitted to question their purposes."[43] Richards later reported that "the rebels are organizing rapidly and will all support the Constitution," and that their leaders were sponsoring Reed meetings. The Conservatives not only used threats and intimidation, but the Reed Republican faction boasted of their employment of force and their control of the election boards. And yet, even though the Negro leader Saunders deserted them, the Radicals remained optimistic of a shift in the tide.[44]

Despite internal party divisions and growing Conservative opposition, the ratification elections resulted in Republican victories in each of the states except Virginia, where the election was postponed. A combination of factors contributed to this victory, but Republican reports particularly stressed the value of the Union League organizations in achieving ultimate victory.[45]

---

[37] J. S. Powell to "The Reconstruction Committee," February 18, 1868, in Stevens Papers.

[38] Joseph McKee to Stevenson [Stevens], April 16, 1868, *ibid.*

[39] J. G. Landes to Stevens, March 28, 1868; Thomas J. Gale to Stevens, March 19, 1868, *ibid.*

[40] J. M. Clement to Edward McPherson, April 21, 1868, in Edward McPherson Papers (Manuscripts Division, Library of Congress).

[41] Samuel Linsley to Stevens, March 15, 1868, in Stevens Papers.

[42] F. A. Dockray to Stevens, March 18, 1868, *ibid.*

[43] Richards to Washburne, April 14, 1868, in Washburne Papers.

[44] Richards to Washburne, April 14, 20, 21, 1868, *ibid.*

[45] H. P. Farrow of Georgia proclaimed that the "Union League has again saved us." J. M. Edmunds, head of the National Union League, announced in a report to Chandler that testimony from every Southern state witnessed the fact that the Union League was responsible for the Republican sweep in the delegate and constitutional elections. In contrast to most estimates, Farrow announced that the Conservatives of Georgia had secured the support of about 20,000 Negroes. Farrow to Chandler, April 28, 1868; Edmunds to Chandler, June 13, 1868, in Chandler Papers.

Meanwhile disaffection continued among the Republicans of strife-torn Florida. Lamenting Reed's victory in that state, Daniel Richards charged that the Reed party had controlled the newspapers, telegraph, mail, and railroads, had used the school fund for campaign purposes, and had perpetrated "enormous and startling frauds" to secure the adoption of their illegal constitution. He reported that General Milton S. Littlefield, notorious lobbyist from Pennsylvania, had been active in buying up votes for the Reed group; and Richards lamented: "If hell has not turned out all its imps against us then it must be a big and roomy place."[46] Liberty Billings also complained of fraud by the Reed faction; he asked: "Is not Congress bound to see that the people of these States are likely to have a loyal government of equal rights in the future secured by decisive and trustworthy majorities? . . . Give us another opportunity, & we will see that the State is reconstructed upon a basis that will secure permanent peace, progress and prosperity."[47]

Assuring congressional Radicals that Reed was preparing to sell out Radical Republicanism to the Democrats, the Florida extremists pleaded for the rejection of the Florida constitution by Congress. Richards warned: "They have swindled and cheated the people and now they mean to try it on with Congress, and defy their wishes and choice in the matter."[48] Liberty Billings referred to the "Rebel Herods and Johnson office-holding Copperhead-Pilates combining to crucify Radical Republicanism,"

and predicted that the acceptance of the constitution by Congress would ruin the Republican party in Florida.[49] Charges that the constitution was the result of a compact between Reed and the rebels were mingled with requests for a new provisional government and summary rejection by Congress of the Reed constitution.[50]

To all pleas from the Florida extremists for congressional action national Radicals turned a deaf ear. On June 8, 1868, Governor Reed was sworn into office, and 17 days later a bill passed over Johnson's veto admitted Florida's representatives to Congress.[51] Apparent party harmony settled over the political scene in Florida, although one prominent Tallahassee Radical described this harmony as "the concord of a gang of slaves lashed by the whip of the enormous appointing power of the Governor."[52] Congressional Republicans, however, apparently chose to accept the Reed constitution in preference to risking the loss of the state electoral vote in the forthcoming presidential election.

With an apparent victory won in the battle for state reorganization, congressional and local Radicals began to show increasing concern over the approaching presidential election. For a time there was some doubt among Southern Radicals as to whether they should support Grant or Chase for the nomination.[53] Grant's nomi-

---

[46] Richards to Washburne, May 6, 1868, in Washburne Papers; Richards to Stevens, May 25, 1868, in Stevens Papers.

[47] Liberty Billings to Washburne, June 7, 1868, in Washburne Papers. Another Radical claimed that the ballot box stuffing and mail-robbing propensities of the Reed forces "incapacitated them for lawmakers," and a Tallahassee Republican protested vigorously to Washburne against the apparent adoption of the constitution by "mail robbing, stealing votes honestly cast against it, ballot box stuffing, etc., etc." Atwood to Washburne, June 11, 1868; Samuel Walker to Washburne, June 12, 1868, ibid.

[48] Richards to Washburne, June 2, 1868, ibid.

[49] Billings to Washburne, June 7, 1868, ibid.

[50] C. L. Robinson to Stevens, May 29, 1868, in Stevens Papers; Atwood to Washburne, June 8, 1868; Richards to Washburne, May 18, June 2, 1868, in Washburne Papers.

[51] Davis, Civil War and Reconstruction in Florida, 528–31.

[52] Samuel Walker to Washburne, June 20, 1868, in Washburne Papers.

[53] Washburne, the central power behind the early Grant boom, was informed of the Chase campaign in the South; a Florida carpetbagger warned that Thomas Conway, Union League agent, on his tour through the South was threatening the curtailment of funds to the local leagues unless they lent their support to Chase. By January, 1868, however, the incipient Chase boom was losing ground. A native of Jacksonville, Florida, just completing a tour of the South, wrote Washburne that the entire region could be swung for Grant if he took a stand "unequivocally with the

nation by the Chicago Republican convention resolved this doubt, but left the Radicals to face the twin difficulties of Conservative opposition in the South and dissension within their own state organizations. A moderate Republican of Florida reported to national party secretary William E. Chandler: "The Rebels are thoroughly organized and are using every means to intimidate and prevent the loyal people black and white from a free expression & exercise of their political rights. . . . It is evident that . . . the Rebels intend to take forcible possession of these State Governments."[54] North Carolina Republicans, blessed with relative party harmony, caused no worry to the national leaders, although a correspondent from Smithfield informed Washburne that "The rebels are more industrious than the bee & the vote on the constitution is not significant of the presidential vote."[55] Virginia Radicals, although unable to participate in the election, expressed an anxiety over the outcome, predicting that "if [Horatio] Seymour & [Francis P.] Blair should be elected, we are satisfied all loyal men would have to leave the State."[56]

Political conditions in South Carolina during the presidential campaign became so chaotic as to justify the dispatch of a special Radical agent and observer to that state. This observer, John M. Morris, reported that the Democrats were very active and well supplied with money—the "rich rebels coax with one breath and threaten with the next." As to intimidation by the Democrats, Morris declared: "All that is said in the North is true. It is not safe for me to go alone unarmed into the up country here. Negroes are daily shot dead or

wounded. Nobody is convicted because no adequate testimony is found or the magistrates don't prosecute. . . . I fear that thousands of voters will be kept away or driven away from the polls."[57] The carpetbag leadership in the state reported that the malignancy of the Democrats was growing and that they were openly proclaiming that no Negro would be allowed to approach the polls.[58] Governor Robert K. Scott warned: "The rebels did not misrepresent the fact when they said they were not whipped but only overpowered."[59] Nor was evidence lacking to corroborate these charges. In Abbeville County, B. F. Randolph, colored state senator and chairman of the Republican state central committee, while on a speaking tour was murdered by a group of undisguised whites.[60] A congressional representative from the state reported: "Three members of the General Assembly and one member of the late Constitutional Convention have been murdered secretly." He added that the "whole upper portion of the State is said to be in such a condition that it is regarded as unsafe for Republicans to go there to speak." It was impossible, he said, to punish the murderers because of the sympathy of their white neighbors.[61]

Faced with this determined Democratic opposition, Morris was concerned over the prospects of a divided state machine. He reported: "There is yet small *party discipline* and self control. . . . Every man nominated by the State Convention was heartily cursed and shamelessly abused by those he defeated." The colored element, the majority in South Carolina, Morris de-

Republican Party & opposed to Johnson's plans of Reconstruction." Deweese to Washburne, October 30, 1867; Richards to Washburne, November 11, 13, 1867; J. B. Stockton to Washburne, January 14, 1868, *ibid.*

[54] S. B. Conover to Chandler, September 3, 1868, in Chandler Papers.

[55] H. G. Gallion to Washburne, April 27, 1868, in Washburne Papers.

[56] Lewis W. Webb to Chandler, September 16, 1868, in Chandler Papers.

[57] John M. Morris to William Claflin, September 14, 1868, *ibid.*

[58] B. F. Wittemore to Chandler, September 16, 1868; N. G. Parker, D. H. Chamberlain, C. C. Bowen to Chandler, September 12, 1868, *ibid.*

[59] R. K. Scott to T. L. Tullock, October 20, 1868, *ibid.*

[60] A. J. Ransier to Tullock, October 19, 1868; Scott to Tullock, October 20, 1868, *ibid.;* Francis B. Simkins and Robert H. Woody, *South Carolina During Reconstruction* (Chapel Hill, 1932), 446.

[61] F. A. Sawyer to Chandler, October 22, 1868, in Chandler Papers.

scribed as "shrewd—but not educated politically. They have not experience and sagacity." Such lack of party harmony in a Northern state would lead to inevitable defeat. "But here," Morris observed, "I think all can be quieted . . . and a victory won."[62]

The position of the party in Georgia caused further anxiety to the national Radicals. The Negroes of that state were of doubtful value to the Republicans, and the white members of the party were hopelessly at odds. The Democrats, on the other hand, were well organized. Ex-governor Joseph E. Brown predicted a difficult campaign to swing the state to Grant, and, in a plea for funds, declared that all the money in Georgia was concentrated in the hands of the Democrats.[63] John H. Caldwell, national Republican committee member from Georgia, reported that the Democrats were spending vast sums on barbecues to lure the colored vote to the Seymour ticket. He believed that the position of the party would improve when Governor Rufus B. Bullock assumed charge of the patronage;[64] but another prominent Republican informed Chandler that the "sadly demoralized" condition of the party was caused by the action of the constitutional convention in nominating Bullock instead of calling a state Republican convention. He wrote: "In order to secure his nomination and to allay opposition to such action by the Cons'l Conv'n Gov. B. had recourse to bargain and sale of all the prominent offices in the State mainly amongst the members of the Convention, which bargains are now being carried into effect in his appointments to the great mortification and disgust of the prominent Republicans of the State."[65]

The success of the Democrats in the newly elected Georgia legislature served to heighten the anxiety of the Radicals. Close division not only made it impossible for the Republican administration to carry out an effective program, but ultimately led to the expulsion of the Negro members of both houses by the Democrats, and thus to an absolute Democratic majority.[66] The Radicals hoped that this move would "arouse the colored race to sense of their danger, and . . . stimulate them in the cause of their own defense, and that of the Republican party."[67] Actually, Democratic assumption of control in the legislature caused talk of calling a "white man's" constitutional convention. A Republican observer declared: "It is manifestly the intention of the Rebel leaders, to defy the power of the U.S. Govt. and to set at naught the laws of Congress."[68]

Democratic success in Georgia brought an increased volume of Republican protests against frauds, violence, and intimidation. An Atlanta Radical informed Chandler that the colored vote could not be trusted:

The Negroes are too dependent upon their employers to be counted upon with certainty. They are without property, and cannot sustain themselves, but a few days at most, without being fed by their Masters; they are without education or sufficient intelligence to appreciate the power the *Ballot* gives them, add to which a system of intimidation persistently practiced by the Rebels, appealing to their fears through their superstitions, and you have a mass of poverty, ignorance, stupidity, and superstition under the influence of fears both real and imaginary, to organize and control, upon whom but little reliance can be placed.[69]

Joseph E. Brown feared that the Negroes would be driven from the polls either by intimidation or by force. In the event of a free election the state would go Republi-

[62] Morris to Claflin, Septemberd 14, 1868, *ibid*.

[63] Joseph E. Brown to Tullock, June 29, 1868, *ibid*.

[64] John H. Caldwell to Claflin, July 4, 1868, *ibid*.

[65] Volney Spalding to Chandler, August 14, 1868, *ibid*.

[66] Caldwell to Claflin, September 1, 3, 1868; J. E. Bryant to [Chandler], October 5, 1868; Spalding to Chandler, September 5, 1868, *ibid*.

[67] Spalding to Chandler, September 1, 1868, *ibid*.

[68] Spalding to Chandler, September 5, 1868, *ibid*.

[69] Spalding to Chandler, September 1, 1868, *ibid*.

can by a 10,000 majority, but, Brown declared: "There is . . . a reign of terror and violence in some parts of the state, and Republicans cannot hold meetings and discuss the questions involved in the canvass without actual violence or such threats of it as drive off the timid from the meetings."[70] Foster Blodgett, notorious Georgia scalawag, echoed the former governor's observations. "The rebellious spirit is more intense and bitter now than in 1860 and 1861," he said. "Negroes are killed almost every day while white Republicans are threatened [with] abuse and maltreated to an extent that is alarming."[71] John H. Caldwell, Republican candidate for Congress, reported that Democratic methods in Georgia included "bribery, threats, and when they can do so unmolested, actual violence, as well as fraud in the election."[72]

When it became increasingly obvious that the Republican organization lacked the strength to carry Georgia for Grant, Radicals begged Congress to intercede. From Dalton came the assertion: "The present Rebellious spirit is greater here now than it was before the late War. Congress have been too lenient toward the Rebels. Give them an inch and they will take a mile. Active measures must be enacted or we are Butchered up and Law & Constitution trampled under foot."[73] Chandler was warned that further congressional inaction would lead to civil war in the state.[74] Blodgett suggested that Georgia be given another provisional government with Bullock as governor and with six regiments of infantry and one of cavalry to support him. When the election returns confirmed the fears of the Republicans, additional charges of corruption were accompanied by pleas for the overthrow of the "rebel" government and the disallowance of the Georgia electoral vote.[75]

The election resulted in a Grant victory in three of the five states. Through intimidation of the Negroes and a tightly knit white organization the Democrats secured the ascendancy in Georgia; Virginia, not yet readmitted to the Union, was not entitled to a vote.

With the Republicans in control in North Carolina, South Carolina, and Florida, and the status of Virginia and Georgia not fully decided, correspondence between the Radicals of the South and congressional Republicans began to dwindle. No longer were Southern Republicans entirely dependent upon Northern arms for their support. And, with Grant safely elected, congressional Radicals were largely content to allow their Southern colleagues free sway in the former rebellious states—their electoral votes would not be required again until 1872.

Only in Virginia and Georgia did Southern Radicals still urgently petition congressional aid. In a bid for further help, a prominent Georgia Republican, early in 1869, reported that "There is no split in the Republican Party of Georgia. . . . There has never been a question as to whether Georgia is reconstructed." His solution of the problem called for the convening of the old constitutional convention to complete the work of reconstruction.[76] The strife in Georgia led Congress, after a year of vacillation, again to impose military rule in that state. Even so, the state Radicals were still unable to cooperate, and a combination of anti-Bullock Republicans and Democrats brought about the overthrow of the Radical administration in the state election of December, 1870.[77] In Virginia, the dis-

---

[70] Brown to Chandler, October 8, 1868, *ibid.*
[71] Blodgett to Chandler, September 13, 1868, *ibid.*
[72] Caldwell to Claflin, July 4, 1868, *ibid.* Caldwell reported that there was a Democratic plot to murder him which failed when rains delayed his campaign trip. Caldwell to Chandler, October 10, 1868, *ibid.*
[73] L. P. Gudger to Chandler, September 7, 1868, *ibid.*
[74] Spalding to Chandler, September 5, 1868, *ibid.*

[75] Blodgett to Chandler, September 13, 1868; Caldwell to Chandler, November 23, 1868, *ibid.*; Francis H. Smith to Washburne, November 8, 1868, in Washburne Papers.
[76] Farrow to Washburne, February 26, 1869, in Washburne Papers.
[77] C. Mildred Thompson, *Reconstruction in Georgia* (New York, 1915), 255–75; M. M. Hale to Chandler, March 25, 1872, in Chandler Papers.

puted sections on disfranchisement in the 1868 constitution delayed the ratification vote until 1869, when a combination of conservative Republicans and Democrats secured the defeat of these provisions and elected a compromise governor and a Democratic legislature.[78]

The presidential election of 1872 brought another attempt to affect a liaison between national Radical leaders and Southern Republicans to assure the reelection of Grant. Southern Republicans again poured forth tales of Democratic violence and intimidation and bemoaned the dissension within the Radical group of the South. From North Carolina came an early request for protection from the outrages of the Ku Klux Klan. A New Bern Republican wrote Benjamin F. Butler: "I can Say to you With Safity that a Union man Chance is slender hear in North Carolina."[79] A prominent carpetbagger of Greensboro wrote:

The old aristocracy and slave owners of the South are soreheaded; thus far they have refused to be comforted by any sanctifying grace flowing from republican sources. Their hostility to the republican party and their hatred of the U.S. government drove them into the Ku Klux organization. They hoped that by means of that wicked order they would get undisputed control of the South, and with the assistance of Tammany they would walk into the White House in 1873.[80]

On the other hand, Joseph C. Abbott, former carpetbag senator from North Carolina, telegraphed from Raleigh that "Prospects looks [sic] bright if fraud can be Prevented we think success certain."[81] The

Radicals of South Carolina bitterly complained of their lot. A prominent Republican editor of Columbia, protesting continued Klan activity, declared: "There has never, during my four years residence here, been a more intolerant and vindictive spirit manifest than is exhibited now. The threat is openly made, that if Mr. Greeley is elected President the northern men will all be driven out of the state, the negroes degraded from office, and all the old Southern rebel element put into power again."[82] Despite the seriousness of a growing party schism in South Carolina, however, national Radicals refused to intercede in aid of either group. William E. Chandler informed Franklin J. Moses that local politics were of no concern to the party leadership so long as the state was won for Grant.[83]

Radical reports from Georgia expressed a more optimistic view of the chances of the party in that doubtful state. In spite of the activity of the Ku Klux Klan and the poll tax requirements for voting—a newly inaugurated Democratic device—informed Republicans were increasingly hopeful of a Democratic party split in the state.[84] The carpetbag president of the local Union League Council reported to Chandler: "Hostility to the Federal Government and dread of 'negro supremacy,' constitute the cement that holds together the discordant elements of the Democratic Party. The refractory are tamed and whipped in by the fear of 'nigger equality'; but for this kind of pressure the Democratic Party would fall in pieces, and the whites would be about equally divided."[85] The development of the "straight-out" Democratic movement in Georgia in opposition to Horace Greeley was a concrete illustration of internal Democratic strife. Georgia Republicans anticipated aid from the "straight-outs" in preventing the intimidation of Negroes at the

[78] L. E. Dudley to Chandler, August 1, 1868, in Chandler Papers; James B. Hope to Washburne, December 21, 1868; J. K. Gilmer to Washburne, January 16, 1869, in Washburne Papers; Hamilton. Eckenrode, *The Political History of Virginia During the Reconstruction* (Baltimore, 1904), 87–128.

[79] E. A. Smith to Butler, March 20, 1871, in Padgett (ed.), "Reconstruction Letters from North Carolina," in *North Carolina Historical Review,* XX (October, 1943), 348.

[80] Thomas B. Keogh to Butler, November 25, 1871, *ibid.,* 358–59.

[81] J. C. Abbott to Chandler, July 29, 1872, in Chandler Papers.

[82] L. Cass Carpenter to Chandler, August 6, September 21, 1872, *ibid.*

[83] F. J. Moses to Chandler, September 1872, *ibid.*

[84] A. B. Ragan to [Chandler?], September 28, 1872, *ibid.*

[85] Isaac Seeley to Chandler, March 26, 1872, *ibid.*

polls, and an Atlanta Radical reported that "where they make no nomination, the agreement is, that they will support our man or else remain neutral."[86]

Republican hopes for the capture of Georgia were dissipated by the results of the state election in August. Democrats again asserted their power. One Radical, reporting to Chandler, declared: "To say that the election was a farce, fails to express the truth, it was a mob, controlled by the Democratic bullies, and ended in *crime*." The "straights," he complained, either stayed at home or were bullied into the Democratic ranks.[87] A South Carolinian observing the Georgia election reported:

Never since the formation of this government was there a more shameful outrage upon free suffrage than the one just perpetrated in Georgia in the name of democracy. The colored men were intimidated and driven away from the polls by the hundred and one devices of the democrats, and where words would not do, bloody deeds soon taught the negroes that to vote against the wishes of their white employers and neighbors was to risk death.[88]

Despite internal Republican dissension, the political picture in Florida was cause for Radical optimism. A Tallahassee carpetbagger wrote of the improving political sagacity of the Negro: "The opposition may talk of the everlasting 'nigger' but it is beginning to learn that it has in the black man a foe whose opinions are born of honesty and whose native instincts assisted by six years' education in the exercise of the suffrage, and his naturally Christian heart, make him at this time their most formidable enemy, and the finest and most progressive friend of the Republican party."[89]

By midsummer of 1872 the party had begun to recover from the effects of attempts to impeach Governor Reed, and the relative harmony displayed at the August state convention gave further hope of continued Radical success.[90] Although Reed continued to press for the support of the national Radicals, his influence steadily declined.[91] Republicans in Florida became more concerned over President Grant's removal from federal office of District Attorney H. Bisbee and Marshal Sherman Conant, two leading carpetbaggers, than with the contentions of Reed. Radicals protested that these removals "cast a damper upon the *honest Republicans* here and the Democrats are in great glee"; and the chairman of the state executive committee informed Chandler that this action would probably throw the state to the Democrats. So insistent were the state leaders that Grant was persuaded to reinstate the two carpetbaggers, a move hailed by the state Radical leadership as responsible for the revival of party harmony.[92]

Notwithstanding the favorable turn of events in Florida, and continued strong Radical influence in North and South Carolina, Republican prospects generally were not thought to be as bright as in 1868. Indeed, a Savannah correspondent declared that the Republican victory of 1868 had brought about the ultimate decline of the party by the elevation of unworthy and corrupt individuals to positions of trust.[93] A

---

[86] William L. Scruggs to Chandler, September 26, 1872, *ibid;* Edward Stanwood, *A History of the Presidency from 1788 to 1897* (Boston, 1928), 349–55.

[87] Scruggs to Chandler, October 5, 1872, in Chandler Papers.

[88] Carpenter to Chairman, National Executive Committee, October 6, 1872, *ibid.*

[89] Sid L. Bates to Chandler, April 15, 1872, *ibid.*

[90] Osborn to [Chandler?], July 11, 1872; W. J. Purman to Chandler, April 25, 1872; Bates to Chandler, April 15, 1872, *ibid.*

[91] In October Reed informed Chandler: "I have not suffered for four years, to now be willing to see my glorious work overthrown & freedom cheated of her triumphs, nor shall I under any circumstances consent to see this great revolution turned back, either for the benefit of rebels, or sneaking traitors." Reed to Chandler, October 24, 1872, *ibid.*

[92] John F. Rollins to Chandler, October 4, 1872; A. A. Knight to Chandler, October 6, 1872; E. M. Cheney to Chandler, October 7, 11, 1872; J. O. Townsend to Chandler, October 7, 1872; Charles Cowlan to Chandler, October 8, 1872, *ibid.*

[93] Hale to Chandler, March 25, 1872, *ibid.*

South Carolina Radical wrote that the main hope of a Grant victory must rest on the Northern states, for "Southern States like Southern chivalry are mighty uncertain."[94] A North Carolina carpetbagger suggested an astute political move by which national Radicals could improve the party position in the South. He proposed that a bill be drawn up for the assumption of the Southern state debts and sent through the House with a great deal of fanfare. Then it could be held in the Senate until after the election, at which time it could be killed or passed as desired. Thus could favorable sentiment be created for the Republicans by subterfuge.[95] More optimistically, the secretary of the National Union Council informed Chandler that with "the Union League in full blast all over the South and South West . . . we can rally all our forces, and control the black vote for Grant" even though there were persistent reports of organized attempts to mislead the Negro.[96]

Doubtless these local Radical apprehensions had a salutary effect upon the activities and contributions of national Republicans, for the efforts of the Democrats and "straight-outs" to recapture these Southern states were in vain except in Georgia. In that state, although it was a center of insurgent Democratic activity, the regular Democrats produced a sizable majority for Greeley.

After the reelection of Grant in 1872, the tie between the congressional Radicals and Southern Republicans rapidly deteriorated. Southern Radicals, gradually losing power through the South Atlantic states, discovered that Congress was reluctant to act except during periods of national party crisis, and their complaints and pleas gradually lessened. Indeed, when in 1874 the Democrats captured the lower house of Congress, Radical congressional action was no longer possible.

As the election of 1876 approached, Democratic leaders displayed a determination to oust the Republicans regardless of methods. A Florida Radical, despairing of victory with two Republican electoral tickets in the field, informed Chandler that the strong opposition was composed of young men who had grown up in postwar conditions and who blamed all the ills of the South on Yankees and Negroes, and a Virginia observer told John Sherman that there was great danger of open revolt in the South if the Democrats failed to win the election.[97] In South Carolina, Governor Daniel H. Chamberlain, candidate for reelection, faced Wade Hampton's formidable "red-shirts," undergoing personal abuse and even threats on his life. Chandler received a report that at one Republican rally in Barnwell County 600 mounted Democrats had taken over the meeting and heaped abuse upon the carpetbaggers and scalawags. The governor was denounced as "a Carrion Crow, a Buzzard who has come down here to prey upon our people and steal from them their substance," and amidst frequent rebel yells it was suggested that the crowd hang him and his entourage on the spot. An observer of the affray declared that the Republicans of the state were no longer willing to undergo such punishment unless the North came to their aid.[98] An Atlanta Republican suggested that Northern speakers be sent South: "The ignorant masses here (mostly Republicans) require instruction in their political rights and duties as free citizens, and encouragement to stand up like men for their rights."[99]

The determination of Southern Democrats plus the dissension within the Southern Republican party ultimately led to the defeat of the Radicals in each of the South

---

[94] Carpenter to Chandler, October 15, 1872, *ibid*.

[95] Keogh to Butler, November 25, 1871, in Padgett (ed.), "Reconstruction Letters from North Carolina," in *North Carolina Historical Review,* XX (October, 1943), 358–59.

[96] Thomas G. Baker to Chandler, May 17, 23, 1872, in Chandler Papers.

[97] Alex River to Sherman, July 25, 1875, in Sherman Papers; Rollins to Chandler, August 9, 1876, in Chandler Papers.

[98] Carpenter to Chandler, August 26, 1876, in Chandler Papers.

[99] Spalding to Chandler, June 26, 1876, *ibid*.

Atlantic states by 1876. Contested election returns from both South Carolina and Florida for a time beclouded the political scene, but the repudiation of the Radical state leaders by the Hayes administration brought a quick collapse of the remaining Radical organizations.

Although Southern Radical Republican correspondence necessarily presents a distorted picture of the full process of Southern Reconstruction, it is nevertheless an invaluable source for a study of that much-disputed period of American history. From no other source is the historian able to secure so complete a picture of the motives, emotions, and reactions of the members of the three factions who composed the Southern wing of the postwar Republican party. This correspondence, along with other contemporary sources, reveals a much more complex social, economic, and political evolution than is found in partisan accounts by historians who neglect material prejudicial to their sectional sympathies.

Several factors of primary importance are disclosed by these Radical letters from the South. In the first place they reveal a problem of adjustment of interests which plagued the party until its overthrow in 1876—a problem which undoubtedly contributed much to that downfall. A contemporary North Carolinian phrased the difficulty thus: "The problem of adjusting the balance between the three constituent elements of the Republican party South is certainly one pregnant with danger, therefore claiming imminent solution from the hands of the national leaders of our party."[100] That the national leaders were either unable or unwilling to undertake this task is evidenced by the inability of the state organizations to follow consistently a policy of cooperation.

These communications further reveal a lack of close cooperation between the leading Radicals of the South and the congressional Radicals. Most frequently the correspondence was from less influential Republicans often in opposition to dominant groups. The urgency of pleas and complaints from these Southern Radicals obviously was important in helping to shape the opinions of congressional leaders, but, after 1868, the pleas received a favorable response only when the strength of the national party was threatened. Intrastate party difficulties were, in the main, left to the solution of local leaders; national leaders refused to become involved in party splits such as occurred in Florida and South Carolina. Central direction was difficult to achieve, particularly as the Southern Radicals became increasingly a burden and an embarrassment to the national party.[101] Personal ambition and differences in ideology worked to produce antagonistic groups within the party in each of the Southern states, and astute Conservative politicians proved to be adept at widening the gaps. This intraparty division ultimately proved disastrous to the Republicans in all of the South Atlantic states, especially in South Carolina, Georgia, and Florida, where conflicting groups struggled for power throughout the Reconstruction years.

Southern Radical correspondence further reveals the effectiveness of the campaign developed by the Redeemers in their struggle to capture control of the state governments. Radical accounts of intimidation, fraud, and violence, while undoubtedly exaggerated, demonstrate an early reinvigoration of local political leadership. The evidence indicates that state Radicals, especially the carpetbag leaders, grossly underestimated the abilities and strength of this Conservative leadership in all of the South Atlantic states. The immigrants from the North seized upon the Reconstruction Acts as an opportunity to revamp Southern political and social standards, but their methods were revolutionary in character and took little

---

[100] E. M. Rosafy to Butler, March 28, 1874, in Padgett (ed.), "Reconstruction Letters from North Carolina," in *North Carolina Historical Review*, XX (October, 1943), 365–70.

[101] C. Vann Woodward, *Reunion and Reaction: The Compromise of 1877 and the End of Reconstruction* (Boston, 1951), deals extensively with this party problem.

account of past development and of national trends in political economy. Ultimately cultural forces of the past, and long-standing mores, in league with newly evolving economic combinations, led to repudiation of Southern Radicalism by the national party leaders and the emergence of conservative whites of the South as the stronger force.

1962

Enforcing the Fifteenth Amendment[*]

EVERETTE SWINNEY

Since 1940 when Howard K. Beale called for a reevaluation of the Reconstruction period in American history, revisionist monographs and articles have been appearing in ever-increasing numbers.[1] Much work, however, remains to be done. For instance, no one has attempted any fundamental research on the federal Enforcement Acts since the days of William A. Dunning and James Ford Rhodes. These acts, which lay at the heart of the Grant administration's Southern policy, were its response to the South's challenge to the Reconstruction program of the radicals.

Begun in March, 1867, and completed by the summer of 1870, the Reconstruction settlement showed signs of crumbling at its foundation even before the edifice was completed. The election of 1868 amply demonstrated the tenuous nature of Republican supremacy upon which the success of the radical program rested. President Andrew Johnson's amnesty proclamations of September 7 and December 25, 1868, restoring the suffrage to most former Confederates did not help matters, and the victory of the Democratic party in 1869 and 1870 at the polls in Virginia, North Carolina, and Georgia was discouraging. But most alarming of all was the way in which the Ku Klux Klan and other similar extralegal bodies were, by violence and intimidation, preventing Negroes from voting.[2]

In the face of these cumulative threats to Republican ascendancy, Congress moved expeditiously, passing within a 12-month period in 1870–71 three laws designed to protect the Negro in the enjoyment of his newly won political and civil rights. The First Enforcement Act, which became law on May 30, 1870, was long and complex. It forbade state officials to discriminate among voters on the basis of race or color in the application of local election laws, outlawed "force, bribery, threats, and in-

* Everette Swinney, "Enforcing the Fifteenth Amendment, 1870–1877," *Journal of Southern History,* XXVII (May 1962), 202–18. Copyright 1962 by the Southern Historical Association. Reprinted by permission of the Managing Editor.

[1] See Howard K. Beale, "On Rewriting Reconstruction History," *American Historical Review,* XLV (July, 1940), 807–27, and Bernard A. Weisberger, "The Dark and Bloody Ground of Reconstruction Historiography," *Journal of Southern History,* XXV (November, 1959), 427–47.

[2] See Charles H. Coleman, *The Election of 1868; the Democratic Effort to Regain Control* (New York, 1933); Jonathan Truman Dorris, *Pardon and Amnesty Under Lincoln and Johnson: The Restoration of the Confederates in Their Rights and Privileges, 1861–1898* (Chapel Hill, 1953), 339–61; and James A. Rawley, "The General Amnesty Act of 1872: A Note," *Mississippi Valley Historical Review,* XLVII (December, 1960), 480–84.

426 THE AGE OF CIVIL WAR AND RECONSTRUCTION

timidation" of voters, and made it a misdemeanor to deprive a citizen of "employment
or occupation" in order to control his vote.
Most important, the law prohibited disguised groups from going "upon the public
highways, or upon the premises of another"
with intent to interfere with constitutional
liberties.[3] The Second Enforcement Act,
passed following the disheartening midterm
elections of 1870, extended further the federal control of the voting process. Supervisors of election, to be stationed in cities
where election irregularities were considered
likely, were to stand guard over and scruti-
nize registration and voting procedures and
to certify returns.[4] The third law, popularly
known as the Ku Klux Act, made it a federal offense to conspire to "overthrow . . .
or destroy by force the government of the
United States" or to conspire to prevent persons from holding offices, serving on juries,
enjoying equal protection of the laws, or
voting.[5] The three laws provided for extensive enforcement machinery. The President
was given authority to call out the Army and
Navy and to suspend the writ of habeas
corpus; United States marshals were authorized to use the *posse comitatus;* and federal troops were empowered to implement
court orders. In the hope of reducing the
effect of local pressures against enforcement,
exclusive original jurisdiction in all suffrage
cases was reserved to the federal courts.

Historians have been far from favorable
in their evaluation of this legislation. William W. Davis, whose study published in
1914 has been somewhat of a standard
account of the enforcement program, wrote,
"The enactment of the law and its enforcement meant the desertion, for the time being,
by the national government of certain principles in political procedure which make
working democracy in America a practical
possibility." He found "considerable similarity between the arbitrary order and mailed
fist in the South during the seventies and

the past oppression of Ireland by England,
of Bohemia and Italy by Austria, of Fin-
land and Poland by Russia, of Alsace and
Lorraine by Germany."[6] His interpretation
has been perpetuated in textbooks where
the terms "harsh," "drastic," or "iniquitous"
are commonly used to describe the laws.

The Acts were comprehensive it is true;
but the fact is that they did not go beyond
the intent of the Fifteenth Amendment,
which took a moderate and statesmanlike
position on voting. The Fifteenth Amendment, unlike the Reconstruction Act of
1867, did not grant the Negro the right to
vote; it merely outlawed the use of race as
a test for voting. The Enforcement Acts
of 1870–71 accorded with the Fifteenth
Amendment in leaving to the state full freedom to restrict suffrage on any basis except
race or color. As a matter of fact, the constitutionality of the Enforcement Acts was
challenged at the time not for any federal
invasion of the states' reserved power to
establish suffrage requirements but for alleged encroachment upon the states' police
power. The opponents of the Acts denied
that the Fifteenth Amendment authorized
the federal government to punish private
citizens who prevented persons from voting
for reasons of race, holding that the amendment limited only state and federal action
and could not be construed as extending
"one hair's breadth further."[7]

Recent developments have gone far to
destroy the force of Davis' argument that the
Enforcement Acts "belonged to a more arbitrary period," suggesting "an autocracy
rather than a democracy."[8] The Civil Rights
Acts of 1957 and 1960, which were hailed
by libertarians, demonstrate that the United
States Congress has returned to the principles of 1870 in its approach to voting, and
by its 1961 report the Civil Rights Commission shows that it has gone far beyond

---

[3] *Statutes at Large of the United States,* XVI
(1871), 140–46.

[4] *Ibid.,* 433–40.

[5] *Ibid.,* XVII (1873), 13–15.

[6] William W. Davis, "The Federal Enforcement Acts," *Studies in Southern History and Politics; Inscribed to William A. Dunning* (New York,
1914), 205.

[7] *Congressional Globe,* 41st Cong., 2d sess.,
pt. 4, 3662.

[8] Davis, "Federal Enforcement Acts," 228.

such principles in its demand for federal supervision of elections.[9] Finally, the provisions for enforcement of the acts of 1870–71—with the exception of the authorization to suspend the writ of habeas corpus, which was done only once—were not innovations but were consistent with traditional usage. Whatever the motives of those who promoted the legislation, the laws as enacted were essentially in accord with the democratic credo.

Under these laws the Department of Justice made a determined effort to enforce the Fifteenth Amendment. Between 1870 and 1896, when the bulk of the legislation was repealed, 7,372 cases were tried, and hundreds of offenders who were never brought to trial were arrested.[10] Despite this widespread activity, the disfranchisement of the Negro proceeded apace. By 1877 the Negro vote had been largely neutralized and a solid Democratic South assured. Complete disfranchisement of the Negro was to follow. The few historians who have attempted to evaluate the operation of the Enforcement Acts have emphasized the fact that there were relatively few convictions. William A. Dunning, who laid down the general lines of interpretation which have since prevailed, wrote,

The proportion of convictions to indictments was ridiculously small and sufficiently illustrated the iniquity of the laws. In the year ending June 30, 1874, for example, there were 102 convictions out of 966 cases, or 10.5 percent, while for all other classes of cases in the same courts . . . the percentage of convictions was 49.9.[11]

E. Merton Coulter, generalizing upon Dunning's calculations, observed that "in all the trials throughout the South for the next few years, only about 10 per cent of the defendants were convicted." He concluded

that "arrests were made more to terrorize the people and to promote the Radical party than to secure actual justice."[12]

These assertions give a distorted picture. The percentages hold true only for the years after 1874. In 1870 the government won 74 percent of its enforcement cases; in 1871 41 percent; in 1872, 49 percent; and in 1873, 36 percent. After 1874, it is true, convictions seldom passed the 10 percent mark and were often considerably below it.[13] If, as Dunning and Coulter aver, the low percentage of convictions proved the iniquity of the laws, one would have to conclude that the laws became iniquitous only after 1874.

The proper explanation is somewhat less absurd and more complex. In the first place, by 1874 the government was ready to pursue a more moderate policy. Attorney General George Williams justified this change in strategy by two arguments, both of which were probably fallacious. He took the position that the worst of the Ku Klux activity had been brought under control and that it was safe for the government to relax its vigilance. The Attorney General wrote in 1874 that "the Government has reason to believe that its general intentions in prosecuting these offenses . . . have been accomplished . . . and that there are good grounds for hoping that it will not return."[14] Most scholars have accepted the view that the backbone of the Klan proper was broken by the initial impact of the prosecutions; it is

[9] *Statutes at Large of the United States,* LXXI (1958), 637; LXXIV (1961), 88–92; U.S. Commission on Civil Rights, *Report, 1961* (5 vols., Washington, D.C., 1961), I (*Voting*), 139–42.

[10] Davis, "Federal Enforcement Acts," 224.

[11] William A. Dunning, *Reconstruction, Political and Economic, 1865–1877* (New York, 1907), 271.

[12] E. Merton Coulter, *The South During Reconstruction, 1865–1877* (Baton Rouge, 1947), 171.

[13] *Annual Report of the Attorney General, 1870, House Exec. Docs.,* 41st Cong., 3rd sess., No. 90 (Serial 1454); 1871, *ibid.,* 42d Cong., 2d sess., No. 55 (Serial 1510); 1872, *Senate Exec. Docs.,* 42d Cong., 3rd sess., No. 32 (Serial 1545); 1873, *House Exec. Docs.,* 43rd Cong., 1st sess., No. 6 (Serial 1606); 1874, *ibid.,* 43rd Cong., 2d sess., No. 7 (Serial 1638); 1875, *ibid.,* 44th Cong., 1st sess., No. 14 (Serial 1686); 1876, *ibid.,* 44th Cong., 2d sess., No. 20 (Serial 1751); 1877, *ibid.,* 45th Cong., 2d sess., No. 7 (Serial 1802); 1878, *ibid.,* 45th Cong., 3rd sess., No. 7 (Serial 1852), *passim.*

[14] Attorney General George Williams to Virgil S. Lusk, April 25, 1874, in Record Group 60 (National Archives), Instructions to United States Attorneys and Marshals, D, 511.

certain, however, that violence continued and that the Negro's position in Southern society was anything but secure. Williams also sought to justify the change in policy on the grounds that the government's enforcement program had proved to be an irritant which provoked disrespect for authority and incited lawlessness. "My intention," Williams announced, "is to suspend these prosecutions except in some of the worst cases, in the hope that the effect will be to produce obedience to the law and quiet among the people."[15] Republican control and Negro equality, not the enforcement program, were the real irritants; and it was unlikely that token concessions on procedure would soothe where major concessions on principle were demanded. The South was determined to have a free hand in settling the Negro question, and nothing approaching real peace would come to that section until this was realized.

The Attorney General's arguments disguised rather than revealed the government's real motivation for instituting a more lenient program. Expediency was the primary consideration. The South had remained obdurate in its opposition to enforcement; and the North, preoccupied with the depression, was beginning to lose interest. Erstwhile friends of coercion like Carl Schurz and E. L. Godkin had become critical before the time of the Liberal Republican revolt. Williams himself, a fairly influential radical at the time of his appointment, was now in 1874 one of the most unpopular men in the country. A congressional committee questioned him about alleged excesses in the use of troops, and he was ridiculed in the press as "Grant's Secretary of State for Southern Affairs"; the year before, in 1873, the Senate had rejected his appointment to the Supreme Court. The point is that the Republicans controlled Congress by a scant 35 votes with the midterm elections approaching. Under the circumstances, it is not surprising that in the spring and summer of 1874 Williams instructed district attorneys to dismiss all indictments "excepting such as involve charges of high crime committed in furtherance of the object of the conspiracy." They were told to "enter a *nolle prosequi*" in all cases in which the charge was "merely that of belonging to the Ku Klux Klan . . . of cooperating in its general purposes, or of committing some minor misdemeanor."[16] Many of the indictments which never came to trial were dismissed as a direct result of changing policy.

A second and perhaps more important reason for the abrupt decline in the number of convictions was that adverse court rulings made successful prosecutions after 1874 almost impossible. The constitutionality of certain portions of the Enforcement Acts had been questioned at the very outset. In the famous Ku Klux trials at Columbia, South Carolina, in 1871 defense attorneys Reverdy Johnson and Henry Stanbery developed a powerful case against the constitutionality of the laws, and several federal judges, notable among whom was Bland Ballard of Kentucky, were known as early as 1872 to view the legislation with suspicion.[17] In 1873 three election judges of Louisville, Kentucky, were brought before Ballard and Circuit Judge Halmor H. Edmunds, in the case of *United States* v. *Reese et al.*, on four counts of violation of sections three and four of the First Enforcement Act. The indictments were found defective, and Ballard in an obiter dictum declared the law invalid; the government appealed to the Supreme Court.[18] Meanwhile, another case

---

[15] Quoted in Homer Stillé Cummings and Carl McFarland, *Federal Justice; Chapters in the History of Justice and the Federal Executive* (New York, 1937), 238.

[16] Williams to Lusk, April 25, 1874, in Instructions, D, 511.

[17] For the Johnson and Stanbery arguments, see U.S. Congress, Joint Select Committee on Condition of Affairs in the late Insurrectionary States, *Report, House Reports,* 42d Cong., 2d sess., No. 22 (13 vols.; Serials 1529–41), also *Senate Reports,* 42d Cong., 2d sess., No. 41 (13 vols.; Serials 1484–96), V, 1615–72. See also Gabriel C. Wharton to Williams, March 27, 1872, in Record Group 60, Selected Records Relating to Reconstruction, Source-Chronological for Kentucky.

[18] Wharton to Williams, November 10, 1873, and Benjamin H. Bristow to Williams, October 24, 1873, *ibid.*

(*United States* v. *Cruikshank et al.*) was taking shape in Louisiana. The bloody Colfax massacre of April, 1873—a by-product of the struggle between the McEnery and Kellogg governments for control of the state —had resulted in the slaughter of about 60 Negroes. At the April, 1874, term of the circuit court for the district of Louisiana more than 100 persons were indicted under sections five and six of the First Enforcement Act.[19] Supreme Court Justice Joseph P. Bradley, who was reputed to believe the law unconstitutional, sat in on the trial. "It was an ill-starred hour for this state when he put in his appearance in this Circuit in time to meddle with the trial," District Attorney James Beckwith complained to Washington. "His presence in the district was to me a nightmare while he remained."[20] In a closely reasoned opinion Bradley questioned the scope of the Fifteenth Amendment. It was clear, he said, that Congress has the power to enforce "every right and privilege given or guaranteed by the constitution" but that the mode of enforcement depends upon the character of the right. Where the right is guaranteed by the Constitution "only by a declaration that the State or the United States shall not violate it," as in the Fifteenth Amendment, the power of affirmative enforcement is retained by the state "as part of its residuary sovereignty." Hence, "the power of Congress . . . to legislate for the enforcement of such a guarantee, does not extend to the passage of laws for the suppression of ordinary crime within the States." The other trial justice, Circuit Judge William B. Woods, did not agree, and the case went to the Supreme Court on a division of opinion.[21]

While the Reese and Cruikshank cases were pending before the Supreme Court (1874–76), the enforcement program was arrested. "As I do not believe any convictions can be obtained under existing circum-

stances," Williams informed district attorneys, ". . . I am of the opinion that criminal prosecution under these acts ought to be suspended until it is known whether the Supreme Court will hold them constitutional or otherwise."[22] The Supreme Court decisions, rendered in the spring of 1876, constituted a major reversal for the radicals. Chief Justice Morrison R. Waite, speaking for the court in both cases, adopted the narrow interpretation of the Fifteenth Amendment adumbrated in Bradley's opinion in the Louisiana case two years before. "The Fifteenth Amendment," he argued, "does not confer the right of suffrage upon any one." The right to vote comes from the states; only "the right of exemption from the prohibited discrimination comes from the United States." Congress can legislate only to prevent official discrimination by the states or the United States but not to prevent obstructions and discriminations generally, as it had done in the First Enforcement Act.[23] Technically, just two sections of the act were declared unconstitutional, but the whole law had been brought under a shadow. The effect of the decisions was to bring to a close the active policy of the government to enforce the Fifteenth Amendment.

By going behind the statistics one discovers that there were other factors which made successful prosecutions difficult. White Southern Democrats insisted from the outset that the enforcement laws were unconstitutional, oppressive, and not worthy of respect. Linton Stephens of Georgia well expressed this view when brought before a United States commissioner for a preliminary hearing on an alleged violation.

I am accused under the Enforcement Act of Congress [Stephens said]. My first position is that this whole act is not a law, but a mere legal nullity. It was passed with the professed object of carrying into effect what are called

---

[19] Robert Selph Henry, *The Story of Reconstruction* (Indianapolis, 1938), 484–92.

[20] James R. Beckwith to Williams, June 24, 1874, in Source-Chronological for Louisiana.

[21] *United States* v. *Cruikshank et al.*, 25 Fed. Cas. 707 (1874), quotation on p. 710.

[22] Williams to W. W. Murray, May 5, 1875, in Instructions, E, 443–44.

[23] *United States* v. *Reese et al.*, 92 U.S. 214 (1875), and *United States* v. *Cruikshank et al.*, 92 U.S. 542 (1875).

the 14th and 15th Amendments to the Constitution . . . and depends on their validity for its own. These so-called amendments are . . . not true amendments of that sacred instrument. They are nothing but usurpations and nullities, having no validity themselves and therefore incapable of imparting any to the Enforcement Act or to any other act whatsoever.[24]

With such a view widely held it was extremely difficult to gather evidence. Native whites were usually uncooperative, and Negroes were often reluctant to testify in the face of white hostility. Those witnesses who were persuaded to testify might find their property and lives in danger. In 1872 G. Wiley Wells, district attorney of the northern district of Mississippi saw his case fall apart when five key witnesses were murdered. "I cannot get witnesses," he reported to Washington, "as all feel it is sure death to testify before the Grand Jury."[25] Frightened witnesses appealed to the President and Department of Justice for protection, but they received little comfort. The best the Attorney General could do was to exhort Negro witnesses to have courage, to "take the position that the country is as much yours as it is theirs—that you have as good a right to live in it as they—and that you are determined to live in it, and enjoy all your rights; or to die in it, bravely asserting your rights."[26]

State and local authorities often failed to cooperate with federal officials; indeed, on numerous occasions they impeded the operation of the federal program. In virtually every Southern state, at one time or another during the decade of the 1870s, federal deputy marshals, supervisors of election, or soldiers were arrested by local law enforcement officers on charges ranging from false arrest or assault and battery to murder. In South Carolina no less a figure than Major Lewis

Merrill, commander of the troops stationed in York County during the period of martial law, was taken into custody for false arrest.[27] A favorite stratagem was to prosecute for perjury Negroes who had testified against Klan members before United States commissioners.[28] The government never worked out a reliable device for combating these practices. Sometimes district attorneys were instructed to sue for a writ of habeas corpus in United States courts, but usually they were directed merely to defend the accused before the state tribunal.[29] The most effective way to protect the federal officer was to get the case removed to a federal court for trial, which could sometimes be done under section eighteen of the First Enforcement Act, but only with "exceeding difficulty."[30]

Securing juries that would convict was a perennial problem. In the words of Judge Amos Morrill of Texas, "Jurors drawn at random from the list of voters . . . would not be convinced that any man had violated the revenue acts or the enforcement acts by any testimony."[31] Consequently, in many districts the marshal was given full authority to select jurors and was advised by the Department of Justice to avoid jurors "unfriendly to the laws and the government."[32] Even ostensibly friendly juries were anything but reliable. In 1876 a grand jury in Mississippi refused to indict several persons

[24] John D. Pope to Williams, February 7, 1871, in Source-Chronological for Georgia.

[25] G. Wiley Wells to Williams, January 17, 1872, in Source-Chronological for Mississippi.

[26] Cummings and McFarland, *Federal Justice*, 238.

[27] Bristow to Wells, September 19, 1871, in Instructions, C, 370.

[28] Williams to Henry P. Farrow, January 4, 1875, *ibid.*, E, 214.

[29] Habeas corpus proceedings in the federal courts to release citizens from state custody were authorized by statutes passed in 1833 and 1867, but not until late in the century was the constitutionality of this procedure fully established. *Statutes at Large of the United States,* IV (1850), 634; XIV (1868), 385; *In re Neagle,* 135 U.S. 1 (1890); *In re Loney,* 134 U.S. 372 (1890).

[30] Williams to George M. Duskin, February 11, 1875, in Instructions, E, 266, and Attorney General Edwards Pierrepont to N. S. McAfee, September 11, 1875, *ibid.*, F, 157.

[31] Amos Morrill to Williams, April 3, 1873, in Source-Chronological for Texas.

[32] Attorney General Amos T. Akerman to James H. Pierce, August 28, 1871, in Instructions, B, 336.

for violations of the Enforcement Acts even though, as the foreman admitted, the evidence was overwhelming. The reason given was that key witnesses, fearful of reprisals, would not agree to testify in open court, and the jury saw little use in involving the government in the expense of an abortive trial.[33] In many districts there was experimentation with part-Negro juries, but the effect fell short of expectations. District Attorney Henry P. Farrow of Georgia placed six Negroes on a petit jury in 1873, only to see the term frittered away in an endless debate as to their qualifications.[34] Only in those districts where officials were willing to impanel all-Negro juries, fully protected by federal troops in the courthouses, could convictions be relied upon. The price paid at the bar of Southern public opinion for such success was, of course, high.

Intimidation of witnesses and juries might have been prevented had marshals enjoyed sufficient power to guarantee protection. Indeed, in theory the marshal had ample resources, but in practice he was often impotent. He could call upon the *posse comitatus,* but social pressure made the bystanders reluctant and undependable. Federal troops were stationed throughout the South, but they were seldom available for routine police duty. Securing troops involved much red tape, and requests for them were turned down as often as they were granted; unless actual riot impended, there was little chance of military aid. District Attorney Gabriel C. Wharton of Kentucky made an urgent request for troops in 1875 and received the terse reply, "not a case yet for United States soldiers . . . send written report." Wharton, by return mail, expressed what must have been the unspoken thoughts of many a federal officer, "When there is a case for United States troops in this state there is not time for a written report." As an afterthought, he added, "The Ku-Klux

never fire on United States soldiers, but they do not hesitate to shoot . . . Marshals whenever an opportunity is presented."[35]

Perhaps more basic in the failure of enforcement than the unavailability of troops to protect witnesses and juries was the lack of money. The enforcement program was expensive, as a sampling of court costs in the South reveals. Between fiscal 1870 and 1873 the cost of maintaining the courts in the western district of North Carolina rose from $35,000 to $125,000, in South Carolina from $41,000 to $128,000, and in northern Mississippi from $9,000 to $84,000. Congress, harried by demands for lower taxes, was reluctant to provide adequate funds. About a million dollars a year, far less than was necessary, was allocated for court expenses under the new program.[36] Consequently, the Attorney General was forced to urge economy from the beginning, and starting in 1873 marshals were required to make financial reports weekly. Soon the necessity for economy affected the program. Because of high costs Attorney Gene-al Williams in 1873 instructed district at or-neys that "no case be prosecuted under the Enforcement Acts . . . unless the public interest imperatively requires it."[37] Emergency requests for money made by marshals and attorneys were halved and sometimes quartered before being approved. After the Democrats gained control of the House in the elections of 1874, a congressional committee was set up to investigate the expense of the Department of Justice, and the judicial appropriation for 1876–1877 was cut by a half million dollars. Attorney General

---

[33] James R. Cavett to Alphonso Taft, August 28, 1876, in Source-Chronological for Mississippi.

[34] Farrow to Williams, March 15 and May 1, 1873, in Source-Chronological for Georgia.

[35] Wharton to Pierrepont, July 7, 1875, in Source-Chronological for Kentucky.

[36] Treasury Department, *An Account of the Receipts and Expenditures of the United States,* 1870–1873, *passim.* See also *Statutes at Large of the United States,* XVII, 134, and *Annual Report of the Secretary of the Treasury on the State of the Finances,* 1870, *House Exec. Docs.,* 41st Cong., 3d sess., No. 2 (Serial 1451); 1873, *ibid.,* 43rd Cong., 1st sess., No. 2 (Serial 1603).

[37] Williams to All Marshals, March 8, 1873, and Williams to William H. Smyth, February 5, 1873, in Instructions, C, 645, 608.

Alphonso Taft saw little alternative but to put each district on a strict budget, allowing only a little more money than had been available prior to 1870.[38] By the end of the Reconstruction period the vigor of the enforcement program was clearly circumscribed by financial considerations.

The enforcement program was further handicapped by the inadequacies of the federal court system. The Enforcement Acts imposed an unmanageable extra burden on an antiquated judicial structure. The attorneys general frequently complained of the inability of courts to clear their dockets. By October, 1870, some 472 persons had been arrested in South Carolina for alleged violation of the Enforcement Act. At the November term of the circuit court, 420 were indicted, but at the end of the one month session only five had been brought to trial.

With the caution and deliberation which the law wisely observes in criminal proceedings [Attorney General Akerman wrote], it is obvious that the attempt to bring to justice . . . even a small portion of the guilty in that state must fail. . . . If it takes a court over one month to try five offenders, how long will it take to try four hundred, already indicted, and many hundreds more who deserve to be indicted?[39]

Similar problems arose in North Carolina and Mississippi. Faced by this dilemma, the Attorney General had little choice but to compromise. District attorneys were instructed in 1871 to prosecute vigorously only such persons "as appear to have been leaders in the conspiracies." Others were ordered to be "released on light bail" and their cases pushed to trial only if time allowed. "Those whose connection with the conspiracies was compulsory and reluctant" were not even to be indicted.[40]

Assuming that Congress had provided adequate machinery for enforcement, the vitality of the program would still have rested, in the last analysis, upon federal officials in the field, i.e., with the United States judges, district attorneys, marshals, and commissioners. It is impossible to generalize about the quality of the Department of Justice bureaucracy except to say that it was uneven. Evaluation of the quality of the work done by individual officeholders is likewise difficult, even when biographical information is available, because of the biased nature of the sources and the conflicting criteria of judgment. Corruption, irresponsibility, and rank political partisanship were to be found, of course, but it is safe to say that the caliber of federal officialdom, with some notable exceptions, was somewhat higher than has usually been acknowledged. Nor were federal appointments in the South the special preserve of the carpetbagger; a perusal of the roster of Department of Justice officers reveals that a majority were Southern born.[41]

Neither is it true that all officials shared the same sociopolitical views. Many, of course, were radicals in the tradition of Charles Sumner and Thaddeus Stevens. Hugh Lennox Bond from Maryland, judge of the fourth judicial circuit, had been a staunch Unionist during the war, supported the politics of Henry Winter Davis, and was one of the founders of the Association for the Improvement of Colored People. As presiding judge at the famous Ku Klux trials at Columbia, South Carolina, in 1870, he showed little leniency toward lawbreakers, and in two notable cases he upheld the constitutionality of the enforcement legislation.[42] Richard Busteed, district judge for Alabama, was considered one of the most obnoxious men in the state because of his equalitarian ideas and his political harangues from the bench. "He taught that the boy who could read and write was worth twice

---

[38] Taft to Robert P. Baker, August 1, 1876, ibid., F, 571–74.

[39] Annual Report of the Attorney General, 1871, 4 5.

[40] Akerman to D. T. Corbin, November 10, 1871, in Instructions, C, 33–34.

[41] Register of the Department of Justice and the Judicial Officers of the United States, 1–5 eds. (1871–76), passim.

[42] United States v. Crosby et al., 25 Fed. Cas. 701 (1871), and United States v. Petersburg Judges of Election, same v. Petersburg Registrars of Election, 27 Fed. Cas. 506 (1874).

as much to himself and to the community as he that could not, and that the public school should know the public weal only . . . with open door to all creeds and all races alike."[43] D. H. Starbuck, district attorney for eastern North Carolina, who won 49 convictions in 1871, saw the Enforcement Acts as a partisan weapon.

We who were born and raised [in the South, he wrote], know too well the terrible outrages committed by these bands of conspirators whose purposes were to destroy the freedom of elections and stab the government at its vitals . . . . We are entitled to the gratitude and thanks of the Republican or Union Party of this nation which it was the purpose of this daring conspiracy to destroy.[44]

The administration was sensitive to charges of partisanship and consistently sought to control overzealous authorities. In November, 1871, Attorney General Akerman tactfully cautioned District Attorney John A. Minnis of Alabama, "I am glad to observe your zeal, and this I trust will never flag as long as the crimes exist, though of course it should be guided by discretion. The government in these matters is not vindictive, and wishes to worry no citizen unnecessarily. . . ." Later the Attorney General spelled out his meaning:

I suggest the expediency of taking great care to keep the administration of the law unconnected with mere party feuds. As a matter of fact, I suppose that the crimes at which the law aims have principally been perpetrated by one party; but if the members of the other party commit the same offenses . . . they must receive the same treatment. In each instance it seems to one that the case should be clear, both for the moral and legal effect of the prosecution.[45]

As the election of 1874 approached, Attorney General Williams urged district attorneys and marshals in Alabama, South Carolina, Louisiana, Kentucky, and Tennessee "to proceed with all possible energy and dispatch to detect, expose, arrest, and punish" Ku Klux marauders, but he added, "You understand, of course, that no interference whatever with any political or party action not in violation of the law" should be undertaken.[46]

Moderates, conservatives, and even a few Democrats were to be found among the federal authorities in the South. The judiciary in particular was dominated by conservative ideas, and several judges endeared themselves to the Southern population by their refusal to embrace doctrines of social equality and constitutional change. William B. Woods, of the fifth judicial circuit, was a former Ohio Democrat who had come to the support of "Lincoln's war" only reluctantly. Ultimately he joined the Union army and served with Sherman; when the war was over he settled in Alabama and became an ardent Republican. His ardor soon cooled, however, and he subsequently became a conservative on civil rights questions.[47] George W. Brooks, judge of the district of North Carolina, was a Johnson appointee with a reputation for industry and sound judgment. In 1870 Governor W. W. Holden declared two counties under martial law and sent in troops; Brooks released the prisoners under writ of habeas corpus basing his action on the Fourteenth Amendment to protect the personal liberties of white men.[48] Of Henry Clay Caldwell, judge of the eastern district of Arkansas, it was said that "during the six years that the carpetbag regime lasted he was the greatest protec-

[43] John Witherspoon DuBose, *Alabama's Tragic Decade; Ten Years of Alabama, 1865–1874,* James K. Greer (ed.) (Birmingham, 1940), 255; *National Cyclopaedia of American Biography,* IV, 531; Walter L. Fleming, *Civil War and Reconstruction in Alabama* (New York, 1905), 394, 744.

[44] Cummings and McFarland, *Federal Justice,* 237.

[45] Akerman to John A. Minnis, November 11 and 24, 1871, in Instructions, C, 22, 64–65.

[46] Williams to District Attorneys and Marshals, September 3, 1874, *ibid.,* F, 13–14.

[47] Alonzo H. Tuttle, "William Burnham Woods," *Dictionary of American Biography,* XX, 505–06. For Woods' opinions, see *United States* v. *Harris,* 106 U.S. 629 (1882), and *Presser* v. *Illinois,* 116 U.S. 252 (1886).

[48] J. G. de Roulhac Hamilton, *Reconstruction in North Carolina* (New York, 1914), 525–30.

tion that the people of the state had. . . ."[49] Other judges like John Erskine of Georgia, who never took an enforcement case when he could avoid it, and Robert A. Hill of Mississippi, who enforced United States laws with as much leniency as possible, won the confidence, respect, and gratitude of the Southern people.

Some marshals and district attorneys were either sensitive to Southern public opinion or in substantial agreement with it. James H. Pierce, Mississippi marshal, was very concerned about Democratic charges early in his term. The Attorney General sought, in instances like this, to bolster morale:

You give greater consideration than I think is due to the censures of a party press. While of course you should give no occasion for grounded censures, yet on the other hand, you should not be deterred by unfounded censures for doing your full duty.[50]

Another Mississippi marshal supported the Democratic ticket in the election of 1872, and the marshal and district attorney of the eastern district of Texas packed juries with Democrats in order to prevent convictions.[51] When such defections became known to the Attorney General, investigations were undertaken, and removal from office usually resulted. Georgia District Attorney John D. Pope, a Johnson appointee, is a case in point. Georgia Republicans early complained that Negroes were receiving no protection from the district attorney's office, and the secret service, investigating Ku Klux disturbances in Georgia in 1871 and 1872, found that Pope would not allow Klan "victims" to testify in court. "If there is not a

United States attorney sent here to prosecute these fellows in earnest," one operative observed, "I can see but little use for us to work them up, run the risk of our lives and bring them to Atlanta, there to see them discharged."[52] Pope was shortly replaced by Henry P. Farrow and prosecutions of klansmen began.

Although the Department of Justice was involved in none of the great scandals of the Grant administration, there was to be found among department personnel some of the low morality characteristic of the age. Extravagance was perhaps the most common failing. Virgil S. Lusk, district attorney of the western district of North Carolina, was repeatedly warned about laxity in financial matters.

So conduct the business of your office [Williams cautioned], that hereafter it will be unnecessary for me to complain of extravagance in its administration. As the Comptroller [of the Treasury] well says, referring to your district, the number of warrants issued appears to be limited only by inability to serve them all . . . . There is ground for suspicion that persons concerned in criminal prosecutions in your district are sacrificing the interests of the government . . . to the accumulation of their fees.[53]

Misconduct was most usually found among minor officials such as commissioners, supervisors of election, and deputy marshals. Drunkenness, arbitrary use of power, and blackmail were the most common complaints lodged against them. Reports of such misconduct were a source of much discomfort to the Attorney General, and marshals were encouraged to select only "prudent and fearless" subordinates. "It is important,"

[49] H. W. Howard Knott, "Henry Clay Caldwell," *Dictionary of American Biography*, III, 408.
[50] Akerman to James H. Pierce, August 28, 1871, in Instructions, B, 336.
[51] Williams to Marshal Robert J. Alcorn, July 8, 1873, *ibid.*, D, 115, and Governor E. J. Davis to Williams, February 2, 1872, in Source-Chronological for Texas.

[52] J. R. W. Johnston to Williams, February 15, 1872, in Source-Chronological for Georgia, and Record Group 60, Hiram G. Whitley, Reports Regarding the Ku Klux Klan, Report Number 2, 9–10.
[53] Williams to Lusk, February 3, 1874, in Instructions, D, 386–87.

Williams emphasized, "that you delegate . . . power to none but careful and responsible persons."[54] The most notorious scandal involving the Department of Justice occurred in the western district of Arkansas. This district, with headquarters at Fort Smith, embraced the "Indian Territory," a lawless area inhabited by cutthroats and renegades. Successive United States attorneys and marshals and Judge William Story were all implicated in fraud, bribery, and other misconduct; not until Isaac C. Parker, the "hanging judge," took office in 1875 was the mess cleaned up.[55]

In attempting to reach a fairer evaluation of the enforcement program, one additional factor must be considered. As in other phases of Southern history it is dangerous to overwork the concept of the "Solid South." Although the South ultimately presented a united front on the race question, there was initially considerable difference of opinion on this matter between the Black Belt planter and the upcountry farmer. The Ku Klux movement was strongest in the former nonslaveholding regions, such as western North Carolina, eastern Kentucky and Tennessee, and northern South Carolina, Georgia, and Alabama. The congressional committee which investigated the Klan tacitly recognized this fact when it limited its investigations to six states, and reports from federal officials in the field show conclusively that life and property were a good deal less secure in some districts than in others.[56] Since the Enforcement Acts were essentially, although not exclusively, designed to combat the Klan, it is not surprising to find that outside of the former nonslaveholding areas there was relatively little activity under the

legislation. The following table shows the number of cases instituted in each of the Southern states during 1870–77.[57]

South Carolina	1,387	Florida	41
Mississippi	1,175	Texas	29
North Carolina	559	West Virginia	27
Tennessee	214	Virginia	16
Alabama	134	Louisiana	4
Kentucky	116	Arkansas	3
Georgia	73	Missouri	3
Maryland	56		

These statistics reveal a correlation between Klan concentration and enforcement activity and suggest that prosecutions were more justified than Coulter, Dunning, and others have admitted.

In conclusion, it may be pointed out that most exciting studies of the federal enforcement policy in the 1870s were written at a time when disfranchisement and Jim Crowism were accepted as the normal state of affairs in both North and South; political and social inequality, it was assumed, was the logical result of racial inferiority. Such attitudes affected the validity of scholarly findings. Today, we may agree with Dunning and Rhodes that unlimited Negro suffrage was a mistake. But we cannot accept the corollary of this, that universal Negro disfranchisement was a valid alternative.

In 1870, measures to preserve the Negro's constitutional rights were desperately needed, and Congress responded with the passage of the Enforcement Acts of 1870 and 1871. These laws, essentially sound, worked fairly well for three or four years. Implementation, however, was difficult. The Grant administration, whose radicalism has perhaps been overemphasized, used federal power conspicuously on a few well-known occasions, but shortages of troops, money, and courts plagued law enforcement officers from the beginning. After 1874, the Acts were virtually dead letter. In the final analy-

---

54 Williams to All Marshals, September 30, 1874, *ibid.*, E, 63.

55 David Y. Thomas. "Isaac Charles Parker," *Dictionary of American Biography*, XIV, 225–26. See also Source-Chronological for Arkansas, *passim.*

56 See, for example, *Message on Political Affairs in the Southern States*, House Exec. Docs., 42d Cong., 2d sess., No. 268 (Serial 1515).

57 *Annual Report of the Attorney General*, 1870–1877, *passim.*

sis, Southern intransigence and Northern apathy together brought about the collapse of the enforcement program; white supremacy proved to be a more vital principle than Republican supremacy. The South, in its determination to win home rule, was willing to face the prospect of race war; the North was not. In the end, the policy of enforcement failed; but this does not mean that the policy was iniquitous nor that its failure was a blessing. A complete re-examination of the subject should tell us much about the later Reconstruction period and might well provide useful object lessons for the present.

CHAPTER 10

The Retreat from Reconstruction

In the case of Reconstruction the roots of failure go deeply into American culture. From the earliest days of the Republic most Southerners *and* Northerners subscribed to racial opinions which denied the democratic creed to Negroes, and only the upheaval of Civil War made the revolutionary dream of emancipation a living possibility. The flight of slaves to Union lines forced federal commanders to ask whether or not they wished to aid the enemy by returning valuable slave property. The desperate need for manpower, the early and successful experiments in the use of Negro troops, and the clamorous antislavery agitation—all helped to bring a skeptical administration gradually to the policy of emancipation. It soon became clear, however, that the Proclamation and the Thirteenth Amendment alone would not make citizenship a reality for the former slaves, and Southern violence followed by presidential blunders stimulated Northern fears that the results of the war would be reversed or damaged without a Reconstruction program.

Unfortunately Reconstruction never progressed far enough to secure land for the freedman. Charles Sumner and a few others saw the importance of providing an economic foundation for freedom but most Radicals, like the overwhelming majority of Americans, regarded conventional property rights as nearly sacred and would not sanction the proposal to turn confiscated plantation lands over to the freedman. In the final analysis the leaders of the Republic proved to be less perceptive than the czar of Russia, who at that very time had begun to allow newly emancipated serfs to purchase land and become landowners. There were several notable exceptions to the general rule, and Willie Lee Rose in 1964 examined the most favorable of the land distribution experiments in a study of the South Carolina Sea Islands. Here at least some of the freedmen gained land which gave them a more hopeful future than most American Negroes were to know in the decades to come. Still, the experiment enjoyed only a limited success. The plots were small and often threatened by further subdivision and legal disputes, and the Sea Islands had to compete with new cotton areas of the world for a declining market. Most importantly, these small enclaves of Negro ownership and independence found survival difficult in the shadow of the larger and unsympathetic communities of South Carolina, the South, and the United States at large.

As Patrick W. Riddleberger indicated in 1960, the abandonment of Reconstruction began as early as the "Liberal Republican" secession from the party in 1872. The Liberal Republicans called for an end to military Reconstruction on the grounds that the three amendments and the various pieces of federal legislation had brought freedom to the Negro, and there was no longer any need for "special assistance." The North grew weary of violence, social conflict, and Southern issues in general, and a spokesman for President Grant indicated that "we are tired of these annual outbursts" of Democratic violence against Negro Republican voters. The spokesman did not mean that the country had become so weary of violence by white men as to act more effectively to stop it, but that the government was tired of having to act and think about the fate of the freedman. Then too, the Republicans had some white Southern voters and politicians were constantly tempted by the possibility of expanding this segment of support. The Radicals had gone to so much trouble to secure the franchise partly because they needed Negro assistance to stay in power, and free elections continued to be an issue until 1896 when the Republicans secured a solid national majority without Negro support. Subsequently Republican leaders ceased to be seriously concerned about Southern support of any kind.

While the withdrawal of federal troops in 1877 struck a damaging blow to the Radical cause, Reconstruction had not yet run its course. As books by Vincent P. De Santis in 1959 and Stanley P. Hirshson in 1962 demonstrated, every president from Hayes to Harrison gave some attention to "the Negro problem," and white Southerners could not be reasonably sure until the 1890s that the nation would not attempt to interfere with Southern racial domination. In 1877 a part of "the bargain" which brought Hayes to the White House was the promise of Southerners to respect the rights of the Negro. Despite all evidence to the contrary, Hayes seems to have seriously believed that the "redeemers," "conservatives," and Democrats who made this pledge would abide by it, and the President urged Congress several times to use federal support of education as a supplementary means of improving the status of the freedman. No doubt some Southern leaders meant to keep the pledges made in 1876, but as the North grew increasingly disinterested and as the concrete pressures lessened, the politicians tended to follow the desire of the white majority for more and more subordination of Negroes. The Republican political creed advocated both moral and material progress, and this belief did not die on Inauguration Day, 1877. As time passed moral idealism did diminish, the desire to have "business as usual" increased, and the amount of real concern for the Negro declined, but Rutherford B. Hayes, Chester A. Arthur, James G. Blaine, and even Benjamin Harrison made proposals relating either to voting rights or to educational opportunities. Hopes for a federal education bill died a lingering death in the decade after 1877, and Senator Henry Cabot Lodge introduced the last serious "force" bill to protect Negro voting rights in 1890.

For nearly 20 years after 1877 at least a few Republican politicians tried to keep alive the grand issues of Civil War and Reconstruction, an effort which led to the creation of another term of political abuse to use along with "carpetbagger" and "scalawag." The phrase "waving the bloody shirt" was applied to Northern politicians who raised the ghost of presumably dead "war" issues (such as Negro voting rights) for purely demagogic purposes. By implication, the new term denied the existence of any real issues, suggested that news of violence and caste subjugation from the South was somehow misleading or false, and impugned the motives of Republicans who made speeches on "war issues." Here is another instance of a rationalization which served to conceal the fact that a single society harbored both democratic values and social oppression. Quite possibly political leaders of the era from 1876 to 1895, men such as John Sherman, James G. Blaine, and George F. Hoar, fell below the high moral standards of Garrison, Douglass, and Phillips and failed to operate on the same plane of momentous political leadership as Sumner and Stevens, but one should not assume that these men were totally devoid of principle and completely hypocritical in their speeches on Southern violence and the status of the Negro. If moral idealism was waning in the North between 1875 and 1895, the fact remained that the Negro had no one else to turn to other than the "wavers of the bloody shirt." Moreover, even if all the motives of the dwindling Republican minority who kept "war issues" alive were bad, did not their speeches refer to the real issue of Negro freedom? Were not the lynchings and acts of terror reported by the "bloody shirt" politicians events which actually took place?

The Supreme Court, which preceded the Republican Party in the abandonment of the Negro, initiated an anti-equalitarian trend of thought as early as 1873. The Court in the Civil Rights cases of 1883 virtually destroyed the Civil Rights Act of 1875, and rendered many parts of the Fourteenth Amendment inoperative. Hostile legal reasoning reached a climax in the Plessy case of 1896 after a fashion which Barton J. Bernstein charted so well in 1963. The "separate but equal" formula was accepted despite the sharp protest of Justice John Marshall Harlan who identified segregation laws as oppressive measures contrary to the Fourteenth Amendment. Did the Court or any other group of informed Northerners or Southerners really imagine that the facilities in any area of Southern life were in fact equal or likely to become so? It seems most improbable, and certainly "the separation of the races" makes sense only in the context of belief in racial superiority and inferiority. The Supreme Court's rationalization that "social equality" between "the races" could not be legislated represented surrender by the national government to regional forces intent on an increasingly firm subordination of Negroes.

The fate to which nation and Congress, Republican Party and Supreme Court abandoned the Southern Negro was defined over a long period of time. Negroes and whites separated with dramatic speed after 1865 in religious and social spheres but, as C. Vann Woodward demonstrated in 1955, the complete system of "Jim Crow" segregation did not spring directly from slavery or from the timeworn customs of many generations. A particular area of segregation was usually the product of a specific state law in 1885 or 1915, an event which very old people in our own times might remember. As late as 1890 a substantial number of Negroes voted and used many public facilities freely. The last Negro did not leave Congress until 1901, and the state constitutions which placed the stamp of approval on the new social arrangements came into existence between 1890 and 1907. The edifice of segregation was still under construction during the 1930's, and in several states even as recently as the fifties. When it became reasonably clear that no significant national institution would intervene, Southern Democrats proceeded to perfect by law and private action a set of social controls which made the South a fortress of white supremacy.

The closure of many choice occupations coupled with the establishment of invariably inferior educational systems sharply curtailed the Negro's hopes for a better life. Joblessness, low wages, and frequent threats to male independence sustained patterns of family instability inherited from slavery, and the assault on Negro dignity in the condescending ridicule or the harsh aggression of stories, songs, and maxims demoralized the lives of both men and women. To prevent or to destroy any form of group unity inimical to the interests of the dominant caste, local authorities generally kept Negro communities under surveillance. The occasional practice of holding any Negro or even an entire community responsible for the actions of one person and the general failure to police Negro neighborhoods encouraged "displaced aggression" by men who lacked the power to direct hostile emotions toward their oppressors and consequently turned against each other.

"Segregation" seems an inadequate word to describe this new system of bondage which developed so many harsh and cruel institutions. The hated practice of using chain gangs for public works and leased convict labor for private wealth were not examples of isolated abuse but part of a complex pattern of social domination. In the midst of general poverty and at a time when wealth was rare, few could resist the temptation to exploit—and often to cheat —the illiterate and helpless sharecroppers and laborers. The system simply did not compel white men to observe agreements faithfully, and the Negro had few means of redress after he had been excluded from the polls, the jury box, and the right to a trial before unbiased judges and juries. Invariably white men transformed Negro losses into personal advantage. The economic benefits to the dominant caste were dramatically evident, and they increased with the passing of every decade. The task of measuring white status gains achieved at the expense of Negro dignity and security is more difficult, but John Dollard in 1937 made an excellent analysis of the whole pattern of caste gain.

The pervasiveness and the frequency of violence provided the most demoralizing aspects of the system, and often lynchings became virtually public ceremonies led by local officials and attended by thousands of men, women, and children. To read the history of Southern racial violence is to read a catalog of the excessive acts of savagery of which humanity is capable—men emasculated, burnt alive, toes and fingers chopped from living persons and corpses to be used as souvenirs, the sustained torture of persons until death came from shock, and the occasional lynching of women and children as well as men. Frequently the killings went beyond the conceivable needs of a system of caste control and served either as a barbarous outlet for the most sadistic segment of the community or as a kind of ritual murder in the religion of white supremacy.

It is quite true that many white citizens regretted these "acts of excess" but few made serious efforts to stop the violence, and juries invariably freed both leaders and members of the mobs. Rayford W. Logan in 1954 traced the web of responsibility far beyond the Mason-Dixon line to a Supreme Court which did not protect constitutional rights, to a Congress which failed to pass anti-lynching laws, and to the general majority of Americans who belonged to the high age of imperialism when white men from America to Germany enjoyed a new peak of power and self-esteem. Most Northerners were perfectly willing to grant that the Southerner, as the man who "knew" the Negro best, should handle "race relations." Americans often acknowledged the inferiority of the Negro and just as frequently conceded that Reconstruction had been a mistake.

The South was the home of most Negroes and the storm center of violence, but men were also lynched elsewhere. The years from 1880 to 1910 also saw a general retrogression in the status of Northern Negroes, as state civil rights bills became hollow pretenses and universities closed doors which had once been open. The abolitionists had always been a minority, death and old age removed many from the political scene and a consequential number of the survivors were gradually persuaded by the new wave of racist opinion which marked the eighties and nineties. Some, without conscious hypocrisy, began to grant the need for more segregation and to recommend "self-help" coupled with "better morale" as the only solution. A history of Negro labor in the North is in large part a history of violent displacement by the most recent and poverty-stricken immigrant group. On the New York docks, for example, Negroes could work as longshoremen until they were driven from their jobs by Irishmen; later they were able to reclaim some of the jobs only to be thrust out again by later waves of immigration. In general the racial concepts which dominated the South ruled the minds of most Americans. Between 1895 and 1919 nearly every major Northern and Middle Western city which contained Negroes experienced the kind of racial violence usually described as a "race riot" but which often represented the effort of a mob of white men to injure or kill Negroes and to destroy their property.

American Negroes moved into the twentieth century as an oppressed minority, deprived in almost every area—education, income, economic opportunity, and individual human dignity. Nevertheless, the Civil War and Reconstruction had created some permanent gains. The old system of slavery had been destroyed; and the freedman had gained a precarious economic independence and mobility of person, the rudiments of an educational system, and the hope for a better future. A small Negro middle class existed even in ante-bellum days, and it grew steadily through the postwar decades. The literacy rate increased with each decade, and modern measures such as social security and general community welfare which were certainly not created with the Negro in mind nonetheless often helped him. The New Deal and the post World War II eras brought a less hostile political climate, a Supreme Court willing to reverse its predecessors, an international situation favorable to the Negro cause, and above all the political movement which broke out among American Negroes in the late fifties and the early sixties.

The old question of when Reconstruction ended might be answered by asking when it began. Was it not a continuation of the old antislavery struggle which began before the Republic itself? The year 1866 did see momentous gains in the struggle for freedom, and the year 1876–77 did see monumental losses, but Reconstruction did not come to a complete halt in 1877. Did it stop in 1896 with the Plessy decision, or in 1901 when the last Negro congressman vacated his seat, or in 1906 when the last of the Southern states completed the new round of hostile constitutions? Or did it ever end? Massive and constant violations did not take the Fourteenth and Fifteenth Amendments from the Constitution, and they continued to have a shadowy existence as ultimate promises of full citizenship. The cause of Negro freedom and equality never went without at least a few defenders, and in the 1950s and 1960s the struggle became a mass movement under dynamic Negro leadership. Martin Luther King, James Farmer, and the young men of SNCC inherited the mantle of leadership from Garrison, Douglass, and Sumner with great hope of achieving that ultimate victory which had eluded the abolitionists and the Radical Republicans.

BIBLIOGRAPHY

Books and Articles Referred to in the Chapter Introduction

Patrick W. Riddleberger, "The Radicals' Abandonment of the Negro During Reconstruction," *Journal of Negro History* (1960).

Vincent P. De Santis, *The Republicans Face the Southern Question; The New Departure Years, 1877–1897* (1959).

Stanley P. Hirshson, *Farewell to the Bloody Shirt; Northern Republicans and the Southern Negro, 1877–1893* (1962).

John Dollard, *Caste and Class in a Southern Town* (1937).

Suggested Reading

All the works by C. Vann Woodward cited in other chapters are pertinent to this chapter. Aside from Woodward's original analyses of Southern politics in the generation after 1876, the most interesting work in the period can be found in the early historical chapters of studies by the sociologist E. Franklin Frazier. See *The Negro in the United States* (1948) and *The Negro Church in America* (1964). De Santis and Hirshson provided much useful information about the Republican party and the Negroes in the last decades after 1877. The earliest Republican revolts against Reconstruction were analyzed by Patrick W. Riddleberger, "The Break in the Radical Ranks: Liberals *vs*. Stalwarts in the Election of 1872," *Journal of Negro History* (1959), and James M. McPherson, "Grant or Greeley? The Abolitionist Dilemma in the Election of 1872," *American Historical Review* (1965). C. Vann Woodward wrote the most provocative account of the election of 1876 in *Reunion and Reaction* (1956). Herbert J. Clancy produced a moderately helpful account of *The Presidential Election of 1880* (1958). On the Blair education bill see Allen J. Going, "The South and the Blair Election Bill," *Mississippi Valley Historical Review* (1957), and on the Lodge election bill of 1890 see John A. Garraty, *Henry Cabot Lodge* (1953). The origins of segregation were discussed by John Hope Franklin in "Jim Crow Goes to School," *South Atlantic Quarterly* (1959); C. Vann Woodward, "The Birth of Jim Crow," *American Heritage* (1964) [which also contains material on the Plessy case]; and Woodward, *The Strange Career of Jim Crow* (1955). For information concerning the help given to segregation by Northern philanthropists, see William P. Vaughn, "Partners in Segregation: Barnas

Sears and the Peabody Fund," *Civil War History* (1964); and Louis D. Rubin (ed.), *Teach the Freeman: The Correspondence of Rutherford B. Hayes and the Slater Fund for Negro Education, 1881–1887* (2 vols.; 1959). On Southern dissenters from the dominant ultra-segregationist point of view, see Charles E. Wynes, "Lewis Harvie Blair, Virginia Reformer," *Virginia Magazine of History and Biography* (1964); Lewis Harvie Blair, *A Southern Prophecy* (1899) (ed.), C. Vann Woodward (new ed.; 1964); and Arlin Turner's collection of essays, written by Cable between 1875 and 1895, George W. Cable, *The Negro Question* (1956). Arthur F. Raper, *The Tragedy of Lynching* (1933) needs to be replaced by a modern study. Ralph Ginzberg (ed.), *100 Years of Lynching* (1962) contains over a hundred news stories on lynching. On Southern violence see Glen S. Sisk, "Crime and Justice in the Alabama Black Belt, 1875–1917," *Mid-America* (1958); Allen D. Grimshaw, "Lawlessness and Violence in America and their Special Manifestations in Changing Negro-White Relations," *Journal of Negro History* (1959); Clarence A. Bacote, "Negro Proscriptions, Protests, and Proposed Solutions in Georgia, 1880–1908," *Journal of Southern History* (1950). Louis R. Harlan revealed in *Separate and Unequal* (1958) that in South Carolina the expenditures on the Negro child fell from ⅛ to ¹⁄₁₂ the amount spent on white children between 1900 and 1915. Herbert Aptheker (ed.), *A Documentary History of the Negro People in the United States* (1951) contains selections on lynching, convict labor, and other forms of violence and exploitation. The best general studies of Negroes during this period are Charles E. Wynes, *Race Relations in Virginia, 1870–1902* (1961); Frenise A Logan, *The Negro in North Carolina, 1876–1894* (1964); George B. Tindall, *South Carolina Negroes, 1877–1900* (1952); and Helen C. Edmonds, *The Negro and Fusion Politics in North Carolina, 1895–1901* (1951). For accounts of Northern proscription and violence, see Irving Dillard, "Civil Liberties of Negroes in Illinois since 1865," *Journal of the Illinois State Historical Society* (1963); Elliott M. Rudwick, *Race Riot at East St. Louis, July 2, 1917* (1964); Leslie H. Fishel, Jr., "The Negro in Northern Politics, 1870–1900," *Mississippi Valley Historical Review* (1955). The hostile situation for Negro workers was discussed by Herman D. Bloch in "The New York City Negro and Occupational Eviction, 1860–1910," *International Review of Social History* (1960), and "Labor and the Negro, 1866–1910," *Journal of Negro History* (1965). On Darwinian racism among Anti-Imperialists, see Christopher Lasch, "The Anti-Imperialists, the Philippines, and the Inequality of Man," *Journal of Southern History* (1958). For a curious piece of historical irony in American Negro history, see Louis R. Harlan, "Booker T. Washington and the White Man's Burden," *American Historical Review* (1966). For discussions of the Supreme Court and racist thought see Robert Harris, *The Quest for Equality* (1960); Hugh Williamson, "The Role of the Courts in the Status of the Negro," *Journal of Southern History* (1955); Sydney Kaplan, "Albion W. Tourgee, Attorney for the Segregated," *Journal of Negro History* (1964). Barton J. Bernstein argued that the Plessy decision was not even good case law, "Case Law in Plessy v. Ferguson," *Journal of Negro History* (1962). Sam Ross wrote an interesting account of a Union veteran and Republican politician who was presumably the worst and latest of the "bloody shirt" wavers. See *The Empty Sleeve: A Biography of Lucius Fairchild* (1964).

1964

The Aftermath of Reconstruction at Port Royal*

WILLIE LEE ROSE

What had gone wrong? The future had seemed so promising back in 1868 when the radical Republican government had begun its course. Part of the initial exhilaration had been sheer relief. All the fears for the freedmen associated with Saxton's last months in office, when he had tried manfully to block President Johnson's land restoration policy, were banished. The colored people had not been relegated to the tyranny of their late owners, and in the islands near Beaufort the freedmen had retained their land. President Johnson had been a poor politician and had understood little of the national sentiment in the year following the war; he had prescribed too mildly for the returning South. In the pivotal election of 1866, the radical reconstructionists had been returned to Congress in such strength that the meager alterations Johnson had conceived were swept from the board, and stern measures were promptly enforced. The radicals had, by a series of acts of 1867 and the enforcement of the Fourteenth Amendment, banished the old leading class from political power and "reconstructed" the South on the basis of an electorate composed, to all practical purposes, of enfranchised Negroes and Northerners in residence.

Back in 1864 James Thompson had written in passionate conviction of the great future in store for South Carolina with the overthrow of slavery. "To make another Massachusetts of South Carolina it is only necessary to give her freedom and education. To these ends we devote our best efforts."[1] For many idealists who converged on Columbia in 1868 to write a new constitution for the state, these words were as meaningful as they had been for young Thompson, a Gideonite. The radicals, who included among their number many of the missionaries sent South by the freedmen's aid societies, wrote an excellent constitution, based upon the most modern concepts of popular government. No good Gideonite could have asked for more. Every disability of race was demolished, and the legal foundation for a universal free system of public education was laid.[2] The evangels had approached their part in the Reconstruction with confidence.

Laura Towne wrote Edward Pierce of her feelings. She congratulated her old friend on a radical speech he had made in the fall elections and said she was sorry to be so far from the great events in the North, where men like Pierce were "moulding the destinies" of America. But she added, "We are doing a little moulding in a small way ourselves. Isn't South Carolina loyal, and are

* Willie Lee Rose, *Rehearsal for Reconstruction: The Port Royal Experiment*, (Indianapolis, Ind.: Bobbs-Merrill Co., 1964).

[1] Beaufort *Free South*, January 2, 1864.

[2] Simkins and Woody, *South Carolina During Reconstruction*, pp. 93–100.

not the states where there are no 'Yankee school-marms' disloyal? Won't we grow in loyalty as the rising generations come up?" The satisfaction of most evangels regarding universal suffrage was strongly predicated upon the assumption that they would remain the controlling political influence among the freedmen. For as Reuben Tomlinson wrote, although he was "a universal suffrage man," he didn't "care a cent for it unless we can keep Northern influence here along with it." The Northern influence would remain, and the radicals would have their chance. E. L. Pierce was exultant. "How great [are] these days!" He thought he could see the end of the contest "concerning the African race in this country" and was confident that there had never been since Christian martyrdom or the Reformation the "opportunity for equal devotion—or like exhilaration of the moral sentiments." The Negroes of the South were "at last upon their feet provided with all the weapons of defense which any class or race can have."[3]

Pierce did not see the danger. The whole North seemingly joined him in thinking that, with the granting of suffrage, the slaves of a few years before were well "on their feet." By 1868, when the radical government of South Carolina went into effect, the Freedmen's Bureau, except for two more years of assistance to education, had already finished its work.[4] The charitable organizations were left alone in the field, and their days were numbered. In fact, the great American Freedmen's Union Commission was hardly organized before it began to disintegrate. In early 1967 the Western branches at Chicago and Cincinnati forsook the nonsectarian commission and joined forces with the American Missionary Association. By fall of that year the American Freedmen's Union Commission was restating its goals in such modest terms that it was possible to claim that the commission had actually done what it had set out to do. It was a bad thing, thought the officers, to continue to press the cause of the black man before the public, because pressure might hasten a reaction against him. The triumph of the Republican party on President-elect Grant's "Let us have peace" slogan in the fall elections and the formation of reconstructed governments in the South were thought to have removed the necessity of Northern efforts for freedmen's schools. The organization had provided a model for the new state governments. "The skeleton of an educational system will be already there, waiting only to be filled up." At the close of its work the officers congratulated the organization mildly, and deceptively, on having "checked, if it has not altogether overcome, that spirit of denominationalism which endangered the whole movement."[5] Honesty should have compelled the officers to admit that the organized churches had triumphed and that nearly all that would be done in the future by the North for Negro education would come through the American Missionary Association and other denominational groups.[6]

Gone were the grand claims of making a new New England of the South. What had happened in the North is much more clearly seen in the statements of the officers of the New England branch of the Commission, a branch that struggled on alone until 1874. As early as the fall of 1866 the editors of its journal, the *Freedmen's Record,* were complaining of public indifference to the cause: "were the tidings to come, as they

---

[3] Laura Towne to E. L. Pierce, December 6, 1867, Pierce MSS; Reuben Tomlinson to J. M. McKim, December 4, 1866, and E. L. Pierce to McKim, April 20, 1867, McKim MSS.

[4] John Cox and LaWanda Cox, "General O. O. Howard and the 'Misrepresented Bureau,'" *Journal of Southern History,* XIX (November, 1953), 442.

[5] See the *American Freedman,* II (November, 1868), *passim,* and quotations from this issue of the *American Freedman* in the *Freedmen's Record,* IV (November, 1868), 169–170; Synopses of School Reports, I, 158, entry 158, Education Division, BRFAL MSS.

[6] Richard Bryant Drake, "The American Missionary Association and the Southern Negro, 1861–1888" (Ph.D. dissertation, Emory University, 1959), pp. 20–24; *A History of the American Missionary Association: Its Churches and Educational Institutions among the Freedmen, Indians and Chinese* (New York, 1874), pp. 13–14.

did last year, that thousands were suffering from hunger, cold, and nakedness, the appeal would probably be responded to as generously as it was then. The great mass of people do not, as yet see that in the education of . . . freedmen is to be found the solution of some of the weightiest public questions of the day." If the freedmen could not even read a newspaper, would they not become political pawns, perhaps in the hands of their late masters?[7] The society rallied, however, and spent an all-time high budget of nearly $76,000 for Southern education in the year 1866-67. The contributions tumbled sharply in the succeeding winter, dwindling to approximately $29,000. The society again recovered some lost ground, but not for long. Edward Hooper, the treasurer, was writing a supporter in early 1873, in great complacency: "The New England Freedmen's Aid Society has had so much money from the good people of Boston during the past ten years that it no longer thinks it fair to urge its friends to continue their gifts. The Society has reduced its work very much, having turned over to the local authorities in the South as many of its schools as they would take." A year later, at the annual meeting, a letter was read concerning the transfer of the society's "Robert Gould Shaw Memorial School" to the city of Charleston. Then the question was put whether the society should disband. The first vote was to continue. The secretary then recorded, "These votes not seeming on the whole to reflect the exact feelings of the meeting[,] they were subsequently reconsidered, and instead it was voted, to discontinue the Society in its present form." Adjournment followed, "*sine die*."[8]

The North had plainly concluded that in granting the franchise the national obligation to the freedmen had been fulfilled. Ed-

ward King pointed out the folly of the federal government's granting voting rights without providing the means for national assistance to education, thrusting upon the impoverished South the responsibility for a public school system that it had not possessed in its flourishing days. By the time King came to South Carolina, the state had been on its own for five years, the state school system was simply one more tool in the hands of the corrupt, and Laura Towne was writing, "The need of education here seems to be greater than ever—the means less, friends fewer. . . ." Editor Thompson posited that "the fault of the North in its treatment of the South seems to us to be an indifference to it. This is a result of a reaction." The North was not completely oblivious of the South and its problems in the early 1870s, but there was an inclination to blame the sad state of affairs in the late slave states on the ignorance of the electorate and on renegade Northerners who used them as tools. The North was not so much indifferent as tired, and the nation seized simple excuses that left the Northern conscience easier. Thompson, however, brought up the point of Northern indifference in order to scold Southern conservative white people who persisted in making no difference between Northerners of honesty and good will and those who were no credit to any section. The editor of the *Republican* was angry because the conservatives had failed to come to the polls to help put in a reform Republican government in South Carolina in 1872. Thompson advised them "to give up looking for extraneous aid. . . . Quit sitting at home, thanking God that you were born between the Pedee and the Savannah, grumbling over the present and sighing for the past. No one cares for a self-made martyr."[9]

What had happened to bring James Thompson to such a pass that he cried out to the old planter class to aid Gideon's Band? He was smarting from the results of

[7] *Freedmen's Record,* II (November, 1866), 198.

[8] Financial statement in Synopses of School Reports, I, 341, Educational Division, BRFAL MSS; Edward Hooper to Miss M. G. Chapman, March 10, 1873, Weston MSS; Minutes of the New England Freedmen's Aid Society, March 20, 1874, NEFAS MSS, Sturgis-Hooper Papers.

[9] Towne to F. R. Cope, April 9, 1873, Towne MSS; Beaufort *Republican,* November 21, 1872; King, *Southern States,* p. 602.

the failure in 1872 to elect his old friend Reuben Tomlinson to the governorship on a reform ticket. The results of the election, at least in Beaufort County, had made a certain matter completely clear, one that should have been foreseen by the Gideonites long ago. Northern "evangels," however high-minded, could not control the Negro vote. Robert Smalls had become the greatest political force in the region; and he had swung the colored vote for the "regular" Republicans, galvanizing the opposition to Tomlinson and his own opponent for the state senatorship, a Northern Negro lawyer named W. J. Whipper, with cries that the freedmen could not trust outsiders, that they should vote for none but Southern men.[10] It had worked. If Tomlinson had been known anywhere in South Carolina as a just and honorable man it would have been at Port Royal, where he had worked with the freedmen since 1862 with much credit and universal acclaim among his fellow evangels. He had received in Beaufort County a meager vote of 1,445 to 4,995 for Franklin J. Moses, as blatant a swindler as ever sat in any gubernatorial chair, and a native white Southerner. In the "Brick Church" precinct, near his old headquarters as General Superintendent under Saxton, Tomlinson received only 62 votes, to 631 for Moses. Editor Thompson saw that the votes had been divided between the two men largely on the basis of color, with the white people voting for Tomlinson and the colored voters, following Smalls, voting for Moses.[11] Smalls had called for reform too, and in the murky waters of Reconstruction it was impossible sometimes for even well-educated men to differentiate between the

degrees of corrupt associations that clouded the reputations of nearly all politicians. To the Negro electorate Smalls was a hero, the brave skipper of the *Planter* and "the smartest *cullud* man in Souf Car-lina."[12] If a Yankee missionary named Reuben Tomlinson, Gideonite, was remembered at all, it was not very distinctly.

It is also impossible to say that the instincts of the Republican majorities were completely wrong. Still being for the most part illiterate, they probably never read the aspersions of Editor Thompson against Smalls in the *Republican*. In truth, although Smalls was identified with the regular Republicans rather than with the reformers, he emerged from the Reconstruction era convicted of only one serious charge, that he had bribed the clerks of the House and Senate to state that a claim of his for $2,250 had been passed and approved. Smalls, self-educated, had become a self-possessed speaker; he was a man of undoubted intelligence and ready wit. The radical politician may well have been as deeply involved as most of his fellows in the depressing round of graft that characterized the government at Columbia; his conduct of the printing committee was at once politically successful and morally blameworthy. To the Sea Islanders, however, it was thrilling to have a leader who spoke to them in their own Gullah dialect, a powerful man who was known to the conservative editor of the Charleston *News* as the "King" of Beaufort County.[13]

On the other hand, the so-called reform wing of the party included in its ranks numerous unsavory characters. In actuality, Tomlinson himself was connected strategi-

---

[10] Beaufort *Republican,* July 11, August 1, 1872; Simkins and Woody, *South Carolina During Reconstruction,* pp. 466–67. The authors list Smalls as among the bolters from the party, but on the local level he worked to defeat the movement, perhaps because his own opponent, Whipper, associated himself more closely with the reformers, and the carpetbag element was, as Thompson put it, "the heart of the reform movement. . . ." Beaufort *Republican,* August 22, 1872, and September 26, 1872.

[11] *Ibid.,* October 24, 1872.

[12] [Justus Clement French], *Steamer Oceanus,* p. 86.

[13] Simkins and Woody, *South Carolina During Reconstruction,* pp. 133, 476, 543; [French], *Steamer Oceanus,* p. 86; George B. Tindall, *South Carolina Negroes 1877–1900* (Columbia, South Carolina, 1952), pp. 54–55; Beaufort *Tribune,* May 12, 1875, quoting the *News.* The printing swindles were not exposed until after the election of 1872. Smalls was chairman of the printing committee. See Beaufort *Republican,* December 5, 1872, and Port Royal *Commercial,* April 9, 1874.

cally with an extremely lucrative swindle. One of the most outstanding grafts of the era was the Greenville and Columbia Railroad operation. Although Tomlinson emerged in the odor of sanctity, he had been State's Attorney General and at the same time treasurer of the Railroad Company when the crucial transactions that so depressed the credit of the state were made. He had been either a great fool or subject to a serious moral lapse. Back home in Pennsylvania Tomlinson had been a bank clerk, and he ought to have been able to read ledgers. The regular Republicans charged also that Tomlinson had bribed the legislature as freely as any "regular" had done when he wanted the body to grant a franchise to a phosphate company that he was promoting. Whether it was true or not, the state gained little from the franchises granted to such companies.[14]

The truth was simple: The voters of Beaufort had less confidence in the white people than in Negroes. Ten years of exposure to the social and political ideas of Northern radicals had not made them more confident of the ultimate intentions of their teachers. Just as the immigrant population of New England in a later day would follow on faith the city "boss" who understood them, so Port Royalists accepted the leadership of their own people who won power. Perhaps nothing illustrates better the naïveté of certain evangels than their failure to foresee this eventuality.

When the Republican party organized on St. Helena Island in 1867, Laura Towne reported that at a meeting of Negroes, with only a handful of whites present, one man rose to say "he wanted no white man on their platform." He was talked down by his more generous fellows, who said, according to Miss Towne, "What difference does skin make, my bredren. *I* would stand side by side with a *white* man if he acted right," and pleaded that the Negroes not be prejudiced "against their color." Another said,

"If dere skins *is* white, dey may have principle."[15]

Laura Towne found it amusing. It was more significant than she imagined. The colored people were speaking the language of New England liberals, but the resentment of the member who "wanted no white man" was more widespread than the generous Miss Towne had reason to know. She had simply assumed that the whites would lead.[16]

The one man who might have challenged Robert Smalls successfully, the most popular of all the evangels with the Sea Islanders, had been Mansfield French. The minister, however, had returned North in 1872, "philanthropy being more his line than politics," in the words of his son, W. M. French, who remained on the islands to edit the Beaufort *Tribune*. It had not always been so, and in 1868 French had been much excited at the prospect of becoming United States Senator from South Carolina. He had written Chief Justice Chase that his friends regarded his "chances of success" as being "*very good.*" The minister's political hopes were bolstered by a formidable array of nation radicals, who had petitioned him to run in the contest. By the time the radicals attained power in the state, however, French's reputation was under a black cloud. He had attended land sales in the low country regularly and seems to have been at the head of an attempt to buy up lapsed soldiers' claims and other cheap property to resell to Negroes. He had the backing of Chase and banker Jay Cooke.[17] There is no good evidence that French did not manage his part with integrity, but many people did not think that he had done so. A reporter for the *New York Times* charged that "in almost all cases the certificates ultimately found their way into Father French's pockets." The reporter venomously labeled French the "Tycoon of all the robbers" and

[14] Simkins and Woody; *South Carolina During Reconstruction*, pp. 204–6; John S. Reynolds, *Reconstruction in South Carolina* (Columbia, 1905), pp. 126, 223.

[15] Holland (ed.), *Towne,* p. 182.

[16] Letter of Laura Towne of June 7, 1867, in *Pennsylvania Freedmen's Bulletin,* III (October, 1867), 8.

[17] Obituary of French, Beaufort *Tribune,* March 22, 1876; French to Chase, June 8, 1868, and same to same, February 7, 1867, Chase MSS.

charged that he had gotten thousands of Negroes in debt to him "on account of his lofty charges for meal and Attleborough jewelry." The reporter of the *Times* was clearly jaundiced, but he was not the only observer who held these opinions. Many schoolteachers in Beaufort thought him dishonest; in the words of Arthur Sumner, "a liar, scoundrel, thief, and hypocrite." It seems most unlikely that the overt charges of fraud had any basis in fact, and it is probable that certain of French's accusers confused the minister with his son, W. M. French, who had remained on the islands as a newspaper editor and was involved in numerous real estate ventures. If French's defenders are correct, the circulation of these charges at the time French was ambitious to become the first radical senator from South Carolina was a calculated stratagem on the part of his rival, and slander was the real cause of the minister's failure to be elected. French was not without friends, however, and Reuben Tomlinson, who had never liked French's methods, was writing to McKim in 1867 that "with all his eccentricities, . . . [French] is true to the colored man, and to the country."[18]

When even Gideonites could not with certainty identify virtue among candidates and good policy among the parties and factions, it is not astonishing that the largely uninformed Negro electorate was at a loss. In an age when corruption was rampant in nearly every state legislature and when "Grantism" came to signify demoralization in the national administration, the Southern states under Reconstruction drew a disproportionate degree of criticism. The opportunities for plunder afforded by the new and

rapid growth of capitalism left the reputations of few public figures a decent covering. The voters of South Carolina were hardly more responsible for the chicanery of the Greenville and Columbia Railroad ring than were the voters of New York State at a time when Jim Fiske and Jay Gould could arrive at Albany and buy the legislature to do the will of the Erie Railroad ring.

The colored voters of Beaufort County did have the real issues placed before them in the spirited contests between 1868 and 1877, and if they could not determine precisely what occurred at Columbia after the successful candidates took office, they were little more confused than the mass of voters over the nation. The three most persistent local issues on the Sea Islands were discussed at nearly every meeting. They were corruption on state and local levels, exorbitant taxes, and the still unresolved controversy over the lands seized and sold under the Direct Tax Laws. On the head of corruption, the voters frequently heard charges flung directly at opposing candidates at political rallies, and staunch "regulars" warned the electorate just as freely as did the "reformers" not to send bad men to the legislature, on the ground that they "might steal." Of such a meeting Editor Thompson fulminated, "No allusion was made to the present splendid financial condition of the State, and no doubt many a hearer went away from the meeting with the impression that everything was going on as smoothly as possible in our State. . . ."[19] The voters of Beaufort County threaded their way through the confusion by trusting the skipper of the *Planter* to recognize the scoundrels, and they regularly returned the men he backed to the state offices. On the local level, the town and county offices usually went to carpetbaggers who managed with indifferent success. John Hunn and H. G. Judd, both of Gideon's Band, were local officers who managed badly but were apparently honest. The town went in and out of bankruptcy, and George Holmes, not of

---

[18] *New York Times*, July 23, 1866; Arthur Sumner to Nina Hartshorn, August 8, 1864, Sumner MSS; Mansfield Joseph Franch, *Ancestors and Descendants of Samuel French the Joiner* (privately printed, Ann Arbor, 1940), pp. 88–92. Tomlinson to McKim, February 19, 1867, McKim MSS. A Union soldier reported that French was not respected or admired by the officers stationed at Port Royal, who called him "Holy Joe" and "Aaron." Henry Hitchcock's diary, *Marching With Sherman* (New Haven, 1927), pp. 227–28, edited by M. A. DeWolfe Howe.

[19] Beaufort *Republican*, July 11, 1872.

Gideon's Band, was certainly guilty of with-holding teachers' salaries under the pretext of low funds and profiting from buying up teachers' pay certificates at a discount.[20]

The problems of taxation and land were closely related, and in this particular the small Negro landowners of Beaufort were in the frustrating position of finding their own interests at cross-purposes with those of most of the colored people in the state. At a Fourth of July political rally in 1872, a politician told the voters that "the object of the [high] tax law and the general legisla-tion" of the previous session "was to take the lands out of the possession of the white people and place them in the hands of the colored people." Editor Thompson lined out the paradox: "We ask our delegation if this is so, [because] if so the tax law has utterly failed of its object, for two-thirds of the lands sold at the tax sales has been the property of colored people. Their little farms have been sold from them, and they are left destitute and homeless. Think of this, you owners of ten and twenty acre lots." Thompson did not exaggerate. What-ever the tax law did for landowners in the state at large, the Beaufort papers were lined with lists of small farms delinquent in taxes. With due warning most Negro farm-ers did scrape up the tax money, however, no matter what the sacrifice, for they well understood the basis of their security.[21]

The incessant litigation over the status of the Direct Tax lands troubled Negroes and whites alike. Throughout the Recon-struction period the dispossessed whites worked under the leadership of Richard DeTreville to break the tax laws under which the confiscation of their estates had been effected. Using the house in Beaufort in which Robert Smalls had been reared as a slave and which the Negro leader had

bought at the government tax sales, De-Treville fought the case through the state courts and lost. When the claim on the Prince Street house came into the posses-sion of William DeTreville upon the death of Richard DeTreville, the case at last, in 1878, reached the Supreme Court, where it was defeated. The freedmen and North-erners who had benefited from the tax sales retained their land, and Port Royal became, in respect of landownership, very much what the Gideonites had hoped it would become. By 1890 Elizabeth Botume reported that three-fourths of the land in Beaufort County was owned by Negroes.[22]

As years passed, the animosities of war cooled, at least as far as the victors were concerned. In Beaufort County nothing demonstrated the mellowing attitude better than the growing sense among many resi-dent Northerners that the local Southern white people had in the loss of their prop-erty, suffered an unfair amount of punish-ment. In January of 1872 Editor James Thompson was still reminding them that there had been a certain "poetic justice" in the fact that "the hot-bed of rebellion" had "received the worst punishment" and that the former owners had no claim to the res-toration of their lands. But he was already speaking of a possible money compensa-tion.[23]

As a representative of those who wished to develop the commercial possibilities of the region, Thompson was especially con-cerned about the depression of property values that had resulted from the continua-tion of "occupance" [sic] of lands and town property by the United States," which he pronounced an "unmitigated nuisance." The sales of government property had been halted in 1866, and the neglected town houses had become eyesores that appalled

[20] Beaufort *Tribune*, June 14, 1876, and Feb-ruary 3, 1875; Sworn affidavit of D. H. Hyatt, March 20, 1875, Education Petitions, State Arch-ives, Columbia; Beaufort *Republican*, November 14, 1872.

[21] Beaufort *Republican*, July 11, 1872. See listing of delinquent properties, *ibid.*, February 22, 1872.

[22] *DeTreville* v. *Smalls*, 98 U.S.; *First Mohonk Conference on the Negro Question, June 4, 5, 6* (Boston, 1890), p. 24. The records of the Direct Tax Commission include a notebook that outlines the tangled legal history of the Direct Tax lands. Records of the Fifth Special Agency, United States Archives.

[23] Beaufort *Republican*, January 11, 1872.

visitors like Edward King. "No improvements can be made upon adjoining property because of the filthy condition of the government ruins, the disgusting character of their inhabitants and the danger from fire." Insurance was expensive and frequently unobtainable at any price. The wreck of Commissioner Brisbane's dream of a property revolution had become an embarassment; Thompson was glad when a plan was effected whereby the old owners were allowed to redeem by paying the tax on those parts of their property that had not been sold, and he explained just how they ought to go about making their claims. Afterward, the government would be free to sell what remained of the property, and Thompson joined the clamor for a financial settlement for those whose property had ben sold outright before the end of hostilities.[24]

There were other signs of peaceful coexistence. Indigent Southern whites accepted positions teaching in the Negro schools. Within the county, of the nineteen teachers reporting in 1870 all but five Negro teachers and two Northern whites were Southern whites. Thomas Chaplin came back to St. Helena; living in an overseers' house on a plantation neighboring his own old home, he taught "a large school for Negro children."[25] The signs of peace were even more pronounced in the religious life of the community. As early as the spring of 1867, the Reverend Mr. Elliott, son of the General Stephen Elliott who had held Fort Sumter for so long against Gillmore's guns, came to St. Helena Episcopal Church and spoke peace to "a crowded house, with about an equal number from each section," North and South. Northerners began to hear that Southerners were ready to "let 'bygones be bygones.'" An ominous sign developed when the Northern white people of St.

Helena Island began to go to the "White Church," apart from the Brick Church of the freedmen, the scene of so many exciting meetings during the war. Much as such a move was resented by so strong an integrationist as Laura Towne, who castigated whilom "army sutlers and low camp followers" for becoming "too uppish" to associate with the Negroes, the signs that the Northerners resident were beginning to conciliate the "native" whites were abundant.[26] Editor Thompson began to regret "the loss during the war, of the names by which the respective streets in the town of Beaufort had been previously designated" and concluded that the "temporary system" had "subserved" its original purpose. The old names were restored. In 1873 Thompson ran a series of articles in his paper written by an old white resident who outlined, presumably for the benefit of the newcomers, the history of the region and the plight and sentiments of the dispossessed "natives." He ended on a note of brotherhood.[27]

Not every white resident shared the amicable spirit; a young Southern white woman wrote in 1876 that spring had come to Beaufort—"Drumfish is scarce, but Yankees abundant. . . ." She had "not the *horror* of being acquainted with one of them." Neither was Laura Towne prepared to conciliate. When an affable young scion of the Rhett family made overtures to Miss Towne and said he was sorry to have been unable to call upon her, she said that that was just as well, for "our ways are not their ways, and it is troublesome to know them."[28] Most Northerners were not responding in like manner. The death of S. C. Millett, a young carpetbagger who had steered clear of politics and advanced the commercial interests of the region by his able management of the

24 *Ibid.*, July 24, 1873, and June 6, 1872; Jan. 25, 1872. W. M. French, editor of the Beaufort *Tribune*, took the same view. See the *Tribune,* May 19, 1875.
25 Teachers' Monthly School Reports, State Archives, Columbia. Chaplin MS diary, final entry, January 1, 1886, relating the salient events of Chaplin's life during the Reconstruction.
26 Botume, *First Days,* pp. 230–31; Towne MS letter to her sisters, March 3, 1867.
27 Beaufort *Republican,* February 13, 1873; the series on the history of the region was written by [Dr.] J. A. J[ohnson] and appeared from February 20, 1873, running through July 3, 1873.
28 [?] to Emily Elliott, April 12, 1876, Elliott–Gonzales MSS; Laura Towne to "L," October 29, 1876, Towne MSS.

new Port Royal railroad, was regretted by all. His eulogy in the *Port Royal Commercial* stated that under Millett's management "all" employees on the road had been "Southern boys of integrity, sobriety, honesty, and position." Millett had "spurned and despised the oppression of our poor South, as much as do the dearest of our own."[29]

The Reverend Mr. Mansfield French's son, W. M. French, had returned to Beaufort to edit the *Tribune,* and although he called himself an "independent" he followed an editorial policy that must have pleased the conservative whites as much as it displeased Laura Towne. Editor French had apparently come to some important and portentous conclusions about Southern Reconstruction. Commenting upon the hearty reception in Boston and New York of the famous rebel military unit, the Washington Light Infantry of Charleston, he saw it as a sign of a reaction:

There can be no doubt but what this reactionary feeling in favor of those who sought the dissolution of the Union, is a manifestation of the sympathy felt by the best classes at the North for a kindred people who, they are convinced, have for the last ten years been subject to state governments forced upon them of the most degraded nature.

Moral? Those same Northerners would help the return of decent government, and

. . . whatever elements obstruct the attainment of so desirable an end, whether ignorance, lust of power or greed of plunder will be thrust aside. If a suspicion gains ground that the colored vote is subversive of the best interests of an important section of the union, because controlled by bad men, the handwriting on the wall indicates that the same power that bestowed the right of suffrage will not hesitate to withdraw it for the benefit of the descendants of those who fought at Eutaw and Bunker Hill a century ago to found this republic.[30]

The nation was preparing to celebrate its centennial, and the spirit of peace and concord was general. On the Fourth of July Laura Towne wrote to a faithful friend in Philadelphia and tried to imagine the excitement that would mark the celebration in her native city. She did not envy her friends there, however, for sitting at her home on the islands she could enjoy the wonderful sea breeze "in utter quiet" and reflect upon "our hundred years of progress. I can imagine it all as glorious as I please." Laura Towne would not enjoy such a complacency again, for although she seemed unaware of the ominous implications of sectional reconciliation, she should have understood that the Sea Islanders were a powder keg in the summer of 1876. Her instincts had been more accurate 15 years before, when she had enjoyed the sea breeze in Newport on a quiet Sunday afternoon, with the thunderheads of civil war looming on the horizon. Then she had sensed that the nation was "waiting for something—some great, terrible time."[31]

Two months earlier, on May 3, 1876, Editor French had informed his readers in the *Tribune* of "an event which seems almost incredible: that the Democracy of Beaufort County, so long dormant has awakened from its slumbers for a sufficient length of time to rub its sleepy eyes, get on its feet and meet in a Convention for the purpose of electing delegates" to the state party convention. French was glad to see that "some of the best citizens of the county" were taking part, welcomed the advent of the two-party system, and rejoiced "that a wealthy and intelligent class of citizens, who for years have abstained from taking part in public affairs are about to abandon their policy of inactivity and thereby add new zest to the next political campaign." Democratic clubs, he observed, were being organized all over the county.[32] Editor French seemed as unaware as Laura Towne of the impending counterrevolution. The Democratic clubs were arming themselves, they were wearing red shirts, and they intended

---

[29] *Port Royal Commercial,* March 19, 1874.
[30] Beaufort *Tribune,* June 23, 1878.

[31] Towne to Francis Cope, July 4, 1876, and Towne MS letter to [?], May 26, 1861, Towne MSS.
[32] Beaufort *Tribune,* May 3, 1876.

to banish the Republican party from South Carolina.

After a fall campaign notorious for the fraudulent practices and violence of both parties, the Democrats, with the cooperation of the federal government, accomplished their purpose. The attempt to remodel South Carolina along the lines of Massachusetts was officially interred. The North would not protest when their "kindred people" snatched the reins of political power from Northerners and Negroes, nor lift a hand to prevent the "redemption" of the state where Reconstruction began first and lasted longest. By 1876 even a few Negroes and carpetbaggers who had been associated with the Port Royal movement seemed ready to acquiesce to the counterrevolution. Tax Commissioner William Brisbane made a public announcement of his conversion in September before the elections: "I intend to vote for [Wade] Hampton. Why? Because I think I can strike more effectually against the combined effort to destroy the material interests of our State; and because he has promised, if he is elected, that the rights of the colored man, as defined in the thirteenth, fourteenth and Fifteenth Amendments, shall be respected. . . ." Martin R. Delany, a talented radical Negro leader who had been prominent on the islands during the war, also backed Hampton for governor. Editor French made his sympathies clear on every page of his journal, remarking with satisfaction that "many men are changing their political faith who were thought to be incorrigible."[33]

But not all evangels were "redeemed," or "reconciled" to the overthrow of their hopes. Reuben Tomlinson went North and attempted to rouse popular indignation against President Rutherford Hayes, the Republican whose elevation to office had been part and parcel of the compromise that returned South Carolina to the rule of the white native population of the state. In vain did Tomlinson suggest that under the ad-

ministration of Republican Governor Daniel Chamberlain the state had already been well on the way to good government and honest reform; in vain did he point to the violence that had marked the overthrow of the Republican party. He was astonished that the North should have acquiesced to a policy "which nullified some of the most important results of the war." For Tomlinson the Southern Question was not settled. Was the federal government not failing in its "promises to protect the millions of colored people at the South in their civil and political rights?" He pointed out that "States rights and home rule in the South mean the right of the rich and intelligent and powerful to trample under foot the poor and ignorant and weak."[34]

Protests availed little, for the nation was almost as weary of Reconstruction as were South Carolina Bourbon Redeemers. Laura Towne write in anger and sadness to Francis R. Cope, a faithful supporter of her school. She drew a mild reproof:

We feel very sorry that the prospect for the colored people of S. Carolina appears to you so dark. But how is it to be helped? Force may for awhile restrain the passions of men, [but] it is at least questionable whether the evil resulting does not overbalance the good. We never contemplated when we took the freed blacks under the protection of the North that the work was to be for an unlimited time. We hoped that if for a few years we lent them a helping hand, self interest, if not a sense of right, would prompt the Southern whites to do their duty by them. That in this we have been disappointed is partly their fault, partly ours in permitting so many disreputable men to take the office of protectors and so bring discredit on the whole system.

Mr. Cope thought that "all protective systems" were "unsatisfactory" and that "no business and no individual can stand firmly

---

33 *Ibid.*, September 27, 1876; Simkins and Woody, *South Carolina During Reconstruction,* p. 511.

34 Tomlinson was active in the North for several years following the campaign of 1876, attempting to draw public attention to the dangers inherent in the triumph of the Democrats in South Carolina for the Negroes. See the Boston *Advertiser,* January 28, 1878, for the speech from which the quotations are taken.

till he learns to stand alone."[35] His attitude was the one most acceptable to men in the North who regarded themselves as moderate and enlightened on public issues.

Reconstruction had begun first on the Sea Islands, and it did not end there, suddenly, with the victory of Wade Hampton for the governorship in 1876. Well into the evening of the century Negroes in Beaufort County were a political force, and the two old rivals, W. J. Whipper, carpetbag Negro, and Robert Smalls, ex-slave, were regularly returned to the state legislature. Smalls was United States Congressman from 1875 to 1879 and served again to complete a vacated term in 1884. He was reelected for his last full term in 1884.[36] Near the end of the century, however, the story of Negro participation in South Carolina political life came to an end. In 1895, under the leadership of Governor Ben Tillman, a constitutional convention was held, and South Carolina effectually nullified the Fifteenth Amendment by erecting such voting requirements for voting that Negroes saw the futility of even trying. True to its reputation as the strongest black district, Beaufort had sent five of the six Negro representatives present at this convention, Whipper and Smalls among them. With wit and skill the two men eventually obliged the delegates to drop the cant about establishing fair practices of universal application with regard to suffrage; they pressed the issue forward until one white delegate said, in exasperation, "We don't propose to have any fair elections. We will get left every time." Robert Smalls had his chance to say the many good things that could be said for the radical constitution of 1868, which had, after all, served nearly 20 years after the resumption of white control. He pleaded no special defense for his race, but asked only "an equal chance in the battle of life." He was proud to be a Negro. "I stand here the equal of any man." It was brave whistling in the wind. The new constitution was adopted, and by 1903 a citizen of Beaufort reported that even though literate male Negroes in the county numbered 3,434 to 927 white voters, the "registration officials do not allow registered Negro voters to outnumber the whites."[37]

There always remained about Beaufort and the islands special reminders of their unique history during the Civil War. Among the school children there was an impressive number of Rufus Saxtons, Matilda Saxtons, and Edward Pierces. There was even a John Andrew. In the great Union cemetery in the center of the town lay the numbers of men who had died in the ineffectual but sanguinary fighting in the Department of the South. Every year at the Memorial Day celebration the remaining Northerners resident gathered to decorate the graves. H. G. Judd contributed an ode, as he had always done; and Laura Towne noted with grim pride the inscription of the monument: "Immortality to thousands of the brave defenders of our Country from the Great *Rebellion*." She admitted that it was "out of fashion now to use such plain words, but there they stand! right in the midst of the rebels, in granite." Gradually, however, time eroded some of the granite even from Laura Towne's heart, and she undertook a few social exchanges with the "native" whites, as she called them. Although she never was "redeemed," Laura Towne became a good neighbor, and her virtues were extolled by "natives" both black and white.[38]

The islanders could no longer vote, but in a signal respect they were more fortunate

---

[35] Francis Cope to Laura Towne, November 19, 1877, Towne MSS.

[36] George Brown Tindall, *South Carolina Negroes, 1877–1900* (Columbia, South Carolina, 1952), p. 55, and Appendix, "Negro Members of the South Carolina General Assembly after Reconstruction," pp. 309–10.

[37] *Ibid.*, pp. 81–89, quotations, in order, from pp. 87, 86, 88.

[38] Laura Towne to her sisters, June 1, 1879, Towne MSS. Lily Ellis Fripp, to her sister-in-law, Emily Fripp, wrote of Miss Towne's neighborly acts to her in an undated letter written sometime shortly after January 18, 1883. The letter is in the Ellis Family Papers in the South Caroliniana Library, University of South Carolina. For names of schoolchildren, see *Freedmen's Record*, IV (March, 1868), 39.

than other Negroes of the South. They owned their own land, and upon it they could support themselves. They came in time to constitute a "black yeomanry," although they did not prosper as their best Northern and Southern white friends had hoped they might. They had been granted a chance to become free and independent in a span of years when even the most able and experienced white Sea Island planters were at a loss to meet the terrible readjustments required of them. They had had to help restore prosperity to a region that had been in an unfavorable competitive position even before the war, and to achieve this in spite of a national depression, the loss of the fine seed that had been the main element in successful long-staple cotton farming, and the capture of the long-staple cotton market by the producers in other parts of the world. Unfortunately for the freedman, these events had coincided with his entry into the political picture, and most observers, North and South, in explaining the problem, had seized the simple but inadequate excuse that the freedmen were not working. The readjustments indicated were exactly what the agricultural experts pointed out: a shift to more diversified farming; the raising of hay and truck produce; and the increasing use of commercial fertilizers. Because of the lack of capital the changes were slow in coming, but they did in time take place. Although the freedmen continued to farm the long-staple crop they knew and understood, taking their chances on getting a sufficient money return to pay taxes while subsisting themselves with their corn and vegetables, the larger farmers began the shift to short-staple cotton very shortly after the war.

The Negroes of the low country were much assisted in maintaining their independent status by the opening in 1867 of phosphate mines along the rivers and estuaries. Frequently the young men went to "the rock," as they called the mines, leaving the farming of the little ten-acre plots to their wives and children. Edward Philbrick had been correct in his prediction that these tiny estates would be encumbered by excessive subdivision and lawsuits and that the acreages would diminish in size to the extent that they were no longer suitable for staple agriculture. But the remedy had appeared with the disease. Even by 1888 a Gideonite who returned to the islands for a visit reported that a New England firm regularly shipped early garden truck from the islands direct to Northern ports. After 1870 truck farming came to be a more and more important economic activity. Two great calamities eventually spurred the readjustment to its final stages; a great tidal wave in 1893, which wreaked havoc upon the central islands; and the arrival of the boll weevil in 1918. Thereafter the long-staple cotton crop disappeared, making room for new crops better suited to the new institutions of freedom and small landownership.[39]

The Sea Islanders had learned the lessons of freedom, and they became, in their own way, as self-governing as many a small New England town. The church remained for them a greater force in the conduct of men than man-made law, a law with which they would not have less and less to do. Scholars who studied the islands closely in the 1920s found that nearly all disputes were settled by committees within the churches and that among "members" the collective wisdom of the elders constituted the recognized law and reduced crime to a minimum. The Baptist church was essentially democratic; its elders were the choice of the local members, and it was the only denomination that had a considerable following on the islands. To the islanders, the secular law was the "unjust" law; the church law was the "just" law.[40]

The efforts of Gideon's Band had not gone for nothing, although Pierce's evangels

---

[39] Charles Howard Family [MS] History, pp. 108–9, 198–99, 201–2; Tindall, *South Carolina Negroes,* p. 93. The Beaufort County Census Report for 1868 (S.C. MS Census, in S.C. State Archives) lists only 220,614 acres planted in long-staple cotton, as opposed to 7,036,957 acres in short-staple. Market garden produce was valued for 1868 at above $2 million.

[40] Johnson, *Social History,* pp. 209–10; T. J. Woofter, *Black Yeomanry* (New York, 1930), pp. 239–40.

might not have understood the fruit of their labor. The freedmen had become self-supporting, if not wealthy. They paid their taxes, and they took care of their local troubles with aplomb. In addition to owning their land, they enjoyed yet another advantage over many American Negroes, North or South, at the end of the century. Living almost isolated from their white neighbors on the mainland, they were spared contacts at a time when race relations in America reached their most disgraceful depths. Perhaps Suzie King Taylor, far away in Boston, experienced more painful knowledge of the frightful abuse of her people than her old neighbors on the islands ever endured. In 1902 she wrote her reminiscences of the life she had led as a little slave girl on St. Simon's Island, how she had come to Beaufort, "liberated," and had worked as a laundress and unofficial schoolteacher for the first Negro troops. She remembered that "glorious day" on the Smith plantation when the Sea Islanders had first heard the Emancipation Proclamation. At the time of writing she knew that Negroes traveling in the South always rode second-class, and that small excuse was required to set off a lynching bee. She knew that in the South the time had come again when there were few liberties of Negroes that white people were bound to respect. She could not understand. "There is no redress for us from a government which promised to respect all under its flag. It is a mystery to me."[41]

There was really no mystery. The nation had forgotten. Thomas Wentworth Higginson, who wrote the introduction to Mrs. Taylor's little book, had even in 1863 feared for the "ultimate fate" of the liberated Negroes, remembering that "revolutions may go backward."[42] The regression had simply taken longer than Higginson had imagined it might.

[41] Suzie King Taylor, *Reminiscences of My Life in Camp* (Boston, 1902), p. 61.
[42] Thomas W. Higginson, *Army Life in a Black Regiment* (Cambridge, 1900), pp. 63–64.

1955

Southern Capitulation to Racism *

C. VANN WOODWARD

Up to the year 1898 South Carolina had resisted the Jim Crow car movement which had swept the western states of the South completely by that time. In that year, however, after several attempts, the proponents of the Jim Crow law were on the eve of victory. The Charleston *News and Courier,*

* C. Vann Woodward, *The Strange Career of Jim Crow* (Copyright © 1955 by Oxford University Press, Inc. Reprinted by permission.

the oldest newspaper in the South and a consistent spokesman of conservatism, fired a final broadside against extremists in behalf of the conservative creed of race policy.

"As we have got on fairly well for a third of a century, including a long period of reconstruction, without such a measure," wrote the editor, "we can probably get on as well hereafter without it, and certainly so extreme a measure should not be adopted and enforced without added and urgent cause." He then called attention to what he considered the absurd consequences to which such a law might lead once the principle of the thing were conceded. "If there must be Jim Crow cars on the railroads, there should be Jim Crow cars on the street railways. Also on all passenger boats. . . . If there are to be Jim Crow cars, moreover, there should be Jim Crow waiting saloons at all stations, and Jim Crow eating houses. . . . There should be Jim Crow sections of the jury box, and a separate Jim Crow dock and witness stand in every court—and a Jim Crow Bible for colored witnesses to kiss. It would be advisable also to have a Jim Crow section in county auditors' and treasurers' offices for the accommodation of colored taxpayers. The two races are dreadfully mixed in these offices for weeks every year, especially about Christmas. . . . There should be a Jim Crow department for making returns and paying for the privileges and blessings of citizenship. Perhaps the best plan would be, after all, to take the short cut to the general end . . . by establishing two or three Jim Crow counties at once, and turning them over to our colored citizens for their special and exclusive accommodation."

In resorting to the tactics of *reductio ad absurdum* the editor doubtless believed that he had dealt the Jim Crow principle a telling blow with his heavy irony. But there is now apparent to us an irony in his argument of which the author was unconscious. For what he intended as a *reductio ad absurdum* and obviously regarded as an absurdity became in a very short time a reality, and not only that but a reality that was regarded as the only sensible solution to a vexing problem, a solution having the sanction of tradition and long usage. Apart from the Jim Crow counties and the Jim Crow witness stand, all the improbable applications of the principle suggested by the editor in derision had been put into practice—down to and including the Jim Crow Bible.

The South's adoption of extreme racism was due not so much to a conversion as it was to a relaxation of the opposition. All the elements of fear, jealousy, proscription, hatred, and fanaticism had long been present, as they are present in various degrees of intensity in any society. What enabled them to rise to dominance was not so much cleverness or ingenuity as it was a general weakening and discrediting of the numerous forces that had hitherto kept them in check. The restraining forces included not only Northern liberal opinion in the press, the courts, and the government, but also internal checks imposed by the prestige and influence of the Southern conservatives, as well as by the idealism and zeal of the Southern radicals. What happened toward the end of the century was an almost simultaneous—and sometimes not unrelated—decline in the effectiveness of restraint that had been exercised by all three forces: Northern liberalism, Southern conservatism, and Southern radicalism.

The acquiescence of Northern liberalism in the Compromise of 1877 defined the beginning, but not the ultimate extent, of the liberal retreat on the race issue. The Compromise merely left the freedman to the custody of the conservative Redeemers upon their pledge that they would protect him in his constitutional rights. But as these pledges were forgotten or violated and the South veered toward proscription and extremism, Northern opinion shifted to the right, keeping pace with the South, conceding point after point, so that at no time were the sections very far apart on race policy. The failure of the liberals to resist this trend was due in part to political factors. Since reactionary politicians and their cause were identified with the bloody-shirt issue and the demagogic exploitation of sectional animosities, the liberals naturally felt themselves strongly drawn toward the cause of sectional reconciliation. And since the Negro was the symbol of sectional strife, the liberals joined in deprecating further agitation of his cause and in defending the Southern view of race in its less extreme forms. It was quite common in the eighties and nineties to find in the *Nation, Harper's*

Weekly, the *North American Review,* or the *Atlantic Monthly* Northern liberals and former abolitionists mouthing the shibboleths of white supremacy regarding the Negro's innate inferiority, shiftlessness, and hopeless unfitness for full participation in the white man's civilization. Such expressions doubtless did much to add to the reconciliation of North and South, but they did so at the expense of the Negro. Just as the Negro gained his emancipation and new rights through a falling out between white men, he now stood to lose his rights through the reconciliation of white men.

The cumulative weakening of resistance to racism was expressed also in a succession of decisions by the United States Supreme Court between 1873 and 1898 that require no review here. In the *Slaughter House Cases* of 1873 and in *United States* v. *Reese* and *United States* v. *Cruikshank* in 1876, the Court drastically curtailed the privileges and immunities recognized as being under federal protection. It continued the trend in its decision on the *Civil Rights Cases* of 1883 by virtually nullifying the restrictive parts of the Civil Rights Act. By a species of what Justice Harlan in his dissent described as "subtle and ingenious verbal criticism," the Court held that the Fourteenth Amendment gave Congress power to restrain states but not individuals from acts of racial discrimination and segregation. The Court, like the liberals, was engaged in a bit of reconciliation — reconciliation between federal and state jurisdiction, as well as between North and South, reconciliation also achieved at the Negro's expense. Having ruled in a previous case *(Hall* v. *de Cuir,* 1877) that a state could not *prohibit* segregation on a common carrier, the Court in 1890 *(Louisville, New Orleans, and Texas Railroad* v. *Mississippi)* ruled that a state could constitutionally *require* segregation on carriers. In *Plessy* v. *Ferguson,* decided in 1896, the Court subscribed to the doctrine that "legislation is powerless to eradicate racial instincts" and laid down the "separate but equal" rule for the justification of segregation. Two years later, in 1898, in *Williams* v. *Mississippi* the Court completed the opening of the legal road to proscription, segregation, and disfranchisement by approving the Mississippi plan for depriving Negroes of the franchise.

Then, in that same year, 1898, the United States plunged into imperialistic adventures under the leadership of the Republican party. These adventures in the Pacific and the Caribbean suddenly brought under the jurisdiction of the United States some 8 million people of the colored races, "a varied assortment of inferior races," as the *Nation* described them, "which, of course, could not be allowed to vote." As America shouldered the White Man's Burden she took up at the same time many Southern attitudes on the subject of race. "If the stronger and cleverer race," said the editor of the *Atlantic Monthly,* "is free to impose its will upon 'new-caught, sullen people' on the other side of the globe, why not in South Carolina and Mississippi?" The doctrines of Anglo-Saxon superiority by which Professor John W. Burgess of Columbia University, Captain Alfred T. Mahan of the United States Navy, and Senator Albert Beveridge of Indiana justified and rationalized American imperialism in the Philippines, Hawaii, and Cuba differed in no essentials from the race theories by which Senator Benjamin R. Tillman of South Carolina and Senator James K. Vardaman of Mississippi justified white supremacy in the South. The Boston Evening *Transcript* of 14 January 1899, admitted that Southern race policy was "now the policy of the Administration of the very party which carried the country into and through a civil war to free the slave." And the *New York Times* of 10 May 1900 reported editorially that "Northern men . . . no longer denounce the suppression of the Negro vote [in the South] as it used to be denounced in the reconstruction days. The necessity of it under the supreme law of self-preservation is candidly recognized."

In the South leaders of the white supremacy movement thoroughly grasped and expounded the implication of the new imperialism for their domestic policies. "No Republican leader," declared Senator Tillman, "not even Governor Roosevelt, will now dare to wave the bloody shirt and preach a crusade against the South's treatment of the negro. The North has a bloody shirt of its own. Many thousands of them have been made into shrouds for murdered Filipinos, done to death because they were fighting for liberty." And the junior senator from South Carolina, John J. McLaurin, thanked Senator George F. Hoar of Massachusetts "for his complete announcement of the divine right of the Caucasion to govern the inferior races," a position which "most amply vindicated the South." Hilary A. Herbert, an advocate of complete disfranchisement of the Negro in Alabama rejoiced in May, 1900, that "we have now the sympathy of thoughtful men in the North to an extent that never before existed."

At the dawn of the new century the wave of Southern racism came in as a swell upon a mounting tide of national sentiment and was very much a part of that sentiment. Had the tide been running the other way, the Southern wave would have broken feebly instead of becoming a wave of the future. . . .

Such resistance to proscription and segregation as had lingered in the older states of the seaboard South crumbled rapidly. The Richmond *Times* in 1900 demanded that a rigid principle of segregation be "applied in every relation of Southern life" on the ground that "God Almighty drew the color line and it cannot be obliterated." The conservative old Charleston *News and Courier,* quoted at the beginning of this chapter as heaping ridicule upon the Jim Crow movement and the absurdity of its consequences, was of another opinion by 1906. "The 'problem' is worse now than it was ten years ago," wrote the editor. Far from being ridiculous, segregation did not now seem sufficient. Mass deportation was the remedy. "Separation of the races is the only radical solution of the negro problem in this country. . . . There is no room for them [the Negroes] here," declared the paper.

Within this context of growing pessimism, mounting tension, and unleased phobias the structure of segregation and discrimination was extended by the adoption of a great number of the Jim Crow type of laws. Up to 1900 the only law of this type adopted by the majority of Southern states was that applying to passengers aboard trains. And South Carolina did not adopt that until 1898, North Carolina in 1899, and Virginia, the last, in 1900. Only three states had required or authorized the Jim Crow waiting room in railway stations before 1899, but in the next decade nearly all of the other Southern states fell in line. The adoption of laws applying to new subjects tended to take place in waves of popularity. Streetcars had been common in Southern cities since the eighties, but only Georgia had a segregation law applying to them before the end of the century. Then in quick succession North Carolina and Virginia adopted such a law in 1901, Louisiana in 1902, Arkansas, South Carolina, and Tennessee in 1903, Mississippi and Maryland in 1904, Florida in 1905, and Oklahoma in 1907. These laws referred to separation within cars, but a Montgomery city ordinance of 1906 was the first to require a completely separate Jim Crow streetcar. During these years the older seaboard states of the South also extended the segregation laws to steamboats.

The mushroom growth of discriminatory and segregation laws during the first two decades of this century piled up a huge bulk of legislation. Much of the code was contributed by city ordinances or by local regulations and rules enforced without the formality of laws. Only a sampling is possible here. For up and down the avenues and byways of Southern life appeared with increasing profusion the little signs: "Whites Only" or "Colored." Sometimes the law prescribed their dimensions in inches, and in one case the kind and color of paint. Many appeared without requirement by law —over entrances and exits, at theaters and boarding houses, toilets and water foundations, waiting rooms and ticket windows.

A large body of law grew up concerned with the segregation of employees and their working conditions. The South Carolina code of 1915, with subsequent elaborations, prohibited textile factories from permitting laborers of different races from working together in the same room, or using the same entrances, pay windows, exits, doorways, stairways, "or windows [sic]" at the same time, or the same "lavatories, toilets, drinking water buckets, pails, cups, dippers or glasses" at any time. Exceptions were made of firemen, floor scrubbers, and repair men, who were permitted association with the white proletarian elite on an emergency basis. In most instances segregation in employment was established without the aid of statute. And in many crafts and trades the written or unwritten policies of Jim Crow unionism made segregation superfluous by excluding Negroes from employment.

State institutions for the care of the dependent or incapacitated were naturally the subject of more legislation than private institutions of the same sort, but ordinarily the latter followed pretty closely the segregation practices of the public institutions. The fact that only Mississippi and South Carolina specifically provided for general segregation in hospitals does not indicate that non-segregation was the rule in the hospitals of other states. The two states named also required Negro nurses for Negro patients, and Alabama prohibited white female nurses from attending Negro male patients. Thirteen Southern and border states required the separation of patients by races in mental hospitals, and ten states specified segregation of inmates in penal institutions. Some of the latter went into detail regarding the chaining, transportation, feeding, and working of the prisoners on a segregated basis. Segregation of the races in homes for the aged, the indigent, the orphans, the blind, the deaf, and the dumb is the subject of numerous state laws.

Much ingenuity and effort went into the separation of the races in their amusements, diversions, recreations, and sports. The Separate Park Law of Georgia, adopted in 1905, appears to have been the first venture of a state legislature into this field, though city ordinances and local custom were quite active in pushing the Negro out of the public parks. Circuses and tent shows, including sideshows, fell under a law adopted by Louisiana in 1914, which required separate entrances, exits, ticket windows, and ticket sellers that would be kept at least 25 feet apart. The city of Birmingham applied the principle to "any room, hall, theatre, picture house, auditorium, yard, court, ball park, or other indoor or outdoor place" and specified that the races be "distinctly separated . . . by well defined physical barriers." North Carolina and Virginia interdicted all fraternal orders or societies that permitted members of both races to address each other as brother.

Residential segregation in cities developed along five different patterns in the second decade of the century. The type originating in Baltimore in 1910 designated all-white and all-Negro blocks in areas occupied by both races. This experiment was imitated in Atlanta and Greenville. Virginia sought to legalize segregation by a state law that authorized city councils to divide territories into segregated districts and to prohibit either race from living in the other's district, a method adopted by Roanoke and Portsmouth, Virginia. The third method, invented by Richmond, designated blocks throughout the city black or white according to the majority of the residents and forbade any person to live in any block "where the majority of residents on such streets are occupied by those with whom said person is forbidden to intermarry." This one was later copied by Ashland, Virginia, and Winston-Salem, North Carolina. A still more complicated law originated in Norfolk, which applied to both mixed and unmixed blocks and fixed the color status by ownership as well as occupancy. And finally New Orleans developed a law requiring a person of either race to secure consent of the majority of persons living in an area before establishing a residence therein. After these devices were frustrated by a Supreme Court decision in 1917, attempts continued to be made to circumvent the decision. Probably the most effective of these was the restrictive covenant, a private contract limiting the sale of property in an area to purchasers of the favored race.

The most prevalent and widespread segregation of living areas was accomplished without need for legal sanction. The black ghettos of the "Darktown" slums in every Southern city were the consequence mainly of the Negro's economic status, his relegation to the lowest rung of the ladder. Smaller towns sometimes excluded Negro residents completely simply by letting it be known in forceful ways that their presence would not be tolerated. In 1914 there were six such towns in Texas, five in Oklahoma, and two in Alabama. On the other hand there were by that time some 30 towns in the South, besides a number of unincorporated settlements, inhabited exclusively by Negroes. In August, 1913, Clarence Poe, editor of the *Progressive Farmer,* secured the unanimous endorsement of a convention of the North Carolina Farmer's Union for a movement to segregate the races in rural districts.

The extremes to which caste penalties and separation were carried in parts of the South could hardly find a counterpart short of the latitudes of India and South Africa. In 1909 Mobile passed a curfew law applying exclusively to Negroes and requiring them to be off the streets by 10:00 P.M.

The Oklahoma legislature in 1915 authorized its Corporation Commission to require telephone companies "to maintain separate booths for white and colored patrons." North Carolina and Florida required that textbooks used by the public-school children of one race be kept separate from those used by the other, and the Florida law specified separation even while the books were in storage. South Carolina for a time segregated a third caste by establishing separate schools for mulatto as well as for white and Negro children. A New Orleans ordinance segregated white and Negro prostitutes in separate districts. Ray Stannard Baker found Jim Crow Bibles for Negro witnesses in Atlanta courts and Jim Crow elevators for Negro passengers in Atlanta buildings.

A search of the statute books fails to disclose any state law or city ordinance specifying separate Bibles and separate elevators. Right here it is well to admit, and even to emphasize, that laws are not an adequate index of the extent and prevalence of segregation and discriminatory practices in the South. The practices often anticipated and sometimes exceeded the laws. It may be confidently assumed—and it could be verified by present observation—that there is more Jim Crowism practiced in the South than there are Jim Crow laws on the books. . . .

BIBLIOGRAPHICAL NOTES

A most helpful synthesis of modern scholarship in the field is a collaborative work directed by the Swedish scholar, Gunnar Myrdal, *An American Dilemma: The Negro Problem and Modern Democracy* (2 vols.; 1944). John Hope Franklin, *From Slavery to Freedom* (1947) is the best-informed brief history of the Negro. A critical period of Southern history is treated in C. Vann Woodward, *Origins of the New South, 1877–1913* (1951).

Of particular importance for their original investigation of special subjects are Vernon L. Wharton, *The Negro in Mississippi, 1865–1890* (1947), and George B. Tindall, *South Carolina Negroes, 1877–1900* (1952). The desertion of Northern liberals, a neglected subject, is stressed by R. W. Logan, *The Negro in American Life and Thought: The Nadir, 1877–1901* (1954). Legal aspects of race relations are treated in Charles S. Mangum, Jr., *The Legal Status of the Negro* (1940); Franklin Johnson, *The Development of State Legislation concerning the Free Negro* (1919); Gilbert T. Stephenson, *Race Distinctions in American Law* (1910); and Pauli Murray, *State Laws on Race and Color* (1952).

Sociological phases are the subject of Bertram W. Doyle, *The Etiquette of Race Relations in the South* (1937); Arthur F. Raper, *The Tragedy of Lynching* (1933); and E. Franklin Frazier, *The Negro in the United States* (1949). Various works of John Dollard, particularly *Children of Bondage* (with Allison Davis, 1940), are illuminating. A most helpful essay is one by Guion G. Johnson, "The Ideology of White Supremacy, 1876–1910," in Fletcher M. Green, *Essays in Southern History, The James Sprunt Studies in History and Political Science,* Vol. 31, (1949).

Race factors in politics are astutely examined in V. O. Key, Jr., *Southern Politics in State and Nation* (1949); and there is much of value in Paul Lewinson, *Race, Class, and Party, A History of Negro Suffrage and White Politics in the South* (1932). William A. Mabry, *The Negro in North Carolina Politics since Reconstruction* (1940) is an able work.

A few guides to recent developments, out of a vast number of publications, are recommended. Howard W. Odum, *Race and Rumors of Race* (1944) gives an account of racial tension during World War II. Lee Nichols, *The Breakthrough on the Color Front* (1954) outlines the history of desegregation of the American armed services. Harry S. Ashmore, *The Negro and the Schools* (1954) brings the story of the attack upon segregated schools up to the Supreme Court decision of 17 May 1954. Other aspects of the school situation are treated by Truman Pierce, *Bi-Racial Education in the Southern States* (1955); Ernest W. Swanson and John A. Griffin, *Public Education in the South Today and Tomorrow* (1955); and Robin M. Williams, Jr., and Margaret W. Ryan, *Schools in Transition* (1954). Morroe Berger, *Equality by Statute: Legal Controls over Group Discrimination* (1952) traces the interplay of pressure group, legislative body, and court decision. Able assessments and evaluations of recent developments in desgregation are to be found in Kenneth B. Clark, "Desegregation: An Appraisal of Evidence," *Journal of Social Issues,* Vol. IX, No. 4 (1953); *The Negro Yearbook of The Journal of Negro Education* for 1954 and 1955; David Loth and Harold Fleming, *Integration North and South* (1956); and Ira De A. Reid (ed.), *Racial Desegregation and Integration,* which is Vol. 304 of *The Annals of the American Academy of Political and Social Science* (March, 1956), Of inestimable value are the files of the *Southern School News,* published monthly by the Southern Education Reporting Service.

Caste Responses in the North[*]

RAYFORD W. LOGAN

Three of the leading literary magazines —*Harper's New Monthly Magazine, Scribner's* (*Century* after 1881), and the *Atlantic Monthly*—mirrored the refined tastes of the upper classes. Frederick Lewis Allen, editor of *Harper's* from 1941 to 1953, wrote in

* Rayford W. Logan, *The Negro in American Life and Thought* (New York: Dial Press, 1954).

1950 a penetrating evaluation of *Harper's* in 1891:

To us today some of the *Harper's* fiction of 1891 seems naive, some of its verse weakly sentimental, some of its pen-and-ink illustrations too daintly photographic; we wonder at its comparative neglect of the vital social and economic issues of the day, at its preoccupation with the safely remote, and the respectably classical, the second-hand literary; and its careful propriety. We have to remind ourselves that the public for which it was edited was the victim of an attractive but academic and timorous genteelism.

Harper's from 1877 to 1901 varied little from this sharply focused picture of 1891. Like *Harper's,* the *Atlantic* and *Century,* according to Commager, "made few concessions to the contemporary scene and none to vulgar taste."[1] Readers had to go to magazines like the *North American Review* and to *Forum,* established in 1886, for regular discussion of the vital issues of the day.

The editors of these five magazines were Northerners except Walter Hines Page, editor of *Forum* from 1886 to 1895 and of the *Atlantic* after 1897. It would be difficult to ascertain a substantial difference between the portrayal of the Negro under Northern editorship and under Page's. In fact, the largest number of derogatory stereotypes appeared in *Harper's, Scribner's,* and *Century,* partly because they contained drawings and cartoons that vividly depicted the antics of Negroes and more short stories in dialect than did the *Atlantic.* Most of the authors of fiction and poetry about Negroes were Southerners whose lives were more closely associated, unavoidably, with Negroes than were those of Northerners. Most of the essays in all five magazines, however, were written by Northerners. It may be safely assumed that the majority of readers were Northerners. The composite picture of the Negro that emerges from this chapter is, therefore, that which appealed to editors who were overwhelmingly Northern, to writers who were largely Northern except in the case of fiction and poetry, and to readers who were predominantly Northern. A modern reader wonders why Northern devotees of the Genteel Tradition found such evident delight in the lampooning of Negroes. Perhaps these New World aristocrats gloried

all the more in their own faultless language, polished maners, and physical attractiveness because of the outlandish speech, crude behavior and "ugliness" of those Americans who were most different from them.

Harper's, Scribner's, Century, and to a less degree the *Atlantic,* regularly employed derisive terms that are rarely used today except in local color fiction, in private conversation, and by the most rabid of "woolhat" politicians. Many stories, anecdotes, poems, and cartoons referred to Negroes as nigger, niggah, darkey, coon, pickaninny, mammy, aunt, uncle, buck, light-complected-yaller man, yaller hussy. Pralines were "nigger candy." Thomas Nelson Page had an article in the Editor's Drawer of *Harper's* entitled "All the Geography a Nigger Needs to Know." The *North American Review* rarely if ever permitted in its staid pages such uncomplimentary terms; when it published an article by General Sherman that refered to Negroes as "Darkies," the word was placed in quotation marks. The word Negro was practically never capitalized, and the dialect was generally strained, showing variations sometimes in the same story. But as the most eminent colored novelist, Chesnutt, himself explained: "The fact is, of course, that there is no such thing as a Negro dialect; that what we call by that name is the attempt to express, with such a degree of phonetic correctness as to suggest the sound, English pronounced as an ignorant old southern Negro would be supposed to speak it, and at the same time to preserve a sufficient approximation to the correct spelling to make it easy reading."[2]

Negroes were described as being black, ebony, midnight black, black as a crow, or black as a total eclipse. A little white girl asked her mother whether God had made an "ebony" little boy. When her mother replied in the affirmative, the girl queried: "Mama, do you suppose God thought he was *pretty?*" Negroes were thick-lipped; they had flat noses, big ears and feet, kinky or woolly hair. An anonymous traveler in the "great

---

[1] "One Hundred Years of *Harper's*," *Harper's Magazine* (Centennial Issue, 1850–1950), CCI (October, 1950), 32; Commanger, *American Mind,* pp. 74–75.

[2] Chesnutt, *Chesnutt,* p. 95.

black" regions of the South pictured "the uncouth, strangely shaped animal-looking Negro or mulatto, who seems mentally, even more than by his physical characteristics, to belong to a race entirely distinct from that of the white race around them." The writer of the article understood why white women were afraid of Negroes, since they were "a race alien, animal, half savage, easily made sullen or aroused to fury."[3]

Negroes were made ludicrous by the bestowal of titles, names of famous men or of folk expressions. Among the choice ones were Colonel, Senator, Sheriff, Apollo Belvedere, George Washington, Webster, Abraham Lincum, Napoleon Boneyfidey Waterloo, Venus Milo Clevins, Columbus, Pomp, Caesar, Lady Adeliza Chimpanzee, Prince Orang Outan, Hieronymous, Ananias, Solomon Crow, Piddlekins, Sosrus Dismal, Asmodeus, Bella Donna Mississippi Idaho, Violetta Marie Evaline Rose Christian, Nuttin 'Tal, Had-a-Plenty, and Wanna-Mo. The ultimate was achieved in Henri Ritter Demi Ritter Emmi Ritter Sweet-potato Cream Tarter Caroline Bostwick.

Virtually every derogatory stereotype was affixed upon the Negro. Sometimes several appeared in one passage or the same story. Thus, one colored woman was described as being a "typical Negro," since she was improvident, emotional, gossipy, kindhearted, high-tempered, vain, dishonest, idle, working only two or three days a week, and " 'res'n' " up the rest of the week, with always a hearty appetite and " 'miz'ry in de bres'.' " The Negro of Barbados was *sui generis,* for

There is nothing like him on earth, above it, or under it. He will lie, cheat, and steal beyond all comprehension. He is impudent to a degree hardly to be understood by an American. They are outwardly very devout, but it never enters their heads to practice what they preach. As an English clergyman living among

them once said, "They will go to communion, and steal yams on the way home."[4]

In various articles, stories, anecdotes, poems, and cartoons, the Negro was made to appear superstitious, dull and stupid, imitative and hence not creative, ignorant, suspicious, happy-go-lucky, improvident, lazy, immoral, criminal; he was a liar, a thief, and a drunkard. He used big words which he did not understand. He liked fine clothes and trinkets, chickens, " 'watermillions,' " " 'Sweet- 'tators,' " and " ' 'possum.' " The inevitable razor-totin' Negro made his appearance. Preachers, and to a less degree lawyers, were the frequent butt of jokes. The Negro was portrayed in the plantation tradition as a faithful slave and servant. But he could not adapt to freedom. Occasionally he was revealed as the "tragic mulatto." While some articles and other contributions treated Chinese, Indians, Irish, Germans, and other immigrants in general in an unfavorable light, these aliens and the oldest Americans fared better than did the Negro. Jews, partly because articles about them were written by Jews, received more kindly treatment than did other minorities. . . .

The emigration of Negroes, which had been frequently advocated during the 1880s, again became a favorite theme in the 1890s. Page saw no need in 1892 for deportation since the Negro race in the United States would soon die out. Blyden opposed large-scale emigration until a new generation of both whites and blacks developed different ideas. At the turn of the century, John Roach Straton of Macon, Georgia, argued that conditions elsewhere should be made so inviting that Negroes would want to emigrate.[5]

Toward the latter part of the century, however, all other topics were submerged

---

[3] Editor's Drawer, *Harper's,* LXXIV (May, 1887), 993 (italics as in the original); Unsigned, "Studies in the South," *Atlantic Monthly,* XLIX (February, 1882), 183.

[4] A. Van Cleef, "Barbadoes," *Harper's,* LIV (February, 1877), 387.

[5] Thomas Nelson Page, *A Southerner on the Negro Question,* pp. 411–12; Edward W. Blyden, "The African Problem," *North American Review,* CLXI (September, 1895), 327–39; John Roach Straton, "Will Education Solve the Race Problem?," *ibid.,* CLXX(June, 1900), 800–01.

by the plethora of articles on American expansion. Social Darwinists[6] enjoyed the advantage of a generally accepted American belief in the inherent inferiority of the Negro when they justified that expansion on racial grounds. Reciprocally the failure of Negroes and other dark peoples in distant lands to match strides with Europeans and Americans was invoked to justify the inability of the American Negro to exercise rights which the Constitution conferred upon him. As early as 1879 a writer in *Scribner's* concluded that the colored pupils in Richmond, Virginia, public schools showed quite as good progress as the white pupils until the two groups reached the age of 14, at which time there apeared a marked difference in favor of the latter. (It would be interesting to discover whether this pontifical assertion that the Negro's brain "closed up" at this age had its roots, knowingly or not, in the Freudian association with the age of puberty and virility.) The personality of a colored man who had advanced from slavery to freedom, from freedom to a high position during Reconstruction, evoked this declaration: "There are aspects of evolution in the man which would astonish and possibly terrify Darwin himself." Still another article in *Century* endorsed the theory that the half-caste was lower mentally and morally than the parent stock. Brazil was also cited in 1879 as "proof" that "the mixed races are invariably bad; they seem to combine all the worst characteristics of the two parent stocks. . . . A light mulatto or an almost black one may be a very decent sort of fellow; but the brown half-and-half is nearly always lazy, and stupid and vain." But shortly before this, another writer had offered Haiti as a "discouraging commentary on the theories of those humanitarians who believe in the ultimate elevation of the negro to the level of the Caucasian race. There is a backward tendency of which barbarism

seems to be the inevitable goal unless a new people take possession of the soil."[7]

One of the most amazing examples of early Darwinism appeared in *Harper's* in 1877. Lady Adeliza Chimpanzee became alarmed when she noticed that she was turning white. Her mother reassured her by pointing out that this turning of color was evidence of the fact that she was of a superior race. Prince Orang Outan, who had been selected to marry her, was even whiter than she. The Prince realized his superior ancestry because he had no caudal appendage. But the child of Lady Adeliza and Prince Orang had no tail and no hair; on the other hand, he had flat feet and a white skin. Since no one knew what to call this strange creature, Lady Adeliza named him Man. An accompanying pictures showed "the new species" as being quite similar to the caricatures of Negroes that frequently appeared in *Harper's*.[8]

Several articles in the *Atlantic* during this early period also revealed evidence of belief in the superiority of the Anglo-Saxon. But the *North American Review* surpassed all others in publishing articles which presented similar views. Typical of these was the prediction by Gayarré in 1877 that, "if contrary to the teachings of history and science, the negro should rise to an equality of intelligence and energy with the Caucasian," there would be a final struggle between the two races from which the Caucasian would emerge victorious.[9]

The revived creed of racial superiority was nurtured in the 1880s by agitation for Chinese exclusion, the wiping out of the Indian frontier, and the growing momentum for the scramble for Africa. A review in the *Atlantic* of Francis Galton's *Inquiries*

---

[6] Richard Hofstadter, *Social Darwinism in American Thought, 1860–1915* (Philadelphia and London, 1944); Josiah Strong, *Our Country* (New York, 1885).

[7] R. W. Wright, "Richmond Since the War," *Scribner's,* XIV (July, 1877), 311–12; Herbert H. Smith, "The Metropolis of the Amazons," *ibid.,* XVIII (May, 1879), 65–77; Edmund Clarence Stedman, "Christophe," *Century,* XXIII (November, 1881), 34–35.

[8] Editor's Drawer, "The Origin of Man by Darwin," *Harper's* LV (October, 1877), 637–38.

[9] Gayarré, *op. cit.,* pp. 494–97.

into Human Faculty and Its Development
agreed, 1883, that Chinese, Indians, and
Negroes should be excluded from the earth
and the sooner the better. But Social Darwinism continued to find a sturdy rationale
in the growing deterioration of the Negro's
status in the United States. A writer in the
Review, 1881, asserted that "in no time or
clime have the Caucasian race ever consented to live with inferior ones *save as
rulers*." Numerous articles supporting the
concept of the inherent inferiority of the
American Negro appeared in the *Review*
and *Century*. John Fiske's famous lecture,
"Manifest Destiny," which glorified the
progress made by the Teutonic and "Aryan"
races and praised English imperialism was
published in *Harper's* in 1885.[10]

The refrain continued in the 1890s, re-
enforced undoubtedly by some of the
speeches by Southerners who opposed the
Lodge bill. Bryce argued that the Negro had
not been able to protect himself in the exercise of suffrage because he was naturally
inferior to the white man. Thomas Nelson
Page contended: "The Negro has not progressed, not because he was a slave, but because he does not possess the faculties to
raise himself above slavery. He has not yet
exhibited the qualities of any race which has
advanced." He also cited Liberia, Haiti, and
the Dominican Republic in order to establish the "fact" that the Negro did not possess the qualifications to conduct his own
government. Theodore Roosevelt affirmed
in 1895: "A perfectly stupid race can never
rise to a very high plane; the negro, for instance, has been kept down as much by
lack of intellectual development as anything else." Marion L. Dawson, former
Judge Advocate-General of Virginia, explained in 1897 that the South was influenced by the same ruling spirit which had
characterized the Anglo-Saxon from the beginning of his history to that time. He believed that the whole problem of the South

was "whether the negro or the white man
should occupy the seat of power; whether
the inferior should dominate the superior,
and whether ignorance should rule intelligence." Straton in 1900 declared that the
Negro showed all the defects of a degenerate
race—lessened fertility, prevalence of venereal and other diseases caused by immorality
and resulting in a large infant mortality.
The Negro would not, therefore, be able to
adapt to Anglo-Saxon civilization. Two articles by obscure authors, one in 1884 and
another in 1889, probably did little to offset
the barrage of articles by much better
known authors. In 1900 Washington cited
Jamaica as an example of the increase of
Negro population in contact with white
races. In the United States, he added, Negroes enjoyed advantages and incentives
that were not possessed by the colored Ja-
maicans.[11]

A natural consequence of the acceptance
of the concept of the inherent inferiority of
the Negro was advocacy of the "White
Man's Burden." Bryce, however, wanted it
clearly understood that assumption of the
burden did not involve mixing of the races.
On the contrary, he assured, white colon-
izers, especially in the Union of South Africa, repudiated the idea. (Bryce could
hardly have been ignorant of the existence
of the "Cape Coloured.") He also sought
to dispel fear that the inferior race would
predominate there any more than in the
Southern states of the United States. *Harper's* ran in serial form "A White Man's
Africa" by Poultney Bigelow, a well-known
New York journalist and lawyer, which also
gave the assurance that the English in South
Africa were not mixing their blood with that
of the natives. But the "degeneracy" of the
Portuguese in Africa stemmed from the fact
that since the fifteenth century they had

---

[10] W. Henry Holland, "Heredity," *Atlantic
Monthly*, LII (October, 1883), 452; H. H. Chal-
mers, *op. cit.*, pp. 239–48, italics as in the original;
Hofstadter, *Social Darwinism*, p. 153.

[11] Bryce, *op. cit.*, pp. 641–60; Thomas Nelson
Page, *A Southerner on the Negro Question*, pp.
411–13; Theodore Roosevelt, "Kidd's 'Social
Evolution,'" *North American Review*, CLXI
(July, 1895), 94–109; Dawson, "Will the South
Be Solid Again?," *ibid.*, CLXIV (February, 1897),
193–98; Straton, *op. cit.*, pp. 784–801; Washing-
ton, *A Reply*, pp. 221–32.

intermarried with Negroes. The *North American Review,* as usual, presented articles praising and condemning European imperialism in India, China, and Africa, but the majority extolled the blessings of civilization that were being carried to the benighted heathen. The most effective answer may be summed up in the sarcastic conclusion of the Marquis of Lorne: "Truly it is a wonderful phenomenon—this pouncing of Northern eagles and lions upon the abodes and realms of the black man. And why is it? Oh, for their good, of course! We shall stop their mauling and enslaving each other, and they ought to be grateful, and would be so if they only knew what unselfish intentions we one and all of us have." Most readers, however, probably agreed with the Reverend W. Garden Blaikie that European imperialism would "issue in great good to the Dark Continent." Even conditions in the Belgian Congo found favor in the eyes of a contributor to *Century* in 1896 and 1897. Stanley urged in 1896 that European partitioning of Africa should be looked upon as "civilization" rather than as "colonization." Another writer endorsed Rudyard Kipling's well-known views. There were, finally, undertones and overtones of racism in the "Anglo-Saxon mystique" which led Captain Alfred T. Mahan, Andrew Carnegie, Sir Charles Beresford, and others to favor an alliance between the United States and Great Britain and their eventual unification.[12]

The way had thus been prepared for the acceptance of American imperialism on racial and moral grounds. One writer, reversing a position that he had taken in 1896,

urged in 1898 permanent American intervention in Cuba in order to prevent the domination of the whites by the blacks. While most of the writers in the *Review,* including General Leonard T. Wood, found the Cuban Negroes industrious, there was a tendency to emphasize that they constituted only about 30 percent of the population (an estimate that is probably considerably too low). Several articles supported the annexation of Hawaii and the Philippines by the plea that it was the duty of the United States to assume the obligation of civilizing backward peoples. An article in the *Atlantic* described most Cuban Negroes as ignorant, boastful, untruthful, ungrateful, fond of trinkets; "docility, except under abuse, is their most marked trait." Several editorials in *Century* emphasized the "purity" of the motives of the United States and endorsed the assumption of responsibility toward backward races.[13]

But opposition to American expansion also stemmed from racial considerations. Senator Vest (Democrat) condemned the idea of conferring citizenship upon the "half-civilized, piratical, muck-running inhabitants of two thousand islands, seven thousand miles distant." A less well-known author added that American expansion would bring vexing problems similar to those in the South. "Pitchfork" Ben Tillman naturally expressed opposition to annexation on racial grounds in the most extreme language. There would always be racial antagonism, he contended, because the Anglo-Saxon walked on the necks of every race with which he came in contact and resistance to his will meant destruction to the weaker race. Since the United States had its

---

12 Poultney Bigelow, "White Man's Africa," *Harper's,* XCIV (January, 1897), 775–89; Marquis of Lorne, "The Partition of Africa," *North American Review,* CLI (December, 1890), 701–12; W. Garden Blaikie, "Central Africa Since the Death of Livingstone," *ibid.,* CLXV (September, 1897), 318–32; E. J. Glave, "Glave in the Heart of Africa," *Century,* LII (October, 1896), 918–33; Glave, "New Conditions in Central Africa," *ibid.,* LIII (April, 1897), 900–15; Henry M. Stanley, "The Story of the Development of Africa," *ibid.,* LI (February, 1896), 500–09; Henry Rutgers Marshall, "Rudyard Kipling and Racial Instincts," *ibid.,* LVIII (July, 1899), 375–77.

13 Leonard Wood, "The Existing Conditions and Needs in Cuba," *North American Review,* CLXVIII (May, 1899), 593–601; see other articles listed in Betty R. Jordan, "The Negro as Portrayed in the *North American Review,* 1877–1900" (M.A. thesis, Howard University). See also Herbert Pelham Williams, "The Outlook in Cuba," *Atlantic Monthly,* LXXXIII (June, 1899), 827–36 and Queen C. Green "The Negro as Portrayed in *Scribner's Monthly* and *Century,* 1877–1901" (M.A. thesis, Howard University).

own race problem, it would be foolhardy to incorporate 9 million more brown men under the flag. How could the Republicans, he inquired, defend their abandonment of the Negroes at home, and at the same time defend McKinley's policy of subjugating the Filipinos with greater hardships than Southern Negroes had to endure. Probably more in triumph than in sorrow, Tillman concluded: "And no Republican leader . . . will now dare to wave the bloody shirt and preach a crusade against the South's treatment of the negro. The North has a bloody shirt of its own. Many thousands of them have been made into shrouds for murdered Filipinos, done to death because they were fighting for liberty." Even Carl Schurz, whom Du Bois has called "the finest type of immigrant American," and who had written a report shortly after the Civil War castigating the South, wrote in 1898:

We are vexed by a very troublesome race problem in the United States now. That race problem is still unsolved, and it would be very sanguine to say that there is a satisfactory solution in near prospect. Cool-headed men think that we have enough of that. What will be the consequence if we indefinitely add to it by bringing under this republican government big lots of other incompatible races—races far more intractable, too, than those with which we have so far had to deal?[14]

Two of the best-known advocates of the Social Gospel revealed their astigmatism on the plight of the American Negro. Walter Rauschenbusch, who was born of German parents in Rochester, New York, on April 15, 1861, was equally unconcerned during the period under investigation about the political condition of Negroes in the South. Purvis M. Carter, who made a detailed study of his writings, including *For the Right* in the Yale University Library, *Dawn* and *In-*

dependent, found that the great Baptist leader devoted practically no attention prior to 1901 to this subject. In May, 1890, Rauschenbusch urged that a petition be circulated in behalf of the downtrodden people of Russia. But in September of the same year, when Mississippi was revising its constitution and the fate of the Lodge bill hung in the balance, he wrote in *For the Right,* the organ of the Brotherhood of the Kingdom:

Our institutions are the admiration and the inspirational beaconlight of noblemen from the Straits of Gibraltar to the bleak huts of Siberian exiles. Whenever a hand seeks to rear the banner of liberty, it is nerved by the thought of a great nation beyond the sea, in which men are free and equal.

He recognized that social equality had not been achieved: "Political liberty is ours, now let us use it to secure social equality."[15]

Lyman Abbott went further than did Gladden or Rauschenbusch, for he explicitly endorsed some Southern viewpoints. This endorsement is all the more significant because of his previous views and activities. He had publicly favored emancipation before Lincoln issued his preliminary Emancipation Proclamation. He had opposed granting Negroes immediate political responsibility because he would confine the administration of government "always to the moral and the intelligent." Since the South possessed neither the free schools nor the free churches necessary to develop these qualities, he believed as early as 1864 that the North should supply them. As corresponding secretary of the American Union Commission and as general secretary of the American Freedmen's Union Commission from 1865 to July 1, 1869, he had "performed a useful service in co-ordinating the efforts of the non-denominational benevolent societies, in acting as an intermediary between them and the Freedmen's Bureau, and in general stimulating interest in moral

---

[14] G. G. Vest, "Objections to Annexing the Philippines," *North American Review,* CLXVII (January, 1899), 112–20; B. R. Tillman, "Causes of Southern Opposition to Imperialism," *ibid.,* CLXXI (October, 1900), 439–46; Carl Schurz, "Thoughts on American Imperialism," *Century,* LVI (September, 1898), 781–88.

[15] Purvis M. Carter, "The Astigmatism of the Social Gospel, 1877–1901," (M.A. thesis, Howard University).

reconstruction." While he believed that children in the South might choose to attend school with companions of their own race, he insisted that no child should be barred from any Commission school because of his color. He was a gradualist as far as the abolition of segregation was concerned, but he was convinced that, once segregation was accepted, it could not be abolished. But in the 1880s Abbott began to be an apostle of the "New South." It is probable that his "conversion" was prompted by Henry W. Grady's speech which he heard in 1886. The *Christian Union,* which became the *Outlook* in 1891, and which frequently reflected Abbott's views, supported the Blair bill in 1884 and 1888, but it took a positive stand against the Lodge bill. By 1890 Abbott had come to believe that the wisest policy was to allow the South to administer her own future. "The negro problem," averred an editorial in the *Christian Union* on June 12, 1890, "must be worked out by the negroes and the white men of the South with the aid of the North, not by the North or the Federal government over the heads of the negroes and the white men."[16] His conversion is also apparent in an article in the *North American Review* in 1898 in which he discussed the Indian problem in the United States. He advocated the abolition of reservations and urged that the Indian be treated as a man. He then added:

Treat them [the Indians] as we have treated the negro. As a race the African is less competent than the Indian, but we do not shut the negroes up in reservations and put them in charge of politically appointed parents called agents. The lazy grow hungry; the criminal are punished; the industrious get on. And though the sporadic cases of injustice are often tragic, they are the gradually disappearing relics of a slavery that is past, and the negro is finding his place in American life gradually, both as a race and as an individual.

Three years later, after touring South Atlantic schools and attending the conference of the Southern Educational Board at Winston-Salem, North Carolina, he again gave explicit endorsement of Southern points of view. He approved the Southern suffrage amendments. The Southerner, he found, had less prejudice against the Negro and more interest in his welfare than did the Northerner. The South desired education for the Negro but felt, realistically, that it should be industrial rather than literary. Attempts to force political or social equality would inflict "uncalculable" injury on the Negro and on the nation.[17] Professor William Warren Sweet, perhaps the most authoritative historian of the church in the United States, has concluded that "no religious leader in modern times has exercised a more abiding influence than has Lyman Abbott."[18] Professor Sweet was not, of course, endorsing the contributions, positive and negative— not one of some 100 magazine articles by Abbott between 1890 and 1900 bore a title referring specifically to the Negro—that Abbott made to the development of the concept of the "New South" that religious and other intellectual molders of American thought were implanting in the minds of the American people.

---

[16] Ira V. Brown, "Lyman Abbott and Freedmen's Aid, 1865–1869," *Journal of Southern History,* XV (February, 1949), 22–38. Professor Brown generously permitted the author to use relevant parts of his manuscript which is now being published by the Harvard University Press.

[17] Lyman Abbott, "Our Indian Problem," *North American Review,* CLXVII (December, 1898), 719–28; *Outlook,* LXVII (April, 1901), 948.

[18] William Warren Sweet, *Makers of Christianity* (New York, 1937), III, 320.

1963

The Supreme Court Defers to Racism[*]

BARTON J. BERNSTEIN

The felt necessities of the time, the prevalent moral and political theories, intuitions of public policy, avowed or unconscious, even the prejudices which judges share with their fellow-men, have had a good deal more to do than the syllogism in determining the rules by which men should be governed.

OLIVER WENDELL HOLMES,
The Common Law

For 58 years *Plessy* v. *Ferguson*,[1] the federal source of the "separate but equal" doctrine, had escaped judicial challenge. When the 1954 Supreme Court in effect overruled the *Plessy* doctrine in the *Segregation Cases*,[2] the Warren tribunal's decision was attacked as sociological jurisprudence.[3] Implicit in

this criticism was an assumption that *Plessy* was free of social theory and allegedly based upon the more solid grounds of precedent and constitutional law.

However, recent studies of the tangled history of the Fourteenth Amendment establish that the Amendment did not require the Supreme Court's decision in *Plessy*.[4] And a careful examination of the case law cited by the *Plessy* court reveals that only through distortion could these cases have been used to support the court's holding.[5] In view of this research the court's opinion

---

not be equal; the "separate but equal" doctrine was self-contradictory.

Criticism of the *Segregation Cases* as sociological jurisprudence has been based on three propositions: the Fourteenth Amendment was not intended to prohibit Jim Crow education, and the framers' intent should be followed; the court should have followed the precedent, *Plessy*, and later segregation cases whose broad holdings could be interpreted as Supreme Court approval of "separate but equal"; and social theories should not be the basis for a legal decision.

[*] Barton J. Bernstein, *"Plessy* v. *Ferguson:* Conservative Sociological Jurisprudence," *Journal of Negro History,* Vol. No. 7 (1963).

[1] 163 U.S. 537 (1896).

[2] *Brown et al* v. *Board of Education et al.,* 347 U.S. 483, has since been called the *Segregation Cases.* Since only in a case identical in material facts to *Plessy* v. *Ferguson,* a transportation case, could the Supreme Court overrule *Plessy.* The overruling did not occur until such a transportation case came before the Warren court. *Gayle* v. *Browder,* 352 U.S. 903 (1956).

[3] In *Brown* the court had announced that "we cannot turn the clock back to 1868 when the Amendment [Fourteenth] was adopted, or even to 1896 when *Plessy* v. *Ferguson* was written. We must consider public education in the light of its full development and its present place in the American life throughout the nation." The court did not seek to erect an impressive legal argument, buttressed by case law, to overturn *Plessy.* Case law was deemed inapplicable, and the history of the original meaning of the Fourteenth Amendment was judged "inconclusive." The high court cited sociological and psychological studies to establish that separate educational facilities can-

[4] John Frank and Robert Munro, "The Original Understanding of 'Equal Protection of the Laws,'" *Columbia Law Review,* L, No. 1 (January, 1950), 131; Jacobus Ten Brock, *The Antislavery Origins of the Fourteenth Amendment* (Cal., 1951); Howard Graham, "The Anti-Slavery Backgrounds of the Fourteenth Amendment," *Wisconsin Law Review,* 1950, No. 3 (May, 1950), No. 4 (July, 1950), 479, 610; Alfred Kelly, "The Fourteenth Amendment Reconsidered," *Michigan Law Review,* LIV, No. 8 (June, 1956), 1049; Robert Harris, *The Quest for Equality* (Louisiana State University, 1960); and Jack Greenberg, *Race Relations and American Law* (Columbia, 1959).

[5] Bernstein, "Case Law in *Plessy* v. *Ferguson,*" *Jour. of Negro Hist.* XLVII, No. 3 (July, 1962), 192–98.

merits analysis to determine whether social theories shaped the "separate but equal" position.

I

Homer Plessy, part Negro, had been arrested in Louisiana where he had violated the state law requiring separate accommodations for the races in intrastate travel. Plessy's contention that the Louisiana statute was unconstitutional was rejected by the state court and appealed to the United States Supreme Court. With only Justice John Marshall Harlan dissenting, the Supreme Court held that the state law was a reasonable exercise of the state police power and therefore constitutional.

Before the Supreme Court, counsel for Plessy had attacked the segregation provision as unreasonable. In an argument which Harlan adopted in his dissent, the counsel had argued that a decision against Plessy and for segregation would authorize the states to require separate cars for people with different colors of hair, aliens, or Catholics or Protestants, or to required colored people to walk on one side of the street and white people on the other side, or to demand that white men's homes be painted white and black men's homes black. These analogies were close enough to the case at bar to compel the court to distinguish these fact situations and justify its reasoning in *Plessy*.[6]

Judge Henry Billings Brown, writing the court's opinion, replied that "every exercise of the police power must be reasonable, and extend only to such laws as are enacted in good faith for the promotion of the public good, and not for the annoyance or oppression of a particular class." He relied upon two arguments to establish the contention that the Louisiana statute was a reasonable exercise of the state police power. Each revealed that sociological and psychological theories controlled the court's decision.

First, Brown maintained that the Louisi-

ana act was not designed as an "annoyance or oppression" and should not have been so considered. He contended that the laws requiring racial segregation did not "necessarily imply the inferiority of one race to the other." The underlying fallacy of the plaintiff's argument was "the assumption that enforced separation of the two races stamps the colored race with a badge of inferiority." Such reasoning, Brown explained, would mean that if a Negro legislature separated whites, the whites would feel inferior. He concluded that they would not.[7]

Harlan might have attacked Brown's analogy. Or the dissent might have noted that the court avoided relevant facts: the white race outnumbered the Negro in the nation; Negroes had only recently been freed from servitude and awarded legal equality; their alleged inferiority was attested to by a host of pseudoscientific theories. Harlan, however, simply asserted that candor demanded recognition "that the statute in question had its origin in the purpose . . . to exclude colored people from the coaches" of white people. The Louisiana statute, he maintained, was designed as an annoyance and intended as oppression. "The brand of servitude and degradation" was placed upon a large class of fellow citizens. Harlan concluded: "The thin disguise of equal accommodation for passengers . . . will not mislead anyone, nor atone for the wrong this day done."[8] Harlan's statement about the law's purpose leads to the conclusion that the Louisiana act was unreasonable—by Brown's criteria.

Brown's second argument wrote conservative theory and the prevailing social science "truths" into law. The court explained that the standard of reasonableness is determined "with reference to the established usages, customs, and traditions of the people." This is the underlying social doctrine upon which the case is erected. Law is reasonable when it follows custom. The court implied that law is unreasonable when it violates custom

---

[6] S. F. Phillips and F. D. McKenney, *Brief for Plaintiff in Error in Plessy* v. *Ferguson*, 13.

[7] 163 U.S. 537 at 551.
[8] 163 U.S. 537 at 562, 3.

or tradition or seeks to change the folk-ways of the people. Judge Brown denied that "social prejudices may be overcome by leg-islation. . . . 'This end can neither be accom-plished nor promoted by laws which con-flict with the general sentiment of the com-munity upon whom they are designed to operate.' " Brown concluded that "legisla-tion is powerless to eradicate racial instincts. . . . If one race be inferior to the other socially, the Constitution of the United States cannot put them upon the same plane."[9]

The court believed that it was only within the duty and capacity of government to guarantee the races equal civil and political rights, and that state laws requiring racial segregation did not constitute a violation of these rights. Brown considered Jim Crow laws an abridgement of social equality.[10] Social equality could not be legislated, and the court approved that it should not be legislated. "If the two races are to meet upon terms of social equality," the court concluded, "it must be the result of natural affinities, a mutual appreciation of each other's merits and a voluntary consent of individuals."[11]

II

At least four questionable factual allega-tions or dubious legal and scientific theories

were employed by the court to justify the legislation of prejudice: racial segregation is a custom or tradition; law is reasonable when it follows custom and unreasonable when it does not adhere to custom; a con-trary decision in *Plessy* would have meant the enforcement of social equality; and law cannot "eradicate [the] racial instincts." Each of these reflects the underlying theo-ries and prejudices upon which the decision rests.

Contrary to the *Plessy* court's contention, segregation in transportation was not con-sistent with custom or tradition. Racial seg-regation in the Old South had been un-known.[12] The system of slavery would have been virtually inoperative had Jim Crow prevailed.[13] Nor did Jim Crow spontane-ously arise after the war. Negroes and whites frequently shared the same coaches; al-though sometimes the freedmen were barred from the first-class cars, the races did share the same second-class coaches. A South Carolinian remarked in 1877 that Negroes in his state "were permitted to, and fre-quently do ride in first-class railway and street cars." At first this had caused trouble, but it was then "so common as hardly to provoke remarks."[14] One reporter observed that Negroes rode "exactly as white people . . . and in the same cars" in Virginia.[15] When the *Plessy* court judged it custom, Jim Crow transportation was but a recent Southern creation. By 1896 only eight

---

[9] 163 U.S. 537 at 550, 1. The quote within the quote is persuasive authority from *People* v. *Gallagher,* 93 N.Y. 438 at 448 (1883). Earlier in the *Plessy* opinion the Supreme Court had recog-nized that Negroes were considered inferior. Brown had written: "the reputation of belonging to the dominant race, in this instance the white race, is property, in the same sense that a right of action, or of inheritance is property. . . . If he be a white man assigned to a colored coach he may have his action for damages against the company for being deprived of his so-called property. Upon the other hand, if he be called a colored man [and he is]. . . , he has been deprived of no property since he is not lawfully entitled to the reputation of being a white man." 163 U.S. 537 at 545.

[10] John Marshall Harlan contended that the issue was a violation of a civil right, not a social right. A railroad, he reasoned, was a public high-way, and all rights pertaining to its use were con-sequently civil rights.

[11] 163 U.S. 537 at 551.

[12] Speaking about the Old South, W. E. B. Du Bois later noted, the two races sometimes "lived in the same house, shared in the family life, often attended the same church, and talked and con-versed with each other." *The Souls of Black Folks* (McClure, 1903), 184.

[13] Three southern states—Florida and Mis-sissippi in 1865, and Texas in 1866—did enact Jim Crow transportation laws. The last of these was repealed in 1873. Franklin Johnson, *The Development of State Legislation Concerning the Free Negro* (Arbor, 1918), 13–16.

[14] Belton O'Neall Townsend, "South Carolina Society," *Atlantic Monthly,* XXXIX (June, 1877), 676.

[15] George Cable, *Silent South* (New York, 1885), 85–86, quoted by C. Vann Woodward, *Origins of the New South, 1877–1913* (Vol. IX, *A History of the South,* Louisiana State Univer-sity, 1951), 210.

Southern states had such laws, and seven of the statutes were less than eight years old.[16] These regulations were frequently the enactment of codes of recent practice. The caste system was not yet a custom or tradition; it was a new pattern. Institutionalized prejudice had not hardened; that was the promise of *Plessy* v. *Ferguson.* By its decision the Supreme Court constitutionalized the state enactment of race prejudice.

Laws severely violating custom and tradition are usually unenforceable and may therefore be judged unreasonable. This proposition does not, however, mean that custom must be reflected in law. Customs can exist independently of law, and custom is not violated if it is not enacted in law. If the *Plessy* court had declared the Louisiana statute unconstitutional, custom would not have been violated. The court was right in stating that social equality cannot be enforced, because social relations constitute an area of free selection, and when human relations are legislated by government, they cease to be social and are transformed into political relations.

But if the court had decided that the law was unconstitutional, it would not have been enforcing social equality. The court's illogical predictions to the contrary, enforced commingling of the races would not have occurred. The practices of railroads and the social habits of passengers would not have been immediately affected. The prevailing policy would have been maintained: where informal segregation existed, it would have remained; where commingling occurred, it would have continued. However, the court's decision that "separate but equal" facilities were constitutional did enforce political inequality. Those of each race who were in the habit of mingling with members of the other were denied this right by law.

The court argued that social attitudes cannot be shaped by law.[17] While this was poor

history, it was consistent with the popular sociology which emerged after the Civil War. All good Spencerians—most sociologists—agreed that society, the organism of evolution, could not be refashioned by legislation. William Graham Sumner explained that "legislation cannot makes mores" and stateways cannot change folkways. Franklin Henry Giddings, Columbia University's counterpart of Sumner, had emphasized "consciousness of kind," a new guise for the "racial instincts" concept, to explain segregation. The implication in *Plessy* was that this social custom, the desire for racially segregated facilities, was grounded in "race instincts." These instincts were unchangeable before man-made law.[18]

The vague theory of "racial instincts," requiring the separation of the races, provided the "scientific" means for justifying the Southern system of white superiority which had been threatened by the abolition of slavery. One Southerner succinctly stated the new ideology as scientific fact: "there is an instinct, ineradicable and positive, that will keep the races apart."[19] Inferiority of the Negro was an article of Southern faith to which many clung. To yield their position of superiority and accept the Negro as an equal would have overturned the habits nurtured by many decades of slavery. However, only some Southern whites felt threatened by the rising status of Negroes. It was the lower class white who demanded Jim Crow laws when the Negro competed with him for subsistence wages.[20] White

---

16 See Johnson, *op. cit.,* 15, 54, 62–207, and Gilbert Stephenson, *Race Discrimination in American Law* (New York, 1910), 216–17.

17 The Massachusetts high court in *Roberts* v. *City of Boston,* 59 Mass. (5 Cush) 198 (1849),

the source of the "separate but equal" doctrine, had stated that race prejudice "is not created by law, and probably cannot be changed by law."

18 It is to be noted that the court did not tilt against anti-miscegenation laws. Obviously if a "racial instinct" required segregation, such laws were unnecessary; by instinct everyone would refrain from interracial marriage.

19 Quoted by Paul Buck, *The Road to Reunion, 1865–1900* (Vintage, 1959), 299, from Joel Chandler Harris, *Life, Writings, and Speeches of Henry W. Grady* (New York, 1890), 299 ff.

20 Woodward speaks of this process as "one of the paradoxes of Southern history that political democracy for the white man and racial discrimination for the black were often products of the same dynamics." Negroes understood that eco-

superiority could be guaranteed by this new enforced relationship between whites and blacks. For the poor white, caste would protect class. Jim Crow was designed as an "annoying oppression," contrary to the *Plessy* opinion. Separation of the two races would constitute a constant and visible affirmation of the continuing inferiority of blacks to whites.

Out of earlier American doubts and theories a new doctrine had arisen to justify segregation. It merged the discoveries of older thought and the contemporary science.[21] "Racial instinct" and white supremacy were intertwined theories promoted by the Frenchman, Joseph Gobineau,[22] who had not awaited the appearance of Darwinism. Shortly after Gobineau, "survival of the fittest," the popular catchword summary of Darwin's theory of organic evolution, was invoked to establish white superiority over

the Negro. Biologists and anthropologists readily confirmed Negro inferiority. The Negro's skull was weighed and his brain measured. Elaborate scientific studies were said to demonstrate that in brain size, pelvic expanse, and a great variety of physiological and psychological traits Negroes were inferior to whites. Comparative disease rates and criminality percentages, always favorable to the whites, "scientifically" established this superiority. It was demonstrated that the Negro's intelligence did not control his actions.[23] Studies showed that he was "light-hearted and carefree," seldom allowing "responsibility to weigh on his mind."[24] Obviously whites were more mature and civilized; they had advanced higher on the evolutionary scale. The Negro's inferiority made him a child while the white was an adult. Some racists sought to modify this bastard offspring of Darwinism by accenting the supremacy of the Anglo-Saxon or Aryan, terms more specific in the categories they excluded than those included. A German strain of racism, born in Romanticism and carried to America by German seminar-trained students, advanced this theory.[25] Either explicitly or implicitly, the Negro was always relegated to hopeless inferiority by the scientific "truths."

The influence of these ideas was apparent in *Plessy* v. *Ferguson,* and probably reflected the dominant thoughts and fears of an uneasy American society. At the same time sectional tensions were being eliminated at

---

nomic pressures were creating the pressures for Jim Crow. "It took a lot of ritual and Jim Crow to bolster the creed of white supremacy in the bosom of a white man working for black man's wages. . . . A North Carolina Negro wrote: 'The best people in the South do not demand this separate car business . . . and, when they do, it is only to cater to those of their race who, in order to get a big man's smile, will elevate them to place and power.' " Quoted by Woodward, *op. cit.,* 211, from Editorial, *Southland* (Salisbury, N.C.), 1 (1890), 166–67.

[21] See William Stanton, *The Leopard's Spots* (University of Chicago, 1960); Oscar Handlin, *Race and Nationality in American Life* (Little, Brown, 1957), c. 1–4; William Jenkins, *Pro-Slavery Thought* (University of North Carolina, 1935); Charles Wesley, "Negro Inferiority in American Thought," *Journal of Negro History,* XXV, No. 4 (October, 1940). 540; and Leon Litwack, *North of Slavery* (University of Chicago, 1961).

[22] In his *Essai sur l'inegalité des races humaines* (1853), he had demonstrated the alleged superiority of the white race over the other races, and Aryans over other whites. A translation of his work appeared in America in 1856, with some notes by an admirer, *Moral and Intellectual Diversity of the Races . . . with an Analytic Introduction and Copious Historical Notes, by H. Hotz to which is Added an Appeal Concerning a Summary of the Latest Scientific Facts Bearing Upon the Question of Unity or Plurality of Species,* by J. C. Nott (1856). For a brief discussion of Gobineau, see Handlin, *op. cit.,* c. 4, and Jacques Barzun, *Race: A Study in Modern Superstition* (Meuten, 1938).

[23] Tests measuring the speed of mental reactions showed that the Negro reacted more rapidly than the white. From this it was concluded that intelligence did not control the black man's actions; actually he was close to the savage. R. M. Burke, "Reaction Time with Reference to Race," *Psychological Review,* 11 (1895), 474.

[24] Charles Johnson and Horace Bond, "Investigation of Racial Differences Prior to 1910," *Journal Negro Education,* 111, No. 3 (July, 1934), 337.

[25] The late nineteenth century germ theory of politics, promoted by Herbert Baxter Adams and John Burgess, the dominant intellectual figures at Johns Hopkins and Columbia, respectively, provided respectable garb for racism. Richard Hofstadter, *Social Darwinism in American Thought* (Boston, 1959), c. 9.

the price of abandoning the Negro. The Negro was sacrificed "on the altar of reconciliation, peace and prosperity." The Supreme Court had anticipated this movement in earlier decisions. Southern writers had contributed their efforts. Thomas Nelson Page, Joel Chandler Harris, and their associates in the South, with the aid of Northern editors and publishing houses, had created an image of a friendly South where the childlike Negroes loved the white folks."[26] Northerners seeking sectional reconciliation with the South put the "bloody shirt" in their trunks and were mouthing the shibboleths of white supremacy and Negro inferiority.[27] Most Northerners who advocated Negro rights embraced a philosophy of segregation and wanted to improve the black man's status within this framework. The aggressive Negro leadership of Frederick Douglass had been replaced by a new movement more concerned about Negro advancement than integration. The year before the *Plessy* decision became the law of the land, Douglass had died and Booker T. Washington, the spearhead of the new order, delivered the famous Atlanta address calling for a program of racial coexistence grounded in racial separation: "The opportunity to earn a dollar in a factory just now is worth infinitely more than an opportunity to spend a dollar in an opera-house."[28] Social advancement, it was hoped, would occur within the context of segregation.

III

While the most respected Negro leader was counseling patience and gradual progress through economic advancement, the Supreme Court, in constitutionalizing racial separation, had condemned the Negro to an inferiority confirmed by the legal recognition of contemporary biological and social science "truths." By not acknowledging that social attitudes could be shaped by law, the court assured that Jim Crow would become custom and treatment of Negroes as second-class citizens habit.[29] The seeds of race hatred were sown. It was Harlan, the constant champion of Negro rights, who predicted that the decision would stimulate "aggressions, more or less brutal or irritating, upon the admitted rights of colored citizens." "What," he added, "can more certainly arouse race hatred?"[30]

26 See Buck, *op. cit.*, for a discussion of sectional reconciliation, particularly the literature of the period.

27 C. Vann Woodward, *The Strange Career of Jim Crow* (Oxford, 1955), 52–53. Such expressions frequently appeared in *Nation, Harper's Weekly, North American Review,* and *Atlantic Monthly* of the period. Illustrative of the change in Northern attitudes is the case of Thomas Wentworth Higginson. As a young man he had led a mob to free a fugitive slave from jail, and in the Civil War he had commanded a regiment of Negro troops. Thirty years after Appomattox he shed tears as he read of the death of a slaveowner in a popular story. Buck, *op. cit.*, 244. See also Vincent De Santis, *Republicans Face the Southern Question* (Johns Hopkins, 1959), and Stanley Hirshson, *Farewell to the Bloody Shirt* (University of Indiana, 1962).

28 In the same address he explained, "The wisest among my race understand that the agitation of questions of social equality is the extremist folly. . . ." *Up From Slavery* (Doubleday, 1901), 223–24.

29 A half century later the brief submitted for the Negro children in *Brown* v. *Board of Education* surveyed the success of the *Plessy* decision: "Without the 'constitutional' sanction which *Plessy* v. *Ferguson* affords, racial segregation could not have become entrenched in the South. . . . The doctrine of *Plessy* v. *Ferguson* was essential to the successful maintenance of a racial caste system in the United States." Herbert Hill et al., *Brief for Appellants in Brown* v. *Board of Education et al.*, 62.

30 Harlan concluded: "State enactments, regulating the enjoyment of civil rights, upon the basis of race, and cunningly devised to defeat legitimate results of war, under the pretense of recognizing equality or rights, can have no other result than to render permanent peace impossible, and to keep alive the conflict of the races, the continuance of which must do harm to all concerned." 163 U.S. 537 at 560–61.

Index of Authors

Bernstein, Barton J. (Stanford University) is the author of several articles on the Supreme Court and the retreat from Reconstruction.

Carpenter, John A. (Fordham University) provided evidence for the rejection of long standing stereotypes about Southern politics after the Civil War.

Coben, Stanley (Princeton University) has written about the Reconstruction era but is best known for his book on A. Mitchell Palmer.

Cochran, Thomas C. (University of Pennsylvania), a prominent economic historian, has written many essays and books including *Railroad Leaders, 1845-1890, The American Business System, 1900-1955;* and a *Basic History of American Business.*

Cox, John H. and La Wanda (City College of New York and Hunter College) are the authors of several articles on postwar politics and of *Politics, Principles, and Prejudice, 1865-1866.*

Current, Richard N. (University of North Carolina at Greensboro) has written a number of books over the past two decades on the Civil War era including *The Lincoln Nobody Knows* and *Lincoln and the First Shot.*

Degler, Carl N. (Vassar College) produced a widely used interpretative study of American life and thought, *Out of Our Past.*

Duberman, Martin (Princeton University), the author of *Charles Francis Adams* and the editor of *The Anti-Slavery Vanguard,* is also the author of the play, *In White America.*

Elkins, Stanley M. (Smith College), the co-author with Eric L. McKitrick of several interpretative essays on the Revolution and on the frontier, provided a recent analytical account of *Slavery.*

Franklin, John Hope (University of Chicago), the author of the standard work on Negro history, *The Slavery to Freedom,* has written recently on themes such as *The Militant South* and *Reconstruction after the Civil War.*

Govan, Thomas P. (New York University) has written on historiography and is the author of *Nicholas Biddle.*

Hyman, Harold M. (University of Illinois) is the author of *To Try Men's Souls: Loyalty Tests in American History* and the co-author of *Stanton: The Life and Times of Lincoln's Secretary of War.*

Isaacs, Harold R. (Massachusetts Institute of Technology), who has made several studies on racial images and ideas, is best known for *The New World of Negro Americans.*

Johnson, Ludwell H. (College of William and Mary), a specialist in Civil War military history, has written several essays and *The Red River Campaign.*

Jordan, Winthrop D. (University of California at Berkeley), the author of *White Over Black: The Development of American Attitudes Toward the Negro,* has written a number of articles about slavery and the Negro in the colonial period.

Korngold, Ralph, a professional writer, is the author of *Thaddeus Stevens: A Being Darkly Wise and Rudely Great* and several other biographies.

Litwack, Leon F. (University of California at Berkeley), the author of *North of Slavery: The Negro in the Free States, 1790-1860,* is working on a study of the Negro in Reconstruction.

Logan, Rayford W. (Howard University), an authority on American Negro history, is the author of *The Negro in American Life and Thought, 1877-1901.*

Lynd, Staughton (Yale University) is the author of several interpretative essays on the Revolution and on the Civil War era as well as the editor of *Non-Violence in America: A Documentary History.*

McKitrick, Eric L. (Columbia University) is the author of *Andrew Johnson and Reconstruction.* (See the Elkins entry.)

McLaughlin, Wayman B. (Winston-Salem College), a scholar in philosophy and religion, has analyzed the slave songs.

McPherson, James M. (Princeton University), the author of several essays on the abolitionists, has written *The Abolitionists in Civil War and Reconstruction* and *The Negro's Civil War.*

Morrow, Ralph E. (Washington University), who has written several essays on the ante-bellum and Reconstruction eras, is best known for his book *Northern Methodism and Reconstruction.*

Porter, Kenneth W. (University of Oregon) has established himself as the leading authority on the Negro under pioneer conditions in several dozen articles and in books such as *Relations Between Negroes Within the Present Limits of the U.S.*

Potter, David M. (Stanford University) has written extensively about the Civil War era in books such as *Lincoln and His Party in the Secession Crisis* and is also the author of a study of the American character, *People of Plenty.*

Puzzo, Dante A. (City University of New York), the author of an essay on the origins and nature of racism, wrote *Spain and the Great Powers, 1936-1941.*

Rose, Willie Lee (University of Virginia) is the author of *Rehearsal for Reconstruction: The Port Royal Experiment* and the editor of *Slavery in America.*

Ruchames, Louis (University of Massachusetts at Boston), who has written several articles on Charles Sumner and on Negro history, is the editor of *The John Brown Reader.*

Schlesinger, Arthur M., Jr. (City University of New York) first won recognition for *The Age of Jackson* but has devoted most of his attention to a three volume study of the Franklin Roosevelt era and, more recently to an account of the Kennedy administration, *A Thousand Days.*

Scroggs, Jack B. (North Texas State College) has written about Reconstruction politics in the South.

Sellers, Charles G. (University of California at Berkeley) is best known for his work on Polk and on Jacksonian topics but he has also dealt with Southern themes in articles and as the editor of *The Southerner as American.*

Silver, James W. (University of Notre Dame), for many years a Mississippi scholar and a commentator on Southern history, is the author of *Mississippi: The Closed Society.*

Stampp, Kenneth M. (University of California at Berkeley), the author of many articles and books including a definitive study of slavery, *The Peculiar Institution,* recently wrote an interpretative study of Reconstruction, *The Era of Reconstruction, 1865-1877.*

Strout, Cushing (Cornell University) is best known for his books, *The Pragmatic Revolt in American History* and *American Images of the Old World.*